lonely planet

London

Steve Fallon

LONELY PLANET PUBLICATIONS
Melbourne • Oakland • London • Paris

London
3rd edition – March 2002
First published – March 1998

Published by
Lonely Planet Publications Pty Ltd ABN 36 005 607 983
90 Maribyrnong St, Footscray, Victoria 3011, Australia

Lonely Planet Offices
Australia Locked Bag 1, Footscray, Victoria 3011
USA 150 Linden St, Oakland, CA 94607
UK 10a Spring Place, London NW5 3BH
France 1 rue du Dahomey, 75011 Paris

Photographs
Many of the images in this guide are available for licensing from
Lonely Planet Images.
email: lpi@lonelyplanet.com.au

Front cover photograph
Big Ben strikes again (Neil Setchfield)

ISBN 1 86450 353 X

text & maps © Lonely Planet 2002
photos © photographers as indicated 2002

Printed by The Bookmaker International Ltd
Printed in China

**Although the authors
and Lonely Planet try
to make the informa-
tion as accurate as
possible, we accept
no responsibility for
any loss, injury or
inconvenience sus-
tained by anyone
using this book.**

Contents – Text

PLACES TO STAY   247

PLACES TO EAT   269

ENTERTAINMENT   303

SHOPPING   328

THE MARKETS OF LONDON   340

EXCURSIONS   346

INDEX   371

MAP SECTION   383

MAP LEGEND   back page

METRIC CONVERSION   inside back cover

The Author

Steve Fallon

A native of Boston, Massachusetts, Steve graduated from George-town University with a Bachelor of Science in modern languages and then taught English at the University of Silesia near Katowice in Poland. After he had worked for several years for an American daily newspaper and earned a master's degree in journalism, his fascination with Asia took him to Hong Kong, where he lived for over a dozen years, working for a variety of publications and running a travel bookshop. Steve lived in Budapest for 2½ years from where he wrote *Hungary* and *Slovenia* before moving to London in 1994. He has written or contributed to a number of other Lonely Planet titles, including the Lonely Planet Journeys travelogue *Home with Alice: Travels in Gaelic Ireland*.

From the Author

A number of people helped in the research of this edition of *London*, but colleague and friend Neal Bedford, who did much of the walking while I did the talking, stands head and shoulders above everyone else (as he usually does). In the Lonely Planet London office, special thanks go to transport supremo Rachel Suddart for help with the Getting There & Away chapter, Matt Begg for updating the Canterbury section in the Excursions chapter, Tom Hall for his tips and infallible knowledge of 'the great game' and Imogen Franks for her enviable organisational skills. Sophie Howells and Emma Sangster offered restaurant and other ideas. I am grateful to Pelin Thornhill in the Oakland Lonely Planet office and to Leonie Mugavin in the Melbourne office for vetting certain sections of the Getting There & Away chapter. Thanks, too, to editor Heather Dickson for her sharp eye and even sharper stylus.

As always, I'd like to state my admiration, gratitude and great love for my partner, Michael Rothschild.

For the 2nd edition of *London* I wrote the following dedication: 'It may seem a very long time ago to many people but, well, *plus ça change…* This book is dedicated to the more than 30,000 people killed in the defence of London during WWII and about whom we thought a lot as we walked the streets of their beloved city. It is largely due to these grannies and brothers and daughters and lovers of decent, ordinary people that we can enjoy London past, present and future. They shall never be forgotten.'

The dedication remains, of course, but I'd like to add an addendum. During the production of this edition of *London*, terrorists attacked key targets in the USA, killing untold numbers of people, including many Britons. Londoners as always rose to the fore and one expatriate American, with no more connection to the holocaust or its hapless victims than a shared passport, received messages and words of condolence and kindness from friends, colleagues, neighbours and even strangers. I'd like to express my heartfelt gratitude to this incomparable city, to a people without match.

This Book

This is the 3rd edition of LP's *London* city guide and was written and updated by Steve Fallon. It also incorporates material written by Pat Yale for the 1st and 2nd editions.

From the Publisher

This edition of *London* was produced in Lonely Planet's London office. Heather Dickson was the coordinating editor and Ian Stokes handled the design and layout. Ed Pickard produced the maps with help from Rachel Beattie, Jimi Ellis, Liam Molloy, Jolyon Philcox and David Wenk. Abigail Hole and Jenny Lansbury helped with editing and proofreading. Annika Roojun designed the cover, James Timmins drew the climate chart and Lachlan Ross drew the back-cover map. Lonely Planet Images provided the photographs, and illustrations were drawn by Asa Andersson and Jane Smith.

Thanks to Amanda Canning and Paul Piaia for their expert advice.

Thanks

Many thanks to the travellers who used the last edition and contacted us with helpful hints, advice and interesting anecdotes:

Jennifer Alexander, Dave Allen, Kerry Barker, Antonella Barretos, Christian Bergner, Helen Bissland, Dirk Borowski, Douglas Broadbent, Edward Burke, Bee Chen, Ray Coe, Yochana Coleman, Beth Cooke, Diana Cotter, Mavis Coxon, Pete Cull, Nathan Bruyn, Emma De Souza, Gene Denison, Cathie Desjardins, Natalie Doherty, Patricia Dorrington, Hugh Elsol, Jennifer Ethington, Kirsty Ew, David Ewing, Jeff Gabello, Gary M Garfield, David Golshevsky, Chris Gossip, Meagan Graham, Ronalie Green, G Grimandi, Ben Guezentsvey, Sabine Haller, Susan M Haskell, T Henry, Gavin Hewitson, Edith Hofer, Paul Holt, Steffi Hombach, Harald Horvei, Jan Hruza, Sonya Hui, Doug Journeay, Max Kamenetsky, Mme Lemoine, Barbara Lewis, M Lovell, Bruce Lyon, John Mabon, Dr Paul Macnamara, Diane Matray, Carolina Miranda, Marie-Christine Munos, Doron Nof, Reeves Novak, Richard Nunns, Shona Otswald, Jane Perry, Stuart Pritchard, Habib Rathle, Mark Roddick, Ian David Row, Scott Ryan, Jeff Schildhorn, Kurt H Schindler, Edward Sim, Stephen Simon, Pauline Simpson, Frank Sitchler, Joan Smith, Rebecca Smith, Andy Sparrow, Shelly Spence, Judy Straalsund, Ka Lun Tam, Isabelle Terrier, Nigel Thornley, Niels Vrolijk, Michael W, Angela Walton, Monica Willett, Adele Wyers and Dan and Annette Youngberg.

Foreword

ABOUT LONELY PLANET GUIDEBOOKS

The story begins with a classic travel adventure: Tony and Maureen Wheeler's 1972 journey across Europe and Asia to Australia. There was no useful information about the overland trail then, so Tony and Maureen published the first Lonely Planet guidebook to meet a growing need.

From a kitchen table, Lonely Planet has grown to become the largest independent travel publisher in the world, with offices in Melbourne (Australia), Oakland (USA), London (UK) and Paris (France).

Today Lonely Planet guidebooks cover the globe. There is an ever-growing list of books and information in a variety of media. Some things haven't changed. The main aim is still to make it possible for adventurous travellers to get out there – to explore and better understand the world.

At Lonely Planet we believe travellers can make a positive contribution to the countries they visit – if they respect their host communities and spend their money wisely. Since 1986 a percentage of the income from each book has been donated to aid projects and human rights campaigns, and, more recently, to wildlife conservation.

Although inclusion in a guidebook usually implies a recommendation we cannot list every good place. Exclusion does not necessarily imply criticism. In fact there are a number of reasons why we might exclude a place – sometimes it is simply inappropriate to encourage an influx of travellers.

UPDATES & READER FEEDBACK

Things change – prices go up, schedules change, good places go bad and bad places go bankrupt. Nothing stays the same. So, if you find things better or worse, recently opened or long-since closed, please tell us and help make the next edition even more accurate and useful.

Lonely Planet thoroughly updates each guidebook as often as possible – usually every two years, although for some destinations the gap can be longer. Between editions, up-to-date information is available in our free, quarterly *Planet Talk* newsletter and monthly email bulletin *Comet*. The *Upgrades* section of our website (**w** www.lonelyplanet.com) is also regularly updated by Lonely Planet authors, and the site's *Scoop* section covers news and current affairs relevant to travellers. Lastly, the *Thorn Tree* bulletin board and *Postcards* section carry unverified, but fascinating, reports from travellers.

Tell us about it! We genuinely value your feedback. A well-travelled team at Lonely Planet reads and acknowledges every email and letter we receive and ensures that every morsel of information finds its way to the relevant authors, editors and cartographers.

Everyone who writes to us will find their name listed in the next edition of the appropriate guidebook, and will receive the latest issue of *Comet* or *Planet Talk*. The very best contributions will be rewarded with a free guidebook.

We may edit, reproduce and incorporate your comments in Lonely Planet products such as guidebooks, websites and digital products, so let us know if you don't want your comments reproduced or your name acknowledged.

How to contact Lonely Planet:
Online: **e** talk2us@lonelyplanet.com.au, **w** www.lonelyplanet.com
Australia: Locked Bag 1, Footscray, Victoria 3011
UK: 10a Spring Place, London NW5 3BH
USA: 150 Linden St, Oakland, CA 94607

Introduction

It's no exaggeration to say that London offers visitors more than any other city in Europe. Not only is it home to such familiar landmarks as Big Ben, St Paul's Cathedral, Tower Bridge, the timeless Thames and now the ever-present London Eye Ferris wheel, it also boasts some of the greatest museums and art galleries anywhere and more parkland than any other world capital. And the opportunities for entertainment after dark? From pubs and live music to theatre and dance, they go on and on and on again.

London is an amazingly tolerant place for its size, its people pretty much unflappable. 'As long as you don't scare the horses, mate, you'll be all right here,' as they say. It is also an increasingly multicultural city, with a quarter of all Londoners belonging to almost three dozen ethnic minorities, most of whom get along fairly well together. It is not hyperbole to suggest that visitors will encounter more mixed-race couples on the streets of central London in a single day than they will in a year in New York.

Of course, it's not *all* sweetness and light – never is (especially the latter). Mid-week afternoons in London seem to stretch on, from early November to sometime in March, with the cold and drizzly perma-darkness weighing down even more heavily as the months go by. The number of homeless people in the streets is not just a stain but an adulteration on the rich robes of this, Europe's richest city, and the gulf between very poor and super-affluent at times seems unbridgeable. The public transport system is an exhausting, debasing grind for most commuters, and when a yobbo in a car – radio on full blast, mobile glued to the ear, indicator controls untouched – nearly runs you over at a pedestrian crossing and you protest, he dissolves into road rage as only

London's beckoning charm and famous cityscape have lured visitors for centuries.

7

Londoners know it. And let's face facts: a city where most pubs and many restaurants close at a time when the rest of Europe is choosing its first course cannot claim to be the 'coolest city' in the world.

But then April – 'with his shoures', as Chaucer wrote – brings spring, turning the city's glorious open spaces into an Impressionist tapestry of indigo, gold and green. Shortly after your man the motorist threatens to 'punch your lights out' (ie, do untold damage to you), your fellow passengers on the Underground apologise to *you* for your having stepping on *their* toes or a shopkeeper abandons the till and leads you out to the pavement to give you more precise directions. And once you find one of the many clubs with extended licences, you will party like you've never partied before. Clubbing is not just a form of entertainment here but a career at which Londoners work very, very hard.

As much as anything else, London is the link that unites all of us who were rocked in the soft cradle of the English language or slept on its comfortable cushions for the first time at a later age. Our common language is the tie that binds an Irishman from Boston with a Bombay-wallah and a Chinese Vancouverite with a Jew from Sydney, and this is both our tongue's birthplace and its epicentre. And as the Internet and new developments in communications technology send English even farther afield, we'll be welcoming an increasing number of people 'home'.

London is not, and never will be, the 'museumland' that is Paris or a tidy, flower-bedecked Amsterdam or the impossibly polite Berlin. Gritty and savvy, London exhilarates and intimidates, stimulates and irritates. It offers different things to different people and in abundance. Breathe deeply in this world-class city and – once the coughing fit subsides – you will have ingested enough history, culture, sleaze, joys and disappointments to last half a lifetime.

'London; a nation, not a city'
Benjamin Disraeli (*Lothair,* 1870)

Facts about London

HISTORY

London was settled by the Romans and the area, particularly the City of London, has been inhabited continuously ever since. As a result, archaeologists have had to dig deep to discover the city's past, relying more often than not on redevelopment to allow excavations. The building boom of the 1980s revealed an astonishing number of finds, and the practice continues.

In 1999 archaeologists from the Museum of London, excavating the area around Spitalfields Market prior to redevelopment, unearthed an unusual 4th-century stone sarcophagus containing a lead coffin and the remains of a wealthy young Roman woman, now on display in the Museum of London. The latest forensic tests for DNA and isotope analysis show that she came from the western Mediterranean but her final resting place was Roman London. A year later the remains of what is believed to have been a woman gladiator were found just outside the walled Roman cemetery near Southwark's Old Kent Rd,

the main thoroughfare in Roman London. It is thought that she died in combat at the Roman amphitheatre, which was discovered, in 1987, 6m below what is now Guildhall Yard in the City of London. And in the summer of 2001 archaeologists unearthed two outstanding Roman waterwheels beneath Gresham St in the City and close to the amphitheatre. The wheels, powered by a treadmill and capable of bringing some 227,500L of water to the surface each day via bucket chains, are to be reconstructed in the Museum of London.

The Celts & the Romans

Certain areas along the River Thames had already been occupied by the Iron Age however. The misleadingly named Caesar's Camp, an earthwork fort on Wimbledon Common, was probably constructed in the 3rd century BC by the Celts, who had arrived from Europe about 500 years before. A beautiful shield found in the Thames near Battersea Bridge (and now in the British Museum) also dates from that period.

ANGUS OBORN

Tower Bridge, a spectacular emblem of the city's architectural prowess, spans the River Thames.

The Celts settled round a ford in the Thames, which – being twice as wide as it is today – probably served as a barrier separating tribal groups. Under the Celts London failed to develop into a major centre such as Colchester (Camulodunum in Latin) had; for that London had to wait for the arrival of the Romans.

Armies of Romanised Gauls under Caesar's lead made short reconnaissance trips to the British Isles in 55 and 54 BC and presumably traded with the Celts, judging from the Roman artefacts found in Iron Age burial sites. But the Romans did not arrive in large numbers until almost a century later.

In AD 43, an invasion force led by Claudius established the port of Londinium, the first real settlement at what is now London, and used it as a springboard to capture the tribal centre of Camulodunum. They constructed a wooden bridge across the Thames near today's London Bridge, and this became the focal point for a network of roads fanning out around the region.

In AD 60 or 61, members of the Iceni tribe from what is now East Anglia were outraged when Roman soldiers, trying to expropriate their property, flogged their queen, Boudicca (or Boadicea), and raped her daughters. The Iceni overran what had now become the capital of Roman Britannia at Camulodunum and then turned south-west to Londinium, massacring the settlement's inhabitants and burning it to the ground. If you dig deep enough in London, they say, you'll find a layer of rubble and soft red ash dating from that great conflagration.

Because of the Thames' deep anchorage for their fleet and the relative ease in defending the area, the Romans rebuilt Londinium around Cornhill, the highest elevation north of the bridge, between AD 80 and 90 and wrapped a defensive wall some 2.7m thick and 6m high around it about a century later. Towers were then added to strengthen it. Excavations in the City have shown Londinium, a centre for business and trade but not a fully fledged *colonia* (settlement), to be an imposing city whose massive buildings included a basilica, an amphitheatre, a forum and the governor's palace.

By the middle of the 3rd century AD Londinium was almost as multicultural as modern London, with some 30,000 people of various ethnic groups (but all Roman citizens, of course) and temples dedicated to a large number of cults. When Roman Emperor Constantine converted to Christianity in 312, the fledgling religion became the Empire's – and London's – official cult, seeing off its rival Mithraism.

Mithras & the Great Sacrifice

Mithraism, the worship of the god Mithras, originated in Persia. As Roman rule extended into Asia, the religion became extremely popular with traders, Imperial slaves and mercenaries of the Roman army and spread rapidly throughout the Empire in the 2nd and 3rd centuries AD. It was the principal rival of Christianity until Constantine came to the throne in the 4th century.

Mithraism was a mysterious religion with devotees sworn to secrecy. What little is known of Mithras, the god of the sun, justice and social contract, has been deduced from reliefs and icons found in sanctuaries and temples, such as the temple in Queen Victoria St in the City of London, and on exhibit in the Museum of London. Most of these portray Mithras clad in a Persian-style cap and tunic, sacrificing a white bull. From the bull's blood and semen sprout grain, grapes and living creatures. The bull is then transformed into the god Soma, the moon, and time is born.

Mithraism and Christianity were close competitors partly because of the striking similarity in many of their rituals. Both involve the birth of a deity on 25 December, shepherds, death and resurrection, and a form of baptism. Devotees knelt when they worshipped and a common meal – a 'communion' of bread and water – was a regular feature of both liturgies.

ELLIOT DANIEL

Dig this: archaeologists continue to reveal ancient remains, such as the Temple of Mithras in the City.

The Saxons & the Danes

In the 4th century, the Roman Empire in Britain began to decline, with attacks by the Picts and Scots in the north and the Saxons, Teutonic tribes originating from north of the Rhine, in the south-east. In 410, when the embattled Emperor Honorius refused them military aid, the Romans abandoned Britain, and Londinium was reduced to a sparsely populated backwater. Little firm evidence from this period survives – there's no written record whatsoever of the town from 457 to 604 – although it is clear that Saxon settlers established farmsteads and small villages in the area during this time.

In the late 6th century, Ethelbert, king of the East Saxons (who controlled an area that included what was left of London), converted to Christianity. In the following years London received a new bishop from Rome and the first church to be built on the site of today's St Paul's Cathedral was erected in 604. Saxon settlement was predominantly outside the city walls to the west, towards what is now Aldwych and as far as Charing Cross. This infant community, called Lundenwic, appears to have traded with Frisia, France and the Rhineland, but as it grew in importance it attracted the attention of the Vikings from Denmark. They attacked in 842 and again nine years later, burning Lundenwic to the ground.

Under the leadership of King Alfred the Great of Wessex, the Saxon population fought back and the Danes were driven out. Alfred resettled the old Roman city, now known as Lundunburg or Lunduntown, farther east towards the River Lea, with a trading wharf at Billingsgate, and south of the Thames to Sudwerke (south work), today's Southwark.

Saxon London grew into a prosperous and well-organised town divided into 20 wards, each with its own alderman, and resident colonies of German merchants and French vintners. But attacks by the Danes continued apace and the Saxon leadership was weakening; in 1016 Londoners were forced to accept the Danish leader Canute (Cnut) as king of England. With the death of Canute's son Harold in 1042, the throne passed to the Saxon Edward the Confessor, who went on to found an abbey and palace at Westminster on what was then an island at the mouth of the River Tyburn (see the boxed text 'London's Underground Rivers' later in this chapter). When Edward moved his court to Westminster, a division of the city's labour began that would continue to our day: the port became the trading and mercantile centre of London, with Westminster its seat of justice and administration.

The Normans

By the turn of the first millennium, the Vikings, who were also known as the Norsemen or Normans, were in control of much of the north and west of today's France. In 1066 they mounted a successful invasion – the so-called Norman Conquest – of England under the leadership of William, the duke of Normandy.

After the watershed Battle of Hastings, London at first held out against William, but when all of south-eastern England capitulated, London followed suit and William the Conqueror was crowned king on Christmas Day in Westminster Abbey, which had been consecrated less than a year before.

William found himself in control of a city that was by far the largest, richest and most powerful in the Saxon kingdom. He distrusted the 'vast and fierce populace' of London and built several strongholds, including the White Tower, the core of the Tower of London, but he also confirmed the city's independence and its right to self-government.

Medieval London

In 1154 Stephen, the last of the Norman kings, died and the throne passed to Henry II of the powerful House of Plantagenet, which would rule England for the next two and a half centuries. According to an account written by the monk William Fitz Stephen, London was a 'flourishing city a prey to frequent fires' (in 1087 fire had consumed the third St Paul's Cathedral).

Always short of a penny, Henry's successors were happy to let the City of London keep its independence so long as its merchants continued to finance their wars or building projects. When Richard I (known as 'the Lionheart') needed funds for his crusade, he recognised the city as a self-governing commune in return for cash. The City's first mayor, Henry Fitz Aylwin, was elected sometime around 1190.

In 1215, Richard's successor, John (nicknamed 'John Lackland' because he'd lost Normandy and almost all the other English possessions in France), was forced to cede some say in government to the powerful barons he had alienated and to cease making excessive demands for money without their consent. Among those pressing him to seal (he did not *sign*) the Magna Carta at Runnymede was the powerful mayor of the City of London, the privileges of which were also guaranteed.

Old London Bridge and the fourth St Paul's were built in stone towards the end of the 12th century. The descendants of the Runnymede barons built themselves sturdy houses with riverside gardens along what is now the Strand linking Westminster to the City. The area flourished on trading wine, furs, cloth and other goods with Europe.

By this time, the population of London was 40,000 and the Palace of Westminster was firmly established as the centre of royal power. In 1295 a model parliament with representatives of the barons, clergy and knights and burgesses had met for the first time in Westminster Hall, but by the 14th century the embryonic House of Lords was meeting in the Palace of Westminster and the House of Commons in the Westminster Abbey Chapter House. To raise more revenue the Crown levied taxes on City merchants and moneylenders, notably the Jews, in exchange for its 'protection'. When the kingdom's entire Jewish population was expelled in 1290, the king turned to the Italian bankers who had followed them and had based themselves on and around today's Lombard St in the City.

Though fire was a constant threat in the cramped and narrow houses and lanes of 14th-century London, disease – exacerbated by unsanitary living conditions and the impurity of drinking water carried up from the Thames – posed a greater risk. In 1348, rats carrying the bubonic plague unleashed a Black Death that left between a third and a half of the total population (around 100,000 at the time) dead within a year.

Along with fire and disease there was the danger of violence, with tradesmen fighting over turf or wages. In 1381, when the king tried to impose a poll tax on everyone in the realm, the soldier Wat Tyler and the priest Jack Straw led a horde of some 60,000 peasants from Essex and Kent to London. Several ministers were murdered and many buildings, including John of Gaunt's grand Savoy Palace on the Strand, were razed before the so-called Peasants' Revolt ended. Tyler himself was stabbed to death by the mayor; Straw was beheaded at Smithfield.

London gained wealth and stature under the Houses of Lancaster and York in the 15th century, which saw an increase in the power of craft guilds known as livery companies (see the boxed text 'The City's Livery Companies' in the Things to See & Do chapter), the tenure of the charitable mayor Dick Whittington and the arrival of the first printing press in England, set up by William Caxton at Westminster in 1476 (and moved to Fleet St after his death 15 years later). It was also a time of much political intrigue.

In 1483 12-year-old Edward V of the House of York reigned for only two months before vanishing with his younger brother into the Tower of London, never to be seen or heard from again. Whether or not Richard III, the boys' uncle and the next king, had them murdered has been the subject of much conjecture over the centuries. (In 1674 workers found a chest containing the skeletons of two children near the White Tower, which were assumed to be the princes' remains and were reburied in Innocents' Corner in Westminster Abbey.) Few tears were shed, however, when Richard himself was deposed from the throne by Henry Tudor, first of the dynasty of that name, at the end of the 15th century.

Tudor London

By the time Henry Tudor was crowned Henry VII in 1485, London was the largest and wealthiest town in England. During Henry's reign commerce continued to flourish (the trade in wool was a mainstay of the economy) and the population started

---

A Boy, a Puss & City Hall

Ken Livingstone, London's mayor since May 2000, may be enjoying a certain popularity as he does battle with the national government over how to modernise the city's transport, but he's yet to gain anything like the same respect and affection Londoners had (and still have) for his 15th-century predecessor, Dick Whittington.

Legend tells us that Dick was a country lad who came to the city to seek his fortune with his faithful feline in tow. Soon disillusioned with the Big Smoke, he was about to turn back when he heard the bells of St Mary-le-Bow ringing out the message 'Turn again, Whittington, thrice mayor of London'. Dick did just that and went on to find fame and fortune. A 19th-century stone on Highgate Hill, at the point where he is said to have heard the bells, features a bronze cat and makes reference to the 'thrice' mayor 'Sir' Richard Whittington.

It's a nice story but almost entirely inaccurate or just plain untrue. Dick Whittington was the third son of an affluent Gloucestershire family who arrived in London in a 'cat', as coastal boats were then called. He may indeed have heard those bells but they told lies too: he was in fact mayor *four* times between 1397 and 1419. Oh, and Dick was never knighted.

ASA ANDERSSON

GUY MOBERLY

Fit for a king: glorious Hampton Court Palace caught the envious eye of Henry VIII.

to rise again, reaching some 75,000. Most manufacturing industry was concentrated south of the River Thames in Southwark and Bermondsey.

Between 1536 and 1540, Henry's son and successor, Henry VIII, dissolved London's monasteries and priories during his quarrel with the pope over his right to divorce his queen, Catherine of Aragon, and marry Anne Boleyn, although this move had as much to do with getting his hands on the Church's tax-free property (church revenue at the time went directly to Rome). Some 50 London churches and monastic buildings were shut – some became warehouses, hospitals or private houses, while others were demolished. Church plate was expropriated by the king – most of it melted down and refashioned – and Church land was requisitioned as royal hunting ground.

The peripatetic Henry VIII lived in dozens of palaces during his 38-year reign but spent much of his time at Richmond, Whitehall, Greenwich and Nonsuch palaces – the last a castle 'without compare' (it was originally called 'Nonesuch') near today's Cheam in Surrey, south-west of central

London. When his lord chancellor, Cardinal Thomas Wolsey, had the temerity to build himself a grand palace at Hampton Court that caught Henry's eye, he was cajoled into gifting it to the king. This did not prevent Henry from charging Wolsey with high treason in 1529 because of his opposition to Henry's divorce. (Wolsey died the following year, before the trial could commence.) Keen on public display, Henry brought skilled craftsmen from Europe to decorate his palaces; Leeds Castle in Kent and parts of Hampton Court Palace are superb examples that survive to this day.

Because of his propensity for settling differences with the axe (two of his six wives – Anne Boleyn and Catherine Howard – as well as Wolsey's replacement as lord chancellor, Thomas More, were all beheaded) and his persecution of both Catholics and those of his fellow Protestants who maintained his changes had not gone far enough, Henry VIII gets a very bad press. But he was responsible for building most of today's St Bartholomew's Hospital and the docks at Woolwich and Deptford, and for establishing the Royal

Navy. He remained a popular monarch until his death in 1547.

The reign of Mary I, Henry's daughter by Catherine of Aragon, saw an attempt to return England to the Catholic fold, although London seems to have been particularly unsympathetic to the return of Catholicism. Some 200 Protestants were

Monarchs & Rulers

The following table traces the royal lineage from its beginnings to the present day and gives the length of rule of monarchs and rulers.

Saxon & Danish Kings
Alfred the Great 871–99
Edward 899–924
Athelstan 924–39
Edmund 939–46
Edred 946–55
Edwy 955–59
Edgar 959–75
Edward the Martyr 975–79
Ethelred (the Unready) 979–1016
Canute (Cnut) 1016–35
Harold I 1037–40
Harthacnut 1040–2
Edward the Confessor 1042–66
Harold II 1066

Normans
William I (the Conqueror) 1066–87
William II (Rufus) 1087–1100
Henry I 1100–35
Stephen 1135–54

House of Plantagenet
Henry II 1154–89
Richard I (the Lionheart) 1189–99
John 1199–1216
Henry III 1216–72
Edward I 1272–1307
Edward II 1307–27
Edward III 1327–77
Richard II 1377–99

House of Lancaster
Henry IV (Bolingbroke) 1399–1413
Henry V 1413–22
Henry VI 1422–61 & 1470–71

House of York
Edward IV 1461–70 & 1471–83
Edward V 1483
Richard III 1483–85

House of Tudor
Henry VII (Tudor) 1485–1509
Henry VIII 1509–47
Edward VI 1547–53
Mary I 1553–58
Elizabeth I 1558–1603

House of Stuart
James I 1603–25
Charles I 1625–49

Commonwealth & Protectorate
Oliver Cromwell 1649–58
Richard Cromwell 1658–59

House of Stuart (Restored)
Charles II 1660–85
James II 1685–88
William III (of Orange) 1689–1702 &
  Mary II 1689–94
Anne 1702–14

House of Hanover (Regent from 1811)
George I 1714–27
George II 1727–60
George III 1760–1820
George IV 1820–30
William IV 1830–37
Victoria 1837–1901

House of Saxe–Coburg–Gotha (Windsor from 1917)
Edward VII 1901–10
George V 1910–36
Edward VIII 1936
George VI 1936–52
Elizabeth II 1953–

FACTS ABOUT LONDON

burned at the stake at Smithfield. Though naturally humane, Mary sanctioned the persecutions and was therefore nicknamed 'Bloody Mary'.

By the time Elizabeth I, Henry VIII's daughter by Anne Boleyn, began her 45-year reign, the Catholic cause had effectively been lost and their persecution resumed, with hundreds carted off to the gallows at Tyburn. London began to expand physically (in the half-century up to 1600 the population doubled to 200,000) and economically, establishing itself as the premier world trade market with the opening of the Royal Exchange in 1572.

It was also a time of literary renaissance, especially in theatre, with the works of William Shakespeare, Christopher Marlowe and Ben Jonson staged at new playhouses such as the Rose (built in 1587) and the Globe (1599). Both of these were built in Southwark, which was outside the jurisdiction of the City and notorious for its brothels, bear-baiting and prisons. The first recorded map of London was published in 1558, and John Stow produced *A Survey of London*, the first history of the city, in 1598.

Early-Stuart London & the Civil War

When Elizabeth died without an heir in 1603, she was succeeded by her second cousin, James VI of Scotland, who was crowned James I of England. James was the son of the Catholic Mary Queen of Scots but when he was slow to improve conditions for England's Catholics, Guy Fawkes and his co-conspirators concocted an unsuccessful plot to blow up the Houses of Parliament on 5 November 1605 – an event still marked annually throughout Britain with bonfires and fireworks. Public outrage saw to it that London remained firmly in the Protestant camp.

James was succeeded by Charles I in 1625, and a period of great animosity began between the Crown and Parliament. After Charles had recalled the dissolved Parliament, following a recess of 11 years, he attempted to arrest five antagonistic Members of Parliament (MPs) who fled to the City. The Puritans, extremist Protestants who wanted to rid the Church of England of any vestiges of Roman Catholic ritual, and the City's expanding merchant class (who had everything to gain) threw their support

Burnt offerings: the Great Fire of London started in a bakery on Pudding Lane in 1666.

Oliver Cromwell ruled with a rod of iron and ordered Charles I's execution in 1649.

behind Oliver Cromwell and the Parliamentarians (the so-called Roundheads) in the ensuing Civil War. Charles surrendered in 1646 and was beheaded outside Banqueting Hall in Whitehall three years later.

After Charles' execution, the Commonwealth held sway for over a decade (1649–60), during which time the Puritans closed down theatres and rampaged through churches, smashing stained glass and destroying anything they regarded as idolatrous. As Lord Protector, Cromwell took up residence in Whitehall but his popularity was short-lived. In 1660 Parliament invited Charles I's son to reclaim the throne, and Charles II was reinstated at the Royal Exchange.

Plague & Fire

In mid-17th-century London, the shout 'garde loo' alerted all passers-by that a chamberpot was about to be emptied into the street from an upstairs window. Crowded, filthy London had suffered from recurrent outbreaks of bubonic plague since the 14th century, but nothing had prepared it for the Great Plague of 1665, in which around 100,000 people died.

The beginning of the end of the plague in London was spurred by another disaster that proved to be a watershed in the city's physical development. On 2 September 1666 a fire broke out at a bakery in Pudding Lane in the City. At first it was regarded as a local fire and the lord mayor himself dismissed it as 'something a woman might pisse out' before going back to bed. But the hot, dry conditions that summer and rising winds fanned the flames and it soon raged out of control. Samuel Pepys, who watched the blaze from the steeple of All Hallows-by-the-Tower, provided a wonderful eyewitness account of the conflagration in his diary. It was, he proclaimed, 'the saddest sight of desolation' though he was 'afeared to stay there long'.

By the time the fire was finally brought under control four days later, some 80% of London had burned to the ground. But though damage to property was great – 88 churches, including St Paul's, the halls of 44 livery companies and 13,000 houses had

Wren's Churches

After the Great Fire of 1666 had destroyed 88 of London's churches, Sir Christopher Wren (1632–1723) was commissioned to rebuild 51 of them, as well as to create a new St Paul's Cathedral. The money for the work was raised by putting a tax on all the coal imported through the Port of London. Perhaps the most striking features of Wren's new designs were the graceful Renaissance steeples that were to take the place of the solid square towers of the previous medieval churches.

Wren later built another three churches in London, but some 19 of his churches have been destroyed since 1781. For a partial list of some of the surviving churches and their locations, see Maps 6 & 9. For more details check **w** www.london-city-churches.org.uk.

been destroyed – only eight people died in the fire.

The fire removed almost all traces of medieval, Tudor and Jacobean London in less than a week, but it did have two long-lasting benefits. First, it finally cleansed the city of plague; and second, it gave architects such as Sir Christopher Wren the chance to redesign a modern city. Wren had his plans for a new London ready within a week of the fire, but with no powers of compulsory purchase it proved impossible to force reluctant landowners to give city planners leeway.

A special Fire Court composed of 22 judges was established to settle disputes over property, and by 1671 some 9000 houses – around 70% of those destroyed – had been rebuilt, this time of stone and brick instead of combustible wood, pitch and plaster. Wider streets were paved for the first time, and large open squares ensured it would be harder for any future fire to spread so easily. The fire also accelerated the movement of the wealthy away from the City and into what is now the West End. In 1710 the present St Paul's Cathedral, Wren's masterpiece, opened as the crowning moment of the 'Great Rebuilding'.

Restoration London

With the work almost complete, including a great column topped with a golden blaze of flames commemorating the conflagration raised in 1677 – the so-called Monument – London again turned to trade and manufacturing, which began attracting much-needed workers from other parts of the British Isles and abroad. In 1685, after Louis XIV of France revoked the Edict of Nantes, which had granted freedom of worship to French Protestants for almost a century, some 1500 Huguenot refugees arrived in London, most of them quickly turning their hand to the manufacture of luxury goods – including clocks and watches, silks and silverware – in and around Spitalfields. Italian artisans flocked to the area around Clerkenwell.

In 1688 the Glorious – ie, bloodless – Revolution brought the Dutch king William of Orange to the English throne with his wife Mary, daughter of the very same James II whom the couple had deposed. When William's asthma was badly affected by the proximity of Whitehall Palace to the Thames, they moved into a house in Kensington Gardens and had it converted into a new palace. In 1694 William's need to raise loans to wage war with France led to the creation of the Bank of England, backed by the security of the state and an institution for which London merchants had long been clamouring.

By 1700 London was Europe's largest city, with some 600,000 inhabitants. The influx of foreign workers brought expansion to the east and the south, while the more affluent headed for the north and the west to escape the pollution, disease and violence of innercity life. These divisions remain more or less in place in 21st-century London.

Georgian London

William and Mary had no heir and were succeeded by Mary's sister Anne. Although she had 17 pregnancies only one of Anne's children survived and then not to adulthood. Since the 1701 Act of Settlement forbade a Roman Catholic to ascend the throne, the hunt was on for any Protestant relative suitable for the crown when Anne died in 1714. Eventually the search produced one George of Hanover, who arrived in London speaking no English.

London was increasingly becoming a financial rather than a commercial centre, with all the gains and losses that that role carries. Sure enough, it had its first major financial disaster in 1720, an incident known as the South Sea Bubble, when an orgy of speculation in a company set up to trade with South America ended with its collapse

SIMON BRACKEN

Majestic Kensington Palace has been the fancy of many royals, including William of Orange.

and the ruination of thousands. It was only through the intervention of Robert Walpole, George I's prime minister and the first resident of 10 Downing St, that the government was saved.

At the same time London was becoming ever more segregated and lawless; indeed, contemporary newspapers suggest it was the most crime-ridden city in Europe, and even George II was mugged in the gardens of Kensington Palace by a robber who, 'with a manner of much deference, deprived the King of his purse, watch and buckles'.

This was the London of the artist William Hogarth (see the boxed text 'Of Rakes & Harlots: Hogarth's World' later in this chapter), in which the wealthy built fine new houses in attractive squares while the poor huddled together in appalling slums, downing an average of two pints of gin a week per person. Dram shops enticed them with signs such as 'Drunk for a penny, dead drunk for twopence', while the wealthy sipped a curious new drink from Turkey at coffee-houses such as the Jamaica (now a pub called the Jamaica Wine House) in St Michael's Alley in the City. The advent of street lighting helped reduce crime but, more importantly, in 1751 two magistrates at Bow formed a private police force of a half-dozen 'thief-takers'. The 'Bow Street Runners' would become the capital's first effective police force (though the Metropolitan Police force didn't come into existence until 1829).

Until Westminster Bridge opened in 1750, the horse ferry between Lambeth and Millbank was the only crossing on the Thames apart from London Bridge, not counting the water 'taxis' whose rowers would attract customers with the shout 'Oars? Oars?' (According to contemporary accounts, some visitors from the countryside mistook this for an offer of more carnal services.) But as the population grew, so did the pressure to make it easier to move around. The bulging, higgledy-piggledy shops and houses on the old London Bridge, which severely restricted the movement of traffic from one bank to the other, were torn down, as was much of the medieval city wall and the gates that led into it; these days the latter survive only in place names such as Bishopsgate, Broadgate, Aldgate and Ludgate.

In 1780 Parliament proposed lifting the law that prevented Catholics from buying or inheriting property, but one MP, the demented Lord George Gordon, led a 'No Popery' demonstration that turned into the so-called Gordon Riots, when a furious mob of at least 30,000 burned Newgate and Clink prisons, 'Papishe dens' (ie, chapels) and several law courts. Between 300 and 850 people died during the riots, including at least 20 who drank themselves to death after breaking into a distillery in Holborn.

As George III descended into dementia towards the end of the 18th century, his son, the Prince Regent, set up an alternative and considerably more fashionable court at Carlton House in Pall Mall. When George III died in 1820, his son attempted to divorce his wife Caroline on the grounds of adultery, only to have her try to force her way into his coronation at Westminster Abbey. The public generally sided with the queen, but she died shortly afterwards and her funeral sparked street riots.

Georgian London saw a great surge in creativity in music, art and architecture. Court composer George Frideric Handel wrote his *Water Music* (1717) and *The Messiah* (1742) while living in London, and in 1755 Dr Johnson produced the first dictionary of the English language. Hogarth, Gainsborough and Reynolds were producing some of their finest engravings and paintings, and many of London's most elegant buildings, streets and squares were being erected or laid out by the likes of John Soane, his pupil Robert Smirke and the incomparable John Nash.

Victorian London

In 1837 the 18-year-old Victoria ascended the throne. During her long reign London would become the nerve centre of the largest and richest empire the world had ever known, covering a quarter of the world's surface area and ruling more than 500 million people. New docks were built

NEIL SETCHFIELD

The striking Clock Tower (aka Big Ben) first rang in the New Year in 1924.

to meet the needs of the booming trade with the colonies and, as congestion in the capital worsened, railways began to fan out from London, linking it with all the major cities by 1850. The world's first underground railway opened between Paddington and Farringdon Rd in 1863 and was such a success that other lines followed in quick succession.

The development of London's infrastructure continued apace; the year 1843 saw the opening of the first tunnel under the Thames (from Shadwell to Rotherhithe). And while his name may not be instantly recognisable, London owes more than it realises to Sir Joseph Bazalgette, who modernised the city's sewage system, shored up the river banks on the southern side and built some of London's finest bridges. Many of London's most famous buildings and landmarks were also built at this time: the Clock Tower at the Houses of Parliament known as Big Ben (1859), the Royal Albert Hall (1871) and Tower Bridge (1894).

As a result of the Industrial Revolution and rapidly expanding trade and commerce, the population of London jumped from just under one million in 1801 (the year of the first national census) to 6.5 million a century later. The result was the steady growth of both sprawling innercity slums for the poor and leafy suburbs for the affluent.

Though the Victorian age is chiefly seen as one of great Imperial power founded on industry, trade and commerce, intellectual achievement in the arts and sciences was enormous. The greatest chronicler of Victorian London was Charles Dickens, whose *Oliver Twist* (1837) and other works took as their themes the poverty, hopelessness and squalor of working-class London. In 1859 Charles Darwin published his seminal and immensely controversial *On the Origin of Species* here.

Some of the UK's most capable prime ministers served during the course of Victoria's 64-year-long reign, including William Gladstone (four terms between 1868 and 1894) and Benjamin Disraeli (who served in 1868 and again from 1874 to 1880).

Queen Victoria – she of 'We are not amused' fame – is often seen as a dour, humourless old curmudgeon but was in fact a highly intelligent, progressive and passionate woman. She lived to celebrate her Diamond Jubilee in 1897, but died four years later aged 81 and was laid to rest in Windsor. In retrospect, the reign and achievements of this remarkable woman can be seen as the climax of British world supremacy.

Edwardian London & WWI

Victoria's dissolute son Edward, the Prince of Wales, was already 60 by the time he was crowned Edward VII in 1901. By now change was occurring in London at breakneck speed. With the creation of the London County Council (LCC) in 1889, London had its first-ever directly elected government. The first motor buses went into service in 1904 and, within seven years, they had completely replaced the horse-drawn omnibuses introduced in 1829. Edwardian London saw a legion of new luxury hotels (such as The Ritz in 1906) and department stores (such as Selfridges in 1909) open their doors.

What became known as the Great War broke out in August 1914 and the first Zeppelin bombs fell near the Guildhall a year later, killing 39 people. Planes were soon dropping bombs on the capital, killing in all some 650 people (half the national total of civilian casualties). Tragic as these deaths were, however, they were but a drop in the ocean compared with the carnage that would follow a generation later during the Blitz of WWII.

The Interwar Period

After the war ended in 1918, London's population started to rise again, reaching nearly 7.5 million in 1921. Universal franchise was extended to all men over the age of 21 and to women over 30 (lowered to 21 in 1928). The LCC started clearing the slums and creating new housing estates, while the suburbs spread ever deeper into the countryside. Unemployment was rising steadily, and May 1926 saw a wage dispute in the coal industry erupt into the nine-day General Strike, in which so many workers downed tools that London virtually ground to a halt and the army was called in to keep the buses and Underground running, and to maintain order. This heavy-handed action set the stage for the labour unrest that would plague the UK for the next half-century.

The 1920s were the heyday of the so-called Bloomsbury Group, among them the writers Virginia Woolf and Lytton Strachey and the economist John Maynard Keynes, but in the next decade the centre of London's intellectual life shifted westwards to Fitzrovia, where George Orwell, Thornton Wilder, Dylan Thomas and Cyril Connolly lived and/or clinked glasses at the Fitzroy

---

Prince Albert & the Great Exhibition

In 1851 Victoria's beloved consort, the German-born Prince Albert, organised a huge celebration of new technology from around the world in Hyde Park. The so-called Great Exhibition was held in a 7.5-hectare iron-and-glass hothouse, a 'Crystal Palace' designed by gardener and architect Joseph Paxton. Some two million people flocked from throughout the country and abroad to marvel at the more than 100,000 exhibits; the Great Exhibition was also where, among other things, croquet – 'the world's most vicious game' as it's been called – was played for the first time. So successful was this first world fair that Albert arranged for the profits to be ploughed into building two permanent exhibitions, which eventually became the Science Museum and the Victoria & Albert Museum. The original (and revolutionary) structure itself was moved to Sydenham, where it burned down in 1936, but the area in south-east London – and its popular football club – retain the name. Exactly 10 years after the exhibition the 42-year-old prince died of typhoid and the queen was so prostrate with grief that she wore mourning clothes until her death in 1901.

Tavern in Charlotte St. This was the great age of cinema and radio, and the British Broadcasting Corporation (BBC), which had been established in 1922, broadcast the first television programme from Alexandra Park 14 years later.

The world economic slump of the late 1920s ushered in a decade of misery and political upheaval. Even the royal family took a knock when Edward VIII abdicated in 1936 to marry a woman who was not only twice divorced but – egad! – an American. The less-than-charismatic George VI succeeded his brother Edward. The scandal hinted at the prolonged trial by media that the royal family would start to undergo some 50 years later.

In the same year as the abdication Oswald Mosley attempted to lead the British Union of Fascists on an anti-Jewish march of Blackshirts from the Tower of London through the East End. In Cable St he was repulsed by a mob of around half a million. By 1938 the German threat looked sufficiently alarming for the city's children to be evacuated to the north and west of London.

WWII & the Blitz

In September 1939 WWII broke out when Germany invaded Poland, with which the UK was allied. The first year was one of anxious waiting; although over 600,000 women and children had been evacuated from London and 1600 members of Clerkenwell's Italian community had been interned as aliens, no bombs fell to disturb the blackout. But on 7 September 1940 this 'Phoney War' came to a swift and brutal end when German planes dropped hundreds of bombs on the East End, killing 430 people and injuring over three times that number.

This *Blitzkrieg* (German for 'lightning war'), or 'Blitz', continued for 57 nights, and the Underground was turned into a giant bomb-shelter. For six months after that bombs continued to rain down, if less frequently. Westminster Abbey, Buckingham Palace, St Paul's Cathedral, the Guildhall, Broadcasting House and innumerable City churches were all hit, some of them completely destroyed. The air raids finally

stopped in May 1941, only to start up again in January 1944 when pilotless V-1s – popularly known as doodlebugs – began to fly overhead, slyly dropping their bombs when their humming engines stopped. London then became the target of some 500 V-2s, the first long-range ballistic missiles.

When Nazi Germany capitulated in May 1945, up to a third of the East End and the City had been flattened, including a 16-hectare site where the Barbican complex now stands. In all, almost 32,000 Londoners had been killed and a further 50,000 seriously wounded. It was during these appalling times that Queen Elizabeth (now the Queen Mother) ventured out of the partially bombed Buckingham Palace to inspect the ravaged streets and earned the enduring admiration of Londoners when she said: 'I'm glad we've been bombed – now I can look the East End directly in the face.'

Winston Churchill, prime minister from 1940, orchestrated much of the nation's war strategy from the Cabinet War Rooms deep below Whitehall and it was from here that he made such stirring wartime speeches as the one later that year at the height of the Battle of Britain that concluded: 'Never in the field of human conflict was so much owed by so many to so few.'

Postwar London

After the war, low-cost developments and ugly high-rise housing were thrown up on bomb sites in Pimlico, the East End and Roehampton, and the character of the city began to change as immigrants from the West Indies and the Indian subcontinent arrived in London. Notting Hill, Ladbroke Grove and Brixton acquired a Caribbean feel, Southall became markedly Sikh and the old Jewish East End vanished as Jews moved north to Golders Green and were replaced by Bengalis. Finsbury saw an influx of Cypriots; Chinese from Hong Kong settled in Soho.

The Festival of Britain took place in London in 1951 both to recall the Great Exhibition 100 years before and to boost postwar morale. Its only permanent legacy is the ugly concrete arts buildings of the South

CHARLOTTE HINDLE

Launched in 1938, the powerful cruiser HMS *Belfast* saw extensive action during WWII.

Bank. Rationing of most goods ended in 1953, the year of Elizabeth II's coronation. The first civil flight left Heathrow airport in 1946 and the first red double-deck Routemaster bus appeared on the streets in 1956.

During the 1960s, 'Swinging London' was very much the place to be, with flamboyantly dressed young people flocking to Carnaby St and the King's Rd, bringing colour and vitality to the streets, The Beatles recording in Abbey Rd in north London, and The Rolling Stones playing for free before 500,000 fans in Hyde Park. In 1965 London's local government was reformed as the Greater London Council (GLC), whose jurisdiction covered a much wider area than the LCC's.

Even during the harsher 1970s and early '80s London was spared much of the economic hardship experienced by northern England and Scotland, although the docks never recovered from the loss of the Empire, the changing needs of modern container ships and poor labour relations, disappearing altogether between 1968 and 1981. Shipping moved 26 miles east to

Tilbury, and the Docklands declined to a point of decay, only to be rediscovered by property developers in the 1980s.

The 1970s was a nondescript decade squeezed in between the rampant optimism of the 1960s and the disastrous recession of the early '80s. In 1973 a bomb went off at the Old Bailey (the Central Criminal Court), signalling the arrival on English soil of the IRA's (Irish Republican Army's) campaign for a united Ireland. But the mid-1970s were at least brightened up by the spike-haired punks, pogoing their way to fame at clubs such as the Marquee on Charing Cross Rd.

The Thatcher Years

In 1979 the Conservative (or Tory) leader Margaret Thatcher became the UK's first female prime minister. Her monetarist policy soon sent unemployment skyrocketing; an enquiry following the Brixton riots of 1981 found that an astonishing 55% of men aged under 19 in that part of London were jobless. Riots flared in Tottenham in 1985, and again unemployment and heavy-handed policing were seen as contributing factors.

Meanwhile, the GLC, under the leadership of Ken Livingstone, fought a spirited campaign to bring down the price of public transport in London. Thatcher responded by abolishing the GLC in 1986, which would not see the light of day again for 14 years (see the Government & Politics section later in this chapter for more information).

While poorer Londoners suffered under Thatcher's assault on socialism, things had rarely looked better for the business community. Riding on a wave of confidence partly engendered by the deregulation of the Stock Exchange in 1986 (the so-called Big Bang), London underwent explosive economic growth in the latter part of the decade. New property developers proved to be only marginally more discriminating than the Luftwaffe during WWII, though some outstanding modern structures, including the Lloyd's of London building (see the special section 'London's Contemporary Architecture'), went up amid all the other rubbish.

Like previous booms, the one of the late 1980s proved unsustainable. As unemployment started to rise again and people found themselves living in houses worth much less than what they had paid for them, Thatcher introduced a flat-rate poll tax. Protests all round the country culminated in a march on Trafalgar Square, ending in a fully fledged riot in 1990. Shortly afterwards Canary Wharf, the flagship of the much-hyped Docklands redevelopment scheme, went into receivership. Thatcher was sent packing and John Major was named prime minister.

The 1990s

In 1992 the Conservatives were elected for a fourth successive term in government. Unfortunately for them, the economy went into a tailspin shortly thereafter, and the UK was forced to withdraw from the European Exchange Rate Mechanism (ERM), a humiliation from which it was impossible for the government to recover. To add to the government's troubles, the IRA exploded two huge bombs, one in the City in 1992 and another in the Docklands four years later, killing several people and damaging millions of pounds' worth of property.

The May 1997 general election returned a Labour government to power for the first time in 18 years, but it was a much changed 'New Labour' party, one that had shed most of its socialist credo and supported a market economy, privatisation and integration with Europe. Although Tony Blair and his government came under much criticism in the media soon after coming to power for what was seen as their 'third way revisionism' and their failure to deliver on election promises, the capital's booming economy and low unemployment, a feeble and divided opposition and the charisma and statesmanship (particularly on the world stage) of the prime minister himself kept Labour high in the popularity polls among Londoners.

The New Millennium

At the start of the third millennium London was without a doubt headier and more confident than it had been at any time since the 1960s. The year 2000 was ushered in by a 'wall of fire' – the biggest fireworks display

PAUL KENNEDY

Wheel of fortune: at over 135m high the London Eye offers impressive city views.

the city had ever seen – on the Thames, though sadly it turned out to be a bit of a letdown, with only some of the jets shooting up flames and few spectators able to see it. Throughout the year a pride of new and improved buildings and attractions opened – from the British Airways (BA) London Eye and the Tate Modern to the Great Court at the British Museum – and in May Ken Livingstone returned to head up the newly created Greater London Authority (GLA).

But pink elephants turned white throughout the year and for many Londoners the millennium was a damp squib. The much-touted and enormously expensive Millennium Dome pulled in visitors but attracted nowhere near the number expected and closed – abandoned but hardly forgotten – a year later; the Millennium Bridge linking Bankside and the City was closed to pedestrian traffic two days after its debut due to structural problems.

As universally predicted, Prime Minister Tony Blair was re-elected in June 2001, with Labour scoring 42% of the vote against the Conservative Party's paltry 31%. Charisma-challenged William Hague resigned as Tory leader immediately, leaving behind a party deeply divided and in disarray; it was not until late September that the party-wide electorate chose their new head, right-wing Euro-sceptic Iain Duncan Smith, former shadow defence secretary. Blair's victory was a boost for a city that had given him their overwhelming support. However, a virtual collapse of the Underground, the disastrous effect the countrywide foot-and-mouth epidemic had on tourism in London, renewed IRA bombings in Shepherd's Bush in March and in Ealing in August, and some of the hottest temperatures on record this century had many Londoners yearning for the 'summer of discontent' to come to an end.

GEOGRAPHY

The 607 sq miles of Greater London that are enclosed by the M25 ring road lie in the south-east of England on the River Thames (see the special section 'The River Thames'), which divides the city into its northern and southern halves.

London's Underground Rivers

The Thames is not London's only river: many have been culverted over the centuries and now course underground. Some survive only in place names: the Fleet, Hole Bourne, Wells, Tyburn, Walbrook and Westbourne, which was dammed up in 1730 to form the Serpentine in Hyde Park. The most famous of all, the Fleet, rises in Hampstead and Kenwood ponds and flows southwards through Camden Town, King's Cross, Farringdon Rd and New Bridge St, where it empties into the Thames at Blackfriars Bridge. It had been used as an open sewer and as a dumping area for entrails by butchers for centuries; the Elizabethan playwright Ben Jonson describes a voyage on the Fleet on a hot summer's night in which every stroke of the oars 'belch'd forth an ayre as hot as the muster of all your night-tubs discharging their merd-urinous load'. After the Great Fire, Christopher Wren oversaw the deepening and widening of the Fleet into a canal, but this was covered over in 1733 and the rest of the river three decades later.

London is divided into 33 widely differing boroughs (13 of them in central London), which are run by local councils with significant autonomy. The 'square mile' of the City of London at the heart of the conurbation is known simply as 'the City' and is counted as a borough. Boroughs are subdivided into districts, which generally tally with the first group of letters and numbers of the postcode (see the boxed text 'London's Bewildering Postcodes' in the Facts for the Visitor chapter). The richest borough in terms of per capita income is Richmond in the west, the poorest is Barking in the east.

Districts and postcodes often appear on street signs and are quoted when giving directions; this is vital since names are frequently duplicated (there are 48 Station Rds, for example, and almost as many Park Rds) or cross through a number of different districts. To further confuse visitors, many streets change name (Holland Park Ave becomes Notting Hill Gate, which turns into Bayswater Rd before becoming Oxford St) or duck and weave like the country lanes they once were. Street numbering can also be bewildering: in large streets the numbers on opposite sides can be way out of kilter – 315 might be opposite 520 – or go up one side and down the other.

At the same time some London suburbs well within the M25 don't even give London as a part of their addresses and don't use London postcodes. Instead they're considered part of a county – perhaps Surrey, which still exists, or Middlesex, which was absorbed into Greater London in 1965.

GEOLOGY

The chalk basin upon which London sits is filled with the famous London clay, a stiff, grey-blue muck reaching up to 130m in depth that supports most of the city's tunnels and deeper foundations. Topping the subsoil are rock and pebbles, gravel and brick earth, a mix of clay and sand that is often excavated for building material. The legacy of centuries of continuous human habitation can be seen in deposits averaging 5.5m to 6.5m in the oldest parts of the City and Westminster.

CLIMATE

The old adage that 'London doesn't have a climate, it has weather' refers to the fickleness of the atmospheric conditions in this part of the world. Plan a picnic in a park in the morning and it will be raining by noon; go to a film to escape a wet and dreary afternoon, and you'll emerge to bright sunshine in a blue cloudless sky. You just never know.

But London does have a climate – in fact, among the mildest in England – known as temperate maritime, with mild and damp winters and moderate summers. It's wise to expect cloudy weather and rain even in the height of summer.

In July and August temperatures average around 18°C but can occasionally soar to 30°C or more. You'll wish they hadn't as the tube turns into the Black Hole of Calcutta and the heat concentrates the traffic fumes in the streets. Also a good many public buildings and venues are not air-conditioned, even though average annual temperatures rise year by year. During most summers, however, you'll be lucky if the mercury tops the lower 20s.

In spring and autumn, temperatures drop to between 11° and 15°C. In winter they hover just below 6°C; it very rarely freezes in London these days and snow is a very infrequent visitor. That may seem mild, but the dampness can often make it feel twice or three times as cold. Fortunately, most of the capital's main attractions are safely undercover, with heating systems geared to keeping the cold at bay.

For the Greater London weather forecast ring Weathercall on ☎ 0906 850 040.

ECOLOGY & ENVIRONMENT

London's most serious environmental problems will be apparent to visitors on even the shortest of stays. With some 145,000 cars driving into the centre of London – 17% of all commuters – every day to join the cars, taxis and lorries already there, traffic moves at an average 11mph – about what it did when horses and coaches clogged the city's narrow streets in the 19th century. Whether the problem will be alleviated – much less solved – if Mayor Livingstone's £5 'congestion charge' (see Car & Motorcycle in the Getting Around chapter) goes into effect in 2003 is yet to be seen.

The traffic congestion is also largely responsible for the other obvious problem: poor air quality. Eight of the 10 most polluted streets in the UK are in London, and many cyclists wear masks to protect themselves from breathing in the toxic fumes.

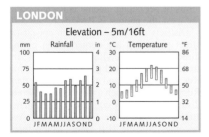

The areas of London that have the highest levels of nitrogen dioxide pollution are Mayfair, Knightsbridge, Kensington and Hyde Park.

Smog, a word coined by the Victorians to describe the poisonous combination of smoke from coal-fuelled furnaces and London's ubiquitous fog, is a thing of the past, thanks to the Clean Air Act promulgated in 1956 after around 4000 Londoners died from the effects of the notorious winter smog of 1952 to 1953. However, these days anyone with asthma or other respiratory problems should take note of the air-quality forecasts attached to weather bulletins.

To look at the Thames' murky waters you'd assume it was another pollution black spot, but in fact things have improved remarkably on that front (see the special section 'The River Thames').

FLORA & FAUNA

London boasts more parks and open spaces than any city of its size in the world – from the neatly manicured (Holland Park, St James's Park) to the semi-wild (Richmond Park, Bushy Park). Between them they provide suitable habitats for a wide range of animals and birds.

Flora

Plant-lovers won't want to miss Kew Gardens in west London (see the Kew section in the Things to See & Do chapter) but if you're more interested in less exotic plants, London's parks boast a variety of common or garden trees, shrubs and flowers. Many Londoners also take pride in their private gardens, which range from handkerchief-sized back yards to sprawling mini-estates, some of which open for a few days each

Old MacDonald's London Farms

To demonstrate to young Londoners that cows' udders are not shaped like milk bottles, farms have been set up all over the city in the last decade with real, live bovines (as well as ovines and porcines) on display, chewing and mooing and doing what barnyard animals are supposed to do. The farms are more popular with local people than visitors so they also offer a way of getting off the beaten track.

Coram's Fields
(Map 4; ☎ 7837 6138)
93 Guildford St WC1
(⊖ Russell Square)
Open 9am–7pm daily in summer,
9am–4.30pm in winter

Freightliners Farm
(Map 2; ☎ 7609 0467)
Sheringham Rd N7
(⊖ Highbury & Islington)
Open 10am–1pm, 2pm–5pm Wed, Sat–Sun
during school holidays

Hackney City Farm
(Map 2; ☎ 7729 6381)
1a Goldsmith's Row E2
(⊖ Bethnal Green)
Open 10am–4.30pm Tues–Sun

Kentish Town City Farm
(Map 11; ☎ 7916 5420)
Cressfield Close, Grafton Rd NW5
(⊖ Kentish Town)
Open 9.30am–5.30pm Tues–Sun

Mudchute Park Farm
(Map 12; ☎ 7515 5901)
Pier St E14
(DLR Mudchute)
Open 9am–5pm daily in summer,
10am–5pm daily in winter

Spitalfields Farm
(Map 4; ☎ 7247 8762)
Weaver St E1
(⊖ Shoreditch)
Open 10.30am–5pm Tues–Sun

Stepping Stones Farm
(Map 2; ☎ 7790 8204)
Stepney Way E1
(⊖ Stepney Green/DLR Limehouse)
Open 9.30am–6pm Tues–Sun

Surrey Docks Farm
(Map 12; ☎ 7231 1010)
South Wharf, Rotherhithe St SE16
(⊖ Rotherhithe)
Open 10am–1pm, 2pm–5pm Wed–Thur &
Sun.

year (generally between May and September) through the National Gardens Scheme (NGS). Admission costs between £1.50 and £2, which goes to charity. For a pamphlet listing dates and participants (*London Gardens*; 50p) contact the NGS (☎ 01483-211535, **w** www.ngs.org.uk) at Hatchlands Park, East Clandon, Guildford GU4 7RT.

Fauna

The mammal you're most likely to spot in London is the grey squirrel, a North American import that has colonised every big park and decimated the indigenous red squirrel population. Hedgehogs also live here, though their numbers are dwindling, perhaps due to the increased use of slug pellets. Foxes also make their home in London, though their nocturnal habits make them difficult to spot except in the very wee hours. Badgers lurk amid the bracken of Richmond Park, which, along with Bushy Park, boasts herds of red and fallow deer.

Bird-watchers, especially those keen on waterfowl, will have a field day in London. There are ducks, pelicans and the Queen's swans in St James's Park, and more ducks and beautiful, chestnut-headed great crested

---

A Regal Bird

Range all thy swannes, faire Thames, together on a ranke,
And place them duly one by one upon thy stately banke

Michael Drayton (*Poly-Olbion*; 1612–22)

How many times have we stood by a park lake or a canal in London looking out at those long-necked, cantankerous hissers that look so pretty as they glide along, only to hear a mum or dad tell their kids: 'Did you know that all the swans in England belong to the Queen?' But why does Liz covet swans and not bustards or titmice or yellow-bellied sapsuckers?

Swans *(Cygnus olor)* have always had royal associations, and they feature in mythologies as far back as ancient Greece. In the early Middle Ages they were also regarded as a delicacy; a roasted swan, often stuffed with smaller birds, was a main course on many medieval menus. Ownership of 'game' swans became a mark of noble privilege and prestige, conferred by the Crown, which also retained ownership of all swans on open and common waters.

In the 17th century two city livery companies (see the boxed text 'The City's Livery Companies' in the Things to See & Do chapter), the Dyers and the Vintners, were given the concession to keep swans and today, along with the monarch, they are the only ones allowed to own swans on the Thames 'from the towne of Gravesende to Cicester'. In July the Queen's Keeper of the Swans presides over the ceremony of 'swan upping' in which the swans are 'upped' (herded). Traditionally the beaks of all young swans and cygnets between Sunbury-on-Thames and Abingdon were 'nicked' – one nick for the Dyers, two for the Vintners and none for the Queen – and their particulars entered on a swan roll. Today they are just weighed and ringed – a job not as easy as it sounds. During the annual avian rodeo in 2001, one of the cranky creatures, apparently unhappy with the way she was being handled, attacked a swan upper. She might have heard about the ancient tradition of ending the ceremony with a banquet of roasted swan meat.

grebes in Hyde Park's Serpentine. Herons can often be seen feeding in the Thames, which also attracts cormorants, especially as you head eastwards into the Docklands. London's canals are also happy hunting grounds for spotting waterfowl.

Garden birds, such as long-tailed and great tits, sparrows, robins and blackbirds, roost in all the parks, but some parks attract more interesting migrants. In Holland Park in spring, for example, you might be lucky enough to glimpse flocks of tiny goldcrests. Kestrels also nest around the Tower of London. Other birds can be seen at reservoirs, particularly Staines Reservoir on Stanwell Moor Road, west of central London and accessible from Hampton train station. The open stretches of the commons in Barnes and Wimbledon also harbour a rich assortment of birds and mammals.

The London Wildlife Trust (LWT) maintains more than 50 nature reserves in the city, which offer the chance to see a range of birds and occasionally small mammals. Battersea Park Nature Reserve has several nature trails for visitors, while the Trent Country Park (⊖ Cockfosters) even boasts a Braille trail through the woodlands. Parts of Hampstead Heath have been designated a Site of Special Scientific Interest for their wealth of natural history. Other important LWT reserves, easily accessible from central London, are Camley St Natural Park (⊖ King's Cross); Chase Nature Reserve, Romford (⊖ Dagenham East); Crane Park Island, Whitton (Station: Whitton); Gunnersbury Triangle (⊖ Chiswick Park); and Sydenham Hill (or Dulwich) Wood (Station: Sydenham Hill).

For more information on nature reserves and wildlife habitats contact the LWT (☎ 7261 0447, Ⓦ www.wildlondon.org.uk) at Harling House, 47–51 Great Suffolk St, London SE1 0BS.

GOVERNMENT & POLITICS
National Government
The UK is a constitutional monarchy with no written constitution; instead it operates under a mixture of parliamentary statutes, common law (ie, a body of legal principles based on precedents, often dating back centuries) and convention. As the capital city of the United Kingdom of England, Scotland, Wales and Northern Ireland, London is home to almost all the national offices of state except those that fall under the jurisdiction of the Scottish Parliament in Edinburgh, the Welsh National Assembly in Cardiff and the Northern Ireland Assembly in Belfast.

Parliament has three separate elements: the monarch, who is head of state but in effect a figurehead who takes advice from ministers and Parliament; the House of Commons, a national assembly of 659 constituencies (or seats) that is directly elected every four to five years; and the House of Lords, which at present consists of the Lords Spiritual (two archbishops and two dozen bishops of the Church of England), 573 life peers (whose titles cannot be passed on) and 92 hereditary peers. The 12 Lords of Appeal (or Law Lords) act as the highest court in the country and have the power of final adjudication. Members of the House of Lords are chosen, not elected by general suffrage.

In practice, the supreme parliamentary body is the House of Commons and the prime minister is the leader of the majority party sitting there. The 20 or so ministers responsible for government departments – from foreign affairs to agriculture and transport – are appointed by the prime minister and make up the Cabinet. The current prime minister is Tony Blair with his Labour Party filling 413 seats against 166 for the Conservatives, 52 for the Liberal Democrats and 28 to other parties and independents.

The partially reformed House of Lords has a certain amount of power but it is tempered by democratic processes. If, for example, the House of Lords vetoes a bill but it is passed twice by the Commons, it is sent to the Queen for her automatic assent, and the bill becomes law. In 1999 more than 1000 hereditary peers were tossed out of the House of Lords in the first stage of reform; as a compromise, 92 of the peers, who were selected by the entire House of Lords before most members left, were allowed to remain. In the second stage of Lords reform (for which there is no time frame), elected peers will enter the upper house for the first time and hereditary peers will be swept away altogether.

Local Government

History records that when the 12th-century king Richard the Lionheart sold London the right to self-government for a little travelling money (see Medieval London in the History section earlier), supporters of the move cried 'Londoners shall have no king but their mayor'. That's been true for the City of London since at least the late 12th century, but not always for Greater London, where the vast majority of the population lives and works. After Prime Minister Thatcher abolished the GLC in 1986, London remained the only major capital city in the world without a self-governing authority and elected mayor (or equivalent) for some 14 years.

That all changed in May 2000 when independent Ken Livingstone, the former head of the erstwhile GLC, was elected by popular vote to lead the new GLA, the city's regional government. The 25-member London Assembly, with certain authority over transport, economic development, strategic planning, the environment, the police, fire brigades, civil defence and cultural matters, is elected from newly created GLA constituencies (14 members) and by London as a whole (11 members). It is not a conventional opposition, but can reject the mayor's budget, form special investigation committees and hold the mayor to account publicly and in the media. At present it is made up of nine Conservatives, nine Labour Party members, four Liberal Democrats and three members of the Green Party. The assembly is expected to move into its new headquarters in the futuristic GLA building in Southwark, immediately south-west of Tower Bridge, in 2003.

The City of London has its own government in the form of the Corporation of London, headed by the Lord Mayor and an assortment of oddly named (and even more oddly dressed) aldermen, beadles and sheriffs; it sits at the Guildhall. These men – and they usually *are* male – are elected by the City of London's freemen and liverymen (see the boxed text 'The City's Livery Companies' in the Things to See & Do chapter). Though its government may appear out of time and obsolete in the third millennium,

RICHARD I'ANSON

The neo-Gothic Palace of Westminster has been a hotbed for political debate since the 19th century.

the Corporation of London still owns roughly a third of the supremely wealthy 'square mile' and has a good record for patronage of the arts in the City.

Different areas (boroughs) of London also have democratically elected local councils, which deal with education and less absorbing matters such as road sweeping and rubbish collecting. Some do a better job than others; at least one was on the verge of bankruptcy at the time of writing.

ECONOMY

London is Europe's richest city and has become a mecca both for those in search of jobs and international corporations drawn by the city's reputation as a financial hub. London's wealth might not be obvious as you pass endless blocks of high-rise housing on a crawling bus or travel along in a dirty Underground carriage. But London comes ahead of, for example, Hamburg and Vienna in terms of wealth per head of population. If the city were a country, its £169 billion gross domestic product – the total output of all goods and services for every man, woman and child – would be higher than that of Sweden, Belgium, Denmark or Ireland.

One out of every eight Britons now lives in London and people keep pouring in, with the population growing at 1.4% each year, five times higher than the national average. They're drawn by wages that are 30% higher than those in the rest of the country, as well as access to the city's cultural and social life. A teacher typically earns £30,000 per year against £27,150 nationally; a corporate manger makes £47,000 – £10,000 more than the average elsewhere.

Living in the capital city, though, is expensive, and eats away at the higher salary. The Centre for Economics and Business Research estimates that the standard of living is actually lower for Londoners than for people in the rest of Britain. Rents, for example, are as much as 56% more expensive. Going out will set you back more, with drinking about 5% more costly than it is outside the city. What's more, almost a quarter of all Londoners have to commute 51 minutes or more to get to work, which is a higher proportion than anywhere else in the country.

It's not only the fat bonuses paid to bankers and lawyers based in the City that add to London's wealth. A quarter of Londoners are employed in business services. More than half of the UK's jobs in the film industry and in media are based here. And people work hard. The statutory working week is 48 hours against 40 in most of the rest of Europe and 35 hours in France.

Some of London's biggest employers are its airports. Heathrow, the world's busiest commercial airport, Gatwick and Stansted together provide some 35,000 jobs. Heathrow, in particular, has grown as a hub for tourists and businesspeople flying to and from Europe, the Americas and Asia.

Pockets of industry and manufacturing can still be found around London, though shipping – the city's mainstay for centuries – was dead as a doornail as long ago as 1981. Greenwich residents might be overpowered from time to time by the less-than-sweet smells coming from the 120-year-old Tate & Lyle sugar refinery across the river, but at least it still provides jobs.

Sweatshops in east London continue to churn out cheap garments – you can still find locally made bargains at Petticoat Lane Market and in the streets leading off Brick Lane and Commercial Rd in the East End. Now they're more likely to be staffed by Bengali workers than the Jews and Cockneys employed until the 1960s.

Trendy pub microbreweries such as the Orange Brewery in Pimlico and the Mash chain have replaced traditional ones such as the massive Truman Brewery in fashionable Spitalfields, while the printing shops of Clerkenwell have been converted to lofts and are now London's most expensive pieces of property.

Despite Europe's attempts to unify its economies by introducing a single currency, the euro, an increasing number of multinational companies use London as their regional base. They're drawn by a common language and not a common currency; the UK has decided not to join the 11 nations that banded together to establish the euro –

at least for now. London attracted over twice as many foreign investment projects than its nearest European rival, Paris. Sony Corp, the world's second-largest maker of consumer electronics, said it was moving its financial headquarters to London by June 2002, consolidating offices in Tokyo, New York and Singapore.

If anything, London's high cost of living could drive jobs out of the city. The strong pound and interest rates that are higher than in the USA or continental Europe add more to the cost of buying goods or taking out mortgages.

This could change if the UK finally elects to join the European Monetary Union (EMU) and drop the pound sterling in favour of the euro, bringing interest rates into line with those in the rest of Europe. But it is a fair bet that sterling will continue to rule Britannia and her finances for some time to come.

POPULATION & PEOPLE

Roughly 12 million people live in Greater London, some 7.4 million of them in central London. Population is growing by 1.4% per year and the average age is decreasing (36 compared with 38 nationally). Another 28 million people visit London every year.

While most residents are white and of Anglo-Saxon stock, the capital becomes more multicultural by the year. Ever since the Industrial Revolution, London has been attracting – if not always welcoming – people from all round the British Isles. Since the late 17th century there have also been significant numbers of refugees from abroad. Huguenots arrived from France after 1685 to avoid religious persecution. Around the same time, Jews were welcomed back from France, Flanders and the Rhineland by the restored Stuarts (after having been booted out *in toto* in 1290) and some 20,000 fled the pogroms of Russia and Poland in the late 19th century. Immigrant Italians began to cluster in Clerkenwell and Holborn, Chinese at Limehouse in the Docklands and Irish in Wapping and Camden in the early 20th century.

Since the 1950s there has also been significant immigration from many of the nation's former colonies, including those in Africa and the West Indies as well as Pakistan and India. Ethnic Indians arrived here in large numbers in the 1960s and '70s, after having been expelled from a number of African countries. Both immigrant and refugee groups have tended to settle in specific areas together: Cypriots, Turks and Kurds in Stoke Newington, Sikhs in Southall, Bengalis in Spitalfields and Shoreditch, Chinese in Soho, West Indians in Brixton, Africans in Hackney and Dalston, Irish in Kilburn, Vietnamese in Hackney and Jews in Golders Green, Hendon and Finchley. Many refugees and other victims of conflict and persecution – from Kurds and Somalis to Bosnians and Kosovans – have settled here in the past two decades.

Just under 25% of all Londoners are from ethnic minorities, according to a survey conducted by the London Research Centre (LRC) in 1999. London has a total of 33 ethnic communities of more than 10,000 people who were born outside England. These range from the largest groups such as the Irish, with some 214,000 people born in Ireland now living in London, and Indians (151,000) to smaller ones such as those from Trinidad and Tobago (around 10,000). The LRC counted around 300 languages regularly spoken in the capital.

EDUCATION

Schooling is compulsory in the UK up to the age of 16 and an increasing number of young people stay on at school (or further education college) until they're 18. Education is free for all until age 18. The number of people going on to university is also on the increase, putting such pressure on funding that the government now expects students to pay part of their own tuition fees and living costs by taking out loans.

In London, primary and secondary education is usually the responsibility of the city's boroughs. Some 92% of all children attend state schools, with the remainder at fee-paying private schools (such schools providing secondary education are called 'public schools' in the UK). Among the oldest and most prestigious are Westminster,

St Paul's, Highgate and the City of London, as well as Dulwich College.

The most famous of Greater London's numerous universities are the 34 colleges of the University of London (founded 1826), which includes the London School of Economics and Political Science, King's College, University College London and the Imperial College of Science, Technology and Medicine, whose research excellence is celebrated around the world.

SCIENCE & PHILOSOPHY

The contributions made by Londoners – or those with a strong London link – to diverse fields of science and technology have been innumerable. Isaac Newton (1642–1727), who legend tells us promulgated the law of gravity after an apple conked him on the noggin, moved from Cambridge to London in 1701 and was president of the Royal Society of London from 1703. He is buried in Westminster Abbey. Edmund Halley (1656–1742), the scientist who first observed the comet that now bears his name, and James Bradley (1693–1762), who provided direct evidence for the revolution of the earth around the sun, were the second and third Astronomers Royal at Greenwich between 1720 and 1762.

The evolutionary theorist Charles Darwin (1809–82) lived for more than four decades at Down House in south-east London. Here he wrote *On the Origin of Species* (1859), in which he used his experiences during a five-year voyage to South America and the Galapagos Islands to develop the theory of evolution by natural selection. The chemist and physicist Michael Faraday (1791–1867), a pioneer in electromagnetism and inventor of the electric battery (1812), spent much of his adult life in Islington and is buried in Highgate Cemetery.

Twentieth-century London residents who made a great impact on science include the Scot Alexander Fleming (1881–1955), who

CHARLOTTE HINDLE

Time and tide waits for no man at the Royal Observatory in Greenwich, the root of GMT.

discovered penicillin more and less by mistake while working as a research immunologist at St Mary's Hospital, Paddington, and John Logie Baird (1888–1946), who invented TV and gave the first public demonstration of the newfangled medium in a room above a Greek St restaurant in Soho in 1925.

In the field of philosophy, London can claim a link to Thomas Hobbes (1588–1679), author of *The Leviathan* and the first thinker since Aristotle to develop a comprehensive theory of nature including human behaviour. He was tutor to the exiled Prince Charles and a great favourite at court when the latter assumed the throne as Charles II in 1660. Karl Marx (1818–83), Friedrich Engels (1820–95), George Bernard Shaw (1856–1950) and Mahatma Gandhi (1869–1948) all studied, thought and wrote in the British Museum Reading Room. The influential thinker, pacifist and Nobel Prize-winner Bertrand Russell (1872–1970) was a lecturer at the London School of Economics at the end of the 19th century and was elected to the Royal Society of London in 1908.

ARTS

London has a flourishing cultural life. It doesn't matter whether you're talking about art as it is found in the National Gallery, the two Tates, the Victoria & Albert Museum or present-day works by the likes of Damien Hirst, Tracey Emin, Rachel Whiteread and Gilbert & George – London still manages to cream off the best.

Dance

John Playford (1623–86), a musician and clerk at the Temple Church, thoroughly democratised dance with the publication of *The English Dancing Master* (1651), in which he outlined more than 100 choral dances of rustic origins that could be enjoyed by everyone, with no discrimination by social class. As suggested by such names as the 'Hide Park', 'Mayden Lane' and 'Nonesuch', many of these 'country dances' were directed at urban dwellers in London.

The morris dance, England's most popular folk dance, is believed to have been introduced to England by John of Gaunt,

duke of Lancaster (1342–62), erstwhile resident of the ill-fated Savoy Palace (see Medieval London in the History section earlier) and the patriot of that name in Shakespeare's *Richard II*, after a visit to Spain. It apparently takes its name from the blackened (ie, *morisco* or 'Moorish') faces of some of the original dancers.

Cecil Sharp (1859–1924), founder of the English Folk Dance and Song Society based in Camden (see Folk, Traditional & World Music in the Entertainment chapter), collected country dances from around England when they were just about to die out and was instrumental for their revival in the 20th century.

Ballet originated in Italy and was first imported to France in the late 16th century by Catherine de' Medici. But classical ballet as we know it today only emerged in the 18th century, followed by romantic ballet in the 19th century. London embraced the latter more than most and 1845 saw the *Pas de Quatre*, in which French choreographer Jules Perrot brought to the English capital four of the greatest ballerinas of the era.

Today London is home to five major dance companies and a host of small and experimental ones. The most celebrated corps

ASA ANDERSSON

Tutu fruity: Prima ballerinas prance their way around the London dance circuit.

de ballet is the Royal Ballet, created in 1956 from Ninette de Valois' Vic-Wells Ballet (1931) and based at the Royal Opera House in Covent Garden. Some modern dance troupes worth seeking out include the Richard Alston Dance Company at The Place, the London Contemporary Dance Theatre and the Rambert Dance Company at Sadler's Wells (see under Ballet & Dance in the Entertainment chapter).

Music

Classical Music Although Britain in general is not known for its great composers, London is passionate about classical music and has five symphony orchestras, various smaller groups, a brilliant array of venues, relatively reasonable prices and high standards of performance.

Handel moved to London in 1712 and became a naturalised citizen in 1726, dying on Brook St in Soho in 1759; many of his operas and oratorios, including the *Messiah* (1741), were written in the capital. JS Bach's youngest son, Johann Christian, was named composer to the King's Theatre in London in 1762 and wrote many successful Italian operas for it until his death 20 years later. He is sometimes called 'the English Bach'. Haydn, too, visited London on two occasions (1791–2 and 1794–5), composing his last 12 symphonies here; his *Symphony No 104 in D* is also called the 'London Symphony'. Mozart visited London for 15 months in the mid-1760s with his parents and it was here that he composed his first symphonies (three of which survive).

When it comes to home-grown composers, however, the ones really worth mentioning are few: Henry Purcell (1659–95), organist at Westminster Abbey; Thomas Augustus Arne (1710–78), composer to the Drury Lane Theatre; Edward Elgar (1857–1934), whose moustachioed mug can be seen on the £20 note; and Ralph Vaughan Williams (1872–1958), who composed his own *London Symphony* on the eve of WWI in 1914. Other virtuosos from the 20th century include Benjamin Britten (1913–76), who wrote the opera *Peter Grimes* (1945), and William Walton (1902–83), who also composed for the ballet and opera and lived with the Sitwell brothers (poets Osbert and Sacheverell) for years in Chelsea.

Gilbert & Sullivan They're neither classical nor pop but the distinctly English comic operas or operettas of WS Gilbert (1836–1911), who wrote the words, and composer Arthur Sullivan (1842–1900) between 1871 and 1896 deserve a mention since their authors were Londoners; from 1882 onwards all their works were produced at the Savoy Theatre. The *Yeoman of the Guard* (1888) is the only musical (to date) to be set inside the Tower of London.

Popular Music After Elvis Presley sold his soul for bejewelled white jump suits and Vegas, Britain quickly snatched the musical baton from the USA. The swinging '60s produced The Beatles, The Rolling Stones, The Who and The Kinks, all of whom had strong links to the capital. The Stones got their first gig at the old Bull & Bush in Richmond in 1963 (they were paid £22) and in April of that year The Beatles came to hear them play. The Fab Four themselves recorded 80% of their albums at Apple Studios in Abbey Road in St John's Wood. The late '60s and the glam years of the early '70s brought stardust-speckled heroes such as David Bowie, Marc Bolan and Bryan Ferry, and bands like Fleetwood Mac, Pink Floyd, Deep Purple, Led Zeppelin and Genesis. Then came punk and its best-known spokesmen, The Sex Pistols, The Clash and The Jam.

The turbulent, ever-changing music scene of the 1980s brought the new romantics and left-wing 'agit-pop'; a frenetic club and rave scene featuring house and techno music also developed. New bands that made it big included the Police, the Eurythmics, Wham!, Duran Duran, Dire Straits, UB40 and the Smiths. And who will ever forget forever beau/belle Bexley-born Boy George, band leader of Culture Club? Thanks for the memories, Boy.

The Americans snatched back the cutting edge with Seattle grunge at the start of the 1990s, but further down the decade saw a renaissance of the quintessentially English

SIMON BRACKEN

On the beat: whether you fancy hip-hop, funk, jazz or folk, London has a music scene for everyone.

Brit-pop band: Elastica, Oasis, Suede, Pulp and Blur. London bands to keep an eye (and ear) out for include the hot indie rock group Turin Brakes, Faithless (pumping house/dance, fantastic live) and Asian Dub Foundation – or ADF (a rocking crossover act).

Literature

The history of English literature is peppered with writers for whom London provided the greatest inspiration – and not all were native to the city or even British. Literally thousands of books take London as their setting; we can only highlight a short selection. For a much more detailed listing, consult *Waterstone's Guide to London Writing* (£3.99), available at Waterstone's bookshops everywhere.

The first literary reference to London comes in Chaucer's *Canterbury Tales*, written between 1387 and 1400, where the pilgrims gather for their trip to Canterbury at the Tabard Inn in Southwark. William Shakespeare lived in London from the age of 21, acted in several Southwark theatres and probably wrote his greatest tragedies – *Hamlet*, *Othello*, *Macbeth* and *King Lear* – for the original Globe, though only *Henry IV: Part II* includes a London setting: a tavern called the Boar's Head in Eastcheap. Daniel Defoe wrote *Robinson Crusoe* (1720) and *Moll Flanders* (1722) while living in

Church St in Stoke Newington; his *Journal of the Plague Years* is a celebrated account of the Black Death in London during the summer and autumn of 1665.

Two early 19th-century poets found inspiration in London. In 1819, Keats wrote his *Ode to a Nightingale* while living near Hampstead Heath and his *Ode on a Grecian Urn* after inspecting the Portland Vase in the British Museum. Wordsworth visited London in 1802, which inspired him to write the poem *On Westminster Bridge*.

Perhaps no writer is more closely associated with London than Charles Dickens (1812–70). Although Dickens had been born into a middle-class family, his father eventually wound up in the Marshalsea, a debtors' prison in Southwark; only the 12-year-old Charles and one of his sisters managed to avoid joining the rest of the family there. His novels most closely associated with the city are *Oliver Twist*, with its story of a gang of boy thieves organised by Fagin in Clerkenwell; *Little Dorrit*, whose heroine was born in the Marshalsea and married in nearby St George the Martyr on Borough High St (there's a road called Little Dorrit Court almost opposite the church); and *The Old Curiosity Shop*. An Old Curiosity Shop still exists just off Lincoln's Inn Fields in Portsmouth St, but it has nothing to do with Dickens' story. The later *Our Mutual Friend* is a scathing criticism of contemporary London values – both monetary and class – and the corruption, complacency and superficiality of 'respectable' London society are fiercely attacked.

Forever associated with 221b Baker St is Sir Arthur Conan Doyle's unflappable detective Sherlock Holmes and his sidekick Dr Watson. Indeed, some 20 letters a week still arrive there addressed to our hero.

Towards the end of the 19th century Jerome K Jerome inserted a memorably witty description of visiting the maze at Hampton Court Palace into his *Three Men in a Boat*. At the turn of the century Joseph Conrad chose Greenwich as the setting for *The Secret Agent*; HG Wells' *War of the Worlds* has wonderful descriptions of the London of that epoch. Somerset Maugham's first novel, *Liza of Lambeth*, was based on his experiences as an internee in the slums of south London; his *Of Human Bondage* provides a truer portrait of late Victorian London than any other work we can think of.

Of the Americans writing about London at the end of the 19th century, Henry James, who settled and died here, stands supreme with his *Daisy Miller* and *The Europeans*. *The People of the Abyss* by the American socialist writer Jack London is a sensitive portrait of the poverty and despair of life in the East End. And who could forget Mark Twain's *Innocents Abroad* in which the inimitable humorist skewers both the Old and the New Worlds? St Louis-born TS Eliot settled in London in 1915, where he published his poem *The Love Song of J Alfred Prufrock* almost immediately and moved on to his groundbreaking epic *The Waste Land*.

For a taste of Chelsea between the wars read *The Naked Civil Servant* by the late Quentin Crisp. Graham Greene's wartime *The End of the Affair* takes place in and around Clapham Common; for a look at how people coped during the Blitz, read Elizabeth Bowen's melodramatic but sensitive *The Heat of the Day*. Colin MacInnes described the bohemian, multicultural world of 1950s Notting Hill in *City of Spades* and *Absolute Beginners*. Doris Lessing painted a picture of 1960s London in *The Four-Gated City*, part of her *Children of Violence* series.

Some of the funniest and most vicious portrayals of 1990s Britain come in Lessing's *London Observed*, a collection of stories set in the capital. *London Fields* by the insufferable Martin Amis uses the capital as a backdrop but is pretty heavy going. His more acclaimed *Money* takes place in Notting Hill. In *Metroland*, Julian Barnes wrote of growing up in the suburbs connected to

PAUL BIGLAND

Thumb the pages of London's literary past and encounter Dickens and Chaucer, the moguls of prose.

London by the Metropolitan line. Nick Hornby immortalised Arsenal Football Club in the virtually unreadable – for non-football fans anyway – *Fever Pitch*. His *High Fidelity*, about a fanatical vinyl-music lover, is a much easier read.

Other modern writers look at London from the perspective of its ethnic minorities. Hanif Kureishi writes about the lives of London's young Pakistanis in *The Black Album*, and his *The Buddha of Suburbia* is set in Bromley. Caryl Phillips describes the Caribbean immigrants' experience in *The Final Passage*, while Timothy Mo's *Sour Sweet* has Soho's Chinatown of the 1960s as its backdrop. David Leavitt's *While England Sleeps*, set in 1930s London and loosely based on the life of poet Stephen Spender, tells the story of an upper-class young writer who falls in love with a self-educated Underground train conductor. A recent runaway bestseller was Zadie Smith's *White Teeth*, the story of an English family and an immigrant Muslim one in north London.

Architecture

London retains plenty of architectural reminders from every part of its long history, but they are often hidden: a Roman wall in the shadow of a utilitarian building from the 1970s, for example, or a perfect galleried coaching inn dating from the Restoration tucked away in a courtyard off a high street. This is a city for explorers. Remember that and you'll be surprised at every turn.

Few traces of Londinium – Roman London – survive outside museums, although you can see the relocated Temple of Mithras built in AD 240 (see the boxed text 'Mithras & the Great Sacrifice' earlier in this chapter) at the eastern end of Queen Victoria St in the City. Stretches of the Roman wall also survive, as foundations to a medieval wall outside Tower Hill Underground station and in a few sections below Bastion Highwalk, just south of London Wall and the Museum of London.

Excavations by archaeologists from the Museum of London during renovations at the Royal Opera House uncovered extensive traces of Ludenwic, the Saxon settlement,

including wattle and daub housing. But the best place to see what the Saxons left behind *in situ* is the church of All Hallows-by-the-Tower, north-west of the Tower of London, which boasts an important archway and the walls of a 7th-century Saxon church.

Complete Norman buildings are also rare in London. The finest survivor from the period is arguably the sturdy White Tower, the Norman keep at the heart of the Tower of London. The church of St Bartholomew-the-Great at Smithfield also has Norman arches and columns marching down its nave; the western door and elaborately moulded porch at the Temple Church in Inner Temple is a very fine example of Norman architecture.

CHARLOTTE HINDLE

Parts of All Hallows-by-the-Tower date from Saxon times, surviving the Great Fire and Blitz.

SIMON BRACKEN

Don't lose your head at the Tower of London, once refuge, fortress and place of execution.

Although the Great Fire of 1666 obliterated many of the city's medieval churches, Westminster Abbey is a splendid reminder of what the master masons of the Middle Ages were capable of. Temple Church as a whole illustrates the transition from the round-arched, solid, Norman Romanesque style to the pointed-arched delicateness of Early English Gothic, but most surviving medieval churches in London reflect centuries of rebuilding and additions. What you see before you now is a hotchpotch of different Gothic styles from Early English to perpendicular. Perhaps the finest surviving medieval church in the City of London is the 13th-century St Ethelburga-the-Virgin in Bishopsgate, which fell victim to the powerful IRA bombs of 1992 and 1993 but has since been restored. The 15th-century Church of St Olave in Hart St, north-west of Tower Hill, is one of the City's few remaining Gothic parish churches, while the crypt at the largely restored St Etheldreda church in Ely Place, north of Holborn Circus, dates from about 1250.

Traces of the medieval city's secular buildings are even more scarce, although the ragstone Jewel Tower opposite the Houses of Parliament dates from 1365, and most of the Tower of London goes back to the Middle Ages. Staple Inn in Holborn dates back to 1378, but the half-timbered facade is mostly Elizabethan and comprises London's only remaining domestic architecture of the 16th century.

The finest London architect of the first half of the 17th century was Inigo Jones (1573–1652), whose *chefs-d'oeuvre* include the Banqueting House in Whitehall and the Queen's House at Greenwich. Often overlooked is the much plainer church of St Paul's in Covent Garden, which he designed to go with the new piazza and described as 'the handsomest barn in England'.

But the greatest architect ever to leave his mark on London – thus far – was Sir Christopher Wren (1632–1723), who was responsible not just for St Paul's Cathedral but for many of central London's finest churches (see the boxed text 'Wren's Churches' earlier in this chapter) as well as for the Royal Hospital in Chelsea and the Old Royal Naval College at Greenwich. His neoclassical buildings are taller, lighter and generally more graceful than their medieval predecessors, which is immediately apparent at his masterpiece and monument, St Paul's.

Nicholas Hawksmoor (1661–1736) was a pupil of Wren who worked with him on several churches before going on to design his own masterpieces. The restored Christ Church at Spitalfields, St George's Bloomsbury, St Anne's Limehouse, St George-in-the-East at Wapping, St Alfege at Greenwich and the City's St Mary Woolnoth are among his finest works.

A few domestic buildings dating from before the 18th century still survive, among them the half-timbered Prince Henry's Room and several old pubs on Fleet St and along the Strand. But the Great Fire effectively wiped out most of the old cityscape and many more secular buildings survive from the 18th century, when some of London's finest squares were laid out.

The Georgian period saw the revival of classicism. John Nash (1752–1835), whose contribution to London's architecture compares favourably with that of Sir Christopher Wren, was responsible for the layout of Regent's Park and its surrounding elegant crescents. He also planned Trafalgar Square and Regent St, although his facades there have long since been replaced. His hand is also visible in some of the more attractive rooms of Buckingham Palace.

John Soane (1753–1837) was the architect of the Bank of England (though much of his work was lost during the rebuilding by Herbert Baker between 1921 and 1939) and the Dulwich Picture Gallery. His pupil, Robert Smirke (1780–1867), designed the British Museum, one of the finest expressions of the Greek Revivalist style anywhere.

Other 18th-century architects who made their mark on the city were Robert Adam (1728–92), whose work can be seen at Syon, Kenwood and Osterley houses; George Dance the Younger (1741–1825), who designed Mansion House in the City; James Gibbs (1682–1754), who designed the church of St Mary-le-Strand; William Kent (1685–1748), who worked on both Kensington Palace and Chiswick House; and William Chambers (1726–96), whose works include Somerset House and the Japanese-style Pagoda in Kew Gardens.

In the next century a reaction set in as the highly decorative neo-Gothic style got into its stride. Champions of this style were George Gilbert Scott (1811–78), Augustus Pugin (1812–52), Charles Barry (1795–1860)

DAVID TOMLINSON

Floodlit fountain in Trafalgar Square with the age-old church of St Martin-in-the-Fields behind

and Alfred Waterhouse (1830–1905). Scott was responsible for the elaborate Albert Memorial, Waterhouse designed the flamboyant Natural History Museum, and Pugin and Barry worked together on the Houses of Parliament.

The Arts & Crafts movement of the late 19th century – 'British Art Nouveau', for lack of a better term – was founded by William Morris (1834–96). It incorporated both design and architecture and stressed the importance of manual processes over machines. The fire station (1902) at the corner of Euston Rd and Eversholt St, opposite St Pancras New Church, is a wonderful example of Arts & Crafts architecture.

The Edwardian Baroque styles of the early 20th century are best exemplified by the works of Aston Webb (1849–1930), who designed the Queen Victoria Memorial and Admiralty Arch and worked on the front of Buckingham Palace. Edwin Lutyens (1869–1944), whose work is classified as British Art Deco, designed the Cenotaph on Whitehall, the Reuters building on Fleet St and Britannic House (formerly Lutyens House) at Finsbury Square. The elegant and humorous Penguin Pool at London Zoo, designed by the Russian-born architect Berthold Lubetkin in 1934, is one of London's earliest modernist structures.

Some unfortunate rebuilding took place immediately after WWII, partly in the rush to make good the bomb damage as quickly and cheaply as possible. But one person's muck is another's jewel; the Royal Festival Hall, designed for the Festival of Britain (1951) by Robert Matthew and J Leslie Martin, attracts as many accolades as brickbats, although hardly anyone has a good word for Denys Ladun's bunker-like Royal National Theatre (1967–77), a stone's throw away.

The 1960s saw the ascendancy of the workaday glass-and-concrete high-rises exemplified by the unspeakable Centre Point (1967) on New Oxford St, above Tottenham Court Road tube station. Fortunately, since the mid-1980s London has seen the erection of some outstanding modern buildings. For more information see the special section 'London's Contemporary Architecture'.

Painting & Sculpture

Although London is home to many extremely rich art collections, British artists have never dominated any particular epoch or style like Italian, French and Dutch artists have. It's not unfair to say that the romantic landscape painter JMW Turner (1775–1851) is the only British artist who can consistently and universally be counted among the greats of the international art world.

There are a few medieval gems around, notably the 14th-century Wilton Diptych in the National Gallery, which depicts Richard II with three saints receiving the blessing of Mary and the Christ Child. But art in London only really got into its stride under the Tudors. The German artist Hans Holbein the Younger (1497–1543) lived in London on two occasions and was court painter to Henry VIII; one of his finest works, *The Ambassadors* (1533), can be seen in the National Gallery. The English miniaturist Nicholas Hilliard (1547–1619) had similar access to the court of Elizabeth I and did portraits of Sir Francis Drake and Sir Walter Raleigh.

The 17th century saw a batch of great portrait artists working at court. Best known is probably Anthony Van Dyck (1599–1641), a Belgian artist who spent the last nine years of his life in London and painted some hauntingly beautiful portraits of Charles I, including *Charles I on Horseback* (1638), now in the National Gallery.

Charles I was himself a great art lover; it was during his reign that many great paintings, including the Raphael Cartoons now in the Victoria & Albert Museum, came to London. Van Dyck was succeeded as court artist by Peter Lely (1618–80), a Dutchman who moved to London in 1641 and was a prolific painter of Baroque portraits, many of them on display in Hampton Court Palace. He was succeeded as court artist by German-born Godfrey Kneller (1646–1723), whose portraits of the Stuart kings can be seen in the National Portrait Gallery.

The 18th century saw art move away from court portraits painted by imported talent, and local artists began to emerge. Thomas Gainsborough (1727–88) still went for portraits in a big way, but at least some were of the gentry rather than the aristocracy; he was the first great British landscapist even though most of his landscapes are backgrounds to portraits. William Hogarth (1697–1764), in contrast, is best known for his moralising serial prints of London lowlife, especially *The Rake's Progress* and *The Harlot's Progress* (see the boxed text below). Thomas Rowlandson (1756–1827) went for gentler cartooning that nonetheless packed a punch; some of his works are on display in the Courtauld Gallery.

Perhaps the diffused (some might say washed-out) quality of the light helps, but England has a fine tradition of watercolourists, beginning with the poet and engraver William Blake (1757–1827); some of his romantic paintings and illustrations (he illustrated Milton's *Paradise Lost*, for example) hang in the Tate Britain. In contrast, John Constable (1776–1837) did landscapes on Hampstead Heath as well as the countryside around the Essex-Suffolk border. He worked for years in a studio on Charlotte St in Fitzrovia and influenced a whole generation of French Impressionists. Turner was equally at home with oils, and he increasingly subordinated detail to the effects of light and colour. By the 1830s, with paintings such as *Snow Storm: Steam-*

boat off a Harbour's Mouth and the later *Rain, Steam, Speed* (1844), his compositions seemed entirely abstract and were widely vilified at the time.

Members of the Pre-Raphaelite Brotherhood (1848–54) – painters Holman Hunt, John Everett Millais, Dante Gabriel Rossetti and Edward Coley Burne-Jones – threw aside pastel-coloured rusticity in favour of big, bright, detailed invocations of medieval legends and biblical stories that go hand-in-hand with the gilded neo-Gothic architecture of men such as Augustus Pugin.

In the 20th century the monumental sculptures of Henry Moore (1898–1986), the contorted, almost surreal, paintings of Francis Bacon (1909–92) and Lucian Freud (b. 1922), and the stylish, pop-art realism and flat, shadowless paintings of friends, swimming pools in California and dachshunds of David Hockney (b. 1937), have ensured the place of British art in the international arena.

Londoner Richard Hamilton's photo and oil montage of pin-ups lounging in a suburban living room, *Just what is it that makes today's homes so different, so appealing?* (1956), launched the pop-art movement in Britain. Recently, attention has been focused on artists like Damien Hirst, the late Helen Chadwick, the mysterious duo

Of Rakes & Harlots: Hogarth's World

William Hogarth (1697–1764) was an artist and engraver who specialised in satire and what these days might be considered heavy-handed moralising on the wages of sin. His plates were so popular in his day that they were actually pirated, leading Parliament to pass the Hogarth Act of 1735 to protect copyright. They provide us with an invaluable look at life (particularly among the lowly) in Georgian London.

The *Marriage à la Mode* series satirises the wantonness and marriage customs of the upper classes, while *Gin Lane* was produced as part of a campaign to have gin distillation made a crime (as it became under the Gin Act of 1751). It shows drunkards lolling about in the parish of St Giles, with the church of St George's Bloomsbury clearly visible in the background. His eight-plate series *The Harlot's Progress* traces the life of a country lass from her arrival in London to convicted (and imprisoned) whore; some of the plates are set in Drury Lane. In *The Rake's Progress*, the debauched protagonist is seen at one stage being entertained in a Russell St tavern by a bevy of prostitutes, one of whom strokes his chest while the other relieves him of his pocket watch. The women's faces are covered with up to a half-dozen artificial beauty marks, which were all the rage at the time.

Hogarth's works can be seen in Sir John Soane's Museum in Holborn, Hogarth's House in Chiswick, Tate Britain and the National Gallery.

Gilbert & George and the Chapman brothers, all of whom seem as interested in shocking – cows sawn in half and preserved in formaldehyde (Hirst), flowers sculpted from urine streams (Chadwick), self-portraits of the artists defecating (G&G) – as in pleasing. Other names to watch out for include Rachel Whiteread, who unveiled a concrete cast of an East End terrace house in 1993 only to see it knocked down, and who installed what looked to many like an empty fish tank atop the empty plinth in Trafalgar Square in 2001, and Tracey Emin, who erected a tent with the names of everyone she'd ever slept with sewn into it. For works in more conventional media, such as oils, look out for the names Cecily Brown, Martin Maloney, Dexter Dalwood and Machiko Edmondson. The best places to view contemporary art are the Tate Modern, the Royal Academy of Arts during the Summer Exhibition and the Saatchi Gallery. See the Things to See & Do chapter for details.

Cinema

Surprisingly for its size and stature, London is not as familiar as, say, New York or Los Angeles to cinema-goers, though the number of films that have been based and shot here is legion. For a much more detailed listing than we can provide, see Colin Sorensen's *London on Film: 100 Years of Filmmaking in London*, published by the Museum of London and on sale at the bookshop there.

The first sighting of London on film was a jerky, primitive glimpse of Trafalgar Square shot by Wordsworth Donisthorpe in 1889. A few pre-talkie films of the 1920s were set in London, but it was a London of the back lot rather than actual locations. For films using real London sets you have to jump forward a few decades and even then there can be deceptions: *My Fair Lady* (1964) with Audrey Hepburn and Rex Harrison, was shot in a mock-up of Covent Garden in California.

Leytonstone-born Alfred Hitchcock shot several of his films in London, including *The Lodger*, *Sabotage*, *The Man Who Knew Too Much*, *The Lady Vanishes* and *Stagefright* – mostly at the now defunct Gainsborough Studios, on the border of Islington

and Hackney – and the much later *Frenzy* (1972), his return to Covent Garden. The villain in Hitchcock's *Blackmail* (1929), his first talking picture, comes crashing through the massive glass dome of the British Museum Reading Room in the film's climax.

Absolute Beginners (1986), a dreadful film based on the book by Colin MacInnes, was set in 1950s Soho and Notting Hill, but more films have celebrated the 'Swinging London' of the 1960s. Foremost among these is Nicholas Roeg's *Performance* (1969) with Mick Jagger and James Fox, but Michelangelo Antonioni's *Blow-Up* (1966), starring David Hemmings as the photographer, is a much better film; the dead body scenes were filmed in Maryon Park in Charlton. *Alfie* with Michael Caine, *Georgy Girl* with Lynn Redgrave and *To Sir with Love* with new face Lulu (all 1966) homed in on the social changes that were taking place on a more workaday level.

Many film-makers have used London as a backdrop for crime and horror stories. One of the earliest was *The Ladykillers* (1955), starring Alec Guinness, which focused on a rather less dodgy-looking King's Cross than *Mona Lisa* (1986), which starred Cathy Tyson as a high-class lesbian call girl who runs rings around her would-be suitor Bob Hoskins. In *Dance with a Stranger* (1984), Miranda Richardson plays Ruth Ellis, the last woman to be hanged in the UK, and Rupert Everett is her faithless lover whom she finally kills. John Landis' campy comic horror film *An American Werewolf in London* (1981) ends with a fabulous chase scene in Piccadilly Circus.

Other film-makers have looked at London's 'villages' and neighbourhoods. Harold Pinter's *The Pumpkin Eater* (1964), with Anne Bancroft, focused on St John's Wood and London Zoo, while Mike Leigh in *Life is Sweet*, *Naked* and *Secrets and Lies*, has preferred to concentrate on the more down-at-heel corners. Scenes at Kew Gardens and Syon House crop up in *The Madness of King George* (1994). A more modern romance was the one portrayed in Stephen Frears' *My Beautiful Laundrette* (1985), in which an ex-member of the National Front

(Daniel Day Lewis) helps his young Asian friend (Gordon Warnecke) create his commercial dream, a glittering laundrette, and falls in love with him in the process. It's an immensely funny and touching film, and a grand indictment of Thatcher's London. Some of the hilarious cult film *Withnail and I* (1987) was shot in Camden.

The Docklands has provided a setting for all sorts of films, including *The Long Good Friday* (1979) with Bob Hoskins as an East End hood, which preceded the redevelopment; *A Fish Called Wanda* (1988), with one of the most attractive riverside flats we've ever seen; and the touching black-and-white *Elephant Man* (1980), about a deformed man (John Hurt) who was exhibited as a fairground freak in Victorian London; much of it was filmed in Shad Thames opposite the Tower of London.

Not surprisingly several of Dickens novels have wound up on celluloid; the lengthy, two-part version of *Little Dorrit*, filmed in 1987, is regarded as the best of the genre, although David Lean's *Oliver Twist* (1948) does an excellent job at recreating the horrors of Victorian slum life. Shakespeare, too, has found his way onto film, although not always in the way one might expect. In *Richard III* (1995) the action has shifted to pre-war London, with sets including Bank-

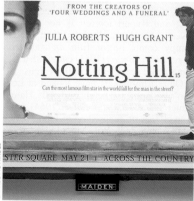

A class act: London's diversity makes it perfect for the movie world.

side Power Station (now the Tate Modern) and St Pancras station.

Some films include vignettes of a London long since lost. The old police epic *The Blue Lamp* (1949), for example, preserves footage of the area around Paddington Green that was levelled to make space for the Westway elevated motorway. Others present a futuristic look at the city, as in Stanley Kubrick's notoriously violent *A Clockwork Orange* (1971), which was shot in and around the grim Thamesmead housing estate in southeast London and banned in the UK shortly after its release. It was not shown again (legally) here until 2001. The film *1984*, released in the year of its title and Richard Burton's last movie, is full of monochromatic shots of how Orwell imagined London would look in the mid-1980s when he wrote his book in 1948, including a looming, sinister-looking Battersea Power Station.

Some children's films with London settings include *Mary Poppins* (1964), in which our heroine floats across the city borne by her umbrella and hooks up with a virtually unintelligible 'Cockney' chimney sweep, Dick Van Dyke, and the original *101 Dalmatians* (1960), with scenes of Scotland Yard. The 1996 remake has Glenn Close as the evil Cruella de Vil, with the base of her world empire at the postmodern Gothic monstrosity Minster Court on Mark Lane in the City. *102 Dalmatians* (2000) features St Pancras station, Borough Market, Westminster Bridge and Lambeth Palace.

More recent films portray London in its many, many guises. Hettie MacDonald's *Beautiful Thing* (1996) is a feel-good film about two working-class teenage boys living in Thamesmead who happen to fall in love with one another; the soundtrack featuring the late Mama Cass was a stroke of genius. The highly recommended *Shakespeare in Love* (1998) is an excellent evocation of Elizabethan London and includes great shots of Bankside. *Lock, Stock and Two Smoking Barrels* (1998), starring ex-Wimbledon footballer Vinnie Jones, has Battersea Bridge as the setting for its cliff-hanging climax. In *Notting Hill* (1999), Richard Curtis' lightweight comedy about an improbable romance between nerd Hugh Grant and delectable Julia Roberts, you get to see Portobello Rd Market, The Ritz hotel and the Strand – but that's about all.

The Millennium Dome made its cinematic debut in the James Bond film *The World Is Not Enough* (1999), with Pierce Brosnan falling from a helicopter on to its roof. The film of Oscar Wilde's *An Ideal Husband* (1999), with Rupert Everett and Kate Blanchett, was filmed partly at the Old Royal Naval College in Greenwich and at the Old Vic.

The East End and Ealing were the perfect locations for *Snatch* (2001) starring Brad Pitt and Vinnie Jones; one scene was filmed in Ye Olde Mitre pub in Ely Court in Holborn. *Harry Potter and the Philosopher's Stone* (2001), with John Cleese, Robbie Coltrane and Maggie Smith, used Australia House in the Strand and King's Cross station.

But perhaps no film in recent memory has provided such a whirlwind cellulose tour of London as the blockbuster *Bridget Jones's Diary* (2001), starring Renee Zellweger, Colin Firth and Hugh Grant. From Borough Market and Shad Thames to the Tate Modern and Piccadilly Circus, it's got it all. Problem is, when the protagonists (we're not telling which) embrace romantically at the finale on a generic (and grimy) street corner and the snow begins to fall, it feels more like New York than London.

Theatre

London has been the centre of English drama ever since James Burbage built its first theatre – called the Theatre, appropriately enough – in Shoreditch in 1576.

Little is known about drama before then, when rowdy theatres were banned from the City and exiled to the east (eg, the Theatre, the Curtain on Curtain Rd and the Fortune on Fortune St) and to Southwark. The Globe was just one of a cluster of theatres on the southern side of the Thames; others included the Swan, the Hope and the Rose. The remains of the Rose, where Shakespeare's *Titus Andronicus* and *Henry VI* were first performed, were recently excavated and are now open to public view (see the Bankside section in the Things to See & Do chapter).

Other playwrights working in Southwark included the duo Francis Beaumont and John Fletcher, Thomas Middleton *(A Chaste Maid in Cheapside)*, Philip Massinger, Ben Jonson *(The Alchemist, Bartholomew Fair)* and Christopher 'Those who don't like boys and tobacco are fools' Marlowe *(Dr Faustus, Edward II)*, who was killed in a tavern brawl in Deptford in 1593. Southwark Cathedral was the parish church for these theatres and contains a memorial to Shakespeare as well as the tombs of his actor-brother, Edmond, and the dramatists Fletcher and Massinger.

The Puritans closed the theatres as dens of iniquity, but with the return of the Stuarts came a revival with a spate of comedies. Among the new writers of these Restoration comedies were William Congreve (1670–1729), whose masterpiece, *The Way of the World*, is still staged occasionally, the outstanding John Dryden (1631–1700) and John Vanbrugh (1664–1726), who wrote *The Provoked Wife*.

By the 18th century the theatre was well established in London and largely respectable. These were the years when John Gay wrote his *Beggar's Opera* (1728), a sort of early *Les Misérables* set in Newgate Prison and the basis for Bertold Brecht's *Threepenny Opera*. In 1773 Oliver Goldsmith's uproarious farce *She Stoops to Conquer* was first staged, followed in 1775 by Richard Sheridan's *The Rivals* and, two years later, *The School for Scandal*.

The 19th century saw the great comedies of Oscar Wilde (1854–1900) hit the stage, including his *chef-d'oeuvre*, *The Importance of Being Earnest*, and *An Ideal Husband*, although his popularity was soon eclipsed by scandal, persecution and a jail sentence for homosexuality. George Bernard Shaw (1856–1950) produced such evergreen plays as *Pygmalion*, *Major Barbara*, *Androcles and the Lion* and *Saint Joan*. Shaw and Wilde were both Irish by origin but moved to London for much of their working lives, as had Goldsmith (1731–74) before them.

Of the playwrights working in the first half of the 20th century who have remained popular, first and foremost is Noël Coward (1899–1973), *bon vivant* author of *Private Lives*, *Blithe Spirit* and *Brief Encounter*. These witty, brittle and sophisticated comedies are still given regular airings in the capital. *An Inspector Calls* by JB Priestley (1894–1984) is rarely off the stage for long.

Despite the tendency to err on the side of conservatism and guaranteed success at the box office, London's theatres (especially the subsidised ones) still stage a wide range of plays by modern writers. Harold Pinter is known for his obscure language and story lines; *The Caretaker* and *The Homecoming*, the latter set in north London, are two of his best-known works. Plays by David Hare *(Plenty, The Judas Kiss)* and the late John Osborne *(Look Back in Anger, A Patriot for Me)* will be more accessible for those who don't go to the theatre regularly.

Alan Ayckbourn and Michael Frayn continue to turn out genuinely entertaining farces; *Absurd Person Singular* and *The Norman Conquests* are two of Ayckbourn's finest, *Noises Off* and *Donkey's Years* among Frayn's best. Like Goldsmith, Shaw and Wilde, Irish playwrights continue to take London by storm and in recent years plays by Martin McDonagh *(The Cripple of Inishmaan, The Beauty Queen of Leenane, The Lieutenant of Inishmore)*, Conor McPherson *(The Weir)* and Marie Jones *(Stones in His Pockets)* have been among the most popular and successful in town.

Musicals The signs were already in place in the 1960s when *Hair* and *Jesus Christ Superstar* achieved phenomenal success on the London stage. Then, during the cash-strapped 1980s, London theatres started to fill up with blockbuster musicals, proven favourites with audiences (especially tourists) and a safe bet for paying the bills. It sometimes seems as if they're all by Andrew Lloyd-Webber *(Cats, The Phantom of the Opera* and so on*)* but there have also been musicals by Lionel Bart *(Oliver!)*, Boublil and Schönberg *(Les Misérables, Miss Saigon* and *Martin Guerre)*, Willy Russell *(Blood Brothers)* and Jonathan Larson *(Rent)*. Among the most popular at the

time of writing were *Chicago*, *The King and I*, and *Mamma Mia!* based on songs by the pop group Abba, and a Lloyd-Webber remake of *The Sound of Music*.

SOCIETY & CONDUCT

It's difficult to generalise about a city of 12 million people, but we're going to give it a go. The most common preconceptions about Londoners – reserved, inhibited and stiflingly polite – are not far off the mark, and visitors are often amazed at the silence on the tube and trains, where the general approach is to get in, grab a seat, open a newspaper or book (studiously avoiding catching anyone's eye) and keep your mouth shut. But London is among the planet's most crowded places, and such behaviour is partly a protective veneer, essential for coping with the constant crush of people.

Londoners rise to the fore in a crisis or emergency; older people still reminisce about the 'good old days' during WWII when no-one had anything and people helped each other with accommodation, rationing and/or mourning loved ones killed by German bombs. Fall down or have your wallet pinched and people will descend on you, offering advice, solace and calling the police or an ambulance. But if you're here for a relatively short time, don't expect to make friends with many Londoners; they're too absorbed in their own world of workmates, friends and family to ask anything 'personal', such as where you're from, if you're married or even how you are. We hasten to add, however, that when you do *really* befriend a Londoner, you'll have made one of the most loyal, supportive and understanding friends of your life.

Londoners are a tolerant bunch, unfazed by outrageous dress or even behaviour (we know – we've been there), and seem to take pride in ignoring anyone who appears to be trying to draw attention to themselves – it just ain't on to show any interest. On the whole, this tolerance means relatively low levels of chauvinism, racism, sexism or any other 'ism' you can think of. Race riots, such as those that occurred in Leeds and Bradford in June 2001 have been unknown in London for decades. The annual Mardi Gras Festival in late June/early July is a vast celebration of homosexual culture that passes off without incident, and London has a long history of absorbing wave after wave of new immigrants and refugees.

Of course the picture is never completely rosy. Loutish behaviour, road rage, some of the coarsest language you'll ever hear spoken in the English language and the peculiarly Anglo-Saxon predilection to urinate in public can be both irritating and threatening. There are pockets of bigotry all over the capital, and the south-east, in particular, has been the scene of unprovoked, vicious racist attacks, even murders. Nor are the police – London's celebrated 'bobbies' – always as colour-blind as people would like to believe.

Dos & Don'ts

It's not especially easy to cause offence in London – unless you're trying to, of course. Having said that, it's worth remembering that most Londoners would no more speak to a stranger in the street than fly to the moon. If you're obviously a tourist in need of directions, that's no problem. But try starting a general conversation at a bus stop or on a tube platform and you'll find most people reacting as if you were mad. It's OK to eye people up, but don't stare, particularly on the tube. Some people take offence and react accordingly.

Queuing The British have always been addicted to queuing, and some comedy sketches depend on the audience accepting that people might actually join a queue without knowing what it's for. The order of the queue at banks, post offices, newsagents and so on is sacrosanct – few things are more calculated to spark an outburst or clucks of disapproval than an attempt to 'push in' to a queue. Queues at bus stops in the very centre of London (eg, along Oxford St) are not taken so seriously as they are elsewhere because of the number of buses that service any one stop.

The Underground Given the vital role it plays, it's hardly surprising that the tube has its own relatively rigid etiquette that starts

CHARLOTTE HINDLE

The tube can be a tight squeeze but it's the oldest and busiest metro system in the world.

as soon as you pass through the turnstile. Where there's an escalator you absolutely *must* stand on the right so that people in a hurry or keen to get in some exercise can rush up or down on the left. This is an extremely important rule – we kid you not – and should you break it, you risk getting pushed aside or verbally abused. Once on the platform you should move along, away from the entrance (this is vital for safety as crowds blocking doorways could cause someone to fall onto the rails). When the train pulls in you should stand aside until everybody inside has got off.

Once in the carriage, it's acceptable to rush for a seat. In theory you're supposed to surrender it to anyone in greater need than you (eg, the elderly, disabled, pregnant women), but as the years go by Londoners get steadily worse at doing this. Putting your feet (or your bags) on the seats is anti-social but happens all the time. And if you see an unattended parcel or bag you should wait until you've reached the next station and *then* pull the communication cord to alert a guard. In general, it's considered a 'nicety' – even a social service – to leave behind a newspaper in the morning. It's plain litter in the evening.

Dress In some countries what you wear or don't wear in churches can get you into trouble. In general, London is as free and easy about this as it is about how you dress in the streets. Bear in mind, however, that if you go into any of the city's mosques or temples you may be expected to take off your shoes and cover your arms, legs and/or head. Men should take care to uncover their heads when visiting Christian churches.

A few classy restaurants and many clubs operate strict dress-codes. In restaurants that usually means a jacket and tie for men and no jeans or trainers (runners/sneakers) for anyone; in clubs it means whatever the management and their bouncers choose it to mean and can vary from place to place and night to night.

RELIGION

The Church of England, a Christian church that split from Rome in the 16th century, is the largest, wealthiest and most influential in the land; about 55% of the population are adherents. It's an 'established' church, meaning that it's the official church of the country, and it has a close relationship with the state: the monarch appoints archbishops and bishops on the prime minister's advice and they sit in the House of Lords as the Lords Spiritual.

It's difficult to generalise about the form of worship, which varies from High Church – full of pomp, ceremony and incense and sometimes almost indistinguishable from Roman Catholicism – to Low Church, which is less traditional and austere and has been more influenced by Protestantism. The first women were ordained as priests in 1994 after many years of debate.

Both the Anglican and Roman Catholic hierarchies administer their flocks through cathedrals north and south of the Thames. The Anglicans have St Paul's to the north and Southwark to the south. The Catholics have Westminster Cathedral to the north and St George's Southwark to the south.

Other significant Protestant churches include the Methodists, the Baptists, the United Reformed Church and the Salvation Army. Evangelical and charismatic churches are the only Christian movements that still appear to be gaining converts, though the proselytising Mormons, Jehovah's Witnesses and Scientologists are all having some success.

At various times since the 16th century Roman Catholics have been terribly persecuted here. They didn't gain political rights until 1829 or a formal structure until 1850, but today about 16% of all Britons call themselves Catholics. An estimated 225,000 Jews make London their home but by no means all of them claim to be religious. They too have not always been treated fairly; they were expelled en masse from England in 1290 by Edward I and not allowed to return for almost four centuries.

Recent estimates suggest that there are now well over a million Muslims in Britain, as well as significant congregations of Sikhs and Hindus. Nowadays it appears that more non-Christians worship regularly than Christians.

LANGUAGE

The English language is by far England's greatest contribution to the modern world. It is astonishingly rich, containing an estimated 600,000 uninflected words (compared with, for example, Indonesian's or Malay's 60,000), and particularly abundant in descriptive words such as nouns and adjectives, as you'll discover pretty fast (quickly, swiftly, speedily, rapidly, promptly) by looking in a thesaurus. These days, however, you'll encounter a veritable Babel of languages – around 300, in fact – being spoken in London, and there are pockets of the capital where English is very much in the minority (eg, Shoreditch in the East End, Soho's Chinatown, Dalston and Stoke Newington). You might even bump into residents who can't understand English at all – though this is usually only the case among older people and housewives of the more conservative communities, who depend on children or grandchildren as translators.

The types of English spoken in London run the gamut from posh Chelsea to low-rent Cockney, with the standard of south-east England – so-called 'Estuarine English' – in between. For more information, see Lonely Planet's *British Phrasebook*.

The River Thames

Measuring just 215 miles long, the River Thames is hardly the boundless Styx of the ancient Greeks, a channel that was said to have flowed seven times around the infernal regions of Hades. And it also comes up short when compared with waterways upon which other world capitals sprouted, grew and prospered. The Danube, for example, which washes the banks of both Vienna and Budapest, follows a course of some 1772 miles from its source in the Black Forest of south-western Germany before emptying into the Black Sea in Romania. Paris' Seine is 480 miles long and even the Potomac in Washington, hardly what you would call a mighty effluent, measures 284 miles from source to mouth.

But size doesn't always matter when it comes to things geographical, and 'Father Thames' enjoys a special place in the hearts and minds of Londoners for many reasons. Along its non-tidal upper reaches, it is every bit the English

Lechlade

Kempsford

Thames

Cricklade

JULIA WILKINSON

idyll of the imagination. Robert Herrick, the 17th-century poet, called it 'the most lov'd of all the Oceans sons' while his contemporary, Michael Drayton, wrote of 'our flouds-queen, Thames, for ships and swans is crowned'. The tidal Thames, on the other hand, is hailed as the historical workhorse that attracted the Romans and then Saxons to tarry and settle and build the Empire that contributed to the economic strength of the present-day city. Could its watery mouth speak, it would tell epic tales of kings and queens, rogues and assassins across the centuries. The Thames is, in almost a real sense, 'liquid history'.

Highs & Lows

The Thames rises in a remote Gloucestershire meadow called Trewsbury Mead north-west of London. But the so-called Thames Head is not a very dramatic start to a river of such stature; there is no waterfall cascading from on high, no bubbling source yearning to run free. In fact, the Thames is not really a river at all until it reaches the town of Cricklade to the south-east, where Alfred the Great, king of Wessex and England's first monarch, built a *burg*, or fortified enclosure, in defence against the Danes in the 9th century. From here the Thames meanders along for more than 124 miles, passing some 44 locks, scores of 'eyots' (as islets in the Thames are called), and a textbook rundown of historic towns, cities and sites: Oxford, where the river is temporarily known as the Isis; the Roman city of Dorchester; Reading, final resting place of Henry I; genteel Henley, famous for its summer regatta held there since 1839; Eton,

Title Page: The river gateway: Tower Bridge (1894) (Photograph by Richard I'Anson)

Top: Boating on the river: an idyllic way to spend a summer's day celebrated for its college; Windsor, home to the aristocratic family of that name; Runnymede, where a reluctant King John fixed his seal to the Magna Carta in 1215; and Hampton, erstwhile stomping grounds of King Henry VIII and his court.

A few miles farther downstream, the river changes its character. From Teddington, a corruption of 'Tide-end-town', according to Rudyard Kipling, to its estuary on the North Sea, some 64 miles to the east, the Thames then turns into a clay- and gravel-lined tidal river. On spring tides the tidal effect holds back the river twice a day, giving the strange impression that

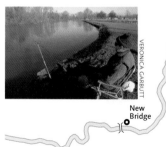

VERONICA GARBUTT

New Bridge

Oxford

Abingdon

Thames

Dorchester

the river is flowing backwards. From here the locks are exchanged for piers and docks and the tree-lined banks for concrete embankments. Father Thames has put on his work clothes.

Wallingford

DAVID TOMLINSON

Springing from the Past

Apart from providing water for drinking and food in the form of fish, rivers offer an easy form of travel and a cheap means of transporting goods. These facts were not lost on the Romans, who called the river Tamesis, the second-oldest place name in England after Kent. In the first half of the 1st century AD, they established the riverside trading centre of Londinium and built a series of long wharves to take advantage of the tides and move goods.

Goring

The Romans also constructed a wooden bridge over the Thames between what is now Southwark and the City of London – the only two places on opposite sides of the river that could support bridge-heads. The first stone bridge spanning the river (more or less on the same spot) did not appear until the late 12th century and until Westminster Bridge opened in 1750, London Bridge was the only crossing on the Thames, apart from the horse ferry between Lambeth and Millbank and the many water 'taxis' offering their services.

The Thames was both London's lifeline and its watery road to riches in the Middle Ages; not only could the swinging tides help the merchant

Top: You'll catch more than an old boot these days: fishing near Runnymede.

Bottom: St Helen's Church, Abingdon

Top: All aboard: hob-nobbing at Henley Royal Regatta

Bottom: Hambledon Mill near Henley

ships along, but its upper reaches, nontidal but navigable, passed through some of the country's most productive land. Control of the river was a coveted prize over which the Crown and State battled.

In 1197, Richard I, who had recognised the City of London as a self-governing commune seven years earlier in return for cash to finance the Third Crusade, sold the Corporation of London control of the river for 1500 marks. The agreement basically granted little more than fishing rights and the authority to remove weirs in the river to open all shipping lanes to traffic, but the City remained in control of the Thames until 1857 when the Crown challenged the lord mayor and successfully wrestled ownership of the river away from the Corporation. The Thames Conservancy Act of that year allowed for a conservation board to oversee the entire length of the navigable river, from Cricklade to the sea. The situation remained more or less the same until 1909, when the Port of London Authority took charge of the tidal river downstream from Teddington, while the conservancy board oversaw the tideless upper reaches.

Fun & Scum

Along with providing the city with food, water and a cheap means of transport from earliest times, the Thames also offered many forms of recreation. In medieval times, jousting matches, in which young men faced one another with lances while standing in the bow of long rowing skiffs, were popular as was ice skating in winter, with animal bones lashed to boots serving as skates. If the river had flooded in the autumn (as it often did before the embankments were built in the 19th century),

the skating carried on as far as Chelsea and on the frozen marsh between Lambeth and Kennington. During the hard winter of 1683 to 1684, the river froze so solidly that a Frost Fair was held throughout the month of January, with football and hockey matches, horse and coach races, food stalls and even a printing press selling commemorative cards. Another Frost Fair took place in 1698, but with the replacement of a new and more streamlined London Bridge (1823–31), the Thames flowed more freely and never again froze so solidly.

But it wasn't all fun and games. From the Middle Ages until the 19th century, waste disposal systems were virtually nonexistent in London; the Thames and its erstwhile tributaries (see the boxed text 'London's Underground Rivers' in the Facts about London chapter) served as the city's open sewers. In 1807, the Romantic poet Robert Southey wrote in *Letters from England*: 'When it is considered that all the filth of this prodigious metropolis is emptied into the river, it is perfectly astonishing that any people should consent to drink it... In its state of fermentation, it is said to be inflammable.'

But drink they did – there was no other alternative and the Thames today still provides some two-thirds of the capital's drinking water – and sick they got. Cholera outbreaks from 1848 to 1849, 1853 to 1854 and 1865 to 1866 killed some 30,000 people – as many as died during the Blitz in WWII. In the summer of 1858, when temperatures exceeded 35°C, the stench from human and industrial waste in the river was so bad that the windows of the Houses of Parliament had to be covered in sheets soaked in lime chloride; even carbolic acid dumped in the river had no effect on what became known as the 'Great Stink'. As the fish died out, the river banks became a purple-pink mass of writhing, uneaten tube worms.

Maidenhead

Eton

Windsor

Kew

Mortlake

Richmond

Runnymede

Staines

Teddington

Kingston Upon Thames

Thames

Hampton

Chertsey

Top: Palatial waterfront housing, Hampton Court

JULIET COOMBE

In 1855, the chief engineer of the new Metropolitan Board of Works, Joseph Bazalgette, set his sights on cleaning up the mess. He supervised the installation of more than 1240 miles of tunnels and pumps to deal with the sewage outflow responsible for the recurrent cholera outbreaks. He also oversaw the reclamation of 15 hectares of foreshore mud and the construction of almost 4 miles of the Victoria, Albert and Chelsea embankments to protect the capital's streets from flooding. He also drew up the plans for Hammersmith (1887) and Battersea (1890) bridges and strengthened the Albert Bridge in 1884.

Ups & Downs

It was the Romans who first built London's docks, or 'hithes' (from the Saxon word *hyth* for 'haven') as they became known, but until two centuries ago the city counted only two large enclosed docks: one at Blackwall and the other at Rotherhithe. Until then most ships anchored in the Pool of London below London Bridge and unloaded their cargoes onto lighters (flat-bottomed barges), which then brought them to shore.

The 19th century saw a frenzy of dock construction as the British Empire grew and London became the economic powerhouse of the

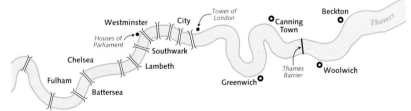

strongest nation on earth. West India, London, Surrey and East India docks were all built in the first decade of the new century. Others, such as St Katharine's (1828), Royal Victoria (1855) and Royal Albert (1880), followed and the huge docks complexes stretched from Tower Bridge to Gallions Reach, a distance of more than 10 miles. Most were built and run privately.

Top: Waterloo Bridge with the city skyline behind

London remained the world's most important port until well into the 20th century – King George V Dock was built in 1921 – but after WWII a series of events forced their closure: the end of the Empire, labour disputes, competition from foreign ports and the advent of container ships, which require deep moorings and a quick turnaround (unloading cargo in 24 hours as opposed to four weeks) – neither of which could be had by sailing up a crowded tidal river. Shipping moved to Tilbury and central London's last working docks – the so-called Royal Group of Docks (Victoria, Albert and George V) – closed in 1981.

Thames Today

As an economic artery for goods and business, the Thames today is dead, and there is very little likelihood it will ever play an important role in the commerce of the city again. Instead, it offers an increasingly attractive backdrop to an increasingly attractive city.

Below the surface, however, the Thames is anything but dead and the cleanup of the river in the last quarter-century has been nothing short of phenomenal. By 1962 the combined impact of untreated sewage and industrial pollution had killed off virtually every sign of life in the river. Efforts to decontaminate the Thames began in 1974, and today the river is home to some 115 species of fish, including shad, sea lamprey and even salmon – last seen in the Thames in 1833 – for which special ladders over the weirs have been built. With them have come 10,000 herons, cormorants and other waterfowl which feed on the fish; even otters have been spotted on the river's upper reaches. The reason why the Thames looks so murky in central London is that it is the brackish centre of two zones: a marine and a freshwater one.

At the same time, development along the river bank, especially south of the river and on the Isle of Dogs, has continued apace. Throughout the first year of the new millennium and into 2001, more than 50 institutions within a 10-minute walk of the Thames (many

Thamesmead

Rainham

Erith

Thames

Purfleet

Dartford

Grays

Tilbury

Gravesend

Top: St Katharine's Dock is a symbol of London's 19th-century trading glory.

DAVID TOMLINSON

normally closed to the public) took part in the London String of Pearls Millennium Festival (☎ 7665 1540, **w** www.stringofpearls.org.uk) in a bid to bring the river 'back to the people'. It proved so popular that a repeat, involving 80 places, was scheduled for Queen Elizabeth's Golden Jubilee in 2002 and could become a permanent fixture.

The best view of the Thames – and riverine London – is from Waterloo Bridge facing eastwards, but for a much better 'on the ground' feel for how the river and city work together, stroll along the Queen's Walk from Waterloo Bridge to Southwark Bridge. Continue on to Southwark Cathedral to see The Long View of London multimedia show (see under Southwark Cathedral in the Things to See & Do chapter) for an idea of how much the river has changed over the centuries. Those who are more interested in the pastoral upper Thames should check out the Environment Agency's Thames Web site at **w** www.visitthames.co.uk.

The truly ambitious (and indefatigable) will hike the Thames Path National Trail, which opened in 1996, from source to mouth. It's some 172 miles long, though of course you can do just a section of it, such as the 16-mile leg from Battersea to the Thames Flood Barrier. For more information see under Walking in the Getting There & Away chapter.

London's most extravagant event using the Thames as a backdrop is the annual Thames Festival (**w** www .thamesfestival .org), the highlight of which is the Great River Race and the riverside pyrotechnic finale. For further information, see Special Events in the Facts for the Visitor chapter.

Canvey Island
○

North Sea

○
Allhallows
on-sea

East
Tilbury
○

Thames

Top: The flourishing city still takes pleasure from the Thames today.

Facts for the Visitor

WHEN TO GO

London is a year-round tourist centre, with few of its attractions closing or significantly reducing their opening hours in winter. Your best chance of good weather is, of course, at the height of summer in July and August, but there's certainly no guarantee of sun even in those months and that is when you can expect the biggest crowds and highest prices.

April/May and September/October are good times to visit the British capital: there's a better chance of good weather and queues for popular attractions are shorter. Choosing these off-peak times will also reduce the cost of getting to London by plane or ferry and may mean cheaper room rates in hotels. If you don't mind braving the winter winds and aren't particularly partial to light, the cheapest travel fares and hotel prices are in force between November and March.

You may want to schedule your visit for a certain event – the London Open House days in September, say, when more than 500 buildings and other sites not normally accessible to visitors open their doors, the Trooping of the Colour in mid-June or the Chelsea Flower Show in late May. See Public Holidays & Special Events later in this chapter for more details.

ORIENTATION

'Goodness me, but isn't London big?' exclaims Bill Bryson in his *Notes from a Small Island*. Bill's right: London does sprawl over an enormous area but at least it has a helpful defining element.

The city's main geographical feature is the Thames, a sufficiently deep (for anchorage) and narrow (for bridging) tidal river that enabled the Romans to build a port that was easily defended from any North Sea attack. Running from west to east, it divides the city into its northern and southern halves. But because it flows in wide bends, creating a series of peninsulas in its wake, it is not always clear on what side of the river you are – especially in the far west and east.

Where next? Central London bursts with attractions in every direction.

Despite London's great size, the Underground system, known as the 'tube' to Londoners, makes most of it easily accessible, and the official and ubiquitous – though geographically misleading – Underground map is easy to use. Most important sights, theatres, restaurants and even affordable places to stay lie within a reasonably compact rectangle formed by the tube's Circle Line (colour-coded yellow), which girds central London just north of the river.

In this chapter, the nearest tube (including the DLR; Docklands Light Railway) or train station has been given for each address; in a few instances bus routes are given as an option. Map 2 shows the location of tube stations and the areas covered by the detailed district maps. The boxed text 'London's Bewildering Postcodes' and accompanying map later in this chapter will also be helpful, especially for locating outlying suburbs.

Most of London's airports lie some distance from the centre but transport in is easy (if not cheap). See under Getting Around for details on how to get to and from them.

MAPS

A good map is vital for getting around London. The ones in this book will help but you should also arm yourself with a single-sheet map so you can see all of central London at a glance. Lonely Planet's *London City Map*

FACTS FOR THE VISITOR

What's in a Name?

Do you know the muffin man, the muffin man, the muffin man?
Do you know the muffin man who lives on Drury Lane?

That ditty was sung to us on our mother's bouncing knee sometime in the early Dark Ages in a far-off English-speaking outpost in New England. We were American-Irish, without a drop of 'Limey' blood coursing through our veins but thanks to nursery rhymes such as 'Drury Lane', the film Mary Poppins and The Beatles, London place names – from Trafalgar and Berkeley Squares to Carnaby St and Piccadilly Circus – were as familiar to us as those in Boston. But what's behind those names? Many City street names still recall the goods that were traded there (eg, Poultry, Cornhill, Fish St Hill, Sea Coal Lane and Milk and Bread Sts). Other meanings are not so obvious.

The '-wich' or '-wych' in names such as Greenwich, Aldwych and Dulwich comes from the Saxon word wic, meaning 'settlement'. Ea or ey is an old word for 'island' or 'marsh'; thus Chelsea (Island of Sand), Bermondsey (Bermond's Island), Battersea (Badric's or Peter's Island) and Hackney (Haca's Marsh). In Old English ceap meant 'trade' or 'market'; hence Eastcheap is where the plebs shopped in medieval times, while Cheapside (originally Westcheap and sometimes still called this by taxi drivers) was reserved for the royal household. 'Borough' comes from burg, Old English for 'fort' or 'town'. And the odd names East Ham and West Ham came from the Old English hamm or 'hem'; they were just bigger enclosed – or 'hemmed-in' – settlements than the more standard hamlets.

And Drury Lane? At first glance it has a rather pedestrian etymology, having been named after one Thomas Drury, who built a house here in the 16th century. But that family name comes from the Middle English druerie, meaning 'love token' or 'sweetheart'. And since Drury Lane was notorious for its prostitutes in the 18th century – Hogarth set one of the plates of *The Harlot's Progress* here – our man the muffin man may have been selling more than something tasty you eat at teatime.

(£3.99) has three separate maps at different scales plus an inset map of Theatreland and a street index. More detailed single-sheet maps are the *AA London Street Map* (£3.99) and *Collins London Street Plan* (£2.99).

For a longer stay you might want to invest in the *A-Z Map of London* (£2.25) or the *A-Z Visitor's Atlas & Guide* (£2.95). The foldout map has an advantage in that the place you want is never on the join between two pages, but the map books are easier to use. If you're staying longer invest in a *Mini A-Z* (£4.25) or the *A-Z London Street Atlas*, which comes in variously sized editions costing from £4.95 to £6.25. They show the city down to its smallest side street.

Two other maps are important for taking public transport. The first is the map of the Underground reproduced in this book; it's a design classic (for details see the boxed text

'Mapping the Underground' in the Getting Around chapter) and shows not just where the stations are in relation to one another but which zone they lie in, something you really need to know in order to buy the right ticket. Some people prefer the newfangled Underground geographical map, showing the tube lines and stations in relation to streets, train stations and other points of interest above ground. It is published as *The Way Out Tube Map* by Drumhouse Ltd and costs £1.50.

To identify all of London's bus routes you'd need to cart around 35 separate map sheets. Luckily the whole of central London is covered on the Central London bus guide (free), which is available from most transport travel information centres (see the Getting Around chapter for locations). If you need a local bus map, ring ☎ 7371 0247 or write to London Buses (CDL), Freepost Lon7503, London SE16 4BR.

RESPONSIBLE TOURISM

London is a very (sometimes intolerably) crowded city, even before the peak season brings yet more millions to the streets. Anything you can do to minimise your impact as a tourist is a good thing.

Traffic congestion on the road – and its polluting effects – is a major problem, and visitors will do themselves and residents a favour if they forgo driving and use public transport (though many Londoners would thank you for avoiding the tube at the worst of the rush hour – 8am to 9.30am and 5pm to 6.30pm). See the Ecology & Environment section in Facts about London for details.

Some 'fragile' attractions (eg, Westminster Abbey and certain gardens) are strained to capacity and have had to go so far as to institute a timed-ticket system, with tickets sold only on the day of your visit or for a day selected in advance at the ticket office. Unless you are really keen on the subject matter, opt for something else.

If you'd like to know more about the problems caused by tourism, contact Tourism Concern (☎ 7753 3330, **W** www.tourism concern.org.uk) at Stapleton House, 277–281 Holloway Rd, London N7 8HN (⊖ Holloway Road). It has a library of press cuttings and other source materials.

TOURIST OFFICES

London is a major travel centre, so along with information on London, tourist offices can help with England, Scotland, Wales, Ireland and most countries worldwide.

Local Tourist Offices

Britain Visitor Centre This comprehensive information and booking centre (Map 7; ⊖ Piccadilly Circus), 1 Regent St SW1, includes the tourist boards of Wales, Scotland, Northern Ireland, the Irish Republic and Jersey as well as a branch of Stanford's map and guide-book shop on the ground floor.

On the mezzanine level you'll find a First Option outlet, where you can arrange accommodation and tours as well as train,

air and car travel, Globaltickets theatre ticket agency, a bureau de change, international telephones and a few computer terminals for accessing tourist information on the Web.

It can get *very* busy but opens 9.30am to 6.30pm Monday, 9am to 6.30pm Tuesday to Friday, and 10am to 4pm Saturday and Sunday (to 5pm on Saturday June to September). The centre deals with direct queries and walk-in customers only; telephone enquiries are not possible. If you're not in the area and need information about Britain or Ireland ring British Tourist Authority (BTA) general enquiries on ☎ 8846 9000 or consult the BTA Web site at **W** www.visitbritain.com.

Tourist Information Centres Like the Britain Visitor Centre, the tourist information centres (TICs) run by London Tourist Board (LTB) handle walk-ins only. Otherwise, phone LTB general enquiries (☎ 7932 2000) or make use of their London Line (☎ 09068 663344; premium-rate calls cost 60p per minute), which can fill you in on everything from tourist attractions and events (such as the Changing of the Guard) to river trips and tours, accommodation, eating, theatre, shopping, children's London and gay and lesbian venues. Written enquiries should be sent to the London Tourist Board & Convention Bureau, Glen House, Stag Place, London SW1E 5LT (or fax 7932

ASA ANDERSSON

A brush with the law: if in doubt ask a London bobby.

FACTS FOR THE VISITOR

0222). The LTB's comprehensive Web site is at W www.londontouristboard.com.

As well as providing information, London's main TIC, on the forecourt of Victoria train station (Map 11; ↔ Victoria), handles accommodation and travel bookings and can arrange national coach and theatre tickets. It opens 8am to 8pm Monday to Saturday and 8am to 6pm on Sunday, April to October, and 8am to 6pm Monday to Saturday and 9am to 4pm on Sunday the rest of the year. It can get positively mobbed in the peak season and the staff are not very welcoming.

There are much more helpful TICs in the arrivals hall at Waterloo International Terminal (Map 6; ↔ Waterloo), open 8.30am to 10.30pm daily, and at Liverpool Street station (Map 9; ↔ Liverpool Street), open 8am to 6pm daily. The TIC at the Heathrow Terminals 1, 2 & 3 Underground station opens 8am to 6pm daily. Gatwick, Stansted, Luton and London City airports, Paddington train station and Victoria coach station all have information desks.

The Corporation of London also has an information centre (☎ 7332 1456, fax 7332 1457, W www.cityoflondon.gov.uk) in St Paul's Churchyard EC4, opposite St Paul's Cathedral (Map 9; ↔ St Paul's). It opens 9.30am to 5pm daily, April to September, and 9.30am to 5pm Monday to Friday (to 12.30pm on Saturday) the rest of the year.

A few London boroughs and neighbourhoods have their own TICs, including:

Clerkenwell
(☎ 7251 6311, fax 7689 3661) 53 Clerkenwell Close EC1R 0EA
Greenwich
(☎ 0870 608200, fax 8853 4607) Pepys House, Old Royal Naval College, King William Walk SW10 9NN
Richmond
(☎ 8940 9125, fax 8940 6899) Old Town Hall, Whittaker Ave, Richmond,Surrey TW9 1TP
Southwark
(☎ 7403 8299, fax 7357 6321, W www.southwark-online.co.uk) London Bridge, 6 Tooley St, SE1 2SY
Tower Hamlets
(☎ 7364 4971, fax 7375 2539) 18 Lamb St, E1 6EA

Tourist Offices Abroad

The BTA stocks masses of information about London and the rest of Britain, much of it free. Be sure to contact the BTA *before* you leave home; some discounts and offers are only available to people who book before arriving in Britain. Travellers with specific needs (such as those with a disability or dietary restrictions) should also contact their nearest BTA office for information. Overseas tourist offices include the following:

Australia
(☎ 02-9377 4400, fax 9377 4499, e visitbritain aus@bta.org.uk) Level 16, The Gateway, 1 Macquarie Place, Sydney, NSW 2000
Belgium
(☎ 02-646 3510, fax 646 3986) Luizalaan 306 Avenue Louise, 1050 Brussels
Canada
(☎ 905-405 1840 or 1-888 VISIT UK toll free, fax 405 1835,) Suite 120, 5915 Airport Rd, Mississauga, Ontario L4V 1T1
France
(☎ 01 44 51 56 20, fax 01 44 51 56 21) Maison de la Grand Bretagne, 19 rue des Mathurins, 75009 Paris
Germany
(☎ 069-97 1123, fax 97 112 444, e soswald@ bta.org.uk) Westendstrasse 16–22, 60325 Frankfurt-am-Main
Ireland
(☎ 01-670 8000, fax 670 8244) 18–19 College Green, Dublin 2
Netherlands
(☎ 020-607 0002, fax 618 6868, e britinfo .nl@bta.org.uk) Aurora Gebouw (5e), Stadhouderskade 2, 1054 ES Amsterdam
New Zealand
(☎ 09-303 1446, fax 377 6965) 17th floor, NZI House, 151 Queen St, Auckland 1
South Africa
(☎ 011-325 0343, 325 0344) Lancaster Gate, Hyde Park Lane, Hyde Park 2196
Spain
(☎ 91 541 13 96, fax 91 542 81 49) Torre de Madrid 6/5, Plaza de España 18, 28008 Madrid
USA
(☎ 212-986 2200 or 1-800 GO 2 BRITAIN toll free) Suite 701, 551 5th Ave, New York, NY 10176-0799
(☎ 310-470 2782, fax 470 8549) Suite 570, 10880 Wiltshire Blvd, Los Angeles, CA 90024

TRAVEL AGENCIES

London has countless travel agencies, not all of them of stellar reputation. Among the best and most reliable are STA Travel, Trailfinders and usit Campus, whose staff understand what a budget is and can offer competitive, reliable fares. You don't have to be a student to use their services. Following is a list of these travel agencies and their London branches:

STA Travel
(Map 10; ☎ 7361 6161 for European enquiries, 7361 6262 for worldwide enquiries or 7361 6160 for tours, accommodation, car hire or insurance, **W** www.statravel.co.uk, 86 Old Brompton Rd SW7, ⊖ South Kensington). Open 10am to 6pm weekdays, and 11am to 5pm Saturday.
Other branches include:
(Map 8; 85 Shaftesbury Ave W1, ⊖ Tottenham Court Road)
(Map 3; 117 Euston Rd NW1, ⊖ Euston)
(Map 6; 38 Store St WC1, ⊖ Goodge Street)
(Map 6; 11 Goodge St W1, ⊖ Goodge Street)

Trailfinders
(Map 5; ☎ 7938 3939 for long-haul travel or 7938 3444 for 1st- and business-class flights, **W** www.trailfinders.com, 194 Kensington High St W8, ⊖ High Street Kensington). Open 9am to 6pm Monday to Saturday (till 7pm on Thursday) and 10am to 6pm Sunday. This branch also has a visa and passport service (☎ 7938 3848), immunisation centre (☎ 7938 3999), foreign exchange (☎ 7938 3850) and information centre (☎ 7938 3303).
Other branches include:
(Map 5; ☎ 7937 5400 for transatlantic travel or 7937 1234 for European travel, 215 Kensington High St W8, ⊖ High Street Kensington)

usit Campus
(Map 11; ☎ 0870 240 1010, **W** www.usitcampus .co.uk, 52 Grosvenor Gardens SW1, ⊖ Victoria). Open 9am to 6pm weekdays, and 10am to 5pm Saturday and Sunday.
Other branches include:
(Map 5; 174 Kensington High St W8, ⊖ High Street Kensington)
(Map 7; 28a Poland St W1 ⊖ Oxford Circus)

Plenty of other agencies advertise in the travel sections of the weekend newspapers, *Time Out* and *TNT Magazine*. All agencies should be covered by an Air Travel Organiser's Licence (ATOL; **W** www.atol.org.uk). This scheme, operated by the Civil Aviation Authority (CAA), means that if either the agency or airline goes bust you are guaranteed a full refund or, if you are already abroad, to be flown back more or less on schedule. It's worth noting that, under existing consumer-protection legislation, the only way you can lose out is if you book directly through an airline; using a travel agency gives you more protection. To be covered by the scheme, however, you must be given either the ticket or an official ATOL receipt showing the agency's number when you hand over the cash.

VISAS & DOCUMENTS

Unlike most other countries within Europe, people in the UK are not required by law to carry identification, but it's always a good idea to have your passport or some other sort of photo ID on your person. Also, with very few exceptions, London is an excellent place to gather information about and visas for other countries worldwide.

Visas

At present, citizens of Australia, Canada, New Zealand, South Africa and the USA are given 'leave to enter' the UK at their point of arrival for up to six months but are prohibited from working unless they secure a work permit. If you're a citizen of the European Union (EU), you don't need a visa to enter the country and may live and work here freely for as long as you like.

Visa regulations are always subject to change, so it's essential to check with your local British embassy, high commission or consulate before leaving home.

The immigration authorities in the UK are tough; dress neatly and be able to prove that you have sufficient funds to support yourself. A credit card and/or an onward ticket will help.

Several travel companies provide quick foreign visa services for a fee. Trailfinders (see Travel Agencies) handles visas for more than a dozen countries and can usually deliver within five working days. Rapid Visa Worldwide (☎ 0870 727 4384 or 7373 3026, **W** www.rapidvisas.com) at Top Deck Travel (Map 10; ⊖ Earl's Court), 131–135 Earl's

Court Rd SW5, is popular with Australians and New Zealanders. Global Visas (Map 7; ☎ 7734 5900 or 7317 9491, Ⓦ www.global visas.com, ⊖ Oxford Circus), 3rd floor, 181 Oxford St W1, can obtain visas for a number of countries – from the Czech Republic, France and Australia to Egypt and India.

Visa Extensions Tourist visas can only be extended in clear emergencies (eg, an accident, death of a relative etc). Otherwise you'll have to leave the UK (perhaps going to Ireland or France) and apply for a fresh one, although this tactic will arouse suspicion after the second or third visa. To extend (or attempt to extend) your stay in the UK, ring the Visa & Passport Information Line (☎ 08706 067766 or 8649 7878) of the Home Office's Immigration & Nationality Directorate, Lunar House, 40 Wellesley Rd, Croydon CR9 2BY (Station: East Croydon), *before* your current visa expires. It opens 10am to noon and 2pm to 4pm weekdays.

Student Visas Nationals of EU countries can enter the country to study without formalities. Otherwise you need to be enrolled in a full-time course of at least 15 hours per week of weekday, daytime study at a single educational institution to be allowed to remain as a student. For more details, consult the British embassy, high commission or consulate in your own country.

Work Permits EU nationals don't need a work permit to work in London but everyone else does. If the *main* purpose of your visit is to work, you have to be sponsored by a British company.

However, if you're a citizen of a Commonwealth country aged between 17 and 27 (inclusive), you may apply for a Working Holiday Entry Certificate, which allows you to spend up to two years in the UK and take work that is 'incidental' to a holiday. You're not allowed to engage in business, pursue a career or provide services as a professional sportsperson or entertainer.

You must apply to the nearest UK mission overseas – Working Holiday Entry Certificates are *not* granted on arrival in Britain. It is not possible to switch from being a visitor to a working holiday-maker nor can you claim back any time spent out of the UK during the two-year period. When you apply, you must satisfy the authorities that you have the means to pay for a return or onward journey and that you will be able to maintain yourself without recourse to public funds.

If you're a Commonwealth citizen and have a parent born in the UK, you may be eligible for a Certificate of Entitlement to the Right of Abode, which means you can live and work in Britain free of immigration control.

If you're a Commonwealth citizen with a grandparent born in the UK, or if the grandparent was born before 31 March 1922 in what is now the Republic of Ireland, you may qualify for a UK Ancestry Employment Certificate, which means you can work full time for up to four years in the UK.

Students from the USA who are at least 18 years old and studying full time at a college or university can get a Blue Card permit allowing them to work for six months in the UK. It costs US$250 and is available through the British Universities North America Club (BUNAC; ☎ 203 264 0901, ℮ wib@bunacusa), PO Box 430, Southbury CT 06488. Once in the UK, BUNAC can help Blue Card holders find jobs, accommodation and so on. BUNAC also runs programmes for Australians, Canadians and New Zealanders but you must apply before leaving home. For more details visit the Web site Ⓦ www.bunac.org.

If you have any queries once you're in the UK, contact the Home Office's Immigration & Nationality Directorate (see under Visa Extensions earlier).

Travel Insurance

Whichever way you're travelling, make sure you take out a comprehensive travel insurance policy that covers you for medical expenses and luggage theft or loss, and for cancellation of or delays in your travel arrangements. Ticket loss should also be included but make sure you have a separate record of all the details – or better still, a photocopy of the ticket. There are all sorts of policies but the international student travel policies handled by STA and other student travel organisations are usually good value. Some policies offer lower and higher medical expense options – unless you're eligible for free NHS treatment (see Health later in this chapter), go for as much as you can afford. Other policies are cheaper if you forgo cover for lost baggage.

Buy insurance as early as possible. Otherwise you may find that you're not covered for delays to your flight caused by strikes or other industrial action. Always read the small print carefully for loopholes.

Paying for your ticket with a credit card often provides limited travel accident insurance, and you may be able to reclaim the payment if the operator doesn't deliver. In the UK, credit-card providers are required by law to reimburse consumers if a company goes into liquidation and the amount in contention is more than £100.

Driving Licence & Permits

Your normal driving licence is legal for 12 months from the date you last entered the UK. You can then apply at post offices for a British licence, which is now an EU-style photo licence, though (in typical British bureaucratic fashion) you must by law also carry the cumbersome, A3-sized Counterpart Driving Licence. For information contact the Driving & Vehicle Licensing Agency (DVLA; ☎ 0870 240 0009, fax 01792-783071), Swansea SA6 7JL. If you are carrying a foreign driving licence, it's still a good idea to carry an International Driving Permit (IDP) as well. This should be obtainable from your local motoring association for a small fee.

Hostel Cards

To stay in one of London's eight Youth Hostels Association/Hostelling International (YHA/HI) hostels you must be a member of the organisation. If not you'll be charged a £2 surcharge for the first six nights, which adds up to the £12 joining fee. See under YHA Hostels in the Places to Stay chapter.

Student, Youth & Teachers' Cards

Most useful of these is the International Student Identity Card (ISIC), a plastic ID-style card with your photograph that costs £6 in the UK and provides cheap or free admission to museums and sights, inexpensive meals in some student restaurants and discounts on many forms of transport.

There's a worldwide industry in fake student cards, and many places now stipulate a maximum age for student discounts or simply substitute a 'youth discount' for a 'student' one. ISTC has introduced a similar card, the International Youth Travel Card (IYTC), which gives people aged 25 and under benefits and access to special travel deals. The card can be obtained from usit (who call it IYC) or similar outlets. Teachers can apply for an International Teacher Identity Card (ITIC).

Seniors' Cards

Many attractions reduce their admission price for people aged over 60 or 65; it's always worth asking even if you can't see a discount listed.

London Pass

The London Pass (☎ 0870 242 9988, W www .londonpass.com) allows free admission to over 50 museums and other attractions, including the Tower of London, London Dungeon and Kensington Palace, and unlimited travel on the tube (Zones 1 to 6), buses and trains within central London for one/two/three/six days. Passes (including transport) cost £24/44/55/89 for adults and £16/27/34/45 for those aged five to 15. Other benefits include commission-free currency exchange, restaurant discounts, free Internet access and reduced telephone charges.

Copies

Copy your passport, air tickets, insurance policy and serial numbers of your camera and travellers cheques before you leave home. Take one set of copies with you (keeping it separate from the original documents) and leave a second set with someone you can rely on back home.

CHARLOTTE HINDLE

Australia House on the Strand is topped by Bertram Mackennal's *The Horses of the Sun*.

It's also a good idea to store details of your vital travel documents in Lonely Planet's free online Travel Vault in case you lose the copies or can't be bothered with them. Your password-protected Travel Vault is accessible online anywhere in the world – create it at W www.ekno.lonelyplanet.com.

EMBASSIES & CONSULATES
British Embassies, Consulates & High Commissions Abroad

British missions overseas include those listed below. If you need details of others, consult the Foreign & Commonwealth Office Web site at W www.fco.gov.uk.

Australia
High Commission: (☎ 02-6270 6666, fax 6270 6653, W www.uk.emb.gov.au) Commonwealth Ave, Yarralumla, Canberra, ACT 2600
Consulate-General: (☎ 02-9247 7521, fax 9251 6201) Level 16, The Gateway, 1 Macquarie Place, Sydney, NSW 2000

Belgium
Embassy: (☎ 02-287 6211, fax 287 6270, W www.british-embassy.be) 85 rue d'Arlon, 1040 Brussels

Canada
High Commission: (☎ 613-237 1530, fax 232 2533, W www.britain-in-canada.org) 80 Elgin St, Ottawa, Ontario K1P 5K7
Consulate-General: (☎ 416-593 1290, fax 593 1229) Suite 2800, 777 Bay St, College Park, Toronto, Ontario M5G 2G2

France
Embassy: (☎ 01 44 51 31 00, fax 01 44 51 31 28, W www.amb-grandebretagne.fr) 35 rue du Faubourg Saint Honoré, 75008 Paris

Germany
Embassies: (☎ 030-204 570, fax 20457 579, W www.britischebotschaft.de) Wilhelmstrasse 70, 10117 Berlin (☎ 0228-916 70, fax 9167 241) Argelanderstrasse 108A, 53113 Bonn

Ireland
Embassy: (☎ 01-205 3822, fax 205 3890, W www.britishembassy.ie) 29 Merrion Rd, Ballsbridge, Dublin 4

Netherlands
Embassy: (☎ 070-427 0427, fax 427 0345, W www.britain.nl) Lange Voorhout 10, 2514 ED The Hague
Consulate-General: (☎ 020-676 43 43, fax 675 83 81) Konigslaan 44, 1075 AE Amsterdam

New Zealand
High Commission: (☎ 04-472 6049, fax 471

1974, W www.britain.org.nz) 44 Hill St,
Wellington 1
Consulate-General: (☎ 09-303 2973, fax 303
1836) 17th floor, NZI House, 151 Queen St,
Auckland 1

South Africa
High Commission: (☎ 021-461 7220, fax 461
0017, W www.britain.org.za) 91 Parliament St,
Cape Town 8001
Consulate-General: (☎ 011-325 2133, fax 325
2132, W www.britain.org.za) Dunkeld Corner,
275 Jan Smuts Ave, Dunkeld West, Johannesburg 2196

Spain
Embassy: (☎ 91 700 82 00, fax 91 700 83 09,
W www.ukinspain.com) Calle de Fernando el
Santo 16, 28010 Madrid

USA
Embassy: (☎ 202-588 6500, fax 588 7850,
W www.britainusa.com) 3100 Massachu-
setts Ave, NW, Washington, DC 20008
Consulate-General: (☎ 212-745 0200, fax 745
0444) 845 Third Ave, New York, NY 10022

Embassies, High Commissions & Consulates in London

It's important to realise what your own embassy – the embassy of the country of which
you are a citizen – can and *cannot* do to help
you if you get into trouble.

Generally, it won't be much help if the
trouble you're in is remotely your own
fault. Remember that while in London you
are bound by British law. Your embassy
will not be sympathetic if you end up in
prison after committing a crime locally,
even if such actions are legal in your own
country.

In genuine emergencies you might get
some assistance, but only if other channels
have been exhausted. For example, if you
need to get home urgently, a free ticket
home is highly unlikely – the embassy
would expect you to have insurance. If you
have all your money and documents stolen,
it might assist with getting a new passport
but a loan for onward travel is almost always out of the question.

The following is a list of selected foreign
embassies and high commissions in London. For a more complete list check under
'Embassies & Consulates' in the *Central
London Yellow Pages* (W www.yell.com).

Australia
High Commission: (Map 6; ☎ 7379 4334,
fax 7240 5333, W www.australia.org.uk)
Australia House, Strand WC2 (⊖ Holborn)

Belgium
Embassy: (Map 11; ☎ 7470 3700, fax 7259
6213) 103 Eaton Square SW1 (⊖ Victoria)

Canada
High Commission: (Map 6; ☎ 7258 6600,
fax 7258 6506, W www.canada.org.uk)
Macdonald House, 1 Grosvenor Square W1
(⊖ Bond Street)

France
Consulate-General: (Map 10; ☎ 7838 2055,
fax 7838 2046) 6a Cromwell Place SW7
(⊖ South Kensington)

Germany
Embassy: (Map 5; ☎ 7824 1300, fax 7824
1435) 23 Belgrave Square SW1 (⊖ Hyde
Park Corner)

Ireland
Embassy: (Map 6; ☎ 7235 2171, fax 7245
6961) 17 Grosvenor Place SW1
(⊖ Hyde Park Corner)
Chancery: (Map 10; ☎ 7255 7700) Montpelier
House, 106 Brompton Rd SW3
(⊖ South Kensington)

Netherlands
Embassy: (Map 5; ☎ 7590 3200, fax 7590
3334) 38 Hyde Park Gate SW7
(⊖ High Street Kensington)

New Zealand
High Commission: (Map 7; ☎ 7930 8422,
fax 7839 4580, W www.newzealandhc.org.uk)
New Zealand House, 80 Haymarket SW1
(⊖ Piccadilly Circus)

South Africa
High Commission: (Map 8; ☎ 7451 7299, fax
7451 7284, W www.southafricahouse.com)
South Africa House, Trafalgar Square WC2
(⊖ Trafalgar Square)

Spain
Embassy: (Map 6; ☎ 7235 5555)
39 Chesham Place SW1 (⊖ Hyde Park
Corner)

USA
Embassy: (Map 6; ☎ 7499 9000, fax 7495
5012, W www.usembassy.org.uk) 5 Upper
Grosvenor St W1 (⊖ Bond Street)

CUSTOMS

Like other nations belonging to the EU, the
UK has a two-tier customs system: one for
goods bought duty free and one for goods
bought in another EU country where taxes
and duties have already been paid.

Duty Free

Duty-free sales to those travelling from one EU country to another were abolished from July 1999. For goods purchased at airports or on ferries *outside* the EU, you are allowed to import 200 cigarettes, 50 cigars or 250g of tobacco; 2L of still wine plus 1L of spirits over 22% or another 2L of wine (sparkling or otherwise); 50g of perfume; 250cc of toilet water; and other duty-free goods to the value of £145.

Tax & Duty Paid

Although you can no longer bring in duty-free goods from another EU country, you can bring in goods from another EU country, where certain goods might be cheaper, if taxes have been paid on them. The items are supposed to be for individual consumption but a thriving business has developed, with many Londoners making day-trips to France to load up their cars with cheap grog and smokes, which they often sell back in the UK. The savings can more than pay for the trip.

If you purchase from a normal retail outlet on the continent, customs uses the following maximum quantities as a guideline to distinguish personal imports from those on a commercial scale: 800 cigarettes, 200 cigars, 1kg of tobacco, 10L of spirits, 20L of fortified wine, 90L of wine (of which not more than 60L is sparkling) and 110L of beer.

MONEY
Currency

Unlike the majority of EU members, whose single currency is the euro, Britain has retained its own monetary system – the pound sterling – and will continue to do so for the foreseeable future. The pound (£) is divided into 100 pence (p and pronounced 'pee'). Coins of 1p and 2p are copper and the 5p, 10p, 20p and 50p ones are silver. The heavy £1 coin is a brassy gold and the £2 one is gold-coloured on the edge with a silver centre. Notes come in £5, £10, £20 and £50 denominations and vary in colour and size. The £50 notes can be difficult to change – avoid them.

Exchange Rates

The following currencies convert at these approximate rates:

country	unit		sterling
Australia	A$1	=	£0.36
Canada	C$1	=	£0.44
euro zone	€1	=	£0.62
Japan	¥100	=	£0.57
New Zealand	NZ$1	=	£0.29
USA	US$1	=	£0.70

Exchanging Money

Cash Nothing beats cash for convenience – or risk. It's still a good idea, however, to travel with some cash in sterling, if only to tide you over until you get to an exchange facility. There's no problem if you arrive at any of London's five airports; all have good-value exchange counters open for incoming flights (see Moneychangers later in this section).

Travellers Cheques A good way of protecting your money from theft is by using travellers cheques. Ideally your cheques should be in pounds and preferably issued by American Express (Amex) or Thomas Cook, which are widely recognised, well-represented and don't charge for cashing their own cheques (though they often offer less-than-stellar exchange rates). Both have offices and bureaux de change all over London; see Moneychangers later in this section or look in the *Yellow Pages* under 'Bureaux de Change' for the nearest branch.

Bring most of your travellers cheques in large denominations. It's only towards the end of a stay that you may want to cash a small cheque to make sure you don't get left with too much local currency. Travellers cheques are rarely accepted outside banks or used for everyday transactions in London as they are in, say, the USA so you usually need to cash them in advance.

The cost of buying travellers cheques varies considerably, depending on the seller. Amex is often the cheapest, charging 1% commission with no minimum charge. Main post offices also offer very competitive rates. The banks are usually more expensive and often want advance warning: National Westminster (NatWest) charges 1% commission for sterling travellers cheques, with a £3 minimum charge; Lloyds and Barclays all charge 1.5% commission, again with a minimum charge of £3.

Lost or Stolen Travellers Cheques Keep a record of the numbers of your cheques and which cheques you have cashed, then if they're lost or stolen you will be able to tell the issuing agency exactly which cheques are gone. Keep this list separate from the cheques themselves.

As soon as you realise any cheques are missing, contact the issuing office or nearest branch of the issuing agency. Thomas Cook (☎ 01733-318950) and Amex (☎ 029-2066 6111), both of which operate 24 hours a day, seven days a week, can often arrange replacement cheques within 24 hours.

ATMs Plastic cards make the perfect travelling companions: they're ideal for major purchases, let you withdraw cash from selected banks and automatic teller machines (ATMs), they don't snore and they never want the window seat.

London ATMs are usually linked up to international money systems such as Cirrus, Maestro, GlobalAccess or Plus, so you can insert your card, punch in your personal identification number (PIN) and get instant cash. But ATMs aren't fail-safe and it's always safer to go to a human cashier. It can be a major headache if an ATM swallows your card.

Some credit cards may not be hooked up to ATM networks unless you specifically ask your bank to do this for you and request a PIN. You might also ask which UK banks' ATMs will accept your particular card and whether you pay a fee to use them.

Credit Cards Carrying credit cards such as Visa, MasterCard, Amex and Diners Club is a good option as they are widely accepted in London, though some small businesses such as B&Bs still prefer cash. Businesses sometimes make a charge for accepting payment by credit card so this isn't always

the most economical way to go. You can get cash advances using your Visa card at HSBC and Barclays banks, or with your MasterCard at NatWest, Lloyds and Barclays. If you have an Amex card, you can cash up to £500 worth of personal cheques at Amex offices in any seven-day period.

If you plan to use a credit card, make sure you have a high-enough credit limit to cover major expenses such as car hire or airline tickets. Alternatively, leave your card in credit when you start your travels. And don't just carry one card, go for two different ones: an Amex or Diners Club card with a MasterCard or Visa card. Better still, combine cards and travellers cheques so you have something to fall back on if an ATM swallows your card or the bank won't accept it.

Lost or Stolen Credit Cards If a card is lost or stolen you must inform both the police (see Emergencies later in this chapter) and issuing company as soon as possible; otherwise, you may have to pay for the purchases that the unspeakable scoundrel has made using your card. Here are some 24-hour numbers for cancelling your cards:

American Express	☎ 01273-689955
	or 696933
Diners Club	☎ 0800 460800
	or 01252-516261
JCB	☎ 7499 3000
MasterCard	☎ 0800 964767
Visa	☎ 0800 895082

International Transfers A fast and efficient way of accessing your money is via international telegraphic transfer. If you instruct your bank back home to send you a draft, be sure you specify the bank and the branch to which you want your money directed, or ask your home bank to tell you where a suitable one is located. The whole procedure is easier if you've authorised someone back home to access your account.

Money sent to you by telegraphic transfer should reach you within a week; by mail, allow at least two weeks. When it arrives, it will most likely be converted into local currency – you can then take it as is or buy travellers cheques. The charge for this service is usually around £20.

You can also transfer money using Amex or Thomas Cook or by post office Money-Gram. Americans can also use Western Union (☎ 0800 833833), although it has fewer offices in London from which to collect, and charges 10% plus commission.

Eurocheques If you have a European bank account, Eurocheques are an option. They are guaranteed up to a certain amount and when cashing them you will be asked to show your Eurocheque card bearing your signature and registration number, as well as your passport or ID card. Eurocheques are not as commonly used in the UK as they are in continental Europe.

Personal Cheques Paying by personal cheque, which is validated by a cheque guarantee card, is a good option in the UK.

Current Accounts If you plan to stay a while in London, you may want to open a current account, but it's no simple matter. Building societies tend to be more welcoming than banks and often have better interest rates. You'll need a permanent address in the UK, and it will smooth the way if you have a reference or introductory letter from your bank manager at home, plus bank statements for the previous year. Owning credit/charge cards also helps.

Make sure you look for a current account that pays interest (however tiny) and gives you a cheque book, a cheque guarantee/debit card and access to ATMs.

Moneychangers Changing your money is never a problem in London, with banks, bureaux de change and travel agencies all competing for your business. Just make sure you're getting the best deal possible. Be particularly careful using bureaux de change; they may seem to offer good exchange rates but frequently levy outrageous commissions (branches of Chequepoint charge up to 8% to cash a sterling travellers cheque) and fees. Check the exchange rate,

the percentage commission and any minimum charge very carefully.

The exchange desks at the international airports charge less than most high-street banks and will cash sterling travellers cheques for free; for other currencies they charge about 1.5% with a £3 minimum. They can also sell you up to £500 worth of most major currencies on the spot.

There are 24-hour exchange bureaus in Heathrow Terminals 1, 3 and 4. The one in Terminal 2 opens 6am to 11pm daily. Thomas Cook has branches at Terminals 1 and 3, and Amex is at Terminal 4. There are 24-hour exchange desks in Gatwick's South and North Terminals and at Stansted; at Luton and London City airports bureaux de change open for arrivals and departures.

The main Amex office (Map 7; ☎ 7484 9610), 30–31 Haymarket SW1 (✆ Piccadilly Circus), opens for currency exchange 8.30am to 7pm Monday to Friday, 9am to 5.30pm (till 6.30pm in July and August) on Saturday, and 10am to 4pm (till 5pm June to September) on Sunday. Amex has a dozen other branches scattered throughout London. The Amex branch (☎ 7706 7127) at Paddington station, near the entrance to the tube, opens 7.30am to 7.30pm weekdays and 8am (9am on Sunday) to 6pm at the weekend.

The main Thomas Cook office (Map 6; ☎ 7853 6400), 30 St James's St SW1 (✆ Green Park), opens 9am (10am on Wednesday) to 5.30pm weekdays, and 10am to 4pm on Saturday (usually in summer only but call to check). There are 100 other branches throughout central London, including many inside HSBC branches and even a branch in Debenhams (☎ 7707 2000), the basement, 334–348 Oxford St W1. The Thomas Cook office on the 1st floor of the Victoria Place shopping centre at Victoria station opens 7.30am to 8pm Monday to Saturday and 8am to 6pm on Sunday.

Security

Whichever way you decide to carry your funds, it makes sense to keep most of it out of easy reach of thieves in a money belt or something similar. It always makes sense to keep around £50 apart from the rest of your cash for use in an emergency.

Take particular care in crowded places such as the Underground, Piccadilly Circus and Oxford St; never leave wallets sticking out of trouser pockets or bags. Also watch out on buses and around popular attractions such as the Tower of London and the big museums. Be warned that pickpocketing is a growing problem at airports.

Costs

The writer William Shenstone remarked more than two centuries ago that 'Nothing is certain in London but expense'. Indeed, London may not be the world's most expensive city but it certainly feels that way most of the time. Prices can be horrific, especially for those trying to stick to a tight budget. The only silver lining in this very dark £-shaped cloud is that most major museums in London will be free by the time you read this.

You will need to budget at least £30 per day for bare survival in London. Dorm accommodation alone will cost an absolute minimum of £12 per night, a one-day Travelcard for Zones 1 & 2 is £4, and drinks and the most basic sustenance will cost you at least £10, with any sightseeing or nightlife on top. There's not much point visiting if you can't enjoy some of the city's life, so if possible add another £20 per day.

Costs will be even higher if you choose to stay in a central B&B or hotel and eat restaurant meals. B&B rates start at around £30 for a single (less per person in a double) and a very cheap restaurant meal costs £10. Add a couple of pints of beer (£4.50 to £5.50) and admission fees to a tourist attraction or club and you could easily spend £60 per day without being extravagant.

Tipping & Bargaining

Many restaurants now add a 'discretionary' service charge to your bill, but in places that don't you are expected to leave a 10 to 15% tip unless the service was unsatisfactory. Waiting staff are often paid derisory wages on the assumption that the money will be supplemented by tips. It's legal for restaurants to include a service charge in the bill but this should be clearly advertised. You needn't add a further tip. You never tip to have your pint pulled in a pub but staff at bars now often return change in a little metal dish, expecting some of the coins to glue themselves to the bottom.

You can tip taxi drivers up to 10% but most people round up to the nearest 50p or pound. It's less usual to tip minicab drivers as you have (or should have) already established the fare. If you take a boat trip on the Thames you'll find the guides and/or drivers importuning for a tip in return for their commentary. Whether you pay is up to you.

Bargaining is virtually unheard of in London, even at markets (though haggling is often in order at the Bermondsey antique market on Friday). It's fine to ask if there are discounts for students, young people or hostel members, and some 'negotiation' is also OK if you're buying a vehicle.

Taxes & Refunds

Value-added tax (VAT) is a 17.5% sales tax levied on most goods and services except food, books and children's clothing. Restaurants must by law include VAT in their menu prices.

It's sometimes possible for visitors to claim a refund of VAT paid on goods – a considerable saving. You're eligible if you have spent fewer than 365 days out of the two years prior to making the purchase living in the UK, and if you're leaving the EU within three months of making the purchase.

Not all shops participate in the VAT refund scheme, called the Retail Export Scheme or Tax-Free Shopping, and different shops will have different minimum purchase conditions (normally around £75 in any one shop). On request, participating shops will give you a special form (VAT 407). This must be presented with the goods and receipts to customs when you depart (VAT-free goods can't be posted or shipped home). After customs has certified the form, it should be returned to the shop for a refund (minus an administration or handling fee), which takes about eight to 10 weeks to come through.

Several companies offer a centralised refunding service to shops and participating shops carry a sign in their window (eg, Tax-Free Shopping). You can avoid bank charges for cashing a sterling cheque by using a credit card for purchases and asking that the VAT refund be credited to your account. Cash refunds are often available at airports.

POST & COMMUNICATIONS
Post
When Londoners get dispirited about the way things work (or rather don't work) in a city that often feels like it's held together with paste, string and a bit of tape, they need only think about Royal Mail, the national postal service, to get all cheered up. It's a cracker, with 90% of letters with a 1st-class stamp posted before noon delivered the following morning *anywhere* in the country! Try to get a letter across town in, say, New York and we'll see you in a week, pal.

For general postal enquiries ring ☎ 0845 722 3344 or visit W www.royalmail.co.uk.

Postal Rates Domestic 1st-class mail is quicker but more expensive (27/41p per letter up to 60/100g) than 2nd class (19/33p).

Postcards and letters up to 20g cost a uniform 36p to anywhere in Europe; to almost everywhere else, including the Americas and Australasia it's 45/65p up to 10/20g. Packets and parcels up to 100/200g cost 87p/£1.32 to Europe and £1.15/2–2.10 to everywhere else. They must be taken to the post office for weighing.

Airmail letters to the USA or Canada generally take three to five days; to Australia or New Zealand, allow five days to a week.

Poste Restante Unless you (or the person writing to you) specify otherwise, poste restante mail sent to London ends up at the Trafalgar Square post office (Map 8; ⊖ Charing Cross), 24–28 William IV St, WC2. It opens 8am to 8pm Monday to Saturday and 9am to 8pm on Saturday. Mail will be held for four weeks; ID is required.

Amex offices will also hold clients' mail for free (see Moneychangers earlier in this chapter for addresses and opening hours).

Telephone
British Telecom's (BT's) famous red phone boxes survive in conservation areas only (notably Westminster), while some private phone companies have painted theirs black and installed them around Piccadilly and Charing Cross. More common these days are the glass cubicles with phones that accept coins, phonecards and/or credit cards.

All phones come with reasonably clear instructions. BT offers phonecards denominated at £3, £5, £10 and £20 that are widely available from all sorts of retailers, including most post offices and newsagents. A digital display on the telephone indicates how much credit is left on the card.

The following are some important telephone numbers and codes. For emergency numbers see the Emergencies section later in this chapter.

International Dialling Code	☎ 00
Local & National Directory Enquiries	☎ 192
International Directory Enquiries	☎ 153
Local & National Operator	☎ 100
International Operator	☎ 155
Reverse-Charge/Collect Calls	☎ 155
Time	☎ 123
Weathercall (Greater London)	☎ 0906 850 0401

Be advised that some of the numbers above are charged calls. Some special phone codes worth knowing include:

Toll-free	☎ 0500/0800
Local call rates apply	☎ 0845
National call rate applies	☎ 0870
Premium rates apply (from 60p per minute)	☎ 09

Calling London London's area code is 020 followed by an eight-digit number beginning with 7 or 8. You only need to dial the 020 when you are calling London from elsewhere in the UK.

To call London from abroad, dial your country's international access code, then 44 (the UK's country code), then 20 (dropping the initial 0) followed by the eight-digit phone number.

London's Bewildering Postcodes

And they say the French make life difficult for themselves... just take a look at the 20 *arrondisse-ments* in Paris that spiral clockwise from the centre in such a lovely – and logical – fashion. If you've got a letter for someone in the 5th, you simply write 75005. And then take a look at London's codes on the map below. How on earth can SE23 border SE6? If there's a north (N), a west (W) and an east (E) why isn't there a south (S)? And what happened to the north-east (NE)?

When they were introduced in 1858, the postcodes were fairly clear, with all the compass points represented, along with an east and west central (EC and WC). But not long afterwards NE was merged with E and S with SE and SW and the problems began. The real convolution came during WWI when a numbering system was introduced for inexperienced sorters (regular employees were off fighting in 'the war to end all wars'). No 1 was the centre of each zone but other numbers related to the alphabetical order of the postal districts' names. Thus anything starting with a letter near the beginning of the alphabet, such as Chingford, would get a low number (E4), even though it was miles from the centre at Whitechapel (E1), while Poplar, which borders Whitechapel, is E14.

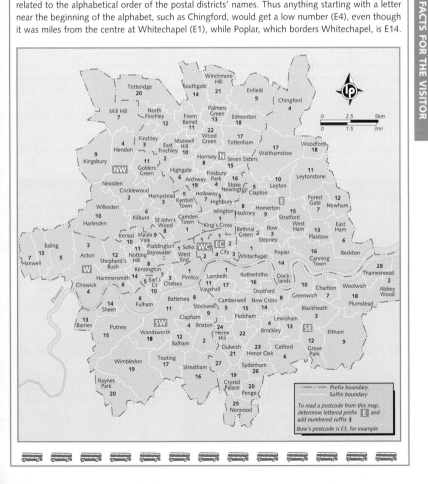

Local & National Calls & Rates Local calls are charged by time alone; regional and national calls are charged by both time and distance. Daytime rates apply from 8am to 6pm Monday to Friday; the cheap rate applies from 6pm to 8am Monday to Friday; and the cheap weekend rate applies from midnight Friday to midnight Sunday. The latter two rates offer substantial savings.

Calls to local and national directory enquiries cost 11p per minute (minimum deposit: 20p) from public phones and 40p from private ones.

International Calls & Rates International direct dialling (IDD) calls to almost anywhere can be made from nearly all public telephones. To call someone outside the UK dial 00, then the country code, the area code (you usually drop the initial zero if there is one) and the number. For example, to ring Melbourne, where the area code is 03 and the code for Australia is 61, you would dial 00-61-3-1234 5678. To reach Boston, where the area code is 617 and the code for the USA is 1, dial 00-1-617-123 4567.

Direct dialling is cheaper than making a reverse-charge (collect) call through the international operator (☎ 155). International directory enquiries (☎ 153) cost a whopping £1.50 per minute from private phones.

Some private firms such as Callshop offer cheaper international calls than BT. You can find a branch of Callshop (Map 10; ☎ 7390 4549, ⊖ Earl's Court) at 181a Earl's Court Rd SW5. It opens 9am to 11pm daily. In such shops you phone from a metered booth and then pay the bill. Some cybercafes and Internet access shops, such as Internet Lounge in Earl's Court, also offer cheap rates for international calls.

It's also possible to undercut BT international call rates by buying a special card (usually denominated £5, £10 or £20) with a PIN that you use from any phone, even a home phone, by dialling a special access number. There are dozens of cards available – with bizarre names such as Alpha, Omega, Banana Call, First National and Swiftlink – available from newsagents and grocers. To decide which is best you really have to compare the rate each offers for the

London pride: you'll still see a few famous red telephone boxes in Westminster.

particular country you want – posters with the rates of the various companies are often displayed in shop doors or windows.

eKno Communication Service Lonely Planet's eKno Communication Card is aimed specifically at travellers and provides cheap international calls, a range of messaging services and free email – you're usually better off with a local card for local calls. You can join online at **W** www.ekno .lonelyplanet.com or by calling ☎ 0800 376 1704 from London. To use eKno from the UK dial ☎ 0800 376 1705 .

Check the eKno Web site for joining and access numbers from other countries and updates on super-budget local access numbers and new features.

Mobile Phones The UK uses the GSM 900 network, which covers the rest of Europe, Australia and New Zealand, but is not compatible with the North American GSM 1900 or the totally different system in Japan (though many North Americans have GSM 1900/900 phones that do work here). If you have a GSM phone, check with your service provider about using it in the UK, and beware of calls being routed internationally (very expensive for a local call). You can also rent one from various companies, including Mobell (☎ 0800 243524, **W** www .mobell.com) and Cellhire (☎ 0870 561 0610, **W** www.cellhire.com) from around £20 per week, depending on the hire period. In this case, however, you can't use your existing number.

Fax & Telemessage
One of the easiest place from which to send faxes is the business services chain Kinko's (see Doing Business later in this chapter), which has four branches in central London open 24 hours a day. They charge 50p per page for sending faxes in London, £1 (50p for each additional page) elsewhere in the UK, £2 (50p) to the rest of Europe, the USA and Canada and £3 (50p) to everywhere else. It costs 50p per page to receive faxes there. You can also send and receive faxes at many cybercafes, including Cyberg@te.

If you need to get a message somewhere in the UK or overseas urgently, call ☎ 0800 190190 to send a telemessage. It costs £8.99 for up to 50 words in the UK, delivered by post. If you want guaranteed delivery by noon the next day, it costs about £13.

Email & Internet Access
Most hotels, hostels and even some pubs nowadays are geared up for Internet access. If you can't access the Internet from where you're staying, London is chock-a-block with cybercafes. The following list includes some of the most conveniently located ones.

Buzz Bar
(Map 5; ☎ 7460 4906, **W** www.buzzbar.co.uk.) 95 Portobello Rd W11 (⊖ Notting Hill Gate). Upstairs from the Portobello Gold Hotel, Buzz Bar has ten terminals available (£1.50 per half-hour) 10am to 7pm Monday to Saturday.
Cyberg@te
(Map 4; ☎ 7387 3810, **W** www.c-gate.com) 3 Leigh St WC1 (⊖ Russell Square). Access costs £1 for 20/30 minutes for adults/students. It opens 9am to 11pm Monday to Saturday, noon to 8pm Sunday. The branch at STA Travel (Map 3; ☎ 7383 2282), 117 Euston Rd NW1, opens 10am to 5pm weekdays, 11am to 5pm Saturday.
Cyberia
(Map 6; ☎ 7681 4223, **W** www.cyberiacafe.net) 39 Whitfield St W1 (⊖ Goodge Street). The first Internet cafe in London, Cyberia has ten terminals; access costs 50p for 15 minutes. It opens 9am to 8pm weekdays, 11am to 7pm Saturday.
easyEverything
(Map 11; ☎ 7233 8456, **W** www.easyeverything .com) 12–14 Wilton Rd SW1 (⊖ Victoria). This chain of cybercafes, a division of the no-frills airline easyJet, opens 24 hours, seven days a week and costs £1 for 20 minutes to an hour, depending on the time of day. Other branches (☎ same) are in Fitzrovia (Map 7; 9–16 Tottenham Court Rd W1, ⊖ Tottenham Court Road); Kensington (Map 5; 160–166 Kensington High St W8, ⊖ Kensington High St); Oxford St (Map 6; 358 Oxford St W1, ⊖ Oxford Street); and the Strand (Map 8; 7 Strand WC2, ⊖ Charing Cross).
Internet Exchange
(Map 7; ☎ 7437 3704, **W** www.internet-exchange .co.uk, ⊖ Piccadilly Circus) London Trocadero, 1st floor, Piccadilly Circus W1. This chain, with branches as ubiquitous as those of easyEverything, charges £3/4.20 per hour from 10am to noon/noon to midnight, or £1.50 for 20 minutes

anytime. It opens 10am to midnight. Branches include Covent Garden (Map 8; ☎ 7836 8636, 37 The Market WC2, ⊖ Covent Garden) and Bayswater (Map 5; ☎ 7792 5790, 47–49 Queensway W2, ⊖ Bayswater).

Internet Lounge
(Map 10; ☎ 7370 5742, ⊖ Earl's Court) 24a Earl's Court Gardens SW5. This place charges £1 for 50 minutes access. It opens 9am till midnight daily.

usit Campus
(Map 11; ☎ 870 240 1010, **w** www.usitcampus .co.uk) 52 Grosvenor Gardens SW1 (⊖ Victoria). This popular student travel agency (see Travel Agencies in the Getting There & Away chapter) charges £1 per hour for access, available 9am to 6pm weekdays, 10am to 5pm on Saturday and 11am to 3pm on Sunday.

Vibe Bar
(Map 9; ☎ 7247 3479, 7377 2899, **w** www.vibe bar.co.uk) The Brewery, 91–95 Brick Lane E1 (⊖ Shoreditch/Aldgate East). Seven terminals are available at no charge to customers. It opens 11am to midnight Monday to Saturday and noon to midnight on Sunday.

Virgin Megastore
(Map 7; ☎ 7631 1234) 14–30 Oxford St W1 (⊖ Tottenham Court Road). This huge record store has access on 20 terminals available 9.30am to 10pm Monday to Saturday and noon to 6pm Sun. It costs £2/4 per hour for members/nonmembers (lifetime membership costs £6).

Webshack
(Map 7; ☎ 7439 8000, **w** www.webshack-cafe .com) 15 Dean St W1 (⊖ Tottenham Court Road). This central Internet cafe has 40 terminals (£50p/£1.25/£2 for 10/40/60 minutes, or £1.25 per hour after 8pm). It opens 10am to 11pm Monday to Saturday and 1pm to 9pm on Sunday.

DIGITAL RESOURCES
Web Sites
Britain is second only to the USA in its number of Web sites, and there are lots of sites of interest to travellers. An increasing number of attractions, hotels and transport companies have their own sites, which have been listed in this book when they would be of use to travellers.

There's no better place to start your Web explorations than the Lonely Planet Web site **w** www.lonelyplanet.com. Here you'll find summaries on travelling to most places on earth, postcards from other travellers and the Thorn Tree bulletin board, where you can ask questions before you go or dispense advice when you get back. You can also find travel news and updates to many of our most popular guidebooks, and the subWWWay section links you to the most useful travel resources elsewhere on the Web.

Useful (and general) London sites include:

w www.6thsenselondon.com
  A guide to London through the five senses
w www.buzzlondon.co.uk
  Virtual tour of London
w www.freshdirection.co.uk
  Complete student guide to London
w www.londononline.co.uk
  Useful sight for London
w www.streetmap.co.uk or **w** www.multimap.com
  London's streets and byways online
w www.thisislondon.com
  The *Evening Standard* guide to London

JULIET COOMBE

Get connected: British Telecom Tower rises out of Fitzrovia

CitySync

CitySync London is Lonely Planet's digital city guide for Palm OS handheld devices. With CitySync you can quickly search, sort and bookmark hundreds of London's restaurants, hotels, attractions, clubs and more – all pinpointed on scrollable street maps. Sections on activities, transport and local events mean you get the big picture plus all the little details. Purchase or demo City-Sync London at **W** www.citysync.com.

BOOKS

London has innumerable good book and map shops (see Books in the Shopping chapter), with a wide range of books, maps, videos etc focusing on the capital. If you are in search of London titles before you arrive, be aware that most books are published in different editions by different publishers in different countries. As a result, a book might be a rarity in one country while it's readily available in another. Fortunately, bookshops and libraries search by title or author, so your local bookshop or library can advise you on the availability of the following recommendations.

Lonely Planet

Lonely Planet also publishes *Britain*, *Walking in Britain*, *England*, *Scotland*, *Edinburgh* and *Wales*, which provide information for those planning to travel around the rest of the island. The *London City Guide* video provides a visual complement to this book. *London Condensed* is a pocket guide written for those on shorter visits to the capital. *Cycling Britain* is the perfect companion for those wanting to see the island by bike. Lonely Planet's *Ireland* guide covers Northern Ireland and the Irish Republic. Those who want to get to grips with British English – Cockney in particular – should get hold of Lonely Planet's *British Phrasebook*.

Guidebooks

Guides to London cover every aspect and specialist interest; we can provide just a brief sampling.

If you want to get to know London better than most Londoners, you might browse through a copy of *The London Encyclopaedia* by Ben Weinreb & Christopher Hibbert. But don't even *think* of taking a copy along with you; it's got 1072 pages and weighs more than your average infant.

Culture vultures who want to find out more about the city's art should look for Abigail Willis' *Museums & Galleries of London*, which tours you through the capital's leading collections. *A Guide to the Architecture of London* by Christopher Woodward & Edward Jones is a seminal, complete work with fine illustrations, but using the computer-manual-style index is frustrating. Samantha Hardingham's *London: A Guide to Recent Architecture* (5th edition), is an excellent, pocket-sized introduction to the capital's contemporary buildings. Hardingham's *Eat London* is a look at London restaurants with architectural and/or design merit.

For hidden corners of the capital and a host of interesting trivia, look for anything by Geoffrey Fletcher (eg, *London: A Private View*, *London Overlooked*), whose books often come with pleasing sketches. Sadly, many of Fletcher's works are now out of print, though you can usually find copies through Internet booksellers. Visitors from North America should look out for *American Walks in London* by Richard Tames, which describes 10 itineraries covering places with links to Canada and the USA.

London for Free by Brian Butler is the cheapskate's bible, though *Harden's London for Free* by Richard & Peter Harden gives Butler a run for his, ah, money.

Food Lonely Planet's *Out to Eat: London* covers a wide selection of London's best eateries, with almost 400 restaurants reviewed. *Cheap Eats in London* by Sandra Gustafson lists more than 170 budget pubs, restaurants, wine bars and tearooms.

For noncarnivores, there's the useful *Vegetarian London* by Alex Bourke et al. Travellers who keep kosher should get a hold of a copy of *The Really Jewish Food Guide* published by the London Beth Din Kashrut Division.

Travel

London doesn't seem to have inspired too many modern-day travel writers to set pen to paper though they were pretty thick on the ground in the last century with the likes of Mark Twain and others (see Literature in the Facts about London chapter). American Bill Bryson's exploits in the capital are as witty and quirky as those elsewhere in Britain in his wonderful bestseller, *Notes from a Small Island.*

London, England is an irreverent and quite excellent portrait of 'cool London' by Derek Hammond, journalist and ex-punk musician. Iain Sinclair's *Lights Out for the Territory*, subtitled 'Nine Excursions in the Secret History of London', is another kettle of fish: dark, brooding and as difficult to put down once you've got going as it is to get into in the first place.

History & Politics

Traveller's History of London by Richard Tames is an excellent and highly readable introduction to London's history – from Roman Londinium to the London Eye. Christopher Hibbert's *London* is a longer (though now outdated) social history of the British capital with excellent illustrations and colour plates. Peter Ackroyd's *Biography of London*, part history and part fiction, tells the story of London's dark past in chapters with themes such as childhood, drinking, theatre, poverty, sex and so on.

It's a bit of a paperweight, but anyone interested in 17th-century London (eg, the Great Fire and all the bawdy goings-on) should try battling through *Samuel Pepys' Diary*. Written in shorthand between 1660 and 1669, it contains enough references to women other than his wife to confirm that London was lewder and less inhibited during the Restoration than it is even today. It comes in several chunky volumes; you might be more successful wading through *The Concise Pepys*, though this still has some 800 pages. *Restoration London* by Liza Picard, a social history of the same decade, covers a lot more ground – from cooking, shopping and laundry to medicine, crime and sex. *The Dreadful Judgement:*

The True Story of the Great Fire of London by Neil Hanson is a blow-by-blow account of the dreadful conflagration that reduced most of London to ashes in 1666. Closer to our time is *London in the Twentieth Century: A City & Its People* by Jerry White.

Longitude by Dava Sobel tells the riveting story of John Harrison, an 18th-century clockmaker who established longitude and thus helped to keep sailors on course. It may sound something of a niche subject but, hey, it all happened right in Greenwich.

NEWSPAPERS & MAGAZINES
Newspapers

'I read the news today, oh boy...' Most major newspapers in the UK are national though many are published outside the capital. The only daily (published Monday to Friday) that is well and truly a Londoner is the *Evening Standard*, a widely read afternoon tabloid that can vacillate from being right-wing to radical (usually when matters directly affecting London are concerned) from page to page and week to week. Its restaurant reviews (particularly those by Fay Maschler) are worth reading and its entertainment supplement *Hot Tickets*, published on Thursday, is an excellent and eclectic source of information. The *Standard* publishes a précis of its stories in *Metro* (available at tube stations on weekday mornings).

At the very bottom end of the newspaper market in terms of content – though tops in circulation – are the *Sun, Mirror, Daily Star* and *Daily Record* tabloids. The middle-level *Daily Mail* and *Express* tabloids are very right wing. Most have Sunday editions.

Of the broadsheets, the *Daily Telegraph* far outsells its rivals. It's sometimes thought of as an old-fogeyish, Conservative paper but it nonetheless features excellent writing and world coverage. *The Times* is still conservative and influential and has good travel and sports sections. The mildly left-wing *Guardian* is read by the so-called chattering classes (the liberal middle class). Its review of the world media called *The Editor*, which comes out as a supplement every Saturday, is required reading for anyone who wants to know what's happening outside Old Blighty.

The *Guide* entertainment supplement (also with Saturday's *Guardian*) is worthwhile. The *Independent* tries to live up to its name but is struggling to stay afloat. It is drier than an old bone in the Sahara and too politically correct for words. The business-oriented *Financial Times* has a great travel section in its weekend edition.

The Sunday papers are an institution in the UK, but are often so full of trashy gossip, star-struck adulation, fashion extras and mean-spirited diatribes directed at government officials, foreigners (especially the French) and anyone who's 'made it' as to rankle the least flappable of readers. The *Sunday Times* must destroy at least one rainforest per issue, but most of it can be tossed in the recycling bin upon purchase. The Sunday-only *Observer* is similar in tone and style to the *Guardian*, which owns it. In fact, almost every daily has a Sunday stable mate, which usually – but not always – shares its political views.

You can also buy the Paris-based *International Herald Tribune*, arguably the best brief source of international news available, and many foreign-language papers in central London. For a particularly good selection, try the newsstands in the Victoria Place shopping centre at Victoria train station, along Charing Cross Rd, in Old Compton St and along Queensway.

Magazines

London sells – and Londoners consume – an astonishing range of magazines: from political weeklies to girl-band fanzines. Good places to stock up are the kiosks in the main-line stations, where *Time* and *Newsweek* are also available.

Time Out (£2.20), the London events magazine published every Wednesday, is a complete listing of what's on and where.

The weekly freebies *TNT Magazine*, *Southern Cross* and *SA Times* have Australasian and South African news and sports results, but are invaluable for any budget traveller, with entertainment listings, travel sections and useful classifieds covering jobs, cheap tickets, shipping services and accommodation. They can be picked up

'Read all about it!' With newsstands dotted all over the city you can catch up on the latest.

outside tube stations, mainly in Earl's Court, Notting Hill and Bayswater. *TNT Magazine* (W www.tnt-live.com) is the glossiest and most comprehensive; ring ☎ 7373 3377 for the nearest distribution point.

Loot (£1.30), which appears five times a week, is a paper made up of classified ads that are placed free by sellers. You can find everything from kitchen sinks to cars, as well as an extensive selection of flat and house-share ads.

RADIO & TV
Radio

London's radio stations include Capital FM (95.8kHz FM), the commercial equivalent of the BBC's Radio 1 and the most popular pop station in the city, and Capital Gold (1548kHz AM), which plays oldies from the 1960s, '70s and '80s. BBC London Live (94.9kHz FM) is a talk station with a London bias. Xfm on 104.9kHz FM bills itself as an alternative radio station and plays indie music.

There are many other commercial radio stations, sometimes offering local news and chat alongside the music. Virgin (105.8kHz FM) is a pop station while Choice FM (96.9kHz FM) and Kiss 100 (100kHz FM) are the soul and dance stations respectively. Classic FM (100.9kHz FM) does classical music with commercials, and the excellent Jazz FM (102.2kHz FM) caters for middle-of-the-road jazz and blues aficionados. Talk Sport (1089kHz AM) is self-descriptive; LBC (1152kHz AM) is a talk-back channel. Magic FM (105.4kHz FM) plays mainstream oldies. News Direct (97.3kHz FM) is an all-news station with full reports every 20 minutes.

While in London you'll be able to pick up all the national BBC services. Radio 1 (98.8kHz FM), the main public pop, rock and dance station, has undergone a revival after some years in the doldrums. At the same time, Radio 2 (89.1kHz FM) has broadened its outlook and now plays gooey '60s, '70s and '80s stuff alongside even older tracks.

Radio 3 (91.3kHz FM) sticks with classical music and plays, while Radio 4 (720kHz AM, 93.5kHz FM) offers a mixture of drama, news, current affairs and talk; its *Today* programme (6am to 9am Monday to Friday and from 7am on Saturday) is particularly popular. Radio 5 Live (909Hz AM), sometimes known as 'Radio Bloke', provides a mix of sport and news, with emphasis on the former.

The BBC World Service (648kHz AM) offers brilliant news coverage and quirky bits and pieces from around the globe.

TV

Britain still turns out some of the world's best TV, padding out the decent home-grown output with American imports, Australian soaps, inept sitcoms and trashy chat and game shows of its own. There are five regular TV channels. BBC1 and BBC2 are publicly funded by a TV licensing system and, like BBC radio stations, don't carry advertising; ITV, Channel 4 and Channel 5 are commercial channels and do. These are now competing with the satellite channels of Rupert Murdoch's BSkyB – which offers a variety of channels with less-than-inspiring programmes – and assorted cable channels.

JULIET COOMBE

Four-ward thinking: for a fresh approach to programme-making switch to Channel 4.

VIDEO SYSTEMS

The UK, like most of Europe, uses the PAL system, which is incompatible with the American and Japanese NTSC system. Since souvenir kiosks at many tourist attractions sell both PAL and NTSC videos, make sure you select the right one.

PHOTOGRAPHY & VIDEO
Film & Equipment

Although print film is widely available, slide film can be more elusive; if there's no specialist photographic shop around, Boots, the chemist chain, is likely to have what you want. At Jessops photo centres, which offer a discount if you buy 10 rolls of film at once, a roll of 36-exposure print film costs just £2.69 for ISO 100 to £3.49 for ISO 400. With slide film it's usually cheapest to go for process-inclusive versions; at Jessops 36-exposure slide film costs from £5.79 for ISO 100. The most central Jessops branch (Map 8; ☎ 7240 6077, ⊖ Tottenham Court Road) is at 63–69 New Oxford St WC1.

Technical Tips

With dull, overcast conditions common in London throughout the year, high-speed film (ISO 200 or 400) is the way to go. When the sun does make an appearance in summer, the best times of day for photography are usually early in the morning and late in the afternoon, when the sun's glare has passed.

Restrictions

Many tourist attractions such as museums and galleries prohibit photography or levy a fee for taking snaps. Use of a flash is often banned to protect light-sensitive paintings and fabrics. Video cameras are sometimes forbidden because of ths inconvenience they can cause to other visitors.

Airport Security

You will have to put your camera and film through the X-ray machine at all airports in the UK. The machines are supposed to be film-safe, but you may feel much happier putting exposed films in a protective lead-lined bag.

TIME

A century ago the sun never set on the British Empire, so the British could be forgiven for thinking that London (or more precisely Greenwich) was the centre of the universe. Greenwich is still the location for the prime meridian, which divides the world into eastern and western hemispheres.

Wherever you are in the world, the time on your watch is measured in relation to the time at Greenwich – Greenwich Mean Time (GMT) – although strictly speaking GMT is used only in air and sea navigation and is otherwise referred to as universal time coordinated (UTC).

British Summer Time, the UK's form of daylight-saving time, muddies the water so that even London is ahead of GMT from late March to late October. To give you an idea, San Francisco is usually eight hours and New York five hours behind GMT, while Sydney is 10 hours ahead of GMT. Phone the international operator on ☎ 155 to find out the exact difference.

ELECTRICITY

The standard voltage throughout Britain is 230/240V AC, 50Hz. Plugs have three square pins, but adapters to fit European-style plugs are widely available.

WEIGHTS & MEASURES

In theory, the UK has now embraced the metric system. All vendors are now required by law to display metric along with their imperial equivalents but the latter are likely to be used by much of the population for some time to come. Distances continue to be given in miles, though builders and younger people tend to use metres and centimetres over yards, feet and inches. Most liquids – apart from milk and beer (which come in half-pints and pints) – are now sold in litres. In this book we use the metric system but give distances in miles to make reading local maps and signposts easier. For conversion tables, see the inside back cover.

LAUNDRY

'Time weighs heavily in a laundrette', as the saying goes, but you're going to have to face washing your gear at some stage. Many hostels and some hotels have self-service washing machines and dryers, and virtually every high street has its own laundrette – with rare exceptions, a disheartening place to spend much time. The average cost for a single load is £2 to £2.60 for washing and from 60p to £1.20 for drying. Hours vary but laundrettes usually open 6.30am or 8am to 8pm or 9pm daily.

The following is a selected list of laundrettes that may be within striking distance of your hotel or hostel:

Bayswater
Laundrette Centre (Map 5) 5 Porchester Rd W2
Sandwich Bar Laundrette (Map 5) 28 Craven Terrace W2
Bloomsbury
Red & White Laundrette (Map 4) 78 Marchmont St WC1
Red & White Laundrette (Map 6) 88 Cleveland St WC1
Camden
Forco (Map 3) 60 Parkway NW1
Chelsea, South Kensington & Earl's Court
Cremorne Launderers (Map 10) 395 King's Rd SW3
Bobo's Bubbles (Map 10) 111 Earl's Court Rd SW5
Wash & Dry (Map 10) 34 Harrington Rd SW7
Hampstead
Hampstead Laundrette (Map 12) 57 South End Rd NW3
Islington
Upper St Laundrette (Map 4) 177 Upper St N1

TOILETS

Although many toilets in central London are still pretty grim, those at main train stations, bus terminals and attractions are generally good and usually have facilities for disabled people and those with young children. At the train and bus stations you usually have to pay 20p to use the facilities, which is pretty irksome when you consider how much rail fares are. You also have to pay to use the self-cleaning concrete pods in places such as Leicester Square (and, yes, they do open automatically after a set amount of time, so no hanky-panky – or make it snappy).

In theory it's an offence to urinate in the streets (and men could be arrested for

indecent exposure). However, as everywhere, those who've passed the evening in the pub happily make use of alleyways, thereby rendering them unpleasant for others.

Many disabled toilets can only be opened with a special key obtainable from tourist offices or by sending a £3 cheque or postal order to RADAR (see the Disabled Travellers section later in this chapter), together with a brief statement of your disability.

LEFT LUGGAGE

All the train stations (with the exception of London Bridge) and Victoria Coach Station (see the Getting There & Away chapter) have left-luggage offices or lockers, as do the airports (see the Getting Around chapter). They cost between £2.50 and £8 per day, depending on the size of the bag or locker. Be advised that left-luggage facilities at the main bus and train stations may close without notice for security reasons.

HEALTH

Aside from the threats posed by the wild nightlife and widely available liquids, herbs and chemical substances, London presents no major health risks. Care about what you eat and drink and good personal hygiene should see you through. Serious problems are unlikely but mild stomach upsets as a result of a change in diet are not unknown.

Tap water is always safe (though with a very high lime content) so there's no need to pay the high prices restaurants ask for bottled water. No jabs are needed to visit Britain. Whether you eat British beef or lamb after the bovine spongiform encephalopathy (BSE or 'mad cow disease') scare and the foot-and-mouth epidemic is up to you, but most carnivorous Londoners still do.

Medical Services

Reciprocal arrangements with the UK allow residents of Australia, New Zealand nationals and residents and nationals of several other countries to receive free emergency medical treatment and subsidised dental care through the National Health Service (NHS; ☎ 0845 4647, ⓦ www.nhsdirect.nhs.uk); they can use hospital emergency departments, GPs and dentists (check the *Yellow Pages* phone directory). Visitors of 12 months or longer with the proper documentation will receive care under the NHS by registering with a specific practice near where they live. Again check the phone book for one close to you. EU nationals can obtain free emergency treatment on presentation of an E111 form that has been validated in their home country.

Travel insurance, however, is advisable as it offers greater flexibility over where and how you're treated and covers expenses for an ambulance and repatriation that won't be picked up by the NHS (see Travel Insurance earlier in this chapter).

For addresses of local doctors or hospitals, look in the phone book or call ☎ 100.

Hospitals The following hospitals have 24-hour accident and emergency departments:

Charing Cross Hospital
(Map 2; ☎ 8846 1234) Fulham Palace Rd W6 (✪ Hammersmith)
Chelsea & Westminster Hospital
(Map 10; ☎ 8746 8000) 369 Fulham Rd SW10 (✪ South Kensington, then bus No 14 or 211)
Guy's Hospital
(Map 9; ☎ 7955 5000) St Thomas St SE1 (✪ London Bridge)
Homerton Hospital
(Map 2; ☎ 8919 5555) Homerton Row E9 (Station: Homerton)
Royal Free Hospital
(Map 12; ☎ 7794 0500) Pond St NW3 (✪ Belsize Park)
Royal London Hospital
(Map 9; ☎ 7377 7000) Whitechapel Rd E1 (✪ Whitechapel)
University College Hospital
(Map 3; ☎ 7387 9300) Grafton Way WC1 (✪ Euston Square)

Dental Services To find an emergency dentist phone the Dental Emergency Care Service on ☎ 7955 2186 between 8.45am and 3.30pm weekdays or call into Eastman Dental Hospital (Map 4; ☎ 7915 1000, ✪ King's Cross), 256 Gray's Inn Rd WC1.

Chemists (Pharmacies) Chemists can advise on minor ailments such as sore throats, coughs and earache. There's always one local chemist that's open 24 hours; other chemists should display details in their window or doorway, or you can look in a local newspaper or the *Yellow Pages*. Since all medication is readily available, either over-the-counter or on prescription, there's no need to stock up.

Immunisation Services
Several travel agencies offer immunisation services for your onward travels but at very different prices. Trailfinders (Map 5; ☎ 7938 3999, ✪ High Street Kensington) has a clinic at 194 Kensington High St W8, offering a full range of travel vaccines. It opens 9am to 5pm (to 6pm on Thursday) weekdays and 10am to 5.15pm on Saturday. The Vaccination Clinic (☎ 7259 2180) has an immunisation clinic at Top Deck Travel (Map 10; ☎ 7370 4555, ✪ Earl's Court) 131–135 Earl's Court Rd SW5. Nomad Traveller's Store & Medical Centre (☎ 8889 7014, ⓦ www.nomadtravel.co.uk, ✪ Turnpike Lane) 3–4 Wellington Terrace, Turnpike Lane N8, gives immunisations on Thursday and Saturday evenings. They'll jab you during the week at their immunisation centre at STA Travel at 40 Bernard St WC1.

HIV/AIDS
Infection with the human immunodeficiency virus (HIV) may lead to acquired immune deficiency syndrome (AIDS), which is a fatal disease. Any exposure to blood, blood products or body fluids may put the individual at risk. The disease is often transmitted through sexual contact or dirty needles; vaccinations, acupuncture, tattooing and body piercing can be potentially as dangerous as intravenous drug use. HIV/AIDS can also be spread through infected blood transfusions; blood used for transfusions in London hospitals is screened for HIV and should be safe.

HIV/AIDS Organisations
Help and support are available from the National AIDS Helpline (☎ 0800 567123) and the Terrence Higgins Trust (Map 6; ☎ 7831 0330) at 52–54 Gray's Inn Rd WC1 (✪ Chancery Lane).

Sexually Transmitted Diseases (STDs)

HIV/AIDS and hepatitis B can be transmitted through sexual contact. Other STDs include gonorrhoea, herpes and syphilis; sores, blisters or rashes around the genitals and discharges or pain when urinating are common symptoms. In some STDs, such as wart virus or chlamydia, symptoms may be less marked or not observed at all, especially in women. Chlamydia infection can cause infertility in men and women before any symptoms have been noticed. Syphilis symptoms eventually disappear completely but the disease continues and can cause severe problems in later years. While abstinence from sexual contact is the only 100% effective prevention, using condoms is also effective. The treatment of gonorrhoea and syphilis is with antibiotics. Different STDs each require specific antibiotics.

Women's Health

Gynaecological Problems Antibiotic use, synthetic underwear, sweating and contraceptive pills can lead to fungal vaginal infections, especially when in hot weather. Fungal infections are characterised by a rash, itch and discharge and can be treated with a highly-diluted vinegar or lemon-juice douche, or with yoghurt. Nystatin, miconazole or clotrimazole pessaries or vaginal cream are the usual treatment. Maintaining good personal hygiene and wearing loose-fitting clothes and cotton underwear may help prevent these infections.

Sexually transmitted diseases are a major cause of vaginal problems. Symptoms include a smelly discharge, painful intercourse and sometimes a burning sensation when urinating. Medical attention should be sought and male sexual partners must also be treated. For more details see the section on Sexually Transmitted Diseases earlier. Besides abstinence, the best thing is to practise safer sex using condoms.

WOMEN TRAVELLERS

In general, London is a fairly laid-back place, and you're unlikely to have too many problems provided you take the usual city precautions. Apart from the occasional wolf-whistle and unwelcome body contact on the tube, women will find male Londoners reasonably enlightened. There's nothing to stop women going into pubs alone, though this is usually not a comfortable experience even in central London.

Safety Precautions

Solo women travellers should have few problems, although common-sense caution should be observed, especially at night. It's particularly unwise to get into an Underground carriage with no-one else in it or with just one or two men, and there are a few tube stations, especially on the far reaches of the Northern Line, where you won't feel comfortable late at night. The same goes for some of the main-line stations in the south (such as Lambeth) and south-east (such as Bromley), which may be unstaffed and look pretty grim. In such cases you should hang the expense and take a black taxi.

Condoms are now often sold in women's toilets as well as men's. Otherwise, chemists and many service stations stock them. The contraceptive pill is only available on prescription in the UK, though the emergency contraceptive pill or 'morning-after' pill (actually effective for up to 72 hours after unprotected sex) is now available to women aged over 16 over-the-counter at chemists.

Information & Organisations

The Well Women Centre (Map 6; ☎ 0845 300 8090), Marie Stopes House, 108 Whitfield St W1 (⊖ Warren Street), offers advice on contraception and pregnancy. It opens 9am to 5pm (till 8pm on Tuesday and Wednesday) Monday to Saturday.

The Rape & Sexual Abuse Helpline (☎ 8239 1122) operates noon to 2.30pm and 7pm to 9.30pm Monday to Friday and 2.30pm to 5pm Saturday and Sunday.

GAY & LESBIAN TRAVELLERS

London has a flourishing gay and lesbian scene. Certainly it's possible for people to acknowledge their homosexuality in a way that would have been unimaginable two decades ago. The current government has several openly gay MPs as well as a Cabinet minister; the BTA has advertised overseas under the slogan 'You don't know the half of it' in a bid to attract more 'pink pound' tourists; and, most importantly, the age of consent has been lowered to 16 to bring it into line with that of heterosexuals.

Having said that, pockets of out-and-out hostility remain – you only need read the scurrilous tabloids to realise the limits of toleration – and overt displays of affection are not necessarily wise away from acknowledged gay venues and areas such as Soho (and Old Compton St in particular).

For more details on the homosexual scene in London, see Gay & Lesbian Venues in the Entertainment chapter.

Information & Organisations

To find out what's going on in London pick up a free listings magazine such as the *Pink Paper* or *Boyz*, or buy a copy of the *Gay Times* (£2.95), which also has listings. *Diva* (£2.25) is for lesbians. The freebies are available at most gay bars, clubs and saunas, and the magazines can be bought at Gay's the Word bookshop (see Books in the Shopping chapter). *Gay London: a Guide* by Will McLoughlin takes up where the simple (and often confusing) listings in the *Spartacus International Gay Guide* leave off.

Another useful source of information is the 24-hour Lesbian & Gay Switchboard (☎ 7837 7324), which can help with most enquiries, general and specific. London Friend (☎ 7837 3337) offers similar help but only from 7.30pm to 10pm daily.

A few Web sites that are worth checking out include: **W** www.gaylondonguide.co.uk; **W** www.queenscene.com; **W** www.heymickey.com/gaylondon; and the lesbian guide http://www.gingerbeer.co.uk.

DISABLED TRAVELLERS

For many disabled travellers, London is an odd mix of user-friendliness and downright disinterest. These days new hotels and modern tourist attractions are usually accessible by wheelchair, but many B&Bs and guesthouses are in older buildings that are hard

(if not impossible) to adapt. This means that travellers who have mobility problems may end up having to pay more for accommodation than those who don't.

It's a similar story with public transport. Some newer trains and buses have steps that lower for easier access (eg, the Stationlink buses that follow a similar route to that of the Circle Line and are described in the Getting Around chapter), but it's always wise to check before setting out. Transport for London's Unit for Disabled Passengers (☎ 7918 3312, **e** lt.udp@ltbuses.co.uk) can give you detailed advice and it publishes *Access to the Underground*, which indicates which tube stations have ramps and lifts (all DLR stations do). To receive a copy ahead of your visit write to the Transport for London Unit for Disabled Passengers, 172 Buckingham Palace Rd, London SW1 9TN.

Many ticket offices, banks and so on are fitted with hearing loops to help the hearing-impaired; look for the ear symbol.

Certain toilets equipped for the disabled can only be opened with a special key. For information on how to obtain one, see the Toilets section earlier in this chapter.

Information & Organisations

The LTB has accessibility information for the disabled on its Web site (**W** www.londontouristboard.com). A highly recommended publication is *Access in London* by Gordon Couch, William Forrester & Justin Irwin (£7.95), a comprehensive guide for disabled people in the capital and a great source for disabled visitors. General information on wheelchair access to theatres, cinemas and other cultural venues is also available from Artsline (☎ 7388 2227), which takes calls from 9.30am to 5.30pm weekdays.

The Royal Association for Disability and Rehabilitation (RADAR; ☎ 7250 3222, **W** www.radar.org.uk), Unit 12, City Forum, 250 City Rd, London EC1V 8AF, is an umbrella organisation for voluntary groups for the disabled and a useful source of information. The Holiday Care Service (☎ 01293-774535, **W** www.holidaycare.org.uk), 2nd floor, Imperial Buildings, Victoria Rd, Horley, Surrey RH6 7PZ, publishes *Accessible*

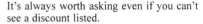

Britain (£6.50) in conjunction with RADAR and can offer general advice from 9am to 1pm weekdays.

A Disabled Person's Railcard (£14) is available, providing discounts on fares of 34%, but it isn't easy to get hold of. First you must fill out a form published in a booklet (coded RTDP2) available from staffed stations, branches of the Citizens Advice Bureau, some post offices and libraries. You then post it to the Disabled Person's Railcard Office, PO Box 1YT, Newcastle-upon-Tyne NE99 1YT. It can take up to three weeks to process so apply well in advance.

SENIOR TRAVELLERS

Senior citizens are entitled to discounts on things such as public transport and museum admission fees, provided they show proof of their age. Sometimes they need a special pass. The minimum qualifying age is generally 60 to 65 for men, 55 to 65 for women.

It's always worth asking even if you can't see a discount listed.

In your home country, there may be a lower age entitling you to special travel packages and discounts (on car hire, for instance) through organisations and travel agencies that cater for senior travellers. Start hunting at your local senior citizens advice bureau.

LONDON FOR CHILDREN

Although London's crowds, traffic and pollution might be off-putting to some parents, the city is jam-packed with things to entertain the young 'uns.

People travelling with children can turn to a number of titles, including *In and Around London for Kids* by Judith Milling and *Help! I've Got Kids – London* by Sheila Harries & Pauline Dale. Lonely Planet's *Travel with Children* provides general information as well as advice on travel health for younger children.

To see some farm animals doing their stuff see the boxed text 'Old MacDonald's London Farms' in the Facts about London chapter.

The following attractions are particularly recommended for children. For details, prices and opening hours, see the Things to See & Do chapter.

BA London Eye Ferris wheel
Battersea Park Children's Zoo
Bethnal Green Museum of Childhood
Brass Rubbing Centre, St Martin-in-the-Fields church
Cutty Sark clipper ship
HMS *Belfast* cruiser
Horniman Museum
Imperial War Museum
London Aquarium
London Dungeon (not for very young children)
London IMAX Cinema
London Transport Museum
London Trocadero
London Zoo
Madame Tussaud's & Planetarium
National Maritime Museum
Natural History Museum
Pollock's Toy Museum
Science Museum
Tower of London (for older children)

CHARLOTTE HINDLE

Legends of the deep: splash out at the London Aquarium, County Hall.

London has several theatres specially aimed at children:

Little Angel Theatre
(Map 4; ☎ 7226 1787, Ⓦ www.littleangel theatre.com) 14 Dagmar Passage N1 (✪ Angel)

Pleasance Theatre
(Map 2; ☎ 7609 1800), Carpenter's Mews, North Rd N7 (✪ Caledonian Road)

Polka Theatre for Children
(☎ 8543 4888, Ⓦ www.polkatheatre.com), 240 The Broadway SW19 (✪ South Wimbledon/ Wimbledon)

Unicorn Theatre for Children
(Map 2; ☎ 7700 0702), St Marks Studios, Chill-ingworth Rd N7 (✪ Holloway Road)

Most hotels in London will be able to rec-ommend a babysitter if you want to escape during the day or want a night out *sans* kids. Or contact any of the following:

Childminders
(Map 6; day ☎ 7935 2049 or night 7935 3000, Ⓦ www.babysitter.co.uk), 6 Nottingham St W1 (✪ Baker Street). This large agency can organ-ise you a babysitter – they have over 1500 reg-istered – for £6.80 per hour by day and between £5.20 and £6.40 in the evening, depending on the night. Membership (required) costs £59 per year, excluding VAT; renewals are £45.

Pippa Pop-Ins
(Map 10; ☎ 7385 2458, fax 7385 2458), 430 Fulham Rd SW6 (✪ Fulham Broadway). This nursery and kindergarten offers day care and holiday activities for kids aged two to 12. It opens 8am to 6pm weekdays and rates are around £32/48 for a half-/full day.

USEFUL ORGANISATIONS

Membership of English Heritage (EH) and the National Trust (NT) are worth consider-ing if you plan to travel a lot around the UK and are interested in stately homes and other historical buildings. Both are nonprofit org-anisations dedicated to the preservation of the environment, and care for hundreds of spectacular sites. If you're just sticking to London, however, they're of limited use.

Drifters
(Map 5; ☎ 7262 1292), 22a Craven Terrace W2 (✪ Lancaster Gate). This club offers back-up

services such as luggage storage, mail holding, local information, freight forwarding and equip-ment purchase, and cheap tours. It's mainly aimed at Aussies and Kiwis but anyone is wel-come. Membership costs from £10 to £15.

English Heritage
(☎ 0870 333 1181 or 7973 3434, Ⓦ www .english-heritage.org.uk). EH properties cost nonmembers between £1.50 and £6 to visit. Membership gives free admission to all EH properties, and half-price entry to Historic Scot-land and Cadw (Wales) properties during the first year (free with membership thereafter), and an excellent guidebook and map. Adult mem-bership is £31, a couple pays £50 and family membership is £55. Those aged under 16 pay £13; it costs £18 for those aged 16 to 20.

Globetrotters Club
If you'd like to meet other travellers it's worth going along to Globetrotters, which holds meet-ings at 2.30pm on the first Saturday of every month at the Church of Scotland Crown Court (Map 3; ☎ 7836 5643 or 8674 6229), Russell St WC2 (✪ Covent Garden). Admission costs £2/4 for members/nonmembers.

Great British Heritage Pass
This pass gives you access to hundreds of NT, EH and other properties open to the public. It's available overseas (ask your travel agent or con-tact the nearest Thomas Cook office) and costs US$54 for a week, $75 for 15 days and $102 for a month. It can also be purchased in London (eg, at the Britain Visitor Centre) for £35/46/60.

National Trust
(☎ 0870 458 4000 or 8315 1111, Ⓦ www .nationaltrust.org.uk). Most NT properties cost nonmembers up to £5.50 to enter. Membership for those aged over/under 26 is £31/15; mem-bership for a couple is £52.50 and for a family £58. It provides free admission to all the NT's English, Welsh and Northern Irish properties as well as an excellent guidebook and map. You can join at most major sites. There are recipro-cal arrangements with NT organisations in Scot-land, Australia, New Zealand and Canada and the Royal Oak Foundation in the USA.

LIBRARIES

London's most important library is the British Library in St Pancras. This is the UK's main copyright library and receives one copy of every British publication. The library has 11 reading rooms accommodat-ing more than 1200 people. However, access is limited to those with specific research needs, and there is a stringent application procedure; for details contact the Reader Admissions Office, British Library (Map 3; ☎ 7412 7677, e reader-admissions@bl.uk, w www.bl.uk, ⊖ King's Cross St Pancras), 96 Euston Rd NW1. It opens 10am to 8pm Monday, 9.30am to 8pm Tuesday to Thursday, and 9.30am to 5pm Friday and Saturday.

You're free to use any local library for reading or consulting newspapers, magazines and books provided you don't want to take them away; look in the *Yellow Pages* for the nearest branch. The Westminster Central Reference & Business Library (Map 8; ☎ 7641 4634, ⊖ Charing Cross), 35 St Martin's St WC2, is a public reference library with all sorts of publications, including newspapers and telephone directories on three floors. It opens 10am to 8pm Monday to Friday and 10am to 5pm on Saturday.

The Chamber of Commerce & Industry (Map 9; ☎ 7248 4444), 33 Queen St EC4 (⊖ Mansion House), stocks all manner of commercial materials and information.

UNIVERSITIES

For general information about London's universities, see Education in the Facts about London chapter. The University of Westminster and many colleges of the University of London, including the London School of Economics and Political Science and the Imperial College of Science, Technology and Medicine, let their residence halls to nonstudents during the holidays, which usually run from the end of June to mid-September. See Student Accommodation in the Places to Stay chapter for details.

Most student unions will allow foreign students admission to their bars and other amenities provided they have some form of student identification, such as an International Student Identity Card (ISIC); see the Documents section earlier in this chapter.

CULTURAL CENTRES

The main role of the British Council (Map 7; ☎ 7930 8466, w www.britishcouncil.org.uk, ⊖ Charing Cross), 10 Spring Gardens SW1, is to provide English-language classes and community access to British expertise in the areas of science and technology. It produces a free list of accredited colleges that meet minimum standards for facilities, qualified staff and pastoral back-up. The council can also offer general advice to overseas students on educational opportunities in the UK.

JULIET COOMBE

Good with figures? From fashion to economics, life drawing to maths you're sure to find the right course in London.

The Institut Français (Map 9; ☎ 7838 2144, W www.institut.ambafrance.org.uk), 17 Queensberry Place SW7 (⊖ South Kensington), promotes French culture abroad and has a library, cinema called Ciné Lumière showing French-language films (see Cinema in the Entertainment chapter) and, predictably, an excellent restaurant (Brasserie de l'Institut; see the Places to Eat chapter).

For German books, films and the chance to meet a fellow German speaker, contact the Goethe Institute (Map 9; ☎ 7596 4000, W www.goethe.de/london), 50 Princes Gate, Exhibition Rd SW7 (⊖ South Kensington).

DANGERS & ANNOYANCES
Crime
Considering its size and the great disparities in wealth, London is a remarkably safe city; most visitors will spend their two weeks in the capital without anything worse happening than being overcharged for an ice-cream cone. Though violent crime rose by 20% between 1995 and 1999 and use of handguns in crimes by 40% over the same time, London has one of the lowest murder rates in the developed world, with 2.36 per 100,000 inhabitants. Compare that with Washington's 50.82, Moscow's 18.20 and even Amsterdam's 5.37.

You should take the usual precautionary measures against pickpockets, who operate in crowded public places such as the Underground and major tourist attractions. Always carry your bags in front of you and don't put them down without keeping an eye on them, especially in a crowded pub or outside at a cafe. Never put a wallet in a back pocket – the thieves will be laughing all the way to the shops.

Take particular care at night. When travelling by tube, choose a carriage with other people in it and avoid some deserted suburban stations; a bus or a taxi is a safer choice.

The most important things to protect from theft are your passport and other papers, tickets, money and credit cards – in that order. It's always best to carry these next to your skin or in a sturdy leather pouch on your belt. Try to keep them separate; lose that one bag and you've lost the lot.

Be careful even in hostels and hotels; use your own padlock if lockers are provided and don't leave valuables lying around in your room. Never leave valuables in a car and remove all luggage overnight. Report thefts to the police and ask for a statement. Otherwise, your travel insurance won't pay.

Traffic
Remember that since cars drive on the left in the UK you need to look to the *right* at pedestrian crossings; most crossings in central London will remind you of this. Couriers on motorcycles, scooters and bicycles, who belt down London's roads at full tilt, weaving in and out of the traffic at death-defying speeds, can be even more of a menace than motorists. Keep your wits about you while crossing the road, even with the traffic lights in your favour.

Terrorism
The IRA has not struck a major target in London since 1996, when a bomb exploded in the Docklands. In 1999 a right-wing extremist, apparently acting alone, planted nail bombs that exploded in crowded areas of Brixton, Brick Lane in the East End and Old Compton St in Soho. The bombs had been quite clearly directed at blacks, Asians and gays respectively. Three people were killed instantly and more than 100 injured, many of them very seriously. In March 2001 a car bomb exploded outside the BBC's main news centre in west London and in August of that year another exploded in Ealing, injuring several people; they were thought to have been the work of the dissident Irish republican terror group, the Real IRA. It could happen again so it's just as well to restate the ground rules.

Never leave your bag unattended in case you trigger a security alert. If you see an unattended package, keep calm and alert those in authority and anyone nearby as quickly as possible. Do *not* touch it.

There is a much higher sense of security in London than in many other world capitals, and precautions are taken regularly – and seriously. If asked to open your bag for inspection in museums or other public places, do so willingly – it's for your own safety ultimately.

Petty inconveniences due to terrorism include transport delays while suspicious packages are inspected, the 'ring of steel' around 75% of the City with police periodically checking cars and other vehicles as they enter or leave, and, at times, the sealing of left-luggage lockers at bus and train stations and post boxes and the removal of rubbish bins.

Lost Property

Every year thousands of items are lost by their owners in London: mobile phones, keys, bags of money, jewellery – even sets of false teeth. Eventually most items found on buses and Underground trains find their way to the Transport for London's Lost Property Office (Map 5; ☎ 7486 2496 for recording, fax 7918 1028), 200 Baker St, NW1 5RZ (◉ Baker Street), where you can call in person to collect them 9.30am to 2pm Monday to Friday. A charge of £3 per item is made; it's £2 if you retrieve it from the bus garage where it was found instead.

Items left on main-line trains usually end up back at the main terminals; ring ☎ 7928 5151 and you will be connected to the proper number. If you leave something in a black taxi, phone Taxi Lost Property on ☎ 7918 2000.

Touts & Scams

Hotel and hostel touts descend on backpackers at tube and main-line stations such as Earl's Court, Liverpool Street and Victoria. Treat their claims with scepticism and don't accept any offers of free lifts unless you know exactly where you're going.

Every year foreign men are lured into Soho strip clubs and hostess bars and are efficiently separated from huge amounts of money; refuse to pay and things may rapidly turn nasty. Do yourself a favour and give them a wide berth.

Beggars

These days London has a depressing number of beggars and street sleepers, and it's difficult to know how best to deal with

them. All the arguments against giving to beggars in developing countries apply in London too; it's probably better to donate something to a recognised charity than give directly. Shelter (☎ 7505 2000), 88 Old St EC1Z 9HU, is a charity that helps the homeless and gratefully accepts donations. Also consider buying the *Big Issue* (£1), a weekly magazine available from homeless street sellers who receive 60p of every copy sold.

Racism

London is not without its racial problems, particularly in some of the more deprived areas of the East End and south London, but tolerance generally prevails. Visitors are unlikely to have problems because of their skin colour but please let us know if you find otherwise.

Smoking

Smoking is banned in cinemas, theatres, all forms of public transport and most shops; most restaurants have no-smoking sections, which you should request when booking. Pubs remain one of the last strongholds of the smoker, though the Wetherspoon chain sets aside corners for nonsmokers.

Litter

Many first-time visitors are shocked at how dirty the capital is, with rubbish strewn everywhere. The excuse would be to say that litter bins are periodically removed in large parts of central London in response to the threat of bombs. In reality, however, Londoners seem to be a bunch of litterbugs. Dog owners are particularly irresponsible here.

Britain as a whole ranks at the bottom of the EU recycling league tables, with 25% of glass containers collected against 42% in Portugal, 55% in France and 81% in Germany.

EMERGENCIES

In the event of an emergency phone ☎ 999 (toll-free) for the fire service, the police or an ambulance. See the Health section earlier in this chapter for a list of hospitals with 24-hour accident and emergency departments and information on dental services.

LEGAL MATTERS

Should you face any legal difficulties while in London visit any one of the Citizens Advice Bureaux (**W** www.nacab.org.uk) listed under 'Counselling & Advice' in the *Yellow Pages* or contact the Community Legal Services Directory (**☎** 0845 608 1122, **W** www .justasl.org.uk).

Drugs

Illegal drugs of every type are widely available in London, especially in clubs. Nonetheless, all the usual drug dangers apply and there have been several high-profile deaths associated with ecstasy, the purity of which is often dubious. Cannabis has recently been reclassified as a Class C drug, which means possessing small quantities will not result in the user being arrested. There are still stiff penalties for dealing and handling large amounts of the drug. No other drugs have been reassessed and be warned that other drugs are treated much more seriously.

Driving Offences

The laws against drink-driving have got tougher and are treated more seriously than they used to be. Currently you're allowed to have a blood-alcohol level of 35mg/100mL but there's talk of reducing the limit. The safest approach is not to drink anything at all if you're planning to drive. For information about current speed limits and parking violations, see Car & Motorcycle in the Getting Around chapter.

Fines

In general you rarely have to cough up on the spot for an offence. The exceptions are trains, the tube and buses, where people who can't produce a valid ticket for the journey when asked to by an inspector can be fined there and then: £5 on buses and £10 on trains and the tube. No excuses are accepted.

BUSINESS HOURS

Offices usually open 9am to 5pm or 5.30pm Monday to Friday, with shops opening on Saturday as well and often staying open much later. A growing number of shops and most department stores also open for six hours (the maximum allowed by law) on Sunday, typically from 10am to 4pm or noon to 6pm. Late-night shopping in the West End is on Thursday.

Post office hours vary slightly but most open from 9am to 5pm or 5.30pm Monday to Friday, with main ones also open 9am to noon on Saturday. The post office facing Trafalgar Square (see Post & Communications earlier in this chapter), where poste restante is usually sent unless a different address and/or postcode is provided, opens 8am to 8pm Monday to Friday and 9am to 8pm on Saturday.

Bank hours vary considerably but you'll be safe if you visit between 9.30am and 3.30pm on weekdays; Friday afternoon can be very busy. A few banks also open 9.30am till noon on Saturday.

PUBLIC HOLIDAYS & SPECIAL EVENTS

Public Holidays

Britons don't get a lot of holidays compared with other developed countries, although things are definitely a lot better than they were before the Bank Holidays Act was passed in 1871. Until then the only two days when employers allowed their workers time off was Christmas Day and Good Friday.

Most banks and businesses are closed on the following eight public holidays: New Year's Day (1 January), Good Friday and Easter Monday (late March/April), May Day Holiday (first Monday in May), Spring Bank Holiday (last Monday in May), Summer Bank Holiday (last Monday in August), Christmas Day and Boxing Day (25 & 26 December).

Museums and other attractions may well observe the Christmas Day and Boxing Day holidays but they generally stay open for the other ones. Exceptions are those that normally close on Sunday; they're quite likely to close on bank holidays too. Some smaller museums close on Monday and/ or Tuesday, and several places close on Sunday morning.

Special Events

Countless festivals and events are held in and around London. Look out for the LTB's bimonthly *Events in London* or its *Annual Events* pamphlet; you can also find special events listed on their Web site **w** www .londontouristboard.com. And don't forget the LTB's London Line (☎ 09068 663344), which can fill you in on all the ongoing and upcoming events.

New Year (1 January)
London Parade – the mayor of Westminster leads a parade of 10,000 musicians and street performers, as well as floats and carriages, from Parliament Square to Berkeley Square.
Early to mid-January
International Boat Show – Earl's Court Exhibition Centre.
Late January/early February
Chinese New Year – with lion dances and other colourful celebrations in Soho.
Late February/March
Shrove Tuesday Pancake Day Races – Spitalfields, Covent Garden and Lincoln's Inn Fields.

Last week in March
Oxford & Cambridge Boat Race – the traditional rowing race on the Thames, from Putney to Mortlake.
Head of the River Race – a less well-known race from Mortlake to Putney, with some 400 teams.
London International Book Fair – Olympia.
Late March/April
Easter Fair – Battersea Park.
London Marathon – a 26-mile race from Greenwich Park to the Mall via the Isle of Dogs and Victoria Embankment.
Mid-/late May
Royal Windsor Horse Show – show-jumping event.
Chelsea Flower Show – Royal Hospital Chelsea.
June
Spitalfields Festival – three-week celebration at Spitalfields Market with music, theatre, talks and walks.
First week in June
Royal Academy Summer Exhibition – unique art exhibition, which runs till August.
Beating of the Retreat – military bands and marching in Horse Guards Parade, Whitehall.

DAVID WALL

In a spin: fusing West Indian vibes with garage, reggae and salsa at the annual, multicultural Notting Hill Carnival

Second Saturday in June
Trooping of the Colour – celebrates the Queen's official birthday with parades and pageantry in Horse Guards Parade, Whitehall.
Late June/early July
Wimbledon Lawn Tennis Championships – runs for two weeks.
City of London Festival – top-notch performances of music, dance, theatre and so on in City churches and squares.
London Pride March & Mardi Gras – gay and lesbian march from Hyde Park and huge festival in Finsbury Park.
Early July
Greenwich & Docklands International Festival – dance, theatre and music on either side of the Thames.
Hampton Court Palace International Flower Show – flowers galore in one of London's finest gardens.
Henley Royal Regatta – posh boating race on the Thames.
Mid-July
Clerkenwell Festival – fun and games around Farringdon.
Vintners' Company Procession – vintners in traditional dress parading from Upper Thames St to St James's Garlickhythe church.
Promenade Concerts (or 'Proms') – start of the world's greatest musical festival, which runs till mid-September, at the Royal Albert Hall.
Late August
Notting Hill Carnival – Europe's biggest outdoor festival, a vast Caribbean carnival in Notting Hill, held over the Summer Bank Holiday weekend.
Mid-September
Thames Festival – London's foremost event focused on the Thames, with a funfair, street theatre, food stalls, fireworks and, as the centrepiece, the Great River Race.
Great River Race – barges, dragon boats and long ships racing 22 miles from Ham House in Richmond to Island Gardens on the Isle of Dogs opposite Greenwich.
Late September
London Open House – the public is admitted to some 550 buildings and other sites normally closed.
Horseman's Sunday – a vicar on horseback blesses more than 100 horses outside the Church of St John & St Michael, Hyde Park Crescent W2, followed by horse jumping in Kensington Gardens.
Early October
Dance Umbrella – British and international dance companies perform at venues all across London for five weeks.

Punch & Judy Festival – a gathering of puppet fanatics in Covent Garden piazza.
Pearly Harvest Festival Service – over 100 Pearly Kings and Queens attend a service in St Martin-in-the-Fields church.
Late October
Trafalgar Day Parade – marching bands descend on Trafalgar Square to lay wreaths commemorating Nelson's victory over Napoleon in 1805.
November
London Film Festival – at the National Film Theatre, South Bank.
London to Brighton Veteran Car Run – pre-1905 vintage cars line up in Serpentine Rd, Hyde Park, to race to Brighton.
Early November
State Opening of Parliament – the Queen visits Parliament by state coach amid gun salutes to summon MPs back from their rather long summer recess.
November 5
Guy Fawkes Night – also called Bonfire Night, this festival commemorates an attempted Catholic coup with bonfires and fireworks around town but especially in Battersea Park, Primrose Hill, Blackheath, Clapham Common and Crystal Palace Park.
Mid-November
Lord Mayor's Show – the newly elected mayor of the City of London travels in a state coach from Mansion House to the Royal Courts of Justice, amid floats, bands and fireworks.
Remembrance Sunday – the Queen, members of the government and other notables lay wreaths at the Cenotaph to remember the dead of the two world wars, and everyone wears a red poppy.
World Travel Market – the world's largest travel show, at Earl's Court Exhibition Centre.
December
Lighting of the Christmas Tree & Lights – switches are flipped on a huge Norwegian spruce in Trafalgar Square and all the festive lights along Oxford, Regent and Bonds Sts.

DOING BUSINESS

Roughly five million people per year come to do business in London, one of the world's major commercial centres and home to almost a quarter of the head offices of Europe's 500 largest companies. As a result most of London's biggest hotels depend on business travellers for their livelihood and come equipped with business centres with ISDN lines, faxes, secretarial services and Internet access and so on. More countries can be dialled direct from London than from anywhere else in Europe and international call rates are cheaper here too. In any given week there are flights to more than 160 different destinations worldwide served by some 90 different airlines.

The main source of general information for businesspeople in London is the staid, pink-tinged *Financial Times*, published Monday to Saturday, while *The Economist* is a more detailed weekly magazine (though it calls itself a newspaper). Other useful sources of information include:

Bank of England
(Map 9; ☎ 7601 4878, fax 7601 5460, **W** www .bankofengland.co.uk) Threadneedle St EC2R 8AH (✪ Bank)

Board of Inland Revenue
(Map 10; ☎ 7605 9800, **W** www.inlandrevenue .gov.uk) Charles House, 375 Kensington High St W14 (✪ Kensington-Olympia)

Confederation of British Industry
(Map 8; ☎ 7395 8195, fax 7379 0945) Centre Point, 103 New Oxford St WC1A 1DU (✪ Tottenham Court Road)

Department of Trade & Industry
(Map 6; ☎ 7215 5000, fax 7222 0612, **e** dti .enquiries@imsv.dti.gov.uk) 1 Victoria St SW1H 0ET (✪ St James's Park)

London Chamber of Commerce & Industry
(Map 9; ☎ 7248 4444, fax 7489 0391, **W** www .londonchamber.co.uk) 33 Queen St EC4R 1AP (✪ Mansion House)

Office of the European Commission
(Map 6; ☎ 7973 1992, fax 7973 1900) 8 Storey's Gate, London SW1P 3AT (✪ Westminster/ St James's Park)

Trade Partners UK
(formerly Board of British Trade International; Map 6; ☎ 7215 5444, fax 7215 4231, **W** www .tradepartners.gov.uk), Department of Trade & Industry, Kingsgate House, 66–74 Victoria St, London SW1E 6SW (✪ Victoria)

For word processing or secretarial services go to Typing Overload (Map 6; ☎ 7404 5464, **W** www.typingoverload.com), 1st floor, 67 Chancery Lane WC2 (✪ Chancery Lane). For photocopying, computer services such as scanning, computer rentals and video-conferencing, try Kinko's (Map 6; ☎ 7539 2900, **W** www.kinkos.com), a reliable chain open 24 hours with a branch at 326–328 High Holborn WC1 (✪ Chancery Lane). Other Kinko's are at 29–35 Mortimer St W1 (Map 6; ☎ 7643 1900; ✪ Goodge Street) and at 1 Curzon St W1 (Map 6; ☎ 7717 4900; ✪ Green Park).

WORK

If you're prepared to work long hours at menial jobs for relatively low pay, you'll almost certainly find work in London. The trouble is that without skills, it's difficult to find a job that pays well enough to save money. You should be able to break even but will probably be better off saving in your home country. And remember you will be competing with recent arrivals from Eastern Europe, particularly Poles and nationals of the former Yugoslav republics. See Work Permits under Visas & Documents earlier in this chapter for more details.

Traditionally, unskilled visitors have worked in pubs and restaurants and as nannies. Both jobs often provide live-in accommodation, but the hours are long, the work exhausting and the pay not so good (and then there are all those pissheads to deal with). A minimum wage (now £4.10 per hour; £3.20 for those aged 18 to 21) was introduced in April 1999, but if you're working under the table no-one's obliged to pay you even that. Before you accept a job, make sure you're clear about the terms and conditions, especially how many (and which) hours you will be expected to work.

Accountants, health professionals, journalists, computer programmers, lawyers, teachers and clerical workers with computer experience stand a better chance of finding well-paid work. Even so, you'll probably need some money to tide you over while you search. Don't forget copies of your qualifications, references (which will probably be checked) and a CV (résumé).

Teachers should contact the individual London borough councils, which have separate education departments, although some schools recruit directly. To work as a trained nurse or midwife you have to register (£56) with the United Kingdom Nursing & Midwifery Council, a long process that can take up to three months; write to the Overseas

Registration Department, UKNMC, 23 Portland Place, London W1N 4JT, or phone ☎ 7333 9333 (fax 7636 6935). If you aren't registered then you can still work as an auxiliary nurse.

The free *TNT Magazine* is a good starting point for jobs and agencies aimed at travellers. For au pair and nanny work buy the quaintly titled *The Lady*. Also check the *Evening Standard*, the national newspapers and government-operated Jobcentres, which are scattered throughout London and listed under 'Employment Services' in the phone directory. Whatever your skills, it's worth registering with a few temporary agencies.

For details on all aspects of short-term work consult the excellent *Work Your Way Around the World* by Susan Griffith. Other good sources are *Working Holidays Abroad* by Mark Hempshall and the *Directory of Summer Jobs in Britain*, edited by David Wentworth.

If you play a musical instrument or have other artistic talents, you could try working the streets. As every Peruvian pipe-player (and his fifth cousin once removed) knows, busking is fairly common in London. It is now legal to perform in certain train and Underground stations provided the busker secures a licence (£20 per year) from Transport for London, which requires an audition. Buskers are assigned a marked pitch, where they can perform at specified times. The borough councils are also moving to license buskers at top tourist attractions and popular areas like Covent Garden and Leicester Square. You will still be able to play elsewhere, but those areas will be off-limits to anyone without a permit.

Tax

As an official employee, you'll find income tax and National Insurance are automatically deducted from your weekly pay-packet. However, the deductions will be calculated on the assumption that you're working for the entire financial year (which runs from 6 April to 5 April). If you don't work as long as that, you may be eligible for a refund. Contact the Board of Inland Revenue (see the Doing Business section earlier in this chapter) or use one of the agencies that advertise in *TNT Magazine* (but check their fee or percentage charge first).

Getting There & Away

London is one of the world's busiest air transport hubs and with intense competition between airlines there are always plenty of opportunities for finding cheap flights. In addition, there is a range of bus, ferry and rail services between Europe and the UK, including those using the Channel Tunnel.

The national weekend newspapers and the *Evening Standard* carry ads for cheap fares. Also look out for *TNT Magazine*; you can often pick it up free outside main train and tube stations. For recommended travel agencies, see Travel Agencies in the Facts for the Visitor chapter.

AIR

Greater London has five airports: Heathrow is the largest, followed by Gatwick, Stansted, Luton and London City. For information on getting to and from these airports, see The Airports in the Getting Around chapter.

Departure Tax

All domestic flights and those to destinations within the EU from London carry a £10 departure tax. For flights to other cities abroad you pay £20. This is usually built into the price of your ticket.

Other Parts of the UK

Almost all regional centres in the UK are linked to London. However, unless you're travelling from the outer reaches of Britain, and in particular northern Scotland, planes are only marginally quicker than trains if you include the time it takes to get to and from the airports.

The main operators are British Airways (BA; ☎ 0845 773 3377, W www.british-airways.com) and British Midland (☎ 0870 607 0555, W www.flybmi.com). Smaller companies offering very competitive fares include easyJet (☎ 0870 600 0000, W www.easyjet.com), Go (☎ 0845 605 4321, W www.go-fly.com) and Ryanair (☎ 0870 156 9569, W www.ryanair.com). Most airlines offer a

range of tickets, including full-fare (very expensive but flexible), Apex (for which you must book at least 14 days in advance) and, on some services, special offers. There are also youth fares (usually for under-26s), but Apex and special-offer fares can often be cheaper as youth fares are discounted on full-fare tickets.

Prices vary enormously. For example, at the time of writing a return ticket from Edinburgh or Glasgow to London with BA costs £162/304 one-way/return full fare, but just £92 Apex or £70 with a BA World Offer fare. British Midland charges £259 for a full-fare return from Edinburgh or Glasgow, but this can drop to as low as £49 (£56 at the weekend) if you book in advance and stay over on Saturday night. The no-frills airline easyJet has one-way flights between Edinburgh or Glasgow and Luton from £17.50 to £117.50; easyJet tickets are only sold directly by phone or via their Web site. Tickets are sold on a first-come, first-served basis; when the £17.50 fares are gone the price jumps up to the next level and so on up to £117.50. Most cheap fares carry restrictions that a travel agency or the airline will explain; staying over on Saturday night or travelling midweek are two of the most common.

BA also offers connections between Belfast and Heathrow; fares range from £96 to £330. British European (☎ 0870 567 6676, W www.british-european.com) have fares from Belfast to Gatwick, Stansted or London City costing between £69 and £320.

Other Countries

Ireland Dublin is linked to all the major London airports. BA fares from Dublin to Gatwick range from around €104 to €528, British Midland fares to Heathrow from around €77.50 to €413. On price-cutting Ryanair, one-way tickets are sometimes available for as little as €24, including tax.

Continental Europe Typical discount return fares to London include: Amsterdam

Air Travel Glossary

Alliances Many of the world's leading airlines are now intimately involved with each other, sharing everything from reservations systems and check-in to aircraft and frequent flyer schemes. Opponents say that alliances restrict competition. Whatever the arguments, there is no doubt that big alliances are the way of the future.

Cancelling or Changing Tickets If you have to cancel or change a ticket, you need to contact the original travel agent who sold you the ticket. Airlines only issue refunds to the purchaser of a ticket – usually the travel agent who bought the ticket on your behalf. There are often heavy penalties involved; insurance can sometimes be taken out against these penalties.

Courier Fares Businesses often need to send urgent documents or freight securely and quickly. Courier companies hire people to accompany the package through customs and, in return, offer a discount ticket which is sometimes a bargain. However, you may have to surrender all your baggage allowance and take only carry-on luggage.

Fares Airlines traditionally offer 1st class (coded F), business class (coded J) and economy class (coded Y) tickets. These days there are so many promotional and discounted fares available that few passengers pay full fare.

Lost Tickets If you lose your airline ticket an airline will usually treat it like a travellers cheque and, after enquiries, issue you with another one. Legally, however, an airline is entitled to treat it like cash and if you lose it then it's gone forever. Take good care of your tickets.

Onward Tickets An entry requirement for many countries is that you have a ticket out of the country. If you're unsure of your next move, the easiest solution is to buy the cheapest onward ticket to a neighbouring country or a ticket from a reliable airline which can later be refunded if you do not use it.

Open-Jaw Tickets These are return tickets where you fly out to one place but return from another. If available, this can save you backtracking to your arrival point.

Overbooking Since every flight has some passengers who fail to show up, airlines often book more passengers than they have seats. Usually excess passengers make up for the no-shows, but occasionally somebody gets 'bumped' onto the next available flight. Guess who it is most likely to be? The passengers who check in late. If you do get 'bumped' you are normally offered some form of compensation.

Reconfirmation Some airlines require you to reconfirm your flight at least 72 hours prior to departure. Check your travel documents to see if this is the case.

Restrictions Discounted tickets often have various restrictions on them – such as needing to be paid for in advance and incurring a penalty to be altered or cancelled. Others are restrictions on the minimum and maximum period you must be away.

Round-the-World Tickets RTW tickets give you a limited period (usually a year) in which to circumnavigate the globe. You can go anywhere the carrying airlines go, as long as you don't backtrack. The number of stopovers or total number of separate flights is decided before you set off and they usually cost a bit more than a basic return flight.

Ticketless Travel Airlines are gradually waking up to the realisation that paper tickets are unnecessary encumbrances. On simple one-way or return trips, reservations details can be held on computer, and the passenger merely shows ID to claim his or her seat.

Transferred Tickets Airline tickets cannot be transferred from one person to another. Travellers sometimes try to sell the return half of their ticket, but officials can ask you to prove that you are the person named on the ticket. On an international flight tickets are always compared with passports.

€122.50; Frankfurt-am-Main €204.50, Madrid €159; Paris €137; and Rome €159. EasyJet offers one-way fares from Barcelona to Luton in the range €54 to €90 and from Nice in the range €53.50 to €120, while Go has nonflexible return fares from Naples or Rome to Stansted for around €133. Another good airline to consider for cheap fares is Buzz (☎ 0870 240 7070, **w** www.buzzaway.com) with flights from (among other European destinations) Paris (€107), Frankfurt (€128) and Geneva (€180) to Stansted. Standard tickets with carriers such as BA can cost much more.

Last Minute, at **w** www.lastminute.com, is a UK Web site selling late deals. Other sites for cheap tickets include **w** www.ebookers.com, **w** www.travelocity.com and **w** www.bargainholidays.com.

USA & Canada Council Travel (**w** www.counciltravel.com) and STA (**w** www.statravel.com) have offices throughout the USA. At the time of writing, a New York–London return costs around US$450 in the low season and US$650 in the high season. Equivalent fares from the West Coast are US$100 to US$200 higher.

Priceline (**w** www.priceline.com) is a 'name your price' service on the Web. You enter your destination, dates of travel and the price you'll pay for a ticket and if one of the participating airlines has an empty seat for which it would rather get something than nothing, it will email you back within 15 minutes. Bear in mind that you will not know the time or the specific airline for your flight until after you have purchased your ticket. Whole Earth Travel (☎ 212-864 2000, **w** www.4standby.com) is worth contacting for one-way tickets and can get you to London for around US$175/225/250 from the East Coast/Midwest/West Coast.

Another option is a courier flight, where you accompany a parcel or freight to be picked up at the other end. A New York–London return, at the time of writing, costs around US$300 in low season. You can also fly one-way. The drawbacks are that your stay in Europe may be limited to one or two weeks, your luggage is usually restricted to hand luggage (the parcel or freight you carry comes out of your luggage allowance) and you may have to be a US resident to work for some courier companies.

You can find out more about courier flights from the International Association of Air Travel Couriers (IAATC; ☎ 352-475 1584, fax 475 5326, **w** www.courier.org), Now Voyager Travel (☎ 212-431 1616, fax 334 5243, **w** www.nowvoyagertravel.com) or As You Like It Travel (☎ 212-216 0644, fax 947-6117, **w** www.asulikeit.com).

Travel CUTS (☎ 800-667 2887 or ☎ 866-246 9762, **w** www.travelcuts.com) has offices in all major cities in Canada. Whole Earth Travel has stand-by fares to/from Toronto, Montreal and Vancouver. Their typical discount return fares to London include C$600 from Montreal or Toronto and C$800 from Vancouver.

Australia & New Zealand STA Travel and Flight Centres International are major antipodean dealers in cheap air fares. STA Travel (☎ 03-9349 2411) has its main office at 224 Faraday St, Carlton, in Melbourne, with offices in all major cities and on many university campuses. Call ☎ 131 776 Australiawide for the location of your nearest branch or visit **w** www.statravel.com.au. Flight Centre (☎ 131 600 Australiawide, **w** www.flightcentre.com.au) has a central office at 82 Elizabeth St, Sydney, and there are dozens of offices throughout Australia.

Discounted return fares on mainstream airlines through STA cost between A$1800 (low season) and A$2350 (high season). Flights to/from Perth are a couple of hundred dollars cheaper.

In New Zealand, Flight Centre (☎ 09-309 6171, **w** www.flightcentre.co.nz) has a large central office in Auckland at National Bank Towers (corner Queen & Darby Sts) and many branches throughout the country. STA Travel (☎ 09-309 0458, **w** www.sta travel.co.nz) has its main office at 10 High St, Auckland, and other offices in Auckland as well as in Hamilton, Palmerston North, Wellington, Christchurch and Dunedin.

Round-the-world (RTW) fares for travel to or from New Zealand are usually the best value, often cheaper than a return ticket in the high season. Depending on which airline you choose, you may fly across Asia, with possible stopovers in India, Bangkok or Singapore, or across the USA, with stops in Honolulu, Australia or one of the Pacific Islands.

Expect to pay around NZ$2199 for a return in the low season or NZ$2599 in the high season.

Africa Nairobi and Johannesburg are probably the best places in Africa to buy tickets to London. A typical discounted return fare from Johannesburg to London is R4800 to R7150.

In Johannesburg, STA Travel (☎ 011-447 5414) at 27a Mutual Square, Oxford Rd, Rosebank are worth trying for cheap tickets.

Asia Hong Kong, Bangkok and Singapore are all discount air-fare centres. Shop around and ask the advice of other travellers before buying a ticket. STA Travel has branches/affiliates in all three cities as well as in Tokyo, Jakarta and Kuala Lumpur. Khao San Rd in Bangkok is a mecca for travellers seeking budget airfares.

From Hong Kong, Singapore Airlines has a return fare to London of HK$3500 on its morning flight (via Singapore), though this usually costs HK$6000 to HK$7000. At the time of writing, Virgin Atlantic and British Airways were offering 30-day return tickets for HK$4500, but prices are generally HK$5600/8000 in the low/high season. On Malaysia Airlines, Gulf Air or Emirates Airlines, count on HK$4800 to HK$7000.

From India, the cheapest flights tend to be with Aeroflot or one of the Middle Eastern airlines such as Kuwait Airways and Gulf Air. Mumbai is the air transport hub, with many transit options to/from South-East Asia, but cheap fares are more widely available in Delhi, especially from the discount travel agencies near Connaught Place.

Airline Offices

All major airlines have ticket offices in London. The following are the ones you're most likely to want, but others can be found in the *Yellow Pages* (W www.yell.com), a business directory available at hotels and libraries, or check directory enquiries online at W www.192.com.

Aer Lingus	☎ 0845 973 7747
Aeroflot	☎ 7355 2233
Air Canada	☎ 0870 524 7226
Air France	☎ 0845 084 5111
Air New Zealand	☎ 8741 2299
Alitalia	☎ 0870 544 8259
American Airlines	☎ 0845 778 9789
British Airways	☎ 0845 773 3377
British European	☎ 0870 567 6676
British Midland	☎ 0870 607 0555
Canadian Airlines	
International	☎ 0870 524 7226
Cathay Pacific	
Airways	☎ 7747 8888
Continental Airlines	☎ 0800 776464
Delta Air Lines	☎ 0800 414767
El Al Israel Airlines	☎ 7957 4100
Iberia	☎ 0845 601 2854
KLM uk	☎ 0870 507 4074
Lufthansa Airlines	☎ 0845 773 7747
Olympic Airways	☎ 0870 606 0460
Qantas Airways	☎ 0845 774 7767
Ryanair	☎ 0870 156 9569
Sabena	☎ 0845 601 0933
Scandinavian	
Airlines (SAS)	☎ 0845 607 2772
Singapore Airlines	☎ 0870 608 8886
South African	
Airways	☎ 7312 5000
TAP Air Portugal	☎ 0845 601 0932
Thai Airways	
International	☎ 0870 606 0911
Turkish Airlines	☎ 7766 9300
United Airlines	☎ 0845 844 4777
Virgin Atlantic	☎ 01293-747747

BUS

Most long-distance express buses (called coaches in the UK) leave London from Victoria Coach Station (Map 11; ☎ 7730 3466), an attractive 1930s-style building at 164 Buckingham Palace Rd SW1 (⊖ Victoria), about 10 minutes' walk south of Victoria train and tube stations. The arrivals terminal is in a separate building across Elizabeth St from the main coach station.

There are information desks in the main entrance hall (open 7.30am to 9pm daily) and near Gate 11 (open 10am to 6pm daily). The ticket hall, behind Gate 11, opens 6am to 11pm daily. To avoid queuing, you can book tickets up to two hours before departure by phone on ☎ 7730 3499 (open 9am to 7pm Monday to Saturday). You must pick up the tickets at least 30 minutes before the coach is due to depart. The left-luggage office, behind Gate 6, opens 6am to 11pm in summer and 7am to 11pm in winter. It charges £1 for deposits of less than two hours and £2 to £2.50 for periods between two and 24 hours, prices depend on the size of baggage.

Other Parts of the UK
Buses in the UK are almost always privately owned and run. National Express (☎ 0870 580 8080, W www.gobycoach.com) runs the largest network – it completely dominates the market and is a sister company to Eurolines (see the Other Countries section). However, there are often smaller competitors as well on the main routes.

Generally speaking, if you want to travel by coach it's cheaper to do so midweek. Booking a week ahead can also result in a discount. Oddly, there are some routes where it can be several pounds cheaper to buy two one-way tickets than a return.

National Express Discount Coachcards (£9 per year, £19 for three years), which allow 30% off the standard adult fare, can be bought from all National Express agencies and are available to full-time students and those aged between 16 and 25 or over 50. A passport photo is required; ISIC cards are accepted as proof of student status.

Other Countries
Even without using the Channel Tunnel, you can still get from/to Europe by bus with a short ferry ride as part of the deal. Eurolines (Map 11; ☎ 0870 514 3219, W www.eurolines.com), 52 Grosvenor Gardens SW1 (⊖ Victoria), an association of more than 30 bus companies linking London with points all over Western and Central Europe, Scandinavia and Morocco. Buses are slower and less comfortable than trains but they are cheaper, especially if you qualify for the

10% discount available to young people (under 26) and seniors (over 60) or take advantage of the discount fares on offer from time to time.

You can book Eurolines tickets through any National Express office, including Victoria Coach Station, and at many travel agencies. Eurolines-affiliated companies can be found across Europe, including in Amsterdam (☎ 020-560 87 88), Barcelona (☎ 93 490 40 00), Berlin (☎ 030-86 09 60), Brussels (☎ 02 203 0707), Budapest (☎ 1-317 2562), Copenhagen (☎ 33 25 12 44), Frankfurt (☎ 069-23 07 35), Hamburg (☎ 040-24 98 18), Madrid (☎ 91 528 11 05), Paris (☎ 01 43 54 11 99 or ☎ 0836 69 52 52), Prague (☎ 02-2421 3420), Rome (☎ 06-44 23 39 28 or ☎ 06-44 04 009), Vienna (☎ 01-712 0453) and Warsaw (☎ 022-870 5940).

The following one-way/return adult fares and journey times in summer are representative: Amsterdam €48/79 (9½ to 12 hours); Barcelona €88/158.50 (22 to 24 hours); Brussels €44/68 (7½ hours); Frankfurt €70/112 (10½ to 18½ hours); Paris €69/110 (seven to 10 hours) and Rome €114/186 (31 to 36 hours). At peak times (ie, in summer), you should make reservations a few days in advance.

TRAIN
The former British Rail has been privatised into some 25 separate train-operating companies (TOCs), organised under the Association of Train Operating Companies (ATOC; ☎ 7904 3077). In this book, when you should use a train to get to or from somewhere, we differentiate this from the tube by using the word 'station'.

Each company is able to set whatever fare it chooses. Thus on routes served by more than one operator, passengers can buy a cheaper ticket for a more circuitous journey or pay more for a faster or more direct service.

Other Parts of the UK
The main routes are served by InterCity trains that travel at speeds of up to 140mph and can quickly whisk you from London to Edinburgh, say, in just over four hours.

Main-Line Terminals London has 10 main-line terminals, each serving a different geographical area of the UK:

Charing Cross
South-eastern England (Kent, Sussex, south and south-west London)

Euston
North Wales, north-western England, Scotland, north London

King's Cross
Hertfordshire, Cambridgeshire, northern and north-eastern England, East Anglia, Scotland, north London, Luton airport

Liverpool Street
East Anglia, Stansted airport, east and north-east London

London Bridge
South-eastern England (Kent, Sussex, Hertfordshire)

Marylebone
The Chilterns, north-west London,

Paddington
South Wales, western and south-western England, southern Midlands, Heathrow airport, Scotland

St Pancras
East Midlands, south Yorkshire

Victoria
Southern and south-eastern England (Kent, Sussex), Gatwick airport, Channel ferry ports

Waterloo
Southern and south-western England (Surrey, Hampshire, Dorset), Wales, south-west London

Most stations have left-luggage facilities (around £4), toilets (20p) with showers (around £3), newsstands and bookshops, and a range of eating and drinking outlets. Some (eg, Victoria and Liverpool Street stations) have shopping centres attached.

Rail Classes There are two classes of rail travel: 1st class and what is officially referred to as standard class (though everyone calls it 2nd class). You'll pay 30% to 50% more in 1st class, depending on the line and journey time. In general it is not worth the extra money except on very crowded trains.

On some overnight trains there are sleeping compartments, which must be booked

GETTING THERE & AWAY

ELLIOT DANIEL

A first-class masterpiece: the neo-Gothic St Pancras station designed by Sir George Gilbert Scott in advance. The additional costs for these berths are £35/25 for 1st/2nd class between Exeter, Plymouth and Penzance and London (Great Western ☎ 0845 700 0125) and £39/33 on the routes from Scotland (ScotRail ☎ 0845 755 0033).

Tickets The ticketing system in the UK is very complex, so finding the best fare for your journey isn't easy. The best thing to do is to keep asking; you'll soon discover that everyone does that in London.

Children aged under five travel free; those aged between five and 15 pay half-price for most tickets, and full fare for Apex tickets.

If you're planning a long journey, the cheapest tickets on offer must be bought at least one week in advance. Buying an Apex ticket includes a reserved seat. Phone the 24-hour National Rail Enquiries (☎ 0845 748 4950) for timetables, fares and the numbers to ring for telephone bookings, as they differ according to the train operator. For shorter journeys, it's not really necessary to purchase tickets or make seat reservations in advance; just buy them at the station before you embark.

You can also check domestic timetables and frequencies on the Internet. Enter your departure and arrival stations online at

Ⓦ www.rail.co.uk/ukrail/planner/planner.htm, and it will give you the best route and departure times – though not fares.

Other Countries

Since the advent of the Channel Tunnel (see the boxed text below), London's main terminus for trains from Europe has been Waterloo International, though there are plans to transfer it to St Pancras in a few years' time.

Two separate services operate through the tunnel: a high-speed shuttle train known as Eurotunnel for cars, motorcycles, bicycles, coaches and freight from Coquelles (3 miles south-west of Calais) to Folkestone, and a high-speed passenger service, known as Eurostar, between Paris, Brussels and London, connecting London with cities all over Europe.

Rail/ferry links generally arrive at Victoria, Liverpool Street and Charing Cross train stations, depending on the European departure point. There are information centres at all the main stations. For enquiries about European trains contact Rail Europe (☎ 0870 584 8848, Ⓦ www.raileurope.co.uk or Ⓦ www.eurostarplus.com) or visit the Web sites of individual European rail companies – the international Deutsche Bahn (German Rail) Web site, for example, is Ⓦ www.bahn.de while the one for SNCF, the French national railroad company, is Ⓦ www.sncf.fr.

Eurotunnel Specially designed Eurotunnel trains (☎ 0870 535 3535 in the UK, ☎ 03 21 00 61 00 in France, Ⓦ www.eurotunnel.com) run 24 hours a day, every day of the year, with up to four departures an hour during peak periods (once an hour from 1am to 6am).

Eurotunnel terminals are clearly signposted and linked to motorway networks. Customs and immigration formalities are carried out before you drive on to the train. Total travel time from motorway to motorway, including loading and unloading, is estimated at one hour; the train journey itself takes about 35 minutes.

Prices vary depending on the time of year, time of day and type of vehicle, but

---

The Channel Tunnel

The Channel Tunnel, inaugurated in 1994 after massive cost overruns, is the first dryland link between England and France since the last Ice Age. The three parallel, concrete-lined tunnels – two rail tunnels and one for servicing both – were bored between Folkestone and Calais through a layer of impermeable chalk marl 25 to 45m (27 to 49 yards) below the floor of the English Channel and completed in seven years. The tunnels are 31 miles long, with about 24 miles directly under the Channel. Just under US$15 billion in private capital was invested in the project, the fourth real attempt at linking the two countries underground (efforts in 1880, 1922 and 1974 were eventually abandoned).

the standard one-way fare for a car, including all passengers, ranges from around €198 to €259. Same-day returns cost around €99 to €267, five-day returns from €259 to €320. Cheap excursion fares valid for one to five days (eg, €120 for a three-day-return) are sometimes available. For returns valid for more than five days, count on anything between €381 and €534. The fee for a bicycle, including its rider, is about €23; advance booking is required.

You can make an advance reservation by phone or simply pay by cash or credit card when you arrive at the toll booth.

Eurostar The Eurostar passenger trains (☎ 0870 518 6186 or 01233-617575 in the UK, ☎ 08 36 35 35 39 in France, **W** www .eurostar.com) run up to 25 times daily between Paris' Gare du Nord and Waterloo International in London, with half that number linking Brussels and London. Some trains stop at Lille and Calais in France and Ashford in Kent. Immigration formalities are now usually completed at the stations.

The Paris–London journey takes almost exactly three hours (which will drop to just 2½ hours when the high-speed track through Kent is *finally* completed). The journey from Brussels to London takes two hours and 40 minutes; this will be reduced to two hours and 10 minutes.

You can buy tickets from travel agencies, major train stations, the Eurostar Ticket Shop at Amex, 102–104 Victoria St SW1 (⊖ Victoria), or by calling Eurostar directly. The normal one-way/return flexible fare from Paris is a whopping €259/412, but special offers and advance-purchase tickets can reduce the return fare to around €151. The normal one-way/return fare from Brussels is about €235.50/461, falling to around €108 return with discounts and special deals. There are also discount fares for children aged five to 12 and those aged under 26 and over 60.

Rail/Ferry Eurostar has eclipsed many of the long-established rail/ferry links, but they continue to provide the cheapest means of cross-channel travel.

CHARLOTTE HINDLE

Zoom to London from the Continent on the high-speed Eurostar.

There are train-boat-train services in association with Hoverspeed (☎ 0870 524 0241 in the UK, ☎ 0820 00 35 55 in France, **W** www.hoverspeed.co.uk) and others to Charing Cross station from Paris' Gare du Nord via Dover that take about nine hours and cost from about €76 for a five-day return. These are cheaper than Eurostar but take a lot longer, and you've got to mess around transferring by bus between the train station and the ferry terminal on both sides.

From Ostende in Belgium you arrive at Charing Cross station, from Germany at Harwich in Essex. Direct services from the Netherlands will bring you to Liverpool Street station via Harwich. DFDS Seaways ships coming from Hamburg and Esbjerg in Denmark also arrive in Harwich.

CAR & MOTORCYCLE
Getting to London by car or motorcycle couldn't be easier, but do you really want to

Cycle fever is catching on in London and can help ease the traffic jams.

add to the traffic in this overly congested city? See Car & Motorcycle in the Getting Around chapter for the discouraging details.

From France or Belgium you can use the Eurotunnel or the ferries detailed in the Boat section, which also operate from other European countries. See the preceding Train section for information on services through the tunnel. The Getting Around chapter has information about buying a car or camper van as well as road rules in the UK.

Once in the UK there are good road connections from all the ports to London, which is ringed by the M25, useful for getting close to the area you want before trying to deal with normal city streets. If you are thinking of driving in or out of London, it might be worth buying the *A-Z M25 Main Road London* map (£4.45), which highlights the arterial red routes where no stopping is allowed.

BICYCLE

Bringing a bicycle to London is pretty straightforward. Trains, boats and planes all transport them but usually for a fee (eg, €23 on Eurotunnel, €30.50 on Eurostar). Folding bikes usually go free though. You need to contact the carrier directly to check what arrangements you are required to make.

HITCHING

Hitching is never entirely safe, and we can't recommend it as a way of getting to or from London. Having said that, if you're determined to risk it, you can minimise the likelihood of problems by hitching with someone else and making sure someone knows where you're going and when you expect to arrive.

Some ferry and all Eurotunnel fares include extra passengers. This should make it easier to persuade a driver to give you a lift.

BOAT

There is a bewildering choice of ferries and other seagoing vessels between Britain and Ireland and mainland Europe. This section outlines the main options but doesn't give a complete listing. The bible for sea travel is the *DG&G Travel Information Cruise & Ferry Guide*, which comes out four times a year and is published by DG&G Travel Information (☎ 0800 731 0163, Ⓦ www.dgg travelinfo.co.uk), 3rd floor, Dukeminster House, Church St, Dunstable, Bedfordshire LU5 4HU. Many travel agencies have copies.

Competing companies operate on the main routes, and the resulting range of services is comprehensive but complicated. The same ferry company can have a host of different prices for the same route, depending on the time of day or year, the validity of the ticket or the size of vehicle. Five-day returns are generally among the cheapest options. Return tickets may be much cheaper than two one-way fares, and vehicle tickets may also cover a driver and passenger (or passengers). Dirt-cheap day-return tickets are also available, but ferry companies usually make it hard on people who use them for one-way passage. A large backpack is a dead give-away that you're not on the ferry for an afternoon in Dover.

It's worth planning (and booking) ahead where possible as there are often special reductions on off-peak crossings. The ferries all carry cars, motorcycles and bicycles.

Ireland

There are many ferry services from Ireland to Britain using car ferries. Figures quoted are one-way fares; there are often special deals, return fares and other money-savers worth investigating.

There are services from eight ports in the Irish Republic and Northern Ireland to 12 ports in England, Scotland and Wales. Details of the most popular routes to and from

DALE BUCKTON

London are given here; for details of the others see Lonely Planet's *Ireland, Britain, England, Wales* and *Scotland* guides.

You can get from Rosslare in Ireland to Fishguard or Pembroke in Wales. These popular short crossings take 3½ hours to Fishguard with Stena Line (☎ 01-204 7777 in Dublin, ☎ 0870 570 7070, Ⓦ www.stena line.co.uk) or about four hours to Pembroke with Irish Ferries (☎ 01-638 3333 in Dublin, ☎ 0870 517 1717 in the UK, Ⓦ www .irishferries.com). Foot passengers to Fishguard pay between €21.60 and €28 one-way (€16.50 to €23 for students with a current ISIC card), while a car with driver and up to four passengers costs from €119 to €208 one-way; five-day returns cost €170 to €284. The Stena Lynx catamaran to Fishguard, which makes the crossing in just 99 minutes, costs €28 to €38 (€23 to €32 for ISIC cardholders) for foot passengers one-way and €145 to €253 for a car with driver and up to four passengers. The five-day return fare for the same car would be from €227 to €328.

Foot passengers on the Irish Ferries' Rosslare to Pembroke service pay €23 to €33 one-way, while a car plus driver costs

€100 to €202 one-way and €126 to €253 for a five-day return. Extra passengers cost €12.70/6.35 (adult/child aged four to 15).

Foot passengers on Irish Ferries' 3½-hour crossing from Dublin to Holyhead pay the same fare as for Rosslare to Pembroke, while taking a car with passengers on this route costs from €125 to €240 one-way, depending on the date and type of boat. Again, there are five-day return specials are the cheapest at between €151 and €329.

Stena Line has fast services linking both Dublin Port and Dun Laoghaire, south of Dublin, with Holyhead. From Dublin Port, foot passengers pay between €23 and €28 one-way, and a car with driver and up to four passengers costs from €145 to €234. A five-day return costs €195.50 to €310. From Dun Laoghaire, foot passengers pay €28 to €35.50 (students: €23 to €30.50) and a car costs €176.50 to €240 one-way. Count on between €234 and €360 for a five-day return.

France
The shortest ferry links between France and Britain is Calais to Dover, and Dover is the most convenient port for those going on to

Rough and ready: a more traditional approach to crossing the channel

London by bus or train. P&O Stena Line (☎ 08 25 01 00 20 in France or 0870 600 0600 in the UK, **W** www.posl.com), Sea-France (☎ 0870 571 1711 in the UK, **W** www.seafrance.com) and Hoverspeed (☎ 08 20 00 35 55 in France or 0870 241 2737 in the UK, **W** www.hoverspeed.co.uk) run between Calais and Dover every one or two hours. It's worth checking prices for all three.

Fares are extremely volatile, but at the time of writing Hoverspeed was charging adult foot passengers from Calais to Dover €37 one-way and children aged four to 15 €18; a car and up to nine passengers cost €154 to €280, depending on the time of the day and day of the week. A five-day return for the same car cost €178 to €337.

Other routes across the Channel include Boulogne to Folkestone; Dieppe to Newhaven; Cherbourg to Poole; Ouistreham (Caen) or Le Havre in Normandy or St Malo in Brittany to Portsmouth; Roscoff to Plymouth; and St Malo to Weymouth.

Belgium & the Netherlands
Both P&O Stena Line and Hoverspeed operate ferries between Ostende and Dover. The fares on the latter's service between Belgium and the UK are exactly the same as those on its Calais to Dover run.

Stena Line ferries (☎ 017-431 58 11 in the Netherlands) link the Hook of Holland with Harwich in 3½ hours. Foot passengers pay €63.50/45 (adult/child). A car with driver costs €236 to €377 one-way and €168 to €313 for a five-day return.

Scandinavia & Germany
DFDS Seaways (☎ 79 17 79 17 in Denmark, ☎ 031-650650 in Sweden, ☎ 040-389 03 71 in Germany, **W** www.dfdsseaways.com or **W** www.scansea.com) operates a number of ferry services to Britain. The ferry between Esbjerg in Denmark and Harwich runs every other day in summer and twice a week in winter; the trip takes 19 hours. The 20-hour Hamburg-Harwich service runs every two days in summer and three days a week in winter. The service from Gothenburg in Sweden to Newcastle

(via Kristiansand in Norway) operates twice weekly and takes 25 hours.

Spain
Brittany Ferries (☎ 94 236 06 11 in Bilbao, **W** www.brittanyferries.com) operates a car ferry twice a week from Santander on the northern coast of Spain to Plymouth from mid-March to mid-November. The journey takes 24 hours. P&O Portsmouth (☎ 94 423 44 77 in Spain, ☎ 0870 242 4999 in the UK, **W** www.poportsmouth.com) operates a twice-weekly service year round between Santurtzi, 8½ miles north-west of Bilbao, and Portsmouth; the journey takes 29 hours from Spain and 35 hours from the UK. Foot passengers pay from €69 to €179 one-way and €93 to €156 for a 10-day return. A car plus driver costs €258 to €481 one-way and €385 to €690 for a 10-day return.

WALKING
Although Dick Whittington (see the boxed text 'A Boy, a Puss & City Hall' in the Facts about London chapter) supposedly had no problem with it, walking to London would not have seemed a very bright idea until recently. But with the Thames Path National Trail fully up and running, there's nothing to stop you hiking all the way from its source near Kemble in the Cotswolds to the Thames Barrier, a distance of 172 miles. For the less intrepid, the 16-mile section from Battersea to the barrier takes about 6½ hours. Full details can be found in Lonely Planet's *Walking in Britain* or visit **W** www.thamesvalleyguide.co.uk.

Alternatively you could walk Britain's first National Waterway Walk, which follows the Grand Union Canal from Gas St Basin in Birmingham to Little Venice in London, a distance of 144 miles. Contact British Waterways (☎ 01923-201120, **W** www.british-waterways.co.uk) for a leaflet outlining the route.

ORGANISED TOURS
Companies with trips pitched at a young crowd include the following: Top Deck Travel (Map 10; ☎ 7370 4555, **W** www.topdecktravel.co.uk), 131–135 Earl's Court

Warning

The information in this chapter is particularly vulnerable to change: Prices for international travel are volatile, routes are introduced and cancelled, schedules change, special deals come and go, and rules and visa requirements are amended. Airlines and governments seem to take a perverse pleasure in making price structures and regulations as complicated as possible. You should check directly with the airline or a travel agent to make sure you understand how a fare (and ticket you may buy) works. In addition, the travel industry is highly competitive and there are many lurks and perks.

The upshot of this is that you should get opinions, quotes and advice from as many airlines and travel agents as possible before you part with your hard-earned cash. The details given in this chapter should be regarded as pointers and are not a substitute for your own careful, up-to-date research.

Rd SW5 (☮ Earl's Court); Drifters Travel (Map 5; ☎ 7262 1292), 22a Craven Terrace W2 (☮ Lancaster Gate); and Contiki Travel (Map 6; ☎ 7637 0802, Ⓦ www.contiki .com), Royal National Hotel, Bedford Way WC1 (☮ Russell Square).

If you don't fit into that category then try Shearings Holidays (☎ 01942-824824, Ⓦ www.shearingsholidays.com), Miry Lane, Wigan, Lancashire WN3 4AG, which has a wide range of four- to 12-day coach tours covering the whole country. They also offer Club 55 holidays for more mature holiday-makers.

For the over-60s, Saga Holidays (☎ 0800 300500 or 0800 300456 for a brochure, Ⓦ www.saga.co.uk), Saga Building, Middleburg Square, Folkestone, Kent CT20 1AZ, offers holidays ranging from cheap coach-tours and resort holidays to luxury cruises around the UK and abroad. Saga also operates in the USA as Saga International Holidays (☎ 800-343 0273 or 617-262 2262, Ⓦ www.sagaholidays.com), 222 Berkeley St, Boston MA 02116.

Getting Around

London is served by five airports, ranging in size from massive Heathrow to the small London City.

THE AIRPORTS
Heathrow Airport

Heathrow (LHR; ☎ 0870 000 0123, W www.baa.co.uk/heathrow), 15 miles west of central London, is the world's busiest commercial airport, handling upwards of 63 million passengers per year. It currently has four terminals, with a fifth one on its way. Two Piccadilly Line tube stations serve the airport: one for Terminals 1, 2 and 3, the other for Terminal 4. Make sure you know which terminal your flight is departing from when leaving London (see the boxed text below for details).

Heathrow's Terminals

The two tube stations at Heathrow on the Piccadilly Line serve the following airlines. Please note that this is a guide only to which station to disembark at; you should always check the exact terminal your flight is using with the airline or your travel agent.

Terminal 4
Air Malta
British Airways intercontinental flights
British Airways flights to Amsterdam, Athens, Basle, Moscow and Paris
Emirates Abu Dhabi flights operated by BA
KLM Royal Dutch Airlines
Kenya Airways
Qantas Airways
Sri Lankan Airlines

Terminals 1, 2, 3
British Airways domestic and most other European flights
British Airways flights to Capetown, Lagos and Miami
All other flights

Heathrow can appear chaotic and very overcrowded, though there are the requisite pubs and bars, restaurants and duty-free outlets (for those flying to and from non-EU countries only). Each terminal has competitive currency-exchange facilities, information counters and accommodation desks.

There are some 15 international hotels – none particularly cheap or noteworthy – at or near Heathrow, should you be leaving or arriving at a peculiarly early or late hour. To reach them you must take the Heathrow Hotel Hoppa bus (☎ 0870 574 7777) costing £2.50. The buses run between 6am and 11pm, with a service every 10 minutes at peak times, every 15 minutes otherwise, for the first three terminals. Services from Terminal 4 run every 30 minutes.

There are left-luggage facilities at Terminal 1 (☎ 8745 5301), open 5am to 11pm daily; Terminal 2 (☎ 8745 4599), open 5.30am to 10.30pm; Terminal 3 (☎ 8759 3344), open 24 hours; and Terminal 4 (☎ 8745 7460), open 5am to 11pm. The charge is £3.50 per item for the first 12 hours and £4 per item for up to 24 hours. All branches can forward baggage.

To/From Heathrow The fastest way to get to central London is via Heathrow Express (☎ 0845 600 1515, W www.heathrowexpress.co.uk), an ultramodern train that whisks passengers from Heathrow Central station (serving Terminals 1 to 3) and Terminal 4 station to Paddington station (Map 5; ⊖ Paddington) in 15 minutes. At £12/23 one-way/return in express class (£20/40 in 1st class), it's a pricey way to go, though you can save £1/3 one-way/return by booking in advance. There is also a 'meetergreeter', same-day return fare of £13. Up to four children under 16 accompanying a fare-paying adult travel free. Trains leave Paddington every 15 minutes, with the first train at 5.10am, the last at 11.40pm. From the airport, the first train of the day leaves Terminal 4 station Monday to Saturday/

In a flash: stylish Heathrow Express trains connect the airport to Paddington station.

last departure from Terminal 4 is at 9.45pm. Tickets are valid for three months and cost £7/10 (adult) and £3.50/5 (child) one-way/return. The trip takes about 1¾ hours.

A metered black taxi to/from central London (Oxford St) will cost about £35.

Gatwick Airport

Gatwick (LGW; ☎ 0870 000 2468, ⓦ www .baa.co.uk/gatwick), some 30 miles south of central London, is smaller and better organised than Heathrow. The North and South terminals are linked by an efficient monorail service; journey time is about two minutes.

The left-luggage office at the North Terminal (☎ 01293-502013) opens 6am to 10pm daily, the one in the South Terminal (☎ 01293-502014) round the clock. The charge is £3.50 per item for the first six hours and £4 per item for up to 24 hours.

To/From Gatwick The Gatwick Express (☎ 0870 530 1530, ⓦ www.gatwickexpress .co.uk) trains link the station near the South Terminal with Victoria station (Map 10; ⊖ Victoria) every 15 minutes from 5.20am to 12.50am; they then run hourly from 1.35am till 4.35am. from Victoria, trains leave every 15 minutes from 5am until just after midnight; they then go hourly between 12.30am and 4.30am. One-way/return fares are £10.50/20 in express class and £17/34 in 1st class; under-16s pay half-fare. The journey takes about 30 minutes. BA and American Airlines passengers can check in at Victoria station.

The Connex South Central train service (☎ 0845 748 4950, ⓦ www.connex.co.uk) from Victoria, which runs every 15 to 30 minutes (once an hour from 1am to 4am), takes a little longer but costs only £8.20/4.10 one-way. There's also a Thameslink service (☎ 0845 748 4950, ⓦ www.thameslink.co .uk) from King's Cross, Farringdon and London Bridge costing from £9.80/4.95.

Airbus No 5 (☎ 0807 574 7777, ⓦ www .gobycoach.com) runs from Victoria Coach Station to Gatwick 16 times a day between 6am and 11pm (between 4.15am and 9.15pm from the airport to central London). A one-way/return ticket valid for three months

Sunday at 5.07/5.03am (5.12/5.08am from Heathrow Central); the last is at 11.32pm (11.37pm). Many airlines, including American Airlines, BA and United Airlines, now have check-in facilities at Paddington.

The Underground remains the cheapest way of getting to Heathrow costing £3.60/1.50 (adult/child aged five to 15). It runs between 5.30am and 11.45pm daily. To use a Travelcard (see Fares in the London Underground section later in this chapter), it must be valid for all six zones. Be advised that you can buy tickets for the tube from machines in the baggage reclaim areas of the Heathrow terminals so you don't have to queue up in the station itself. The journey to/from central London takes about an hour.

Airbus A2 (☎ 0807 574 7777, ⓦ www .gobycoach.com) links King's Cross station with Heathrow some 30 times a day, making several stops along the way, including Baker Street tube station, Marble Arch and Notting Hill Gate. The first bus leaves King's Cross at 4am, the last at 8pm daily. The first bus bound for London leaves Terminal 4 at 5.30am via Terminal 3, 2 & 1 (6.10am/6.20am weekdays/weekends). The costs £8.50/10; children aged five to 15 pay half-price. The journey takes 1½ hours.

A black cab to/from central London will cost around £70.

Stansted Airport

Some 35 miles north-east of central London, Stansted (STN; ☎ 0870 000 0303, **W** www.baa.co.uk/stansted), London's third busiest international gateway, is its most ambitious, with a 30% growth in the annual number of passengers it handles (currently almost 13 million), and attractive. The futuristic terminal building was designed by Norman Foster.

To/From Stansted The Stansted Express (☎ 0845 748 4950, **W** www.standsted express.com) trains link the airport and Liverpool Street station (Map 8; ⊖ Liverpool Street). Trains depart Liverpool Street station every 15 to 30 minutes from 5am (4.45am on Saturday) to 11pm; the journey takes 45 minutes. From the airport, the first train goes at 6am, the last just before midnight. Standard fares are £13/21 one-way/return (half-price for children); business class costs £18/31. If you need to connect with the tube, change at Tottenham Hale for the Victoria Line or stay on to Liverpool Street station for the Central Line.

Airbus A6 (☎ 0807 574 7777, **W** www .gobycoach.com) links Victoria Coach Station some 40 times a day round the clock and the journey takes about 1½ hours. They depart the coach station every half-hour between 4.05am and 11.35pm and then hourly. From the airport buses leave every half-hour between 3.30am and 11.30pm and then once an hour. A one-way/return ticket valid for three months from Victoria costs £7/10; children pay half-price.

A black taxi to/from central London will cost £70 to £80.

London City Airport

London City (LCY; ☎ 7646 0000, **W** www .londoncityairport.com), 6 miles east of central London, is in the Docklands by the Thames. Seen as a businessperson's airport and under-utilised until recently, London City now has flights to 20 continental European cities as well eight destinations in the British Isles (Aberdeen, Belfast, Dublin, Dundee, Edinburgh, Glasgow, Isle of Man and Jersey).

To/From London City The blue airport Shuttlebus (☎ 7646 0088, **W** www.london cityairport.com/shuttlebus) connects London City with Liverpool Street station via Canary Wharf between 6.50am (11am on Sunday) and 10pm (1.15pm on Saturday). One-way/return tickets to Liverpool Street cost £6/12 (adult) and £2/4 (child) or £3/6 and £1/2 to Canary Wharf. The first bus leaves Liverpool Street at 6.15am (10.30am on Sunday); the last departs at 9pm weekdays (12.45pm on Saturday). Services are every 10/15 minutes on weekdays/at the weekend, and the journey takes 25/10 minutes from Liverpool Street/Canary Wharf. The green airport Shuttlebus links London City and Canning Town station, which is on the Jubilee tube, the DLR and Silverlink lines, every 10 minutes from 6am (10.05am on Sunday) until 10.20pm (1.15pm on Saturday). The one-way fare costs £2/1 (adult/child) and the trip takes five minutes.

A black taxi costs around £20 to/from central London.

Luton Airport

By London standards a small, remote airport some 35 miles to the north, Luton (LTN; ☎ 01582-405100, **W** www.london-luton.co.uk) caters mainly for cheap charter flights, though the discount airline easyJet (see Air in the Getting There & Away chapter) operates scheduled services from here.

To/From Luton Thameslink (☎ 0845 748 4950, **W** www.thameslink.co.uk) runs trains from King's Cross and other central London stations to Luton Airport Parkway station, from where an airport shuttle bus will take you to the airport in eight minutes. Trains depart every five to 15 minutes from 7am to 10pm, the journey takes 30 to 40 minutes and costs £9.50/4.75 (adult/child) one-way.

Green Line bus No 757 (☎ 0870 608 7261, **W** www.greenline.co.uk), which runs from Buckingham Palace Rd south of Victoria station, serves Luton and costs £8/13 (adult) or £4.50/7.50 (child) one-way/return. Buses leave every half-hour from 7.05am (7.35am at weekends) to 10pm and hourly till 6.30am. They depart Luton every half-hour 8am to 8pm and hourly till 7.30am.

A black taxi costs £70 to £80 to/from central London.

LONDON UNDERGROUND

The London Underground, or 'tube', first opened in 1863 (it was then essentially a roofed-in trench) and sometimes it feels like not a whole lot has changed since then; it is slow, unreliable, and, as the ageing system has suffered from decades of underfunding and, in some places, neglect, breakdowns are common. Sometimes entire sections of the tube are closed, and there's the constant threat of strikes by operators and other staff opposed to the government's proposed privatisation. Worst of all, it's terribly expensive: compare the cheapest one-way fare in central London of £1.50 with those charged on the Paris Métro (€1.2/76p), the New York Subway (US$1.50/£1.10) and the Hong Kong Mass Transit Railway HK$4/38p. And in Paris and New York you can travel on the entire system for the flat fare; in London £1.50 gets you around central London (Zone 1) only.

Still, the tube is normally the quickest and easiest way of getting round London and extends as far afield as Amersham in Buckinghamshire to the north-west, Epping in Essex to the north-east, Heathrow airport in the south-west and, via the DLR, Beckton to the south-east. An estimated 2.5 million tube journeys are made every day.

Information

Underground travel information centres sell tickets and provide free maps. There are centres at all Heathrow terminals and at Euston, King's Cross St Pancras, Liverpool Street, Oxford Circus, Piccadilly Circus, St James's Park and Victoria tube and mainline train stations. There is also an information office at Hammersmith bus station. For general information on the tube, buses, the

DLR or trains within London ring ☎ 7222 1234 or visit the Underground Web site at ⓦ www.thetube.com or the Transport for London site at ⓦ www.transportforlondon .gov.uk. For news of how services are running, call Travelcheck (☎ 7222 1200).

Network

Greater London is served by 12 tube lines, along with the independent (though linked) and privately owned DLR and an interconnected rail network (see the DLR & Train section later). The first tube train operates at around 5.30am Monday to Saturday and around 7am on Sunday; the last train leaves between 11.30pm to 12.30am depending on the day, the station and the line.

Remember that any train heading from left to right on the map is designated as eastbound, any train heading from top to

> ## Mapping the Underground
>
> The London Underground map is so familiar that it's often used as a symbol for the city itself. Millions of people refer to it every year without giving a thought to one Harry Beck (1902–74), the engineering draughtsman responsible for designing the map in 1931.
>
> It was Beck who realised that the entire network could be fitted into a realistic amount of space and still be perfectly usable – even if strict geography had to be ignored. After all, once you're underground you don't really need to know exactly where places are, just so long as you understand where they lie in relation to each other in the network.
>
> Beck expanded the space devoted to the central London stations, redrew all the lines until they were horizontal, vertical or at 45 degrees to each other and devised the colour-coding system for the different lines. For his efforts he was paid the grand sum of five guineas (about £5.25 today), but every London Underground map still carried his name until 1960. Even now the map is basically unchanged, except for the addition of new lines and stations.

GETTING AROUND

The Tube: Fun Facts to Know & Tell

The London tube is the world's oldest (1863), most extensive (253 miles of track serving 275 stations) and busiest (18 million passengers per year) underground transport system. With breakdowns every 16 minutes on average, it is also the most unreliable, and for the journey between Covent Garden and Leicester Square (£1.50 for less than ¼ mile, or 250m), the per-mile price makes taking the tube more expensive than flying Concorde. But those aren't the tube's only superlatives and oddities:

- The longest line is the Central Line (46 miles), with the Piccadilly Line running a close second at 46 miles; the shortest is the Waterloo & City Line (1½ miles), known as 'the Drain' that links Bank with Waterloo.
- The Jubilee Line is the only one in the entire system to connect with all the other lines as well as the Docklands Light Railway.
- The longest journey possible *without* changing trains is from West Ruislip to Epping on the Central Line (34 miles), which would take you about 1½ hours.
- The longest distance between stations is from Chesham to Chalfont & Latimer on the Metropolitan Line (4 miles); the shortest is between Leicester Square and Covent Garden (less than ¼ mile/250m).
- The deepest station is Hampstead on the Northern Line (58.5m).
- The District Line has the most stations with 60, followed by the Piccadilly (52) and Central (49) lines; the Waterloo & City Line has but two.
- The busiest station is Victoria, with 7.6 million passengers per year, followed by Oxford Circus, King's Cross, Liverpool Street and Baker Street.
- There are 408 escalators on the Underground and 112 lifts. Waterloo has the most escalators, with 25, while the one at Angel on the Northern Line is the longest (60m, up a vertical rise of 27.5m).
- There are some 40 'ghost' (disused) stations on the Underground, including British Museum on the Central Line (closed in the 1930s); Down Street near Hyde Park Corner on the Piccadilly Line, used by Churchill and his family during WWII; Marlborough Street on the Metropolitan Line near Lord's; South Kentish Town near Camden on the Northern Line, which closed during a power cut and never reopened; and Hounslow Town on the District Line, which functioned from 1883 to 1886 and then again from 1903 to 1909, when it closed permanently through lack of use.
- The stations with the gappiest gaps, which are caused by curvatures in the platform, are Embankment and Bank.
- Unproven but assumed: every Londoner has complained about the tube at some stage in their life.

CHARLOTTE HINDLE

Playing the waiting game: you wait all day and then three tubes turn up at once.

bottom is southbound – no matter how many squiggles and turns it makes. If your two stations are not on the same line, you need to note the nearest station where the two lines intersect, where you must change trains (transfer).

Tube lines vary in their reliability and the Circle Line, which links most of the main-line stations and is therefore much used by tourists, has one of the worst track records. Other lines low in the league tables are the Northern Line (though improving), the Central Line (despite the millions of pounds spent on a new signalling system in recent years) and the Hammersmith & City (often referred to as the 'Hammersmith & Shitty') Line. The Piccadilly Line to/from Heathrow is usually pretty good and the Victoria Line, linking the station with Oxford Circus and King's Cross, is particularly fast. The Jubilee Line, which was extended by 10 miles in 1999, gained a further 11 stations. Each was designed by a different architect, and many are ultramodern works of art in themselves.

If you're caught on the Underground without a valid ticket (and that includes crossing into a zone that your ticket doesn't cover) you're liable for an on-the-spot fine of £10. If you do get nabbed, do us all a favour: shut up and pay up. The inspectors – and your fellow passengers – hear the same stories every day of the year.

Fares

The London Underground divides London into six concentric zones. The basic (ie, cheapest) fare for adults/children aged five to 15 years for Zone 1 is £1.50/60p, for Zones 1 & 2 £1.90/80p, for three zones £2.20/1, for four zones £2.70/1.20, for five zones £3.30/1.40 and for all six zones (eg, to/from Heathrow) £3.60/1.50. If you're travelling through a couple of zones or several times in one day, you should consider a travel pass or some other discounted fare.

Travel Passes & Discount Fares A Travelcard valid all day offers the cheapest way of getting about in London and can be used after 9.30am on weekdays and all day at weekends and public holidays on all forms of transport in London: the tube, suburban trains, the DLR and buses (including night buses). Most visitors will find that a Travelcard covering Zones 1 & 2 card (£4) will be sufficient, but a card for Zones 1, 2, 3 & 4 costs £4.30 and one for Zones 2, 3, 4, 5 & 6 £3.50. A card allowing travel in all six zones costs £4.90, just £1.30 more than a single-journey all-zone ticket – and you get to use it all day. A one-day Travelcard for children aged five to 15 costs £2 regardless of how many zones it covers but those aged 14 and 15 need a Child Photocard to travel on this fare. You can buy Travelcards several days ahead but not on buses.

If you plan to start moving before 9.30am on a weekday, you can buy a Zones 1 & 2 LT Card for £5.10/2.50 (£6.20/3 for Zones 1, 2, 3 & 4 and £7.70/3.30 for all six zones), valid on the tube, the DLR and buses (but *not* suburban trains) for one day with no time restrictions.

At £6/3 (adult/child) in Zones 1 & 2 and £7.30/3 in all six zones, Weekend Travelcards valid on Saturday, Sunday and public holidays are 25% cheaper than two separate one-day cards. Family Travelcards are also available for one or two adults and up to four children aged five to 15 (who need not be related to them); they start at £2.60 per adult and 80p per child for Zones 1 & 2 up to £3.20/80p for all six zones.

Weekly Travelcards are also available but require an identification card with a passport-sized photo. A Zone 1 card costs £15.90/6.60 (adult/child aged five to 15); Zones 1 & 2 £18.90/7.70; Zones 1, 2 & 3 £22.40/10.30; Zones 1, 2, 3 & 4 £27.60/12.80; Zones 1, 2, 3, 4 & 5 £33.30/14.10; all six zones £36.40/15.40. These allow you to travel at any time of day and on night buses as well, but before buying one decide whether you're really likely to travel much early in the morning or at night; five one-day Travelcards for all zones plus a weekend card for a total of £31.80 is about 12% cheaper than a weekly pass. Monthly and annual Travelcards can also be purchased for between one and six zones (between £61.10 and £139.80 for a month, between £636 and £1456 for a year).

If you will be making a lot of journeys within Zone 1 *only*, you can buy a carnet of 10 tickets for £11.50/5 (adult/child), a saving of £3.50/1. But do remember that if you cross over into Zone 2 (eg, from King's Cross St Pancras to Camden Town for the weekend market) you'll be travelling on an invalid ticket and liable for a penalty fare.

BUS

If you're not in much of a hurry, travelling round London by double-decker bus can be more enjoyable than using the tube. Even though they were privatised in 1994, London's 5500-odd buses are under the Transport for London umbrella. About 3.5 million people travel on them every day.

Information

There are some three dozen separate (and free) bus guides available to areas as far-flung as Harrow, Romford and Hounslow. Most visitors, however, will find the Central London bus guide, essentially a map and available from most transport travel information centres, sufficient. If you can't get to a centre, ring ☎ 7371 0247 to have one sent or write to London Buses (CDL), Freepost Lon7503, London SE16 4BR. For general information on London buses call ☎ 7222 1234 (24 hours). For more information on how services are running, phone Travelcheck on ☎ 7222 1200.

Rove the city on a Routemaster bus; it's a great way to see the sights on a budget.

DENNIS JOHNSON

Network & Useful Routes

One of the best ways to explore London is to buy a Travelcard and jump on a bus (especially the double-decker Routemaster ones, with a conductor and an access platform at the rear that makes the jumping on and off so easy).

From north to south (or vice versa) the No 24 is especially good. Beginning at South End Green in Hampstead Heath, it travels through Camden and along Gower St to Tottenham Court Rd. From there it goes down Charing Cross Rd, past Leicester Square to Trafalgar Square, then along Whitehall, past the Palace of Westminster, Westminster Abbey and Westminster Cathedral. It reaches Victoria station and then carries on to Pimlico, which is handy for the Tate Britain.

Another north–south route worth trying is the No 19, which departs from Finsbury Park tube station, travels down Upper St in Islington, through Clerkenwell, Holborn and Bloomsbury, then along New Oxford St and down Charing Cross Rd and Shaftesbury Ave to Piccadilly. It then travels along the northern edge of Green Park to Hyde Park Corner, before carrying on down Sloane St and along King's Rd. If you get off at the southern end of Battersea Bridge, you'll be well placed for Battersea Park.

From east to west, or the reverse, try the No 8. This is a Routemaster bus and comes from Bow in east London. It goes along Bethnal Green Rd and passes the markets at Spitalfields and Petticoat Lane, Liverpool Street station, the City, the Guildhall and the Old Bailey. It then crosses Holborn and enters Oxford St, travelling past Oxford Circus and turning down New Bond St to Piccadilly, Hyde Park Corner and Victoria.

Other good tour buses are Nos 9 and 10, which leave from Hammersmith and go through Kensington and Knightsbridge, passing the Albert Memorial, Royal Albert Hall and Harrods before reaching Hyde Park Corner. The No 9 then goes along Piccadilly to Piccadilly Circus and Trafalgar Square before carrying on down the Strand to Aldwych (good for Covent Garden), where it terminates. The No 10 heads northwards from Hyde Park Corner to Marble

Arch and heads down Oxford St and then up Tottenham Court Rd to Euston, King's Cross and eventually Archway tube station.

The wheelchair-accessible Stationlink buses (☎ 7941 4600), which have a ramp operated by the driver, follow a similar route to that of the Circle Line, joining up the main-line stations – from Paddington, Euston, St Pancras and King's Cross to Liverpool Street, London Bridge, Waterloo and Victoria. People with mobility problems and those with heavy luggage may find this easier to use than the tube, although it only operates once an hour. From Paddington there are services clockwise on the SL1 from 8.15am to 7.15pm, and anticlockwise (the SL2) from 8.40am to 6.40pm.

Night Buses

Trafalgar Square is the focus of two-thirds of the more than 60 night buses (prefixed with the letter 'N') that come on duty when the tube shuts down and the daytime buses return to the barn; if you're not familiar with the routes, head there. Night buses run from about midnight to 7am, but services can be infrequent and only stop on request, meaning you must signal clearly to the driver to stop.

Fares

Though the bus network is divided into four zones, this only effects holders of passes valid for a week or longer. Single-journey bus tickets, which are sold on the bus by the driver or a conductor (both of whom can give you change) cost either £1 in central London (Zone 1) and 70p from any point to any point elsewhere in London; night bus fares are now the same as day ones. Children aged five to 15 pay a uniform 40p. The Travelcards described earlier in the London Underground section are valid on buses.

Stationlink buses cost £70/40p (adult/child aged five to 15) though Travelcards, including those for Zone 1, are also valid.

Travelcards are now valid on all night buses.

Travel Passes & Discount Fares A Saver ticket (£3.90) is a book of six bus tickets valid on all buses, including those in central

London and night buses. They are transferable but valid for one journey only.

If you plan to use buses and buses alone during you stay in London, you can buy a one-day bus pass valid throughout London for £2/1 (adult/child). Unlike the one-day Travelcards, these are valid before 9.30am. All-zone weekly/monthly passes are also available for £9.50/36.50 (adult) and £4/15.40 (child).

DLR & TRAIN

The independent, driverless Docklands Light Railway links the City at Bank and Tower Gateway at Tower Hill with Beckton and Stratford to the east and north-east and the Docklands (as far as Island Gardens at the southern end of the Isle of Dogs), Greenwich and Lewisham to the south. The DLR runs from 5.30am to 12.30am weekdays, from 6am to 12.30am on Saturday and from 7.30am to 11.30pm on Sunday. Fares are the same as those on the tube though there is a host of daily, weekly, monthly and annual passes valid uniquely on the DLR. For example, the one-day Rail & River Rover ticket costs £7.80/3.90/20.50 (adult/child/family) and allows unlimited travel on the DLR and City Cruises (see River Shuttle under Boat later in this chapter), which links central London with Greenwich. For general information on the DLR phone ☎ 7363 9700 or visit ⓦ www.dlr.co.uk. For news of how services are running, call Travelcheck on ☎ 7222 1200.

Several rail companies also operate passenger trains in London, including the Silverlink (or North London) line (☎ 01923 -207258, ⓦ www.silverlinktrains.com), which links Richmond in the south-west with North Woolwich in the south-east via Kew, West Hampstead, Camden Road, Highbury & Islington and Stratford stations, and the crowded Thameslink (☎ 0845 748 4950, ⓦ www.thameslink.co.uk) 'sardine line', which goes from Elephant & Castle and London Bridge in the south through the City to King's Cross and as far north as Luton. Most lines connect with the Underground system, and Travelcards can be used on them.

GETTING AROUND

Ghost train: the driverless DLR runs from the City to the Docklands.

If you're staying in south-east London, where suburban trains are usually much more useful than the tube, it may be worth buying a one-year Network Railcard, which offers one-third off most rail fares in south-east England and on one-day Travelcards for all six zones. Travel is permitted only after 10am on weekdays and at any time at weekends. The card costs £20 and is available at most stations.

CAR & MOTORCYCLE

By all means, avoid bringing a car into London. The roads are horribly clogged, drivers can be extremely aggressive, road rage is common and parking space is at a premium. Traffic wardens and wheel clampers operate with extreme efficiency. If your vehicle is clamped you won't see much change from £100 (release fee plus fine) to get it back; if you do get clamped, ring the 24-hour Clamping & Vehicle Section hotline (☎ 7747 4747). If the car has been removed it's going to cost you at least £125 to get it back.

If all that doesn't discourage you, Mayor Ken Livingstone's bright idea just might: he wants a £5 congestion charge levied on every private car entering central London between 7am and 7pm on weekdays. Cars' licence plates will be checked by fixed and mobile digital cameras and a £80 fine levied on those flouting the code. Motorcycles, taxis, minicabs, buses, post vans, emergency vehicles and vehicles driven by the disabled would be exempt.

Road Rules

Vehicles drive on the left-hand side of the road. Wearing seat belts in the front is compulsory and, if they are fitted in the back, passengers there must wear them as well. You give way to your right at roundabouts (traffic already on the roundabout has the right of way). Motorcyclists must wear helmets at all times.

The current speed limits are 30mph in built-up areas, 60mph on single carriageways and 70mph on motorways and dual carriageways. Other speed limits will be indicated by signs. Many side streets now have speed humps ('sleeping policemen'), aimed at reducing the traffic flow to a crawl.

If you do plan to drive in London you should obtain the *Highway Code*, which is available at AA and RAC outlets as well as some bookshops and tourist information centres (TICs). A foreign driving licence is valid in Britain for up to 12 months from the time of your last entry into the country. If you bring a car from Europe make sure you're adequately insured.

For drink-driving rules see Legal Matters in the Facts for the Visitor chapter.

Motoring Organisations

The two largest in the UK, both of which offer 24-hour breakdown assistance, are the Automobile Association (AA; ☎ 0800 028 8540 for information or 0800 887766 for breakdown, ⓦ www.theaa.com) and the Royal Automobile Club (RAC; ☎ 0800 550550 for information or 0800 828282 for breakdown, W www.rac.co.uk). One year's membership starts at £42/39 for AA/RAC, and both can also extend their cover to include continental Europe. Your motoring organisation at home may have a reciprocal arrangement with one or the other.

Parking

Try to avoid driving at peak hours (from 7.30am to 9.30am, and from 4.30pm to 7pm) and plan ahead if you need to park in central London.

Look out for yellow lines along the roadside. A single line indicates that parking restrictions are in force; you need to find the nearby sign that spells out exactly what they are. A double line means no parking at all; a broken line means more limited restrictions. Single red lines on main routes in and out of central London indicate a ban on stopping, loading or parking between 7am and 7pm, while a double red line means no stopping, loading or parking at all.

There are 'short-stay' and 'long-stay' car parks. Prices are often the same for stays of up to two or three hours, but for lengthier ones the short-stay car parks rapidly become more expensive. The long-stay car parks may be slightly less convenient, but they're much cheaper. Phone National Car Parks (NCP; ☎ 7499 7050, W www.ncp.co.uk) for car park addresses in London.

The City of London Information Centre (☎ 7332 1456) can supply a leaflet on parking in the City for people with disabilities.

Rental

Car hire rates are very expensive in the UK; often you'll be better off making arrangements in your home country for some sort of package deal. The big international rental companies charge around £40/120/200 per day/three-day 'weekend'/week for their smallest cars (such as a Ford Fiesta).

Among the main players are Avis (☎ 0870 606 0100, W www.avis.co.uk), Budget (☎ 0800 181181, W www.go-budget.com), Europcar (☎ 0870 607 5000, W www.europcar.co.uk), Hertz (☎ 0870 599 6699, W hertz.com) and Thrifty Car Rental (☎ 0800 731 1366, W www.thrifty.co.uk).

Holiday Autos (☎ 0870 530 0400, W www.holidayautos.com) operates through a number of rental companies and offers excellent deals, starting at £135 per week. For other cheap operators check *TNT Magazine*.

If you'd prefer a motorbike to a car, try Scootabout (☎ 7833 4607, ⊖ King's Cross St Pancras), 1–3 Leeke St WC1, which has a wide range of bikes available, starting at about £15 per day.

Purchase

If you're planning to tour around when you leave London you may want to buy a vehicle. It's possible to get something reasonable for around £1000. Check *Loot* (W www.loot.co.uk), published five times per week, the weeklies *Autotrader* (W www.autotrader.co.uk) and *Exchange & Mart* (W www.exchangeandmart.co.uk) for ads or visit W www.whatcar.co.uk or W www.autosave.co.uk for ads and price guidelines.

All cars require a Ministry of Transport (MOT) safety certificate valid for one year and issued by a licensed garage; full third-party insurance (expect to pay at least £300); a registration form signed by the buyer and seller, with a section to be sent to the MOT; and a licence disc proving you've paid your Vehicle Excise Duty (VED), a tax of £88/160 for six months/one year (£57.75/105 for a vehicle with an engine of 1200cc or less). The discs are sold at post offices on presentation of a valid MOT certificate, registration document and proof of insurance.

You're strongly advised to buy a vehicle with a valid MOT certificate and a VED disc; both remain with the car through a change of ownership until the end of its validity. Third-party insurance goes with the driver rather than the car, so you'll still have to arrange this; beware of letting others drive the car unless they are listed on the policy. For more details contact a post office or a Vehicle Registration Office for leaflet V100 and sheet V149 for current rates.

Camper Van You'll find that camper vans provide a popular method of touring around the UK and the rest of Europe, particularly for shoestring travellers. Often three or four people will band together to buy or rent a van. Look at the classified ads in *TNT Magazine* if you wish to form or join a group.

Vans usually feature a fixed high-top or elevating roof and from two to five bunk beds. Apart from the essential camping gas cooker, professional conversions may include a sink, fridge and built-in cupboards. You will need to spend a minimum of £1500 to £2000 for something reliable enough to get you around for any length of time.

Autotrader and *Loot* carry ads for vans.

TAXI

The black London taxi cab (**W** www.london blackcabs.co.uk) is as much a feature of the cityscape as the red bus, although these days it comes in a variety of colours, bespattered with advertising. A new, streamlined black version has also been introduced.

Taking a taxi can be worthwhile for a group of three or four people and can avoid the sometimes long waits for trains and buses. They also come into their own at night, although prices are higher. Cabs are available for hire when the yellow sign above the windscreen is lit; just stick your arm out to signal one. Fares are metered, with a minimum charge of £1.40, and increments of 20p for each 219m (after the first 438m). Additional charges include 40p for each additional passenger, 10p for any baggage stored in the front seat next to the driver, 60p for journeys made between 8pm and midnight, and 90p for those between midnight and 6am, though there is talk of adding a surcharge of £3 between 8pm and 6am to encourage more drivers to work at night. You can tip up to 10% but most people round up to the nearest 50p or £1.

The Knowledge Is with Them

When you climb into one of London's 24,000 black cabs you can rest assured you'll get where you want to go by the quickest possible route because all drivers must complete a rigorous learning and testing process known as 'The Knowledge' before they can hit the streets. For an All London licence, this means buying or renting a moped, getting hold of a good map or street atlas and spending up to four years studying and memorising 25,000 streets within a 10km-radius of Charing Cross.

But it's not just about learning how to get from street A to street Z. Drivers are expected to know the locations of hospitals, clubs, hotels, theatres, train stations, places of worship – the list is endless. All this culminates in a series of 15-minute interviews and tests that may take months to pass. It takes a lot of time, money and patience – which, according to the Public Carriage Office, means only committed cabbies will join the 'noble trade'. But this is not a perfect world and in the event that you get a less-than-noble driver you can voice your grievance at the Public Carriage Office on ☎ 7230 1631 between 9am and 4pm Monday to Friday.

ASA ANDERSSON

To order a cab by phone try Radio Taxis on ☎ 7272 0272; they charge what it costs to get to you, up to £3.80. Do not expect to hail a taxi in popular nightlife areas of London such as Soho late at night (and especially after pub closing time at 11pm). If you do find yourself in any of those areas, signal even taxis with their lights off and try to look sober. Many drivers are very choosy about their fares at this time of night.

Minicabs, some of which are now licensed, are cheaper, freelance competitors of black cabs, but they are driven by untrained individuals who are often not insured. Minicabs cannot legally be hailed on the street but must be hired by phone or directly from one of the minicab offices (every high street has at least one). You'll probably be approached by minicab drivers seeking fares in Soho and around Victoria at night; these cowboys are the worst of the lot.

Some minicab drivers have a *very* limited idea of how to get around efficiently (and safely) – you may find yourself being pressed to navigate. They don't have meters, so it's essential to fix a price before you start. Bargain hard – most drivers start at about 25% higher than the fare they're prepared to accept. Minicabs can carry up to four people.

Ask a local for the name of a reputable minicab company, or phone a large 24-hour operators (☎ 7387 8888, 7272 2222, 7272 3322 or 8888 4444). Women travelling alone at night can choose Ladycabs (☎ 7254 3501), which has women drivers. Gays and lesbians can choose Freedom Cars (☎ 7734 1313).

BICYCLE

Cycling around London is one way of cutting transport costs but it can be grim, with heavy traffic and fumes detracting from the pleasure of getting a little exercise. The London Cycling Campaign (LCC; ☎ 7928 7220) is working towards improving conditions, not least by campaigning to establish the London Cycle Network, which is up and running in parts on the South Bank and in Bankside. Plans to realise some 1240 miles of cycle routes throughout the city by 2004 have been put on hold, however, following funding cuts by Transport for London. The

LCC produces the map called *Central London Cycle Routes* (£5). It's advisable to wear a helmet and increasingly Londoners wear face-masks to filter out pollution.

If you want to buy a bike it might be worth heading for the Lloyd's Auctioneers (☎ 8788 7777) at 118 Putney Rd SW15 (Station: East Putney/Putney Bridge). This is where the police offload lost or stolen bikes every other Wednesday at 3pm (viewing starts at 10.30am). Second-hand bikes are also advertised in *Cycling Weekly*, online at W www.cyclingweekly.co.uk, *Loot* and *Exchange & Mart*.

Rental

If you prefer to rent a bicycle, the following places offer mountain or hybrid bikes in mint condition. Each demands deposits of between £100 and £200 (credit-card slips are accepted), however short or long the rental period.

Bikepark Covent Garden
(Map 8; ☎ 7430 0083, W www.bikepark.co.uk) 11 Macklin St WC2 (✛ Holborn).
Bikepark Chelsea
(Map 10; ☎ 7731 7012) 63 New Kings Rd SW6 (✛ Fulham Broadway). The minimum charge at both Bikeparks is £12 for the first day, £6 for the second day and £4 for subsequent days. The first week costs £38 and subsequent ones £28.
London Bicycle Tour Company
(Map 6; ☎ 7928 6838, W www.londonbicycle .com) 1a Gabriel's Wharf, 56 Upper Ground SE1 (✛ Blackfriars). Rentals cost £2.50 per hour, £12 for the first day, £6 for subsequent days, £36 for the first week and £30 per week after that. It also offers daily three-hour bike tours of London at 2pm on Saturday and Sunday for £12 including the bike or £9 if you have your own. The routings are on their Web site.

Bikes can be taken only on the District, Circle, Hammersmith & City and Metropolitan tube lines outside rush hour (ie, from 10am to 4pm and after 7pm on weekdays). Folding bikes can be taken on any line. Bikes can also travel on the above-ground sections of some other tube lines and the Silverlink line. Bikes are banned on the DLR.

Restrictions on taking a bike on suburban and main-line trains vary from company to company so you need to check with the relevant one before setting out. For details call ☎ 0845 748 4950.

PEDICAB

These three-wheeled conveyancers that seat two or three people arrived on the scene in Soho in 1998 and have gained in popularity (and numbers) since then. Starting at around £2 per person for a short trip within Soho to £15 for a ride to King's Cross, they're really for tourists and other pleasure-trippers rather than a cheap form of transport as they are in Asia. The best-known company is the nonprofit Bugbugs (☎ 8675 6577, **W** www.bugbugs.co.uk), which operates from 7pm to 2am (5am at the weekend), although daytime trips can be booked in advance.

WALKING

Many of the main sights are relatively close together in central London, so grab a good street map (see Maps in the Facts for the Visitor chapter) and you'll be on your way.

You can also buy several booklets detailing self-guided walks. A good one is *The London Wall Walk* (Museum of London; £1.95) by Hugh Chapman, which takes in 21 landmarks on a 2-mile walk along the old Roman and medieval city walls. The TICs may have copies of a map (£1.50) showing the route of the 12½-mile Silver Jubilee Walkway, which starts in Leicester Square and runs through the City, along the South Bank and round Westminster, with silver boards describing the sights on the way. The free *Explore London's Canals*, available from British Waterways (see Walking in the Getting There & Away chapter), details six walks along London's canal towpaths.

You'll find other ideas for self-paced walks in the Things to See & Do chapter. For guided walks see Organised Tours later in this chapter. A good Web site for walks is **W** www.londonwalking.com run by the London Walking Forum (☎ 7582 4071).

BOAT
River Shuttle

With the drive to bring London's often overlooked 'liquid artery' closer to the city,

Blue Plaques

The system of placing so-called Blue Plaques on the houses (or sites of houses in this forever developing city) of distinguished people originated in 1867, and you can even buy a guidebook – *The London Blue Plaque Guide* by Nick Rennison – identifying some 700 of them now in place. The candidate must have been dead for at least two decades or have been born 100 years before and be known to the 'well-informed passer-by'. Guess we're not as smart as we thought we were; we never recognise the vast majority of the names, many of which must surely belong to people occupying the footnotes of history. But not all of them... Two quite different musical greats are honoured with plaques on neighbouring houses in Soho's Brook St W1. American rock musician Jimi Hendrix (1942–69) lived at No 23 from 1968 until his death, while German composer George Frideric Handel (1685–1759) died at No 25, after living there for around 36 years.

companies running shuttle boats on the river have been sprouting up in recent years. Even better news is that Travelcard holders get one-third off all fares listed below.

City Cruises (☎ 7740 0400, **W** www.citycruises.com) operates a year-round ferry service from Westminster Pier to Tower Pier, and Tower Pier to Greenwich Pier for £5/2.50 (adult/child aged five to 16) oneway or £6/3 return, and Westminster Pier to Greenwich for £6/3 one-way (adult/child) or £7.50/3.75 return. A River Red Rover Day Ticket costs £7.50/3.75/19.50 (adult/child/family), allowing you to hop off and on. Schedules vary widely depending on the route and the season but leave around every 20 to 40 minutes from 10am or 10.30am to 5pm or 6pm, with later departures in summer (June to August) and fewer sailings in winter (November to March).

Catamaran Cruisers (☎ 7987 1185 or 7925 2215, **W** www.catamarancruisers.co.uk) offers a similar service linking Embankment, Tower and Greenwich Piers that costs

£5.70–9 (adult) and £3.50–5.50 (child) depending on the stage and season, the return fare is included. The River Pass, allowing one day unlimited use of the service costs £10.50–11.50 (adult) and £5.50–6.50 (child). Schedules vary according to season but usually run every 30 minutes from 10am to 6pm, with six or seven daily departures in winter.

Canal Trips

London has 40 miles of innercity canals, most of them constructed in the early 19th century to transport goods from the industrial Midlands to the Port of London. After years of neglect, the canals are being given a new lease of life as a leisure resource for boaters, walkers, anglers and cyclists. For details contact British Waterways (Map 5; ☎ 7286 6101, Ⓦ www.british-waterways .co.uk, ⊖ Warwick Avenue), Toll House, Delamere Terrace W2.

Regent's Canal loops round north London for about 2½ miles from Little Venice to Camden Lock, passing London Zoo and Regent's Park. The London Waterbus Company (☎ 7482 2660 for details or 7482 2550 for bookings) runs 90-minute trips on an enclosed boat between Camden Lock (⊖ Camden Town) and Little Venice (⊖ Warwick Avenue). From April to October boats leave Camden and Little Venice every hour from 10am and 5pm (last return trip is at 4pm) and every 30 minutes on Sunday and public holidays (last return trip is at 4.30pm). From November to March boats run only at weekends, hourly, from 10am from Camden Lock

and 11am from Little Venice to 3pm or 4pm. One-way trips cost £4.20/2.80 (adult/child) or £5.60/3.60 return.

If you want to go to the zoo, a one-way ticket from Little Venice, including admission for one hour, costs £11/8.20 or £10.50/8 if you want to be ferried from Camden Lock. If you'd like to spend more time at the zoo a later boat to Camden Lock is £2.60/2, while to Little Venice it's £3.90/2.70. Boats from the zoo to Camden Lock leave at 10.35am, then hourly until 5.35pm (till 3.35pm in winter); to Little Venice they leave at 10.15am, then hourly to 5.15pm (between 11.15am and 4.15pm in winter). From June to September there are services every 30 minutes on Sunday.

Alternatively you can travel the same route on an open-sided canal cruiser with Jason's Canal Trips (☎ 7286 3428, Ⓦ www .jasons.co.uk). Boats leave Little Venice at 10.30am, 12.30pm and 2.30pm April to early November, and at 4.30pm at weekends and on public holidays in July and August but no 10.30am departure in October or November. Tickets cost £5.95/4.75 one-way (adult/child aged three to 14) or £6.95/5.50 return; a return family ticket costs £20.

Jason's Canal Trips (Map 5) operates from opposite 60 Blomfield Rd W9 in Little Venice. The London Waterbus Company (Map 5) boats leave from a little farther east across the Westbourne Terrace bridge.

Jenny Wren (Map 3; ☎ 7485 4433) offers a service aboard the *My Fair Lady* from the Garden Jetty next to the Waterside Cafe, 250

Messing about on the river: boating on the Thames is a fun way to see the city.

Camden High St NW1 for £5.80/3.50 (adult/ child). You can also book a dinner (£21.95) or Sunday lunch (£18.95) cruise. The dinner cruise dates are not fixed but usually depart at 8pm and return three hours later. Sunday lunch cruises board at 12.30pm.

Along the River Lea in east London, a number of cruises are available on the *Pride of Lea*. Contact the Environmental Education Centre (☎ 8983 1689, fax 8983 7476), The Miller's House, Three Mill Lane E3 (⊖ Bromley-by-Bow). Schedules vary but

options include one-hour cruises for £4/3 (adult/senior & child aged five to 15) and a four-hour East London Ring cruise costing £12/9 or £16/15 (with lunch), as well as trips to Waltham Abbey (£24/22 with lunch), the London Canal Museum (£17.50/15.50 including admission) and the Ragged School Museum (£9/7 including admission).

ORGANISED TOURS

If you're short of time and you prefer to travel in a group, there are plenty of

London Bridges Up & Down

London counts 15 bridges between the neo-Gothic Tower Bridge in the east and Battersea Bridge in the south-west. The one with the longest and most interesting history – going back to Roman times – is London Bridge, which spans the Thames between Southwark and the City. The newest is the beautiful but ill-fated Millennium Bridge, linking Bankside and the City.

The *Anglo-Saxon Chronicle* tells us that a convicted witch was thrown off London Bridge (Map 9) in the 10th century, and the words of that grating children's ditty – 'London Bridge Is Falling Down' – refer to an attack on it by King Olaf of Norway in support of King Ethelred the Unready in 1014. In 1176 Peter of Colechurch began work on what is believed to have been the first post-Roman stone bridge in Europe; the work wasn't completed until 1209. The new bridge stood on 19 piers but was only just wide enough for two carts to pass each other. Nevertheless, by 1358 there were already 139 shops clinging to its sides.

Until 1749, when Westminster Bridge was built, London Bridge was the sole crossing point on the Thames, and less than a decade later the old shops were pulled down to ease traffic congestion. In 1823 work began on a new London Bridge designed by Sir John Rennie and worked on by his son. In 1973 this bridge was, in turn, replaced with another, this time a flattened concrete number with three arches, designed by Harold Knox King. Rennie's old bridge was carefully dismantled and shipped to the USA where it now forms the centrepiece of a park at Lake Havusu in Arizona.

The Millennium Bridge (Map 9) was designed by Norman Foster and Anthony Caro, and was the first bridge to be built over the Thames in central London (not counting replacements) since Tower Bridge was completed in 1894. It is 350m (just under ¼ mile) long and 4m wide, hovers 9.5m above the water, weighs some 360 tonnes and takes five minutes to cross on foot. Sadly, relatively few people got the chance to make that crossing during the bridge's first year of existence.

Shortly after the Millennium Bridge opened to a great fanfare in June 2000, it was discovered that the platform of the bridge wobbled and swayed (sometimes violently) as more and more people passed over it. It was closed just two days later and tests were carried out, which determined that a series of dampers would have to be installed to absorb the vibrations. Repair work began exactly a year later. Luckily the dampers won't affect the bridge's beautiful design but they've succeeded in dampening enthusiasm for what was thought to be the most useful of London's millennium projects.

The Jubilee Bridge, a wobble-proof glass-and-steel structure, built onto an existing walkway alongside Cannon St railway bridge, will open at the end of 2002, linking Southwark and the City. It will be the first covered bridge built in London since the 1176 London Bridge, and 3.4 million pedestrians are expected to use it each year. Another footbridge spanning the Thames, farther upriver and linking Battersea and Pimlico, is also on the cards.

companies offering organised sightseeing tours, many of them of the hop-on, hop-off variety and often in open-top buses. For organised tours to sights on London's periphery and beyond see the Excursions chapter.

Air

If you can stump up the dosh, Aeromega Helicopters (☎ 01708-688361, **W** www .aeromega.co.uk) at Stapleford Aerodrome in Essex has 30-minute helicopter 'flightseeing' tours over London (£99 per person) on the first and third Sunday of every month. Cabair Helicopters (☎ 8953 4411, **W** www.cabair.com) at Elstree Aerodrome in Borehamwood, Hertfordshire, offers the same thing for £125 every Sunday.

Bus

The Original London Sightseeing Tour (☎ 8877 1722, **W** www.theoriginaltour .com), the Big Bus Company (☎ 7233 9533, **W** www.bigbus.co.uk) and London Pride (☎ 01708-631122, **W** www.londonpride.co .uk) all offer tours around the main sights on double-decker buses (sometimes open-top ones) that allow you to loop round London without getting off, or to hop on and off at along the way and reboard the next bus. They cost £12.50–14 (adult) and £5.50–7.50 (child) and tickets are usually valid for 24 hours. Departures are from 8.30am or 9am to 7pm or 8pm in summer, and from 9am or 9.30am to 5pm or 6pm in winter.

Convenient starting points are in Trafalgar Square next to St Martin-in-the-Fields, in front of Baker Street tube station near Madame Tussaud's, on Haymarket southeast of Piccadilly Circus and in Grosvenor Gardens opposite Victoria train station.

Boat

The main starting points for cruises along the Thames are the piers at Westminster, Embankment (also called Charing Cross Pier) and Waterloo.

Eastwards along the Thames Circular Cruise (☎ 7936 2033) offers a service from Westminster Pier as far as St Katharine's Pier in Wapping every 30 to 40 minutes

between 11am and as late as 7pm, April to September; daily departures during the rest of the year are at 11am, 12.20pm, 1.40pm and 3pm. Vessels call at London Bridge City Pier and, in the summer season at weekends, at Festival Pier on the South Bank. Tickets cost £6/5/3/15.80 (adult/student & senior/ child aged five to 15/family). Fares are cheaper between just two stages (eg, Westminster to/from London Bridge City piers costs £4.30/3.20/2.20/11).

Catamaran Cruisers (☎ 7987 1185, **W** www.catamarancruisers.co.uk) has a circular cruise leaving Embankment Pier and returning from the Tower of London hourly from 10.15am to 5.15pm and hourly from 6.30pm to 8.30pm (with possible sailings at 9.30pm and 10.30pm in summer) between April and October. There are hourly departures from Waterloo Pier from 10.45am to 6.45pm during the same period. Cruises depart at 11.45am, 12.45pm, 1.45pm, 3.45pm, 4.45pm and 5.45pm November to March from Waterloo Pier only. The cruise lasts 50 minutes and costs £6.70–7/4.70–5 (adult/ child) depending on the season.

Cruise boats run by Westminster to Greenwich Thames Passenger Boat Service (WGTPBS; ☎ 7930 4097, **W** www.west minsterpier.co.uk) leave Westminster Pier for Greenwich every 30 minutes from 10am to 4pm or 5pm (peak season), passing the Globe Theatre, stopping at the Tower of London and continuing under Tower Bridge and past the docks. The last boats return from Greenwich at about 5pm (6pm in summer). One-way tickets cost £64.80/3/15.75 (adult/senior/child/family) and returns cost £7.50/6/3.77/19.50. For £6.50/5/3.40/17.25 one-way and £8/6.50/4.25/21 return, passengers can stay onboard and carry on to the Thames Barrier before returning to Greenwich (and Westminster if they purchase a return ticket). There are two or three daily Thames Barrier sailings in summer (at 11am, 1pm and sometimes at 2pm) and one at 11am daily the rest of the year.

Westwards along the Thames Boats run by Westminster Passenger Service Association (☎ 7930 4721, **W** www.wpsa.co.uk) go upriver from Westminster Pier, an enjoyable excursion although it takes much longer and is not, perhaps, as interesting as the trip east. The main destinations are Kew Gardens and Hampton Court Palace. It's possible to get off the boats at Richmond in July and August. No boats run in this direction from the end of October until the end of March.

Boats to the Royal Botanic Gardens at Kew sail from Westminster Pier via Putney up to five times a day from 10.15am to 2pm from late March to September with limited services in October. They take about 1½ hours and a one-way/return fare costs £7/11 (adult), £6/9 (senior) and £3/5 (child).

Boats to Hampton Court leave Westminster Pier at 10.30am, 11.15am and noon April to September/October. The journey takes 3½ hours and one-way tickets cost £10/8/4 (adult/senior/child) and £14/11/7 return.

Walking

Discover London on Foot (☎ 01494-888520, **W** www.tourlondon.com) proposes a day-long (8.30am to 4pm) tour that takes in Westminster Abbey, St Paul's Cathedral and the Tower of London and passes a dozen other major sights. The price, which includes admission fees as well as a tube and bus ride but not lunch, is £58/53/48 (adult/senior & student/child aged under 15).

Several companies offer themed guided walking tours; popular ones include London at the time of certain writers – be they Shakespeare, Dickens or Pepys – and other such themes as a Beatles' Magical Mystery Tour, Jewish London and, inevitably, a following in the footsteps of the dastardly Jack the Ripper through Whitechapel.

Walks take place throughout the year but the choice is greatest between April and October. They usually last around two hours and cost £5/4 (adult/senior & student) and leave from outside tube stations.

Probably the best company is The Original London Walks (☎ 7624 3978, **W** www .walks.com), which has at least a dozen different themed walking tours on offer daily – from several Beatles tours and walks around old Bloomsbury to interesting ghost- and spy-themed walks.

Other companies that offer themed guided walks include:

Ray's Route of Rock (☎ 7733 5347)
Historical Tours (☎ 8668 4019)
Capital Walks (☎ 8650 7640)
Cityguide Walks (☎ 01895-675389)

Among the most fascinating tours are those run by Architectural Dialogue (☎ 7267 7697), which examine London's architecture – from Georgian and contemporary to the regeneration of the Docklands. Half-day tours cost £18.50/13 (adult/senior & student) and depart from outside the Royal Academy, Burlington House, Piccadilly W1 (⊖ Green Park), at 10.15am on Saturday and 10.45am on Sunday and last three hours. Full-day tours costing £20–39 are scheduled a few times a month.

Clerkenwell & Islington Guides (☎ 7622 3278) offers regular walks round Clerkenwell, leaving from outside Farringdon tube at 11am on Wednesday and 2pm on Sunday. They also have a Smithfield Trail walk, leaving from outside Barbican tube station at 11am on Tuesday and 2pm on Saturday, an Angel Trail leaving from the Angel tube ticket-barrier at 2pm on Sunday and a Canonbury Trail leaving from Highbury & Islington tube at 11am on some Sundays (call for exact dates). All walks cost £4.50/3.50.

For guided walking tours in Greenwich, see the Things to See & Do chapter.

La crème de la crème are the 900 knowledgeable guides of the Association of Professional Tourist Guides (APTG) who study for two years and have to take both written and practical examinations before being awarded their coveted 'Blue Badge'. You can decide where you want to go and for how long. They're not cheap (eg, £85/128 for a half-/full day of guiding in English or £97/154 in a foreign language), but it can work out cheaper if there's a group. For details and a copy of their pamphlet *Registered Guides* contact the APTG (☎ 7403 2962, **W** www.touristguides.org.uk). You can also book Blue Badge guides through the APTG-approved Tour Guides Ltd (☎ 7495 5504, **W** www.tourguides.co.uk).

London's Contemporary Architecture

RICHARD I'ANSON

The 'shock of the new' has always knocked the UK (and by extension London) sideways. This is the capital of a country where things old – from buildings to pub names – are traditionally venerated, regardless of their aesthetic value or current usefulness. On the other hand, everything new is immediately suspect.

Of course everything old had to be new once and Londoners have generally reacted in a predictable fashion. Christopher Wren's dome for St Paul's Cathedral was rejected twice before he got the green light in 1675. John Nash was harpooned – literally – in the press by the graceful spire of his All Souls Church, Langham Place (Map 6), when it was completed in 1824, and the beloved Eros statue in Piccadilly Circus (1892; Map 7) was so ridiculed that its designer, Alfred Gilbert, went into self-imposed exile for the next 30 years. In more recent years the graceful British Library (Colin St John Wilson, 1998; Map 3), with its warm red-brick exterior and Asianesque touches and its wonderfully bright interior, has met with a very hostile reception (even though the original design was almost 25 years old by the time the building was completed).

Unlike, say, Paris, Washington or Budapest, very little of London has ever been planned; instead it has developed in an 'organic' (for which read: haphazard) fashion. There has always been an aversion to the set piece here, and until recently buildings were rarely used as parts of a larger town or district plan.

The 1970s saw very little building in London (apart from roads), and the recession of the late 1980s and early 1990s brought much of the development and speculation in the Docklands and the City of London to a standstill. In 1990 the publication of *A Vision of Britain*, a reactionary tract by Prince Charles, in which the self-proclaimed architecture expert argued for a synthetic 'English tradition', helped polarise traditionalists and modernists still further. For these and other reasons the London skyline has little to compare to that of New York, Hong Kong or even Singapore, though change is in the air.

DOUG McKINLAY

Title Page: A cut above the rest – Canary Wharf (Photograph: Doug McKinlay)

Top left: The shocking St Paul's Cathedral – well, it was once!

Left: After years in the pipeline the British Library opened in 1998.

The problem has not been a lack of talent. Britain has produced some of the world's most talented architects since WWII and one only has to go to Hong Kong and enter the Hongkong Shanghai Bank building (1985) or to Nîmes and visit the Carrée d'Art (1993) to see the remarkable work of Norman Foster, or to Paris and the Pompidou Centre (1977) for Richard Rogers' creation. In recent years the construction boom in the capital, thanks to large-scale private sector investment and proceeds from the National Lottery Fund, has brought the work of this modern-day Wren and Hawksmoor and that of equally talented (but less well-known internationally) British architects closer to home.

London's contemporary architecture was born in the Docklands and the City some 15 years ago. Taking pride of place in the Docklands (Map 13), Britain's 'enterprise culture development, was Cesar Pelli's 244m-high One Canada Square (1991), commonly known as Canary Wharf and easily visible from central London. It is now flanked by two new neighbours: Foster's twin-tower HSBC Holdings building and the Citigroup headquarters. The residential Cascades building (CZWG

Right: Canary Wharf – the tallest building in the UK – can be seen from all over London.

DOUG MCKINLAY

Architects) and the former Financial Times Print Works by Nicholas Grimshaw (both 1988) were just two other examples of innovative (and controversial) architecture from that period.

The architectural centrepiece in the City (Map 9) was Lloyd's of London (1986), Rogers' 'inside-out' masterpiece of ducts, pipes, glass and stainless steel. Two other City buildings (both by GMW Partnership) breaking new ground included Minster Court (1991), a postmodern Gothic structure that Cruella de Vil used as her headquarters in the film *101 Dalmatians*, and 54 Lombard St (1993), a monolith that manages to remain sensitive to (and reflective of) its neighbouring buildings.

Not everything new and different was restricted to the Docklands and the City, of course. Embankment Place (Terry Farrell, 1990; Map 8) took advantage of its invaluable position atop Charing Cross station to offer 32,000 sq metres of new office space. The symmetrical Vauxhall Cross (Farrell, 1993; Map 2), better known as the MI6 Building, was erected south of the river in Vauxhall, an area not celebrated for its cutting-edge architecture at the time. Far-flung Hammersmith was chosen as the site for Ralph Erskine's boat-like London Ark (1991; Map 2). The independent television station Channel 4 was considered very bold indeed when it moved from the media ghetto of Soho to its new horseshoe-shaped, glass-clad and very asymmetrical headquarters (Rogers, 1994; Map 11) in Victoria.

Bottom left: I spy the MI6 Building, Vauxhall.

Bottom right: Inside out Richard Rogers' uncompromising Lloyd's of London building

If modern architecture in London was not restricted by area, it was also not limited by use; there is plenty of innovative architecture to be seen away from the mammoth office blocks and media centres. The Mound Stand at Lord's Cricket Ground (Michael Hopkins, 1987; Map 3) is a tent-like structure of stretched PVC-coated fabric built for spectators; as it is only used during the warmer months, it is open on all sides and recalls a ship at sea. The NatWest Media Centre at Lord's (Future Systems, 1999), an aluminium and glass pod on stilts, is reminiscent of a 1960s vision of the future – a gigantic alien 'eye' peering down on the field. For such a conservative organisation as Marylebone Cricket Club, these structures standing side by side with older buildings are highly adventurous.

LONDON'S CONTEMPORARY ARCHITECTURE

DOUG MCKINLAY

JULIET COOMBE

ELLIOT DANIEL

Top left: Gateway to Europe: Waterloo International Terminal

Top right: The eco-friendly London Ark finds itself next to the A4's roaring traffic.

Bottom: The London IMAX Cinema, housing the biggest screen in Europe

Other interesting buildings with nonstandard uses include Waterloo International Terminal (Grimshaw, 1993; Map 6), a glass and steel arch over a concrete viaduct supporting 800-tonne trains and a brilliant solution for a site 400m long and only 30 to 50m wide; the Sainsbury's supermarket (Grimshaw, 1988; Map 3) in Camden Town; the unique Buckingham Palace Ticket Office (Hopkins, 1994; Map 6) on the edge of Green Park, with its bizarre flyaway roof; and the award-winning public lavatory with its cantilevered Art Deco-ish glass roof (CZWG Architects, 1993; Map 5) on the corner of Westbourne Grove and Colville Rd. The London IMAX Cinema building (Brian Avery, 1999; Map 6) in Waterloo is impressive from an engineering perspective: it's shaped like a drum, sits on 'springs' to reduce vibrations and traffic noise, and the exterior changes colour at night. Whether or not the doomed Millennium Dome (Richard Rogers, 1998; Map 13), the world's largest such structure, was a success as an attraction is immaterial; it was and remains everything that modern architecture should and can be: innovative, complementary and startlingly beautiful.

Given the propensity here for hanging on to every reminder of the past, it's not surprising to find that many interesting architectural developments of recent years have been adaptations of existing buildings for new uses. Fine examples are the old Michelin factory built in 1911 on Fulham Rd, which houses the Bibendum restaurant (Conran Roche, 1987; Map 10); the Oxo Tower, a one-time meat warehouse on the South Bank converted into a mixture of restaurants, shops and flats by Lifschutz Davidson in 1996 (Map 6); the Cochrane Theatre (Map 6) in Bloomsbury, tranformed by Nigerian-born Abiodun Odedina in 1991 from a faceless 1960s playhouse; the redesigned Bankside Power Station, which now houses the Tate Modern (Herzog & De Meuron, 1999; Map 9) and won the Pritzker award, architecture's Nobel Prize, in 2000; and the Imagination Building (Herron Associates, 1989; Map 6) in Bloomsbury, whose unassuming facade (an Edwardian school) hides a dazzling, multipurpose interior.

Buildings and other structures to look out for include the Millennium Bridge (Map 9) – Norman Foster's magnificent 'blade of light' – and his Greater London Authority building (Map 9) immediately southwest of Tower Bridge, a striking concrete structure with a distinctive glass globe to house the London

Top: An expensive architectural triumph: the £750 million Millennium Dome

Bottom: Art Deco by night: the Oxo Tower

Assembly and the mayor's offices. The British Museum's Great Court (Foster, 2000; Map 6), with its spectacular glass and steel roof, is a triumph, and Broadwick House (Rogers, 2001; Map 7) is a diamond in the rough Berwick St Market area of Soho.

Though you can't admire them from afar, the 11 stations (1998–9) of the Underground's Jubilee Line extension were each designed by a different architect. Especially notable are Southwark station (Map 6), with its luminous glass walls, arches and silver tubes, by Richard Mac-Cormac; the elegant, curving canopy of Chris Wilkinson's Stratford station; and Will Alsop's North Greenwich station (Map 1), whose blue tiles and hull-shaped interior recall Greenwich's maritime past.

One building that we can't wait to see is David Libeskind's on-again, off-again curvaceous extension of the Victoria & Albert Museum (Map 10) called the Spiral. No doubt this innovative modern structure – if it ever materialises – will do for London what American architect Frank Gehry's Guggenheim Museum did for Bilbao in Spain. In the meantime we'll have to be content with Foster's 40-floor, glass-and-steel Swiss Re building on the site of the City's Baltic Exchange, which was blown up by the IRA in 1992. The building has been nicknamed the 'erotic gherkin'; no prizes (Pritzker or otherwise) for guessing its shape.

Right: City hall: the striking new Greater London Authority building

COURTESY OF FOSTER AND PARTNERS

Things to See & Do

London: The Best & the Worst

Highlights
- British Museum
- St Paul's Cathedral
- National Portrait Gallery
- Victoria & Albert Museum
- Boat trip on the Thames
- London's parks, especially St James's
- Waterloo Bridge, with the best views in London
- Tate Modern
- Greenwich, especially the National Maritime Museum
- Hampton Court Palace

Lowlights
- 11pm pub closing – still!
- Most of the Underground & its horrendous service
- A visit inside Buckingham Palace
- Soulless Leicester Square
- The cacophonous London Trocadero
- The worst road rage in the world
- Bad signposting on many streets
- Low value for money in restaurants
- Heathrow airport
- Scurrilous tabloid newspapers

SUGGESTED ITINERARIES

Depending on how much time you have in London, there will be some hard choices to make about what to see and do. The following is a suggested itinerary for a first-time visitor with a week to spend in this fair city:

First Day
Visit Westminster Abbey and view the Houses of Parliament and Big Ben. Walk up Whitehall, passing Downing St, the Cenotaph and Horse Guards Parade. Cross Trafalgar Square to visit the National Gallery or the National Portrait Gallery. Walk to Piccadilly Circus to see the statue of Eros.

Second Day
Visit the British Museum and walk/shop along Oxford St.

Third Day
Visit the Natural History, Science or Victoria & Albert museums in South Kensington, then take a bus to Harrods. Have a quick look at Buckingham Palace from the outside and stroll around St James's Park.

Fourth Day
Visit St Paul's Cathedral and the Museum of London.

Fifth Day
Visit the Tower of London and Tower Bridge. Take the Docklands Light Railway (DLR) to the Isle of Dogs and view Greenwich from Island Gardens.

Sixth Day
Cross the Thames to visit the new Globe Theatre and the Tate Modern. Walk along the South Bank.

Seventh Day
Spend the day in Greenwich, visiting the National Maritime Museum, the *Cutty Sark*, Greenwich Market and other sites. Take a boat to the Thames Flood Barrier, passing the disused but still impressive Millennium Dome on the way.

With another week you could explore some of London's markets, go to the zoo and Camden Lock, and visit some of the smaller museums such as the wonderful Wallace Collection in Marylebone, Sir John Soane's Museum in Lincoln's Inn Fields, Leighton House in Holland Park or the Old Operating Theatre near London Bridge. You could also head north to Hampstead to explore the heath and Freud's and Keats' houses or take a boat westwards to Hampton Court Palace.

A third week would let you explore some of the outer suburbs such as Chiswick and Richmond, perhaps taking in Ham House and Osterley House. You could also take one or two day-trips to any of the places outside London listed in the Excursions chapter.

Please note that all the hours listed in this chapter are literally the opening and closing times. Last admission to most museums and attractions is 30 minutes or even an hour before closing time.

Central London

TRAFALGAR SQUARE (Map 8)

Trafalgar Square *(WC2; ⊖ Charing Cross)* is the heart of visitors' London. This is where many great marches and rallies take place, and where the new year is seen in by thousands of revellers. It's also where you'll fight for space with flocks of pigeons. Though a city ordinance now bans the sale of bird feed in the square, an estimated 2000 of the dirty flying rats are being sustained by visitors on titbits bought at nearby shops.

The square was designed by John Nash in the early 19th century on the site of the King's Mews, and carried out by Charles Barry, who was also partly responsible for the Houses of Parliament. The 43.5m-high **Nelson's Column**, which incorporates granite from places as far apart as Cornwall and the Scottish Highlands, was raised in 1843 and commemorates the admiral's victory over Napoleon off Cape Trafalgar in Spain in 1805. The four bronze lions at its base were designed by Edwin Landseer and added

in 1867. If you glance up at the statue of Nelson, you'll see that he is facing south-westwards, surveying his fleet, some say, of ships atop the lampposts lining The Mall.

Three of the four plinths in the square support worthies such as George IV on horseback, but the one in the north-west corner remains empty. Local artists have been invited to exhibit their work on it in recent years. Rachel Whiteread's *Monument*, an aquarium-like resin work meant to reflect the plinth itself (but upside down), was not to everyone's taste.

Trafalgar Square is flanked by many imposing buildings and important thoroughfares fan out from it. To the north is the **National Gallery** and behind that the **National Portrait Gallery; Pall Mall**, which was named after a croquet-like Italian game called *palla a maglio* (ball to mallet) played here by Charles II and his court, runs south-west from the top of the square. The church of **St Martin-in-the-Fields** is to the north-east, and directly east stands **South Africa House** (1933), where the stone heads of African wildlife have gazed down on anti-apartheid

RICHARD I'ANSON

Take a breather by the pools in Trafalgar Square and watch the world (and traffic) go by.

protesters in the square for decades. To the south, the square opens out and you can catch glimpses of the Houses of Parliament down Whitehall through the traffic. To the south-west stands **Admiralty Arch**, erected in honour of Queen Victoria in 1910, with the Mall leading to Buckingham Palace beyond it. To the west is **Canada House** (1827), designed by Robert Smirke.

National Gallery

The National Gallery's porticoed facade extends along Trafalgar Square's northern side. With more than 2000 European paintings on display, the gallery *(☎ 7747 2885, W www.nationalgallery.org.uk, Trafalgar Square WC2; ⊖ Charing Cross; admission free; open 10am-6pm Thur-Tues, 10am-9pm Wed)* is one of the largest – and finest – in the world and everyone knows that: it attracts some 4.65 million visitors a year. The lovely Sainsbury Wing on the gallery's western side was added only after considerable controversy; Prince Charles, not known for his cutting-edge sense of design in architecture, dismissed one proposal as 'a carbuncle on the face of a much loved friend'. Oh dear. Outside the gallery – rather incongruously in this, the heart of London and capital of the erstwhile British Empire – is a statue of the man who 'robbed' England of its colonies in the New World, the heroic General George Washington. It was presented by the state of Virginia in 1921.

The paintings in the National Gallery are hung in a continuous time-line; by starting in the Sainsbury Wing and progressing eastwards you can take in a collection of pictures painted between the mid-13th and early 20th centuries in chronological order. If you're keen on the real oldies (1260–1510), head for the 2nd floor of the Sainsbury Wing; for the Renaissance (1510–1600), go to the West Wing in the museum's main building. Rubens, Rembrandt and Caravaggio are in the North Wing (1600–1700); if you're after Gainsborough, Constable, Turner, Hogarth and the French Impressionists visit the East Wing (1700–1900). For a larger collection of paintings by British artists you should visit the Tate Britain (see

National Gallery Highlights

- *The Arnolfini Portrait* – van Eyck
- *The Rokeby Venus* – Velásquez
- *The Wilton Diptych*
- *Bathers* – Cézanne
- *Venus & Mars* – Botticelli
- *The Leonardo Cartoon* – da Vinci
- *The Battle of San Romano* – Uccello
- *The Ambassadors* – Holbein the Younger
- *Equestrian Portrait of Charles I* – Van Dyck
- *Portrait of Susanna Lunden* – Rubens
- *The Hay Wain* – Constable
- *Sunflowers* – Van Gogh
- *Bathers at La Grenouillère* – Monet
- *The Fighting Temeraire* – Turner

the following Westminster & Pimlico section). The basement of the Sainsbury Wing is where special exhibits take place, which usually incur a charge of £8/6/4/16 (adult/senior/student/family).

The highlights listed in the boxed text will give you an idea of the *crème de la crème* at the National Gallery but if you want to know a lot more, borrow an audioguide (£4 donation recommended) from the Central Hall just beyond the Trafalgar Square entrance. Each painting is numbered; punch it into the machine and it will skip to the appropriate place on the CD-ROM. There are also highlights audioguide tours (featuring 30 paintings) in six languages and activity sheets for kids (50p). Free one-hour guided tours, which introduce you to a manageable half-dozen paintings at a time, leave at 11.30am and 2.30pm daily; there's another tour at 6.30pm on Wednesday. The *Gallery Café* is in the basement of the West Wing; *Crivelli's Garden* (see the Places to Eat chapter) on the 1st floor of the Sainsbury Wing serves more elaborate meals.

National Portrait Gallery

A visit to the National Portrait Gallery *(☎ 7312 2463, W www.npg.org.uk, St Martin's Place WC2; ➜ Charing Cross/Leicester Square; admission free; open 10am-6pm Mon-Wed, Sat & Sun, 10am-9pm Thur & Fri)* is not so much about art as history – to put faces to the famous and infamous names in British history from the Middle Ages to the present day. The gallery, founded in 1856, houses a primary collection of some 9000 works on five floors, and there is no restriction on media used; there are oil paintings, watercolours, charcoal drawings, sculptures, silhouettes, photographs and even electronic art. Being the subject of one of the 40-odd annual acquisitions is said to be more prestigious than making it onto the Queen's Honours List.

The pictures are displayed in chronological order, starting with the early Tudors on the 2nd floor and descending to the present day on the ground floor. The portraits of Elizabeth I from 1575 in all her finery and of Byron in romantic oriental garb (1813) by Thomas Phillips are as wonderful as the more recent works: Elizabeth II as seen by Andy Warhol; Prince Charles posing under a banana tree; photographs of Oscar Wilde, Virginia Woolf and Diana, Princess of Wales.

Audioguides (a £2 to £3 donation is suggested) highlight some 200 portraits and allow you to hear the voices of some of the people portrayed. The new Ondaatje Wing has expanded the display from the 16th century to the Regency period. The *Portrait Café* and bookshop are in the basement, the *Portrait Restaurant* is on the top floor.

Edith Cavell Memorial

On a traffic island outside the entrance to the National Portrait Gallery is a statue of Edith Cavell (1865–1915), a British nurse who helped Allied soldiers escape from Brussels during WWI and was executed by the Germans. The statue is the work of George Frampton, who also designed the Peter Pan statue in Hyde Park.

St Martin-in-the-Fields

An influential masterpiece by James Gibbs (1682–1754) completed in 1726, the 'royal parish church' of St Martin-in-the-Fields *(☎ 7766 1199 or 7930 9306 for brass-rubbing, W www.stmartin-in-the-fields.org, Trafalgar Square WC2; ➜ Charing Cross/Leicester Square; admission free; open 8am-6.30pm daily; brass-rubbing centre open 10am-6pm Mon-Sat, noon-6pm Sun)* occupies a prime site at the north-eastern corner of the square. The wedding-cake spire (wonderfully floodlit at night) is off-set by the splendid white stone used for both the church and the National Gallery.

St Martin's has a tradition of tending to the poor and homeless that goes back to

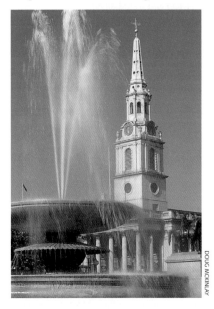

DOUG McKINLAY

Fancy a rub down? Then head for the brass-rubbing centre at St Martin's-in-the-Fields.

WWI. There's a craft market in a lane just north of the church, and in the crypt you'll find a brass-rubbing centre, bookshop and popular *Café in the Crypt* (see the Places to Eat chapter). For details of concerts, see Church Venues under Classical Music in the Entertainment chapter.

WESTMINSTER & PIMLICO (Maps 2, 6 & 11)

While the City of London (known simply as 'the City') has always concerned itself with trade and commerce, Westminster is the centre of political power and most of its places of interest are linked with the monarchy, Parliament or the Church of England.

Pimlico, to the south and south-west, has never been as smart as, say, Belgravia, but contains some wonderful early-19th-century houses and the incomparable Tate Britain.

Whitehall (Map 6)

Whitehall *(SW1; ✆ Charing Cross/Westminster)* and its extension, Parliament St, is the wide avenue that links Trafalgar Square with Parliament Square. It is lined with so many government buildings, statues, monuments and other historical bits and pieces that the best way to take it all in is to follow the short walk described in the Whitehall walking tour. Those interested in only the most important sights – including Westminster Abbey and the Houses of Parliament – can read on.

Westminster Abbey (Map 6)

Westminster Abbey *(✆ 7222 5152, ⒲ www .westminster-abbey.org, Dean's Yard SW1; ✆ Westminster; adult/senior & student/ child aged 11-17/family £6/3/2/12; open 9.45am-4.45pm Mon, 9.30am-4.45pm Tues & Thur-Sat, 9.30am-4.45pm & 6pm-7pm Wed)* is one of the most visited churches in Christendom. It has played a pivotal role in the history of both England and the Anglican church and, with the exception of Edward V and Edward VIII, every sovereign has been crowned here since William the Conqueror in 1066. Most of the monarchs from Henry III (died 1272) to George II (1760) were buried here as well, but since

the death of George III in 1820 they have been laid to rest at Windsor.

The abbey, though a mixture of various architectural styles, is the finest example of Early English Gothic (1180–1280) still extant. The original church was built by the King (later St) Edward the Confessor in the 11th century; he is buried in the chapel behind the main altar. Henry III (ruled 1216–72) began work on the new building but didn't complete it; the French Gothic nave was finished in 1388. Henry VII's huge and magnificent chapel was added in 1519.

Unlike St Paul's, Westminster Abbey has never been a cathedral. It is what is called a 'royal peculiar' and is administered directly by the Crown.

Orientation The main entrance to the nave and royal chapels is through the north door. Immediately past the barrier you come to the **Statesmen's Aisle**, where politicians and eminent public figures are commemorated, mostly by staggeringly large marble statues. The Whig and Tory prime ministers who dominated late Victorian politics, Gladstone (who is buried here) and Disraeli (who is not) have their monuments uncomfortably close to one another. Nearby is a monument to Robert Peel who, as home secretary in 1829, created the Metropolitan Police force. They became known as 'Bobby's boys' and later simply 'bobbies'. Above them is a rose window, designed by James Thornhill, depicting 11 of the Apostles (Judas is absent).

On your left as you turn and walk eastwards are several small chapels with fine 16th-century monuments, including a lovely Madonna and Child in alabaster in Crewe Chapel. Opposite the Islip Chapel in the northern ambulatory are three wonderful medieval tombs, including that of Edmund Crouchback, youngest son of Henry III and founder of the House of Lancaster. Farther on are the tombs of Edward I and Henry III.

At the eastern end of the sanctuary, opposite the entrance to the Henry VII Chapel, is the rather ordinary-looking **Coronation Chair**, upon which almost every monarch is said to have been crowned since 1066. In fact, the oaken chair 'only' dates from the late 13th century – it must have been another chair before. Below it used to sit the Stone of Scone (pronounced skoon) – the Scottish coronation stone pilfered in 1297 by Edward I. It was finally returned to Scotland in 1996, though the Scots are required to hand it back for all future coronations.

Up the steps in front of you and to your left is the narrow **Queen Elizabeth Chapel**. Technically it's not a chapel at all since it doesn't have its own altar – it's actually the northern aisle of the Henry VII Chapel (but let's not quibble). Here Elizabeth I, who gave the abbey its charter, and her half-sister 'Bloody Mary' share an elaborate tomb. In front of the altar are memorials to James I's daughters who died in childhood; the effigy of Princess Sophia, a baby in her cradle, is reflected in a mirror.

The **Henry VII Chapel**, in the easternmost part of the abbey, is an outstanding example of late-perpendicular architecture (a variation of English Gothic), with spectacular circular vaulting on the ceiling. The magnificently carved wooden choir stalls, reserved for the Knights of the Order of the Bath, feature colourful headpieces bearing their owners' chosen symbols: dragons, roosters, lions and so on.

Behind the chapel's altar, with a 15th-century *Madonna and Child* by Vivarini, is the elaborate sarcophagus of Henry VII and his queen, Elizabeth of York, designed by the Florentine sculptor Pietro Torrigiano. Beyond this is the **Royal Air Force Chapel** and a stained-glass window commemorating the Battle of Britain. Next to it a plaque marks the spot where Oliver Cromwell's body lay for two years until the Restoration, when it was disinterred, hanged at Tyburn and beheaded.

The chapel's southern aisle contains the **tomb of Mary Queen of Scots** (beheaded on the orders of her cousin Elizabeth and with the acquiescence of her son, the future

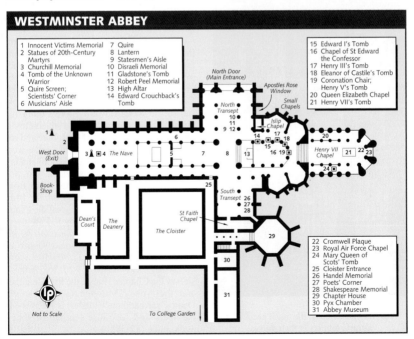

WESTMINSTER ABBEY

1 Innocent Victims Memorial	15 Edward I's Tomb
2 Statues of 20th-Century Martyrs	16 Chapel of St Edward the Confessor
3 Churchill Memorial	17 Henry III's Tomb
4 Tomb of the Unknown Warrior	18 Eleanor of Castile's Tomb
5 Quire Screen; Scientists' Corner	19 Coronation Chair; Henry V's Tomb
6 Musicians' Aisle	20 Queen Elizabeth Chapel
7 Quire	21 Henry VII's Tomb
8 Lantern	
9 Statesmen's Aisle	
10 Disraeli Memorial	
11 Gladstone's Tomb	
12 Robert Peel Memorial	
13 High Altar	
14 Edward Crouchback's Tomb	

North Door (Main Entrance)

Apostles Rose Window

Small Chapels

North Transept

Islip Chapel

West Door (Exit)

The Nave

Henry VII Chapel

Book-Shop

South Transept

Dean's Court

The Deanery

St Faith Chapel

The Cloister

22 Cromwell Plaque	
23 Royal Air Force Chapel	
24 Mary Queen of Scots' Tomb	
25 Cloister Entrance	
26 Handel Memorial	
27 Poets' Corner	
28 Shakespeare Memorial	
29 Chapter House	
30 Pyx Chamber	
31 Abbey Museum	

Not to Scale

To College Garden

James I) and the stunning tomb of Lady Margaret Beaufort, mother of Henry VII. Also buried here are Charles II, William and Mary, and Queen Anne.

The **Chapel of St Edward the Confessor**, the most sacred spot in the abbey, lies just east of the sanctuary and behind the high altar; access may be restricted to protect the 13th-century floor. St Edward was the founder of the abbey and the original building was consecrated a few weeks before his death. His tomb was slightly altered after the original was destroyed during the Reformation. On the casket that lies below the green wooden canopy there are still some original mosaics and niches, in which pilgrims prayed for cures and left votives.

Some of the surrounding tombs in the chapel – those of Henry III, Edward I, Edward III, Richard II, Henry V and four queens – are visible from the northern and southern ambulatory. **Eleanor of Castile**, the wife of Edward I, lies in one of the oldest and most beautiful bronze tombs, designed by goldsmith William Torel in 1291. The abbey's south transept contains **Poets' Corner**, where many of England's finest writers are buried, a precedent established with Geoffrey Chaucer (although he was buried here because he had been clerk of works to the Palace of Westminster, not because of his literary efforts). The practice of burying literati here began in earnest in 1700.

In front of medieval wall-paintings of the doubting apostle St Thomas and of St Christopher carrying the Christ Child on the eastern wall stands the **William Shakespeare memorial** (although like Byron, Tennyson, William Blake, TS Eliot and various other luminaries, he wasn't actually buried here). Here, too, you'll find memorials to Handel (holding a score of his *Messiah*), Edmund Spenser and Robert Browning, as well as the graves of (or memorials to) Charles Dickens, Lewis Carroll, Rudyard Kipling and Henry James. St Faith Chapel is reserved for private prayer.

Just north of Poet's Corner is the **Lantern**, the heart of the abbey, where coronations take place. If you face eastwards while standing in the centre, the **sanctuary** is in front of you. The ornate **high altar** was designed by George Gilbert Scott in 1897. Behind you (ie, to the west) Edward Blore's **quire** (or chancel) dating from the mid-19th century is a breathtaking structure of gold, blue and red Victorian Gothic. Where monks once worshipped, boys from the Choir School and lay vicars now sing the daily services.

The entrance to the **Cloister** dates from the 13th century, the rest of it from the 14th. Eastwards down a passageway off the Cloister are **three museums** run by EH *(w www .english-heritage.org.uk; admission to all three with abbey ticket adult/senior & student/child aged 11-17 £1/80p/50p, without abbey ticket £2.50/1.90/1.30)*. Admission to the Chapter House, the Pyx Chamber and the Abbey Museum (accessible via Dean's Yard and the Cloister) is free for EH members and for those renting an abbey audioguide (£2.50).

Westminster Abbey, the 'royal peculiar', attracts tourists in their droves.

DOUG MCKINLAY

THINGS TO SEE & DO

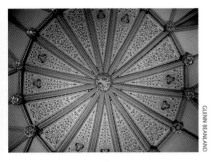

GLENN BEANLAND

**Elaborate circular ceiling decoration
at Westminster Abbey**

The octagonal **Chapter House** *(open 9.30am-5pm Apr-Sept, 10am-5pm Oct, 10am-4pm Nov-Mar)* has one of Europe's best-preserved medieval tile floors and retains traces of religious murals. It was used as a chamber by the king's council and as a meeting place by the House of Commons in the second half of the 14th century. The **Pyx Chamber** *(open 10.30am-4pm daily)* was once the Royal Treasury and contains the pyx, a chest with standard gold and silver pieces for testing coinage weights. It now houses the abbey's treasures and liturgical objects as well as the abbey's oldest altar.

The **Abbey Museum** *(open 10.30am-4pm daily)* exhibits the death masks of generations of royalty, and there are wax effigies representing Charles II and William III (who is on a stool to make him as tall as his wife Mary) as well as armour and stained glass.

To reach the 900-year-old **College Garden** *(open 10am-6pm Tues-Thur Apr-Sept, 10am-4pm Tues-Thurs Oct-Mar)*, enter Dean's Yard and the **Little Cloisters** off Great College St.

A walk around the Cloister brings you to the western end of the nave. Set in the floor is the **Tomb of the Unknown Warrior**, surrounded by poppies in memory of those who died on the WWI battlefields. Just before it is a stone commemorating **Winston Churchill**, prime minister during WWII.

Straight up the aisle is a screen separating the nave from the quire; built in 1834, it is the fourth one to be put here. Against

this stand monuments to Isaac Newton, Charles Darwin, Lord Stanhope, Michael Faraday and four Nobel laureates, including Lord Kelvin and Ernest Rutherford; the area is known as **Scientists' Corner**. Above the screen is a magnificent organ (1730). Look up at the beautiful stone vaulted ceiling in the nave and at the fan-vaulted aisles.

A section of the northern aisle of the nave is known as **Musicians' Aisle**, with memorials to music-makers who served the abbey. Look out for memorials to the composer Henry Purcell, who served as an organist at the abbey, as well as to Vaughan Williams, Edward Elgar and Benjamin Britten.

The two towers above the west door, through which you exit, were designed by Nicholas Hawksmoor and completed in 1745. Just above the door, perched in 15th-century niches, are the latest sacred addition to the abbey: 10 stone statues of **20th-century martyrs**, which were unveiled in 1998. They include US civil rights leader Martin Luther King; the Polish priest St Maximilian Kolbe, who was murdered by the Nazis at Auschwitz; St Elizabeth of Russia, who founded an order of charitable nuns in Moscow in the early 20th century and was shot by the Bolsheviks in 1918; and Wang Zhiming, a pastor killed by the Chinese Communists during the Cultural Revolution in 1972. Protestant or Catholic, they were all Christians.

To the right as you exit is a memorial to innocent victims of oppression, violence and war around the world. 'All you who pass by, is it nothing to you?' it asks poignantly. Give it some thought.

Guided Tours Abbey tours last about 1½ hours and cost £3. They operate Monday to Saturday (departing three to six times a day from April to October, three or four times a day November to March); call for exact times). There's also an audioguide (£2) available but it's not very comprehensive.

One of the best ways to visit the abbey is to attend a service, particularly evensong (5pm Monday to Friday, 3pm Saturday and Sunday). Sung Eucharist is held at 11.15am on Sunday.

WHITEHALL

What was once the administrative heart of the British Empire remains the focal point for British government today. Start at the southern end of Trafalgar Square as it leads into White-hall. On the traffic island is an **equestrian statue of Charles I (1)**, which was cast in 1633, buried in a garden during the Com-monwealth and not erected until after the Restoration. As you walk south you'll see **Admiralty Arch (2)** (1910), **Old Admiralty (3)** to the east (right) and farther on, to the west (left), the **Ministry of Defence (4)**.

In the north-western corner of the latter is **Banqueting House (5)** (☎ 7930 4179, Ⓦ www.hrp.org.uk; adult/senior & student/child aged 5-15 £3.90/3.10/2.30; open 10am-5pm Mon-Sat), the only surviving part of the Tudor Whitehall Palace, which once stretched along White-hall but burned down in 1698. Built in 1622 on a design by Inigo Jones, it was England's first purely Renaissance building. Its claim to fame is that it was on a scaffold built against a 1st-floor window here that Charles I, accused of treason by Cromwell, was executed on 30 Jan-uary 1649. After Whitehall Palace burned down, Banqueting House became the Chapel Royal. It is still used for state banquets and con-certs. Inside there's a video of its history and on the 1st floor is a huge, virtually unfurnished hall with nine ceiling panels (1635) by Rubens.

Opposite Banqueting House is **Horse Guards Parade (6)**, where the mounted troopers of the Household Cavalry are changed at 11am Monday to Saturday and at 10am on Sunday, offering a more accessi-ble version of the ceremony than the one outside Buckingham Palace. The less visually exciting dismounted guards are changed at 4pm daily. Ring the London Line on ☎ 09068 663344 for the latest information.

South of Horse Guards Parade is **Downing St**, traditional site of the British PM's official residence since 1732, when George II gave **No 10 (7)** to Robert Walpole. Tony Blair and his family now live in the larger apartments at No 11, while Chancellor of the Exchequer Gordon Brown, uses the smaller flat at No 10. Recently, Blair commandeered the offices at No 12, traditional base of the chief whip, claiming the need for more work space. During Thatcher's leadership the gates were erected for fear of IRA attacks. Visit online at Ⓦ www.number10.gov.uk.

A short distance farther on in the middle of Whitehall is the **Ceno-taph (8)** (Greek for 'empty tomb'), a memorial to Commonwealth cit-izens who were killed during the two world wars. The Queen and other public figures lay poppies at its base on 11 November.

To the west of the Cenotaph is the restored **Foreign & Common-wealth Office (9)** (FCO; 1872) by Sir George Gilbert Scott and Matt-hew Digby Wyatt. In a bid to rid itself of its reputation as a highly secretive ministry, the FCO has now opened a visitor centre (☎ 7270 1500; admission free; open 10am-4.30pm Mon-Fri), which has an information-technology centre, exhibition gallery and cinema explain-ing how the FCO projects Britain through its global diplomatic posts.

If you walk west along King Charles St and descend the Clive Steps to Horse Guards Rd, you'll reach the **Cabinet War Rooms (10)** (☎ 7930

distance: about 1 mile

start: Trafalgar Square
⊕ Charing Cross

finish: Broad Sanctuary
⊕ Westminster

6961; admission free; open 9.30am-5.15pm Apr-Sept, 10am-5.15pm Oct-Mar), now a branch of the Imperial War Museum, where the British government took refuge underground during WWII, conducting its business beneath 3m of solid concrete. It was from here that Winston Churchill made some of his most stirring speeches. Particularly notable are the room where the Cabinet held over 100 meetings during the war; the Map Room with charts showing the movements of troops and ships; and the Telegraph Room, its door marked with a borrowed 'vacant/engaged' sign to suggest it was a lavatory. A £10 million museum dedicated to Churchill will open adjacent to the Cabinet War Rooms in 2005.

Whitehall ends at **Parliament Square**, where swirling traffic makes it hard to appreciate the statues of past prime ministers, such as **Winston Churchill (11)**, and other worthies, including **Abraham Lincoln (12)**. To the north-east along Bridge St is the ultramodern **Parliament Building (13)** atop Westminster tube station. Farther east along this street is **Big Ben (14)** and, by Westminster Bridge, a **statue of Queen Boudicca (15)** with her daughters in a chariot.

To the south and south-east of the square are **Westminster Abbey (16)** and the **Houses of Parliament (17)**. Just in front of the former is **St Margaret's, Westminster (18)** *(☎ 7222 5152,* **W** *www.westminster-abbey.org; open 9.30am-4.30pm Mon-Fri, 9.30am-2.45pm Sat, 2pm-5pm Sun)*, consecrated in 1523. It is the House of Commons' church and famous for high-society weddings. Notice the **bust of Charles I (19)** in a niche of the church's outside wall facing the Houses of Parliament and (more appropriately) the statue of **Cromwell (20)**, his nemesis, erected in 1899. To the west stands the elaborate neo-Gothic **Middlesex Guildhall (21)** (1913), which houses Middlesex Crown Court.

An interesting building on Storey's Gate is **Westminster Central Hall (22)**, built in 1911 in 'ornate French style' and the seat of the Methodist Church. It hosted the first assembly of the United Nations in 1946 and is used for concerts and religious services. Tours *(☎ 7222 8010)* depart 11am to 3.30pm Tuesday, Wednesday and Thursday; and half-hourly from 1.30pm to 5.30pm Sunday early May to early October. *Wesley's Café* (open 10am to 2.30pm daily) is a good spot for lunch.

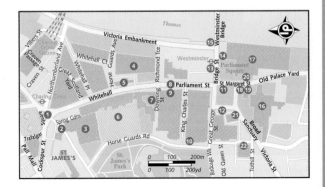

Houses of Parliament (Map 6)

Parliament, comprising the House of Commons and House of Lords, is housed in the **Palace of Westminster** (**W** *www.parliament .uk, Parliament Square SW1;* **⊖** *Westminster*). It was built by Charles Barry and Augustus Pugin in 1840 when the neo-Gothic style was all the rage in London, and a good clean has revealed the soft golden brilliance of the original structure. The most famous feature *outside* the palace is the Clock Tower, commonly known as **Big Ben** (the real Ben, a bell named after Benjamin Hall, who was commissioner of works when the tower was completed in 1858, hangs inside). Big Ben has rung in the new year since 1924. The best view of the whole complex is from the eastern side of Lambeth Bridge. The great clock gets its hands and face washed by abseiling cleaners once every five years.

At the opposite end of the building is **Victoria Tower**, completed in 1860; the medieval-looking little structure with the colourful tile roof in triangular Victoria Tower Gardens to the south is a **monument to the emancipation of slaves** in the British Empire and was erected in 1834.

The **House of Commons** is where Members of Parliament (MPs) meet to propose and discuss new legislation and to question the prime minister and other ministers. The layout of the Commons Chamber is based on that of St Stephen's Chapel in the original Palace of Westminster. The current chamber, designed by Giles Gilbert Scott, replaced the earlier one destroyed by a 1941 bomb. Although the Commons is a national assembly of 659 MPs, the chamber has seating for only 437 of them. Government members sit to the right of the Speaker and Opposition members to the left. The Speaker presides over business from a chair given by Australia while ministers speak from a despatch box donated by New Zealand.

When Parliament is in session, visitors are admitted to the **House of Commons Visitors' Gallery** (**☎** *7219 4272, St Stephen's Entrance, St Margaret St SW1; admission free; open 2.30pm-7.30pm Mon-Wed, 11.30am-7.30pm Thur, 9.30am-3pm Fri*). Expect to queue for at least an hour. Parliamentary recesses (ie, holidays) last for three months over the summer and another couple of weeks over Easter and Christmas, so it's best to ring in advance to check whether Parliament is in session. To find out what's being debated on a particular day, check the notice board posted beside the entrance or

DOUG MCKINLAY

Ayes to the right! If you want to see politicians in action then head to the Palace of Westminster.

look in the *Daily Telegraph* or the freebie *Metro* newspaper under 'Today in Parliament'. Bags and cameras must be checked at a cloakroom before you enter the gallery, and no large suitcases or backpacks are allowed through the airport-style security gate. The **House of Lords Visitors' Gallery** (☎ *7219 3107; admission free; open from 2.30pm Mon-Wed, from 3pm Thur, from 11am Fri)* is also open to outsiders, but unless you want to nap the afternoon away, give it a miss. The closing time varies.

Guided tours *(☎ 7344 9966)* cost £3.50 and are available 9.15am to 4.30pm Monday to Saturday early August to late September from St Stephen's Entrance on St Margaret St.

As you're waiting for your bags to go through the X-ray machines, look left at the stunning roof of **Westminster Hall**, originally built in 1099 and today the oldest surviving part of the Palace of Westminster, the seat of the English monarchy from the 11th to the early 16th centuries. Added between 1394 and 1401, it is the earliest known example of a hammer-beam roof and has been described as 'the greatest surviving achievement of medieval English carpentry'. Along with being used for coronation banquets in medieval times, Westminster Hall also served as a courthouse until the 19th century. The trials of William Wallace (1305), Thomas More (1535), Guy Fawkes (1606) and Charles I (1649) all took place here. In the 20th century monarchs and Winston Churchill lay in state here.

Jewel Tower (Map 6)

Once part of the Palace of Westminster, the Jewel Tower *(☎ 7973 3479 or 7222 2219, **w** www.english-heritage.org.uk, Abingdon St SW1; adult/student & senior/child aged 5-15 £1.60/1.20/80p; open 10am-6pm daily Apr-Sept, 10am-5pm daily Oct, 10am-4pm daily Nov-Mar)* opposite the Houses of Parliament and beside Westminster Abbey, was built in 1365 to house Edward III's treasury. Originally it was surrounded by a moat but this was filled in 1664. Later the tower served as an office for clerks of the House of Lords. Nowadays it houses exhibitions

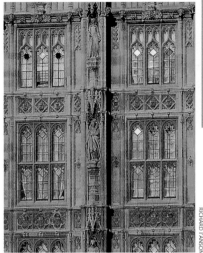

Marvel at the Palace of Westminster's ornately sculpted decoration.

RICHARD I'ANSON

describing the history of Parliament and showing how it works. There's also a 25-minute explanatory video in which you can see some of the present-day MPs in action. It's well worth visiting before attending a Commons debate so you'll understand more of what you're seeing.

Westminster Cathedral (Map 11)

Completed in 1903, Westminster Cathedral *(☎ 7798 9055, **w** www.westminstercathedral .org.uk, Victoria St SW1; ⊖ Victoria; cathedral admission free, tower admission adult/ senior & child/family £2/1/5; open 7am-7pm daily; tower open 9am-5pm daily Apr-Nov, 9am-5pm Thur-Sun Dec-Mar)* is the headquarters of the Roman Catholic Church in Britain and is the only good example of neo-Byzantine architecture in London. Its distinctive candy-striped red-brick and white-stone tower features prominently on the west London skyline, although remarkably few people think to look inside. Audio-guides are available for £2.50.

The interior is part splendid marble and mosaic and part bare brick; the money ran out and the cathedral was never completed. The highly regarded stone carvings of the 14 Stations of the Cross (1918) by Eric Gill and the marvellously sombre atmosphere, especially in early evening when the mosaics glitter in the candlelight, make this a welcome haven from the traffic outside. The views from the 83m-tall **Campanile Bell Tower**, served by a lift, are impressive.

Seven Masses are said daily from Monday to Friday, five on Saturday and seven on Sunday. There's a gift shop and a *cafe* here open 10am to 4.30pm daily.

Tate Britain (Map 2)

The Tate Britain (☎ 7887 8008 or 7887 8888, ⓦ www.tate.org.uk, Millbank SW1; ✈ Pimlico; admission free, major exhibitions adult/concession/family £5/3.50/13.50; open 10am-5.50pm daily) serves as the historical archive of British art from the early 16th century to the present day. Its sister gallery, the Tate Modern, is at Bankside (see that section later in this chapter).

The Tate Britain, built in 1897, has expanded in recent years and the new Linbury Galleries, mostly reserved for temporary exhibits, have increased space by over a third. With all the moving about it is impossible to say what will be on display (and where) but likely highlights include the Constable Gallery, the Gainsborough Octagon, the Reynolds, Spencers and Hockneys in the Painters in Focus Gallery and the Portrait Gallery, with works by Whistler, Bacon and Spencer. The Tate Modern also has important works by Blake, Hogarth and Rossetti.

Adjoining the main building is the **Clore Gallery**, James Stirling's stab at acceptable, postmodern architecture, where the bulk of JMW Turner's paintings can be found.

One-hour guided tours of the museum are available 11.30am, 2.30pm and 3.30pm Monday to Friday, and 3pm on Saturday. An audioguide to the collection called Tate Inform is available for £1. The *Tate Restaurant* (☎ 7887 8825), with a splendid mural by Rex Whistler, is enormously popular. It opens for lunch only noon to 3pm daily (to 4pm on Sunday). The *Tate Café & Espresso Bar* keeps the same hours as the museum.

CHRISTINE OSBORNE

The world's most extensive collection of British art can be viewed at Tate Britain.

ST JAMES'S & MAYFAIR (Map 6)

St James's is a mixture of exclusive clubs (eg, the Army & Navy, Reform and Carlton clubs), historic shops and elegant buildings; indeed, there are some 150 historically noteworthy buildings within its 36 hectares. It has largely escaped the redevelopment that has taken place in much of London.

Mayfair is the area bordered by Oxford St to the north, Piccadilly to the south, Park Lane and Hyde Park to the west and Regent St to the east. Regent St owes its original design to John Nash (see Architecture in the Facts about London chapter), who tried to separate refined Mayfair from teeming, working-class Soho. Nash's architectural blueprint, the closest London has ever come to a grand plan, was for Regent St to reach all the way from the Mall to Regent's Park. He was unable to continue with his plan north of Oxford St due to the intractability of property owners, but his immaculate stuccoed terraces around the perimeter of Regent's Park survive.

Bordering the south-eastern corner of Hyde Park, Shepherd's Market – the 'village centre of Mayfair' – is today a tiny enclave of pubs, restaurants and bistros but was once a very busy red-light district.

Institute for Contemporary Arts

The Institute for Contemporary Arts *(ICA;* ☎ *7930 3647 or 7930 6393,* **W** *www.ica .org.uk, The Mall SW1;* ⊖ *Charing Cross/ Piccadilly Circus; day pass £1.50/2.50 Mon-Fri/Sat & Sun; open noon-11pm Mon, noon-1am Tues-Sat, noon-10.30pm Sun)* has a reputation for being at the cutting edge of all kinds of arts. In any given week this is the place to come for obscure films, dance, photography, art, theatre, music, lectures, multimedia works and book readings.

The complex includes a bookshop, gallery, cinema, bar, theatre and the *ICA Café* (see the Places to Eat chapter), which is also a licensed restaurant.

Up the steps beside the ICA into Waterloo Place you'll see the **Duke of York Column**, commemorating a son of George III. It was erected in 1834 but never quite caught the public imagination like Nelson's Column in Trafalgar Square, though it's just 6m shorter.

St James's Park & St James's Palace

St James's Park, *(*☎ *7930 1793, The Mall SW1;* ⊖ *St James's Park; open 5am-dusk daily)* is the neatest and most royal of London's royal parks and has the best vistas, including those of Westminster, St James's Palace, Carlton Terrace and Horse Guards Parade; the best view of Buckingham Palace in London is from the footbridge spanning St James's Park Lake. In summer, the flower beds are sumptuous and colourful, some of them newly replanted to mimic John Nash's original 'floriferous' beds that mixed shrubs, flowers and trees. But what makes St James's so special is its large lake and the waterfowl that inhabit it, including a group of pelicans. Pelicans have lived here since the reign of James I, when the Russian ambassador presented some of the birds to him as a gift. This lot, however, comes from Florida and can be vicious.

The striking Tudor gatehouse of **St James's Palace**, the only surviving part of a building initiated by the palace-mad Henry VIII in 1530, is best approached from St James's St to the north of the park. It is the residence of Prince Charles and his sons, the princes William and Harry, and is never open to the public. Princess Diana, who hated the place, did time here until her divorce from Charles and her move to Kensington Palace in 1996. Ironically, the powers-that-be thought St James's Palace the most suitable place for her body to lie in state after her death in 1997. Foreign ambassadors to the UK are still accredited to 'the Court of St James'. Next door is **Clarence House** (1828), the residence of the Queen Mother.

PAUL BIGLAND

Swan around St James's Park, the royal gem of London's green spaces.

Spencer House

Just outside the park, Spencer House (☎ 7499 8620, ⓦ *www.spencerhouse.co .uk, 27 St James's Place SW1;* ◉ *Green Park; adult/student & under-16s £6/5; open 10.30am-5.30pm Sun only Feb-July & Sept-Dec)* was built for the 1st Earl Spencer, an ancestor of Diana, Princess of Wales, in the Palladian style between 1756 and 1766. The Spencers moved out in 1927 and eventually their grand house became an office, but a recent £18 million restoration by Lord Rothschild has returned it to its former glory. The house can be visited by guided tour only. The gardens open only between 2pm and 5pm a couple of Sundays in summer. Tickets cost £3.50.

Buckingham Palace

Buckingham Palace (☎ 7839 1377, ⓦ *www .the-royal-collection.org.uk;* ◉ *St James's Park/Victoria; adult/senior/under-17s/family £11/9/5.50/27.50; open 9.30am-4.30pm daily early Aug-Sept)* is at the end of The Mall, where St James's Park and Green Park meet at a large roundabout. In the centre of the circle is the **Queen Victoria Memorial**, close to where Marble Arch stood until it was moved to its present location in 1851. The memorial (1911), by Thomas Brock, is almost 25m high and portrays the seated Regina, carved from a single block of white marble, facing eastwards and surrounded by a number of allegorical figures representing everything from Charity, Truth and Justice, near the plinth, to Progress, Painting, Shipbuilding and so on farther out.

Buckingham Palace was built in 1705 as Buckingham House for the duke of Buckingham and has been the royal family's London home since 1837, when St James's Palace was judged too old-fashioned and insufficiently impressive. A total of 19 State Rooms (out of 661), including the enomous Ballroom, are open to visitors for eight weeks each summer, but don't expect to see the Queen's bedroom or privy. She and her consort, Philip, the duke of Edinburgh, share a suite of 12 rooms in the northern wing overlooking Green Park. Many people find the visit overpriced and disappointing.

The tour starts in the **Guard Room**, which is too small for the Ceremonial Guard, who are deployed in adjoining rooms, and includes a peek at the **State Dining Room** (all red damask and Regency furnishings, with a portrait of George III looking fetching in fur); **Queen Victoria's Picture Gallery** (a full 76.5m long, with works by Van Dyck, Rembrandt, Canaletto, Poussin and Vermeer); the **Blue Drawing Room**, with a gorgeous fluted ceiling by John Nash; the **White Drawing Room**, where the monarch receives foreign ambassadors; and the Ballroom, where official receptions and state banquets are held. But most visitors will get the biggest kick out of the **Throne Room**, with his-and-hers pink chairs initialled 'ER' and 'P' sitting smugly under what looks like a theatre arch. In the past, visitors have been allowed to stroll along the southern side of the huge Palace Gardens, with views of its pretty lake.

RICHARD I'ANSON

We are not amused: Queen Victoria sits regally atop her white-marble memorial.

NEIL SETCHFIELD

Marching orders: Her Majesty's Foot Guards strut their stuff outside Buckingham Palace.

Tickets to the palace are sold from a futuristic kiosk (open 9am to 4pm daily from a week before the season starts) in Green Park to the north. You can also book by credit card on ☎ 7321 2233.

Changing of the Guard This is a London 'must see' – though, like many visitors, you'll probably go away wondering what all the fuss was about. The old guard (Foot Guards of the Household Regiment) comes off duty to be replaced by the new guard on the forecourt of Buckingham Palace, which gives tourists a chance to gape at the bright red uniforms, bearskin hats (synthetic alternatives are being looked at), shouting and marching. If you arrive early, grab a prime spot by the railings; more likely you'll be 10 rows behind. The ceremony takes place daily at 11.30am sharp from April to August and on alternate days (usually odd dates – eg, 1, 3, 5 September) at the same time during the rest of the year. This can change so ring London Line on ☎ 09068 663344 for up-to-the-minute details (60p per minute). For the schedule of the changing of the Horse Guard in Whitehall, see the Whitehall walking tour earlier in this chapter.

Queen's Gallery Works from the extensive Royal Collection of paintings, drawings, cartoons, miniatures and engravings usually go on display in regularly changing exhibitions held in The Queen's Gallery (☎ 7839 1377 or 7799 2331, W www.the-royal-collection org.uk; southern wing Buckingham Palace, entrance Buckingham Gate). Designed by Nash as a conservatory and converted into a chapel for Victoria in 1843, it was destroyed in a 1940 air raid and reopened as a gallery in 1962. The present gallery is relatively small and has been undergoing a £10 million renovation to enlarge the small entrance hall, add a Greek Doric portico and expand the exhibition space in time for Elizabeth II's Golden Jubilee.

Royal Mews South of the palace, the Royal Mews (☎ 7839 1377 or 7799 2331, W www.the-royal-collection.org.uk, Buckingham Palace Rd SW1; ⊖ Victoria; adult/senior/under-17s/family £4.60/3.60/2.60/11.80; open 10.30am-4.30pm Mon-Thur Aug & Sept, noon-4pm Tues-Thur Oct-July) started life as a falconry but now houses the flashy vehicles the royals use for getting around on ceremonial occasions, including the stunning Gold State Coach of 1762, used for every coronation since that of George III, and the Glass Coach of 1910, which is used for royal weddings. Don't forget to see the stables designed by John Nash in the 1820s and home to the Queen's Cleveland Bays and Windsor Greys.

Green Park

Green Park (*☎ 7930 1793, Piccadilly W1; ⊖ Green Park; open 5am-dusk daily*) adjoins St James's to the north-west across The Mall and is a less fussy, more naturally rolling park, with trees and open space. Once a duelling ground and, like Hyde Park, a vegetable field during WWII, Green Park tends to be quieter than its illustrious neighbour. If you need to get to Hyde Park Corner from, say, Buckingham Palace a stroll through the park is much more enjoyable than taking the tube or bus.

Mayfair

Mayfair is one of London's most exclusive neighbourhoods – as everyone who's ever played the British version of Monopoly will know. At the heart of the district is **Grosvenor Square**, dominated by the US embassy on the western side and a **memorial to Franklin D Roosevelt** in the centre. The statue, showing FDR cloaked and leaning on a stick to hide his disability resulting from polio, was unveiled by Eleanor Roosevelt in 1948. It was paid for by 200,000 British subscribers, whose contributions were limited to five shillings (now 25p) each. Such was the popularity of America's 32nd president after WWII that the sum – £50,000 – was raised within 24 hours.

The other famous Mayfair landmark is **Berkeley Square**, where nightingales might conceivably still sing amid the plane trees, although you'd probably not hear them for all the traffic. The house at No 44, part of the Clermont Club, still retains its fine old iron railings, complete with snuffers for extinguishing the torches carried by footmen.

THE WEST END: PICCADILLY TO SOHO & COVENT GARDEN (Maps 6, 7 & 8)

No two Londoners ever agree on the exact borders of the West End but let's just say it takes in Piccadilly Circus and Trafalgar Square to the south, Oxford St and Tottenham Court Rd to the north, Regent St to the West and Covent Garden and the Strand to the east. A heady mixture of consumerism and culture, the West End is where outstanding museums and galleries rub shoulders with tacky tourist traps, and world-famous buildings and monuments share the streets with some of the capital's most popular shopping and entertainment venues. This is the London of postcard and T-shirt stands and folk memory.

ELLIOT DANIEL

A sign of the times: the flashier, trashier side of Piccadilly Circus

Piccadilly Circus (Map 7)

Piccadilly Circus is home to the statue of the *Angel of Christian Charity*, commonly known as **Eros** and dedicated to Lord Ashley, the Victorian earl of Shaftesbury, who championed social and industrial reform. It was London's first memorial built of aluminium and was despised when it was unveiled in 1893. We prefer the statue on the edge of Piccadilly and Haymarket: the *Horses of Helios*, with their flaring nostrils and all that rushing water. It's a great meeting spot.

Piccadilly Circus used to be the hub of London, where flower girls flogged their wares and people arranged to meet or just bumped into each other. Today it's fume-choked and pretty uninteresting, overlooked by CD supermarkets and the Rock Circus.

The streets fanning out from Piccadilly Circus are another story. Running to the north-east is **Shaftesbury Ave**, named after the eponymous earl and the heart of London's theatreland. To the east Coventry St heads past Planet Hollywood to Leicester Square and Covent Garden. To the south, Regent St runs past the Britain Visitor Centre, while parallel Haymarket passes the main Amex office and New Zealand House, the former Carlton Hotel where the Vietnamese revolutionary leader Ho Chi Minh (1890–1969) worked as a waiter in 1913. To the west the road called Piccadilly itself leads past Fortnum & Mason, the Royal Academy and Green Park to end at Hyde Park Corner. From the north-western corner of the circus Regent St doglegs north towards Oxford Circus and is lined on both sides with elegant arcades of shops.

Rock Circus Funnily enough, the Rock Circus *(☎ 7734 7203 or 0870 400 3030,* **W** *www.rock-circus.com, London Pavilion, Piccadilly Circus W1;* **⊖** *Piccadilly Circus; adult/senior & student/child £8.25/6.95/ 5.95; open 10am-5.30pm Mon & Wed-Sun & 11am-5.30pm Tues late June-early Sept, 10am-8pm Mon, Wed, Thur & Sun, 11am-8pm Tues & 10am-9pm Fri & Sat rest of year)* is one of the capital's most popular attractions, despite the fact that it's one of the tackiest tourist traps in town. Listening and

On a wing and a prayer: the statue of Eros
in Piccadilly Circus

SIMON BRACKEN

viewing posts treat you to a five-minute video of the history of rock and roll and don't-look-alike animated models lip-sync to their music while jerking their limbs around like puppets on strings: Michael Jackson, Bryan Ferry, The Beatles and (shudder) the Spice Girls. It's hardly cutting-edge stuff.

London Trocadero Spread over six levels, the London Trocadero *(☎ 09068 881100,* **W** *www.troc.co.uk, 1 Piccadilly Circus W1;* **⊖** *Piccadilly Circus; admission free; open 10am-1am daily)* is a huge indoor entertainment complex with several high-tech attractions, anchored by the Funland indoor theme park. It's a good place to take youngsters who can't be sold on London's more cultural attractions, but don't expect a peaceful – or cheap – time. There's no admission fee but you must pay £3 for each of the eight rides (or save by buying a two/five/12/26-ride token for £5/10/20/40), including things with names like Max Flight and Cybersled

An eye-widening array of computer games and gadgetry is on offer at the London Trocadero.

as well as go-karting, dodgem cars and bowling. Also inside the Trocadero you can scare yourself half to death on the **Scream Ride** (£3) or see a film at the seven-screen **UGC Trocadero** (☎ *0870 907 0716*). In addition, Funland has upwards of 400 video games to keep the most hyperactive active.

Piccadilly (Map 7)

Piccadilly, the road running westwards from Piccadilly Circus, is said to take its curious name from 'picadils', stiff collars or ruffs popular at court in the 17th century and made by a tailor who built himself a house here. As you leave Piccadilly Circus look on the left for **St James's Piccadilly** (☎ *7734 4511, 197 Piccadilly W1; open 8am-7pm daily*) designed by Sir Christopher Wren after the Great Fire of 1666. It's another of those sociable London churches, with both lunch-time and evening concerts and a small *antiques market* 8am to 6pm on Tuesday and an *arts and crafts fair* 10am to 6pm Wednesday to Saturday.

On the right you'll come to the **Royal Academy of Arts** (☎ *7300 8000, *Ⓦ* www .royalacademy.org.uk, Burlington House, Piccadilly W1; *✆* Green Park; adult/senior & student/child aged 12-18/child aged 9-11 £7/6/2.50/1.50 during Summer Exhibition;* open 10am-6pm Sun, 10am-10pm Fri)*, which has hosted some record-breaking exhibitions in recent years; its *Monet in the 20th Century* in early 1999 saw 800,000 visits over three months and forced the academy to open its doors nonstop for the last 36 hours of the show. From early June to mid-August, the academy holds its traditional Summer Exhibition, an open show that anyone can enter. The quality can be mixed but in the glorious setting of one of London's few remaining 18th-century mansions it never seems to matter much.

Flanking the academy on the western side is **Burlington Arcade** (*51 Piccadilly W1*), which was built in 1819 and recalls a bygone age – selling the kinds of things that only the very rich are likely to want. Watch out for the Burlington Berties, the uniformed guards who patrol the arcade, with a brief to prevent high spirits, whistling and the inelegant popping of chewing gum. As you emerge from the arcade look right on to Burlington Gardens and you'll see an imposing 19th-century Italianate building that was, until recently, home to the Museum of Mankind. It now houses the British Museum's Department of Ethnography.

Head westwards along Burlington Gardens and you'll come to Old Bond St, where many of London's commercial art galleries can be found. The **Royal Arcade** *(28 Old Bond St W1 or 12 Albemarle St W1)*, a covered thoroughfare lined with extremely expensive shops selling such English wares as hunting jackets, pipe tobacco, cashmere jumpers and golfing knickerbockers, runs off it to the west. Built in 1879, it reflects that era's love affair with the neo-Gothic style. A short distance north along New Bond St will take you to a statue of Winston Churchill and Franklin D Roosevelt sitting on a park bench. It's called *Allies* and was cast by Lawrence Holofcener in 1995.

South-west of Old Bond St and bordering Green Park is *The Ritz* (see the Places to Stay chapter), perhaps the most glitzy of London's upmarket hotels. This was one of London's first steel-framed buildings, but that's unlikely to interest you much if you're coming here for tea (see the boxed text 'On the High Teas' in the Places to Eat chapter).

If you follow Piccadilly to the south-west you come to **Hyde Park Corner**.

Regent St (Map 7)

Regent St, originally designed by John Nash as a ceremonial route linking Carlton House, the Prince Regent's long-demolished city dwelling, with the 'wilds' of Regent's Park, later became a buffer between workaday Soho and affluent, residential Mayfair. The street is lined with elegant shop fronts but they date back only to 1925. Here you'll find *Hamleys*, London's premier toy and game store, and the upmarket department store *Liberty* (see the Shopping chapter). Go eastwards along Great Marlborough St and you'll reach the northern end of **Carnaby St**, which runs parallel to Regent St. It was the street for fashion in the 'swinging London' of the 1960s, and the whole area – now a pedestrian shopping zone taking in Beak, Ganton and Kingly Sts – is coming back to life as a place for tourists to visit.

All Souls, Langham Place (Map 6) A

Nash solution for the curving, northern sweep of Regent St was this delightful church *(☎ 7580 3522, Langham Place W1; ⊖ Oxford Circus; admission free; open 9.30am-6pm Sun-Fri)*, with its circular columned porch and distinctive needle-like spire, reminiscent of an ancient Greek temple. The church was very unpopular when completed in 1824; a contemporary cartoon by George Cruikshank shows Nash rather painfully impaled on the spire through the bottom with the words 'Nashional Taste!!!' below it. It was bombed extensively during the Blitz and renovated in 1951.

Broadcasting House (Map 6) Opposite

All Souls to the north is Broadcasting House, from which the BBC began radio broadcasting in 1932. There's a shop stocking any number of videos, CDs, tapes and books relating to BBC programmes (open 9.30am to 6pm Monday to Saturday and 10am to 5.30pm on Sunday). For tours of the BBC Television Centre in west London, see the Shepherd's Bush section later in this chapter.

Oxford St (Maps 6 & 7)

London's most popular shopping street, Oxford St is hardly its finest, especially if you emerge from Oxford Circus tube and head east towards Tottenham Court Rd and the flagship HMV and Virgin record stores. It sometimes feels as if you're running the gauntlet of permanent 'closing down' sales. Things are much better if you head west from Oxford Circus towards Marble Arch; this is where you'll find the famous department stores, including John Lewis and Selfridges (for more information see the Shopping chapter).

Spend, spend, spend: it might not be classiest street in town but it's a shopaholics dream.

Soho (Maps 6 & 7)

East of Regent St and south of Oxford St, with Shaftesbury Ave and Charing Cross Rd to the south and the east respectively, is Soho, one of the liveliest corners of London and the place to come for fun and games after dark. Hard though it is to believe, this area was once a hunting ground; 'So-ho!' was a rallying cry, something like a 'Tally-ho!', hence the name. A decade ago Soho was an extremely sleazy neighbourhood filled with strip clubs and peepshows, where unwary males were easily separated from large sums of cash. A few of the strip joints are still there but these days some of London's trendiest clubs, bars and restaurants (see the Places to Eat and Entertainment chapters for more details) predominate.

Handel Museum (Map 6) The first museum devoted to a composer in London, the new Handel Museum (☎ 7495 1685, 23-25 Brook St W1; ⊖ Bond Street/Oxford

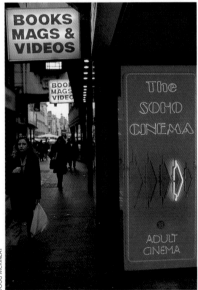

DOUG MCKINLAY

Naughty but...
Soho still aims to please.

Circus; admission adult/senior & student/child £4.50/3.50/2; open 10am-6pm Tue, Wed, Fri & Sat, 10am-8pm Thur, noon-6pm Sun) celebrates the life and times of the German-born composer George Frideric Handel (1685–1759), who lived at No 25 from 1723 until he died 36 years later. Handel moved to London in 1712 and became a naturalised citizen in 1726. As court composer, he wrote many of his most celebrated works in London, including Water Music (1717) and The Messiah (1741). Highlights of the museum include early editions of his operas and oratorios, Mozart's hand-written arrangement of a Handel fugue, and artwork contemporary with Handel's life, including the renowned portraits of the composer by Philip Mercier completed in 1730.

In an odd twist of fate, the house at No 23 (now part of the museum) was home to a musician as different from Handel as could be imagined: the American guitarist Jimi Hendrix (1942–69). He lived there from 1968 until his death.

Leicester Square (Maps 6, 7 & 8)

Despite efforts to smarten it up and the presence of four enormous cinemas, various nightclubs, pubs, bars and restaurants, pedestrians-only Leicester (**les**-ter) Square still feels more like a transit point between Covent Garden and Piccadilly Circus than its own little world. You're bound to pass through here at some point, but it's hard to imagine a time when artists Joshua Reynolds and William Hogarth actually chose to live here.

The patch of green in the middle of the square is a barely acceptable picnic spot if you haven't got the energy to press on to St James's Park. The fountain in the centre commemorates Shakespeare, and there's a small statue of Charlie Chaplin to one side. Plaques in the ground also list the distances from central London to the capitals of various Commonwealth countries. More plaques in the pavement outside incorporate the hand-prints of various Hollywood stars; the cinemas here are where many British film premieres take place.

RICHARD I'ANSON

Peking duck to perk you up: indulge yourself in Chinatown's stir-fry heaven.

Chinatown (Maps 7 & 8)

Immediately north of Leicester Square are Lisle and Gerrard Sts, the heart of London's Chinatown, where street signs are written in both English and Chinese characters, and red lanterns and dragon-adorned moon gates are commonplace. This is the place to come for an after-hours Chinese meal; at least one place is open round the clock (see The West End: Piccadilly, Soho & Chinatown in the Places to Eat chapter). But to see it at its over-the-top best, time your visit for Chinese New Year in late January/early February, when the streets explode with firecrackers and lion dances are staged.

Covent Garden (Map 8)

In the 1630s Inigo Jones converted something that had started life as a vegetable field belonging to Westminster Abbey into the elegant square – or piazza – at Covent Garden. In time it became the haunt of such writers as Pepys, Fielding and Boswell in search of stimulating nightlife, but by Victorian times a fruit and veg market had been set up (immortalised in *My Fair Lady*, the 1964 screen adaptation of George Bernard Shaw's 1912 play *Pygmalion*). When the market was moved out to Nine Elms in Battersea in the 1980s, the old marketplace was transformed into one of central London's liveliest tourist meccas, with shops built into the old arcades. Where stallholders once flogged fresh produce, they now sell antiques, clothes and overpriced bric-a-brac.

Covent Garden (✆ *Covent Garden*) gets horribly overcrowded in summer but remains one of the few bits of London where pedestrians rule, and there's always a corner of relative peace where you can listen to the licensed buskers.

Overlooking the piazza to the south-west is **St Paul's Church** (*✆ 7836 5221, Bedford St WC2; admission free; open 9am-4.30pm Mon-Fri, 9am-12.30pm Sun*), long associated with the theatre and actors; inside are memorials to a number of stars of stage and screen, including Charlie Chaplin and Vivian Leigh, who were born (lest we forget) British. Designed by Inigo Jones in the 1630s, it's little more than a stone rectangle with a pitched roof; 'the handsomest barn in England', he called it. In the square in front, where Samuel Pepys watched England's first Punch and Judy show in 1662, you can still see buskers perform.

To the south-east of the piazza stand Jubilee and Floral halls, where markets are held (see the special section 'To Market, to Market'). Excavations by the Museum of London in the area have uncovered extensive traces of the Saxon settlement of Lundenwic, including wattle-and-daub housing.

Beyond the piazza are lively streets of clothes shops and bars, restaurants and designer gift shops. To the north, Floral St is where swanky designers such as Paul Smith, Joseph, Jones and Agnès B have outlets. Another block north and you're in Long Acre, which boasts Kookaï, Boss, Versace and a requisite Marks & Spencer. Here too you'll find bookshops (including Stanford's for guidebooks and maps) and St Martin's College of Fashion & Design. Neal St, a narrow lane leading from Long Acre to Shaftesbury Ave, is particularly worth exploring for both shopping and eating (see the Places to Eat chapter for details of Neal's Yard).

Tea and symphony: relax after shopping in Covent Garden's South Hall.

To the north-east of the piazza is the redeveloped **Royal Opera House** (☎ 7304 4000, **W** *www.royaloperahouse.org, Bow St WC2*), which is open to the public throughout the day and offers guided tours (£7/6 adult/senior & student) at 10.30am, 12.30pm and 2.30pm Monday to Saturday. For information about buying tickets for performances, see the Opera section in the Entertainment chapter.

London's Transport Museum (Map 8)

Tucked into the corner of Covent Garden between the Jubilee Hall and Tutton's Brasserie, London's Transport Museum (☎ 7565 7299, **W** *www.ltmuseum.co.uk, Covent Garden Piazza WC2; admission adult/senior, student and over-16s £5.95/3.95; open 10am-6pm Sat-Thur, 11am-6pm Fri)* tells how London made the transition from streets choked with horse-drawn carriages to the arrival of the DLR and the ultra-modern Jubilee Line extension, along with streets choked with motor cars. It's a much more interesting and timely story than you might suspect. The kids will love all the

hands-on exhibits and the activities in the interactive KidZones, including an Underground simulator.

Theatre Museum (Map 8)

A branch of the Victoria & Albert Museum, the Theatre Museum (☎ 7943 4700, **W** *www.theatremuseum.org, Russell St WC2; ✪ Covent Garden; admission free; open 10am-6pm Tues-Sun)* displays costumes and artefacts relating to the history of the theatre and more recently opera and ballet, including memorabilia of great actors and actresses such as David Garrick, Edmund Kean, Henry Irving and Ellen Terry, and costumes worn by prima ballerina Margot Fonteyn. Demonstrations highlight how stage make-up is applied, and you can hear recordings from the National Video Archive of Stage Performance before you return along a corridor where famous performers have left their hand-prints in paint.

The Strand (Map 6)

At the end of the 12th century, nobles built sturdy houses of stone with gardens along the 'beach' (ie, strand) of the Thames. The

Strand linked Westminster, the seat of political power, with the City, London's centre of industry and trade, and became one of the most prestigious places in London in which to live; in the 19th century Disraeli pronounced it the finest street in Europe. Today this thoroughfare, stretching nearly a mile, is a hotchpotch of shops, fine hotels, theatres and offices, on the doorsteps of which the homeless lay out their sleeping bags for the night. For things to see along the Strand, see the Fleet St & the Strand walking tour under The City later in this chapter.

Somerset House This splendid Palladian masterpiece (☎ *7845 4600,* Ⓦ *www .somerset-house.org.uk;* Ⓔ *Temple/Covent Garden)* was designed by William Chambers in 1775 and contains three fabulous museums: the Courtauld Gallery, the Gilbert Collection of Decorative Arts and the Hermitage Rooms. The central Great Court, long used as a car park for civil servants, is now a gauntlet of 55 dancing fountains open to the public from 7.30am to 11pm daily. Evening concerts take place here at 7pm on Thursday from late June to late July (£11/9 adult/ concession) and an ice-skating rink appears in winter. There are 45-minute highlight tours (£2.75) of Somerset House available at 11am and 3.15pm on Tuesday, Thursday and Saturday.

Courtauld Gallery Housed in the North Wing (or Strand Block), the Courtauld Gallery (☎ *7848 2526,* Ⓦ *www.courtauld.ac .uk, Somerset House, The Strand WC2; adult/senior & student/under-18s £4/3/free, free admission 10am-2pm Mon, joint ticket to Gilbert Collection & Courtauld Gallery adult/senior & student £8/5; open 10am-6pm daily mid-Apr–Aug plus 10am-9pm Fri late July-early Sept, 10am-6pm Mon-Sat, noon-6pm Sun rest of year)* displays some of the Courtauld Institute of Art's marvellous collection of paintings in grand surroundings after a £25 million architectural refurbishment. Exhibits include works by Rubens *(Moonlight Landscape)*, Bellini, Velásquez, Cranach *(Adam and Eve)* and Botticelli *(The Trinity).* However, for many

visitors the most memorable display is of Impressionist and postimpressionist art by Van Gogh, Cézanne, Rousseau, Gauguin, Toulouse-Lautrec, Manet, Pissarro, Sisley, Renoir, Degas and Monet.

The gallery also has a small exhibition of paintings by the 20th-century Bloomsbury artists Duncan Grant, Vanessa Bell and Roger Fry, together with colourful furniture produced by the Omega Workshops (also in Bloomsbury) and influenced by what were then newly discovered African masks and other ethnographical items.

One-hour guided tours of the gallery are available at noon on Tuesday, Thursday and Saturday (£5.50/5 adult/concession, including admission to the gallery). There's a branch of the *Coffee Gallery* on Museum St (see the Bloomsbury section in the Places to Eat chapter) on the lower ground floor.

Gilbert Collection of Decorative Arts
The vaults beneath the South Terrace, which boasts one of the finest views of the Thames, are home to the Gilbert Collection (☎ *7420 9400,* Ⓦ *www.gilbert-collection .org.uk, Somerset House, The Strand; adult/ senior & student/under-18s £5/4/free, joint ticket to Gilbert Collection & Courtauld Gallery adult/senior & student £8/5, free admission 4.30pm-5.30pm daily; open 10am-6pm daily).* This valuable collection of decorative arts includes such treasures as European silver, gold snuffboxes, Italian mosaics and 18th- and 19th-century English miniature portraits bequeathed to the nation

The eye-catching Somerset House on the Strand houses three top art collections.

PAUL BIGLAND

by London-born American businessman Arthur Gilbert. One-hour guided tours of the collection's highlights are at 2pm on Tuesday, Thursday and Saturday (£5.50/5 adult/concession, including gallery admission).

Hermitage Rooms The Hermitage Rooms (☎ 7845 4630, W www.hermitagerooms .com, Somerset House, The Strand WC2; adult/concessions/under-5s £6/4/free; open 10am-6pm daily mid-Apr–Aug plus 10am-9pm Fri late July-early Sept, 10am-6pm Mon-Sat, noon-6pm Sun rest of year), which shares space with the Gilbert Collection in the South Terrace, displays treasures (Old Masters, medals, jewellery, antique

Woolf at the door: Bloomsbury was once the haunt of London's literati.

GLENN BEANLAND

sculpture and so on) from the State Hermitage Museum in St Petersburg on a rotating basis changing every six to 10 months.

Royal Courts of Justice

At the eastern end of the Strand, where it joins Fleet St, you'll see the entrance to the Royal Courts of Justice (☎ 7936 6000, 460 The Strand; admission free; open 9am-4.30pm Mon-Fri), a gargantuan mélange of Gothic spires and pinnacles and burnished Portland stone, designed by GE Street in 1874. This is where civil cases (eg, libel) are tried and where many famous appeals against conviction have wound up. Criminal cases (murders, bank robberies and so on) are heard at the so-called Old Bailey, near St Paul's (see Central Criminal Court under The City later in this chapter).

Visitors are welcome to watch cases in progress (unless they're closed proceedings). Expect airport-like security checks and note cameras are banned.

BLOOMSBURY (Maps 3, 4 & 6)

East of Tottenham Court Rd and north of High Holborn, south of Euston Rd and to the west of Gray's Inn Rd, Bloomsbury is a peculiar mix of the University of London, the British Museum, beautiful Georgian squares and architecture, literary history, traffic, office workers, students and tourists. **Russell Square (Map 6)**, the very heart of Bloomsbury, is London's largest public square. It was laid out by Humphrey Repton in 1800 and has recently had a £1.4 million facelift, including the addition of a 10m-tall fountain.

Between the world wars these pleasant streets were colonised by a group of artists and intellectuals who became known collectively as the Bloomsbury Group. The novelists Virginia Woolf and EM Forster and the economist John Maynard Keynes are perhaps the best-known members.

The centre of literary Bloomsbury was **Gordon Square (Map 3)** where, at various times, Bertrand Russell lived at No 57, Lytton Strachey at No 51 and Vanessa and Clive Bell, Maynard Keynes and the Woolf family at No 46. Strachey, Dora Carrington and Lydia Lopokova (the future wife of Maynard Keynes) all took turns living at No 41. Not all the buildings, many of which now belong to the university, are marked with blue plaques.

Until recently, lovely **Bedford Square (Map 6)**, the only completely Georgian square still surviving in Bloomsbury, was home to many London publishing houses now swallowed up by multinational conglomerates and moved out to west London. They included Jonathan Cape, Chatto and the Bodley Head (set up by Woolf and her husband Leonard). These publishers were part-conspirators in creating and sustaining the Bloomsbury Group legend, churning out seemingly endless collections of letters, memoirs and biographies.

British Museum Highlights

- Benin Bronzes
- Elgin Marbles
- Egyptian mummies
- Rosetta Stone
- Sutton Hoo Treasure
- Lewis chess pieces
- Mildenhall Treasure
- Battersea shield & Waterloo helmet
- Lindow Man
- Oxus Treasure
- Portland Vase

British Museum (Map 6)

The British Museum (☎ 7323 8000, W www .thebritishmuseum.ac.uk, Great Russell St WC1; ⊖ Tottenham Court Road/Russell Square; admission free, £2 donation suggested; open 10am-5.30pm Sat-Wed, 10am-8.30pm Thur & Fri) is Britain's largest museum and one of the oldest in the world. It's also the most visited tourist attraction in London, with around six million annual visitors.

The collection is vast, diverse and exceedingly rich – so much so that it can seem pretty daunting. To make the most of the museum don't plan on seeing too much in one day; admission is free so you can come back several times to appreciate the museum's exhibits at your leisure.

The museum building is, in itself, striking. It was designed by Robert Smirke in 1823 and completed in 1847, though the central Reading Room with its large copper dome didn't open until 1857. The collections inside originated with the curiosities collected by Sir Hans Sloane (of Sloane Square fame), which the physician sold to the nation in 1753, and were augmented not long afterwards with manuscripts and books from two other major collections.

The British Museum has two entrances: the imposing Smirke-designed porticoed main entrance off Great Russell St to the

south, and a back entrance off Montague Place to the north, which tends to be less congested. If you come in through the front entrance, head straight for one of the information desks to the left or the right in the Great Court and ask for a list of the free eye-opener tours (see Guided Tours later). If you don't want to be shown around by someone else, use the plan of the museum to find your way around. The *Visit Guide* (£2.50) has a highlights tour and a clear plan.

From the main entrance you can choose to go left or upstairs. The following quick tour of the museum assumes you start by turning left to arrive in the galleries housing the ancient Assyrian finds from Nimrud, Nineveh and Khorsabad (rooms 6 to 10). Most striking are the vast human-headed winged lions (9th century BC) that used to guard the royal palace at Nimrud. The carved lion-hunt reliefs dating from the 7th century BC are almost as fascinating. To the east in room 4 are Egyptian sculptures and the **Rosetta Stone**, written in two forms of ancient Egyptian (hieroglyphics and demotic) and in Ancient Greek and discovered in 1799. The Rosetta Stone was the key to deciphering Egyptian hieroglyphics, which had stymied scholars up to that time. The famous **Egyptian mummies** are in rooms 62 and 63 on the upper floor and accessible via the eastern staircase.

West of these rooms on the main floor you'll come to the galleries housing finds from the classical Greek and Roman empires (rooms 11 to 23). Best known of the exhibits here are the **Elgin Marbles**, pilfered from the walls of the Parthenon on the Acropolis in Athens by Lord Elgin from 1801 to 1806, in room 18. The marbles used to provide parts of the frieze round the top of the temple; they are thought to show the great procession to the temple that took place during the Panathenaic Festival but have been pretty battered and beaten over the years. Greece has offered Britain the loan of hundreds of newly discovered classical treasures in exchange for the marbles, which the department of Culture is now considering. Other fine monuments include the reconstructed facade of the **Nereid Monument** from Xanthos in Turkey (room 17).

Avoiding Museum Fatigue

Warm-up exercises, half-hour breathers, a portable seat, bottled water and an energy-providing snack … it might sound as if you're preparing for a mountain trek but these are some of the recommendations for tackling London's museums offered by the experts. And with most major museums in London now free of charge, the temptation to see more and more is greater than ever. Take their advice.

The British Museum alone has more than 2½ miles of corridors, over seven million exhibits in 90 galleries and around six million visitors, all elbowing each other to see what they want to see in a limited amount of time. It's hardly surprising that many people feel worn out almost before they've crossed the threshold.

To avoid museum fatigue wear comfortable shoes and make use of the free cloakrooms. Be aware that standing still and walking slowly promote tiredness; whenever possible, sit down. Reflecting on the material and forming associations with it cause information to move from your short- to long-term memory; your experiences will thus amount to more than a series of visual sound-bites.

Tracking and timing studies suggest that museum-goers spend no more than 10 seconds viewing an exhibit and another 10 seconds reading the label as they try to take in as much as they can before succumbing to exhaustion. Your best bet in a large museum such as the British Museum or the Victoria & Albert is to choose a particular period or section and pretend that the rest is somewhere across town. You can get some useful sneak previews and make your decisions in advance by checking out the 24-Hour Museum Web site at **w** www .24hourmuseum.org.uk; it is linked to hundreds of museums in London, with details of great paintings and other works of art and some virtual-reality tours.

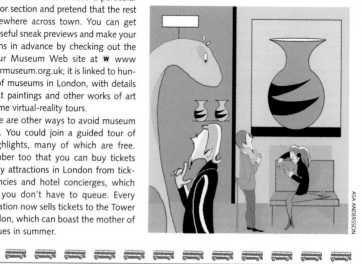

There are other ways to avoid museum fatigue. You could join a guided tour of the highlights, many of which are free. Remember too that you can buy tickets to many attractions in London from ticket agencies and hotel concierges, which means you don't have to queue. Every tube station now sells tickets to the Tower of London, which can boast the mother of all queues in summer.

ASA ANDERSSON

In room 21 you can see sculptures from the Mausoleum of Halicarnassus and in room 22 a carved column drum from the Temple of Artemis at Ephesus. These places were counted among the Seven Wonders of the Ancient World and are in modern-day Turkey.

Tucked away at the foot of the eastern staircase is the Mexican Gallery (room 27), with the fine **Mask of Tzcatlipoca**, with a turquoise mosaic laid over a real skull on display. Beyond that, in rooms 33 and 34, the Asian collections contain the wonderful **Amaravati Sculptures** (room 33A), Indian goddesses, dancing Shivas and serene cross-legged Buddhas in copper and stone.

If you climb the eastern staircase and turn left you'll enter more galleries devoted to western Asia (rooms 51 and 52). Here you'll find the stunning **Oxus Treasure**, a collection of 7th- to 4th-century BC pieces of Persian gold rescued from bandits in a Rawalpindi bazaar. It's believed that they originally hailed from the ancient Persian capital at Persepolis. In room 56 you'll discover the **Ur Treasure** of the Chaldees, including a beautiful model of a goat on its hind legs peering through gold leaves and a remarkable hollow box known as the Royal Standard of Ur. These artefacts are believed to date back to 2500 BC, placing them among the oldest exhibits in the museum.

Rooms 49 and 50 contain artefacts from Roman Britain and from Bronze Age and Celtic Europe (approximately 900 to 100 BC). This is where you'll see the stunning **Mildenhall Treasure**, a 28-piece silver dinner service dating from the 4th century AD, and the Celtic **Snettisham Treasure**, a hoard of gold and silver torques (necklaces). Also here are the **Battersea shield** and **Waterloo helmet** dredged from the Thames near the bridges whose names they bear. The Battersea shield dates from around 350 to 150 BC, the horned helmet, the only one of its kind ever found, from around 150 to 50 BC. The **Hoxne Treasure** is the largest horde of Roman coins ever found in Britain.

This is also where you'll find **Lindow Man**, an Iron Age unfortunate who seems to have been struck on the head with a narrow axe (there are holes in the skull) and then garrotted. His throat was probably slit open to bleed him as part of a ritualistic sacrifice. A Cheshire peat-bog preserved his gruesome, leathery remains until 1984 when he was sliced in half by a peat-cutting machine and uncovered. Poor old sod.

Eventually you'll arrive in rooms 41 to 43, which display medieval European art. Particularly interesting are the fragmentary **murals from St Stephen's Chapel** in the Palace of Westminster, now the Houses of Parliament. The chapel burned down in 1834 – but not before these scenes from the Book of Job were rescued. The two panels from the ceiling of the King's State Bedchamber, known as the Painted Chamber because of its 14th-century murals, were rediscovered in Bristol in 1993. They show a seraph and a prophet.

Here, too, you'll see the finds from **Sutton Hoo** (room 41), an Anglo-Saxon ship burial site dating from AD 620 near Woodbridge in Suffolk, that was excavated in 1939. Inside the remains of the wooden ship wonderful gold and garnet cloisonné shoulder clasps and purse decorations were found. Perhaps the most evocative sight is the helmet of the presumed king, but hurry up and come to see these treasures; the museum is planning to return many of them to the National Trust, which will exhibit the treasures in two purpose-built exhibition halls on the site where they were found.

Also worth seeing are the 67-piece Scandinavian **walrus ivory chess pieces** (room 42) found in the sandbanks on the Isle of Lewis in 1831 and dating from the mid-12th century, and the tiny **Dunstable Swan Jewel**, a 15th-century gold masterpiece with its feathers picked out in white enamel.

The *objets d'art* in rooms 44 to 48 would seem more at home in the Victoria & Albert Museum, but it's worth inspecting the late 16th-century Bohemian **ship-clock** – you'll be hard pressed to spot the clock-face tucked away at the foot of the main mast of a miniature ship. The **Hull-Grundy jewellery collection**, which includes pieces by Tiffany, Boucheron and other masters, should also not be missed.

On the landing leading up from the main stairs you'll see the stunning 4th-century **Roman mosaic** from Hinton St Mary, which incorporates the Christian chi-rho symbol. Look down into the stairwell and on the wall you'll see the 17th-century **Benin Bronzes**, plaques depicting soldiers, musicians and other scenes from everyday life that were stolen from the king and his chiefs in 1897, when a British company seized Benin City and overthrew the ruler.

Across the corridor you'll see more finds from the Greek and Roman Empires in southern Italy and Cyprus (rooms 69 to 73), including the blue and white **Portland Vase** (room 70), one of the first objects made of glass but perhaps most famous for having been smashed into 200 pieces by a visitor in 1845 and then painstakingly put together again. More antiquities from Egypt and from western Asia line the corridor between the eastern and western staircases. Room 66 covers Coptic Egypt, and beyond that and up some stairs lies a temporary exhibition gallery (room 90) that often has fine, free displays from the prints and drawings collection. Beyond that is a gallery devoted to Korean art. Continue upstairs and you'll come to the lovely Japanese Galleries (rooms 92 to 94).

As part of the millennium celebrations, the British Museum underwent a major renovation. The most important change was that the museum's inner courtyard, hidden from the public for almost a century and a half, was covered with a spectacular glass and steel roof designed by Norman Foster, and is now the light-filled **Great Court** *(open 9am-6pm Mon, 9am-9pm Tues, Wed & Sun, 9am-11pm Thur & Sat)*.

In the heart of the Great Court is the **Reading Room** *(open 10am-7.30pm Sat-Wed, 10am-8.30pm Thur-Fri)*, where Mahatma Gandhi and George Bernard Shaw studied, and Friedrich Engels and Karl Marx wrote *The Communist Manifesto.*

The northern end of the Great Court's lower level houses the museum's **African Galleries**. There are other galleries that are devoted to Greek and Roman sculpture and architecture.

Guided Tours The museum offers visitors free eyeOpener tours of individual galleries (eg, World of Asia in room 33, the Islamic World in room 34, Prehistoric and Roman Britain in room 49 and so on). These last 50 minutes and depart at 10.30am, 1.30pm, 2.30pm and 3.30pm daily. One-hour Focus tours cost £5/3 (adult/senior & student) and spotlight some of the museum's most important objects (Parthenon sculptures, Rosetta Stone, Assyrian reliefs etc), leaving at 3.15pm Monday to Saturday and 4.30pm on Sunday, with additional tours at 5pm and 7pm on Thursday and Friday. Ninety-minute Highlights tours (£7/4) leave at 11.30am and 12.30pm daily, with additional tours at 5pm and 7pm on Thursday and Friday.

Those who want to go it alone can rent the Museum Highlights Audio Tour (£2.50) or a more specialised one to the Parthenon sculptures (£3) from the information desk.

St George's Bloomsbury (Map 8)

A short distance south of the British Museum is St George's *(☎ 7405 3044, Bloomsbury Way WC1; ✜ Holborn/Tottenham Court Road; admission free; open 9.30am-5.30pm Mon-Fri, 10.30am-12.30pm Sun)*, another of Nicholas Hawksmoor's creations and finished in 1731. The church is notable not just for its portico of Corinthian capitals but for its steeple, which was inspired by the Mausoleum of Halicarnassus and is topped with a statue of George I in Roman dress. This steeple can just be made out in the background of Hogarth's influential print of the goings-on in *Gin Lane* in the area known as the Rookery (now Clerkenwell).

Dickens' House (Map 4)

This house *(☎ 7405 2127, W www.dickens museum.com, 49 Doughty St WC1; ✜ Russell Square; adult/senior & student/child 5-15/family £4/3/2/9; open 10am-5pm Mon-Sat)* is the only surviving residence of the many houses the great Victorian novelist occupied before moving to Kent. While living here from 1837 to 1839, he wrote *The Pickwick Papers*, *Nicholas Nickleby* and *Oliver Twist*, between bouts of worry over debts, deaths and his ever-growing family.

In Dickens' day, Doughty St was an exclusive neighbourhood with porters in gold-laced livery guarding gates at each end. The house itself has 11 reasonably interesting rooms, including a complete Victorian kitchen and lots of memorabilia, but only the drawing room has been restored to its original condition. Two desks illustrate Dickens' own rags-to-riches story: the rough-hewn wooden table where he worked as a 15-year-old Gray's Inn lawyer's clerk for a pittance and the velvet-topped desk he later used on reading tours of England and America.

HOLBORN & CLERKENWELL (Maps 6 & 8)

Holborn (**hoe**-b'n), the area north of the Strand and Fleet St and wedged between the City to the east, Covent Garden to the west and High Holborn to the north, includes several of the Inns of Court, the defunct Inns of Chancery and the wonderful Sir John Soane's Museum. It is the smallest of London's former metropolitan boroughs and takes its name from a tributary of the River Fleet (see the boxed text 'London's Underground Rivers' in the Facts about London chapter).

Immediately north-west of the City, Clerkenwell (**clarken**-well) gets its name from Clerk's Well in Farringdon Lane (below house Nos 14 to 16) where, according to a contemporary account by the monk William Fitz Stephen in 1174, the Parish Clerks of London performed miracle plays. Known in Victorian times for its appalling slums – the

so-called Rookery – and street crime, Clerkenwell was settled by Italians whose mark can still just be made out in some of the surviving cafes. The Italian revolutionary Mazzini settled here and Garibaldi dropped by in 1836. The great tenor Caruso also performed on the steps of St Peter's Church and Lenin edited the influential newspaper *Iskra* (Spark) from 37a Clerkenwell Green (now the Karl Marx Memorial Library; see Other Attractions later in this chapter), where he lived from 1902 to 1903.

Clerkenwell has become a very trendy corner of the capital in recent years, with the usual batch of pricey restaurants, and expensive property that exceeds Mayfair in cost. The area around Clerkenwell Green is very attractive, with St James's Church looming over the houses. They include the restored 18th-century Old Sessions House, supposedly haunted by a woman whose lover had been transported.

Inns of Court (Map 6)

There are four Inns of Court, clustered around Holborn and to the south of Fleet St: **Lincoln's Inn** (*☎ 7405 1393, Lincoln's Inn Fields WC2; ⊖ Holborn; grounds open 9am-6pm Mon-Fri, chapel 12.30pm-2.30pm Mon-Fri)*; **Gray's Inn** (*☎ 7458 7800, Gray's Inn Rd WC1; ⊖ Holborn/Chancery Lane; grounds open 10am-4pm Mon-Fri, chapel 10am-6pm Mon-Fri)*; **Inner Temple** (*☎ 7797 8250, King's Bench Walk EC4; ⊖ Temple; grounds open 10am-4pm Mon-Fri)*; and

Chim chim cheree! Glance up at the quaint roof-tops and chimney pots along Chancery Lane.

Middle Temple (☎ 7427 4800, Middle Temple Lane EC4; ✪ Temple; grounds open 10am-11.30am & 3pm-4pm Mon-Fri). The last two are part of the Temple complex between Fleet St and Victoria Embankment; for information on Temple Church, see The City later in this chapter.

All London barristers work from within one of the Inns, which boast a roll call of former members ranging from Oliver Cromwell and Charles Dickens to Mahatma Gandhi and Margaret Thatcher. It would take a lifetime spent working here to grasp all the intricacies and subtleties of the arcane protocols of the Inns – they're a lot like the Freemasons (both organisations date from the 13th century) and a lot of barristers are Masons as well.

Both Gray's Inn and the much prettier Lincoln's Inn have chapels and quadrangles as well as peaceful, picturesque gardens with lawns and plane trees that offer the chance for a stroll, especially early on weekday mornings before the hordes of barristers in wigs and gowns have started to rush around.

All four Inns were badly damaged during the war. Lincoln's Inn is relatively intact, with original 15th-century buildings, including the Tudor Lincoln's Inn Gatehouse on Chancery Lane (although the archway leading from the adjoining park, Lincoln's Inn Fields, is a replacement dating from 1957). Inigo Jones helped plan the chapel at Lincoln's Inn, which was built in 1623 and remains pretty well preserved. The less-interesting Gray's Inn chapel, which dates from 1689, was destroyed during WWII and rebuilt and expanded.

Staple Inn (Map 6)

Just opposite the start of Gray's Inn Rd on Holborn stands Staple Inn (1589), one of the eight Inns of Chancery, whose functions were superseded by the Inns of Court in the 18th century. Much of the original structure still stands, including the 16th-century shopfront facade, which was completely restored in the 1950s after wartime bombing. Most of the building is now occupied by the Institute of Actuaries and private offices. On the same side of Holborn but closer to Fetter Lane stood **Barnard's Inn**, redeveloped in 1991. Pip lived here with Herbert Pocket in Dickens' Great Expectations.

Sir John Soane's Museum (Map 8)

Sir John Soane's Museum (☎ 7405 2107, ⓦ www.soane.org, 13 Lincoln's Inn Fields WC2; ✪ Holborn; admission free; open 10am-5pm Tues-Sat, 6pm-9pm first Tues of month) is partly a beautiful – if quirky – house and partly a small museum representing one man's personal taste. Some visitors consider it their No 1 'small' London sight.

John Soane (1753–1837) was a leading architect who designed the Bank of England, Dulwich Picture Gallery and Pitshanger Manor, drawing on ideas he'd picked up while on an 18th-century Grand Tour of Italy. He married into money, which he poured into customising two houses in Lincoln's Inn Fields – this one and the one next door (which the museum hopes to expand into over the next couple of years). The building itself is a curiosity, with a glass dome bringing light to the basement, a lantern room filled with statuary, and a picture gallery where each painting folds away if pressed to reveal another one behind.

Soane's collection of Egyptiana predated the Victorian passion for such things and includes a sarcophagus of Seti I. It also includes the original Rake's Progress, William Hogarth's set of cartoon caricatures of late-18th-century London lowlife (see the boxed text 'Of Rakes & Harlots: Hogarth's World' in the Facts about London chapter).

There's an hour-long lecture tour (£3) at 2.30pm on Saturday.

St Andrew Holborn (Map 6)

This church (☎ 7353 3544, Holborn Viaduct EC4; admission free; open 9am-4.30pm Mon-Fri) on the south-eastern corner of Holborn Circus, which is first mentioned at the end of the 10th century, was rebuilt by Wren in 1686 and was the largest of his parish churches. The interior suffered severe damage during the bombings of 1941; much of what you see inside is original but brought from other churches.

Holborn Viaduct (Map 6)

This fine iron bridge with its four bronze statues was built in 1869 to link Holborn and Newgate St above what had been a valley created by the River Fleet and part of St Andrew Holborn's churchyard. The four statues represent Commerce and Agriculture (on the northern side) and Science and Fine Arts (on the southern side).

St John's Gate (Map 6)

What looks like a toy-town medieval gate cutting across St John's Lane (✆ Farringdon) turns out to be the real thing, dating from the early 16th century but heavily restored 300 years later. During the crusades the Knights of St John of Jerusalem were soldiers who took on a nursing role. In Clerkenwell they established a priory that originally covered around four hectares. Their church, St John's Clerkenwell in St John's Square, had a round nave like the one at Temple Church, and you can still see some of the outline picked out in brick outside.

St John's Gate was built as a grand entrance to the church in 1504. Although most of the buildings were destroyed when Henry VIII dissolved the priory along with all the others in the country between 1536 and 1540, the gate lived on to have a very varied afterlife, not least as a Latin-speaking coffee house run, without much success, by William Hogarth's father during Queen Anne's reign. The restoration dates from the period when it housed the Old Jerusalem Tavern in the 19th century.

Order of St John Museum

Inside St John's Gate is the small Order of St John Museum (✆ 7253 6644, St John's Lane EC1; admission free; open 10am-5pm Mon-Fri, 10am-4pm Sat). It recounts the history of the knights and their properties around the world, and of the modern British Order of St John, which has taken the knights' place as the St John Ambulance brigade.

To get the most out of a visit try to time it for 11am or 2.30pm on Tuesday, Friday or Saturday when you'll be given a guided tour (£4/3 adult/senior & student) of the restored church remains, including the fine Norman crypt with a sturdy alabaster monument commemorating a Castilian knight (1575), a battered monument showing the last prior William Weston as a skeleton in a shroud, and stained-glass windows showing the main figures in the story. You'll also be shown the Chapter Hall where the Chapter General of the Order meets every three months.

Charterhouse (Map 6)

Another remnant of medieval Clerkenwell is Charterhouse (✆ 7253 9503, Charterhouse Square EC1; ✆ Barbican/Farringdon; admission £3; open for guided tours 2.15pm Wed Apr-July or by special arrangement), all that remains of a Carthusian monastery founded in 1371 by Sir Walter de Manny, a knight of Edward III. The Carthusians, the strictest of all Roman Catholic monastic orders, refrained from eating meat, grew their own vegetables and took vows of silence, broken only for three hours on Sunday.

During the Reformation the monastery was oppressed, with at least three priors hanged at Tyburn and then quartered and a dozen monks sent to Newgate, where they were chained upright and died of starvation. Henry VIII confiscated the monastery in 1537 and it was passed on to various members of the nobility as private residences until Thomas Sutton, known at the time as the 'richest commoner in England', bought it in 1611. He opened a school for poor boys, which carried on here till 1872 when it moved to Godalming in Surrey and counted William Thackeray among its pupils. Sutton also opened an almshouse for destitute gentlemen; some three dozen pensioners (known as 'brothers') live here today.

Charterhouse was badly damaged during WWII but some of it has been reconstructed. The two-hour guided tour, which is the only way to visit Charterhouse, begins at the 14th-century gatehouse on Charterhouse Square and goes through Preachers' Court (notice the three original monks' cells in the western wall) and Master's Court. The latter leads on to the Great Hall, with its rebuilt hammer-beam roof, and the Great Chamber, where Queen Elizabeth I stayed on numerous occasions. The remains of the philanthropist Sutton lie within a finely carved marble tomb in the Chapel.

THE CITY (Maps 6 & 9)

The City of London is the 'square mile' on the northern bank of the Thames where the Romans first built a walled community some 2000 years ago. The boundaries of today's City haven't changed much and you can always tell when you're within them because the Corporation of London's coat of arms appears on the street signs, and the small statue of a griffin emblazoned with the motto *Domine Dirige Nos* (God Direct Us) marks the borders. This is the business heart of London where you'll find not only the Bank of England but also the headquarters of many British and overseas banks, insurance companies and other financial institutions.

St Paul's Cathedral and the Tower of London are both in the City. Here too you'll find the headquarters of many of London's livery companies and many of the churches built by Sir Christopher Wren after the Great Fire of 1666. There's been a feverish construction boom in the City over the past 15 years or so, with dozens of blocks and towers either being planned or under way.

A quiet weekend stroll when the offices and banks are closed offers a unique chance to appreciate the architectural richness of its famous buildings and atmopheric alleyways that now separate futuristic office towers. Bear in mind, though, that some City sights close at the weekend, as do the shops in Leadenhall Market and most of the pubs.

Barbican (Map 9)

Tucked into a corner of the City of London, where there was once a watchtower (or 'barbican'), the Barbican *(☎ 7638 8891 for information, 7638 4141 for the switchboard, W www.barbican.org.uk, Silk St EC2; ⊖ Barbican/Moorgate; open 9am-11pm Mon-Sat, 10.30am-11pm Sun)* is a vast urban development built on a large bomb site from WWII.

The original ambitious plan was to create a terribly smart, modern complex for offices, housing and the arts. Perhaps inevitably, the result was a forbidding series of wind tunnels with a dearth of shops, plenty of expensive high-rise flats and an enormous

The City's Livery Companies

In the Middle Ages most crafts-workers belonged to guilds that organised apprenticeships and were the prototypes of today's trade unions. The wealthier guilds built themselves magnificent halls, and their leaders wore suitably fine costumes, or liveries. These same leaders were eligible to stand for a series of offices, with the post of Lord Mayor of the City of London at the pinnacle.

While the old craft guilds may be no more, more than 100 livery companies live on (with a dozen of them considered the principal companies), and their leading lights still stand for office at the Court of Common Council, which runs the Corporation – and thus the City – of London. Although most of the original halls were destroyed in the Great Fire or by the Blitz, some have since been rebuilt and they're impressive, if largely inaccessible, places. One of the most interesting is the Merchant Taylors' Hall in Threadneedle St, which still retains its Great Kitchen in continued use since 1425. The wealthy Vintners' Company occupies the oldest surviving hall. It's on Upper Thames St and dates back to the late 17th century.

If you'd like to visit one of the halls you'll have to inquire at the Corporation of London Tourist Information Centre *(☎ 7332 1456, W www.cityoflondon.gov.uk)*; see Local Tourist Offices in the Facts for the Visitor chapter. They receive stocks of tickets for the Goldsmiths', Fishmongers', Ironmongers', Tallow Chandlers', Haberdashers' and Skinners' halls in February each year but they're snapped up pretty quickly. Otherwise, you can visit the Guildhall, where the liverymen meet to choose two sheriffs in June and again in September to elect the Lord Mayor.

CHARLOTTE HINDLE

Barbican Tower looms boldly over
the City of London

cultural centre lost in the middle. Here you will find the London home of the Royal Shakespeare Company (RSC), the London Symphony Orchestra and the London Classical Orchestra. There are also **two cinemas**, smaller theatrical auditoriums, and the wonderful **Barbican Gallery** (☎ 7638 8891, *Level 3, Barbican Centre, Silk St EC2; adult/senior, student & those aged 12-17 £7/5; open 10am-6pm Mon, Tues & Thur-Sat, 10am-9pm Wed, noon-6pm Sun*) with among the best photographic exhibits in London. But be warned – even Londoners get to the Barbican Centre early to find their way to the right spot at the right time.

For details of the theatres, cinemas and concert halls, see the Entertainment chapter. For details of the highly regarded brasserie **Searcy's**, see the Places to Eat chapter.

Museum of London (Map 9)

Despite its unprepossessing setting amid the concrete walkways of the Barbican (look for gate 7), the Museum of London (☎ 7600 3699 or 7600 0807, [W] *www.museumof london.org.uk, London Wall EC2;* ⊖ *Barbican; admission free; open 10am-5.50pm*

Mon-Sat, noon-5.50pm Sun) is one of the city's finest museums, showing how the city has evolved from the Ice Age to the Internet. It is also the world's largest urban-history museum, with more than a million objects on display and in its archives.

The museum, purpose-built in 1976, is divided into several sections, tracing the history of the city from the prehistoric period to the present day. The Archaeological Archive houses material from archaeological excavations in London; the new World City Gallery looks at the growth of London from a European capital in late 18th century to the nerve centre of a world empire by the early 20th century.

The sections on Roman Britain and Roman Londinium make use of the nearby ruins of a Roman fort discovered during road construction, and examine such finds as the spectacular 4th-century lead coffin and stone sarcophagus containing the remains of a well-to-do young Roman woman that were discovered at a development site at Spitalfields in early 1999. Otherwise, the displays work steadily through the centuries, using audiovisual materials to show such events as the Great Fire of London.

There are items such as one of the two shirts Charles I wore on the morning of his execution in 1649 'lest my shivering be taken as a sign of fear', but the focus is on ordinary people as much as on the buildings and streets; Dickens' London – a city of mass prostitution and sweatshop labour – makes for particularly poignant stories. The museum also has some ace special exhibitions. Part of the museum's stored collection dealing with London's port and the Thames has been transferred to the long-gestating Museum in Docklands (see the Wapping & the Isle of Dogs walking tour).

The pleasant *Museum Café* opposite the entrance serves light meals 10am to 5.30pm (from 11.30am on Sunday). The fine *bookshop* has a wide selection of fictional and factual accounts of London.

Smithfield Market (Map 6)

Smithfield (☎ 7248 3151, *West Smithfield EC1;* ⊖ *Farringdon)* is central London's

THINGS TO SEE & DO

last surviving meat market. For details see the special section 'To Market, to Market'.

St Bartholomew-the-Great (Map 6)

One of London's oldest churches, adjoining one of London's oldest hospitals, St Bartholomew-the-Great *(☎ 7606 5171, W www.greatbarts.com, West Smithfield EC1; ⊖ Barbican; open 8.30am-5pm Tues-Fri, 10.30am-1.30pm Sat, 8am-8pm Sun)* is a stone's throw from the Barbican and worth more than a fleeting visit. The authentic Norman arches and details lend this holy space an ancient calm; approaching from nearby Smithfield Market through the restored 13th-century archway is like walking back in time. Hogarth was baptised here, Benjamin Franklin apprenticed himself as a printer here and scenes from the films *Four Weddings and a Funeral* and *Shakespeare in Love* were shot here.

Three blocks to the south-west, perched atop the corner of Cock Lane and Gilspur St and opposite **St Bartholomew's Hospital** is a small statue of a corpulent boy 'in memory put up for the fire of London occasioned by the sin of gluttony 1666'. It was once the site of the Fortune of War tavern, where 'resurrectionists' (body snatchers) took corpses to be appraised and purchased by surgeons from the hospital.

Central Criminal Court (Old Bailey) (Map 6)

All Britain's major gangsters, serial killers and compulsive liars (eg, Jeffrey Archer eventually – we hope – find themselves at the Central Criminal Court *(public gallery ☎ 7248 3277, Cnr Newgate St & Old Bailey; open 10am-1pm & 2pm-5pm Mon-Fri)*. It's better known as the Old Bailey after the street on which it stands (*baillie* was Norman French for 'fortified church'). Look up at the great copper dome and you'll see the figure of justice holding a sword and scales in her hands; unusually she is *not* blindfolded, which has sparked many a sarcastic comment from those being charged here.

The old Newgate Prison, dating from the 12th century and site of innumerable

JULIET COOMBE

See no evil? The blindfold-free figure of jusitce atop the Old Bailey

hangings, once stood here. Like most London prisons it was burned down during the Gordon Riots of 1780, only to rise again from the ashes to incarcerate yet more prisoners until 1902.

St Paul's Cathedral (Map 9)

St Paul's Cathedral *(☎ 7236 4128, W www .stpauls.co.uk, St Paul's Churchyard; ⊖ St Paul's; admission adult/senior & student/child aged 6-16 £5/4/2.50; open 8.30am-5pm Mon-Sat)* was built, amid much controversy, by Sir Christopher Wren between 1675 and 1710. It stands on the site of four previous cathedrals, the first of which dated from 604.

St Paul's was one of the 50 commissions that Wren was given after the Great Fire of London wiped out most of the city. Plans for alterations had already been made, but the fire presented him with the opportunity to build from scratch. Several plans were spurned before the authorities accepted the current design.

The dome still dominates the City and the only church dome that exceeds it in size is that of St Peter's in Rome. Pictures of the cathedral miraculously surviving the devastation of WWII bombing can be seen in a glass case in the southern choir aisle; fortunately, the dome survived virtually unharmed, although other parts of the cathedral were not left entirely unscathed. The windows were blown out (hence the large quantity of clear glass) and various other parts were also damaged.

A **statue of Queen Anne** stands in front of the Great West Door, which serves as the main entrance. But before you enter, take a moment to walk around to the north of the cathedral (that's to the left as you face the large stairway). A long overdue **monument to the people of London** – not all those warmongers, sabre-rattlers and heroes at rest in the cathedral's crypt – was unveiled in the small garden just outside the north transept in St Paul's Churchyard in 1999. Simple but elegant, it honours the 32,000 civilians killed (and another 50,000 seriously injured) in the defence of the city and the cathedral during WWII. It is largely due to them that you can still stand today and admire the gem that is St Paul's Cathedral. Enjoy, but never forget these brave souls; as the inscription says: 'Remember before God, the people of London 1939–1945'.

From the main entrance, proceed up the northern aisle, past the **All Souls' Chapel** and the **Chapel of St Dunstan**, dedicated to the 10th-century archbishop of Canterbury, and the grandiose **Duke of Wellington Memorial** (1875) on the left, until you reach the central pavement area under the dome. It is decorated in a compass design and bears Wren's epitaph in Latin: *Lector, si monumentum requiris, circumspice* (Reader, if you seek his monument, look around you). Some 30m above the paved area is the first of three domes – actually a dome, inside a cone, inside a dome – supported by eight massive columns. The walkway around its base is called the **Whispering Gallery**, because if you talk close to the wall it carries your words around to the opposite side 32m away.

JULIET COOMBE

The dome of St Paul's, designed by Sir Christopher Wren, is the second largest in the world.

The Whispering Gallery as well as the **Stone Gallery** and the **Golden Gallery** can be reached by a staircase on the western side of the south transept (ie, at about 'five o'clock' on the central paved area as you face the altar). All in all there are 259 steps to the Whispering gallery, another 119 to the Stone Gallery and 152 more steps to the top altar; that's a total of 530 steps to climb up and down. But even if you can't make it right up to the Golden Gallery, it's worth struggling as far as the Stone Gallery for one of the best views of London.

In the north transept chapel is Holman Hunt's celebrated painting *The Light of the World*, which depicts Christ knocking at an overgrown door that, symbolically, can only be opened from the inside. Beyond are the **quire** (or chancel), whose ceilings and arches dazzle with green, blue, red and gold mosaics, and the high altar. The ornately carved **choir stalls** by Grinling Gibbons on either side of the quire are worth a look as

are the **ornamental wrought-iron gates** separating the aisles from the altar by Jean Tijou (both men also worked on Hampton Court Palace). Walk around the altar, with its massive gilded oak canopy, to the **American Memorial Chapel**, a memorial to the 28,000 Americans based in Britain who lost their lives during WWII.

As you walk round the southern side of the ambulatory look for the **effigy of John Donne** (1573–1631), once dean of St Paul's, standing upright in his shroud in a niche. For whomever the bell tolled, it most decidedly tolled for him. Almost opposite is a glass case with photographs of **St Paul's during WWII**.

On the eastern side of the south transept, close to a memorial to the painter JMW Turner, a staircase leads down to the Crypt, Treasury and OBE Chapel, where services (weddings, funerals and so on) reserved for members of the Order of the British Empire are held. The **Crypt** has memorials to up to

ST PAUL'S CATHEDRAL

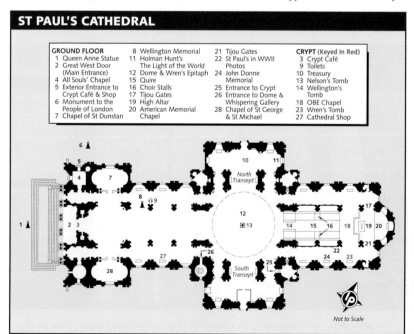

GROUND FLOOR	8 Wellington Memorial	21 Tijou Gates	CRYPT (Keyed In Red)
1 Queen Anne Statue	11 Holman Hunt's	22 St Paul's in WWII	3 Crypt Café
2 Great West Door	The Light of the World	Photos	9 Toilets
(Main Entrance)	12 Dome & Wren's Epitaph	24 John Donne	10 Treasury
4 All Souls' Chapel	15 Quire	Memorial	13 Nelson's Tomb
5 Exterior Entrance to	16 Choir Stalls	25 Entrance to Crypt	14 Wellington's
Crypt Café & Shop	17 Tijou Gates	26 Entrance to Dome &	Tomb
6 Monument to the	19 High Altar	Whispering Gallery	18 OBE Chapel
People of London	20 American Memorial	28 Chapel of St George	23 Wren's Tomb
7 Chapel of St Dunstan	Chapel	& St Michael	27 Cathedral Shop

Not to Scale

RICHARD I'ANSON

Fleet St was once 'London's Street of Shame'.

child with Peter perched on his outstretched hand. The ashes of the architect Edwin Lutyens (1869–1944) rest in a nearby niche.

The **Treasury** displays some of the cathedral's plate, along with some spectacular needlework, including Beryl Dean's Jubilee cope (bishop's cloak) of 1977 showing spires of 73 London churches and its matching mitre. The *Crypt Cafe* and *Refectory* restaurant open 9am to 5pm Monday to Saturday (from 11am on Sunday).

Guided Tours Audioguide tours lasting 45 minutes cost £3.50/3 per adult/senior & student and guided 90-minute tours (adult/senior & student/child aged 6-16 £2.50/2/1) leave the tour desk at 11am, 11.30am, 1.30pm and 2pm. There are organ recitals (free) at St Paul's at 5pm most Sundays, as well as celebrity recitals (adults/concessions £7.50/5) at 6.30pm on the first Thursday of the month between May and October. Evensong takes place at 5pm most weekdays and at 3.15pm on Sunday.

Fleet St (Map 6)

From the time Wynkyn de Worde moved Caxton's printing press from Westminster to a shop beside St Bride's church in 1500, Fleet St (⊖ Blackfriars) has been ink-splattered. In the 20th century it earned the nickname of 'London's Street of Shame', where printing presses, stoked by gossip and half-truths, churned out their scurrilous product: the British tabloid newspaper. But then the mid-1980s brought Rupert Murdoch, new technology and the Docklands redevelopment. Now that the action has moved eastwards only ghosts linger on, such as El Vino's, once the journos' preferred watering hole, and the glamorous former Daily Telegraph building (1928), now occupied by assorted banks.

Like Whitehall in Westminster, Fleet St and its surroundings are so full of interesting sights that the best way to take it all in is to follow the Fleet St & the Strand walking tour later in this chapter. Those interested in only the most important sights – St Bride's church, Dr Johnson's House and Prince Henry's Room – should read on.

300 military demigods, including Wellington, Florence Nightingale, Kitchener and Nelson, who is directly below the dome in a black sarcophagus (originally made for Cardinal Wolsey); on the surrounding walls are plaques in memory of those from the Commonwealth who died in various wars and conflicts in the 20th century: from Gallipoli (1915) through the world wars and Korea to the Falklands (1982) and Kuwait (1991). There are also effigies rescued from the previous cathedral that look rather the worse for wear; a few were saved from the Great Fire but most were damaged by Cromwell's men. A niche exhibits Wren's controversial plans and his actual working model.

The most poignant memorial of all is to Sir Christopher himself. It is south-west of the **OBE Chapel** and is just a simple slab with his name, the year of his death (1723) and his age ('XCI'). An amusing memorial is that to the sculptor George Frampton (1860–1933), who did the statue of Peter Pan in Hyde Park. It shows a very young

FLEET STREET & THE STRAND

This walk takes you from Fleet St to the Strand, the roads that have linked London's two opposing worlds for centuries: the business-minded City of London and political Westminster.

Begin the tour at Ludgate Circus (⊖ Blackfriars) and walk westwards along Fleet St, one-time home to the nation's national newspapers. Almost immediately on the left is a gateway leading to **St Bride's church (1)**, designed by Sir Christopher Wren. The office of the newswire service Reuters is farther along at 85 Fleet St.

On the northern side of the street at No 135 is **Peterborough Court (2)**, the former *Daily Telegraph* building, designed by Elcock and Sutcliffe in 1928 and variously described as 'jazz modern' and 'neo-Greek'. Next door, at 129 Fleet St, is **Salisbury Court (3)**, the Art Deco erstwhile home of the *Daily Express*.

Farther along on the northern side you'll see a narrow alleyway called Wine Office Court (where the excise office stood until 1665), which leads to a famous London pub, **Ye Olde Cheshire Cheese (4)**. Several Georgian buildings line the alleyway.

Walk back to Fleet St and continue westwards along the same side. At No 154 you pass **Bouverie House (5)**, once home to the *Sun* newspaper. Turn right at narrow Johnson's Court, which leads to Gough Square and **Dr Johnson's House (6)**. The wooden chair on which he used to sit while drinking at **Ye Olde Cock Tavern (7)** is preserved on the 1st-floor landing. The tavern, the oldest in Fleet St, is a short distance to the west on the other side of the street at No 22 and was a favourite of the poet TS Eliot. The colourful cockerel on its pub sign is said to have been designed by Grinling Gibbons, whose work adorns many London churches, including St Paul's Cathedral. Pepys, Dr Johnson, Goldsmith and Dickens all drank here – when they weren't knocking them back at Ye Olde Cheshire Cheese.

Opposite the Cock stands **St Dunstan-in-the-West (8)**, which was built by John Shaw in 1832 and boasts a spectacular octagonal lantern tower. Look out for Elizabeth I on the facade, the only such outdoor statue of the Virgin Queen, which stood on Ludgate until it was demolished in 1760. You can't miss Gog and Magog (see the boxed text later in this chapter) in the recess above the clock outside; they swing round and club the bells beside them on the hour.

Farther west at No 17 is **Prince Henry's Room (9)** and beyond that an archway leading to **Temple Church (10)** in the Inner Temple.

In the centre of Fleet St a statue of a griffin bestriding an elaborately carved plinth marks the site of the original **Temple Bar (11)**, where the City of Westminster becomes the City of London. The plinth is decorated with statues of Queen Victoria and her husband, Prince Albert, together with symbols of Art and Science, and War and Peace.

The **Wig & Pen Club (12)** at Nos 229 to 230 on the Strand dates from 1625 and is the only Strand building to have survived the Great Fire of 1666; it's now a restaurant. Have a look at the symbolic wigs and pens in the external plasterwork.

distance: about 1.5miles
start: Ludgate Circus ⊖ Blackfriars
finish: Lancaster Place ⊖ Covent Garden

As you proceed westwards look up to appreciate the fine architecture. A few doors west of the Wig & Pen, at Nos 222 to 225, an Art Deco branch of **Lloyd's Bank (13)** has carved fish twined around its circular windows and elaborate tiles adorning the recess now housing its cash machines. Just beyond on the same side at No 216 is **Twinings (14)**, a teashop opened by Thomas Twining in 1706 and believed to be the oldest company in London still trading on the same site and owned by the same family. The colourful sign above the door incorporates two Chinese and a lion, recalling the name of the original shop: the Golden Lyon. On the northern side of the Strand is the extraordinary neo-Gothic confection of the **Royal Courts of Justice (15)**.

The church in the centre of the road is **St Clement Danes (16)** (☎ 7242 8282; open 8.30am-4.30pm Mon-Fri, 9am-3.30pm Sat, 9am-12.30pm Sun). The original church was designed by Sir Christopher Wren in 1682, with the steeple added by James Gibbs in 1719; only the walls and steeple survived the bombings of 1941. In 1958 the church was rebuilt for the Royal Air Force; 800-plus slate badges of different squadrons and units of the RAF are set into the nave pavement. At 9am, noon, 3pm or 6pm the church bells chime out the old nursery rhyme 'Oranges and Lemons' (see the boxed text 'A Church for All Chimes' later in this chapter). The statue in front of the church is that of the controversial Sir Arthur 'Bomber' Harris, Marshall of the Royal Air Force, who led the bombing raids over Germany, including Dresden in which 10,000 civilians were incinerated, during WWII.

Continue west along the Strand with **Australia House (17)**, designed by Marshall Mackenzie between 1912 and 1918, and **Bush House (18)**, built in 1920, on your right. Part of the latter houses the BBC World Service offices. The pile that is **India House (19)** dates from 1930.

In the centre of the road is **St Mary-le-Strand (20)**, designed by James Gibbs between 1715 and 1724 and the church of the Women's Royal Naval Service.

The elegant building to the south is **Somerset House (21)**, designed by Sir William Chambers in 1774 and completed in 1835. It now houses assorted government offices as well as the **Courtauld Gallery (22)**, **Hermitage Rooms (23)** and **Gilbert Collection of Decorative Arts (24)**.

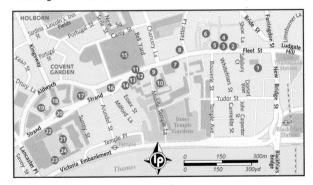

St Bride's, Fleet St This small, perfect church (☎ 7353 1301, Fleet St EC4; open 8am-4.45pm daily) is the eighth on this site. The present structure was designed by Sir Christopher Wren in 1671 and was his tallest (and most expensive) church after St Paul's. The add-on spire (1703) is said to have inspired the design of the tiered wedding cake. The church was hit by bombs in December 1940, and the interior is wood-panelled, modern and not particularly attractive.

St Bride's is still referred to as 'the journalists' church' or 'the printers' cathedral' and a quite moving chapel in the northern aisle honours journalists who have died or been injured in the course of their work. Be sure to descend to the crypt, which contains a small museum of the printing trade amid the foundations of previous churches and Roman remains found during postwar renovations, including traces of a Roman house. On display, too, is the party dress of one Susannah Pritchard, wife of William Rich (1755–1811), the pastry cook credited with modelling his wedding cakes on the steeple.

Dr Johnson's House This well-preserved Georgian town house (☎ 7353 3745, W www .drjh.dirco.co.uk, 17 Gough Square EC4; adult/senior & student/child aged 5-14/ family £4/3/1/9; open 11am-5.30pm Mon-Sat May-Sept, 11am-5pm Mon-Sat rest of year) belonged to Dr Johnson, who lived here from 1748 to 1759. Johnson was a lexicographer who, along with six full-time assistants working in the attic upstairs, compiled the first English dictionary.

Johnson is also famous for his witty, scathing aphorisms, all written down by his amanuensis and fellow Scot, James Boswell. (A modern office building nearby – Boswell House – carries on the latter's memory.) It was Johnson who claimed: 'When a man is tired of London he is tired of life; for there is in London all that life can afford'.

The house is full of pictures of friends and intimates of Johnson, including his black manservant Francis Barber to whom he was very generous in his will – there's a copy on display). A video provides background information on Johnson and Boswell, and the

SIMON BRACKEN

It might be London's financial hub but the City still has many historical offerings.

18th-century antiburglar devices fitted to the front door are interesting. In Gogh Square is a modern statue of Johnson's cat, Hodge, haughtily eating oysters.

Prince Henry's Room Just before the archway leading to Temple Church, and to the left of the outdoor newsstand, is Prince Henry's Room (☎ 7936 2710, 17 Fleet St EC4; admission free; open 11am-2pm Mon-Sat), the 1st-floor room of a building that dates from the 16th century but was extensively remodelled as a tavern with an overhanging half-timbered facade in 1611. Since the overhanging rooms were known as the Prince's Arms, the feathers of the Prince of Wales appear in the external woodwork. The room, with items related to the life and writings of Samuel Pepys, boasts the best Jacobean plaster ceiling in London, some original oak panelling and stained glass.

Temple Church (Map 6)

Temple Church (☎ 7353 8559, Inner Temple, King's Bench Walk EC4; ⊖ Temple/ Blackfriars; open 11am-6pm Wed-Fri, 11am-2.30pm Sat, 12.45pm-2.45pm Sun) is just off Fleet St, under the archway next to Prince Henry's Room. Duck under it and you'll find yourself in the Inner Temple, one of the Inns of Court. Temple Church was originally planned and built by the secretive Knights Templar between 1161 and 1185. They modelled it on the Church of the Holy Sepulchre in Jerusalem, using Purbeck marble for the pillars, and the core of the building is the only round church left in London. In 1240 a more conventional, if elongated, Early English chancel was added.

Although the Knights Templar were eventually suppressed for being too powerful and their lands leased to the lawyers who set up the Inns of Court, stone effigies of 13th-century knights still adorn the floors of the circular nave; some of them are cross-legged but contrary to popular belief this doesn't necessarily mean they were crusaders. Look out, too, for the grotesque faces peeping down from the circular wall just above eye level. In a couple of instances ears are being nibbled by monsters.

Externally the most interesting feature is the Norman western door with its elaborately moulded porch. It's set into a dip that shows how far the ground level has risen over the centuries. The church was badly damaged during WWII but has since been sensitively restored to serve as the private chapel of Middle and Inner temples.

Westminster Abbey and St Paul's Cathedral aside, this is possibly London's most interesting and architecturally important church. Don't miss it.

Guildhall (Map 9)

The Guildhall *(☎ 7606 3030, ⓦ corpof london.gov.uk, Gresham St EC2; ⊖ Bank; admission free; open 10am-5pm daily May-Sept, 10am-5pm Mon-Sat rest of year),* which sits exactly in the centre of the square mile, has been the City's seat of government for nearly 800 years. The present building dates from the early 15th century and the walls have survived both the Great Fire of 1666 and the Blitz of 1940, although the surrounding development makes it hard to appreciate them from the outside.

Visitors can see the **Great Hall** where the mayor and sheriffs are still elected, a vast empty space with church-style monuments and the shields and banners of the 12 principal livery companies of London (see the boxed text 'The City's Livery Companies' earlier in this chapter) lining the walls. The impressive wooden roof is a postwar reconstruction by Giles Gilbert Scott. The

minstrels' gallery at the western end carries statues of Gog and Magog (see the boxed text below), modern replacements of the 18th-century figures destroyed in the Blitz. Among the monuments to look for are those to Winston Churchill, Admiral Nelson, the Duke of Wellington and the two prime ministers Pitt the Elder and Younger.

The Guildhall's stained glass was blown out during the Blitz but a modern window in the south-western corner depicts the City's history; look out for Dick Whittington and his cat, old and new St Paul's, and modern landmarks such as the Lloyd's of London building. Set into two nearby windowsills you can also see standard measures for feet, yards and metres.

Meetings of the Common Council are still held in the hall every third Thursday of each month (except August) at 1pm, and the Guildhall hosts an annual flower show and various ceremonial banquets, including the one for the Booker Prize, the leading British literary prize.

Beneath the Great Hall is London's largest medieval crypt with 19 stained-glass windows showing the livery companies' coats of arms. The crypt can only be seen on a free **guided tour** *(☎ 7606 3030 ext 1463).*

The buildings to the west house Corporation of London offices and the **Guildhall**

Gog & Magog

According to the 12th-century *Historia Regum Britanniae* (History of the Kings of Britain) by Geoffrey of Monmouth, Britain was once inhabited by giants who were conquered by Brutus the Trojan and his compatriot, Corineus. Brutus founded Troia Nova (New Troy), or London, while Corineus established Cornwall after hurling the last of the great giants, the 3.5m-tall chieftain Gogmagog, into the sea.

By the 18th century Gog and Magog were thought to have been the last two surviving giants, forced to work for Brutus in his palace on the site of today's Guildhall. The effigies of the giants there are the third since the reign of Henry V.

Library (☎ 7606 3030, Aldermanbury EC2; open 9.30am-4.45pm Mon-Sat), founded in about 1420 under the terms of Richard 'Dick' Whittington's will. It is divided into three sections for research: Printed Books, Manuscripts and Prints, Maps and Drawings. Also here is the **Clockmakers' Company Museum** (☎ 7332 1868, Guildhall Library, Aldermanbury EC2; admission free; open 9.30am-4.45pm Mon-Fri), which has a collection of more than 700 clocks and watches dating back some 500 years. The clock museum sometimes closes for an hour or two on Monday to wind the clocks.

Guildhall Art Gallery Located to the south-east of the Great Hall, the Guildhall Art Gallery (☎ 7332 3700, ⓦ www.guildhall-art-gallery.org.uk, Guildhall Yard EC2; ☻ Bank; adult/senior & student/family £2.50/1/5; open 10am-5pm Mon-Sat, noon-4pm Sun) contains a small selection of the Corporation of London's collection of more than 4000 works. The museum reopened in 1999 for the first time since WWII, when the original building (1885) was destroyed. Most of the works are of historical interest rather than artistic merit.

Church of St Lawrence Jewry (Map 9)

Along the south-western side of Guildhall Yard stands St Lawrence Jewry (☎ 7600 9478, Gresham St EC2 ☻ Bank; admission free; open 7am-1pm Mon-Fri), the church of the Corporation of London, which explains its excellent condition. It was originally built by Sir Christopher Wren in 1677

A Church for All Chimes

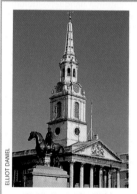

ELLIOT DANIEL

St Martin-in-the-Fields

Oranges & lemons, say the bells of St Clements
Bulls' eyes & targets, say the bells of St Margarets
Pokers & tongs, say the bells of St Johns
Pancakes & fritters, say the bells of St Peters
Two sticks & an apple, say the bells at Whitechapel
Old Father Baldpate, say the bells at Aldgate
Maids in white aprons, say the bells of St Catherines
Brickbats & tiles, say the bells of St Giles
Kettles & pans, say the bells at St Annes
You owe me five farthings, say the bells of St Martins
When will you pay me, say the bells of Old Bailey
When I grow rich, say the bells of Shoreditch
Pray, when will that be, say the bells of Stepney
I'm sure I don't know, says the great bell at Bow
Here comes a candle to light you to bed
Here comes a chopper to chop off your head.

'Oranges & Lemons', the nursery rhyme that incorporates the names of many churches and landmarks in the City and east London, first surfaced in 1744. It's generally agreed that St Clements was St Clement Danes (or perhaps St Clement Eastcheap near the docks where citrus fruit was once unloaded) and St Martins was St Martin-in-the-Fields, while the bells of Old Bailey belonged to St Sepulchre, Holborn, the bells of Shoreditch to St Leonards, and the bells of Stepney to St Dunstan, Stepney. The great bell at Bow belonged to St Mary-le-Bow and was the one whose range decided who was and who was not a Cockney. The rest is just guesswork, and some believe the writer just plucked out of the air the names of saints that happened to rhyme (sort of) with the chosen phrase. That theory is given more credence by the fact that the names of the churches are not always the same. In some surviving versions of the rhyme, for example, Shoreditch is Fleet Ditch and Bow has become Paul.

but was almost completely rebuilt after WWII. The arms of the City of London adorn the organ case at the western end. In the northern **Commonwealth Chapel**, be-decked with the flags of member-nations, a modern (and bad) painting of the Madonna and Child incorporates images of the sins of the modern world: financial greed, use of drugs and pornography, and a preoccupa-tion with living standards.

As the name of the church suggests, this was once part of the Jewish quarter – the centre being Old Jewry, the street to the south-east. The district was ransacked and some 500 Jews were killed in 1262 when a Christian claimed he had been charged too much interest by a Jewish moneylender. Edward I expelled the entire community from London to Flanders in 1290. They did not return until the late 17th century.

Bank (Map 9)

One of the best tube stations for exploring the heart of the City is Bank, which brings you out at the point where seven bank-filled streets converge. Take Prince's St north-westwards to get to the Guildhall or head north-eastwards along Threadneedle St for the Bank of England Museum.

Squeezed in between Threadneedle St and Cornhill to the east is the **Royal Exchange**, the third building on a site originally chosen in 1564 by Thomas Gresham, whose grass-hopper emblem is still on the weather vane. Until 1992 you could watch the London In-ternational Financial Futures Exchange in hectic action. Now however, it has moved to newer concrete-and-glass premises at the **Stock Exchange** farther along Threadneedle St and is closed to the public. The steps of the Royal Exchange provide a great vantage point for observing the citadel that is the Bank of England to the north.

Lombard St, named after the Italian bankers who ran London's money markets between the 13th and 16th centuries after the Jews had been expelled, heads off to the south-east. Notice the large banking signs, some bearing the bank's founding date: a grasshopper (1563), a running mare (1677), a cat and a fiddle. Such signs were commonplace everywhere in London until they started falling in high winds and killing people. They were banned here until 1901 when they were first hung out again to mark Edward VII's coronation.

In the angle between Lombard St and King William St to the south you'll see the twin towers of Hawksmoor's **St Mary Woolnoth** (☎ 7626 9701; open 8am-5pm Mon-Fri), built in 1717. The huge Corin-thian columns of its interior are a foretaste of his even more splendid Christ Church in Spitalfields. St Mary Woolnoth was Hawks-moor's only City church.

Between King William St and Walbrook stands the grand, porticoed **Mansion House** (☎ 7626 2500, W www.cityoflondon.gov.uk), the mid-18th-century work of George Dance the Elder built as the official residence of the Lord Mayor of London. It's not open to the public, though group tours are some-times available when booked in advance.

Walbrook, which heads off to the south, is named after one of London's lost rivers (see the boxed text 'London's Underground Rivers' in the Facts about London chap-ter). Here you'll find **St Stephen Walbrook** (☎ 7283 4444, 39 Walbrook EC3; admission free; open 10am-4pm Mon-Thur, 10am-3pm Fri), built in 1679. Many people (including us) regard St Stephen Walbrook as the finest of Wren's City churches; it's certainly the one where he experimented with a dome before embarking on St Paul's Cathedral. Some 16 pillars with Corinthian capitals rise up to support the dome and ceiling, parting in the middle to provide a central open space now filled with a large creamy-grey boulder, actually an altar by Henry Moore and re-ferred to as 'the Camembert' by early critics who were less than impressed.

Queen Victoria St cuts south-westwards from Bank. A short way along it on the left and in front of Temple Court at No 11 you'll find all that remains of the 3rd-century AD **Temple of Mithras**, excavated from 5.5m below ground in 1954 and moved here from a short distance away. Mithras was a Per-sian god of justice and social contract whose cult travelled round the Roman Empire with its legionaries (see the boxed text 'Mithras

& the Great Sacrifice' in the Facts about London chapter). The finds from the temple – such as sculptures and siver incense boxes – can be seen in the Museum of London.

Due west of Bank is Poultry, which runs into Cheapside, site of a great medieval market (see the boxed text 'What's in a Name?' in the Facts for the Visitor chapter). On the left you'll see another of Wren's great churches, **St Mary-le-Bow** (☎ *7248 5139, Cheapside EC2; admission free; open 6.30am-6pm Mon-Thur, 6.30am-4pm Fri)*, built in 1673 and famous as the church whose bells dictate who is – and who is not – a cockney (see the boxed texts 'A Church for All Chimes' earlier and 'Cockney Rhyme and Royalty' later). Its delicate steeple is one of Wren's finest works and the modern stained glass is striking. There's a good cafe called ***The Place Below*** (see the Places to Eat chapter).

Bank of England Museum The Bank of England (☎ *7601 5545,* W *www.bankof england.co.uk, Bartholomew Lane EC2;* ✚ *Bank; admission free; open 10am-5pm Mon-Fri)* is in charge of maintaining the integrity and value of sterling and of the British financial system. It was set up in 1694 when the government needed to raise money to finance a war with France. At first it was housed in the Mercers' and Grocers' halls, but in 1734 it moved to a new home on the present site. From 1788 to 1833 John Soane, whose statue graces the Lothbury side of what is nicknamed 'the Old Lady of Threadneedle St', was architect to the Bank of England, and although much of his work was destroyed during the rebuilding after WWI, some of it has been reconstructed.

The first room of the museum you come to is a reconstruction of Soane's 18th-century banking hall, the Bank Stock Office, complete with mannequin clerks and customers. A statue of William III, who was king when the Bank was founded, stands to one side. You can also inspect the caryatids that supported Soane's original rotunda in Herbert Baker's later replacement rotunda (room 8).

The museum traces the history of the bank and of bank notes. Highlights include a pair of Roman gold ingots in the rotunda (room

Towering inferno: the Monument marks the spot where the Great Fire began.

ASA ANDERSSON

8) and a diorama showing an attack on the bank during the Gordon Riots of 1780 (room 13). Finally, if you ever fancied a career as a foreign-exchange dealer, an interactive video lets you try your hand (room 24).

The Monument (Map 9)

At the south-eastern end of King William St, near London Bridge, stands the Monument (☎ *7626 2717, Monument St;* ✚ *Monument; adult/child aged 5-15 £1.50/50p; open 10am-5.40pm daily)* designed by Sir Christopher Wren to commemorate the Great Fire of 1666, which started in a bakery on Pudding Lane, east of the Monument. The height of the monument, which was completed in 1677, is 60.6m, the exact distance to the bakery. It is topped off with a gilded bronze urn of flames that looks, to some, like a big gold pincushion. If you're up to it, 311 tight steps lead to a balcony beneath the urn offering panoramic views over the City.

Leadenhall Market (Map 9)

There's been a market on this site in Whittington Ave off Gracechurch St (⊖ Bank) since Roman times when it served as a forum. In the late 14th century, out-of-towners were allowed to sell their goods here and in 1445 the City Corporation made it an official food market. For details of the market in more recent times, see the special section 'To Market, to Market'.

Lloyd's of London (Map 9)

Although it is the most famous house of insurance brokers in the world, where everything from ships, ships' cargoes and planes to film stars' faces and dancers' legs are insured by syndicate underwriters, Lloyd's of London *(☎ 7623 1000, 1 Lime St EC3; ⊖ Aldgate/Bank)* wouldn't be much of a tourist destination were it not for the building that houses it.

In 1986, Richard Rogers, one of the architects of the Pompidou Centre in Paris, created a stunning new building in a part of London not then known for avant-garde architecture. Lloyd's, with its external pipes and ducts of stainless steel, was a triumphant exception, especially at night with its spectacular illuminated framework of yellow and electric blue. Part of the facade of the old Lloyd's building (1925) was retained; you can see it on Leadenhall St.

Access to the equally excellent interior is restricted to professional groups, who must book in advance.

Tower of London (Map 9)

One of London's three World Heritage Sites (the others are Westminster Abbey and its surrounding buildings and Maritime Greenwich) is the Tower of London *(☎ 7709 0765, W www.hrp.org.uk, Tower Hill EC3; ⊖ Tower Hill; adult/senior & student/child aged 5-15/family £11.30/8.50/7.50/34; joint ticket to Tower of London & Hampton Court Palace adult/senior & student/child aged 5-15/family £19/14.50/12.50/55.50; open 9am-6pm Mon-Sat & 10am-5pm Sun Mar-Oct, 9am-4pm Tues-Sat & 10am-4pm Sun & Mon Nov-Feb)*. It has dominated the south-eastern corner of the City since 1078 when William the Conqueror laid the first stone of the White Tower to replace the earth and timber castle he'd built on the site.

William II completed his father's work on the White Tower and between 1190 and 1285 two walls with towers and a moat were built around it. A riverside wharf was later added and since then the medieval defences have barely been altered.

RICHARD I'ANSON

Twilight descends on the Tower of London, the City's hulking stronghold.

Wildlife at the Tower

Ravens, scavengers on the lookout for scraps chucked from the Tower of London's windows – and feasting on the corpses of beheaded traitors that were displayed as a deterrent – have been here for centuries; the first reported sighting was made by no less than Thomas à Becket in the early 13th century. By the 17th century, however, the numbers had become so great that it was proposed to kill them all, until someone remembered the old legend: should the ravens leave it, the White Tower would crumble and a great disaster would befall England. The newly restored Charles II was sufficiently superstitious to take note of this and a compromise was reached. Now there are never fewer than six ravens in residence, all with their wings clipped so that they can't fly away.

While at the tower you're also bound to come across another species with far more colourful plumage: the Yeoman Warders, better known as the Beefeaters, who sport dark-blue (almost black) and red Tudor costumes for everyday wear, and more elaborate gold and red Victorian ones for ceremonial occasions that cost £12,000 a go. They've been guarding the tower for just over 900 years.

The more than three dozen Beefeaters have all spent at least 22 years in the armed services and have reached the rank of sergeant major. They can stay in the job until they're 60 and live within the tower precincts. The Beefeaters conduct engaging tours of the Tower and also enact the age-old Ceremony of the Keys each evening, in which the tower gates are locked and the keys ceremoniously locked away in the Queen's House.

The Beefeaters received a daily ration of beef and beer and, since beef was a luxury well beyond the reach of the poor, this generated jealousy and the envious nickname back in the 17th century.

Until the reign of Henry III (1216–72), the kings had been content to live within the White Tower itself but, along with strengthening the tower's defences, Henry had a palace constructed between the White Tower and the river. He also started the Royal Menagerie, London's first zoo, after Louis IX of France presented him with an elephant in 1255. The menagerie was moved to Regent's Park in the 19th century and became London Zoo.

In the early Middle Ages, the Tower of London acted not just as a royal residence but also as a treasury, a mint, an arsenal and a prison. After Henry VIII moved to Whitehall Palace in 1529, the tower's role as a prison became increasingly important, with Thomas More, queens Anne Boleyn and Catherine Howard, Archbishop Cranmer, Lady Jane Grey, Princess (later Queen) Elizabeth and Robert Devereux, earl of Essex, just some of the famous Tudor prisoners.

After the monarchy was restored in 1660, a large garrison was stationed in the tower and the arsenal was expanded. For the first time the public was admitted to see the coronation regalia and the armoury.

When the Duke of Wellington became constable of the tower in 1826 he was worried that revolution might spread across the Channel from France and so set about reinforcing its military strength. The Royal Menagerie was closed and the public records moved out. A new barracks quickly replaced the Grand Storehouse when it burned down in 1841.

Queen Victoria's husband, Prince Albert, saw things very differently and oversaw the demolition of some of the newer buildings and the repair or reconstruction of the medieval towers. From then on the tower's gruesome and sometimes ferocious history became little more than a tourist attraction, although prisoners were still occasionally housed here right up to WWII, most notably Rudolf Hess in 1941.

These days the Tower is visited by more than two million people a year, with impressive crowds even on cold winter afternoons. The queues move quickly and you won't wait longer than 20 minutes or so to see the Crown Jewels even in summer. You can also buy tickets in advance from most Underground stations.

Orientation You enter the tower via the West Gate and proceed across the walkway over the dry moat between the **Middle Tower** and **Byward Tower**.

Walking along Water Lane between the walls you come to **St Thomas's Tower** on the right. Built by Edward I between 1275 and 1279, it stands immediately above **Traitor's Gate**, the gateway through which prisoners being brought by river entered the Tower of London. Rooms inside the tower show what the king's hall might once have looked like and also how archaeologists peel back the layers of newer buildings to find what went before.

Opposite St Thomas's Tower is the **Wakefield Tower**, built by Henry III between 1220 and 1240. The ground floor was once a guardhouse and shows its original stonework. In sharp contrast the upper floor has been furnished with a replica throne and a huge candelabra to give an impression of how it might have looked in Edward I's day. It is believed that Henry VI was murdered in the tower's chapel in 1471.

Passing under Henry III's Watergate you come to the **Cradle Tower**, the **Well Tower** and the **Develin Tower** on the southern side. On the left is the **Lanthorn Tower**, a Victorian copy of the original, which burned down in 1774. Passing through to the inner ward and turning right you'll come to the **Salt Tower**, built around 1238 and perhaps used to store saltpetre for gunpowder. Some Beefeaters believe the Salt Tower to be haunted. On the 1st floor you can see graffiti carved into the wall by Tudor prisoners.

The Salt Tower gives access to the **Wall Walk** along 13th-century ramparts. Beside the Salt Tower stands the massive red-brick **New Armouries** built in 1664. These display an assortment of exhibits, including old prints of the tower, pictures of the Royal Menagerie, the elaborately carved pediment of the Grand Storehouse, which survived the 1841 fire, and a list of the tower's famous prisoners, from Ranulf Flambard, bishop of Durham, in 1100 to Josef Jakobs, a German spy who was executed by firing squad in 1941. On the lawn opposite are fragments of the **Roman city wall** and a bit farther north

a magnificent Flemish **cannon** built in 1607 and brought from Malta in 1800. It bears the arms of the Order of St John of Jerusalem and of Grand Master Alof de Wignacourt, together with a pewter plaque showing St Paul shipwrecked off Malta. The nearby **Broad Arrow Tower**, built in 1238, has been furnished as the bedchamber of Simon Burley, tutor to the young Richard II.

Passing the **Hospital Block**, completed in 1700 as houses for officials of the Board of Ordnance, you'll see the **Fusiliers Museum** run by the royal Regiment of Fusiliers for which a separate nominal charge is made. It covers the history of the Royal Fusiliers dating back to 1685, and has models of several battles. A 10-minute video gives details of the modern regiment.

The Wall Walk ends at the **Martin Tower**, which houses an exhibition about the original coronation regalia. Here you can see some of the older crowns, designed so that

GLENN BEANLAND

If walls could speak: the Tower of London's gory past still haunts visitors to this day.

TOWER OF LONDON

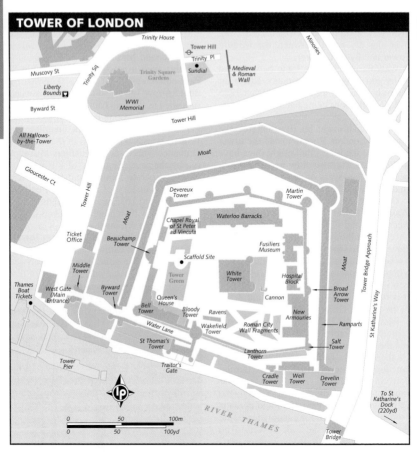

Trinity House

Tower Hill

Trinity Pl

Muscovy St

Minories

Trinity Sq

Trinity Square Gardens

Sundial

Medieval & Roman Wall

Liberty Bounds

WWI Memorial

Byward St

Tower Hill

All Hallows-by-the-Tower

Tower Hill

Gloucester Ct

Moat

Devereux Tower

Martin Tower

Moat

Chapel Royal of St Peter ad Vincula

Waterloo Barracks

Ticket Office

Beauchamp Tower

Scaffold Site

Fusiliers Museum

Middle Tower

Tower Green

White Tower

Hospital Block

Moat

Thames Boat Tickets

West Gate (Main Entrance)

Byward Tower

Queen's House

Cannon

Broad Arrow Tower

Tower Bridge Approach

St Katharine's Way

Bell Tower

Bloody Tower

Ravens

New Armouries

Water Lane

Wakefield Tower

Roman City Wall Fragments

Ramparts

St Thomas's Tower

Lanthorn Tower

Salt Tower

Tower Pier

Traitor's Gate

Cradle Tower

Well Tower

Develin Tower

To St Katharine's Dock (220yd)

RIVER THAMES

0 ——— 50 ——— 100m
0 ——— 50 ——— 100yd

Tower Bridge

the jewels in them could be removed. The oldest surviving crown is that of George I, which is topped with the ball and cross from James II's crown. The crown of George IV (1821) was originally set with some 12,314 cut diamonds. It was from the Martin Tower that Colonel Thomas Blood attempted to steal the Crown Jewels in 1671 while disguised as a clergyman.

The most striking building in the tower complex is undoubtedly the huge **White Tower**, in the centre of the courtyard, with its solid Romanesque architecture and four turrets. It was whitewashed during the reign of Henry III and thus got its name. After extensive renovations lasting eight years, it now houses a collection from the Royal Armouries, based in Leeds, in nine galleries, including a child's suit of armour designed for James I's young son Henry. Another exhibit deals with gruesome implements of torture and punishment, including the block and axe used to execute the 80-year-old Scottish Jacobite Simon Fraser, the 11th Lord Lovat, in 1747. You can also see the restored Line of Kings, a set of models of monarchs on horses, dating from 1660. On the 2nd floor is the **Chapel of St John the**

Evangelist, which dates from 1080 and is therefore the oldest church in London.

Facing the White Tower to the north is the **Waterloo Barracks**, a neo-Gothic structure built while the Duke of Wellington was constable of the tower to house some 1000 soldiers. It now contains the Crown Jewels: orbs, sceptres and the centrepiece, the Imperial State Crown, set with diamonds (2868 of them to be exact), sapphires, emeralds, rubies and pearls. It's quite a bonnet – and insured for £27.5 million. Topping the Sceptre with the Cross is the First Star of Africa diamond weighing in at 530 carats. It's quite a walking stick.

Beside the Waterloo Barracks stands the **Chapel Royal of St Peter ad Vincula** (St Peter in Chains), which can only be visited on a group tour or after 4.30pm; if you aren't already part of a group you can hang around until one shows up and then tag on, or attend a service. This is the third church on the site and a rare example of ecclesiastical Tudor architecture, but it's most interesting as the burial place of those beheaded on the scaffold outside or at nearby Tower Hill. Buried without much care at the time, these bodies were disinterred and reburied with proper memorials in Victorian times. Services take place at 9am on Sunday.

What looks a peaceful, picturesque corner of the Tower is in fact one of its bloodiest. On the green in front of the church stood the **scaffold**, set up during Henry VIII's reign and where seven people were beheaded, including his two allegedly adulterous wives, Anne Boleyn and Catherine Howard, together with Jane Rochford, lady-in-waiting to the latter. Also executed here was Margaret Pole, countess of Salisbury. The fact that she was 70 and guilty of no particular offence except being descended from the House of York couldn't protect her from Henry's wrath.

Lady Jane Grey, on the other hand, was only 16 when she was executed here during the reign of Henry's daughter, Mary I. Proclaimed queen on the death of Edward VI to ensure that a Catholic wouldn't recover the crown, Jane came to the tower to await her coronation but lasted only nine days before Mary's supporters rose against her. From her room overlooking Tower Green, Jane watched her husband being taken away for his execution on Tower Hill before she too was dragged to her own.

These five women were executed within the tower precincts largely to spare the monarch the embarrassment of their public execution. The two men executed here were William, Lord Hastings, in 1483, and Robert

Keeping an eye on the Crown Jewels: there are 2868 diamonds in the State Crown alone.

VERONICA GARBUTT

DOUG MCKINLAY

Beefy Yeoman Warders have watched over the Tower of London for 900 years.

Devereux, earl of Essex, once a favourite of Elizabeth I. Although he had betrayed her it was believed to be a mark of her continued affection that he was spared public execution. The authorities may also have feared a popular uprising in his support.

To the west of the scaffold site is the **Beauchamp Tower**, built around 1281, which takes its name from Thomas Beauchamp, earl of Warwick, who was imprisoned here from 1397 to 1399. The walls, especially of the upper chamber, are densely carved with graffiti. A numbered list is available to help you pick out the most interesting scribbles.

Set around Tower Green are attractive half-timbered Tudor houses that are home to Tower of London staff. The **Queen's House**, where Anne Boleyn is believed to have been imprisoned and etched her signature into the wall of her cell, is now home to the Resident Governor; when Prince Charles or his son, Prince William, succeeds the Queen, its name will change to the King's House.

Beside the Wakefield Tower stands the **Bloody Tower**, probably the best-known part of the complex. On the 1st floor you can see the windlass that controlled the portcullis, the grating that could be dropped down to guard the gateway, with a 17th-century wooden screen separating it from a room furnished with artefacts dating from 1520 to 1620. It was here that Sir Walter Raleigh was imprisoned and where he wrote his *History of the World*, a copy of which is on display. The upstairs room is similarly equipped with 16th-century bedchamber furnishings, including a fine oak four-poster bed.

Once called the Garden Tower, Bloody Tower acquired its unsavoury nickname from the story that the 'princes in the tower', Edward V and his younger brother, were murdered here. The blame is usually laid at the door of their uncle Richard III, but there are those who prefer to finger Henry VII for the crime.

Don't leave the tower without looking at the stretch of green between the Wakefield and White towers where the Great Hall once stood. Here you'll find the Tower's famous ravens (see the boxed text 'Wildlife at the Tower' earlier in this chapter).

Guided Tours Hugely entertaining, hour-long tours led by the Yeoman Warders leave from the Middle Tower every 30 minutes from 9.30am (on Sunday from 10am) to 3.30pm (2.30pm in winter) daily. The Warders also conduct about eight different short talks (35 minutes) and tours (45 minutes) on specific themes. The first is at 9.30am Monday to Saturday (10.15am on Sunday in summer, 11.30am in winter), the last at 5.15pm (3pm in winter). A self-paced audio-guide in five languages is available for £3 from the information point on Water Lane.

Around the Tower (Map 9)

Despite the Tower's World Heritage Site status, the area immediately to the north is fairly disappointing. Just outside Tower Hill tube station, a giant bronze sundial depicts the history of London from AD 43 to 1982. It stands on a platform offering a view of the neighbouring **Trinity Square Gardens**, once the site of the Tower Hill scaffold and now home to Edwin Lutyens' memorial to the marines and merchant sailors who lost their lives during WWI. A grassy area off the steps leading to a subway under the main road lets you inspect a stretch of the medieval wall built on Roman foundations, with a modern statue of Emperor Trajan (ruled AD 98 to 117) standing in front of it. At the other end of the tunnel is a postern (or gate) dating from the 13th century.

All Hallows-by-the-Tower A church by this name (meaning 'all saints') has stood on this site since AD 675. Despite its proximity to the spot where the Great Fire of 1666 started (Samuel Pepys watched the blaze from the brick tower), All Hallows-by-the-Tower (*☎ 7481 2928, Byward St EC3; ✪ Tower Hill; admission free; open 9am-5.45pm Mon-Fri, 10am-5pm Sat & Sun)* survived virtually unscathed, only to be all but flattened by German bombs in 1940.

All that remains of the pre-fire building is the brick tower, the church's outer walls and an important Saxon archway. The copper spire was added in 1957 to make the church stand out more in an area devastated by bombs. Notice the pulpit taken from a Wren church in Cannon St destroyed in the war, the beautiful 17th-century font cover, decorated with three cherubs and a dove by the master woodcarver Grinling Gibbons,

and the memorial brasses dating from the 14th to 17th centuries. Several people executed at the Tower of London or on Tower Hill were buried here – at least for a while – including Thomas More and Archbishop William Laud. William Penn, founder of Pennsylvania, was baptised here in 1644, and John Quincy Adams, sixth president of the USA, was married here in 1797.

The **crypt** *(admission £2.50; open 10am-4pm Mon-Sat, 1pm-4pm Sun)* reveals a pavement of reused Roman tiles and walls of the 7th-century Saxon church. A 45-minute audioguide tour of the church is available (donation requested). At the **brass-rubbing centre** *(open 10am-4pm Mon-Sat, 1pm-4pm Sun)* rubbings cost from £2 to £5.

Tower Bridge (Map 9)

Tower Bridge *(✪ Tower Hill)* was built in 1894 when London was still a thriving port. Until then, London Bridge had been the easternmost crossing point, and congestion was so bad that ship owners were forced to agree to a new bridge equipped with an ingenious bascule (seesaw) mechanism that could clear the way for oncoming ships in three minutes.

MANFRED GOTTSCHALK

An uplifting experience: the bascules of Tower Bridge still rise around 500 times a year.

The 25m-high twin towers were given a steel frame and then faced with stone.

The bridge's walkways afford excellent views across the City and Docklands. For the **Tower Bridge Experience** (☎ 7940 3985, Ⓦ *www.towerbridge.org.uk; adult/senior, student & child aged 5-15/family £6.25/ 4.25/18.25-22.25; open 10am-6.30pm daily Apr-Oct, 9.30am-6pm daily Nov-Mar)*, a lift takes you up from the modern visitors' facility in the north pier, where the story of its building is recounted. Afterwards, the basement engine room and engineers' gallery are well worth visiting, although the re-enactment of the royal opening of the bridge can be skipped if time is tight.

Although London's port days are long over, the bridge still does its stuff, lifting some 500 times a year and as many as 10 times a day in summer. For information on the next lifting ring (☎ 7940 3984).

SOUTH OF THE THAMES: BERMONDSEY TO BATTERSEA

Just a decade ago, the southern part of central London was the city's forgotten underside – rundown, neglected and offering little for visitors once they'd seen the South Bank arts venues. That's all changed now, and parts of London just south of the river can be as exciting as anywhere to the north.

The Globe Theatre, a copy of Shakespeare's original, opened to considerable acclaim in 1997 and the restaurant in the old Oxo Tower helped to bring people to 'the other side'. A spate of new museums and

CHARLOTTE HINDLE

All's well that ends well: the faithul Bankside re-creation of Shakespeare's Globe Theatre

attractions have opened in and around Southwark and the South Bank – from the new Tate Modern to the London IMAX Cinema and the gigantic BA London Eye Ferris wheel. The new pedestrian Millennium Bridge will help bring the two sides even closer together, once it stops wobbling.

This section covers the following areas (from east to west): Bermondsey, Southwark (including Borough and Bankside), Waterloo, the South Bank, Lambeth and Battersea.

Bermondsey (Map 9)

Although parts of Bermondsey still look pretty derelict, there are pockets of refurbishment, even gentrification, especially along the waterfront in the area called Shad Thames. Antique lovers will also want to explore the antiques market in Bermondsey Square on Friday mornings (see the special section 'To Market, to Market').

Design Museum Sir Terence Conran's sparkling white Design Museum (☎ 7940 8790, Ⓦ *www.designmuseum.org, 28 Shad Thames SE1;* ⊖ *Tower Hill; adult/student/ child aged 5-16/family £5.50/4.50/4/15; open 11.30am-6pm Mon-Fri, 10.30am-6pm Sat & Sun)* has displays on how product design has evolved over time and how it can make the difference between success and failure for items intended for mass production. Try a set of chairs for comfort and then use a computer to help you design a new-look toothbrush. Temporary exhibitions on the 1st floor might tell you, for example, how the Dyson cyclonic cleaner – otherwise known as a newfangled vacuum cleaner – was developed, celebrate 40 years of the Mini car or look at new developments in wheelchair and cutlery design. The permanent Collection Gallery on the 2nd floor looks at the past and future development in design of everyday things: from TVs and washing machines to chairs and tableware.

The *Riverside Café* opens 11am to 5.30pm Monday to Friday and 10.30am to 5.30pm on Saturday and Sunday. The *Blue Print Café*, a restaurant rather than a coffee shop, offers sky-high river views and prices to match (see the Places to Eat chapter).

Bramah Museum of Tea & Coffee The story of tea- and coffee-drinking in the UK is traced at the Bramah Museum of Tea & Coffee (☎ 7378 0222, 1 Maguire St SE1; ⊖ Tower Hill; adult/senior & student/family £4/3/10; open 10am-6pm daily); nearby Butler's Wharf once handled 6000 chests of tea in a single day. Teapots abound in every shape you can imagine and many you probably wouldn't – a cactus plant, a ball of wool with knitting needles, a Eurostar train – as well as related silverware and prints. The coffee exhibits (enter from Gainsford St) are outstanding, especially the ones focusing on the coffee houses of the 17th century and the coffee bars of the 1950s but, alas, nowhere is there any explanation as to why Britons still can't manage to make a proper cup of java.

In the excellent Tea Room, your cuppa is served with an egg timer so you can get the infusion just right.

A short distance to the south in Millennium Square at the eastern end of Queen Elizabeth St is a bronze **statue of Jacob**, one of the many Courage drayhorses stabled here in the 19th century. These work horses delivered beer all over London from the brewery on Horselydown Lane, where the poor things rested ('horse lie down') before crossing the bridge. A nag's life, it was.

Southwark (Map 9)

Originally settled by the Romans, Southwark (**suth**-erk) became an important thoroughfare for people travelling to London in the Middle Ages. For centuries London Bridge, with its houses and shops, was the only crossing on the Thames; travellers congregated in Southwark where many inns opened to cater for them. In Tudor times the authorities refused to allow theatres in the City and so it was on Bankside in Southwark that the Globe, the Rose, the Swan and the Hope theatres were built. At that time Southwark had a thoroughly raffish air, with plentiful 'stews' (bathhouses-cum-brothels), several prisons and innumerable bear-baiting pits.

Victorian Southwark flourished on the back of the docks trade. Processing and packaging firms set up nearby, many of them household names in the UK such as

Crosse & Blackwell, Jacob's and Courage. However, Southwark suffered terribly during WWII and even worse in the postwar years when the docks closed and the trade on which it had prospered moved away.

Although Southwark is still pretty rundown it's on the up and up; some say it's London's new Left Bank. The back streets are also well worth exploring for their many small museums and attractions, including HMS Belfast, the London Dungeon and the Britain at War exhibition. In the area known as Borough there's a lovely market (see the special section 'To Market, to Market') and the excellent Old Operating Theatre Museum. The Tate Modern in the Bankside area is the new jewel in the crown – it attracts more visitors than any other contemporary art museum in the UK and ranks just after the British Museum in favourite tourist attractions – but the Globe Theatre and Southwark Cathedral are other major draws.

HMS Belfast The large, light cruiser HMS Belfast (☎ 7940 6300, **W** www.hmsbelfast .org.uk, Morgan's Lane, Tooley St SE1; ⊖ London Bridge; adult/senior & student /under-16s £5/3.80/free; open 10am-6pm daily Mar-Oct, 10am-5pm Nov-Feb) was built with 12 six-inch guns and launched in 1938. It took its name from the Belfast shipyard Harland & Wolff where it was built. During WWII, the Belfast escorted merchant ships on the Arctic convoy but struck a mine in 1939 and was out of action until 1942. It took part in the 1943 Battle of the North Cape off Norway when the German battleship Scharnhorst was sunk during the last largescale gun battle between ships fought in Europe; only 36 of the 1963 men on board the Scharnhost survived. The following year it took part in the Normandy landings, before being moved to Asia to repatriate POWs and internees at the end of the war. It saw 404 days' action during the Korean War.

In 1952 the Belfast returned to the UK and was comprehensively refitted before setting off on a round-the-world voyage. In 1963 it returned to Devonport docks and was only saved from the scrap yard when the Imperial War Museum bought it to serve as a branch in 1971. The *Belfast* was towed to Portsmouth for a paint job and a freshen up in the summer of 1999 – the first time she'd 'put to sea' since she was saved for the nation.

It probably helps to be keen on things naval, but the *Belfast* is surprisingly interesting for what it shows of the way of life on board a cruiser. Finding your way around the eight zones on nine decks and platforms can be rather confusing even with the *Visitors Guide* map supplied, and you need to be prepared for a lot of scrambling up and down steep ladders and steps.

In the Zone 3 Operations Room on the bridge, models and sound effects attempt to bring the Battle of the North Cape to life, while a fixed exhibition, HMS *Belfast* in War and Peace, in Zone 5, gives more details and shows a video of the battle. A second exhibition here, the Modern Royal Navy, has information on Britain's nuclear deterrent. Almost anyone should enjoy looking around Zone 7, where you can see the ship's galley, operating theatre, dental surgery, chapel and laundry. Even more interesting are the mess decks and punishment cells of Zone 4.

London Dungeon Under the arches of London Bridge station, the London Dungeon *(☎ 09001 600066, Ⓦ www.thedungeons .com, 28-34 Tooley St SE1; ⊖ London Bridge; adult/student/senior & under-14s £19.95/9.50/6.95; open 10am-6.30pm daily Apr-Sept, 10am-5.30pm daily Oct-Mar)* was supposedly developed after someone's kid didn't find Madame Tussaud's Chamber of Horrors frightening enough. Here you can watch people hanging on the Tyburn gallows, listen to Anne Boleyn before her head was deftly separated (by a sword – not an axe – wielded by an executioner imported from Calais) from her narrow shoulders, observe Thomas à Becket's murder and wonder at an assortment of ingenious methods of torture. The reconstruction of the French guillotine in action is particularly gruesome but still doesn't hold a candle to the section dealing with Victorian serial killer Jack the Ripper and the five

prostitutes he sliced and diced, depicted in gory detail with their entrails hanging out. The Judgement Day exhibit sees spectators condemned to death and put aboard the executioner's barge for a 'final trip' through Traitors' Gate; Medieval Mayhem sees a city under siege; and The Great Fire of London runs you – literally – through a gauntlet of flames. Love it or leave it, it's your call – but the kids can't get enough.

Be prepared for long queues in July and August unless you've bought advance tickets from a reputable outlet, like the South-wark Visitors' Centre (see Local Tourist Offices in the Facts for the Visitor chapter).

Britain at War Experience Under another Tooley St railway arch is the Britain at War Experience *(☎ 7403 3171, Ⓦ www .britainatwar.co.uk, 64-66 Tooley St SE1; ⊖ London Bridge; adult/senior & student/ under-15s/family £5.95/3.95/2.95/14; open 10am-6pm daily Apr-Sept, 10am-5pm daily Oct-Mar)*. This aims to educate the younger generation about the effect WWII had on daily life while simultaneously playing on the nostalgia of the war generation who sit in the mock Anderson air-raid shelter listening to the simulated sounds of warning sirens and bombers flying overhead with extraordinary detachment. In general it's a tribute to ordinary people, rather than heroes and statesmen, and comes off very well.

You descend by lift to a reproduction of an Underground station fitted with bunks, tea urns and even a lending library (as some of the stations really were) and then progress through rooms that display wartime newspaper front pages, posters and Ministry of Food ration books. Mannequins illustrate the ways in which women tried to get around a shortage of fabric, and there's a model of an iced cardboard wedding cake with a small drawer at the bottom for a tiny piece of real fruit cake. The BBC Radio Studio allows you to hear broadcasts of everyone from Winston Churchill and Edward Murrow to Hitler and Lord Haw Haw; the Rainbow Corner is a mock-up of a club frequented by American GIs 'over here'. Finally, you emerge amid the wreckage of a shop hit by a bomb, with the smoke still eddying around and the injured – or dead – being carried from the rubble.

St Olaf House This diminutive office block fronting the Thames on Tooley St (the name of which is actually a corruption of St Olave's St) was built in 1932 and is one of London's finest Art Deco buildings. Note the gold mosaic lettering on the front and the bronze relief sculptures.

Old Operating Theatre Museum & Herb Garret While the London Dungeon is all about shock and horror, the nearby Old Operating Theatre Museum (☎ 7955 4791, W www.thegarret.org.uk, 9a St Thomas St SE1; ⊖ London Bridge; adult/ senior & student/child/family £3.50/2.50/ 1.75/8; open 10.30am-5pm daily) focuses on the more mundane nastiness of 19th-century hospital treatment. It is at the top of the narrow and rickety, 32-step tower of St Thomas Church (1703). The garret was used by the apothecary of St Thomas's Hospital to store medicinal herbs and now houses an atmospheric medical museum delightfully hung with bunches of herbs that soften the impact of the horrible devices displayed in the glass cases.

Even more interesting is the 19th-century women's operating theatre attached to the garret. An adjoining building used to house the surgical ward of St Thomas's and the church's roof space provided an ideal position for the theatre – high enough to take advantage of the natural light and isolated enough to provide soundproofing. In the days before the importance of an antiseptic environment was understood, students crowded round the operating table in what looks like a modern lecture hall. A box of sawdust was placed beneath the table to catch the blood and guts and contemporary accounts record the surgeons wearing frock coats 'stiff and stinking with pus and blood'. Don't eat lunch before visiting.

Bankside (Maps 6 & 9) This corner of Southwark includes several of south London's most important attractions.

Southwark Cathedral (Map 9) There was already a church on the site of Southwark Cathedral (☎ 7367 6700, W dswark.org, Montague Close SE1; ⊖ London Bridge; admission free, £2.50 donation requested; open 8am-6pm daily) in 1086 but it was rebuilt in 1106 and then for a third time in the 13th century. During the Middle Ages it was part of the Priory of St Mary Overie (from 'St Mary over the Water'), becoming the local parish church in 1539 after the dissolution of the monasteries. By the 1830s it had fallen into decay and much of what you see today is actually Victorian – the nave was rebuilt in 1897 – although the central tower dates from 1520 and the choir from the 13th century. In 1905 the Collegiate Church of St Saviour and St Mary Overie became Southwark Cathedral, with its own bishop. Sometimes referred to as the 'Cinderella of English cathedrals', it is often overlooked but definitely well worth a visit, particularly for its historical associations.

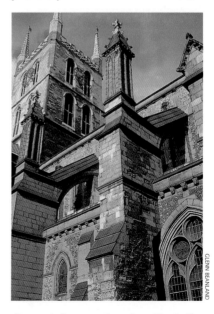

Once a pigsty, now a place of worship: Southwark Cathedral has a potted history.

You enter via the south-west door and immediately to the left is the *Marchioness memorial* to the 51 people who died in 1989 when a pleasure cruiser on the Thames hit a dredger and sank near Southwark Bridge. Against the western wall are a series of 15th-century **wooden bosses** taken from the original nave ceiling; one shows a pelican (Christ) nurturing its young (the faithful) with its own breast blood – a common motif in medieval Christianity.

Walk up the northern aisle of the nave and on the left you'll see the brightly coloured and much renovated canopied **tomb of John Gower** (c.1330–1408), whose *Confessio Amantis* is considered the first poem written in English.

In the northern transept, you'll see several 17th- and 18th-century monuments and a fine 17th-century wooden **sword-rest** from the church of St Olave Old Jewry, demolished in 1888. More interesting is the **memorial tablet to Lionel Lockyer**, a quack doctor celebrated for his pills, and its humorous epitaph. On the eastern side of the north transept is the **Harvard Chapel**, originally the chapel of St John the Evangelist but now named after John Harvard, founder of Harvard University in Cambridge, Massachusetts, who was baptised here in 1607.

In the north choir aisle look for the macabre **medieval tomb** showing a skeleton in a shroud and for the rare but heavily restored 13th-century **wooden effigy** of a knight in chain-mail armour. Immediately opposite is a 17th-century **monument to Richard Humble** that shows him kneeling towards the altar with his two little wives behind him. The lovely inlaid chest nearby is the **Nonsuch Chest**, given to the church in 1588.

Cross the retrochoir – used as a bakery and a pigsty in the 16th century – with its four chapels behind the high altar and return along the southern choir aisle. To the right is the fine **17th-century tomb of Lancelot Andrewes**, last bishop of Winchester, who

SOUTHWARK CATHEDRAL

1 Marchioness Memorial	6 Nonsuch Chest	11 Hunter God Statue
2 Wooden Bosses	7 Knight Effigy	12 High Altar
3 Neo-Gothic Font	8 Richard Humble Monument	13 Edmond Shakespeare's Tomb
4 John Gower's Tomb	9 Great Screen	14 Shakespeare Monument
5 Lionel Lockyer Memorial	10 Lancelot Andrewes' Tomb	15 Sam Wanamaker Memorial

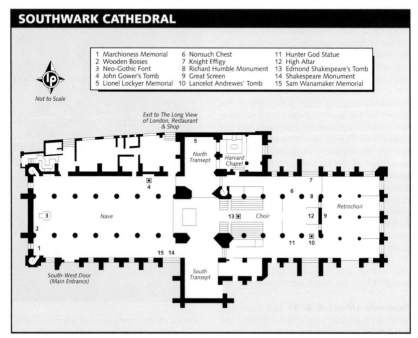

Not to Scale

Exit to The Long View of London, Restaurant & Shop

North Transept

Harvard Chapel

Nave

Choir

Retrochoir

South-West Door (Main Entrance)

South Transept

helped translate the King James version of the Bible. A few steps farther on and you'll see a **Roman statue of a hunter god** found in a nearby well in 1976 and probably dating from the 2nd or 3rd century AD.

Cross into the choir to admire the Early English arches and vaults, and 16th-century **Great Screen** separating the choir from the retrochoir, a gift of the bishop of Winchester in 1520. The statues in the niches were added in 1905. On the choir floor are tablets marking the **tomb of Edmond Shakespeare**, actor-brother of the Bard, who died in 1607. The Jacobean dramatists John Fletcher and Philip Massinger are also buried here.

Return to the southern choir aisle and continue to the south transept, noting the fine **organ** designed by Lewis in 1897 (rebuilt in 1952).

Stand beneath the 16th-century crossing tower and look up at the finely **painted ceiling**. The **brass candelabrum** hanging from it dates from 1680. The crown, mitre and dove incorporated in the design are said to have reflected concern at the time about the relationship between Church and State.

Returning along the southern aisle of the nave, stop and look at the green alabaster **monument to William Shakespeare**, whose works were originally written for the Bankside playhouses. The background depicts the Globe Theatre and Southwark Cathedral, and the **stained-glass window** above shows characters from *Hamlet*, *The Tempest* and *A Midsummer Night's Dream*. Shakespeare is actually buried in Stratford-upon-Avon and this memorial was only erected in 1912. Each year on 23 April a birthday service is held here in his honour. Right beside Shakespeare's monument is a small **memorial to Sam Wanamaker** (1919–93), the American film director and actor who was the force behind the rebuilt Globe Theatre.

Audioguides, featuring the voices of Tommy Steele, Prunella Scales and Zoë Wanamaker and lasting about 40 minutes, are available for £2.50/2/1.25 per adult/senior & student/child. Evensong is at 5.30pm Tuesday and Friday, 4pm Saturday and 3pm on Sunday. Lunch-time concerts usually take place at 1.10pm on Monday and Tuesday.

Like so may other major sights and attractions in London, Southwark Cathedral jumped on the Year 2000 bandwagon and had two Millennium Project Buildings erected adjacent to the church. One of the buildings now has an excellent visitors' centre with an exhibition called **The Long View of London** *(adult/senior & student/child £3/2.50/1.50, with audioguide adult/senior & student/child/family £5/4/2.50/12.50; open 10am-6pm Mon-Sat, 11am-5pm Sun)*, based on Wenceslaus Hollar's definitive panorama of historic London produced in 1638. Multimedia allow visitors to witness the great changes that have occurred from this unique vantage point of London over the past 2000 years. The second Millennium Project Building contains the *Refectory* restaurant (open 10am to 5pm daily) and a shop.

Golden Hinde (Map 9) A replica (1973) of the boat in which Sir Francis Drake circumnavigated the globe between 1577 and 1580, the *Golden Hinde (☎ 7403 0123, Ⓦ www.goldenhinde.co.uk, Cathedral St SE1; ✪ London Bridge; adult/senior & student/child £2.50/2.10/1.75; open 9am-5.30pm daily)* is moored in tiny St Mary Overie Dock. You can go on board and explore the five decks. Buy your tickets at the card and souvenir shop just opposite the *Golden Hinde*. It's quite fun to see the replica Tudor fittings and cannons, but watch your head on the low ceilings of the gun deck. The truly adventurous will want to spend the night aboard this 37m-long ship. It costs £31.50 per person and includes supper of stew and bread and breakfast of bread and cheese. Ring ☎ 0870 011 8700 to book.

Winchester Palace (Map 9) North-west of Southwark Cathedral is Clink St, once the heart of a huge palace complex built for the bishop of Winchester, William Giffard, in 1109; it would remain home to the bishops of Winchester for more than 500 years but was converted into a prison for royalists under Cromwell in 1642. Today the scant remains include a fine 14th-century rose window (discovered in a Clink St warehouse in 1814) from the Great Hall and part of the flooring; you can view the ruins from outside.

Clink Prison Museum (Map 9) Once a private jail in the park of Winchester Palace – a 28-hectare park known as the Liberty of the Clink and under the jurisdiction of the bishops of Winchester and not the City – Clink Prison detained debtors, whores, thieves and even actors. It was burned down during the Gordon Riots in 1780 but hadn't been used for a century in any case. This was the notorious address that gave us the expression 'in the clink', meaning 'in jail'. The small, rather half-hearted Clink Prison Museum (☎ 7378 1558, Ⓦ www.clink.co .uk, 1 Clink St SE1; ⊖ London Bridge; adult/senior, student & child/family £4/3/9; open 10am-6pm daily) reveals the wretched life of the prisoners who were forced to pay for their own food and accommodation and sometimes had to resort to catching and eating mice. It also looks at the history of prostitution; this was, after all, the heart of the red-light district south of the river. Guided tours cost £1/free per adult/child but must be booked in advance.

Vinopolis – City of Wine (Map 9) It might seem an odd attraction in the capital of a country with little in the way of winemaking history and negligible amounts produced from its own vines, but Vinopolis (☎ 0870 444 4777, Ⓦ www.vinopolis.co .uk, 1 Bank End, Park St SE1; ⊖ London Bridge; adult/senior/child aged 5-15 £11.50/ 10.50/5; open 11am-9pm Mon, 11am-6pm Tues-Fri & Sun, 11am-8pm Sat), in a hectare of Victorian railway vaults in Bankside, has cashed in on Londoners' love affair with things red, white and rosé. Hightech exhibits introduce visitors to the history of wine-making, vineyards and grape varietals, regional characteristics and which wine goes with which food. Those aged under 18 must be accompanied by an adult.

The centrepiece is a tour of the wineproducing regions of the world in which you travel through the hills of Chianti on a 'scooter', 'fly' over the Hunter Valley and 'visit' Argentina, Chile, California, Spain and South Africa. The tour ends in the Grand Tasting Halls, where you can sample five different wines from all over the world. There are also **wine-tasting evenings**, a branch of the wine retailer **Majestic**, a **gourmet food and wine shop** and **Cantina Vinopolis**, which opens for lunch daily and for dinner Monday to Saturday.

Rose Theatre (Map 9) Though nothing of the original Globe Theatre has ever been found, the foundations of the nearby Rose Theatre (☎ 7593 0026, Ⓦ www.rosetheatre .org.uk, 56 Park St SE1; adult/senior & student/child aged 5-15/family £4/3/2/10; open 11am-5pm Apr-Sept, 10am-5pm Oct-Mar), built in 1587, were discovered in 1989 beneath an office building at Southwark Bridge. A 25-minute sound-and-light show at the excavation site takes place every 30 minutes daily.

Shakespeare's Globe (Map 9) The Globe Theatre (☎ 7902 1500, Ⓦ www.shakes peares-globe.org, 21 New Globe Walk SE1; ⊖ London Bridge; open 10am-5pm daily) consists of the reconstructed Globe Theatre and, beneath it, an **exhibition** (adult/senior & student/child aged 5-15/family £7.50/6/5/ 23 including guided tour; tours at 9am-noon May-Sept, 10am-5pm Oct-Apr) which focuses on Elizabethan London and the struggle to get the theatre rebuilt. The exhibits devoted to Elizabethan special effects are especially interesting and we love the lifesize cast from the 450-year-old Norfolk oak.

The original Globe (known as the 'Wooden O' after its circular shape and roofless centre) was erected in 1599 with timber from the Theatre (1576) on Curtain St in Shoreditch. The Globe burned down in 1613 and was immediately rebuilt. In 1642 it was finally closed by the Puritans, who regarded theatres as dreadful dens of iniquity, and it was dismantled two years later. Despite the worldwide popularity of Shakespeare, the Globe was barely a distant memory when American actor (later film director) Sam Wanamaker came searching for the Globe in 1949. Undeterred by the fact that the foundations of the theatre had vanished beneath a

For ticket details see Theatre in the Entertainment chapter; it's a popular attraction, with English-speaking foreigners far outnumbering local spectators. The *Globe Café* and *Globe Restaurant* open for lunch and dinner till 10pm or 11pm daily.

Millennium Bridge (Map 9) Though it got off on the wrong, well, footing (see the boxed text 'London Bridges Up & Down' in the Getting Around chapter), the Millennium Bridge linking Bankside and the City of London is now up and running. It pushes off from the southern bank of the Thames in front of the Tate Modern and berths on the northern bank at the steps of Peter's Hill. A footpath leads up to and across Queen Victoria St to St Paul's Churchyard and the cathedral. The bridge is accessible 24 hours a day and, of course, is free.

Tate Modern (Maps 6 & 9) The Bankside Power Station, designed by Giles Gilbert Scott after WWII but decommissioned in 1986, is now home of the vastly popular Tate Modern *(☎ 7887 8008, W www.tate org.uk, Queen's Walk SE1; ⊖ Blackfriars/London Bridge; admission free, special exhibitions £3-10; open 10am-6pm Sun-Thur, 10am-10pm Fri & Sat)*. The museum contains Britain's collection of international 20th-century and modern art and was the surprising winner of the Millennium Projects' popularity contest: by the end of its first year it had attracted 5.2 million visitors, making it the second favourite attraction in London after the august and long-established British Museum.

On display are high-quality works by Picasso, Matisse, Cézanne, Pollock, Rothko, Warhol and many more arranged by theme rather than chronologically or by artist, for instance Still Life, Object, Real Life, Nude, Action, Body, History, Memory, and Society. Tate's reputation for avant-garde special exhibitions – firmly established at its Millbank site (now Tate Britain) – continues south of the river, with recent exhibits focusing on the Italian Arte Povera (Poor Art) school of the late '60s and the sculptures of the late Juan Muñoz. Audioguides,

SIMON BRACKEN

The play's the thing... and nowhere is it better staged than at the Globe Theatre.

row of listed Georgian houses, Wanamaker set up the Globe Playhouse Trust in 1970 and began fund-raising for a memorial theatre. Work started in 1987, but Wanamaker died four years before it opened in 1997.

The new Globe was painstakingly constructed with 600 oak pegs (there's not a nail or a screw in the house), specially fired Tudor bricks and thatching reeds from Norfolk that – for some odd reason – pigeons don't like; even the plaster contains goat hair, lime and sand as it did in Shakespeare's time. Unlike other venues for Shakespearean plays, this theatre has been designed to resemble the original as closely as possible – even if that means leaving the arena open to the skies, expecting the 500 'groundlings' to stand and obstructing much of the view from the seats closest to the stage with two enormous 'original' Corinthian pillars. In winter, plays are staged in the new indoor **Inigo Jones Theatre**, a replica of a Jacobean playhouse connected to the Globe.

with four different tours, are available for £1. Free guided highlights tours depart at 10.30am, 11.30am, 2.30pm and 3.30pm daily. There are *cafes* on levels 2 & 7 open 10am to 5.30pm Sunday to Thursday and till 9.30pm on Friday and Saturday.

The building itself – with its two upper floors shrouded in glass and brightly lit at night and its landmark central chimney – is quite dramatic, especially when viewed from the opposite bank or the Millennium Bridge. The vast Turbine Hall is the most dramatic entrance to any public space in London.

Bankside Gallery (Map 6) This gallery *(☎ 7928 7521, Ⓦ www.banksidegallery .com, 48 Hopton St SE1; ✆ Blackfriars/ Waterloo; adult/senior & student £3.50/2; open 10am-8pm Tues, 10am-5pm Wed-Fri, 11am-5pm Sat & Sun)* is home to the Royal Watercolour Society and the Royal Society of Painter-Printmakers. There's no permanent collection at this friendly upbeat place but there are changing exhibitions of watercolours, prints and engravings. Artists Perspectives at 6.30pm on Tuesday gives you a chance to meet the artists and discuss their work. The gallery's ***bookshop*** is very good.

Waterloo (Map 6)

Waterloo, a less-than-salubrious area where the Eurostar terminates, is where you'll find the £20 million London IMAX Cinema sitting in the middle of a roundabout where bear- and bull-baiting were staged in the Middle Ages. In more recent years the wretched underpass below Tenison Way suffered the nickname 'Cardboard City' because of the number of homeless people living in its soulless confines. With the arrival of the cinema, they've been moved on.

London IMAX Cinema Part of the British Film Institute, the London IMAX Cinema *(☎ 7902 1234, Ⓦ www.bfi.org.uk/imax, 1 Charlie Chaplin Walk SE1; ✆ Waterloo; adult/senior & student/child aged 5-16 £6.95/5.95/4.95, with additional films £4.20; screenings 1.15pm, 2.25pm, 3.25pm, 4.35pm, 5.35pm, 6.50pm and 8pm daily, additional screening 9.15pm Fri & Sat)* is the largest in Europe, with a screen some 10 storeys high and 26m wide. The 485-seat cinema screens the usual 2-D and IMAX 3-D films – documentaries about travel, space and wildlife that thrill, shock and frighten for a while and then get dull and repetitive. Films last from 40 minutes to 1½ hours.

The South Bank (Map 6)

North of Waterloo station and across the Thames from Embankment tube station, the South Bank is a labyrinth of arts venues strung out on concrete walkways between Hungerford Railway Bridge and just beyond Waterloo Bridge. Almost no-one has had a good word to say about the indescribably ugly architecture, but a lot of work is being done to brush things up. In the short term that may make matters worse, but in the long term it can only be good news.

The **Royal Festival Hall** *(☎ 7960 4242, Ⓦ www.rfh.org.uk, Belvedere Rd SE1; ✆ Waterloo)* was built in 1951 for the Festival of Britain and now hosts opera, classical, jazz and choral music. It is currently undergoing a massive £50 million face-lift to celebrate its 50th anniversary. Alongside a range of pricey *cafes* and *restaurants* (including the popular *People's Palace* on level 3 – see the Places to Eat chapter), it also has a foyer where free recitals take place at lunchtime and most evenings. The smaller **Queen Elizabeth Hall** to the north-east and the **Purcell Room** host similar concerts and will also be redeveloped in the next few years.

Tucked almost out of sight under the arches of Waterloo Bridge is the **National Film Theatre** *(NFT; ☎ 7633 0274 for information or 7928 3232 for bookings, Ⓦ www .bfi.org.uk/nft, South Bank SE1; ✆ Waterloo)* built in 1958 and screening some 2000 films a year. Next door, the popular **Museum of the Moving Image** *(Ⓦ www.bfi.org .uk/museum)*, closed for redevelopment till 2003, tells the story of film and television.

The **Riverside Walk Market**, with prints and second-hand books, takes place immediately in front of the NFT under the arches of the bridge. See Books in the Shopping chapter for details.

ELLIOT DANIEL

Concrete evidence of the city's flourishing arts scene can be found at the South Bank complex.

The **Royal National Theatre** (☎ 7452 3000, W www.nationaltheatre.org.uk, South Bank SE1; ⊖ Waterloo), a love-it-or-hate-it complex of three theatres (Olivier, Lyttleton and Cottesloe), is the nation's flagship theatre. Dismissed by Prince Charles as resembling a 'disused power station', the National was designed in 1976 by the modernist architect Denys Lasdun, a great fan of concrete and horizontal lines. A £42 million modernisation was completed in 1999. Backstage tours cost £5/4.25 adult/senior & student and depart three times a day Monday to Saturday; for performance details see Theatre in the Entertainment chapter.

A short walk eastwards along the South Bank is **Gabriel's Wharf**, a cluster of twee craft shops, snack bars, cafes and restaurants that forms part of a successful attempt by local residents to resist further large-scale development in the area. It has more of a continental European than a British feel to it. From the South Bank Walkway you look across the river to stunning views of St Paul's and the City of London.

Hayward Gallery The brutalist Hayward Gallery (☎ 7261 0127 for information or 7960 4242 for bookings, W www.sbc.org .uk, Belvedere Rd SW1; adult/concession usually £8/6; open 10am-6pm Mon & Thur-Sun, 10am-8pm Tues & Wed), built in 1968, is one of London's premier exhibition spaces for blockbuster international art shows. Some love the grey, fortress-like concrete building, others can't say a nice thing about it. Whichever camp you fall into, you can hardly deny that it makes an excellent hanging space for contemporary and 20th-century art. But it's future is also in doubt. Admission prices depend on what's showing.

County Hall Directly across Westminster Bridge from the Houses of Parliament stands County Hall (⊖ Westminster/Waterloo), home to London County Council and then the renamed (1965) Greater London Council until its final disagreement with Margaret Thatcher in 1986. The grand building with its curved, colonnaded facade was built in

1922. After more than a decade of wrangling over its future it's finally started to acquire new life with the opening of a vast aquarium in the basement, a museum devoted to the work of the artist Salvador Dalí, two hotels and a restaurant.

London Aquarium As room after room of fish tanks go, this aquarium (*☎ 7967 8000,* W *www.londonaquarium.co.uk, County Hall, Westminster Bridge Rd SE1, entrance on Albert Embankment;* ✪ *Westminster/ Waterloo; adult/senior & student/child aged 3-14/family £8.75/6.50/5.25/25; open 10am-6pm daily*) is a pretty good one, and one of the largest in Europe. There is an uncomfortable discrepancy between the huge tanks with their sharks and the side tanks, which are so small that it takes only one inconsiderate photographer to block them from view. The coral-reef display and the new terrapin tank are impressive and the pond of Japanese goldfish in the foyer sets the watery mood.

Dalí Universe Cool but slippery is what some might call the Catalan Surrealist painter whose work forms the collection at Dalí Universe (*☎ 7620 2720,* W *www.daliuniverse .com, County Hall, Westminster Bridge Rd SE1;* ✪ *Westminster/Waterloo; adult/senior & student/child aged 5-16/family £8.50/6/ 5/22; open 10am-6.30pm daily*). With more than 500 items on display – from melting clocks and the famous Mae West Lips Sofa to the enormous painting he created for Hitchcock's *Spellbound* (1945) – in three themed areas (Sensuality & Femininity, Religion & Mythology and Dreams & Fantasy) there's something here for everyone, provided they're into Surrealism.

British Airways London Eye Just north of County Hall are the **Jubilee Gardens**, the site of the 1951 Festival of Britain and being extended northwards as far as the Hungerford Bridge. At the south-western corner of the gardens and fronting the Thames rises the British Airways (BA) London Eye *(Millennium Wheel;* ☎ *0870 500 0600,* W *www .ba-londoneye.com, Jubilee Gardens SE1;*

✪ *Waterloo; adult/senior/child aged 5-15 £8.50/6.50/5 Jan-Mar, £9/7/5 Apr-June & Oct-Dec, £9.50/7.50/5 July-Sept; open 10am-7pm daily Oct-Mar, 10am-8pm daily Apr-May & Sept, 10am-10pm daily June-Aug).* At 135m tall, it is the world's largest Ferris wheel. It is a thrilling experience to be in one of the 32 enclosed glass gondolas, enjoying views of some 25 miles (on clear days) across the capital; the Millennium Wheel takes 30 minutes to rotate completely and each capsule holds 25 passengers. Original plans were for the wheel to remain on site until 2005 and then be moved elsewhere, but the wheel has turned into a city icon and most Londoners love it.

Lambeth (Maps 2 & 6)

Lambeth is the district immediately south of Westminster Bridge where you'll find Lambeth Palace, with the Museum of Gardening History just beside it, and St Thomas's Hospital, with the Florence Nightingale Museum inside its grounds.

NEIL SETCHFIELD

A real Eyecon: Londoners love the Millennium Wheel but it might be moved in 2005.

Florence Nightingale Museum (Map 6)

Within walking distance of County Hall and attached to St Thomas's Hospital is the Florence Nightingale Museum (☎ 7620 0374, W www.florence-nightingale.co.uk, 2 Lambeth Palace Rd SE1; ⊖ Westminster/ Waterloo; adult/senior, student & child/ family £4.80/3.60/10; open 10am-5pm Mon-Fri, 11.30am-4.30pm Sat & Sun). It tells the story of the feisty war heroine (1820–1910) who led a team of nurses to Scutari in Turkey in 1854 during the Crimean War, where she worked to improve conditions for the soldiers before returning to London to set up a training school for nurses at St Thomas's Hospital in 1859. Some will find the museum rather wordy, but the video about Nightingale's life is certainly interesting.

Lambeth Palace (Map 2)

The red-brick Tudor gatehouse immediately beside the church of St Mary-at-Lambeth leads to Lambeth Palace (Lambeth Palace Rd SE1; ⊖ Lambeth North), the London residence of the archbishop of Canterbury. Although the palace is not usually open to the public, the gardens occasionally are; check with a TIC (see Local Tourist Offices in the Facts for the Visitor chapter) for details.

Museum of Gardening History (Map 2)

At the southern end of Lambeth Palace is the Museum of Gardening History (☎ 7401 8865, W www.museumgardenhistory.org, Lambeth Rd SE1 ⊖ Lambeth North; admission free; open 10.30am-5pm Mon-Fri & Sun Feb-mid-Dec). It's housed in the church of St Mary-at-Lambeth, which has some lovely stained glass (notice the Peddler of Lambeth, who left the parish an acre of land provided he and his dog were remembered in a church window such as this one) and a font for Baptist-style total immersion (the only one in London). The museum was inspired by the work of John Tradescant (1608–62) and his son, also called John, who were gardeners to Charles I and Charles II respectively. The Tradescants roamed the globe and brought back many exotic plants to London, including the pineapple, together with a collection of 'all things strange and rare' that they housed in The Ark, their house on South Lambeth Rd. This collection eventually formed the basis of the Ashmolean Museum in Oxford (see the Excursions chapter).

Although the church tower dates from the 14th century, the nave was rebuilt in 1852 and now provides exhibition space for information on the Tradescants' lives and on the inspirational 20th-century gardener Gertrude Jekyll. A 17th-century replica knot garden – a formal garden of intricate design – has been planted in the small churchyard, which also shelters the tombs of the Tradescants and of William Bligh (1754–1817), the ship's captain cast adrift during the mutiny on the Bounty in 1789.

Imperial War Museum (Map 2)

Housed in a striking building dating from 1815 and topped with a copper dome (1845), the Imperial War Museum (☎ 7416 5320 or 0891 600140, W www.iwm.org.uk, Lambeth Rd SE1; ⊖ Lambeth North; admission free; open 10am-6pm daily) traces various 20th-century conflicts. The site of the museum was originally the third Bethlehem Royal Hospital, known as Bedlam (the first was established outside Bishopsgate in Liverpool St in 1247, the second in Moorfields in 1676). When the hospital moved to Kent in 1926, Viscount Rothermere bought the old building and gave it to the nation to house a museum. Look out for a chunk of the Berlin Wall to the left of the main entrance.

Although there's still plenty of military hardware on show and the core of the six-floor museum is a chronological exhibition on the two world wars, these days the museum places more emphasis on the social cost of war: the Blitz, the food shortages and the propaganda. The 2nd floor features war paintings by the likes of Stanley Spencer and John Singer Sargent.

Particularly popular exhibits are the Trench Experience, which depicts the grim day-to-day existence of a WWI infantryman in a frontline trench on the Somme, and the Blitz Experience, which lets visitors sit inside a mock bomb-shelter during an air raid and then stroll through ravaged East

End streets. Both are on the lower-ground floor. Another popular one is the Secret War exhibition on the 1st floor, which takes a look at the work of the secret services from 1909 to the present day, with video footage of the 1980 siege of the Iranian embassy in Knightsbridge brought to a dramatic end by balaclava-clad SAS commandos in an 11-minute assault.

The museum's biggest draw, however, is the Holocaust Exhibition, which opened in 2000 on the 3rd floor and has proved so popular that tickets sometimes have to be time-stamped. As inured as one can get after viewing so much holocaust footage, breathing still tightens when Auschwitz's 'welcome mat', 'Arbeit Macht Frei' (Work Will Set You Free), comes into view, bones chill at the sight of piles of abandoned shoes and suitcases, tear ducts open as hundreds of twig-like corpses are shown being bulldozed into mass graves. Never again.

Temporary exhibits cover such topics as war reporting, fashion in the postwar years and the reconstruction – inside and out – of a 1940s-style house that featured in a Channel 4 documentary of that name.

In the museum grounds and facing Lambeth Rd is the **Tibetan Peace Garden** opened by the Dalai Lama in May 1999.

Battersea (Maps 10 & 11)

South-westwards along the Thames from Lambeth is Battersea (Station: Battersea Park), not the most inspiring of London districts but boasting a fine riverside park with a children's zoo, a pagoda and the looming shell of the old Battersea Power Station.

Battersea Power Station (Map 11)

Familiar from a million Pink Floyd album covers, Battersea Power Station is the building with the four smokestacks that somewhat resembles a table turned upside-down, visible from Chelsea Bridge. Built by Giles Gilbert Scott with two chimneys in 1933 (the other two were added in 1955), it ceased operating in 1982 and since then there have been innumerable proposals to give it a new life – from a Disney theme park, Warner multiplex cinema and Cirque du Soleil theatre to a new train station and shopping and hotel complex. Meanwhile, the main hall stands exposed to the elements with its insides ripped out, and the power station's future seems as uncertain as ever.

Battersea Park (Maps 10 & 11)

Stretching between Albert and Chelsea bridges is Battersea Park, (☎ 8871 7534; open dawn-dusk daily) a 50-hectare area of greenery

PAUL BIGLAND

The massive, upside-down table that is Battersea Power Station awaits a transformation.

filled with attractions and distractions, most prominently the **Peace Pagoda (Map 10)**, erected in 1985 by a sect of Japanese Buddhists who aim to complete similar pagodas all over the world. Golden statues of the Buddha sit in the niches on all four sides and a pinnacle soars 10m into the air.

Boats can be hired to get around the small lake (£4.60 per hour); buy tickets from the booth by the running track (☎ 8871 7537). The small **Children's Zoo (Map 10)** *(☎ 8871 7540, Battersea Park SW11; adult/senior & student/child £2/1/1; open 10am-5pm daily Apr-Sept, 11am-3pm Sat & Sun Oct-Mar)* is located in the park. On public holidays there is usually a funfair here, the sound carrying over the river.

CHELSEA, SOUTH KENSINGTON & EARL'S COURT (Map 10)

Much of west London is high-class territory; indeed, Kensington & Chelsea enjoys the highest average gross income of all central London boroughs. Go a bit farther west, though, and you'll reach Earl's Court and Barons Court, less prosperous areas that seem to have been dropped there by accident.

Until the 18th century, Chelsea was a relatively remote village harbouring the grand country houses of the rich. Cheyne Mews was the site of Henry VIII's Chelsea Manor House, built in 1536 and demolished shortly after the death in 1753 of its last resident, Hans Sloane, whose collection was the nucleus of the British Museum. Nowadays, of course, it's well and truly part of London, although its riverside setting ensures that it's still a favoured place for the wealthy to live. During the 1960s Chelsea was fashionable with the trendsetters who frequented King's Rd. The heyday of punk brought a brief, colourful renaissance in the '70s and the Sloane Rangers ruled the '80s from Sloane Square, but even if Chelsea is no longer at the forefront of fashion this is still one of London's classier and most exclusive districts.

Thanks to Prince Albert and the 1851 Great Exhibition (see the boxed text 'Prince Albert & the Great Exhibition' in the Facts about London chapter), South Kensington is first and foremost museumland, boasting

Give peace a chance: the Japanese Buddhist Peace Pagoda in Battersea Park

DOUG McKINLAY

the Natural History, Science and Victoria & Albert museums all on one road. Albert's memorial, fabulously renovated in recent years, is due north of this admirable trio.

Earl's Court is a lively, cosmopolitan part of town, with a large, mobile population, particularly Poles (who stay) and Australians (who don't – usually). It's a funny mix of the smart and the scruffy – one minute you're on Earl's Court Rd watching tall cans of lager being swilled on the street by vowel-wringing ockers, the next you're on Old Brompton Rd with its gay bars and chichi continental-style cafes.

Royal Hospital Chelsea

The Royal Hospital Chelsea *(☎ 7881 5204, Royal Hospital Rd SW3; ⊖ Sloane Square; admission free; open 10am-noon & 2pm-4pm Mon-Sat, 2pm-4pm Sun)* is a superb building (1692) designed by Sir Christopher Wren during the reign of Charles II, whose statue in Roman dress adorns the courtyard facing south. (There are excellent 'framed' views of Battersea Power Station across the Thames from here.) It was a home for veteran soldiers and still houses 337 Chelsea Pensioners, ex-servicemen over 65 who are widowed or single. In 2001 it was announced that ex-servicewomen over the age of 65 who meet the hospital's stringent requirements would be admitted for the first time in history. You may see some pensioners walking around the grounds in their dark blue greatcoats (in winter) or scarlet frockcoats (in summer).

You can stroll in the grounds (enter from West Rd) and visit the elegantly simple **Chapel** with its altar painting, *The Resurrection*, by Sebastiano Ricci, and the **Great Hall**, a refectory bedecked with flags and royal portraits. There's a service at the Chapel at 11am on Sunday. The **Chelsea Flower Show** (☎ 7834 4333) is held in the grounds of the hospital in May.

National Army Museum

Right beside the Royal Hospital but designed in the late 1960s with complete disregard for its elegant neighbour, the National Army Museum (☎ 7730 0717, W www.national-army-museum.ac.uk, Royal Hospital Rd SW3; ⊖ Sloane Square; admission free but donations requested; open 10am-5.30pm daily) does its best to inject life into its military exhibits. Displays deal with the history of weapons, armies, artillery and tactics, but the best one focuses on the life and times of the 'Redcoat', the British soldier from the Battle of Agincourt (1415) to the American Revolution (lower-ground floor). The story continues from the Napoleonic Wars on the 1st floor to the British Army today on the 3rd floor. Outside there is a memorial, in English and Chinese, to the Middlesex Regiment 'who defended Hong Kong with distinction in December 1941'.

Chelsea Physic Garden

The Chelsea Physic Garden (☎ 7352 5646, W www.cpgarden.demon.co.uk, 66 Royal Hospital Rd SW3, entrance Swan Walk; ⊖ Sloane Square; adult/child aged 5-16 £4/2; open noon-5pm Wed & 2pm-6pm Sun Apr-Oct) was created by the Apothecaries' Society, a City livery company, in 1673 to study the ways in which botany related to

medicine (then known as the 'physic art'). It's one of the oldest botanical gardens in Europe and its 1.5 hectares contain many rare trees and plants. Individual corners of the garden are given over to world medicine and plants suitable for dyeing and use in aromatherapy. A number of notable gardeners have worked here over the years, including William Aiton, the first gardener at Kew, and William Forsyth, who gave his name to the forsythia bush.

During the Chelsea Flower Show in May and the Chelsea Festival in June the garden opens noon to 5pm Monday to Friday. On Snowdrop Days (the first two Sundays in February) the garden opens 11am to 3pm.

Carlyle's House

From 1834 until his death in 1881, the great Victorian essayist and historian Thomas Carlyle lived in the three-storey house now known as Carlyle's House (☎ 7352 7087, 24 Cheyne Row SW3; ⊖ Sloane Square; adult/child £3.50/1.75; open 11am-5pm Wed-Sun Apr-early Nov). Here in the attic of this National Trust property he wrote his famous history of the French Revolution and many other works. Legend claims that when the manuscript was complete, a maid accidentally threw it on the fire, whereupon the diligent Thomas duly wrote it all again.

While it's not particularly large, this charming terraced house, built in 1798, has been left much as it was when Carlyle was living here and Chopin, Tennyson and Dickens came to call as guests. There's a small garden at the rear.

Chelsea Old Church

As you walk along Cheyne Walk you'll spot a black and gold **statue of Thomas More** (1477–1535), the lord chancellor who was executed for his opposition to Henry VIII's plans to make himself head of the Church of England after his divorce from Catherine of Aragon and marriage to Anne Boleyn. More and his family used to live in Chelsea, in a property expropriated by Henry after the lord chancellor's execution.

Immediately behind the statue is Chelsea Old Church (☎ 7795 1019, Cheyne Walk,

Old Church St SW3; ⊖ *Sloane Square; admission free; open 1.30pm-5.30pm Tues-Fri & Sun)*, which dates from the late 12th century but was flattened by two bombs in 1941 and later rebuilt. The interior contains many fine Tudor monuments, including the **More Chapel** to the south, which was rebuilt by Sir Thomas in 1528 and retains its wooden ceiling and pillar capitals, examples of the fledgling Renaissance style. At the western end of the southern aisle don't miss the only chained books in a London church (chained, of course, to stop anyone making off with them), including a copy of Foxe's *Book of Martyrs* dating from 1684. They were a gift from Hans Sloane of British Museum fame.

Celebrated former residents of Cheyne Walk also include *Middlemarch* author George Eliot, who lived and died at No 4; the artist Dante Gabriel Rossetti and the poet Algernon Swinburne, who shared the house at No 16; and the painter JMW Turner, who lived at No 119 under the alias Booth.

Albert & Battersea Bridges

One of the most striking of London's bridges, Albert Bridge is a cross between a cantilever and a suspension bridge that was buttressed to strengthen it as an alternative to closure in the 1960s. It was designed by Roland Mason Ordish in 1873 but later modified by the engineer Joseph Bazalgette (see Victorian London under History in the Facts about London chapter). Painted white and pink and with fairy lights adorning its cables, it can look positively festive at night. The booths at either end survive from the days when tolls were charged to cross it.

The Battersea Bridge that featured in the painter Whistler's *Nocturnes* and etchings was an earlier wooden model dating from 1772. It was Bazalgette who once again came up with the designs for the current bridge, which was built in 1890.

King's Rd

In the 17th century, Charles II set up a Chelsea love nest for his mistress, an orange-seller at the Drury Lane Theatre called Nell Gwyn. Returning from her house to Hampton Court Palace, he would make use of a farmer's track that inevitably came to be known as the King's Rd *(*⊖ *Sloane Square/ South Kensington).*

Even today, long after the hippies and the punks have moved on, King's Rd is still a trendy and fashionable place to be. It begins at Sloane Square, to the north of which runs

Albert Bridge, another wonder from the Victorian era, gives the Thames added sparkle.

Sloane St, celebrated for its designer boutiques. At 75 Sloane St is the Cadogan Hotel, where Oscar Wilde was arrested (in room No 118, to be precise) in 1895 and later jailed for his 'friendship' (the euphemism of the time) with Lord Alfred Douglas.

Michelin House

Even if you can't afford to eat at Terence Conran's restaurant **Bibendum** (see the Places to Eat chapter) in Michelin House *(81 Fulham Rd SW3;* ✪ *South Kensington)*, pass by just to take a look at the superb Art Nouveau architecture. It was built for Michelin between 1905 and 1911 by François Espinasse and completely restored in 1985; the famous roly-poly Michelin Man appears in the modern stained glass. The open-fronted ground floor provides space for upmarket fish and flower stalls, while the lobby is decorated with tiles showing early-20th-century cars. The Conran Shop (see Furnishings & Household Goods in the Shopping chapter) is also housed here.

Chelsea World of Sport

Chelsea World of Sport *(*☎ *7915 2222,* **W** *www.chelseaworldofsport.com, Chelsea Village, Fulham Rd SW6;* ✪ *Fulham Broadway; adult/senior & child aged 5-16/family £12.50/8/40; open 10am-6pm Mon-Fri, 9am-6pm Sat & Sun, plus 9am-noon on match days for CFC members only)* is Chelsea Football Club's very pricey paean to itself, tracing, through multimedia displays, the history and achievements of CFC, Stamford Bridge Stadium and the ever-expanding Chelsea Village recreation complex. Other interactive displays generously focus on other sports: tennis, rowing, volleyball, sprinting and climbing.

Brompton Oratory

Also known as the Oratory of St Philip Neri, this Roman Catholic church *(*☎ *7808 0900, 215 Brompton Rd SW7;* ✪ *South Kensington; open 6.30am-8pm daily)* was built in the Italian Baroque style in 1884. There are six daily Masses on weekdays, one at 6pm on Saturday and nine between 7am and 7pm on Sunday.

V&A Museum Highlights

- Raphael Cartoons
- Music Room from Norfolk House
- Morris, Gamble and Poynter Refreshment Rooms
- George Gilbert Scott's Hereford Screen
- Shah Jahan's wine cup
- Throne of Maharaja Ranjit Singh
- Becket Casket
- *Board and Bear Hunt* tapestry
- Henry VIII's writing desk
- Burghley Nef
- Great Bed of Ware
- Antonio Canova's *The Three Graces*

Victoria & Albert Museum

The Victoria & Albert Museum *(V&A;* ☎ *7942 2000,* **W** *www.vam.ac.uk, Cromwell Rd SW7;* ✪ *South Kensington; admission free; open 10am-5.50pm Mon, Tues & Thur-Sun, 10am-10pm Wed & last Fri of every month)* is a vast, rambling, wonderful museum of decorative art and design, part of Prince Albert's legacy to the nation in the aftermath of the successful Great Exhibition of 1851 (see the boxed text 'Prince Albert & the Great Exhibition' in the Facts about London chapter).

Like the British Museum, this is a place that needs careful planning if you're to get the most out of your visit. Again, don't try to see too much in one go; it's free, so you can come back again and again.

As soon as you're through the turnstile look at the floor plan and decide what you're most interested in; then stick to that plan unless you want to find the time has flown by and you're still inspecting the plaster casts of classical statues. Alternatively, take one of the free guided tours that introduce you to the galleries. Amazingly, most of the V&A's collection of some 4 million items is actually on display, but there's no chance of seeing everything – even in several goes.

Orientation The V&A's main entrance is on Cromwell Rd although you can also enter from Exhibition Rd. Level A is mostly devoted to art and design from India, China, Japan and Korea as well as European art. Room 40 is devoted to costume – everything from absurd 18th-century wigs and whalebone corsets to the platform shoes that brought Naomi Campbell crashing to the ground on a Paris catwalk.

The Raphael Gallery (room 48A) is devoted to seven cartoons by Raphael (1483–1520), not early satirical drawings but great paintings commissioned by Pope Leo X as designs for tapestries that now hang in the Vatican Museum. The finest are *Christ's Charge to Peter*, *The Miraculous Drought of Fishes* and *Paul Preaching at Athens*. Also on this floor, beyond the Pirelli Garden and off rooms 13 to 15 of the Italian art section are the V&A's three original refreshment rooms dating from the 1860s. The gorgeous Green Dining Room was designed by William Morris with help from his friend Edward Coley Burne-Jones and is now named after the former. Next to it is the Gamble Room, with elegant tiles, marble statuary and friezes with quotations from Ecclesiastes in the Old Testament. Beyond that is the Poynter Room, designed by Edward Poynter, which retains its original grill for turning out chops. The Canon Photography Gallery (room 38) has excellent rotating exhibits.

On Level B you'll find collections of ironwork (rooms 113 and 114), stained glass (rooms 111 and 116), jewellery (rooms 91 to 93) and a wonderful exhibit of musical instruments (room 40A). In the 15 recently reopened British Galleries, featuring every aspect of British design from 1500 to 1900, you will see the late-6th-century Great Bed of Ware, big enough to sleep five and designed as an early advertising gimmick for an inn in Hertfordshire. The highlights of this floor, though, are the Silver Galleries (rooms 65 to 69); even if silver isn't your thing have a look. The goblets, chalices and assorted other gewgaws are displayed in a lovely Victorian gallery approached up a delightful tiled staircase, which was narrowly saved from destruction in the days when full-blown Victoriana was thought the height of bad taste.

On this floor you'll also find displays of textiles (rooms 95 to 100), arms and armour (rooms 88A and 90) and 20th-century furniture (rooms 70 to 74 and 103 to 106). Up on Levels C and D are more displays of British art and design as well as ceramics, glass and porcelain from Europe and Asia.

The Henry Cole Wing, an add-on at the Exhibition Rd side of the museum, contains the largest collection of Constables gathered under one roof. It was a bequest from the artist's Charlotte St studios and contains mostly watercolours and minor oil paintings. You'll also find displays of prints and printmaking techniques as well as European paintings and miniatures. The exhibition focusing on the work of the American architect Frank Lloyd Wright (1869–1959) is worth the climb.

The *New Restaurant* near the Exhibition Rd entrance serves snacks and meals 10am to 5.30pm daily (10am to 9.30pm on Wednesday).

Guided Tours There are free, one-hour introductory tours of the V&A's various galleries between 10.30am and 3.30pm daily with an additional departure at 4.30pm on Wednesday. Gallery talks on all aspects of art and design take place at 1pm daily and last 45 minutes.

SIMON BRACKEN

With four million items on display you could be at the V&A for quite some time...

Natural History Museum

The Natural History Museum (☎ 7942 5000, W www.nhm.ac.uk, Cromwell Rd SW7; ⊖ South Kensington; admission free; open 10am-5.50pm Mon-Sat, 11am-5.50pm Sun) is housed in one of London's finest neo-Gothic buildings. It was designed by Alfred Waterhouse between 1873 and 1880 with a grand cathedral-like main entrance, a gleaming blue and sand-coloured brick and terracotta facing, thin columns and articulated arches, and carvings of plants and animals crawling all over it. It's a gem.

The Natural History Museum incorporates the old Geological Museum in Exhibition Rd; the two collections are divided between the adjoining Life Galleries (entrance on Cromwell Rd) and Earth Galleries (enter from Exhibition Rd). Where once the former was full of dusty glass cases of butterflies and stick insects, there are now wonderful interactive displays on themes such as Human Biology and Creepy Crawlies, alongside the crowd-pulling exhibition on mammals and dinosaurs, which includes animatronic movers and shakers like the 4m-high Tyrannosaurus Rex. School children flock to see these, but luckily that leaves more space on the wondrous mammal balcony, at the Blue Whale exhibit and in the Ecology gallery, with its replica rainforest.

In some ways, though, it's the Earth Galleries that are the most staggering. As you enter from Exhibition Rd you'll find yourself facing an escalator that slithers up and

DAVID WALL

Long-legged beasties to menacing midges: critters galore at the Natural History Museum

into a hollowed-out globe. Around its base, single fine samples of different rocks and gems are beautifully displayed. Upstairs there are two main exhibits: Earthquake and the Restless Surface, which explains how wind, water, ice, gravity and life itself impact on the earth. Earthquake is an extraordinary trembling mock-up of what happened to one small grocery shop during the Kobe trembler in Japan in 1995 that killed 6000 people. Excellent exhibitions on the lower floors include Earth Today and Tomorrow, which focuses on ecology; Earth's Treasury, which looks at gems and other precious stones; and from the Beginning, which explores how planets are formed.

To avoid crowds during school term-time it's best to visit early morning or late afternoon. The *Waterhouse Café* on the ground floor of the Life Galleries is quite good, with a decent selection of vegetarian dishes.

Natural History Highlights

- Moving & shaking Tyrannosaurus Rex
- Entrance to the Earth Galleries
- Simulated Kobe earthquake
- Creepy Crawlies display
- Minerals and gemstones in the Earth's Treasury
- Diplodocus dinosaur skeleton
- Blue whale model
- Wildlife Garden

Science Museum

The Science Museum (☎ 0870 870 4868, W www.sciencemuseum.org.uk, Exhibition Rd SW7; ✦ South Kensington; admission free, IMAX cinema adult/senior, student & under-16s £6.75/5.75; open 10am-6pm daily) is at the cutting edge of exhibiting items on a subject that could otherwise be quite dull.

On the ground floor, Making the Modern World looks back at the history of the Industrial Revolution via examples of its machinery and then looks forward to the exploration of space. There are enough old trains (including Puffing Billy, a steam locomotive dating from 1813) and vintage cars to keep the kids well and truly happy. Up a floor and you can find out about the impact of science on food, time, telecommunications and weather. Up another one and you're into the world of computers, chemistry and nuclear power. The 3rd floor is the place to come for the old aeroplanes, among them the Vickers Vimy in which Alcock and Brown first flew the Atlantic in 1919, and Amy Johnson's Gipsy Moth, in which she flew to Australia in 1930. On the 4th and 5th floors you'll find exhibits relating to the history of medicine and veterinary science.

Look out for a modern version of Foucault's famous pendulum hanging in the hall. As the day wears on the pendulum seems to change direction. In fact, because the earth is moving beneath it, it really stays in the same place. This is how Foucault illustrated how the earth rotates on its own axis.

The basement has imaginative hands-on galleries for children: the Garden is for three to six-year-olds, Things for seven to 11-year-olds. The Secret Life of the Home, a collection of labour-saving appliances that householders have either embraced or shunned, is for everyone.

The Wellcome Wing, a £50 million extension to the museum, is filled with hands-on displays and is a great place to take kids. Of special interest are Digitopolis, which focuses on digital technology; On Air, which looks at broadcasting; and Flight Lab, where you can test a model in a wind tunnel or try to get a helicopter off the ground. The 450-seat IMAX cinema (entrance on the ground

floor of the Wellcome Wing) has the usual crop of travelogues, space adventures and dinosaur attacks in stunning 3-D.

The **Deep Blue Café** on the ground floor of the Wellcome Wing opens 10.30am to 5.30pm daily.

Science Museum Highlights

- Boulton & Watt's steam engine
- Foucault's Pendulum
- Apollo 10 Command Module
- Robert Stephenson's Rocket
- Gas-drilling rig
- Wells Cathedral clock (1392)
- Hologram displays
- Amy Johnson's Gipsy Moth
- Mr Gibson's pharmacy (1905)
- Digitopolis

KNIGHTSBRIDGE, KENSINGTON & HOLLAND PARK
(Maps 5 & 10)

Knightsbridge is where you'll find some of London's best-known department stores, including Harrods and Harvey Nichols (see Department Stores in the Shopping chapter). To the west and north-west is Kensington, another thoroughly desirable London neighbourhood where you won't get a penny change from a million pounds if you want to buy a house. Its main thoroughfare, Kensington High St, is another shoppers' mecca. North of Kensington High St is Holland Park, a residential district of elegant town houses, in the heart of which is a wooded park, open from 7.30am to dusk. Here you'll find the wonderful Holland Park Theatre (see the Opera and the Ballet & Dance sections in the Entertainment chapter) and a hostel in the Jacobean wing of the former Holland House (see the Places to Stay chapter), some delightful formal gardens (at their most glorious in summer), a playground and a restaurant. The old Orangery is often used as an exhibition space for young artists.

ELLIOT DANIEL

The elegant Albert Memorial stands
opposite the Albert Hall in Hyde Park.

Albert Memorial (Map 5)

On the southern edge of Hyde Park and facing Kensington Gore, the Albert Memorial *(✆ South Kensington/Gloucester Road)* is an over-the-top monument to Queen Victoria's German-born husband Albert (1819–61), which has recently undergone a £11 million renovation lasting eight years. The 52.5m-high memorial was designed by George Gilbert Scott in 1863 and decorated with 178 figures representing the continents (Asia, Europe, Africa and America) as well as the arts, industry and science. The mosaics are the work of the renowned church artists Clayton and Bell. Albert is shown holding a copy of the catalogue of the 1851 Great Exhibition (see the boxed text 'Prince Albert & the Great Exhibition' in the Facts about London chapter). Guided tours (✆ 7495 0916) lasting 35 to 40 minutes depart at 2pm and

3pm on Sunday and cost £3.50/3 (adult/ senior & student). The monument is very impressive at night when it is fully illuminated.

Royal Albert Hall (Map 5)

The huge red-brick amphitheatre facing the Albert Memorial on the other side of Kensington Gore is the Royal Albert Hall *(✆ 7589 3203, W www.royalalberthall.com, Kensington Gore SW7; ✆ South Kensington)*, completed in 1871 and adorned with a frieze of Minton tiles. The hall was never intended as a concert venue but as a 'Hall of Arts and Sciences'; Queen Victoria added the 'Royal Albert' when she laid the foundation stone, much to the surprise of those attending.

The hall is best known for the Promenade Concerts (or 'Proms') held here every summer since 1947 (see Classical Music in the Entertainment chapter). Unfortunately, the only way to see inside is by attending a concert, and the acoustics are horrible; it is said that the only way a British composer can ever hear his work *twice* is by playing at the Royal Albert Hall, so bad is the echo reverberating around the oval structure.

The hall's enormous Victorian organ, built in 1868 and the largest in Britain, is undergoing an overhaul and won't be played again until 2004.

Royal Geographical Society (Map 5)

A short distance to the east of the Royal Albert Hall is the headquarters of the Royal Geographical Society *(RGS; ✆ 7591 3040, W www.rgs.org, 1 Kensington Gore SW7; ✆ South Kensington; admission free, map research adult/student £10/5; open 10am-5pm Mon-Fri)*. This Queen Anne-style red-brick edifice (1874) is easily identified by the statues of explorers David Livingstone (facing Kensington Gore) and Ernest Shackleton (facing Exhibition Rd) outside. The RSG will be closed for renovations until mid-2003

Kensington Palace (Map 5)

Sometime home to Princess Margaret and Diana, Princess of Wales, is Kensington Palace *(✆ 7937 9561, Kensington Gardens*

W8; ✚ *Queensway/Notting Hill Gate; admission to State Apartments adult/senior & student/child aged 5-16/family £8.80/6.90/ 6.50/26.80, park & gardens free; State Apartments open 10am-5pm daily Mar-Oct, 10am-4pm daily Nov-Feb; park & gardens open 5am-30 minutes before dusk daily).* It dates from 1605 when it was home to the 2nd earl of Nottingham. In 1688, when William of Orange arrived to take over as king from James II, he found the old palace at Whitehall confining and too close to the busy river to suit his asthmatic lungs; Queen Mary complained she could 'see nothing but water or wall' from the palace. They bought the house in the park from Nottingham and had it adapted by Sir Christopher Wren and Nicholas Hawksmoor. When George I came from Hanover to succeed Queen Anne, the childless last Stuart monarch, he recruited William Kent to modernise the palace. Much of the decor you see today is Kent's sometimes clumsy handiwork. Queen Victoria was born in a ground-floor room here in 1819, and one room is kept as a memorial.

Tours of the palace are via audioguide and self-paced but should take about 1½ hours. They take you round the small, wood-panelled State Apartments dating from the time of William and the much grander, more spacious apartments of the Georgian period.

Displayed under low lights you'll see costumes from the Royal Ceremonial Dress Collection, including skirts so ludicrously wide that they made it impossible for their wearers to sit down and ensured that rooms had to be sparsely furnished. The major draw here is a striking collection of lovely frocks worn by Diana, Princess of Wales.

Most beautiful of all the rooms is the **Cupola Room**, where the ceremony of initiating men into the exclusive Order of the Garter took place and where Victoria was baptised; you can see the order's crest painted on the *trompe l'œil* 'domed' ceiling, which is essentially flat. The room is ringed with marbled columns and niches in which stand gilded statues in the Roman style. In the centre of the room an ugly clock stands on a stepped plinth. It used to play the music of Handel and Corelli but no more.

The **King's Long Gallery** displays some of the royal art collection, including the only known painting of a classical subject by Van Dyck. On the ceiling William Kent painted the story of Odysseus but slipped up by giving the Cyclops two eyes!

The **King's Drawing Room** is dominated by an extraordinarily ugly painting of *Cupid and Venus* by Giorgio Vasari (1511–74), an Italian mannerist painter better known for his history of Italian Renaissance art. Through the window you can see the **Round Pond**, once full of turtles for turtle soup but now popular for sailing model boats, and a statue of the young Queen Victoria, sculpted by her daughter, Princess Louise.

The **King's Staircase** is decorated with striking murals by William Kent who painted himself in a turban on the fake dome. A prominent figure of a Highlander was included at a time when the threat from the Jacobites in Scotland was by no means dead. Also included is a portrait of Peter, the 'wild child' who had been discovered in the woods of Hanover and brought to England to entertain the jaded court.

The **Sunken Garden** near the palace is at its prettiest in summer. Nearby is the Orangery, designed by Hawksmoor and Vanbrugh with carvings by Grinling Gibbons. Tea here is a pricey treat (see the boxed text 'On the High Teas' in the Places to Eat chapter).

Linley Sambourne House (Map 5)

Tucked away behind Kensington High St is Linley Sambourne House *(☎ 8994 1019, 18 Stafford Terrace W8;* ✚ *High Street Kensington; adult/senior & student/child £3.50/ 2.50/2; open 10am-4pm Wed, 2pm-5pm Sun Mar-Oct),* home from 1874 to 1910 of the *Punch* political cartoonist and amateur photographer Linley Sambourne. This is one of those houses whose owners never redecorated or threw anything away; what you see is the virtually unmodernised home of a fairly well-to-do Victorian family, all dark wood, Turkish carpets and rich stained glass. If you've ever wondered what a real-life 19th-century house looked like, this is it. The house is closed till 2002 due to renovations.

Commonwealth Institute (Map 5)

On the southern side of Holland Park just off Kensington High St, an open space with fountains and flagpoles fronts the Commonwealth Institute (☎ 7603 4535, W www.commonwealth.org.uk, Kensington High St W8; ⊖ High Street Kensington), designed in 1962 to resemble a large tent and created from materials gathered from all over the British Commonwealth. It looks as horrid as it sounds. The rather pedestrian interior has recently been revamped to extol the virtues of the 54 countries making up the Commonwealth and temporary exhibits related to the Commonwealth take place here.

Leighton House (Map 10)

Near Holland Park and Kensington but frequently overlooked is Leighton House (☎ 7602 3316, 12 Holland Park Rd W14; ⊖ High Street Kensington; admission free but donations welcome; open 11am-5.30pm Wed-Mon), a gem of a house designed in 1866 by George Aitchison. It was once the home of Lord Leighton (1830–96), a painter who belonged to the Olympian movement and decorated parts of the house in Middle Eastern style. Finest of all the rooms is the exquisite **Arab Hall**, added in 1879 and densely covered with blue and green tiles from Rhodes, Cairo, Damascus and Iznik (Turkey) and with a fountain tinkling away in the centre. Even the wooden latticework of the windows and gallery was brought from Damascus. The house contains notable pre-Raphaelite paintings by Burne-Jones, Watts, Millais and Lord Leighton himself. Restoration of the back garden has returned it to its Victorian splendour as has work on the stairwell and upstairs rooms.

NOTTING HILL & BAYSWATER (Map 5)

The great popularity of the Notting Hill Carnival on the August Bank Holiday weekend reflects the multicultural appeal of this area of west London. In the 1950s Notting Hill became a focus for immigrants from Trinidad. Today it's a thriving, vibrant corner of London separated from the West End and

Mayfair by the great expanse of Hyde Park and best visited on Saturday for the Portobello Rd Market (see the special section 'To Market, to Market').

There's not a heck of a lot to see in Notting Hill, though you might check out the newly renovated Edwardian **Electric Cinema**, the oldest purpose-built cinema in the UK, at 191 Portobello Rd (see Cinemas in the Entertainment chapter).

The site of a spring (Baynard's Watering) that supplied the City of London with fresh water in the Middle Ages, Bayswater was given a wide berth for centuries due to the proximity of the gallows at Tyburn (see Marble Arch in the Hyde Park Area section). Today it is a fairly well-to-do and convenient residential area sitting uncomfortably close to scruffy Paddington. Its main thoroughfare is Queensway, which has a decent selection of restaurants, many of them Chinese. Come to Bayswater on Sunday to view the paintings (mostly derivative, touristy stuff) on sale on the railings of Hyde Park and Kensington Gardens along Bayswater Rd or to unwind in the Porchester Spa (see Public Baths under Activities later in this chapter).

HYDE PARK AREA (Maps 5 & 6)

At the far western end of Piccadilly, Hyde Park is one of those areas where posh hotels and prestigious shops have long since squeezed out the hoi polloi. If you're driving, you'd do well to avoid the nightmare of the Hyde Park Corner roundabout – although trying to find the right exit from the Underground isn't a whole lot easier.

Hyde Park (Map 5)

At 145 hectares, Hyde Park (☎ 7298 2100; open 5.30am-midnight daily) is central London's largest open space. Expropriated from the Church by Henry VIII in 1536, it became a hunting ground for kings and aristocrats, and then a venue for duels, executions and horse racing. In the early 17th century it opened to the public – the first royal park to do so. In 1851 the Great Exhibition was held here (see the boxed text 'Prince Albert & the Great Exhibition' in the Facts about London chapter) and during

WWII it became an enormous potato bed. More recently, it has served as a concert venue. The park is a riot of colour in spring and full of milk-white to pinkish sunbathers in summer. Boating on the Serpentine is an option for the relatively energetic; see the Activities section in this chapter for details.

Along with sculptures by Henry Moore and Jacob Epstein and a statue of **Peter Pan** by George Frampton, there's also **Serpentine Gallery** (☎ *7402 6075,* **W** *www.serpentine gallery.org;* ✚ *Knightsbridge; admission free; open 10am-6pm daily)*, which is beautifully located south of the Serpentine and just west of the main road that cuts through the park, separating Hyde Park from Kensington Gardens. It sponsors temporary exhibitions and specialises in contemporary art.

Not far from Marble Arch, **Speakers' Corner** *(*✚ *Marble Arch)* started life in 1872 as a response to serious riots 17 years earlier when 150,000 people gathered to demonstrate against the Sunday Trading Bill before Parliament. Every Sunday anyone with a soapbox – or anything else to stand on – can hold forth on whatever subject takes their fancy. Provided you don't go along expecting Churchill-style oratory, it's entertaining.

As with other parks, walkers should keep to the pedestrian paths and watch out for skaters and cyclists.

Marble Arch (Map 5)

In the north-eastern corner of Hyde Park is Marble Arch *(*✚ *Marble Arch)*, a huge arch designed by John Nash in 1827 that was moved here from its original spot in front of

London's grandest bedsit, otherwise known as Marble Arch

Buckingham Palace in 1851. There is actually a one-room flat inside.

At the junction of Edgware Rd and Bayswater Rd stood the so-called **Tyburn Tree**, the three-legged gallows where up to 50,000 people were executed between 1300 and 1783. Many of them had been dragged to the scaffold from the Tower of London or Newgate Prison in the City. Farther west along Bayswater Rd is the Benedictine **Tyburn Convent** (☎ *7723 7262, 8 Hyde Park Place; admission free; open 6.15am-8.30pm daily)*, the chapel of which contains relics of 105 Catholic martyrs executed at Tyburn during the Reformation (notice the victims' coats of arms on the walls). Free 40-minute tours take place at 10.30am, 3.30pm and 5.30pm daily.

Apsley House & Wellington Museum (Map 6)

Striking Apsley House *(149 Piccadilly W1;* ✚ *Hyde Park Corner)*, which once had the prestigious address of 'No 1 London' as it was the first building one saw when entering from the west, but which now overlooks the nightmarish Hyde Park Corner roundabout, was designed by Robert Adam between 1771 and 1778 for Baron Apsley. It was sold in 1817 to the 1st duke of Wellington, victor at the Battle of Waterloo and later prime minister, who lived here until his death in 1852. In 1947 the house was given to the nation and today it houses the Wellington Museum *(*☎ *7499 5676; admission free; open 11am-5pm Tues-Sun)*. Unlike most 18th-century London town houses, Apsley House retains many of its original furnishings and collections, and still has descendants of the original family in residence. Some 10 rooms are open to the public, however.

The ground floor displays an astonishing collection of china, including a dinner service decorated with Egyptian scenes, and some of the Iron Duke's silverware, including the stunning Waterloo Vase and Shield. The stairwell is dominated by Antonio Canova's staggering 3.4m-high statue of Napoleon, naked but for the obligatory fig leaf. 'Rather too athletic,' opined the subject when it was unveiled. The 1st-floor rooms have fine plaster ceilings and a collection of paintings by Velásquez, Goya, Rubens, Brueghel and Murillo. The basement gallery contains Wellington memorabilia, including his medals, some entertaining old cartoons and his death mask.

Wellington Arch (Map 6)

Opposite Apsley House in the little bit of green space being strangled by the Hyde Park Corner roundabout is Wellington Arch *(☎ 7973 3539, W www.english-heritage .org.uk, Hyde Park Corner W2; ✪ Hyde Park Corner; adult/senior & student/child £2.50/1.90/1.30; open 10am-6pm Wed-Sun)*, which was long off-limits to ordinary mortals like us but is now an English Heritage property open to the public. Built in 1826 to commemorate Wellington's victories over Napoleon, the arch was for many years London's smallest police station before falling into disrepair. A £1.5 million refit has given it three floors of exhibition space, including ones devoted to both Wellington and Marble arches, and a viewing platform with spectacular views of Hyde Park and the Houses of Parliament.

MARYLEBONE & REGENT'S PARK (Maps 3, 5 & 6)

Marylebone Rd is north of Oxford St and home to the capital's No 1 tourist trap, Madame Tussaud's. It's also close to Regent's Park, which provides a haven of peace in as well as being home to London Zoo.

Wallace Collection (Map 6)

The Wallace Collection *(☎ 7935 9500, W www.wallace-collection.com, Hertford House, Manchester Square W1; ✪ Bond Street; admission free; open 10am-5pm Mon-Sat, noon-5pm Sun)* is London's finest small gallery and relatively unknown by most – including Londoners. It houses a treasure-trove of high-quality paintings from the 17th and 18th centuries, including works by Rubens, Titian, Poussin and Rembrandt, in a splendid Italianate mansion, which was left to the nation by the widow of fine-art collector Sir Richard Wallace (1818–90). There's also a collection of elaborate armour. The exquisite

classical building is worth a visit in itself, and the staircase is reckoned to be one of the best examples of French interior architecture; it was intended for the Banque Royale in Paris but was bought by Wallace and installed here in 1874. Vast canvases by Frances Boucher adorn the stairwell.

Four new galleries in the basement focus on watercolours and conservation; don't miss the Fakes & Forgeries section in the Reserve Collection. From here you can cross over to the Sculpture Garden or visit the pleasant *Café Bagatelle*, which opens the same hours as the collection.

Free guided tours start around 11.30am or 1pm Monday to Friday, 11.30am Saturday and 3pm Sunday (call for exact times).

Madame Tussaud's (Map 5)

Madame Tussaud's *(☎ 0870 400 3000, W www.madame-tussauds.com, Marylebone Rd NW1; ✪ Baker Street; adult/ senior/under-16s £12/9.50/8.50, including London Planetarium £14.45/11.30/10; open 9am-5.30pm daily June–mid-Sept, 10am-5.30pm Mon-Fri, 9.30am-5.30pm Sat & Sun mid-Sept–May)* is one of London's most popular sights in London (after the British Museum, Tate Modern and National Gallery), counting some 2.7 million visitors a year. In order to avoid the long queues (particularly in summer), arrive early in the morning or late in the afternoon or – better still – buy your tickets in advance from a ticket agency or make a card booking by phone (£2 fee).

Madame Tussaud's – or Madame Tussaud's Waxworks as it was once known – dates back two and a half centuries and Mme T herself started life modelling the heads of people killed during the French Revolution; the 200 Years exhibition shows her working on a death mask from the head of Marie Antoinette in her original studio.

Much of the modern Madame Tussaud's is made up of the **Garden Party** exhibition at the beginning, where you can have your picture taken alongside celebrities – from Pierce Brosnan and Hugh Grant to Whoopi Goldberg. The **Grand Hall** is where you'll come across models of world leaders past and present, including Nelson Mandela and the Royal Family (now minus Sarah 'Fergie' Ferguson, the errant duchess of York, and with a dead-ringer model of Diana, Princess of Wales, on the sidelines) and of pop stars such as The Beatles. And what happens to those whose 15 minutes of fame have ticked by? Their heads are removed as surely as Marie Antoinette's was and stored in a cupboard – just in case they get another stab at those 15 minutes.

In the **Spirit of London** 'time taxi', you sit in a mock-up of a London black cab and are whipped through a five-minute summary of London's history. The models are great but it's irritating if you land the cab whose commentary is still dealing with the Great Fire as you pass the Swinging London panorama.

The **Chamber of Horrors** has models of contemporary prisoners such as Dennis Nilsen (the 'Muswell Hill Murderer') sitting uneasily alongside representations of historic horrors including the mutilated corpse of one of Jack the Ripper's victims. But it all seems somewhat tame compared with the London Dungeon's blood-fest.

London Planetarium (Map 5)

Attached to Madame Tussaud's, the London Planetarium (☎ 0870 400 3000, ☒ www

MANFRED GOTTSCHALK

It's amazing what you can do with a lump of wax, a wig and a pair of outlandish glasses.

.madame-tussauds.com, Marylebone Rd NW1; ⊖ Baker Street; admission adult/senior/under-16s £7/5.60/4.85, including Madame Tussaud's £14.45/11.30/10; open 9am-5.30pm daily June-mid-Sept, 10am-5.30pm Mon-Fri, 9.30am-5.30pm Sat & Sun mid-Sept–May) presents 30-minute spectaculars on the stars and planets livened up with some fairly impressive special effects; the Wonders of the Universe, in which you join a spaceship of travellers on a tour of the solar system is particularly effective. There are wax figures of scientists and other space-related figures – from Copernicus and Stephen Hawkings to American astronauts Buzz Aldrin and Neil Armstrong – greeting you and assorted computer consoles will answer most (if not all) of your questions about space and space travel.

Baker Street Underground Station (Map 5)

The train-spotters among you – and we know you're out there – will be interested to learn that one of the original stations of the first underground train line in the world (the Metropolitan Railway) lies underfoot at Baker Street station and can be visited simply by buying an Underground ticket or using your travel pass. Baker Street, one of the seven original stations on the line that stretched for all of about 3¾ miles from Paddington to Farringdon St, opened in 1863. It's on platform Nos 5 and 6 (Circle and Hammersmith & City lines) and was restored to its dimly lit former self in 1983.

Sherlock Holmes Museum (Map 5)

While the Sherlock Holmes Museum (☎ 7935 8866, ☒ www.sherlock-holmes .co.uk, 221b Baker St; adult/child aged 6-14 £6/4; open 9.30am-6.30pm daily) gives its address as 221b Baker St, the house in which Sherlock Holmes supposedly resided is actually the Abbey National building a bit farther south on the corner with Melcombe St. Fans of the books will enjoy looking at the three floors of reconstructed Victoriana and the new waxworks of various Holmes characters scattered throughout the museum:

Charles Augustus Milverton; the 'Man with the Twisted Lip' (Neville St Clair); and, of course, Professor Moriarty.

Regent's Park (Map 3)

Regent's Park (☎ 7486 7905; open 5am-dusk daily; ⊖ Baker Street/Regent's Park), north of Marylebone and south-west of Camden, was, like many other London parks, once used as a royal hunting ground, subsequently farmed and then revived as a place for fun and leisure during the 18th century.

With the London Zoo, the **Grand Union Canal** along its northern side, an **open-air theatre** (see the Entertainment chapter) where Shakespeare is performed during the summer months, ponds and colourful flower beds, football pitches and summer games of softball, Regent's Park is a lively but serene, local but cosmopolitan haven in the heart of the city. The roses in **Queen Mary's Gardens** are particularly spectacular, and there's an adjoining cafe.

On the western side of the park is the impressive **London Central Islamic Centre & Mosque** (☎ 7724 3363, 146 Park Rd NW8; ⊖ St John's Wood), a huge white edifice with a glistening dome. Provided you take your shoes off and dress modestly you're welcome to go inside, although the interior is fairly stark.

To the north of Regent's Park, across Prince Albert Rd, is **Primrose Hill**, which, besides being less touristy and less conventionally pretty, also has a spectacular view over London.

London Zoo (Map 3)

One of the oldest zoos in the world, London Zoo (☎ 7722 3333, ⓦ www.londonzoo.co.uk, Regent's Park NW1; ⊖ Camden Town; adult/senior & student/child aged 3-14 £10/8.50/7; open 10am-5.30pm daily Mar-Oct, 10am-4pm daily Nov-Feb) is – like the London Underground – a victim of its great age: it was 170 years old in 1998. During WWII, most of the wild animals here were put down as it was feared that they might escape if the zoo was bombed. The rest were evacuated to Ireland. Zoo staff al-

ASA ANDERSSON

Soak up a few rays in one of central London's wide open spaces.

legedly took the tropical fish home for supper.

The zoo is saddled with many buildings that are historically interesting but don't meet the expectations of animal-rights-minded modern visitors. But the zoo is in the middle of a 10-year, £21 million programme to modernise the place; the emphasis is now firmly placed on conservation and education, with fewer species kept, wherever possible in breeding groups.

The **Web of Life**, a glass pavilion containing some 60 live animal exhibits (from termites and jellyfish to the birds and the bees), has interactive displays and, yes, real-life, on-show breeding groups look at. It makes a visit to the zoo worthwhile by itself. Elsewhere don't miss the enclosures housing the big cats, the elephants and rhinos, the apes and monkeys, the small mammals and the birds. The revamped Mappin Terraces houses **Bear Mountain**; the elegant and cheerful **Penguin Pool** is one of London's foremost modernist structures, designed by Berthold Lubetkin in 1934.

The nicest way to get to the zoo is by canal boat from Little Venice or Camden (for details see Canal Trips in the Getting Around chapter), but you can also reach it by walking along the canal towpath.

North London

The northern reaches of central London stretch in a broad arc from St John's Wood in the west to Islington in the east. Those two districts exemplify the great economic divide that exists in the capital: the former is all moneyed gentility, the latter the run-down opposite in areas around Angel, where less than 10% of the area is open public space. In between, Regent's Park and its northerly extension, Primrose Hill, offer the largest expanse of greenery. The Grand Union (or Regent's) Canal wends round the north of the park, offering a pleasant way to avoid the traffic en route to Camden Market. North London's other main attractions are Hampstead Heath, where it's as easy to forget you're in a big city as it is to get completely lost, and that Victorian Valhalla of Highgate Cemetery.

ST JOHN'S WOOD & MAIDA VALE (Maps 2 & 3)

Posh St John's Wood, a leafy suburb of genteel houses to which the comfortably off retreat, is due west of Regent's Park. Art lovers may want to detour here to visit the Saatchi Gallery, one of the more cutting-edge art collections in London, and pop fans will head for 3 Abbey Rd NW8, where The Beatles recorded 80% of their albums, including *Abbey Road* (1969) itself, with the album cover shot taken on the **zebra crossing (Map 3)** outside. Cricket lovers will instead want to hotfoot it to Lord's Cricket Ground. Slightly south-west are Maida Vale and Little Venice, the place to come for canal trips to London Zoo and Camden (see Canal Trips in the Getting Around chapter).

Saatchi Gallery (Map 2)

The Saatchi Gallery (☎ 7624 8299, 98a Boundary Rd NW8; ⊖ Kilburn High Road; adult/senior, student & child aged 12-18 £5/3; open noon-6pm Thur-Sun) is the private collection of contemporary art owned by Charles Saatchi, until recently co-chairman of Saatchi & Saatchi, once the world's biggest advertising agency.

This is not the place to come if your tastes run to Constable or Turner. Here you're more likely to find yourself confronting giant pools of oil reflecting the ceiling or models of human figures so lifelike you're almost afraid they'll jump and start talking. It was Saatchi who patronised Damien Hirst, the formaldehyde king, and Rachel Whiteread, who turned an entire house into a work of sculpture only to see it torn down shortly afterwards, as well as Tracey Emin and Sarah Lucas. The exhibition space is light-filled, airy and large.

DENNIS JOHNSON

Look familiar? This zebra crossing on Abbey Rd was made famous by the Fab Four.

Lord's Cricket Ground (Map 3)

Daily guided tours of Lord's Cricket Ground (☎ 7432 1066, W www.lords.org, St John's Wood Rd NW8; ↔ St John's Wood) take in the famous Long Room, where members watch the games surrounded by portraits of cricket's great and good, as well as a small museum (☎ 7432 1033) with cricket memorabilia. They also offer cricket fans the chance to pose next to the famous little urn containing the Ashes; however many times Australia wins the Ashes, they still remain in English hands. In the grounds look out for the famous weather-vane in the shape of Old Father Time and the lovely modern Mound Stand (see the special section 'London's Contemporary Architecture'). Tours leave from the Grace Gates on St John's Wood Rd at 10am, noon and 2pm daily April to September, and at noon and 2pm only October to March (there are no tours when major matches are on). Tours cost £6.50/5/4.50 (adult/senior & student/child aged 5-16) and last 1¾ hours. The museum (admission £2) can be visited without going on a tour but only on match days, and you have to buy a ticket to the game.

EUSTON & KING'S CROSS (Map 3)

Euston Rd links Euston train station to St Pancras and King's Cross stations. This is not an especially inviting area to visit, although it's one that you're likely to pass through en route to or from the north of England. Attractions are thin on the ground, but the restored St Pancras station is a Victorian masterpiece and the fabulous British Library is open to readers and visitors alike.

Although some effort has been made to clear up the street prostitution and drug-dealing around King's Cross, this is still a distinctly seedy area best avoided after dark.

St Pancras New Church

The striking Greek Revival St Pancras New Church (☎ 7388 1461, Cnr Euston Rd & Upper Woburn Place WC1; admission free; open 9am-5pm Tues-Fri, 9.15am-11am Sat, 7.45am-noon & 5.30pm-7.15pm Sun) has a tower designed to imitate the Temple of the Winds in Athens, a portico with six Ionic columns mirroring the Erechtheion on the Acropolis and a wing decorated with caryatids, again like the Erechtheion. When it was completed in 1822 this was the most expensive new church to have been built in London since St Paul's Cathedral. Within the porch you can see a large tablet in memory of the 31 people who lost their lives in the King's Cross tube station fire of November 1987.

British Library

After 15 years and £500 million (the most expensive building in the UK after the Millennium Dome), the British Library (☎ 7412 7000 switchboard or 7412 7332 visitor services, W www.bl.uk, 96 Euston Rd NW1; ↔ King's Cross St Pancras; admission free; open 9.30am-6pm Mon & Wed-Fri, 9.30am-8pm Tues, 9.30am-5pm Sat, 11am-5pm Sun), designed by Colin St John Wilson, opened its doors in 1998. It is the nation's principal copyright library and stocks one copy of every British publication as well as historical manuscripts, books and maps from the British Museum.

The library counts some 186 miles of shelving on four basement levels and will have some 12 million volumes when it reaches the limit of its storage capacity.

British Library Highlights

- Magna Carta
- Gutenberg Bible
- Shakespeare's First Folio
- Sforza Book of Hours
- Leonardo da Vinci notebook
- *Alice's Adventures Under Ground* manuscript by Lewis Carroll
- Penny Black stamp
- Handel's *Messiah*
- Jane's Austen's *History of England*
- Early Beatles lyrics

Orientation At the heart of the building is the wonderful **King's Library**, the 65,000-volume collection of the insane George III, given to the nation by his son, George IV, in 1823 and now housed in a six-storey, 17m-high glass-walled tower. To the left as you enter are the library's excellent bookshop and exhibition galleries.

Subtitled 'Treasures of the British Library', the **John Ritblat Gallery** spans almost three millennia and every continent. Among the most important documents here are the Magna Carta (1215); the Codex Sinaiticus, the first complete text of the New Testament, written in Greek in the 4th century; a Gutenberg Bible (1455), the first Western book printed using movable type; Shakespeare's First Folio (1623); manuscripts by some of Britain's best-known authors (eg, Lewis Carroll, Jane Austen, George Eliot and Thomas Hardy); and even some of The Beatles earliest hand-written lyrics (including *I Want to Hold Your Hand* and *A Ticket to Ride*). Some of the library's historic recordings (such as the first one ever, made by Thomas Edison in 1877) can be heard from 11am to 1pm and 2pm to 4pm daily. The Turning the Pages exhibit allows you to browse through several important texts – the Sforza Book of Hours, the Diamond Sutra and a Leonardo da Vinci notebook – by touching a computer screen.

The library's **Philatelic Exhibition**, next to the John Ritblat Gallery, is based on collections established in 1891 with the bequest of the Tapling Collection and that now consist of over 80,000 items, including postage and revenue stamps, postal stationery and first-day covers from almost every country and from all periods.

The **Workshop of Words, Sounds and Images** documents the development of writing and communicating through the written word by carefully examining the work of early scribes, printers and bookbinders. The Sound section compares recordings on different media, from early-20th-century wax cylinders to modern CDs. The **Pearson Gallery** hosts some stunning special exhibitions; exceptional recent ones have included 'Oscar Wilde: A Life in Six Acts' and

'Treasures from the Ark: 1700 Years of Armenian Christian Art'.

Guided Tours One-hour guided tours of the library's public areas (£5/3.50 adult/senior & student) and take place at 3pm on Monday, Wednesday, Friday and Saturday, with an extra tour at 10.30am on Saturday. Tours (£6/4.50) that also include one of the reading rooms depart at 6.30pm on Tuesday and at 11.30am and 3pm on Sunday.

St Pancras Station

Together with the Houses of Parliament, St Pancras train station is the pinnacle of the Victorian Gothic revival architecture. There is a dramatic glass-and-iron train shed at the back, engineered by the great Brunel, and a fantastically pinnacled old hotel designed by George Gilbert Scott at the front.

CHARLOTTE HINDLE

Two stations of the cross: St Pancras and King's Cross sit side by side.

St Pancras is expected to be the terminus of Eurostar services to continental Europe by 2004.

ISLINGTON & STOKE NEWINGTON (Maps 1 & 4)

Islington is a residential area of north-east London that you're most likely to visit in order to eat in one of Upper St's many restaurants or visit one of its pubs, bars or clubs. Antique-lovers will also want to explore Camden Passage antiques market (not to be confused with the better known Camden Market in Camden Town), which is described in the special section 'To Market, to Market'. There's also a fine museum of Italian modern art here.

Islington's literary associations are legion. George Orwell was living at 27 Canonbury Square when he published *Animal Farm* in 1945. The playwright Joe Orton (1933–67) had been living at 25 Noel Rd for seven years when his lover, Kenneth Halliwell, bludgeoned him to death and then committed suicide.

Stoke Newington likes to pass itself off as 'village London with an international flavour' and that's more or less true; villages can be dirty and noisy and Stoke Newington Church St is chock-a-block with shops, pubs and ethnic restaurants. Daniel Defoe wrote *Robinson Crusoe* and *Moll Flanders* while living in a house at No 95, and Abney Park Cemetery, the so-called poor man's Highgate, is worth a look.

Abney Park Cemetery (Map 1)

Overgrown and spooky Abney Park Cemetery (☎ 7275 7557, *Stoke Newington Church St N16; Station: Stoke Newington/Bus: No 73, admission free; open 8am-dusk daily*), once the burial ground for nonconformists and laid out in 1840, contains – among many others – the tomb of General William Booth, founder of the Salvation Army.

Estorick Collection of Modern Italian Art (Map 4)

The Estorick Collection (☎ 7704 9522, W *www.estorickcollection.com, 39a Canonbury Square N1, entrance on Canonbury Rd; ⊖ Highbury & Islington; adult/concessions £3.50/2.50; open 11am-6pm Wed-Sat, noon-5pm Sun*), housed in a lovely Georgian town house, focuses on futurism (or *futurismo* in Italian), an early-20th-century artistic movement centred in Italy that responded to the quick pace of technological development. The collection of paintings, drawings, etchings and sculpture, amassed by American writer and art dealer Eric Estorick and his wife Salome, includes works by such greats as Giacomo Balla, Umberto Boccioni, Gino Severini and Ardengo Soffici. It's a fine collection of an arguably minor school of art; you could be forgiven for thinking the museum should be named the Esoteric Collection.

CAMDEN & KENTISH TOWN (Map 3)

From Euston station you can walk up Eversholt St to Camden, a tourist mecca that is especially lively at weekends. Some two decades ago Camden Town was home to a large Irish community, but yuppification has changed all that and nowadays parts of it, at the Chalk Farm end in particular, blend in more with the sedate middle-class character of Hampstead to the north.

North of Camden, Kentish Town has been solidly working class since the 1860s with the arrival of the Midland Railway. Still, it has a few claims to fame. Karl Marx, the artist Ford Madox Ford and the writer George Orwell all lived in Kentish Town at various stages.

Camden Market

In just over 20 years Camden Market has developed into London's most visited 'unticketed' tourist attraction, with some 10 million visitors a year. What started out as a collection of attractive craft stalls by Camden Lock on the Grand Union Canal now extends most of the way from Camden Town tube station to Chalk Farm tube station to the north. How much you like it probably depends on your tolerance for crowds, but the junky stalls at the Camden end and the sight of people gorging themselves on sausages and chips out of

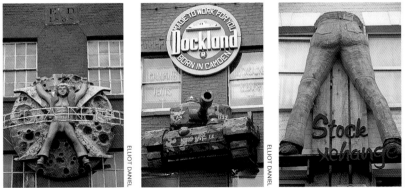

ELLIOT DANIEL ELLIOT DANIEL ELLIOT DANIEL

Camden High St is a hotch-potch of grungy boutiques and off-the-wall shops.

polystyrene boxes are not pretty sights. For more details see the special section 'To Market, to Market'.

Jewish Museum

This branch of the Jewish Museum (☎ 7284 1997, W www.jewmusm.ort.org, Raymond Burton House, 129-31 Albert St NW1; ⊖ Camden Town; adult/senior/student & child aged up to 13/family £3.50/2.50/1.50/8; open 10am-4pm Mon-Thur, 10am-5pm Sun) examines Judaism and Judaic religious practices in the Ceremonial Art Gallery, and the story of the Jewish community in Britain from the time of the Normans till the present day in the History Gallery. There's also a gallery for temporary exhibitions.

The museum's Finchley branch (Map 1) (☎ 8349 1143, W www.jewmusm.ort.org, Sternberg Centre, 80 East End Rd N3; ⊖ Finchley Central; adult/senior, student & child aged up to 13 £2/1/free; open 10.30am-5pm Mon-Thur, 10.30am-4.30pm Sun) houses the museum's social-history collections, including the oral history and photographic archives, and hosts changing exhibitions. Its permanent collection includes reconstructions of tailoring and cabinet-making workshops from the East End, as well as a Holocaust exhibition focusing on the experience of one Jewish Briton who survived Auschwitz.

HAMPSTEAD & HIGHGATE (Maps 3 & 12)

Perched on a hill 4 miles north of the City of London, Hampstead is an exclusive suburb, attached to an enormous, rambling heath, that just about gets away with calling itself a village. You can lose yourself on Hampstead Heath and forget that you're in one of the world's largest, noisiest cities.

Famous people have been making their home in Hampstead since the 17th century, among them the poets Coleridge, Keats and Pope; Charles II's mistress, Nell Gwyn; General Charles de Gaulle during WWII in a convent at 99 Frognal; Sigmund Freud; as well as the painters John Constable and William Hogarth.

Hampstead Heath (Map 12)

Hampstead Heath (☎ 7485 4491; ⊖ Gospel Oak or Hampstead/Station: Hampstead Heath) covers 320 hectares, most of it woods, hills and meadows, and is home to about 100 bird species. Some sections of the heath are laid out for sports such as football and cricket. There are several bathing ponds, but they're only recommended for strong, very competent swimmers (see under Swimming in the Activities section later in this chapter). Walk up Parliament Hill or the hill in North Wood, and on a clear day you'll be able to see Canary Wharf and the Docklands.

For a drink after ambling, the two best-known pubs in the area are the Spaniard's Inn and Jack Straw's Castle (see Pubs & Bars in the Entertainment chapter); both played their part in famous uprisings. Jack Straw's Castle is named after Wat Tyler's brother-in-arms of the Peasants' Revolt (though the building only dates from the 1970s), while some of the Gordon Rioters of 1780 popped into the Spaniard's Inn for a quick one before continuing on to attack Kenwood House.

By night Hampstead Heath is a gay cruising ground and the activities therein are generally overlooked by the authorities. In 1999 the local council approved a plan to renovate a **Victorian lavatory** built in 1897 on South End Green, just opposite Hampstead Heath station. This was gay playwright Joe Orton's lavatory of choice for cottaging (cruising for gay sex). The author George Orwell worked in a bookshop opposite the toilets and doubtless used them once or twice for what they were originally intended.

Kenwood House (Map 12)

On the northern side of the heath lies this magnificent neoclassical mansion *(☎ 8348 1286,* **W** *www.english-heritage.org.uk, Hampstead Lane NW3;* ✆ *Archway/Golders Green, then bus No 210; admission free; house open 10am-6pm daily Apr-Sept, 10am-5pm daily Oct, 10am-4pm daily Nov-Mar; grounds open 8am-8.30 daily Apr-Sept, 8am-4.35pm daily Oct-Mar)*. Remodelled by Robert Adam from 1764 to 1779, it is crammed with paintings by Gainsborough, Reynolds, Turner, Lely, Hals, Vermeer and Van Dyck, and outside has sculptures by Henry Moore (such as *Two Piece Reclining Figure,* 1964) and Barbara Hepworth; it is arguably the finest small collection of European art in London. Adam's Great Stairs and his Library, one of 14 rooms open to the public, are especially fine. A self-paced audio-tour costs £3.50/1.75 adult/concession. There's also a pub-restaurant called the *Brew House and Garden Café* that opens for light snacks and tea daily.

Keats House (Map 12)

A stone's throw from the lower reaches of the heath, this elegant Regency house *(☎ 7435 2062,* **W** *www.keatshouse.org .uk, Wentworth Place, Keats Grove NW3;* ✆ *Hampstead/Station: Hampstead Heath; adult/concession/under-16s £3/1.50/free; open 10am-noon (guided tours at this time by appointment only) & noon-5pm Tues, Thur-Sat, noon-8pm Wed, noon-5pm Sun May-Oct)* was home to the golden boy of the Romantic poets from 1818 to 1820. Never short of generous mates, Keats was persuaded to take refuge here by Charles Armitage Brown, and it was here that he met his fiancée, Fanny Brawne. Sitting under a plum tree in the garden in 1819, Keats wrote his most celebrated poem, *Ode to a Nightingale.* Apart from many mementoes, including original manuscripts and Keats' collection of works by Shakespeare and Chaucer, you can also peek at some of his love letters.

No 2 Willow Rd (Map 12)

Fans of modern architecture may want to visit this nearby NT property *(☎ 7435 6166,* **W** *www.nationaltrust.org.uk, 2 Willow Rd;* ✆ *Hampstead/Station: Hampstead Heath; adult/child £4.30/2.15; open 12.15pm-4pm Thur-Sat Apr-Oct, noon-5pm Sat in Mar & Nov–mid-Dec)*. It's the central house in a block of three designed by the 'structural rationalist' Erno Goldfinger in 1939 as his family home. Though the architect was following Georgian principles in creating it, many people think it looks uncannily like the sort of mundane 1950s architecture you see everywhere. They may look similar now, but 2 Willow Rd was in fact a forerunner; the others were just imitations – and mostly bad ones at that. The interior, with its cleverly designed storage space and collection of artworks by Henry Moore, Max Ernst and Bridget Riley, is certainly interesting and accessible to all. A visit is by one-hour guided tour only.

Burgh House (Map 12)

This late-17th-century Queen Anne mansion houses the **Hampstead Museum** of local history (☎ 7431 0144, New End Square NW3; ❸ Hampstead; admission free; open noon-5pm Wed-Sun) and a small art gallery.

The **Buttery** basement tearoom serves a decent lunch for £5 from 11am to 5.30pm Wednesday to Saturday.

Fenton House (Map 12)

One of Hampstead's oldest houses, Fenton House (☎ 7435 3471, W www.nationaltrust .org.uk, Windmill Hill, Hampstead Grove NW3; ❸ Hampstead; adult/child/family £4.30/2.15/10.50; open 2pm-5pm Sat & Sun Mar, 2pm-5pm Wed-Fri & 11am-5pm Sat & Sun Apr-early Nov) is a late-17th-century merchant's residence with a large walled garden and a fine collection of keyboard instruments, including a harpsichord from 1612 played by Handel.

Freud Museum (Map 3)

Sigmund Freud lived here for the last 18 months of his life after it became clear that it would no longer be safe for him to remain in Nazi-occupied Vienna in 1938. The house (☎ 7435 2002, W www.freud.org.uk, 20 Maresfield Gardens NW3; ❸ Finchley Road; adult/concession/under-12s £4/2/ free; open noon-5pm Wed-Sun), on a quiet, tree-lined residential street, contains the psychiatrist's original couch, together with all his Greek and Asian artefacts and, of course, his books. A photo shows how carefully he attempted to reproduce his Viennese home in the unfamiliar surroundings of London. Later the house was occupied by Freud's daughter, Anna, a child psychologist of note.

A small **shop** sells all sorts of histories, biographies and books to do with every aspect of the psyche.

Highgate Cemetery (Map 12)

Highgate Cemetery (☎ 8340 1834, Swain's Lane N6; ❸ Highgate; eastern sector adult/ child aged 8-16 £2/1; open 10am-5pm Mon-Fri, 11am-5pm Sat & Sun Apr-Oct, 10am-4pm Mon-Fri & 11am-4pm Sat & Sun Nov-Mar) has 20 wild, hectic hectares of absurdly over-decorated Victorian graves

and sombre family tombs linked in a ring, based on ancient Egyptian burial sites, all flanked by spooky cypresses. This is the final resting place for Karl Marx, the novelist Mary Anne Evans (aka George Eliot), the scientist Michael Faraday, the philosopher Herbert Spencer and lots of other ordinary mortals.

The cemetery is divided into two parts. The only way to see the wonderfully atmospheric western section is on a tour at noon, 2pm and 4pm weekdays and on the hour from 11am to 4pm weekends, April to October. The tours leave on the hour from 11am to 3pm, weekends only from November to March. Tours cost £3/1 (adult/child) and an extra £1 charge is made for cameras.

MUSWELL HILL (Map 1)

The hilly, well-to-do northern suburb of Muswell Hill was largely built between 1897 and the outbreak of WWI. As a result, its brick-built terraces with ornamental plasterwork have a uniformity of architectural style (in this case Edwardian) unknown in most other parts of London. In the 1870s, the Great Northern Railway was extended from Highgate to serve the newly opened Alexandra Palace.

Alexandra Park & Palace

Alexandra Park (Station: Alexandra Palace), named in honour of the consort of King Edward VII, before he was king, sprawls over some 88 hectares of what was once Tottenham Wood Farm. There are now public gardens, a nature conservation area, a deer park and various sporting facilities including a boating lake, pitch-and-putt golf course and skate park. The centrepiece of the park, however, lies to the north-west.

Built in 1873 as north London's answer to Crystal Palace, Alexandra Palace (☎ 8365 2121, W www.alexandrapalace.com, Alexandra Palace Way N22; Station: Alexandra Palace) suffered the ignoble fate of burning to the ground only 16 days after opening. Encouraged by attendance figures, investors decided to rebuild and it reopened just two years later. Though it boasted a theatre, museum, lecture hall, library and Great Hall

PAUL BIGLAND

Third time lucky? Alexandra Palace
has burnt to the ground twice.

with one of the world's largest organs, it was no match for Crystal Palace. It housed German POWs during WWI and in 1936 the world's first television transmission – a variety show called *Here's Looking at You* – took place here. The palace burned down again in 1980 but was rebuilt for the third time and opened in 1988.

Today 'Ally Pally' (as it is affectionately known) is largely a multipurpose conference and exhibition centre with a number of additional facilities, including an indoor ice-skating rink, the panoramic ***Phoenix Bar & Beer Garden*** and funfairs on bank holidays and in summer.

NEASDEN (Map 1)

In the unlikely setting of Neasden, a sprawling suburb of north-west London, Britain's Hindu community has built Europe's first traditional mandir, or temple. It really is an astonishing sight with icing-sugar towers and pinnacles.

Shri Swaminarayan Mandir

Shri Swaminarayan Mandir (☎ 8965 2651, 105-19 Brentfield Rd NW10; ⊖ Neasden/ Stonebridge Park; admission free; open 9am-6pm daily) was constructed with 5000 tonnes of Bulgarian limestone and Italian marble, all shipped to India to be carved traditionally and then shipped back to London for erection. Some of the carvings on the pillars seem relatively crude, but the *mandapa* (dome) is a masterpiece, so finely carved it looks more like lace than marble. The work took three years to complete and cost around £7.5 million, with much of the labour provided by volunteers. The temple opened in 1995.

The best time to visit the Hindu temple is from 9am to noon and 4pm to 6pm when the *murtis*, the representations of gods and saints, are on view. You must leave your shoes in racks near the door, and women in short skirts will be asked to wrap up in a sheet.

WALTHAMSTOW (Map 1)

Walthamstow, in north-east London, was a village on the outskirts of the city when the designer William Morris was born here in 1834 on Forest Rd. A fire station now stands on the site.

William Morris Gallery

The William Morris Gallery (☎ 8527 3782, Lloyd Park, Forest Rd E17; ⊖ Walthamstow Central; admission free; open 10am-1pm & 2pm-5pm Tues-Sat, plus first Sun of month) is housed in a delightful Georgian house where the Morris family lived from 1848 to 1856. The downstairs rooms tell the story of Morris' life and his working relationship with pre-Raphaelite artists such as Burne-Jones. They're also full of gorgeous wallpapers, chintzes and furniture designed by Morris and tiles and stained glass designed by his friends. The upstairs gallery houses a good selection of pre-Raphaelite paintings.

To get there, walk northwards along Hoe St for about 15 minutes and turn west (left) on Forest Rd. The gallery is situated just across the street.

East London

The eastern reaches of central London are taken up by the East End – the London of old Hollywood films and Christmas pantomimes – and the sprawl of the Docklands, an odd mix of the old and decaying and the shockingly new.

EAST END (Maps 2, 4 & 9)

The East End districts of Shoreditch, Hoxton, Spitalfields and Whitechapel may lie within walking distance of the City, but the change of pace and style is extraordinary. Traditionally this was working-class London, an area settled by wave upon wave of immigrants, giving it a curious mixture of Irish, French Huguenot, Bangladeshi and Jewish culture, all of which can still be felt

to varying degrees today. Run-down and neglected in the early 1980s, the East End is starting to look up in places, especially where it rubs up against the City and Liverpool Street station in Spitalfields, the nouveau trendy district of Hoxton and the area around Old St.

For anyone interested in modern, multicultural London, it's well worth venturing a look at the East End. Alongside a couple of interesting museums you'll find some of London's best-value Asian cuisine in Whitechapel and, to a lesser extent, Brick Lane (see the Places to Eat chapter) as well as some of its most colourful markets (see the special section 'To Market, to Market'). You may also want to pop into the Whitechapel Art Gallery to see what's on or to eat in its excellent cafe; for details see the East End walking tour.

Cockney Rhyme & Royalty

Some visitors arrive in London expecting to find a city populated by people conversing in cockney. Traditionally the cockneys were people born within the sound of Bow Bells – the church bells of St Mary-le-Bow. Since few people live in the City, that meant most cockneys were East Enders.

The term cockney is often used to describe anyone speaking what is also called estuary English (in which 't' and 'h' are routinely dropped). In fact the true cockney language also uses something called rhyming slang, which may have developed among London's costermongers (street traders) as a code to avoid police attention. This code replaced common nouns and verbs with rhyming phrases. So 'going up the apples and pears' meant 'going up the stairs', the 'trouble and strife' meant 'wife', and would you 'Adam and Eve it?' meant 'would you believe it?' Over time the second of the two words tended to be dropped so the rhyme vanished. Few – if any – people still use pure cockney. You're more likely to come across it in residual phrases such as 'use your loaf' ('loaf of bread' for head), 'ooh, me plates of meat' (feet) or 'e's me best china' ('china plate' for mate).

The cockney monarchs are the Pearly Kings and Queens, who used to be appointed by hawkers to represent them in brushes with the law. In the 19th century an orphan road-sweeper, Henry Croft, dreamed of creating a charity army to help raise money for the poor, and sewed pearly white buttons onto his clothes to attract attention. The kings and queens of the costermongers were duly impressed, and soon they too were decking themselves out in pearls to go fund-raising. The Pearly Harvest Festival Service in early October, when over 100 Pearly Kings and Queens attend a service in St Martin-in-the-Fields church, is a sight you'll never forget. Each suit is made of around 30,000 buttons sewn into sun, moon and star symbols. The most elaborate one has 90,000 buttons.

ÅSA ANDERSSON

EAST END

This walk takes you through the streets of Spitalfields and Whitechapel in east London. Come out of Liverpool Street station and have a look at the high-rise **Broadgate Centre (1)**. Cross Bishopsgate and walk northwards, past the turning for Spital Square, where the medieval hospital (or 'spital') originally stood. Turn right into Folgate St, lined with fine Georgian houses. It was in this area that Protestant Huguenots settled in the late 17th century, bringing with them their skills as silk weavers. Street names such as Fleur-de-Lis St and Nantes Passage recall their presence.

At 18 Folgate St is the **Dennis Severs' House (2)** (☎ 7247 4013, **w** www.denissevershouse.co.uk), named after the late American eccentric who restored it to its 18th-century splendour. The house opens for tours 2pm to 5pm on the first Sunday of each month (£7) and noon to 2pm on the first Monday (£5); advance bookings are not required. Every Monday evening there are 'Silent Night' tours (£10) by candlelight; times vary according to the season and booking is essential.

Turn right (south) along Commercial St and you'll see **Spitalfields Market (3)** on the right, part of which has been snatched from the hands of redevelopers. On Sunday, one of London's more interesting markets takes place in the arena (see the special section 'To Market, to Market').

On Commercial St, virtually opposite the market, you can't miss the striking facade of **Christ Church, Spitalfields (4)** (☎ 7247 7202; admission free; open 12.30pm-2.30pm Mon-Fri, 12.30pm-4.30pm Sun). A magnificent English-Baroque structure, it was designed by Nicholas Hawksmoor and completed in 1729 for the Huguenot weavers who lived in the area. Ongoing restoration work is coming to an end and it's worth timing your visit for the brief opening hours.

Turn down Fournier St, to the left (north) of Christ Church, admiring the beautifully restored Georgian houses with their wooden shutters. Most were built between 1718 and 1728 for wealthy London merchants, only to be taken over by the silk weavers and their families.

At the Brick Lane end of Fournier St is one of the most interesting buildings in Spitalfields. The **New French Church (5)** was built for the Huguenots in 1743. In 1899 the church became the Great Synagogue for Jewish refugees from Russia and central Europe. In 1975 it changed faiths again, becoming the Great Mosque of the Bengali community.

Turn left (north) into Brick Lane, a wonderful street of small curry and balti houses intermingled with shops where you can buy brightly coloured fabrics, all the ingredients for cooking your own curries and the paraphernalia of Islam. In 1550 this was just a country road leading to brickyards; by the 18th century it had been paved and lined with a mixture of houses and cottages inhabited by the Spitalfields weavers. These days many of the Bengalis also make a living from the clothes trade and all the street names are in Bengali too, including Bacon St, which we assume honours the essayist Francis.

Cross over Hanbury St and on the left you come to the **Old Truman's Brewery (6)**, the biggest brewery in London by the mid-18th

---

distance: about 1.5miles

start: Liverpool St
⊖ Liverpool Street

finish: Whitechapel Rd
⊖ Whitechapel

century. The Director's House standing to the left dates from 1740. The brewery closed in 1989 and now there's a modern cafe-bar and arts centre. The old **Vat House (7)**, which dates from the turn of the 19th century and has a hexagonal bell tower, is across the road. Next to it stand the Engineer's House of 1830 and a row of former stables.

Head back down Brick Lane (south) to where it joins Whitechapel High St. If you need a break and a snack it's worth turning right to the **Whitechapel Art Gallery (8)** (☎ 7522 7888 or 7572 7878, **w** www .whitechapel.org; admission free; open 11am-5pm Tues & Thur-Sun, 11am-8pm Wed) at Nos 80 to 82. It has rotating exhibitions and a pleasant *cafe* serving vegetarian dishes (see the Places to Eat chapter).

Whitechapel High St leads east into Whitechapel Rd. At Nos 32 to 34 you'll see the **Whitechapel Bell Foundry (9)** (☎ 7247 2599, **w** www .whitechapelbellfoundry.co.uk), which has been here since 1738, although an earlier foundry nearby is known to have been in business in 1570. The clock bell at St Paul's Cathedral, Big Ben and the Liberty Bell in Philadelphia were cast here. It can be visited by 1½-hour guided tour only at 10am on Saturday (£8, children under 14 not allowed) and booking is essential. The shop opens 9.30am to 5pm weekdays only.

You have now entered **Jack the Ripper territory**. Although the 19th-century serial killer's actual identity remains a mystery, that seems only to have added to the interest in him and his crimes. What is certain is that in 1888 he murdered five prostitutes in the wretched back streets of the Victorian East End; Mary Anne Nichols died in Bucks Row (now Durward St) north of Whitechapel, Annie Chapman in Hanbury St near the Ten Bells pub opposite Christ Church, Spitalfields, Elizabeth Stride in Berner St (now Henriques St) south of Commercial Rd, Catherine Eddowes in Mitre Square near Aldgate and Mary Kelly in Miller's Court.

From here you can walk along Fieldgate St, where you'll find some good *Pakistani restaurants* and the **Fieldgate Great Synagogue (10)**, now part of the modern Whitechapel Mosque. Alternatively continue east on Whitechapel Rd to the junction with Cambridge Heath Rd and you'll see the **Blind Beggar pub (11)** (☎ 7247 6195) at No 337, notorious as the place where Ronnie Kray shot George Cornell in 1966 in a gang war over control of the East End's organised crime. White-chapel tube is a short distance west of the pub.

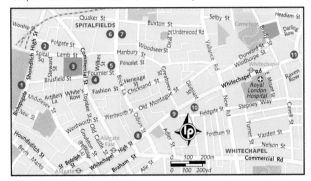

Tower Hamlets Information Centre (see Local Tourist Offices in the Facts for the Visitor chapter) offers free guided tours around Spitalfields at 2.30pm on Sunday.

Geffrye Museum (Map 4)

The 14 almshouses that contain the Geffrye Museum (☎ 7739 9893, W www.geffrye museum.org.uk, 136 Kingsland Rd E2; ✚ Old Street, then bus No 243, or Station: Dalston Kingsland; admission free; open 10am-5pm Tues-Sat, noon-5pm Sun) were originally built by the Ironmongers' Company to provide homes for the elderly poor, with funds bequeathed by Robert Geffrye, a late-16th-century mayor of London who had made a fortune from the slave trade. Today it's devoted to domestic interiors, with each room furnished to show how the homes of the relatively affluent middle class would have looked from Elizabethan times right through to the end of the 19th century. A postmodernist extension (1998), designed by Nigel Coates, contains several 20th-century rooms (a flat from the 1930s, a room in the contemporary style of the 1950s, a 1990s converted warehouse) as well as a gallery for temporary exhibits, a design centre with works from the local community, shop and restaurant. There's also a lovely herb garden at the museum, and the original chapel survives too.

Bethnal Green Museum of Childhood (Map 2)

The Bethnal Green Museum of Childhood (☎ 8980 2415, W www.museumofchild

SIMON BRACKEN

Art and soul: The Whitechapel Art Gallery hosts a variety of exhibitons.

hood.org.uk, Cambridge Heath & Old Ford Rds E2; ✚ Bethnal Green; admission free; open 10am-5.50pm Mon-Thur, Sat & Sun) is guaranteed to bring memories of childhood flooding back. Set in a rather grungy 19th-century building, it's full of dolls, dolls' houses, train sets, model cars, children's clothes, board games, books, toy theatres and puppets from the 17th century to today. The upstairs gallery attempts to provide a context for the toys by tracing the stages of childhood from life as a baby to leaving home.

THE DOCKLANDS (Maps 9 & 13)

London was once the world's greatest port, the hub of the British Empire and its enormous global trade. In the 16th century there were 20 cargo quays to the east of London. By the 18th and 19th centuries these were hard-pressed to cope with the quantity of cargo flowing through, and new docks were opened: West India Dock in 1802, London Dock in 1805, East India Dock in 1806 and Victoria Dock in 1855.

But even these proved inadequate as goods from the Empire poured in and out and a new wave of dock building kicked off, with Millwall on the Isle of Dogs in 1868, followed by the Royal Albert in 1880 and Tilbury in 1886. Each dock catered for a specific type of cargo – from rum and rubber to wool and ivory. King George V Dock opened as late as 1921.

After the Blitz of WWII the docks were in no condition to cope with the postwar technological and political changes as the Empire evaporated. At the same time, enormous new bulk carriers and container ships demanded deep-water ports and new loading and unloading techniques. From the mid-1960s dock closures followed one another as fast as they had opened, and the number of dock workers dropped from as many as 50,000 in 1960 to about 3000 by 1980. Almost 12% of the total land area of London now stood derelict.

In 1981 the London Docklands Development Corporation (LDDC) was set up to rejuvenate the area by encouraging new office and housing development. The builders moved in, the Docklands Light Railway (DLR) was built to link the area with the rest of London, new offices were constructed and new toy-town houses were thrown up beside new marinas. Places such as **Tobacco Dock (Map 9)** in Wapping were transformed into shopping centres full of delicatessen food and designer clothes. But a lack of thought for aesthetics and no planning for open green areas or public spaces left the local community poorly catered for.

When the recession of the early 1990s hit, the Docklands bubble burst first. Offices stood empty, people lost their jobs, flats wouldn't sell and shopping arcades emptied as trendy shops hung up 'For Sale' signs. Over it all towered the flagship development of Canary Wharf on the **Isle of Dogs (Map 13)**, bankrupted by the recession and falling property prices well before the IRA bomb of 1996 devastated the area immediately around it.

Things have turned around since then and 1 Canada Square – the official name of **Canary Wharf Tower** – is full of newspaper people; as the home of the *Daily Telegraph* and *Independent*, it has been described as a 'vertical Fleet St' and is a striking focal point visible in every direction. Neighbouring buildings (see the Wapping & Isle of Dogs walking tour for more details) have helped create a busy financial hub on the Isle of Dogs. Sadly, Tobacco Dock remains an empty shell, awaiting yet another reincarnation.

Getting around was always the Achilles heel of the Docklands. The DLR has got over its teething problems and has even been extended under the Thames in recent years to Greenwich and points south (see DLR & Train in the Getting Around chapter). What's more, the Jubilee Line extension means that for the first time the Isle of Dogs is served by the Underground. Heron Quays station is currently closed for redevelopment; it's due to reopen in autumn 2002, though the new station won't be completely operational until early 2003. Phone the Docklands Travel Hotline (☎ 7918 4000) for up-to-date information.

JULIET COOMBE

The *Traffic Light Tree* near Canary Wharf: waiting for London's 75-road junction.

The Docklands today is a world of contrasts. Eye-catching bridges across docks and futuristic buildings dominate the skyline; it really is today's view of London's future. But it is also an area rich in history. To see both sides, try the Wapping & the Isle of Dogs walking tour (see overleaf).

Museum in Docklands

This long-awaited museum with the slightly odd name *(☎ 7515 1162, W www.museumindocklands.org.uk, Warehouse No 1, West India Quay E14; DLR: West India Quay or ⊖ Canary Wharf; adult/under-16s £5/free; open 10am-6pm daily)* focuses on the history of the Thames, its port and its industries. Multimedia galleries over five floors look at everything from trade under the Romans, the success of the East India company, the decline of the docks in the 20th century and the regeneration of the Docklands in the past two decades. One of the highlights is the *Rhinebeck Panorama* (1810), a huge mural of the upper Pool of London that is exhibited as a painting and as a digitalised interactive display.

WAPPING & THE ISLE OF DOGS

The obvious starting point for a tour of the Docklands is Tower Hill. If you pass under Tower Bridge from the Tower of London on foot you'll come to **St Katharine's Dock (1)**, created in 1828 after up to 1000 houses and a 12th-century church were cleared away. It was the first of the docks to be renovated following its closure in 1968. It's a pleasant – if touristy – haven away from the bustle around the Tower of London, with a marina and the *Dickens Inn* (see Pubs & Bars in the Entertainment chapter).

distance: about 4 miles
start: Tower Hill
⊖ Tower Hill
finish: Island Gardens
DLR: Island Gardens

If you head eastwards along the river from St Katharine's Dock you'll come to Wapping and **Wapping High St**. A quiet cobbled road flanked by restored warehouses, it was described by John Stow in his 16th-century *A Survey of London* as 'a filthy strait passage, with alleys of small tenements or cottages'. As you walk along the street glance to the left down Scandrett St to see the remnants of what was a small community, with a church, a school and – inevitably – a pub.

Your first real port of call though is **Execution Dock (2)** near the old river police station at Wapping New Stairs. This is where convicted pirates were hanged and their bodies chained to a post at low tide, to be left until three tides had washed over them. A nearby *pub* (see Pubs & Bars in the Entertainment chapter) recalls one of the more famous people executed in this way: Captain William Kidd in 1701.

From Wapping High St, head northwards along Wapping Lane and across The Highway to **St George-in-the-East (3)**. It was badly damaged during the Blitz and the shell of the original church, designed by Nicholas Hawksmoor in 1726, now encloses a smaller modern church.

Cannon St Rd leads northwards to Cable St, where ropes were manufactured in the late 18th century. It was once as long as the standard English measure for cable (180m). Head eastwards along Cable St to the **Town Hall building (4)** (now a library). On the outside wall a large mural commemorates the battle that took place here in October 1936 when the British Fascist Oswald Mosley led a bunch of his Blackshirts into the area to intimidate the local Jewish population. Happily, the good guys won.

From here you can enter the **Limehouse** district by following Commercial Rd eastwards or catching the DLR two stops to Westferry. Limehouse became the centre of London's Chinese community – its first Chinatown – after some 300 sailors settled here in 1890. The protagonist of Oscar Wilde's *Picture of Dorian Gray* (1891) passed by this way in search of opium. Today the only reminders are street names such as Ming and Mandarin Sts and a pair of old-style Chinese restaurants on Commercial Rd. Nearby, on the corner of Commercial Rd and Three Colt St, is **St Anne's, Limehouse (5)**, Hawksmoor's earliest church (1724) and boasting the highest church clock in London.

A couple of stops after Westferry on the DLR is Canary Wharf on the Isle of Dogs. Etymologists are still out to lunch over the origin of the island's name. Most likely it's a corruption of the Flemish *dijk* (dike), recalling the island's muddy banks.

Canary Wharf is dominated by Cesar Pelli's 244m **tower (6)** (1991), described as a 'square prism with a pyramidal top'. It's now flanked by two new neighbours: the twin-tower **HSBC Holdings (7)** building and the **Citigroup Headquarters (8)**. On ground level check out **Cabot Square**, at the centre of the complex, which features a shopping centre and hosts art and cultural events. The Jubilee Line Underground station designed by Norman Foster is very impressive indeed (see the special section 'London's Contemporary Architecture'). The new **Museum in Docklands (9)** (see the main entry under The Docklands) is just to the north, in one of the old warehouses next to the West India Quay DLR station.

To the south-west of Canary Wharf, in the centre of a roundabout, is a magnificent modern sculpture by Pierre Vivant called *Traffic Light Tree* **(10)**, composed of 75 sets of flashing red, amber and green lights and looking very much like a Christmas tree gone mad. To the south, a twisting, futuristic **footbridge (11)**, its masts and cables evoking a ship at sea, links Heron Quays with South Quay.

Farther south is the **London Arena (12)**, a huge venue for fairs, conferences and concerts next to the Crossharbour & London Arena DLR station. If you want to see how much of the Isle of Dogs once looked, check out **Mudchute Park & Farm (13)**, a short distance to the southeast (see the boxed text 'Old MacDonald's London Farms' in the Facts about London chapter).

The last DLR station on the Isle of Dogs is **Island Gardens**, from where there are exquisite views of Greenwich's architectural heritage. If you'd like to carry on southwards to Greenwich, take the DLR to Cutty Sark station or, alternatively, use the historic 390m-long **foot tunnel (14)** running under the Thames. The lifts down to the tunnel open 7am to 7pm Monday to Saturday and 10am to 5.30pm on Sunday. Otherwise you're facing between 88 and 100 steps down and – shudder – up.

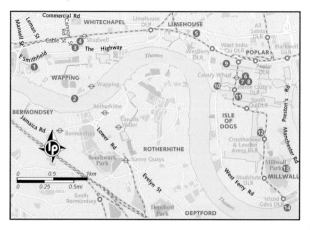

South London

For tourists a major reason to venture south of the Thames is to visit Greenwich, but you can also have fun exploring Brixton's vibrant market or visiting the excellent Horniman Museum in Forest Hill or the Dulwich Picture Gallery designed by John Soane.

GREENWICH (Map 14)

Packed with splendid architecture, Greenwich has strong connections with the sea, science, sovereigns and – of course – time.

Greenwich (**gren**-itch) lies to the southeast of central London, where the Thames widens and deepens. There's a sense of space that is rare elsewhere in the city. Quaint, village-like and boasting the magnificent *Cutty Sark* clipper ship and the fabulous National Maritime Museum, Greenwich has been on Unesco's list of World Heritage Sites (as Maritime Greenwich) since 1997. A trip there will be a highlight of any visit to London, and you should certainly allow a day to do it justice, particularly if you want to head down river to the Thames Flood Barrier, passing the empty Millennium Dome.

The North-South Divide

Londoners still talk as if the Thames was the huge barrier between north and south that it was in the Middle Ages. In fact, the psychological gulf between the two banks is as wide as ever; most people in north London (and that's most Londoners) refuse to believe there's anything of importance across the river. One of the standard questions in Londoner-to-Londoner interviews is 'When was the last time you crossed the river?' (which usually means 'went south') and jokes abound about having to get a visa before crossing the Thames. One wag even called the south the 'B-list side of the Thames', referring – we hope – to the number of place names beginning with that letter (Battersea, Borough, Brixton, Beckton and so on) and not making a biased value judgement.

Greenwich is home to an extraordinary interrelated cluster of classical buildings; all the great architects of the Enlightenment made their mark here, largely due to royal patronage. Henry VIII and his daughters Mary and Elizabeth were all born here. Charles II was particularly fond of the area and had Sir Christopher Wren build both the Royal Observatory and part of the Royal Naval College, which John Vanbrugh then completed in the early 17th century.

It's worth timing your visit for the arts and crafts and antiques markets; see the special section 'To Market, to Market' or ring ☎ 8293 3110 for information.

Virtually everything in Greenwich can be easily reached from the Cutty Sark DLR station. A shuttle bus (£1.50 return) linking Greenwich Pier with the Royal Observatory, Fan Museum and Ranger's House runs 11am to 5pm daily, April to October.

Information

The TIC (☎ 0870 608 2000, fax 8853 4607, **W** www.greenwich.gov.uk), Pepys House, 2 Cutty Sark Gardens SE10 (DLR: Cutty Sark) opens 10am to 5pm daily. The attached Greenwich Gateway (☎ same; admission free; open 10am to 5pm daily), the visitors' centre for the World Heritage Site, has a small exhibition on the history of Greenwich from Roman times till today.

Guided walks (☎ 8858 6169, **W** www .greenwichtourguides.co.uk) to selected sites cost £4/3/free adult/concession/under-14s and depart from the TIC at 12.15pm and 2.15pm daily. There are tours with different themes at other times of the day as well.

Cutty Sark

The *Cutty Sark* clipper ship (☎ 8858 3445, *Cutty Sark Gardens SE10; adult/child aged 5-16/family £3.50/2.50/8.50; open 10am-5pm daily*) is in Cutty Sark Gardens at the top of King William Walk, near the tourist office. It was the fastest ship that had ever sailed the seven seas when launched in 1869, though it was built just as steam and the opening of the Suez Canal were making sailing ships redundant. It remains the sole surviving example of the clippers that

DENNIS JOHNSON

Views of Greenwich's Old Royal Naval College and the city beyond from the Royal Observatory

ominated mid-19th-century trade in tea and wool across both the Pacific and Atlantic oceans and was still carrying cargoes when t was restored in 1922 and retired to Greenwich in 1954.

You can stroll the decks and peep in the teak-panelled cabins, then read up on its history below deck and inspect maritime prints, paintings and the world's largest collection of ship's figureheads in the hold. It's well worth a visit.

Gipsy Moth IV

Just next to the *Cutty Sark* is the *Gipsy Moth IV* (☎ 8858 3445, *Cutty Sark Gardens SE10)*, the 16m-long sailing ketch in which Sir Francis Chichester made the world's first single-handed circumnavigation of the globe (1966-67). Chichester was 64 at the time and endured 226 days in this bathtub-sized craft. He was knighted close to where the boat is now dry-docked by Elizabeth II, using the same sword that Elizabeth I used to knight Francis Drake. Due to its small size, visitors are not allowed on board.

Old Royal Naval College

If you walk southwards along King William Walk from the *Cutty Sark* you'll come to the Old Royal Naval College (☎ 8269 4747 or 800 389 3341, *King William Walk SE10)*. This Wren masterpiece has been largely taken over by the University of Greenwich since the Royal Navy baled out in 1998, but the buildings on the southern side allow vis-

itors to view the fabulous Painted Hall and Chapel *(admission to both adult/senior, student & over-16s £3/2, admission free after 3.30pm and Sun; open 10am-5pm Mon-Sat, 12.30pm-5pm Sun)*.

Work on the college began on the site of the old Greenwich Palace in 1692 when William and Mary ordered the building of a naval hospital for those wounded in the victory over the French at La Hogue. Intended as a retirement home for navy veterans, just as the Royal Hospital Chelsea was for army veterans, it was designed in two separate halves so as not to spoil the view of the river from the Queen's House, Inigo Jones' miniature masterpiece to the south.

You can visit the **Chapel** in the Queen Mary Building, which was completed in 1742, almost two decades after Wren's death, but gutted by fire in 1779 when builders dropped a candle into a room below. When it was redecorated it was in the lighter, airier rococo style. The eastern end of the chapel is dominated by a painting by the 18th-century American artist Benjamin West showing *The Preservation of St Paul after Shipwreck at Malta*. The 'marble' Corinthian columns are actually made of Coade stone, an artificial material manufactured at a site beside Westminster Bridge in the 19th century. The secret of its composition is now lost. Sung Eucharist takes place in the Chapel at 11am on Sunday.

Even more wonderful is the **Painted Hall**, which is made up of the Great (or Lower)

Hall and the Upper Hall, across Upper Grand Square in the King William Building. As soon as you step inside the Great Hall, your eyes will be drawn towards the ceiling to marvel at the painting by James Thornhill (the mirrors on wheels will help you inspect the ceiling without suffering a crick in your neck). It shows William and Mary enthroned amid symbols of the Virtues. Beneath William's feet, you can see the defeated French king Louis XIV grovelling with a furled flag in hand. Up a few steps is the Upper Hall, where George I is depicted with his family on the western wall. In the bottom right-hand corner Thornhill drew himself into the picture, pointing towards his work.

Wren designed the hall as the hospital dining room, but it soon proved too small and was vacated. It stood empty until early 1806, when Admiral Nelson's body was brought here to lie in state.

The *Queen Elizabeth Anteroom Restaurant* is in the basement.

National Maritime Museum

Farther southwards along King William Walk, you'll come to the National Maritime Museum (☎ *8312 6565,* **W** *www.nmm.ac .uk, Romney Rd SE10; admission free; open 10am-6pm daily Apr-Sept, 10am-5pm daily Oct-Mar),* a massive collection of boats, maps, charts, uniforms and marine art designed to tell the long and convoluted history of Britain as a seafaring nation.

As part of the millennium celebrations, the museum's central courtyard, Neptune Court, has been covered with a huge single-span glass roof to provide easy access to some 20 themed galleries on two of the museum's three levels. The galleries have interactive displays and video art that focus on marine ecology and the future of the sea, the tea trade and slavery, and art and the sea.

Videos in the Nelson Gallery on the 3rd level tell the story of the battles of the Nile and Trafalgar, and there's an impressive display of Nelson memorabilia, including his tunic with a hole from the bullet that killed him and the actual bullet itself. All Hands is an on-board interactive display for children on gunnery, signalling and deep-sea diving.

Queen's House

The Palladian Queen's House (☎ *8858 4422, Romney Rd SE10; admission free; open 10am-6pm daily June-early Sept, 10am-5pm daily rest of year)* is attached to the National Maritime Museum on its eastern side and is a stunning exhibition venue. Inigo Jones started work on the house for Anne of Denmark, wife of James I, in 1616 but it wasn't completed until 1635 when it became the home of Charles I and his queen, Henrietta Maria.

Rooms open off the **Great Hall**, which originally had a ceiling painted by Orazio Gentileschi and his daughter Artemisia, one of the few early female artists to achieve much celebrity. Sadly the original was later moved. Most of the original furniture has also been lost and replaced with 17th-century copies so the rooms are perhaps not as exciting as the building's exterior might lead you to expect. You may recognise the Great Hall; it featured in the Ang Lee film *Sense and Sensibility* (1995) starring Emma Thompson. Exhibits focus on illustrious seafarers and historic Greenwich.

St Alfege Church

Designed by Nicholas Hawksmoor in 1714 to replace a 12th-century one, this church (☎ *8858 6828, Church St SE10; admission free; open 10am-4pm Mon-Sat, 1pm-4pm Sun)* is dedicated to St Alfege, archbishop of Canterbury, who was martyred on the site by Vikings in 1012. It suffered fire damage from bombing in WWII and was rededicated in 1953.

Fan Museum

The delightful Fan Museum (☎ *8305 1441, 12 Croom's Hill SE10; adult/concession £3.50/2.50; open 11am-5pm Tues-Sat, noon-5pm Sun),* situated in an 18th-century Georgian town house, exhibits a collection of fans from around the world dating back to the 17th century and examines their role through history. It also has wonderful temporary exhibits. At the back there's a Japanese-style garden with an *Orangery* serving afternoon set-teas (£4.50/3.50 for full/half-tea) 3pm to 5pm Tuesday and Sunday only.

Greenwich Park

Greenwich Park (☎ 8858 2608) is London's largest and one of its loveliest, with a grand avenue, wide-open spaces, a rose garden and rambling, picturesque walks. It's partly the work of Le Nôtre, who landscaped the palace gardens of Versailles for Louis XIV. It contains several historic sights, a *cafe* and a deer park called the **Wilderness**.

If you continue south of the park you come to Blackheath (see Around Greenwich later).

Royal Observatory In 1675 Charles II had the Royal Observatory (☎ 8312 6565, **W** www.nmm.ac.uk, Greenwich Park SE19; admission free; open 10am-6pm daily Apr-Sept, 10am-5pm daily Oct-Mar) built on a hill in the middle of Greenwich Park, intending that astronomy be used to establish

longitude at sea (see the boxed text 'The Longitude Solution'). The Octagon Room, designed by Wren, and the nearby Sextant Room are where John Flamsteed (1646–1719), the first astronomer royal, made his observations and calculations. This is one of the few Wren interiors known to have survived intact.

The globe is divided between east and west at the Royal Observatory, and you can place one foot either side of the meridian line and straddle the two hemispheres. For a small fee a machine will generate a certificate to confirm that you have done just that.

Attached to the observatory **Greenwich Planetarium** (admission free; shows 2.30pm Mon-Fri, 1.30pm & 3.30pm Sat, 2pm & 3pm Sun), where you can see the night sky projected on a dome.

The Longitude Solution

CHARLOTTE HINDLE

A foot in each hemisphere

It was the challenge of the century. Establishing latitude – the imaginary lines that girdle the earth – was child's play; any sailor could do that by looking at the height of the sun or the stars off the horizon. Finding longitude, however, was an entirely different matter and had stumped astronomers from the Greeks to Galileo.

As it takes 24 hours for the earth to complete one revolution of 360°, one hour is 1/24th of a revolution – or 15°. By the 16th century astronomers knew that longitude could be found by comparing local time with the reading of a clock set at the time of a home port or another place of known longitude. But that meant two *reliable* clocks, ones that would keep accurate time as the ship pitched and shook and the temperature rose or fell. Such technology was unavailable until the 18th century.

Reading longitude inaccurately lengthened sea voyages, cost shipping companies money and increased the number of sailors' deaths due to scurvy and accidents, as islands, rocks and reefs appeared from nowhere. In 1714 Parliament offered a prize of £20,000 – a king's ransom in the 18th century – to anyone who could discover a method of finding longitude accurate to within 30 miles. It's a long story – one wonderfully.(and briefly) told in Dava Sobel's *Longitude* – but the English inventor John Harrison was eventually awarded the prize for a marine chronometer tested from 1761 to 1762 by the Royal Observatory at Greenwich.

In 1884 the observatory's contribution in solving the longitude riddle was acknowledged when an international conference in Washington designated 'the meridian passing through the centre of the transit instrument at the Observatory of Greenwich as the initial meridian for longitude', or the prime meridian. Greenwich Mean Time (GMT) was accepted as the universal measurement of standard time.

Ranger's House South-west of the observatory is the Ranger's House (*☎ 8853 0035, Ⓦ www.english-heritage.org.uk, Greenwich Park SE10; adult/senior & student/child £2.50/1.90/1.30; open 10am-6pm daily Apr-Sept, 10am-5pm daily Oct, 10am-4pm Wed-Sun Nov-Mar)*, a stately home built for Admiral Francis Hosier in 1700 and later used to house the park's ranger. The biggest draw at the Ranger's House are the celebrated Luton Hoo art treasures, a rich collection of jewellery and Old Masters amassed by a railway engineer's son who struck it rich in the diamond fields of South Africa in the 19th century. Also here are Jacobean and Stuart portraits, including some by Lely and Kneller, which are striking for their size if nothing else. You can also ascend to Admiral Hosier's rooftop gazebo.

Getting There & Away

Greenwich is now most easily accessible on the DLR; Cutty Sark is the station closest to the TIC and most of the sights. If you happen to be in the Docklands before you visit, you can catch the DLR to Island Gardens and walk through the historic foot tunnel to the southern side of the river (see the Wapping & the Isle of Dogs walking tour earlier).

There are fast, cheap trains from Charing Cross to Greenwich station via London Bridge about every 15 minutes. Maze Hill station, near the north-eastern corner of the park, is more convenient for most of the sights than Greenwich station.

The most pleasant way to get to/from Greenwich if the weather is fine is by boat. For details, see Organised Tours in the Getting Around chapter.

AROUND GREENWICH
Blackheath (Map 1)

What might at first appear on the map as the southern extension of Greenwich Park, Blackheath *(Station: Blackheath)* and its eponymous 'village' to the south-east is very much a world of its own. Known locally as the 'Hampstead of the south', this 110-hectare expanse of open common has played a greater role in the history of London than its much bigger sister to the north.

The Danes camped here in the early 11th century after having captured Alfrege, the archbishop of Canterbury, as did Wat Tyler before marching on London with tens of thousands of Essex and Kentish men during the Peasants' Revolt in 1381. Henry VII fought off Cornish rebels here in 1497, and the heath was where Henry VIII met his fourth wife, Anne of Cleves, in 1540 (he disliked her immediately and divorced her six months later). Later it became a highwaymen's haunt, and it was not until the area's development in the late 18th century – the lovely **Paragon**, a crescent of Georgian mansions on the south-eastern edge of the heath, was built to entice 'the right sort of people' to move to the area – that Blackheath was considered safe. The name of the heath is derived from the colour of the soil, not from its alleged role as burial ground during the Black Death, the bubonic plague of the 14th century.

Today the windswept heath is a pleasant place for a stroll, a spot of kite-flying or a drink at one of a pair of historic pubs to the south: the *Hare and Billet* and the *Princess of Wales*. It's not uncommon to see artists dabbing away at their easels; apparently these Turner wannabes find the light has a special quality on the heath.

Along with the Paragon, other notable buildings include the fieldstone **All Saints' Church** (1858), with its needle-sharp spire to the south, and **Morden College**, the Ritz of almshouses built in 1695 to house 'decayed Turkey Merchants' who had fallen on hard times. The building, now a nursing home and closed to the public, is believed to have been designed by Christopher Wren.

To reach Blackheath from Greenwich park, walk southwards along Chesterfield Walk and past the Ranger's House (or southwards along Blackheath Ave and through Blackheath Gate) and then cross Shooters Hill Rd.

Millennium Dome (Map 14)

The all-singin' and all-dancin' Millennium Dome opened on the first day of 2000 and was the most ambitious building erected in

JULIET COOMBE

On tenterhooks: the future of the Dome is still undecided but it has been a costly venture.

London since St Paul's Cathedral had been completed in 1710. And at more than £750 million, it was also the most expensive, with more than half the cost being paid for with funds from the National Lottery.

Sadly, the dome stumbled from the start, and by the time it closed a year later it had attracted 6.5 million visitors, about half the number predicted. Its future use – indeed, if it has a future – was still undecided at the time of writing; everything from a theme park and a high-tech business park to a sports stadium, giant greenhouse and even a giant billboard visible from aeroplanes had been discussed. One thing is for certain though: the Millennium Dome continues to be an expensive proposition well into the third millennium. It costs £100,000 a week just to keep the damned thing standing.

Thames Flood Barrier (Map 1)

The Thames Flood Barrier between Greenwich and Woolwich was built between 1972 to 1982 to protect London from flooding. It consists of 11 movable gates supported between nine concrete piers with silver roofs that house the operating machinery. They make a surreal sight, straddling the river in the lee of a giant warehouse.

The reason why London needs such a barrier is that the water level has been rising by as much as 75cm per century, while the river itself has been narrowing; in Roman times it was probably around 800m wide at the site of today's London Bridge while now it's barely 250m, with constant pressure to develop the foreshores. The Thames tide rises and falls quite harmlessly twice a day, and once a fortnight there's also a stronger 'spring' tide. The danger comes when the spring tide coincides with an unexpected surge, which pushes tons of extra water upriver. The barrier has been built to prevent that water pouring over the riverbanks and flooding nearby houses. Some 300 people were drowned in 1953 when the Thames burst its banks.

The **Thames Barrier Visitors' Centre** (☎ 8305 4188, Ⓦ www.environment-agency .gov.uk, 1 Unity Way SE18, admission to barrier free, audiovisual show adult/senior & child aged 5-16/family £3.40/2/7.50; open 10am-5pm Mon-Fri, 10.30am-5.30pm Sat & Sun) tells the story of the Thames through history, of the building of the barrier and of attempts in recent years to clean the river up. The audiovisual show lasts for 20 minutes.

The barrier's mechanisms are checked roughly once a month. If you'd like to see this wonder in action, ring the visitor centre for exact dates and times.

CHARLOTTE HINDLE

Since 1982, the Thames Flood Barrier has been raised over 20 times to stop London flooding.

Getting There & Away You can get to within 20 minutes' walk of the barrier by taking a train to Charlton station from Charing Cross or London Bridge. When you get there, turn left (north) out of the station onto Charlton Church Lane, cross Woolwich Rd and follow Anchor & Hope Lane to the Thames Path. Head eastwards along the path for about 800m to the barrier. It's not the path's prettiest stretch, but it's better than walking along busy Woolwich Rd.

To visit the barrier from Greenwich catch bus No 177 or 180 along Romney Rd and get off at the Victoria pub, 757 Woolwich Rd. From there Westmoor St leads northwards to the visitors' centre.

A slower – but nicer – way to get to the barrier from Greenwich is by boat. From late March to October boats run by Campion Launches (☎ 8305 0300) leave Greenwich Pier at 11.15am, 12.30pm, 2pm and 3.30pm daily and take 35 minutes to get there (the last departure doesn't leave time to take in the visitors' centre), passing the Dome along the way (one-way tickets cost £3.55/3/2.25 adult/senior & student/child aged 5-16 and return tickets cost £5/4.25/3.50/3/14 adult/senior/student/child aged 5-16/family). Boats sail at noon, 1.30pm and 3pm daily in November and early December and again from early February to March; there's no service in January. You can also get here from Westminster Pier in central London with Westminster to Greenwich Thames Passenger Boat Service (WGTPBS; ☎ 7930 4097, **W** www.westminsterpier.co

.uk). See under Organised Tours in the Getting Around chapter for details.

If you're up to hoofing it, the barrier is 3½ miles from Greenwich via the Thames Path.

Woolwich Royal Arsenal (Map 1)

A new attraction at Royal Arsenal in Woolwich is **Firepower** (☎ 8855 7755, **W** www.firepower.org.uk, Royal Arsenal, Woolwich SE18; Station: Woolwich Arsenal; adult/senior & student/child aged 5-15 £6.50/5.50/4.50; open 10am-5pm daily), which attempts to recreate the experiences of artillery gunners over the past century in an audiovisual extravaganza called Field of Fire. The History Gallery tells the story of artillery from Roman times till today and the Real Weapons Gallery allows you to try your hand at shooting a tank or a rifle on a simulator. It's loud and it flashes but the kids just can't get enough.

Eltham Palace (Map 1)

Eltham Palace (☎ 8294 2548, **W** www.english-heritage.org.uk, Court Rd SE9; Station: Eltham; admission to grounds only adult/senior & student/child aged 5-16 £3.60/2.70/1.80, grounds & house £6/4.50/3; open 10am-6pm Wed-Fri & Sun Apr-Sept, 10am-5pm Wed-Fri & Sun Oct, 10am-4pm Wed-Fri & Sun Nov-Mar) is an unusual hybrid: part Tudor, part 1930s Art Deco. It started life as a royal palace in 1305 and was for a time the boyhood home of Henry VIII. But the Tudors abandoned it in 1526 in favour of Greenwich and it fell into disrepair. From 1933 to 1937 a member of the Courtauld clan (of Courtauld Institute fame) and his wife built a country home on the palace remains. It was occupied by the Army from WWII until 1995, when English Heritage took it over.

Of what little remains from the Tudor period, the Great Medieval Hall's hammer-beam roof is said to be third only to the ones at Westminster Hall and Hampton Court Palace. However, the main draw is the Art Deco fixtures restored to the way they were when the Courtaulds lived here: from an enormous circular carpet with geometric shapes in the domed entrance hall and a burlwood-veneer fireplace to the black-marble dining room with a silver-foil ceiling, and a heated cage, complete with tropical murals and a bamboo ladder leading to the ground floor, for the couple's spoiled (and vicious) pet lemur, Mah-Jongg.

DULWICH & FOREST HILL (Map 1)

Tucked away in the wide expanse of south London that the tube fails to reach, Dulwich (**dull**-itch) is a leafy, quiet suburb with some fine architecture and an air of gentility. You might want to venture out here to see the Dulwich Picture Gallery, a work of that idiosyncratic 19th-century architect John Soane.

A bit farther off the beaten track and lacking Dulwich's cohesiveness, Forest Hill boasts one attraction well worth venturing onto a suburban train to reach: the Horniman Museum.

Dulwich Picture Gallery

John Soane designed the Dulwich Picture Gallery (☎ 8693 5254, W www.dulwich picturegallery.org.uk, Gallery Rd SE21; Station: West Dulwich; adult/senior & student/ child £4/3/free, admission free Fri; open 10am-5pm Tues-Fri, 11am-5pm Sat & Sun), the country's oldest public art gallery, in 1811 to house paintings collected by dealer Noel Desenfans and painter Francis Bourgeois. Perhaps uniquely, the gallery doubles as this august pair's mausoleum, lit by a moody lumière mystérieuse created with stained glass. The gallery, which underwent a major refurbishment and extension for the millennium, contains masterpieces by Rembrandt, Rubens, Reynolds, Gainsborough, Lely and others. Temporary exhibitions by modern artists generally get more space.

The museum is a 10-minute walk northwards along Gallery Rd, which starts almost opposite West Dulwich station.

Horniman Museum

The Horniman Museum (☎ 8699 1872 or 8699 2339, 100 London Rd SE23; Station: Forest Hill; admission free; open 10.30am-5.30pm Mon-Sat, 2pm-5.30pm Sun) is an extraordinary little place, comprising the original collection of Frederick John Horniman, the son of a wealthy tea merchant, who had the Art Nouveau building with a clock tower and mosaics specially designed to house it in 1901. The main ethnographic hall has undergone major renovation and has emerged as African Worlds, the first permanent gallery of African and Afro-Caribbean art and culture in the UK. The Music Room has a superb collection of musical instruments, each displayed with computerised recordings and headsets. The small Living Waters Aquarium sits rather oddly with the other exhibits, but the way it follows the line of the steps is rather fun.

To get there from Forest Hill station, turn left out of the station along Devonshire Rd and then right along London Rd. The Horniman is on the right.

BRIXTON (Map 15)

There was a settlement on the site of today's Brixton, the southern terminus of the Victoria Line, as early as a year after the Norman Invasion. But Brixton remained an isolated, far-flung village until the 19th century, when the new Vauxhall Bridge (1810) and the railways (1860) linked it with central London. After WWII immigrants from the West Indies settled in large numbers here, giving Brixton a palpable Caribbean flavour that can still be found in the exotic fruits and vegetables on sale at Brixton Market (see the special section 'To Market, to Market'), the reggae blaring from car radios and boom boxes and the never-say-die all-night dance clubs.

Economic decline and hostility between the police and blacks (who accounted for only 29% of the population of Brixton at the time) led to the riots of the 1980s (see History in the Facts about London chapter). Since then the mood has been decidedly more upbeat. Soaring property prices have sent house-hunters foraging in these parts, and pockets of gentrification sit alongside the more run-down streets. Whatever edge is left from the dark days of the 1980s has only added to the excitement of the restaurants and clubs (see Brixton in the Places to Eat chapter and Clubs in the Entertainment chapter) that have sprung up in recent years like mushrooms after rain.

WANDSWORTH (Map 1)

This poorer, working-class sibling of the more affluent Battersea immediately down river was synonymous with quality headgear as early as the 13th century. When the Roman Catholic hierarchy in Rome began to order their mitres and birettas from the newly established Huguenot milliners in the 18th century, Wandsworth hats became famous throughout Europe. If your interests lie in things wet and cool rather than headgear, head for one of the few working breweries still extant in London.

Young's Ram Brewery

Young's Ram Brewery (*☎ 8875 7005, Cnr Wandsworth High & Ram Sts SW18; Station: Wandsworth Town; brewery tour adult/senior & student/child aged 14-17 £5.50/4.50/3, stables tour adult/child aged 6-18/family £3.50/2/9; visitors' centre open 10am-6pm Mon-Sat)* is where to go when you're 'museumed out' and want to digest history with a cup of good cheer. Beer (as in 'ale' or 'bitter', not lager – see the boxed text 'Beer: The National Drink' in the Entertainment chapter) has been brewed at this site since the late 16th century, and tours of the brewery lasting 1½ hours leave at noon and 2pm Monday to Thursday and Saturday; call in advance to book a place. Tours include a pint in the old pub attached. Tours of the stables, where a herd of working shires make their home, are also available but must be booked in advance. Under-18s must be accompanied by an adult.

To get here from Wandsworth Town station (trains from Waterloo station), walk west on Old York Rd, cross over to Armoury Way and then go south along Ram St.

WIMBLEDON (MAP 1)

This leafy southern suburb will be forever associated with the lawn tennis championships that have been held here every June since 1877. You can visit the Wimbledon Lawn Tennis Museum year-round. Wimbledon Common is a great place for a picnic.

Wimbledon Lawn Tennis Museum

This museum (*☎ 8946 6131, W www.wimbledon.org, Gate 4, Church Rd SW19; ⊖ Southfields/Wimbledon Park; adult/concession £5/4; open 10.30am-5pm daily, spectators only during championships)* is of specialist interest, dwelling as it does on the minutiae of the history of tennis playing, traced back here to the invention of the all-important lawnmower in 1830 and of the India-rubber ball in the 1850s. Nonetheless it's a state-of-the-art presentation, with plenty of video clips to let fans of the game relive their favourite moments. The museum houses a ***tearoom*** and a ***shop*** selling all kinds of tennis memorabilia.

Wimbledon Common

Running on into Putney Heath, Wimbledon Common covers 440 hectares of south London, a wonderful expanse of open space for walking, nature trailing and picnicking. There are a few specific sights on the common, most unexpectedly **Wimbledon Windmill** (*☎ 8947 2825, Windmill Rd SW19; ⊖ Wimbledon; adult/child £1/50p; open 2pm-5pm Sat, 11am-5pm Sun Apr-Oct)*, a fine smock windmill dating from 1817. It was during a stay in the mill in 1908 that Baden-Powell was inspired to write parts of his *Scouting for Boys*. On the southern side of the common, the misnamed **Caesar's Camp** is a prehistoric earthwork that proves that Wimbledon was settled before Roman times.

Buddhapadipa Temple

Another unexpected sight, this time in a residential neighbourhood half a mile from Wimbledon Village, is as authentic a Thai temple as ever graced this side of Bangkok. Buddhapadipa Temple (*☎ 8946 1357, 14 Calonne Rd SW19; ⊖ Wimbledon; admission free; complex open 8am-9.30pm daily summer, 8am-6pm daily winter; temple open 1pm-6pm Sat, 8.30am-10.30am & 12.30pm-6pm Sun)* was built by an association of young Buddhists in Britain and opened in 1982. The *wat* (temple compound) boasts a *bot*, or consecrated chapel, decorated with traditional scenes by two leading Thai artists. Remember to take your shoes off before entering the bot.

To get to the temple take the tube or train to Wimbledon and then bus No 93 up to Wimbledon Parkside. Calonne Rd leads off it on the right.

West London

There are many reasons why visitors may consider a foray into the hinterland of west London, including Fulham Palace, Kew Gardens, Syon House, Richmond Park or even a boozy afternoon at one of the riverfront pubs in Hammersmith (see that section under Pubs & Bars in the Entertainment chapter). But the main one should be to visit Hampton Court, the mother of all palaces.

HAMMERSMITH & FULHAM (Maps 1 & 2)

Hammersmith is not an especially inviting borough, dominated as it is by a hideous flyover and chaotic roundabout. There are no specific sights, although you might want to visit the Riverside Studios. With time to spare there's a good set of riverfront pubs on the Chiswick side of Hammersmith Bridge plus a pleasant 2-mile walk along the Thames from the shopping centre beside the bridge to Chiswick itself.

Fulham is more immediately agreeable than Hammersmith; its main draw is Fulham Palace.

Riverside Studios (Map 1)

Riverside Studios (☎ 8237 1000, Crisp Rd W6; ⊖ Hammersmith; open 9am-11pm Mon-Sat, noon-11pm Sun) is west London's equivalent of the ICA (Institute for Contemporary Arts), a mixed-media arts centre with two good-sized auditoriums that present films, theatre, modern dance and about a dozen art shows per year. See also Cinemas in the Entertainment chapter.

Fulham Palace (Map 2)

In Bishop's Park, next to the Thames on the Fulham side of Putney Bridge, stands Fulham Palace (☎ 7736 3233, Bishop's Ave SW6; ⊖ Putney Bridge; museum admission adult/senior & student £1.50/75p; open 2pm-5pm Wed-Sun Mar-Oct, 1pm-4pm Thur-Sun Nov-Feb), summer home of the bishops of London from 704 to 1973. It originally boasted a long moat, making it the largest moated site in Europe. The oldest part to survive is the little red-brick Tudor gateway, but the main building you see today dates from the mid-17th century and remodelled in the 19th century. There's a pretty walled garden and, detached from the main house, a Tudor Revival chapel designed by Butterfield in 1866.

The **Museum at Fulham Palace** describes the history of the palace. Guided tours (£3) usually at 2pm on the second Sunday of every month (call to confirm) take in the Great Hall, the chapel, Bishop Sherlock's dining room and the museum, and last about 1¼ hours.

The Wetland Centre (Map 1)

Europe's largest inland wetland project, the 42-hectare Wetland Centre (☎ 8409 4400, ⒲ www.wetlandcentre.org.uk, Queen Elizabeth's Walk SW13; ⊖ Hammersmith, then bus No 283 known as the 'Duck Bus';

CHRISTINE OSBORNE

Quiet times at the Wetland Centre, which attracts around 130 bird species.

adult/student & senior/child aged 5-15/ family £6.75/5.50/4/17.50; open 9.30am-6pm daily) was created from four Victorian reservoirs in 2000 and attracts some 130 species of birds and 300 types of moths and butterflies – not to mention 100,000 visitors.

CHISWICK (Map 1)

Despite the abomination of the A4, which cuts off the riverside roads from the centre, Chiswick (**chiz**-ick) is still a pleasant west London suburb, with cafes and restaurants with pavement tables on Chiswick High Rd. Most people come to Chiswick to visit Chiswick House and the home of the artist William Hogarth. There's also a very pleasant riverside walk that runs all the way to Hammersmith.

Chiswick House

Chiswick House *(☎ 8995 0508, W www .english-heritage.org.uk, Chiswick Park, off Burlington Lane W4; Station: Chiswick; adult/senior & student/child £3.30/2.50/1.70; open 10am-6pm daily Apr-Sept, 10am-5pm daily Oct, 10am-4pm Wed-Sun Nov-Mar)* is a fine Palladian pavilion with an octagonal dome and colonnaded portico. It was designed by the 3rd earl of Burlington (1694–1753) when he returned from his Grand Tour of Italy, fired up with enthusiasm for all things Roman. Lord Burlington used it to entertain friends and to house his library and art collection.

Inside, the ground floor has details of the recent restoration work and also accommodates several statues brought in from the park to protect them. Upstairs some of the rooms have been completely restored to a grandeur some will find overpowering. The dome of the main salon has been left un-gilded and the walls are decorated with eight enormous paintings. In the Blue Velvet Room look for the portrait of Inigo Jones, the architect much admired by Lord Burlington, over one of the doors. The ceiling paintings are by William Kent, who also decorated the Kensington Palace State Apartments.

Lord Burlington also planned the house's original gardens, now Chiswick Park, but

they have been much altered since then. The restored Cascade waterfall is bubbling again after being out of action for years.

The house is about 1 mile south-west of the station, opposite the start of Burlington Lane.

Hogarth's House

Robbed of its setting by the thundering traffic on the A4, Hogarth's House *(☎ 8994 6757, Hogarth Lane, Great West Rd W4; ⊖ Turnham Green; admission free; open 1pm-5pm Tues-Fri, 1pm-6pm Sat & Sun Apr-Oct, 1pm-4pm Tues-Fri, 1pm-5pm Sat & Sun Nov-Dec & Feb-Mar)* nevertheless offers an opportunity to see inside a small 18th-century house.

William Hogarth lived here from 1749 to 1764 and although very little original furniture remains, the pistachio-coloured walls are decorated with his evocatively named engravings of life in Georgian London (see the boxed text 'Of Rakes & Harlots: Hogarth's World' in the Facts about London chapter) though *The Rake's Progress* is a copy of the original now in Sir John Soane's Museum in Lincoln's Inn Fields.

KEW (MAP 1)

Kew will be forever associated with Kew Gardens, headquarters of the Royal Botanical Society and boasting one of the world's finest plant collections. But central Kew Green is itself a pretty place where cricket is played in summer.

Kew Gardens

One of the most popular attractions on the London tourist itinerary, which means it can get very crowded during summer, especially at weekends, is the Royal Botanic Gardens at Kew *(☎ 8332 5000 or 8940 1171, W www.rbgkew.org.uk, Kew Rd; Kew; ⊖ Kew Gardens; adult/senior, student & over-16s/under-16s £6.50/4.50/free; late entry 45 mins before hothouses close £4.50; gardens open 9.30am-6.30pm Mon-Fri, 9.30am-7.30pm Sat & Sun late Mar-Aug; 9.30am-6pm daily Sept-Oct; 9.30am-4.15pm daily Nov-Feb; glasshouses open 9.30am-5.30pm daily late Mar-Oct; 9.30am-3.45pm*

JULIET COOMBE

Blooming marvellous: Kew Gardens has the world's largest collection of orchids.

daily Nov-Feb). Spring is probably the best time to visit, but at any time of year this 120-hectare expanse of lawns, formal gardens and greenhouses has delights to offer. As well as being a public garden, Kew is an important research centre, and it maintains its reputation as the most exhaustive botanical collection in the world.

If you want a good overview of the gardens, jump aboard the Kew Explorer minitrain (£2.50/1.50), which allows you to hop on and off at stops along the way. the full circuit takes about half an hour.

Orientation Its wonderful plants and trees aside, Kew has several specific sights within its borders. Assuming you come by tube and enter via **Victoria Gate**, you will come almost immediately to a large pond overlooked by the enormous **Palm House**, a hothouse of metal and curved sheets of glass designed by Decimus Burton and Richard Turner (1848) and housing all sorts of exotic tropical greenery. Just north-west of the Palm House is the tiny but irresistible **Water Lily House** (open March to December only), dating from 1852.

If you head northwards, you'll come to the stunning **Princess of Wales Conservatory**, opened in 1987 and housing plants in 10 different computer-controlled climatic zones – everything from a desert to a cloud forest. Beyond that is the **Kew Gardens Gallery** bordering Kew Green, which houses exhibitions of paintings and photos mostly of a horticultural theme.

Heading westwards from the gallery you will arrive at the red-brick **Kew Palace**, a former royal residence once known as Dutch House, dating from 1631. It was very popular with George III and his family (his wife Charlotte died here in 1818). The gardens surrounding the palace are especially pretty. The palace has been closed for extensive renovations.

If you cut southwards from the palace across the lawns you'll pass a long **lake** running roughly west to east. To the southwest is **Queen Charlotte's Cottage**, a wooden summerhouse used, again, by George III and his family and surrounded by bluebells in spring. It opens at weekends in summer only. East of the cottage is the **Japanese Gateway** and the celebrated **Great Pagoda**, designed by William Chambers in 1761.

Heading northwards you'll arrive at the 180m-long **Temperate House**, another wonderful iron-and-glass hothouse (although not so hot this time) designed by Burton in 1860 but not completed until 1899.

Due east of Temperate House is the **Marianne North Gallery**. Marianne North was one of those indomitable Victorian female travellers who roamed the continents from 1871 to 1885, painting their plants and trees along the way. The results of her labour now cover the walls of this small purpose-built gallery.

The **Orangery** near Kew Palace contains a *restaurant*, *cafe* and *shop*.

Note that most of the hothouses close at 5.30pm in summer, earlier in winter.

Getting There & Away You can get to Kew Gardens by tube or train. Come out of the station and walk straight (west) along Station Parade, cross Kew Gardens Rd and continue straight along Lichfield Rd. This will bring you to Victoria Gate.

Alternatively, from March to September (with reduced services in October), boats run by the Westminster Passenger Services Association (☎ 7930 4721, Ⓦ www.wpsa .co.uk) sail from Westminster Pier to Kew Gardens up to five times a day. See under Organised Tours in the Getting Around chapter for details.

RICHMOND & TWICKENHAM (Map 1)

If anywhere in London could be described as a village, Richmond – with its delightful green and riverside vistas – is it. Of Richmond Palace south of the Old Deer Park, where Elizabeth I died in 1603, only a red-brick gatehouse with the name Henry VII on it and a courtyard survive. Best of all, Richmond Park is the largest and most rural of the royal parks. You can get to Richmond on foot from Kew by following the river towards Twickenham, just across the bridge from Richmond.

Twickenham will always be associated with rugby and you'll find one of the few museums in the world devoted to the sport here. Otherwise there's not much to detain you here unless you want to visit the fine Marble Hill House overlooking the Thames.

Richmond Park

One of London's finest and wildest parks, **Richmond Park** (☎ 8948 3209, *Richmond, Surrey;* ⊖ *Richmond; open 7am-dusk daily Mar-Sept, 7.30am-dusk daily Oct-Feb)* covers more than 1000 hectares and is home to all sorts of wildlife, including herds of red and fallow deer, and more elusive foxes and

DOUG MCKINLAY

Richmond Park brims with fauna including herds of red deer.

badgers. It's a great place for bird-watchers too, with a wide range of habitats, from neat gardens to woodland and assorted ponds. The philosopher Bernard Russell (1872–1970) grew up in Pembroke Lodge, now a *tearoom* with fine views from the terrace at the back. Edward VIII was born in the 18th-century White Lodge. The Isabella Plantation is at its most spectacular in April and May when the rhododendrons and azaleas are in bloom.

Getting There & Away To get there from Richmond tube station, turn left along George St, which winds round towards Richmond Bridge and then forks. Take the left fork up Richmond Hill, pausing to soak up views so magnificent that they spurred Gainsborough and Turner to pick up their brushes, until you reach the Royal Star & Garter Home (on the left) for men disabled in 20th-century conflicts from WWI to the Gulf War. Across the road (a dangerous crossing) is Richmond Gate and the main entrance to the park.

Ham House

Ham House (☎ 8940 1950, Ⓦ *www.national trust.org.uk, Ham, Richmond, Surrey;* ⊖ *Richmond, then bus No 371; house & garden adult/child aged 5-15/family £6/ 3/15, gardens only adult/child aged 5-15 £2/75p; house open 1pm-5pm Mon-Wed, Sat & Sun Apr-Oct; gardens open 11am-6pm Mon-Wed, Sat & Sun Apr-Oct),*

'Hampton Court in miniature', was built in 1610 and became home to the 1st earl of Dysart, an unlucky individual who had been employed as 'whipping boy' to Charles I, taking the punishment for all the king's wrongdoings. Inside it's furnished with all the grandeur you might expect; the Great Staircase is a magnificent example of Stuart woodworking. Look out for ceiling paintings by Antonio Verrio, who also worked at Hampton Court Palace, and for a miniature of Elizabeth I by Nicholas Hilliard. Other paintings are by Constable, Reynolds and Kneller. The grounds of Ham House slope down to the Thames, but there are also pleasant 17th-century formal gardens.

Museum of Rugby

A state-of-the-art museum that will appeal to sports lovers but leave everyone else less than impressed, the Museum of Rugby (☎ 8892 8877, W www.rfu.com, Gate K, Twickenham Stadium, Rugby Rd, Twickenham; ⊖ Hounslow East, then bus No 281, or Station: Twickenham; adult/concession £3/2, stadium guided tour & museum £5/3; open 10am-5pm Tues-Sat, 2pm-5pm Sun) is tucked behind the eastern stand of the stadium. Relive those highlights of old matches in the video theatre and then take a tour of the grounds. They depart at 10.30am, noon and 1.30pm (with an additional tour at 3pm on Sunday) but there are no tours on match days.

Marble Hill House

Marble Hill House (☎ 8892 5115, W www .english-heritage.org.uk, Richmond Rd, Twickenham; Station: St Margaret's; adult/senior & student/child aged 5-15 £3.30/2.50/1.70; open 10am-6pm daily Apr-Oct, 10am-4pm Wed-Sun Nov-Mar) is an 18th-century Palladian love nest, built originally for George II's mistress Henrietta Howard and later occupied by Mrs Fitzherbert, the secret wife of George IV. The poet Alexander Pope had a hand in designing the park, which stretches down to the Thames. Inside you'll find an exhibition about the life and times of Henrietta, and a collection of early-Georgian furniture.

To get there from St Margaret's station, turn right along St Margaret's Rd. Then take the right fork along Crown Rd and turn left along Richmond Rd. Turn right along Beaufort Rd and walk across Marble Hill Park to the house.

HAMPTON

Out in London's south-western outskirts, the wonderful Hampton Court Palace (see the Around London map in the Excursions chapter) is pressed up against 400-hectare Bushy Park, a semiwild expanse with herds of red and fallow deer.

Hampton Court Palace

In 1514 Cardinal Thomas Wolsey, lord chancellor of England, decided to build himself a palace in keeping with his lofty sense of self-importance (☎ 8781 9500, W www.frp .org.uk, East Molesey, Surrey; Station: Hampton Court; all-inclusive ticket adult/ senior & student/child aged 5-15/family £10.80/8.50/7.20/32.30; gardens only adult/ child aged 5-15 £2.50/1.30; maze only adult/child aged 5-15 £2.50/1.60; joint ticket to Hampton Court Palace & Tower of London adult/senior & student/child aged 5-15/family £19/14.50/12.50/55.50; open 10.15am-6pm Mon & 9.30am-6pm Tues-Sun mid-Mar-late Oct, 10.15am-4.30pm Mon & 9.30am-4.30pm Tues-Sun rest of year). Unfortunately, even Wolsey couldn't persuade the pope to grant Henry VIII a divorce from Catherine of Aragon and relations between king and chancellor soured rapidly. Given that background, you only need to take one look at Hampton Court Palace to realise why Wolsey felt obliged to present it to Henry, a monarch not too fond of anyone trying to muscle in on his mastery of all he surveyed, some 15 years later. The hapless Wolsey was charged with high treason but died before his trial in 1530.

As soon as he acquired the palace, Henry set to work expanding it, adding the Great Hall, the Chapel Royal and the sprawling kitchens. By 1540 this was one of the grandest and most sophisticated palaces in Europe. In the late 17th century, William and Mary employed Sir Christopher Wren to build extensions. The result is a beautiful blend of Tudor and 'restrained Baroque' architecture.

Today the palace is England's largest and grandest Tudor structure, knee-deep in history, and with superb gardens and a famous 300-year-old maze. You should set aside plenty of time to do it justice, bearing in mind that if you come by boat from central London the trip will have eaten up half the day already.

Orientation At the ticket office by the main **Trophy Gate**, be sure to pick up a leaflet listing the daily programme, which will help you plan your visit; this is important as some of the free guided tours require advance booking.

As you walk up the path towards the palace you'll have a fine view of the lengthy red-brick facade with its distinctive Tudor chimneys and sturdy gateway. Passing through the main gate you arrive first in the **Base Court** and then the **Clock Court**,

RACHEL IMESON

With a maze to amaze and an eye-popping palace, Hampton is set to impress.

named after the fine 16th-century **Astronomical Clock** that shows the sun revolving round the earth. The **Fountain Court** is next. From the Clock Court you can follow signs to the six sets of rooms in the complex.

The stairs inside Anne Boleyn's Gateway lead up to **Henry VIII's State Apartments**, including the Great Hall, the largest single room in the palace, decorated with tapestries and a spectacular hammer-beam roof from which tiny painted faces peep down. A hallway hung with antlers leads to the **Great Watching Chamber** where guards controlled access to the king; this is the least altered of all the rooms dating from Henry's time. Leading off from the chamber is the smaller Pages' Chamber and the Haunted Gallery. Arrested for adultery and detained in the palace in 1542, Henry's fifth wife Catherine Howard managed to evade her guards and ran screaming down the corridor in search of the king. Her woeful ghost is said to do the same thing to this day.

Farther along the corridor you'll come to the beautiful **Chapel Royal**, built in just nine months. A Royal Pew forming part of the state apartments looks down over the altar below. The blue and gold vaulted ceiling was originally intended for Christ Church, Oxford, but was installed here instead, while the 18th-century reredos was carved by Grinling Gibbons.

Also dating from Henry's day are the **Tudor Kitchens**, again accessible from Anne Boleyn's Gateway and originally able to rustle up meals for a royal household of some 1200 people. The kitchens have been fitted out to look as they might have done in Tudor days and palace 'servants' turn the spits and stuff the bustards. Don't miss the Great Wine Cellar, which could originally cope with the 300 barrels of ale and the same again of wine consumed here annually in the mid-16th century.

Returning again to the Clock Court and passing under the colonnade to the right you reach the **King's Apartments**, built by Wren for William III towards the end of the 17th century. These apartments were badly damaged by fire in 1986 but have now been extensively restored.

A tour of the apartments takes you up the grand King's Staircase painted by Antonio Verrio in about 1700 and flattering the king by comparing him to Alexander the Great. You'll emerge into the **King's Guard Chamber**, which is decked out with guns, bayonets and swords and leads to the King's Presence Chamber. This room is dominated by a throne backed with scarlet hangings and by an equestrian portrait of William III by Godfrey Kneller.

Next on the tour is the King's Eating Room where William would sometimes have dined in public, beyond which you'll find the King's Privy Chamber, where ambassadors were received; the chandelier and throne canopy have been carefully restored after suffering terrible damage in the 1986 fire. Beyond this is the King's Withdrawing Room, where more intimate gatherings took place, and the **King's Great Bedchamber**, a splendid room, its bed topped with ostrich plumes, where the king was ceremonially dressed each morning. William actually slept in the Little Bedchamber beyond.

The back stairway beyond the King's Closet leads to three more wood-panelled closets furnished with paintings and more carvings by Grinling Gibbons. You then walk through an orangery to the King's Private Drawing Room and Dining Room, which is decorated with Kneller's paintings of the *Hampton Court Beauties*.

William's wife, Mary II, had her own separate **Queen's Apartments**, which are accessible up the Queen's Staircase, decorated by William Kent. When Mary died in 1694 work on these rooms was incomplete; they were finished under George II's reign. The rooms are shown as they might have been when Queen Caroline used them for entertaining between 1716 and 1737.

In comparison with the King's State Apartments, those for the queen seem rather austere, although the Queen's Audience Chamber has a throne as imposing as that of the king. Pass through the Queen's Drawing Room and you come to the **State Bedchamber**, where the queen took part in levees (royal morning meetings) rather than sleeping. The Queen's Gallery is hung with a set of 18th-century tapestries depicting the adventures of Alexander the Great.

Also upstairs and ringing Wren's graceful Fountain Court are the **Georgian Rooms** used by George II and Queen Caroline on the court's last visit to the palace in 1737. The first rooms you come to were designed to accommodate George's second son, the duke of Cumberland, whose bed is woefully tiny for its grand surroundings. The Wolsey Closet was restored and repanelled in 1888 to give an idea of what one of the palace's smaller rooms might have looked like in Tudor times. The Communications Gallery was built for William III and is decorated with Peter Lely's portraits of the **Windsor Beauties**, the most beautiful women at the court of Charles II. Beyond that is the Cartoon Gallery where the Raphael Cartoons (now in the Victoria & Albert Museum; see that section earlier in this chapter) used to hang; nowadays you have to make do with late-17th-century copies.

Beyond the Cartoon Gallery are the queen's private rooms: her drawing room and bedchamber, where she and the king would sleep if they wanted to be alone. Particularly interesting are the Queen's Bathroom, with its tub set on a floor cloth to soak up any spillage, and the Oratory, with its 16th-century Persian carpet.

Once you're finished with the palace interior there are still the wonderful gardens to appreciate. Look out for the **Real Tennis Court**, dating from the 1620s and designed for real tennis, a rather different version of the game from that played today. The restored 24-hectare **Riverside Gardens** are spectacular. Here you'll find the **Great Vine** planted in 1768 and still producing around 300kg of grapes per year; it's an old vine, no doubt about it, but not the world's oldest, as they say it is here. The Stara Trta (Old Vine) in the centre of Maribor, Slovenia's second city, was planted more than four centuries ago and still produces some 35L of red wine each year. The Lower Orangery in the gardens houses Andrea Mantegna's nine *Triumphs of Caesar* paintings, bought by Charles I in 1629; the Banqueting House was designed for William III and painted by Antonio Verrio. Look out, too, for the iron screens designed by Jean Tijou.

No-one should leave Hampton Court without losing themselves in the famous 800m-long **maze**, which is made up of hornbeam and yew planted in 1690. In case you're wondering, the average visitor takes 20 minutes to reach the centre.

Carriage rides round the gardens cost £9 for 20 minutes.

Getting There & Away There are trains every half-hour from Waterloo to Hampton Court station.

The palace can also be reached from Westminster Pier in central London on one of three river boats operated by Westminster Passenger Services Association (☎ 7930 4721, Ⓦ www.wpsa.co.uk) from April to September, with reduced sailings in October. For details see under Organised Tours in the Getting Around chapter.

ISLEWORTH, BRENTFORD & EALING (Map 1)

Isleworth is a quiet suburb by the Thames without much to draw a visitor except for Osterley House and its fine park. Brentford, equally nondescript, links Kew to Osterley and Ealing and boasts the magnificent Syon House. Parts of Ealing, once known for its film studios, are reasonably leafy and it has Pitshanger Manor, the country retreat designed by John Soane.

Osterley Park & House

Set in 120 hectares of landscaped park and farmland, Osterley House (☎ 8232 5050, Ⓦ www.nationaltrust.org.uk, Osterley Park, off Jersey Rd, Isleworth; ⊖ Osterley; house adult/child aged 5-15/family £4.30/2.15/ 10.50, park free; house open 1pm-4.30pm Wed-Sun Apr-Oct, park open 9am-dusk daily year-round) started life in 1575 as the country retreat of Thomas Gresham, the man responsible for the Royal Exchange, but was extensively remodelled in the mid-18th century by Robert Adam. The wonderful plasterwork, furniture and paintings are all worth seeing, but many people rate the downstairs kitchen and the Tudor Grand Stables as being even more interesting.

To get there from Osterley tube station, walk eastwards along the Great West Rd and turn left into Thornbury Rd, which will bring you to Jersey Rd and the park entrance. The house is about 500m to the north.

Syon House

Syon House (☎ 8560 0881, Ⓦ www.syon park.co.uk, Syon Park, Brentford; Station: Syon Lane; adult/senior, student & child aged 5-15/family £6.25/5.25/15; open 11am-5pm Wed, Thur & Sun mid-Mar–Oct) is a superb example of the English stately home. The house from where Lady Jane Grey ascended the throne for her nine-day reign in 1554 was remodelled by Robert Adam in the 18th century and has plenty of Adam furniture and oak panelling. The

An Englishman's castle: Syon House, still the home of the duke of Northumberland

interior was designed along gender-specific lines, with pastel pinks and purples for the ladies' gallery, and mock-Roman sculptures for the men's dining room. The gardens, including a lake and the 19th-century Great Conservatory, were landscaped by Capability Brown.

Pitshanger Manor

Pitshanger Manor (☎ 8567 1227, W www .ealing.gov.uk/pitshanger, Walpole Park, Mattock Lane W5; ✆ Ealing Broadway; admission free; open 10am-5pm Tues-Sat) was bought by the architect John Soane in 1800 and rebuilt in the Regency style. Parts of the manor now house a collection of pottery, which was designed by the Martin Brothers of Southall in the late 19th century. Not everyone will care for their grotesque designs, although the owl jars with swivel heads are undoubtedly good fun. There is also an adjacent art gallery that houses temporary exhibits.

Other Attractions

MUSEUMS & PUBLIC BUILDINGS

In addition to those listed above, smaller museums and buildings open to the public abound in London. Be warned, however, that some are of specialist interest and have very restricted opening hours.

Alexander Fleming Laboratory (Map 5)
(☎ 7725 6528, St Mary's Hospital, Praed St W2; ✆ Paddington; adult/concession £2/1; open 10am-1pm Mon-Thur). Reconstruction of the laboratory where Fleming discovered penicillin by accident in 1928.

Brunel's Engine House (Map 9)
(☎ 7231 3840 or 8806 4325, Railway Ave SE16; ✆ Rotherhithe; adult/senior, student & child aged 5-15/family £2/1/5; open 1pm-5pm Sat & Sun Apr-Oct, 1pm-5pm Sun Nov-Mar). Engine house designed by Isambard Brunel to drain the Thames Tunnel, the world's first major underwater one (1825–43), which now serves as a railway tunnel. A guided walking tour of Rotherhithe is included in the admission fee.

Faraday Museum (Map 7)
(☎ 7409 2992, Royal Institution, 21 Albemarle St W1; ✆ Green Park; admission £1; open 10am-5pm Mon-Fri). This shrine to Michael Faraday (1791–1867), a pioneer in electromagnetism and inventor of the electric battery, recreates his old laboratory at the institution where he taught.

House Mill (Map 1)
(☎ 8980 4626, Three Mill Lane E3; ✆ Bromley-by-Bow; adult/concession £2/1; open 2pm-4pm Sun May-Oct). The UK's largest surviving tidal mill (1772), used for making flour and powering a distillery. Guided tours are available and there's a small craft market here on the first Sunday of every month.

John Wesley's House, Chapel & Museum of Methodism (Map 4)
(☎ 7253 2262, 49 City Rd EC1; ✆ Old Street; adult/senior, student & child £4/2, admission free Sun; open 10am-4pm Mon-Sat, noon-2pm Sun). Well-kept chapel, museum and house filled to the brim with Wesley and Methodist memorabilia.

Karl Marx Memorial Library (Map 4)
(☎ 7253 1485, 37a Clerkenwell Green EC1; ✆ Farringdon; admission free; open 1pm-6pm Mon, 1pm-8pm Tues-Thur, 10am-1pm Sat). Library where Lenin edited 17 editions of the Russian-language newspaper Iskra (Spark).

Kew Bridge Steam Museum (Map 1)
(☎ 8568 4757, W www.kbsm.org, Green Dragon Lane, Brentford; Station: Kew Bridge; adult/senior & student/child aged 5-15 £3/2/1 Mon-Fri or £4/3/2 Sat & Sun; open 11am-5pm daily). Restored 19th-century pumping station with five Cornish beam engines, two of which steam away at weekends.

London Canal Museum (Map 4)
(☎ 7713 0836, W www.canalmuseum.org.uk, 12-13 New Wharf Rd N1; ✆ King's Cross; adult/senior, student & child £2.50/1.25; open 10am-4.30pm Tues-Sun). Victorian warehouse with small museum about life along London's canals.

Musical Museum (Map 1)
(☎ 8560 8108, 368 High St, Brentford; Station: Kew Bridge; adult/concession £3.20/2.50; open 2pm-5pm Sat & Sun Apr-Oct). Converted church housing a collection of mechanical musical instruments. It also operates a 90-minute tour.

Petrie Museum of Egyptian Archaeology (Map 3)
(☎ 7679 2884, University College London, Malet Place WC1; ✆ Goodge Street; admission free; open 1pm-5pm Tues-Fri, 10am-1pm Sat). Wonderful collection of Egyptian artefacts, particularly mummy portraits.

Pollock's Toy Museum (Map 6)
(☎ 7636 3452, W www.pollacks.cwc.net, 1 Scala St W1; ✪ Goodge Street; adult/under-18s £3/1.50; open 10am-5pm Mon-Sat). Collection of toys in half a dozen cluttered rooms include old model trains and theatres.

Ragged School Museum (Map 2)
(☎ 8980 6405, 46-50 Copperfield Rd E3; ✪ Mile End; admission free; open 10am-5pm Wed & Thur, 2pm-5pm first Sun of month). Small but excellent East End museum with information on the Dr Barnado homes for children and also on education.

Royal Air Force Museum (Map 1)
(☎ 8205 2266, W www.rafmuseum.org.uk, Grahame Park Way NW9; ✪ Colindale; adult/senior/student & child aged 5-15 £7/5.50/4.50; open 10am-6pm daily). Huge museum in the old Hendon Aerodrome displaying 70 planes and flying machines alongside a flight simulator.

Sutton House (Map 2)
(☎ 8986 2264, W www.nationaltrust.org.uk, 2 & 4 Homerton High St E9; Station: Hackney Central; adult/child aged 5-16/family £2.10/60p/4.80; open 11.30am-5.30pm Wed & Sun Feb-Nov). Stunning East End Tudor red-brick house with 18th-century additions and gardens.

GALLERIES

Along with the public art galleries described throughout this chapter, London counts many smaller commercial galleries that host changing exhibitions throughout the year. The freebie *New Exhibitions of Contemporary Art* (W www.newexhibitions.com), published weekly and available at most galleries, will tell you exactly what's on and where.

The galleries in the following list are just suggestions. Go for a stroll up and down Cork St, New Bond St or Old Bond St (all W1) and you will find many other possibilities.

Chinese Contemporary Art Gallery (Map 6)
(☎ 7499 8898, W www.chinesecontemporary .com, 21 Dering St W1; ✪ Bond St). Specialises in contemporary art by young artists from China.

Crafts Council (Map 4)
(☎ 7278 7700, W www.craftscouncil.org.uk, 44a Pentonville Rd N1; ✪ Angel). This is the largest organisation in the UK devoted to crafts.

Lamont Gallery (Map 2)
(☎ 7602 3232, W www.lamontart.com, 3 Swanscombe Rd W11; ✪ Holland Park). This gallery, which has some wonderful sculpture, has eschewed its Roman Rd E2 base for posh Holland Park, which seems to be exactly the opposite direction everyone else is taking.

London International Gallery of Children's Art (Map 12)
(☎ 7435 0903, W www.ligca.org, 02 The Centre, 255 Finchley Rd NW3; ✪ Finchley Road). This is London's only gallery devoted to the artwork of children.

Matt's Gallery (Map 2)
(☎ 8983 1771, 42-44 Copperfield Rd E3; ✪ Mile End). Interesting space that invites artists to come and do what ever they want or, rather, *feel*. Be prepared for anything.

Photographer's Gallery (Map 8)
(☎ 7831 1772, W www.photonet.org.uk, 5-8 Great Newport St WC2; ✪ Leicester Square). Some of the best exhibitions of contemporary photography take place here.

White Cube² (Map 4)
(☎ 7930 5373, W www.whitecube.com, 48 Hoxton Square N1; ✪ Old Street). This flavour-of-the-month gallery in this newly trendy area of East London shows whoever is hot in London at the mo'.

MARTIN MOOS

Get into the swing of things at one of the London golf clubs.

Activities

CLIMBING

Well, it ain't Everest or even the Matterhorn but the **Castle Climbing Centre (Map 1)** (☎ 8211 7000, **W** www.castle-climbing.co .uk, Green Lanes N4; ✪ Manor House or Bus: No 171A or 141) is the country's foremost climbing centre for everyone from beginners to experienced climbers. It opens 2pm to 10pm Monday to Friday and 10am to 7pm on Saturday and Sunday. A similar place is **Mile End Climbing Wall (Map 2)** (☎ 8980 0289, Haverfield Rd, off Grove Rd E3; ✪ Mile End), open noon to 9.30pm Monday to Friday and 10am to 6pm at the weekend.

On the hoof: a discerning
way to travel

GOLF

If you can't bring yourself to leave the clubs behind, the capital has a couple of leafy golf courses on its outskirts. Among the closest is **Chingford Golf Club** (☎ 8529 2107, 158 Station Rd E4; ✪ Chingford), where green fees are £10.80/14.50 on weekdays/at the weekend. Two others are **Brent Valley Golf Course (Map 1)** (☎ 8567 1287, Church Rd, Cuckoo Lane W7; Station: Hanwell) and **Richmond Park Golf Course (Map 1)** (☎ 8876 3205, **W** www.gcmgolf.com, Roehampton Gate, Priory Lane SW15; Station: Barnes).

HORSE RIDING

If you'd like to go riding in Hyde Park, which has 5 miles of bridle paths, horses can be hired from **Hyde Park Stables (Map 5)** (☎ 7723 2813, **W** www.hydeparkstables .com, 63 Bathurst Mews W2; ✪ Lancaster Gate). Rates are £32/35 per hour during the week/at the weekend or £250/270 for 10 hours. Lessons cost £34/300 per hour/10 hours. It opens 10am to 6pm Tuesday to Friday and 8.30am to 4.15pm on Saturday and Sunday.

PUBLIC BATHS

If you're visiting London during a hot, muggy summer you may well want to find a place to cool off. Medieval and Tudor London boasted innumerable public baths, which were called 'stews' and had a distinctly dodgy reputation. Even in the late 19th century the capital still boasted more than a dozen public baths, but today hardly any survive. Those that do are well worth seeking out.

The **Porchester Spa (Map 5)** (☎ 7792 3980, Porchester Centre, Queensway W2; ✪ Bayswater/Royal Oak), where a small plunge-pool sits in the middle of a tiled Art Deco lounge, was built in 1926. You can relax here and then take advantage of the three Turkish hot rooms, two Russian steam rooms, Finnish sauna, whirlpool spa bath and swimming pool; admission costs £18.95 per person or £26.75 for a couple. A full range of massages is also available (£20–36). The spa opens 10am to 10pm (last admission at 8pm) to men on Monday, Wednesday and Saturday and the same hours to women on Tuesday, Thursday and Friday as well as 10am to 4pm on Sunday. From 4pm to 10pm on Sunday both sexes can use the facilities.

A cheaper (but not as classy) possibility is the **Ironmonger Row Baths (Map 4)** (☎ 7253 4011, 1 Ironmonger Row EC1; ✪ Old Street), the closest London gets to a Turkish bath (admission £10 in the afternoon and at weekends, £6.20 in the morning). There's a steam room, sauna, small

DOUG MCKINLAY

Hot wheels: everybody's at it in Hyde Park.

plunge-pool and swimming pool. The baths open 9am to 9.30pm to men on Tuesday and Thursday and 9am to 6.30pm on Saturday, and to women from 9am to 9.30pm on Wednesday and Friday and 10am to 6.30pm on Sunday. From 2pm to 9.30pm on Monday the baths are open to both men and women.

A women-only option is **The Sanctuary** (Map 8) (☎ 7420 5104, *11-12 Floral St WC2;* ✚ *Covent Garden)*, but with a day's membership costing so much this is definitely for that *very* special treat (day membership costs £58 Monday to Thursday, £68 Friday to Sunday, and evening membership 5pm-10pm Thursday to Friday costs £35). It has a sauna, steam room, whirlpool and twin pools. There are all manner of beauty treatments on offer as well. It opens 9.30am to 6pm Monday to Wednesday, 9.30am to 10pm Thursday and Friday and 10am to 6pm Saturday and Sunday.

SKATING

Roller-blade enthusiasts might want to join the weekly two-hour skate around Hyde Park that starts at Wellington Arch, Hyde Park Corner W1 (✚ Hyde Park) at 7pm on Friday; check the Web site at Ⓦ www.citiskate.com for details.

If you arrive in London without your skates, well, you can get on some by renting a pair of in-lines from **Snow & Rock** (**Map 5**) *(*☎ *7937 0872,* Ⓦ *www.snowandrock.com, 188 Kensington High St W8;* ✚ *High Street Kensington)*. Rates (including safety kit) are £10/15 for standard/deluxe (ie, the latest) models for 24 hours, £15/22 for the weekend (3pm on Friday to noon on Monday) and between £30 and £42 for seven days. A deposit of £150 is required (credit cards are accepted). It opens 10am to 6pm Monday to Wednesday and Friday, 10am to 7pm on Thursday, 9am to 6pm Saturday and 11am to 5pm on Sunday.

As for ice skating, the **Broadgate Ice Rink** (**Map 9**) *(*☎ *7505 4608, Broadgate Centre, Eldon St EC2;* ✚ *Liverpool Street)* is one of the very few open-air rinks in the UK and opens from October to April only. Admission costs £5/3 (adult/child) plus £2/1 skate hire. In winter, **Somerset House** *(*☎ *7413 3399 or 7845 4670, The Strand WC2;* ✚ *Temple/Covent Garden)* floods the central Great Court and turns it into a skating rink, which is illuminated at night. Admission costs £6/4 (adult/child) and includes skate hire.

For a rink that is open year-round, you'll have to go farther afield. **Streatham Ice Rink** *(*☎ *8769 7771,* Ⓦ *www.streathamicearena.co.uk, 386 Streatham High Rd SW16; Station: Streatham)* is a large rink where you can also take lessons. It opens 10am to 10pm daily, with half-hour breaks to clean the ice at 3.30pm and 7pm. Admission costs £6.50/5.50 (adult/under-12s) and includes skate hire. The **Lee Valley Ice Centre** (**Map 1**) *(*☎ *8533 3154,* Ⓦ *www.leevalleypark.org.uk, Lea Bridge Rd E10; Station: Clapton, then bus No 48, 55 or 56)* opens noon to 4pm and costs £4.70/3.70 plus £1.20 skate hire.

SKIING

It represents a *very* loose use of the word 'skiing' as we know it, but you can slalom down a 200m slope made out of a substance that looks like the bottom of a bathmat at **Mountaintop Beckton Alps Ski Centre (Map 1)** (☎ 7511 0351, *Alpine Way E6;* ✪ *East Ham, then bus No 101, DLR: Beckton).* A two-hour session before/after 6pm costs £9/10 and lessons cost £25 per hour. It opens 10am to 10pm Monday, Tuesday and Thursday to Sunday and 10am to 11pm Wednesday.

SWIMMING

Almost every London borough has its own swimming pool, and many have several; to find the address of the one nearest to you look under 'Swimming Pools' or 'Leisure Centres' in the *Yellow Pages* or, if you've got time on your hands, try calling Sportsline on ☎ 7222 8000 – it's always engaged. One particularly popular and central pool is at the **Oasis Sports Centre (Map 8)** (☎ 7831 1804, *32 Endell St WC2;* ✪ *Tottenham Court Road),* with both an indoor pool (open 6.30am to 6.30pm Monday to Friday, 9.30am to 5pm Saturday and Sunday) and an outdoor pool (open 7.30am to 9pm Monday to Friday, 9.30am to 5pm Saturday and Sunday). Admission costs £2.90/1.10 adult/child aged five to 15.

From late June to August you can swim at the outdoor **Serpentine Lido (Map 5)** (☎ 7706 3422, *beside the Serpentine in Hyde Park).* It opens 10am to 5.30pm daily and admission costs £2.70/1.70/60p/6 adult/senior & student/child aged 5-15/family.

The indoor **Parliament Hill Lido (Map 12)** (☎ 7485 3873, *Gordon House Rd NW5; Station: Gospel Oak)* opens 7am to 6.30pm, with a half-hour's closure from 9.30am to 10am, daily May to September, and 7am to 9.30am only October to April. Admission is free up to 9.30am but costs £3.50/1.50/7 adult/child aged 5-15/family after 10am.

Hardier souls may head for the nearby **Hampstead Heath Ponds (Map 12)** on the western edge of the heath (☎ 7485 4491, *Hampstead Heath NW3; Station: Hampstead Heath/Gospel Oak).* They're open 7am to dusk daily. Unsurprisingly the ponds are hugely popular in summer.

TENNIS

Although most London parks have tennis courts, they are often booked up for weeks ahead. Check Ⓦ www.londontennis.co.uk for information on where to play in your area. The Lawn Tennis Association (☎ 7381 7000, Ⓦ *www.lta.org.uk, Queen's Club, Palliser Rd W14)* produces a useful series of pamphlets on where to play tennis in London (covered in the Middlesex brochure), which they'll send you on receipt of a stamped and addressed envelope. Alternatively you can call Sportsline on ☎ 7222 8000.

WATERSPORTS

You can go boating on the Serpentine in Hyde Park; the outfit that rents them is called **Bluebird Boats** (☎ 7262 1330) and boats are available in summer for £3.50/5 per half-hour/hour for adults and £1/2 for children.

For a wider range of watersports, the Docklands is the place to go. For details of what's available contact the **Docklands Watersports Club (Map 1)** (☎ 7511 7000, *Gate 14, King George V Dock, Woolwich Manor Way E16; DLR: Gallions Reach).* It opens 10am to 11pm Monday, Thursday and Sunday and 10am to 2pm Saturday and Sunday.

Other places where you can jet ski, water ski and windsurf (boards for rent from about £8–10 an hour) include:

Docklands Sailing & Watersports Centre (Map 13) (☎ 7537 2626, Ⓦ *www.docklandswatersports.co.uk, 235a Westferry Rd, Millwall Docks E14; DLR: Crossharbour & London Arena).* Open 9am to dusk daily.

Peter Chilvers Windsurfing Centre (Map 1) (☎ 7474 2500, *Gate 6, Royal Victoria Dock, Tidal Basin Rd E16; DLR: Royal Victoria).* Open 10.30am till dusk daily.

Royal Victoria Dock Watersports Centre (Map 1) (☎ 7511 2326, *Gate 5, Royal Victoria Dock, Tidal Basin Rd E16; DLR: Royal Victoria).* Open 9am to 6pm Monday and Wednesday, 9am to 8pm Tuesday and Thursday and 9am to 5.30pm Sunday.

Courses

No matter whether you want to study sculpture or Sanskrit, circus skills or computing, someone is going to be running a course somewhere in London that will meet your needs, and your starting point for information should be *Floodlight* (£3.75; **w** www.floodlight.co.uk), published once a year in summer and listing most of the regular courses around town. Another – and cheaper – source is *On Course* (£2.95), issued twice a year.

LANGUAGE

Every year thousands of people come to London to study English and there are centres offering tuition throughout the city. The problem for the prospective student is to identify a reputable one, which is where the resources of the **British Council (Map 8)** *(☎ 7930 8466, 10 Spring Gardens SW1; ⊖ Charing Cross)* come in. It produces a free list of accredited colleges that meet minimum standards for facilities, qualified staff and pastoral back-up. They can also offer general advice to overseas students on educational opportunities in the UK. The British Tourist Authority also produces a brochure for people wanting to study in London.

The following are recognised schools you might find useful. All offer courses aimed at every level that can be studied full-time or part-time. They also offer intensive summer courses and private tuition. A four-week full-time course is likely to cost from £150 to £200, while a 12-week course will cost between £300 and £400, depending in part on how many hours you'll be studying.

Central School of English
*(☎ 7580 2863, **w** www.centralschool.co.uk, 1 Tottenham Court Rd W1; ⊖ Tottenham Court Road)*
Frances King School of English
*(☎ 7870 6533, **w** www.francesking.co.uk, 77 Gloucester Rd; ⊖ Gloucester Road)*
Holborn English Language Services
(☎ 7734 9989, 14 Soho St W1; ⊖ Tottenham Court Road)
London Study Centre
*(☎ 7731 3549, **w** www.londonstudycentre.com, Munster House, 676 Fulham Rd SW6; ⊖ Fulham Broadway)*

COOKING

The long-established **Leith's School of Food & Wine (Map 5)** *(☎ 7229 0177, **w** www.leiths.com, 21 St Alban's Grove W8; ⊖ High Street Kensington)* has courses ranging from a short demonstration matching food and wine (£45) to a year-long diploma in food and wine (£11,600). Contact the school for a brochure describing courses of study.

Places to Stay

Where you choose to stay in London will have an effect on the kind of time you have in the city. You want ethnic London? Stay in Notting Hill or Brixton. If your idea of the British capital is one of stately Georgian houses, Regency crescents and private parks in the centre of leafy squares, book a place in Chelsea or South Kensington. Culture vultures and/or those with literary aspirations should choose a place in Kensington, Bloomsbury or even Fitzrovia. You want workaday London with barrow boys, girls in white-heeled shoes and Cockney accents? Choose somewhere in the East End. And if you want to hang out with your 'mites', Earl's Court (aka Kangaroo Valley) or Shepherd's Bush is for you.

Unfortunately, wherever you stay accommodation in London is going to take a great wad out of your pocket. Demand can outstrip supply – especially at the bottom end of the market – so it's worth booking at least a few nights' accommodation before arriving, particularly in July and August. Remember, too, that single rooms are in short supply here, and places are reluctant to let a double room, even during quiet periods, to one person without charging a hefty supplement or even the full double rate.

Another problem can be quality – even at the mid-range. The bulk of readers' letters sent to Lonely Planet about London and the *London* guide are complaints about the quality and cleanliness of hostels, guesthouses and some B&Bs, 'fauna' in the rooms and the rudeness of staff. Please read the descriptions found in this chapter carefully and make your choices.

Each year, the London Tourist Board & Convention Bureau (☎ 7932 2000, **w** www .londontouristboard.com) publishes *Where to Stay & What to Do in London* (£4.99), which lists approved hotels, B&Bs, guesthouses and apartments. It also produces a

CHARLOTTE HINDLE

If you want deluxe grandeur (and have the bank account to match) then why not try The Savoy?

separate, free pamphlet called *Where to Stay on a Budget*. Also check out W www .frontdesk.co.uk, W www.hotelsoflondon .co.uk and W www.londonlodging.co.uk.

All the places mentioned in this chapter are open year-round unless stated otherwise.

Booking Offices

It's possible to make same-day accommodation bookings for free at most TICs in London; see under Local Tourist Offices in the Facts for the Visitor chapter. Phone or email bookings (☎ 7932 2020, open 9am to 5.30pm weekdays, 10am to 2pm Saturday, e book@londontouristboard.co.uk) cost £5.

The British Hotel Reservation Centre (☎ 0800 282888, W www.bhrconline.com) on the main concourse of Victoria train station opens 6am to 11.30pm daily. The telephone hotline is staffed round the clock.

First Option (☎ 7930 6885), formerly called Thomas Cook Hotel & Travel Reservations Ltd, operates a reservation service and charges about £5. There's a kiosk on the mezzanine level of the Britain Visitor Centre (Map 7) as well as at Euston (☎ 7388 7435) and King's Cross (☎ 7837 5681) stations. You'll find three offices at Victoria station: on platform No 9 (☎ 7828 4646), in a kiosk outside the station (☎ 7233 6754) and upstairs near the taxi rank (☎ 7630 7067). South Kensington tube (☎ 7581 9766) and Gatwick airport train station (☎ 01293-529372) also have outlets.

If you want to stay in a B&B or private home, reservations can be made for a minimum of three nights and a 5% booking fee through London Homestead Services (☎ 8949 4455, fax 8549 5492, e lhs@ netcomuk.co.uk, W www.lhslondon.com), Coombe Wood Rd, Kingston-upon-Thames KT2 7JY. Bed & Breakfast Reservations Service (☎ 01491-578803), PO Box 66, Henley-on-Thames RG9 1XS, specialises in central London. Host & Guest Services (☎ 7385 9922, fax 7386 7575, e acc@ hostguest.co.uk, W www.host-guest.co.uk), 103 Dawes Rd, SW6 7DU, looks for student accommodation and B&Bs. We have heard good things about the London Bed & Breakfast Agency (☎ 7586 2768, fax 7586

6567, e stay@londonbb.com, W www .londonbb.com), 71 Fellows Rd NW3.

For details on Youth Hostel Association reservations see under YHA Hostels.

PLACES TO STAY – BUDGET
Camping

Camping is obviously not a realistic option in the centre of this busy capital, but there are a few options within striking distance.

Abbey Wood Caravan Park (☎ 8311 7708, fax 8311 1465, Federation Rd SE2) **Map 1** Station: Abbey Wood. Tent £2-3.50, caravan £8, plus £4.50/1.20 per adult/under-15s, electricity hook-up £1.25. This park south of the river and east of Greenwich has 360 pitches.

Lee Valley Leisure Centre (☎ 8345 6666, fax 8804 4975, e leisurecentre@leevalleypark .com, W www.leevalleypark.com, Pickett's Lock Lane, Meridian Way N9) **Map 1** Station: Edmonton Green, then bus No W8. Tent & caravan sites £5.65/2.35 per adult/child aged 5-16, electricity hook-up £2.40. Office open 8am-10pm. This site, bordering a reservoir to the north-east, has some 160 pitches for tents and caravans and is close to many leisure and sporting facilities.

Crystal Palace Caravan Club (☎ 8778 7155, fax 8676 0980, Crystal Palace Parade SE19) **Map 1** Station: Crystal Place. Tent & caravan £8, plus £3.75-4.75/1.20 per adult/child aged 5-16, electricity hook-up £1.50-2.25. This site with 150 pitches in south-east London is on the edge of Crystal Palace Park, which offers a number of sporting and leisure options.

YHA Hostels

Seven hostels in the central London area – and another three within striking distance – are members of Hostelling International (HI), which is known in Britain as the Youth Hostels Association (YHA; W www.yha.org .uk). Joining the YHA gives you access to a network of hostels throughout the UK and the rest of the world, and you don't have to be 'young' to belong. Annual membership costs £12/6.25 for 'seniors' (those aged over 18)/'juniors' (under-18s). If you are not a member but wish to stay at a YHA hostel, you'll be given a card to fill up with six nightly stamps, each costing £2 in addition to the rate. When the card's full, you've become a member.

You can join at any YHA Adventure shop (see Camping & Backpacking Equipment in the Shopping chapter) or by contacting the YHA Membership Department, Youth Hostels Association of England & Wales (☎ 0870 870 8808, fax 01727-844126, ℮ customerservices@yha.org.uk), Trevelyan House, 8 St Stephen's Hill, St Albans, Hertfordshire AL1 2DY. Payment can be made by credit/debit card or cheque.

You can also join HI – or its local affiliate – in your home country. National offices include the following:

Australia
(☎ 02-9565 1699, fax 9565 1325, ℮ yha@yha.org.au, ☑ www.yha.org.au) Australian Youth Hostels Association, Level 3, 10 Mallett St, Camperdown, NSW 2050
Canada
(☎ 613-237 7884, fax 237 7868, ℮ info@hostellingintl.ca, ☑ www.hostellingintl.ca) Hostelling International Canada, Suite 400, 205 Catherine St, Ottawa, Ontario K2P 1C3
Ireland
(☎ 01-830 4555, fax 830 5808, ℮ anoige@iol.ie, ☑ www.irelandyha.org) An Óige/Irish Youth Hostel Association, 61 Mountjoy St, Dublin 7
New Zealand
(☎ 0800-278299 or 03-379 9970, fax 365 4476, ℮ info@yha.org.nz, ☑ www.yha.org.nz) Youth Hostels Association of New Zealand, PO Box 436, Level 3, Union House, 193 Cashel St, Christchurch 1
Northern Ireland
(☎ 02890-324733, fax 439699, ℮ info@hini.org.uk, ☑ www.hini.org.uk) Hostelling International Northern Ireland, 22 Donegall Rd, Belfast BT12 5JN
Scotland
(☎ 01786-891400, fax 891333, ℮ info@syha.org.uk, ☑ www.syha.org.uk) Scottish Youth Hostels Association, 7 Glebe Crescent, Stirling FK8 2JA
South Africa
(☎ 021-424 2511, fax 424 4119, ℮ info@hisa.org.za, ☑ www.hisa.org.za) Hostelling International South Africa, PO Box 4402, 3rd floor, St George's House, 73 St George's Mall, Cape Town 8001
USA
(☎ 202-783 6161, fax 783 6171, ℮ hostels@hiayh.org, ☑ www.hiayh.org) Hostelling International/American Youth Hostels, Suite 840, 733 15th St NW, Washington DC 20005

The biggest advantages of staying in hostels are price (although the difference between a very cheap B&B and an expensive hostel is not always so great, particularly if you're sharing) and the chance to meet other travellers. The disadvantages are that you usually sleep in bunks (sometimes in single-sex dorms) and may find the atmosphere somewhat institutional. The rates always include bed linen and sometimes breakfast.

The seven hostels in central London can get very crowded in summer. A less busy (and, unfortunately, less accessible) alternative lies to the north-east of the city in Epping Forest. You can find other YHA hostels in Oxford (☎ 01865-762997, ℮ oxford@yha.org.uk) and Cambridge (☎ 01223-354601, ℮ cambridge@yha.org.uk), as well as Canterbury (☎ 01227-462911, ℮ canterbury@yha.org.uk), Windsor (☎ 01753-861710, ℮ windsor@yha.org.uk) and also Brighton (☎ 01273-556196, ℮ brighton@yha.org.uk).

All YHA hostels take advance credit-card bookings by phone and will hold some beds for those who show up on the same day (arrive early and be prepared to queue). The YHA also operates a central reservations system (☎ 0870 241 2314 or 7373 3400, fax 7373 3455, ℮ lonres@yha.org.uk). Although you can just as easily contact the individual hostels directly for bookings, the staff at the central reservations system will know what beds are available where and when, and they're much easier to contact than the hostels during the busy periods.

Most hostels offer 24-hour access, storage lockers, Internet access for a nominal fee, facilities for self-catering and relatively cheap meals (eg £3.30 for breakfast, £2.90/3.80 for a small/large packed lunch, and £4.90 for a three-course evening meal).

City of London *(☎ 7236 4965, fax 7236 7681, ℮ city@yha.org.uk, 36 Carter Lane EC4)* **Map 6** ⊖ St Paul's. Beds £21.15-27.80/18.90-23.70 senior/junior, including breakfast. This excellent 193-bed hostel stands in the shadow of St Paul's Cathedral. Rooms have mainly two, three or four beds though there are 17 rooms with five to 15 beds. Rates vary according to room type. There's a licensed cafeteria but no kitchen. Remember: this part of town is pretty quiet outside working hours.

Earl's Court (☎ 7373 7083, fax 7835 2034, e earlscourt@yha.org.uk, 38 Bolton Gardens SW5) **Map 10** ⊖ Earl's Court. Beds £18.50/16.50 senior/junior, excluding breakfast. This hostel (155 beds) is in a shabby Victorian town house in quite a buzzy part of town. Rooms are mainly 10-bed dorms with communal showers though there are some rooms with two and four beds. There's a cafe, a kitchen for self-catering and a small garden courtyard. However, we've received quite a few letters complaining about the general standards of this hostel.

Epping Forest (☎ 8508 5971, fax 8508 5161, Wellington Hill, High Beach, Loughton, Essex) ⊖ Loughton. Beds £10/6.90 senior/junior, excluding breakfast. This small hostel (36 beds) is some 12 miles from central London and a good 2-mile walk (or £4 taxi ride) from the nearest tube, so it's only really an option if everything else is full. Accommodation is in four- and six-bed dorms, and the hostel is open to individual travellers from early April to total November.

Hampstead Heath (☎ 8458 9054, fax 8209 0546, e hampstead@yha.org.uk, 4 Wellgarth Rd NW11) **Map 12** ⊖ Golders Green. Beds £19.90/17.70 senior/junior, including breakfast. This 199-bed hostel in a three-storey house built in 1915 has a beautiful setting with a well-kept garden, though it's rather isolated. The dorms are comfortable and each room has a washbasin. There's a licensed cafe and a kitchen.

Holland House (☎ 7937 0748, fax 7376 0667, e hollandhouse@yha.org.uk, Holland Walk, Kensington W8) **Map 5** ⊖ High Street Kensington. Beds £20.50/18.50 senior/junior, including breakfast. This hostel (201 beds) is built into the Jacobean wing of Holland House in the middle of Holland Park. It's large, very busy and rather institutional, but the position can't be beaten. There's a cafe and kitchen.

Oxford St (☎ 7734 1618, fax 7734 1657, e oxfordst@yha.org.uk, 3rd floor, 14 Noel St W1) **Map 7** ⊖ Oxford Circus/Tottenham Court Road. Beds £21.50-23.50/17.50-23.50 senior/junior, excluding breakfast. This most central of the YHA hostels (75 beds) is basic but clean and welcoming. Accommodation is mostly in twins though there are five triples and three family rooms; rates vary according to room type. It has a kitchen but no meals are served apart from breakfast (£3.30).

Rotherhithe (☎ 7232 2114, fax 7237 2919, e rotherhithe@yha.org.uk, 20 Salter Rd SE16) **Map 9** ⊖ Rotherhithe. Beds £23.50/19.90 seniors/juniors, including breakfast; doubles/quads with private bath £51/94. The YHA flagship hostel in London with 320 beds was purpose-built in 1993. It's right by the Thames and recommended, but the location is a bit remote. Most rooms have four or six beds, though there are also 22 doubles (four of them adapted for disabled visitors); all have an attached bathroom. There's a bar and restaurant as well as kitchen facilities and a laundry.

St Pancras International (☎ 7388 9998, fax 7388 6766, e stpancras@yha.org.uk, 79-81 Euston Rd N1) **Map 3** ⊖ King's Cross St Pancras/Euston. Beds £23.50-28/19.90-25.50 senior/junior, including breakfast. This 150-bed place is modern and fairly comfortable, with a kitchen, restaurant, lounge and cycle shed. The 33 more expensive rooms have private bath.

Independent Hostels

London's independent hostels tend to be more relaxed and cheaper than the YHA ones, though standards can be low; some of them are downright grotty. Expect to pay a minimum of £12 per night in a basic dorm.

Most hostels have at least three or four bunks jammed into each small room, a kitchen and some kind of lounge. Some have budget restaurants and a bar attached. Be careful with your possessions; deposit your valuables in the office safe, safe-deposit box or secure locker if provided. Check that fire escapes and stairwells are accessible.

Ashlee House (☎ 7833 9400, fax 7833 9677, e info@ashleehouse.co.uk, w www.ashleehouse.co.uk, 261-5 Gray's Inn Rd WC1) **Map 4** ⊖ King's Cross St Pancras. Beds £19/17/15 in 6-/10-/16-bed dorms, single/twin £36/24 per person, including breakfast. This welcoming place is a clean and well-maintained backpackers' hostel with 180 beds on three floors close to King's Cross station. Dorms (most with bunks) can be cramped, but there is double-glazing on the windows, a laundry, a decent-sized kitchen, a free left-luggage room and Internet access.

Barmy Badger Backpackers (☎/fax 7370 5213, e barmybadger@hotmail.com, 17 Longridge Rd SW5) **Map 10** ⊖ Earl's Court. Beds £13/14 in 6-/8-bed dorms, twins without/with facilities £15/16 per person, including breakfast. A basic but clean family-run hostel, it has a big, sun-filled kitchen, safe-deposit boxes, a back garden and friendly staff. Laundry costs £3.

Curzon House Hotel (☎ 7581 2116, fax 7835 1319, e info@curzonhousehotel.co.uk, w www.curzonhousehotel.co.uk, 58 Courtfield Gardens

SW5) **Map 10** ✆ Gloucester Road. Beds £16/18 in 6-/8-bed dorms, singles/doubles with facilities £35-40/48-52, including breakfast. This relaxed, friendly 62-bed place in Earl's Court is without a doubt one of the better private hostels around. It has a nice TV lounge, kitchen facilities and Internet access.

Dover Castle Hostel (☎ 7403 7773, fax 7787 8654, **w** www.dovercastlehostel.co.uk, 6a Great Dover St SE1) **Map 9** ✆ Borough. Beds £16/15/14/12/10 in 3-/6-/8-/10-/12-bed dorms, £64-75 per week. This 55-bed hostel in a four-storey Victorian terrace house has a Caribbean-theme bar below and is just off Borough High St. It has a TV lounge, kitchen facilities, luggage storage and Internet access.

The Generator (☎ 7388 7655 fax 7388 7644, **e** info@the-generator.co.uk, **w** www.the-generator.co.uk, Compton Place, 37 Tavistock Place WC1) **Map 4** ✆ Russell Square. Beds £22.50/21.50 in 6-/8-bed dorms in high season, £19/20 in low season, twins £53/46, singles £40/36.50, including breakfast. The huge Generator in Bloomsbury is one of the grooviest budget places in central London and the futuristic decor looks like an updated set of Terry Gilliam's film *Brazil*. Along with 213 rooms (833 beds), it has a bar open till 2am, a large lounge

THE GENERATOR

THE ONLY PLACE TO STAY IN LONDON
The Generator, MacKaghton House, Compton Place, London WC1H 9SD
(Off 37 Tavistock Place)
Telephone 0171-388 7655   Facsimile 0171-388 7644

ELLIOT DANIEL

The Generator: neon-lit hostel accommodation in a converted police barracks.

for watching TV or playing pool, a room with Internet access, safe-deposit boxes and a large eating area, but no kitchen.

Hyde Park Hostel (☎ 7229 5101, fax 7229 3170, **e** astorhostels@msn.com, **w** www.astorhostels.com, 2-6 Inverness Terrace W2) **Map 5** ✆ Bayswater. Beds £17.50/16.50/15.50/14/12 in 4-/6-/8-/10-/12-bed dorms, twins £22.50 per person in summer, including breakfast; rates £1-2 less the rest of the year. This Bayswater hostel (283 beds) run by the Astor group is hardly the cleanest or most comfortable place in town, but the building has some character and is conveniently located. There's a cafe, laundry, travel agency, bar (open till 4am) and Internet access.

International Students House (☎ 7631 8310, fax 7631 8315, **e** accom@ish.org.uk, 229 Great Portland St W1) **Map 3** ✆ Great Portland Street. Beds £20/18/12 in 3-/4-/up to 10-bed dorms, with washbasin & breakfast £29.50, singles/doubles £33/52 with bathroom, £31/50 without. This big place in Marylebone feels more like a university hall of residence than a hostel. The single and double rooms are ordinary but clean, and there are excellent facilities and a friendly, relaxed atmosphere.

Leinster Inn (☎ 7229 9641, fax 7229 5255, **e** leinster@astorhostels.com, **w** www.astorhostels.com, 7-12 Leinster Square W2) **Map 5** ✆ Bayswater. Beds £16-11.50 in 4- to 8-bed dorms, depending on floor, singles/doubles/triples £37/27/20 per person with en-suite shower, £27/20/19 without, including breakfast; rates £2-5 less in winter. In a large old house north-west of Bayswater tube station and close to Portobello Rd Market, this 372-bed hostel is the largest in the Astor stable. It has a cafe, laundry, Internet lounge and a bar open till 4am that stages theme parties each month.

Museum Inn (☎ 7580 5360, fax 7636 7948, **e** astormuseuminn@aol.com, **w** www.astorhostels.com, 27 Montague St WC1) **Map 6** ✆ Russell Square/Tottenham Court Road. Beds £15.50/14 in 8-/10-bed dorms, triple/quad £18/16, twin £20-22 per person, including breakfast. This hostel run by the Astor group has an enviable location opposite the British Museum and close to Soho, a small kitchen and TV lounge and Internet access. But it must be said that we have received an alarming number of letters complaining about filthy conditions, rude staff and bookings not being honoured. Be warned.

Quest Hotel (☎ 7229 7782, fax 7727 8106, **e** astorhostels@msn.com, **w** www.astorhostels.com, 45 Queensborough Terrace W2) **Map 5** ✆ Bayswater. Beds £16/15 in 4-/5- to 9-bed dorms, twins £20 per person, including breakfast.

This Astor hostel one block to the east of the Hyde Park Hostel is just as well situated, but with only 90 beds available it gets pretty crowded. There's a kitchen for self-catering.

St Christopher's Village (☎ *7407 1856, fax 7403 7715,* e *bookings@st-christophers.co.uk,* w *www.st-christophers.co.uk, 163 Borough High St SE1)* **Map 9** ⊖ Borough/London Bridge. Beds £18.50/17/16/14 in 4-/6-/8-/10- to 12-bed dorms in high season, £14/13/12/10 in low season, twins £17-23 per person, depending on season, including breakfast. This 164-bed place is the flagship of an excellent hostel chain that has been making a name for itself over the past few years for its basic but cheap and clean accommodation, friendly service and all-round good times. There's a lovely roof garden with sauna, solarium, hot tub and excellent views of the Thames. Nearby branches (same contact details) include *St Christopher's Inn (121 Borough High St SE1)*, with 48 beds, a pub below the hostel, a small veranda and a chill-out room, and the *Orient Expresso (59-61 Borough High St SE1)*, with 36 beds, a laundry and cafe.

St Christopher's Inn Camden (☎ *7388 1012, fax 7388 4200,* e *bookings@st-christophers .co.uk,* w *www.st-christophers.co.uk, 48-50 Camden High St NW1)* **Map 3** ⊖ Camden Town. Beds £17/16/14 in 6-/8-/10-bed dorms in high season, £14/13/12 in low season, twins £17-23 per person, depending on season, including breakfast. This 44-bed branch of the popular Southwark hostel chain is atop *Belushi's*, a popular late-licence bar in Camden.

Victoria Hotel (☎ *7834 3077, fax 7932 0693,* e *astorhostels@msn.com,* w *www.astorhostels .com, 71 Belgrave Rd SW1)* **Map 11** ⊖ Pimlico. Dorm beds £16-20, twins £29-40. This 60-bed place, yet another from the Astor group, is within easy walking distance of the Tate Britain and Westminster Abbey.

Windsor House (☎ *7373 9087, fax 7385 2417, 12 Penywern Rd SW5)* **Map 10** ⊖ Earl's Court. Dorm beds £16, singles/doubles/triples £42/50/63, including breakfast. This 19-room place is not great value but there's a pleasant back garden and a kitchen for guests' use.

Student Accommodation

University halls of residence are let to non-students during the holidays, usually from early July to late September and sometimes over Easter. They're a bit more expensive than the hostels but you usually get a single or double room with shared or en-suite facilities. The price often includes breakfast.

University catering is reasonable and includes bars, cafes, takeaway places and restaurants. Full-board, half-board, B&B and self-catering options are also available.

The London School of Economics and Political Science (☎ 7955 7531, fax 7955 7676, e vacations@lse.ac.uk, w www.lse .ac.uk/vacations), Room B508, Page Building, Houghton St, London WC2A 2AE, lets a few of its halls in summer and sometimes during the Easter break in late March/April.

The main LSE halls are:

159 Great Dover St (☎ *7403 1932, fax 7403 2342,* e *nbha@159gds.ndo.co.uk, 159 Great Dover St SE1)* **Map 9** ⊖ Borough. Singles £29 (£25 students), twins £45. This 280-room hall is a short distance south-east of Borough High St.

Bankside House (☎ *7633 9877, fax 7574 6730, 24 Sumner St SE1)* **Map 9** ⊖ Blackfriars. Basic single £28, singles/twins/triples with facilities £41/55/73, including breakfast. This hall, the largest in the LSE stable with some 800 beds, is located a stone's throw from the Globe Theatre and the Tate Modern.

Butler's Wharf Residence (☎ *7407 7164, fax 7403 0847, 11 Gainsford St SE1)* **Map 9** ⊖ Tower Hill/London Bridge. Basic singles/twins £22.50/40. This 281-bed hall is just below Tower Bridge in Shad Thames.

Carr-Saunders Hall (☎ *7323 9712, fax 7580 4718, 18-24 Fitzroy St W1)* **Map 6** ⊖ Goodge Street/Warren Street. Basic singles £23.50/27 Easter/summer, twins with bathroom £42/50, without £37/45. This 156-bed residence is in a quiet section of Fitzrovia but within easy walking distance of Soho and the West End theatres.

High Holborn (☎ *7379 5589, fax 7379 5640, 178 High Holborn WC1)* **Map 8** ⊖ Holborn. Singles £28-35, twins £47-57, en-suite twins £57-67, en-suite triples £67-77, depending on season, including breakfast. This high rise with 494 beds is just a few minutes' walk from Covent Garden.

Passfield Hall (☎ *7387 3584, fax 7387 0419, 1-7 Endsleigh Place WC1)* **Map 3** ⊖ Euston. Singles/twins/triples £22.50/44/57 at Easter, £25/46/60 in summer, including breakfast. This hall with 195 beds encompasses a terrace of 10 late-Georgian houses in the heart of Bloomsbury.

Rosebery Avenue Hall (☎ *7278 3251, fax 7278 2068, 90 Rosebery Ave EC1)* **Map 4** ⊖ Angel. Singles £26-31, twins £36-46, twins with facilities £57-58, triples £55, including breakfast. This 435-bed hall north of Clerkenwell sometimes has beds available during term-time, with prices about £2 less overall.

The King's Conference & Vacation Bureau (☎ 7848 1700, fax 7848 1717, **e** vac.bureau@ kcl.ac.uk), 3rd floor, Strand Bridge House, 138-142 Strand WC2 (Map 7; ⊖ Holborn), administers bookings for some King's College London halls of residence, including:

Stamford Street Apartments (☎ 7848 2960, fax 7848 2964, 127 Stamford St SE1) **Map 6** ⊖ Waterloo. En-suite singles £33. This 543-bed residence is virtually across the road from Waterloo station, terminus of the Eurostar train to continental Europe.

Hampstead Campus (☎ 7435 3564, fax 7431 4402, Kidderpore Ave NW3) **Map 12** ⊖ Finchley Road. Basic singles/twins £18/31. This 392-bed place is not close to the heath.

Wellington Hall (☎ 7834 4740, fax 7233 7709, 71 Vincent Square SW1) **Map 11** ⊖ Victoria. Basic singles/twins £27.50/42. This 125-bed residence is within easy walking distance of Victoria and Tate Britain.

Other universities and colleges that let out their halls of residence outside of term-time including the following:

Finsbury Residences (☎ 7040 8811, fax 7040 8563, 15 Bastwick St EC1) **Map 4** ⊖ Barbican/Old Street. B&B adult/student £21/19. These residences between Islington and the City comprise two modern halls belonging to City University London.

Imperial College Student Hall (☎ 7594 9507, fax 7594 9504, **e** accommodationlink@ic.ac.uk, Prince's Gardens SW7) **Map 10** ⊖ South Kensington. Singles/twins with shared bathroom £33-38/53.50-61 depending on the season, including breakfast. This college is two minutes from some of London's greatest museums.

John Adams Hall (☎ 7387 4086, fax 7383 0164, **e** jah@ioe.ac.uk, 15-23 Endsleigh St WC1) **Map 3** ⊖ Euston. Basic singles/doubles/triples with breakfast £25/43/60, en-suite twins/triples/quads £49/73/85. John Adams is quite a grand residence in a terrace of Georgian houses in Bloomsbury.

Ramsay Hall (☎ 7387 4537, fax 7383 0843, **e** ramsay.hall@uclac/uk, 20 Maple St W1) **Map 6** ⊖ Goodge Street/Warren Street. Basic singles £22.60, including breakfast. This enormous, 440-room hall in the shadow of the unspeakable British Telecom Tower is one of eight University College London student houses and halls open to visitors at Easter and in summer.

Regent's College (☎ 7487 7483, fax 7487 7524, **e** barnesj@regents.ac.uk, Inner Circle, Regent's Park NW1) **Map 3** ⊖ Baker Street. Singles/doubles/triples £35/52/63. Open mid-May–mid-Aug. This college is in a converted Regency manor house right in the middle of beautiful Regent's Park. Individual guests are rare (they tend to do more groups), and they cannot take such bookings more than a week in advance.

YMCAs

YMCA of England (☎ 8520 5599), 640 Forest Rd, London E17 3DZ, can supply you with a list of all its hostels in Greater London. Its hostels in central London include the following:

Barbican YMCA (☎ 7628 0697, fax 7638 2420, **e** barbicanymca@aol.com, 2 Fann St EC2) **Map 9** ⊖ Barbican. Basic singles/doubles £26/44, including breakfast. This YMCA, a hop and a skip from the Barbican Centre and tube stop, has more than 200 rooms.

Indian Student YMCA (☎ 7387 0411, fax 7383 4735, **e** indianymca@aol.com, 41 Fitzroy Square W1) **Map 6** ⊖ Warren Street. Beds in 4-bed dorms £20, basic singles/doubles £33/46, en-suite doubles £52, including breakfast & dinner. Despite its name, this large property overlooking delightful Fitzroy Square accepts guests of all races and walks of life.

Lancaster Hall Hotel YMCA (☎ 7723 9276, fax 7706 2870, **e** info@lancaster-hall-hotel .co.uk, 35 Craven Terrace W2) ⊖ Lancaster Gate. Basic singles/doubles £25/38, including breakfast. This place, a short walk from Kensington Gardens, is also a business hotel, with mid-range en-suite singles and doubles.

London City YMCA (☎ 7628 8832, fax 7628 4080, **e** housing@london.city.ymca.org.uk, 8 Errol St EC1) **Map 4** ⊖ Barbican. Basic singles £32, en-suite doubles £55, including breakfast. This 111-bed YMCA is within easy walking distance of the trendy Shoreditch and Hoxton areas.

B&Bs, Guesthouses & Hotels

This may come as a shock but anything around £30/50 for a single/double with shared facilities and £40/60 with private bathroom is considered 'budget' in London.

B&Bs are an institution in Britain and are among the cheapest private non-hostel accommodation around. At the bottom end (from around £30 minimum) you get a bedroom in a private house, a shared bathroom and a calorific cooked breakfast. In central London most cheaper accommodation is in guesthouses, often just large converted houses with half a dozen rooms, that tend to be less personal than B&Bs. Double rooms often have twin beds so you don't have to be an 'item' to share a room.

Don't be afraid to ask for the 'best' price or a discount if you're staying out of season or for more than a couple of nights, or if you don't want a cooked breakfast. In July, August and September prices can jump by 25% or more, and it's advisable to book ahead. Be warned: some of the cheaper B&Bs don't accept credit cards.

Pimlico & Victoria (Map 11)
Victoria may not be the most attractive part of London, but you'll be very close to the action, and the budget hotels in this area are better value than those in Earl's Court. Pimlico is more residential though convenient for Tate Britain at Millbank.

Brindle House Hotel (☎ 7828 0057, fax 7931 8805, 1 Warwick Place North SW1) ✆ Victoria. Basic singles/doubles £35/45, en-suite singles/doubles/triples/quads £40/60/75/89. This bluer-than-blue B&B is in an old building in a quiet street; the rooms are small but spick-and-span.

Luna-Simone Hotel (☎ 7834 5897, fax 7828 2474, e lunasimone@talk21.com, w www.lunasimonehotel.com, 47-49 Belgrave Rd SW1) ✆ Victoria. Singles £35-40, doubles £50-60, doubles with private bathroom £60-75, triples with private bathroom £80-100. If all London's budget hotels were like this central, spotlessly clean and comfortable place, we'd all be happy campers (or perhaps not). A full English breakfast is included, and there are free storage facilities if you want to leave your bags while travelling.

Romany House Hotel (☎ 7834 5553, fax 7834 0495, e romany.hotel@virgin.net, 35 Longmore St SW1) ✆ Victoria. Singles/doubles with shared bathroom £30/40, including full breakfast. Part of this hotel is built into a 15th-century cottage that boasts tales – real or imagined – of highwaymen. All rooms have washbasins.

Bloomsbury (Maps 4 & 6)
This area is very convenient, especially for the West End. There are lots of places on Gower and North Gower Sts.

Alhambra Hotel (☎ 7837 9575, fax 7916 2476, e postmaster@alhambrahotel.com, w www.alhambrahotel.com, 17-19 Argyle St WC1) **Map 4** ✆ King's Cross St Pancras. Basic singles/doubles £32/45, with shower £45/50, single/double/triple/quad with shower & toilet £60/60/80/90, including English breakfast. One of the better finds in this area, and very convenient for King's Cross St Pancras tube and the two main-line stations, the Alhambra is a simple but spotlessly clean place with 52 rooms that's been run by a charming family for over 20 years.

Hotel Cavendish (☎ 7636 9079, fax 7580 609, e hotel.cavendish@virginnet.co.uk, w www.hotelcavendish.com, 75 Gower St WC1) **Map 6** ✆ Goodge Street. Singles £38-42, doubles £48-66, both with shared bathroom, including breakfast. This is a clean and pleasant family-run place.

Celtic Hotel (☎ 7837 9258, fax 7837 6737, 61-63 Guilford St WC1) **Map 6** ✆ Russell Square. Basic singles/doubles & twins/triples/quads £38.50/55/74/86. This excellent-value B&B is in the heart of Bloomsbury. The same friendly family owns and runs St Margaret's Hotel (see later under Places to Stay – Mid-Range).

Euston Travel Inn Capital (☎ 7554 3400, fax 7554 3419, w www.travelinn.co.uk, 1 Dukes Rd WC1) **Map 3** ✆ Euston. En-suite room for up to 2 adults & 2 children under 16 £69.95. This is one of those one price, one room deals. It's fairly bare bones, and there are more rules than in a Victorian grammar school, but the rooms are large and – by London standards – reasonable. The hotel faces busy Euston Rd.

Jesmond Hotel (☎ 7636 3199, fax 7323 4373, e reserve@jesmondhotel.org.uk, w www.jesmondhotel.org.uk, 63 Gower St WC1) **Map 6** ✆ Goodge Street. Singles/doubles/triples with shared facilities £36/54/70, with private bath £46/68/80, including breakfast. This B&B is a good choice if you're travelling in a small group.

Quaker International Centre (☎ 7383 5144, e quc1@qic.org.uk, 1 Byng Place WC1) **Map 6** ✆ Goodge Street. Singles/doubles/triples/quads £34/57/60/80, including breakfast. This large centre in a quiet street north of Oxford St has basic but comfortable rooms with washbasins, showers on the hallway and kitchen facilities. Evening meals are available for £4.95.

Repton Hotel (☎ 7436 4922, fax 7636 7045, 31-32 Bedford Place WC1) **Map 6** ✆ Russell Square. Beds £15 in 6-bed dorm. This hotel is good value for a mid-range place but some readers have complained about the lack of hot water in the showers. See also later under Places to Stay – Mid-Range.

Ridgemount Hotel (☎ 7636 1141, fax 7636 2558, 65-67 Gower St WC1) **Map 6** ⊖ Goodge Street. Singles/doubles/triples with shared bath £33/50/66, with shower & toilet £45/65/78, including breakfast. Readers have sent favourable comments about the old-style Ridgemount. It also has a laundry service (£3).

Southwark (Map 6)
The former County Hall doesn't just contain fish tanks and surrealistic paintings; it also has a couple of hotels, including a budget option.

County Hall Travel Inn Capital (☎ 7902 1600, fax 7902 1619, **w** *www.travelinn.co.uk*, *Belvedere Rd SE1)* ⊖ Westminster. Room for up to 2 adults & 2 children under 16 £69.95. With the London IMAX Cinema and the gigantic BA London Eye next door, this may be a good choice if you've got the kids in tow.

Earl's Court (Map 10)
These days African, Arab and Indian immigrants are more conspicuous than Australians in what was

County Hall, the grand location of the
Travel Inn Capital

once known as Kangaroo Valley, but most people seem to be in transit and it shows in the grubby streets (although some smartening up is taking place). It's not really within walking distance of many places of interest, but Earl's Court tube station is a busy interchange, so getting around is easy. There are plenty of places to stay along Warwick Rd.

Boka Hotel (☎ 7370 1388, fax 7912 0515, **e** *enquiries@bokahotel.co.uk, 33-35 Eardley Crescent SW5)* ⊖ Earl's Court. Beds £14-16 in 3–5-bed dorm, basic singles/doubles £25/ 38 Mon-Thur, £35/42 Fri-Sun, doubles with shower/bath £44/48 Mon-Thur, £46/54 Fri-Sun. Guests have access to the kitchen and TV lounge in this relaxed place.

Merlyn Court Hotel (☎ 7370 1640, fax 7370 4986, **e** *london@merlyncourt.demon.co.uk, 2 Barkston Gardens SW5)* ⊖ Earl's Court. Singles £30-35, doubles £50-55, triples £50-60, with private shower and toilet £50-60, £65-75, £75-80. This unpretentious place has a nice atmosphere and lovely location near the tube. Singles and doubles are small but clean; overall it's a good choice.

Regency Court Hotel (☎/fax 7244 6615, **e** *regencycourt@hotmail.com, 14 Penywern Rd SW5)* ⊖ Earl's Court. Beds £20 in 4-bed dorm, basic singles/doubles/quads £35/60/70, singles/triples with private bathroom £40/75, including continental breakfast. This hotel has undergone a much-needed renovation. The bright rooms are small and there's a kitchen for guests.

St Simeon Hotel (☎ 7373 0505, fax 7370 4214, **w** *www.saintsimeonhotel.co.uk, 38 Harrington Gardens SW7)* ⊖ Gloucester Road. Bed £15 in 3- to 5-bed dorm, basic singles £25, doubles £40-46, including breakfast. This less-than-salubrious, not overly welcoming place is within striking distance of the South Kensington museums.

York House Hotel (☎ 7373 7519, fax 7370 4641, **e** *yorkhh@aol.com, 28 Philbeach Gardens SW5)* ⊖ Earl's Court. Basic singles/doubles/ triples £34/54/66, with shower & toilet £47/ 73/86. This friendly place is good value for what and where (on a quiet crescent) it is, and the welcome is warm.

Bayswater, Paddington & Notting Hill (Map 5)
Bayswater is an extremely convenient location though some of the streets immediately to the west of Queensway, which has a decent selection of restaurants (notably Lebanese and other Middle

JULIET COOMBE

PLACES TO STAY

Eastern coffee houses), can be run-down and depressing. Parts of Paddington are pretty seedy too, especially right around the station, but there are lots of cheap hotels and it's a good transit location; you can reach Heathrow in 15 minutes from here (see Airports in the Getting Around chapter). Notting Hill is the opposite – it's upbeat and fun, but budget accommodation is at a premium.

Balmoral House Hotel (☎ 7723 7445, fax 7402 0118, e info@balmoralhousehotel.co.uk, 156 & 157 Sussex Gardens W2) ✆ Paddington. Basic singles £40, en-suite doubles/triples/quads £65/80/100, including breakfast. This immaculate and very comfortable hotel, with two properties directly opposite one another, is one of the better places to stay along Sussex Gardens, a street lined with small hotels but unfortunately a major traffic artery. All rooms have satellite TV.

Cardiff Hotel (☎ 7723 9068, fax 7402 2342, w www.cardiff-hotel.com, 5-7 & 9 Norfolk Square W2) ✆ Paddington. Singles/doubles with shower £45/69, singles/doubles/triples/quads with shower & toilet £55/79/90/99. The family-run, 61-room Cardiff is on the same lovely square as St David's Hotel. It is a green oasis in summer.

Elysée Hotel (☎ 7402 7633, fax 7402 4193, w www.elyseehotel-london.co.uk, 25 Craven Terrace W2) ✆ Lancaster Gate. En-suite singles/doubles £50/60. This hotel is on a quiet street facing Hyde Park but check out one of the rooms first; there have been complaints from readers.

Europa House Hotel (☎ 7723 7343, fax 7402 9331, e europahouse@enterprise.net, w www.europahouse.com, 151 Sussex Gardens W2) ✆ Paddington. Singles/doubles with private bathroom £40-48/60-68. This is another excellent choice, where you're always assured a warm welcome (something not as common as you'd think at small London hotels). The best rooms are the ones in the back.

Garden Court Hotel (☎ 7229 2553, fax 7727 2749, e info@gardencourthotel.co.uk, w www.gardencourthotel.co.uk, 30-31 Kensington Gardens Square W2) ✆ Bayswater. Singles/doubles/triples with shared bathroom £39/58/72, with private bathroom £58/88/99. One of Bayswater's best options and just barely in this category, the Garden Court is a well-run and well-maintained family hotel cobbled from two town houses (1870), and all its 34 rooms have phone and TV. Readers have raved.

Manor Court Hotel (☎ 7792 3361, 7727 5407, fax 7229 2875, 7 Clanricarde Gardens W2) ✆ Notting Hill Gate. Singles/twins with shower £30/50, singles/twins/triples with shower & toilet £50/60/70. Though not a particularly spectacular place, this hotel is in a good location just off Bayswater Rd.

Oxford Hotel (☎ 7402 6860, fax 7262 7574, e info@oxfordhotellondon.co.uk, w www.oxfordhotellondon.co.uk, 13-14 Craven Terrace W2) ✆ Lancaster Gate. En-suite singles/doubles with TV, microwave and kettle £60/66. This hotel is good value and the location is fine.

Portobello Gold Hotel (☎ 7460 4913, fax 7229 2278, w www.portobellogold.com, 95-97 Portobello Rd W11) ✆ Notting Hill Gate. Singles with shared bath £50/55 Sun-Thur/Fri & Sat, doubles with shower £65/70, doubles with shower & toilet £80/85, discount for weekly stays. This somewhat louche hotel has a pleasant restaurant and bar on the ground floor and an Internet cafe (see Email & Internet in the Facts for the Visitor chapter) upstairs that guests can use for free.

Royal Hotel (☎ 7229 7225, fax 7221 8001, 43 Queensborough Terrace) ✆ Bayswater. Doubles/triples/quads with shared bathroom £32/40/48 daily, £192/240/288 weekly, with shower £40/45/52 daily, £240/270/312 weekly. Most of the 17 rooms in this budget place have facilities and some have just received a bit of a face-lift.

Sass House Hotel (☎ 7262 2325, fax 7262 0889, 11 Craven Terrace W2) ✆ Lancaster Gate. Doubles/triples with shower & toilet £56/72, including continental breakfast. This place is fairly threadbare but the price is right for the area.

St David's Hotel (☎ 7723 4963, fax 7402 9061, e info@stdavidshotels.com, w www.stdavidshotels.com, 16-20 Norfolk Square W2) ✆ Paddington. En-suite singles/doubles/triples with TV & phone £49/69/80, including huge breakfast. Right in the centre of the action, this place cobbled from four terraced houses is clean, comfortable and friendly, with the usual over-the-top decor.

Marylebone (Map 5)

Marylebone is very handy for some of London's most popular sights, including Madame Tussaud's and the London Planetarium.

Glynne Court Hotel (☎ 7262 4344, fax 7724 2071, 41 Great Cumberland Place W1) ✆ Marble Arch. Basic singles £40-50, doubles £55-60, en-suite singles £50-60, doubles £60-75, triples £75-90, all with continental breakfast. Fairly typical for this price range and location, the Glynne Court has 14 rooms all with TV and phone.

Hampstead (Map 12)

Hampstead's trump card is the sprawling expanse of the Heath.

Charlotte Guest House (☎ *7794 6476, fax 7431 3584, 195 Sumatra Rd NW6*) ✪ West Hampstead. Singles/doubles with shared bathroom £35/45, with private bathroom £45/55. This is a traditional B&B in the quiet suburb of West Hampstead.

Five Kings Hotel (☎ *7607 3996, fax 7609 5554, 59 Anson Rd N7*) ✪ Tufnell Park. Basic singles/doubles in summer £26/40, in winter £25/38, en-suite singles/doubles in summer £30/46, in winter £29/44, including breakfast. This reasonably priced place is in a nice quiet area but a bit out of the action.

East End (Map 9)

RCA City Hotel & Apartments (☎ *7247 3313, fax 7375 2949*, **e** *info@cityhotellondon.com*, **w** *www.cityhotellondon.co.uk, 12 Osborn St E1*) ✪ Aldgate East. Singles/doubles/twins £70/85/87 Fri-Sun, £95/105/110 Mon-Thur, 1-2 person studios £90-120. This place is well situated for those who have business in the City.

PLACES TO STAY – MID-RANGE

The B&Bs, guesthouses and small hotels in this category offer singles/doubles with shared facilities from £50/70 and from £70/90 with your own bathroom (usually shower or bath and toilet).

Pimlico & Victoria (Map 11)

Pimlico is an attractive area with some good-value accommodation. Victoria is extremely convenient for transport, though it doesn't have a lot of character and can be very noisy.

Hamilton House Hotel (☎ *7821 7113, fax 7630 0806*, **e** *info@hamiltonhousehotel.com*, **w** *www .hamiltonhousehotel.com, 60 Warwick Way SW1*) ✪ Victoria. Singles/doubles with shared bathroom £49/62, with private bathroom, TV & phone £69/85. This friendly place is good value for the area and rooms are a decent size.

Morgan House (☎ *7730 2384, fax 7730 8842*, **w** *www.morganhouse.co.uk, 120 Ebury St SW1*) ✪ Victoria. Singles/doubles with shared bathroom £42/62, with private bathroom £68/80. This hotel is owned by the same people who run nearby Woodville House and neither place affords a particularly warm welcome. You'll find plenty more places to stay on Ebury St.

Winchester Hotel (☎ *7828 2972, fax 7828 5191, 17 Belgrave Rd SW1*) ✪ Victoria. Doubles & twins/triples/quads with private bathroom & TV £85/110/140. This clean, comfortable and welcoming place is also good value for the area. Breakfast is served in a sunny dining room.

Windermere Hotel (☎ *7834 5163, fax 7630 8831*, **e** *windermere@compuserve.com*, **w** *www .windermere-hotel.co.uk, 142-4 Warwick Way SW1*) ✪ Victoria. Singles/doubles with shared bathroom £69/89, with private bathroom £84-96, £104-139, including huge breakfast. The Windermere has 22 small but individually designed and spotless rooms in a sparkling white mid-Victorian town house. Unusually for a hotel of this size, it has eight nonsmoking rooms and its own restaurant called the **Pimlico Room**.

Woodville House (☎ *7730 1048, fax 7730 2574*, **w** *www.woodvillehouse.co.uk, 107 Ebury St SW1*) ✪ Victoria. Basic singles/doubles £42/62. The Woodville, within the same stable as Morgan House, has 12 simple but comfortable rooms with shared bathroom, use of a kitchen and a lovely back patio.

The West End & Covent Garden (Maps 7 & 8)

Moderately priced hotels in the town centre are like hen's teeth. For the most part you should look elsewhere; you'll almost always get more for your money anyway.

Fielding Hotel (☎ *7836 8305, fax 7497 0064*, **e** *reservations@the-fielding-hotel.co.uk*, **w** *www .the-fielding-hotel.co.uk, 4 Broad Court, Bow St WC2*) ✪ Covent Garden. En-suite singles £76,en-suite doubles & twins £100-115, double with sitting room £130. This place, named after the novelist Henry Fielding (1707–54) who lived on now pedestrianised Broad Court, is remarkably good value, clean and well run. It's a block away from the rejuvenated Royal Opera House.

Manzi's (☎ *7734 0224, fax 7437 4864, 1-2 Leicester St WC2*) ✪ Leicester Square. En-suite singles £65-70, doubles £68-77, triples £107. This place above a seafood restaurant just north of Leicester Square is no great shakes but central and atmospheric; Johann Sebastian Strauss (1804–49) stayed here in 1838 when it was the Hôtel de Commerce.

Regent Palace Hotel (☎ *0870 400 8703, fax 7734 6435; Piccadilly Circus, Cnr Glasshouse St W1*) ✪ Piccadilly. Singles with shared bathroom Sun-Thur/Fri & Sat £64/75, doubles £69/89, en-suite singles/doubles £119/129. Gasping for a

PLACES TO STAY

face-lift but pretty good value for its position right beside Piccadilly Circus, this enormous hotel is as frenetic as you'll find in London.

Bloomsbury (Maps 3 & 6)

Bloomsbury is a haven of B&Bs and guesthouses. Tucked away in leafy Cartwright Gardens (Map 3), to the north of Russell Square and within easy walking distance of the West End, you'll find some of London's best-value small hotels. The hotels along nearby Gower St (Map 6) are also pretty good value, but not all of them have double-glazing, which is essential if you're sensitive to traffic noise.

Arran House Hotel (☎ 7636 2186, fax 7436 5328, e arran@dircon.co.uk, 77-9 Gower St WC1) **Map 6** ⊖ Goodge Street. Basic singles/doubles/triples £45/55/73, with shower & toilet £55/75/93, including breakfast. This welcoming place has a lovely garden as well as laundry facilities. The front rooms are sound-proofed, and all have TV and phone.

Crescent Hotel (☎ 7387 1515, fax 7383 2054, w www.crescenthoteloflondon.com, 49-50 Cartwright Gardens WC1) **Map 3** ⊖ Russell Square. Singles without/with shower £44/49,

DOUG McKINLAY

When the lights of Piccadilly start to blur head for a bed in Bloomsbury.

singles/doubles with private bath & toilet £71/85. This friendly, family-owned hotel built in 1810 is maintained at a very high standard.

Euro Hotel (☎ 7387 4321, fax 7383 5044, e reception@eurohotel.co.uk, w www.euro hotel.co.uk, 53 Cartwright Gardens WC1) **Map 3** ⊖ Russell Square. Singles/doubles/ triples with shared bathroom £49/69/85, with shower & toilet £70/89/105, including breakfast. The 35-room Euro can be recommended for its location and standard.

Haddon Hall (☎ 7636 2474, fax 7580 4527, e haddonhall@grangehotels.co.uk, 39-40 Bedford Place WC1) **Map 6** ⊖ Russell Square/Holborn. Singles/doubles & twins/triples with shared bathroom from £50/65/90, singles/doubles & twin with private bath & toilet £65/90, triples with private bath and toilet £90-105. This is one of the better-maintained places to stay in this area.

Jenkins Hotel (☎ 7387 2067, fax 7383 3139, e reservations@jenkinshotel.demon.co .uk, w www.jenkinshotel.demon.co.uk, 45 Cartwright Gardens WC1) **Map 3** ⊖ Russell Square. Single with shared bathroom £52, en-suite singles/doubles/triples £72/85/105, including breakfast. This nonsmoking, 13-room place has comfortable, stylish renovated rooms equipped with TV, phone and fridge. Guests get to use the tennis courts in the gardens across the road.

Morgan Hotel (☎ 7636 3735, fax 7636 3045, 24 & 40 Bloomsbury St WC1) **Map 8** ⊖ Tottenham Court Road. Singles/doubles/triples with private bathroom £58-68/78/130. This friendly place has 20 small but nicely decorated rooms at two locations near the British Museum.

Repton Hotel (☎ 7436 4922, fax 7636 7045, 31-32 Bedford Place WC1) **Map 6** ⊖ Russell Square. Singles £52, doubles £69-75, triples £79-85, all with TV, phone & bath. This hotel is scruffy but pretty good value considering that Bedford Place is much more tranquil than nearby Gower St. See earlier under Places to Stay – Budget.

Ruskin Hotel (☎ 7636 7388, fax 7323 1662, 23-24 Montague St WC1) **Map 6** ⊖ Holborn/ Russell Square. Singles/doubles with shared bath £47/67, en-suite doubles £84. The location of this fairly basic place is very good.

St Margaret's Hotel (☎ 7636 4277, fax 7323 3066, 26 Bedford Place WC1) **Map 6** ⊖ Russell Square/Holborn. Doubles & twins with shower/shower & toilet £78/95 for the first two nights and then £75/90. This 60-room family-run hotel is in a classic Georgian town house. It's not particularly inspiring but it is exceedingly friendly and clean. All rooms have TV and phone and some have private bathrooms. The same family owns the nearby Celtic Hotel (see earlier under Places to Stay – Budget).

Chelsea & South Kensington (Map 10)

Classy Chelsea and 'South Ken' offer easy access to some of London's best museums and shopping.

Hotel 167 (☎ *7373 0672, fax 7373 3360,* **e** *enquiries@hotel167.com,* **w** *www.hotel167 .com, 167 Old Brompton Rd SW5)* ✷ Gloucester Road. Singles £72-85, doubles & twins £90-99, with private bathroom, including continental breakfast. This small hotel is stylish and has an unusually uncluttered and attractive decor.

Amber Hotel (☎ *7373 8666, fax 7835 1194,* **e** *theamberhotel@yahoo.com, 101 Lexham Gardens W8)* ✷ Earl's Court. Singles/doubles/ twins/triples £65/85/90/100 in low season, 95/ 110/120/130 in high season. This hotel is excellent value for its location halfway between Kensington and Earl's Court.

Annandale House Hotel (☎ *7730 5051, fax 7730 2727, 39 Sloane Gardens SW1)* ✷ Sloane Square. En-suite singles/doubles £65/95. This discreet, traditional hotel is an excellent choice for the noise-sensitive. All rooms have a TV and phone.

Swiss House Hotel (☎ *7373 2769, fax 7373 4983,* **e** *recep@swiss-hh.demon.co.uk,* **w** *www.swiss-hh.demon.co.uk, 171 Old Brompton Rd SW5)* ✷ Gloucester Road. Singles with shower £48, singles/triples/quads with shower & toilet £68/ 114/128, doubles & twins with shower and toilet £85-99, including continental breakfast. The Swiss House is a clean and welcoming hotel that has something of a country feel about it.

Kensington (Map 5)

These hotels are well placed for Kensington Gardens, Notting Hill and Kensington High St.

Abbey House (☎ *7727 2594, fax 7727 1873,* **w** *www.abbeyhousekensington.com, 11 Vicarage Gate W8)* ✷ High Street Kensington. Singles/doubles/triples/quads with washbasin & shared bathroom £45/74/90/100, including English breakfast. Abbey House is a particularly good-value small hotel, with well-proportioned and well-decorated rooms and a very high standard of service. Readers seem to love this place.

Vicarage Hotel (☎ *7229 4030, fax 7792 5989,* **e** *reception@londonvicaragehotel.com,* **w** *www .londonvicaragehotel.com, 10 Vicarage Gate W8)* ✷ High Street Kensington. Singles/doubles & twins/triples/quads with shared bathroom £45/74/90/98, doubles & twins with shower &

toilet £98. The Vicarage is pleasant and well kept, with good showers and rooms slightly larger than usual.

Earl's Court (Map 10)

Mid-range places in Earl's Court are usually perfectly acceptable; if the one you've set your heart on is full, there will be plenty more nearby.

London Town Hotel (☎ *7370 4356, fax 7370 7923,* **e** *townhotel@compuserve.com, 15 Penywern Rd SW5)* ✷ Earl's Court. En-suite singles/ doubles & twins/triples/quads £78/98/110/122, including buffet breakfast and 10% discount after three nights' stay. This friendly place in a quiet street has small but clean and comfortable rooms.

Philbeach Hotel (☎ *7373 1244, fax 7244 0149,* **w** *www.philbeachhotel@freeserve.co.uk, 30-31 Philbeach Gardens SW5)* ✷ Earl's Court. Basic singles £35-50, doubles/triples £69/75, with shower & toilet £60/90/100. This is an especially fine hotel popular with gays and lesbians. It has a lovely garden restaurant called *Wilde about Oscar* and a super bar that hosts a transvestite night on Mondays.

Bayswater, Paddington & Notting Hill (Map 5)

Bayswater is residential and convenient for busy Queensway. Though central, Paddington is a bit scruffy at the best of times. Notting Hill has become increasingly trendy and expensive but it is still a great place to stay, with lots of good bars and restaurants in the area.

Gate Hotel (☎ *7221 0707, fax 7221 9128,* **e** *gatehotel@thegate.globalnet.co.uk,* **w** *www .gatehotel.com, 6 Portobello Rd W11)* ✷ Notting Hill Gate. En-suite singles £60-70, doubles £85-95, triples £105, including continental breakfast. The rooms in this old town house with a classic, frilly English decor and lovely floral window boxes, all have a fridge and TV.

Gresham Hotel (☎ *7402 2920, fax 7402 3137,* **e** *sales@the-gresham-hotel.co.uk,* **w** *www .the-gresham-hotel.co.uk, 116 Sussex Gardens W2)* ✷ Paddington. En-suite singles/doubles £60-70/85. This less-than-welcoming place is nevertheless a stylish small hotel with bright and cheery rooms.

Hillgate Hotel (☎ 7221 3433, fax 7229 4808, e hillgate@lth-hotels.com, 6-14 Pembridge Gardens W2) ✆ Notting Hill Gate. En-suite singles/doubles & twins/triples £80/110/134, including breakfast. Set in a quiet street off Notting Hill Gate, the Hillgate's 66 rooms are spread over five Victorian terraced houses. It's now part of the Comfort Inn group of hotels.

Inverness Court Hotel (☎ 7229 1444, fax 7706 4240, e info@cghotels.com, w www.cghotels .com, Inverness Terrace W2) ✆ Queensway. En-suite singles/doubles £86/110. This impressive 183-room hotel was commissioned by Edward VII for his 'confidante' (ie mistress), the actress Lillie Langtry, and came complete with a private theatre (now the Theatre Bar). The panelled walls, stained glass and huge open fires of the public areas give it a Gothic feel but most of the rooms – some of which overlook Hyde Park – are modern and pretty ordinary.

Pavilion Hotel (☎ 7262 0905, fax 7262 1324, e hotelpavilion@aol.com, w www.msi.com.mt/ pavilion/, 34-36 Sussex Gardens W2) ✆ Paddington. En-suite singles £60-85, en-suite doubles & twins/triples £100/120, including breakfast. This place boasts 30 individually themed rooms (Moorish, 1970s, 'Enter the Dragon' chinoiserie, 'Highland Fling', 'Casablanca Nights') to reflect its slogan/motto: 'Fashion, Glam & Rock 'n' Roll'. It's *rather* over the top but refreshingly different from the standard chintz and tartan carpet of so many London hotels.

Marylebone (Map 5)

Marylebone is convenient for shopping in the west and for West End nightlife.

Edward Lear Hotel (☎ 7402 5401, fax 7706 3766, e edwardlear@aol.com, w www.edlear.com, 28-30 Seymour St W1) ✆ Marble Arch. Singles/doubles & twins/triples with shared bathroom £49/69.50/83, with shower £58/81.50/ 91.50, doubles & twins/triples with bath & toilet £93/105. Once the home of the eponymous Victorian painter and poet (well, limerick writer), the 31 rooms in this comfortable place have TV, tea & coffee facilities and phone. There's also free Internet access.

Wigmore Court Hotel (☎ 7935 0928, fax 7487 4254, e info@wigmore-court-hotel.co.uk, w www.wigmore-court-hotel.co.uk, 23 Gloucester Place W1) ✆ Marble Arch. Singles/ doubles with shared bathroom £55/80, singles/ doubles & twins/triples/quads with private bathroom £62/80/120/132. This well-organised place has a kitchen and self-service laundry for guests.

Hampstead (Map 12)

Classy Hampstead certainly retains a village atmosphere although it can feel cut off from central London.

La Gaffe (☎ 7435 8965, fax 7794 7592, e la-gaffe@msn.com, w www.lagaffe.co.uk, 107-11 Heath St NW3) ✆ Hampstead. Singles £65-80/ doubles & twins £90-125, with private bathroom. La Gaffe, above a popular Italian restaurant of the same name (see the Hampstead section in the Places to Eat chapter), is an eccentric but nonetheless comfortable hotel in an 18th-century cottage.

PLACES TO STAY – TOP END

In this section singles/doubles cost from £130/150 – and more. Of course, in this category you can always count on a private bath/shower and toilet, phone and TV as well as such extras as minibars, hairdryers and, increasingly, Internet access.

Trafalgar Square (Map 8)

What is the true centre – in every sense – of London has only one hotel, and it is brand new.

Trafalgar Hilton (☎ 7870 2900, fax 7870 2911, w www.thetrafalgar.hilton.com, 2 Spring Gardens SW1) ✆ Charing Cross/Embankment. Singles & doubles £270-380, suites from £420. This 129-room property overlooking Trafalgar Square is the Hilton chain's first 'lifestyle' hotel and attracts the young, the hip and the fashionable.

Victoria (Map 11)

The following two places are (probably) as close as you'll ever get to staying with Her Maj, Queen Elizabeth II.

41 (☎ 7300 0041, fax 7300 0141, e reservations @41club.redcarnationhotels.com, w www.red carnationhotels.com, 41 Buckingham Palace Rd SW1) ✆ Victoria. Singles & doubles £295-325, suites from £400 including all meals, drinks and services. This new 18-room hotel situated in a lovely old town house opposite the Royal Mews has started what looks like might become a trend: all-in pricing, including meals and drinks served round the clock, a personal butler, laundry service and laptop and mobile rental.

Rubens at the Palace (☎ 7834 6600, fax 7233 6037, e reservations@rubens.redcarnation hotels.com, w www.redcarnationhotels.com, 39

Buckingham Palace Rd SW1) ⊖ Victoria. Singles £126-170, doubles £160-220, suites from £220. This 173-room branch of the Red Carnation hotel group next door to the 41 has a brilliant position overlooking the Royal Mews and Buckingham Palace. It's popular with groups, though.

Mayfair (Map 6)

If you want a deluxe hotel at top-end prices in one of London's most exclusive neighbourhoods, choose the following.

Chesterfield (☎ *7491 2622, fax 7491 4793,* e *reservations@chesterfield.redcarnation hotels.com,* w *www.redcarnationhotels.com, 35 Charles St W1)* ⊖ Green Park. Singles £130-195, doubles £150-375, suites from £230. With 110 rooms and just a block west of Berkeley Square, the Chesterfield has some fine outlets, particularly the lush *Conservatory* restaurant.

The West End: Soho, Piccadilly & Covent Garden (Maps 7 & 8)

There are tremendous advantages to staying in the centre of town, but such a privilege doesn't come cheap.

Hazlitt's (☎ *7434 1771, fax 7439 1524,* e *reservations@hazlitts.co.uk,* w *www.hazlitts hotel.com, 6 Frith St W1)* Map 7 ⊖ Tottenham Court Road. Singles/twins £155/195, doubles £180-195, suite £300. Built in 1718 and comprising three original Georgian houses, this is one of central London's finest hotels, with efficient personal service. All 23 rooms are named after former residents or visitors to the house – which is named after essayist William Hazlitt (1778–1830), who died here – and are individually decorated with antique furniture and prints. Booking is mandatory, particularly since Bill Bryson let the cat out of the bag and introduced it to the world in his bestselling *Notes from a Small Island.*

Strand Palace (☎ *7836 8080, fax 7836 2077,* e *housemanager.sph@forte-hotels.com,* w *www .forte-hotels.com, Strand WC2)* Map 8 ⊖ Charing Cross. Singles/doubles & twins/triples £160/ 180/195, suites from £350. This monstrous place (783 rooms) has an excellent location near Covent Garden and has a number of snappy bars and restaurants, but the prices for rooms without breakfast are pretty steep and the lengthy queues checking in and out depressing.

Thistle Piccadilly (☎ *7930 4033, fax 7925 2586,* e *piccadilly@thistle.co.uk,* w *www .thistlehotels.com, Coventry St W1)* Map 7 ⊖ Piccadilly Circus. Singles/doubles £135/ 161. This 91-room is indistinguishable from other hotels in the same group but its location is very central.

Fitzrovia (Maps 6 & 7)

This area is quieter than Soho but still within easy walking distance of the clubs, theatres and restaurants of the West End.

Charlotte Street Hotel (☎ *7806 2000, fax 7806 2002,* e *charlotte@firmdale.com,* w *www .charlottestreethotel.com, 15 Charlotte St W1)* Map 7 ⊖ Goodge Street. Singles £175, doubles £195-280, suites from £330. This wonderful 52-room hotel, where Laura Ashley goes postmodern and lives to tell the tale, has become a favourite of visiting media types.

Langham Court Hotel (☎ *7436 6622, fax 7436 2303,* e *langham@grangehotels.co.uk,* w *www .grangehotels.co.uk)* Map 6 ⊖ Oxford Circus. Singles £140-160, doubles £160-180, triples £205. This 60-room hotel has lovely tile facing, but rather ordinary rooms.

Bloomsbury (Map 6)

These hotels are handy for both the shopping on Oxford St and the British Museum.

Academy Hotel (☎ *7631 4115, fax 6636 3442,* e *res_academy@etontownhouse.com,* w *www .etontownhouse.com, 21 Gower St WC1)* ⊖ Goodge Street. Singles & doubles £130-185, suites from £205. The renovated Academy has 49 individually decorated rooms and a pleasant back garden.

My Hotel (☎ *7667 6000, fax 7667 6001,* e *guest_services@myhotels.co.uk,* w *www.my hotels.co.uk, 11-13 Bayley St WC1)* ⊖ Tottenham Court Road/Goodge Street. Singles £150-170, doubles £185-245, studios from £325. This hotel with the less-than-inspired name is somewhat overpriced for what it is, but it's convenient for Soho, Fitzrovia and Bloomsbury, and has an all-day bar and cafe and a branch of *Yo! Sushi.*

Clerkenwell (Map 6)

One of London's most up-and-coming areas was devoid of quality accommodation until the following opened in 1999.

PLACES TO STAY

The Rookery (☎ 7336 0931, fax 7336 0932, e reservations@rookery.co.uk, w www.rookery hotel.com, Peter's Lane, Cowcross St EC1) ⊖ Farringdon. Singles £175-190, doubles £205, suites from £265. This 33-room hotel has been built in a row of once derelict 18th-century Georgian houses and fitted out with period furniture (including a museum-piece collection of Victorian baths, showers and toilets), original wood panelling shipped from Ireland and open fires.

Chelsea, South Kensington & Earl's Court (Map 10)

Gracious Chelsea and South Kensington present London at its elegant best. Lexham Gardens, where you'll find the London Lodge Hotel, feels more like Kensington than Earl's Court.

Blakes (☎ 7370 6701, fax 7373 0442, e blakes @easynet.co.uk, w www.blakeshotels.com, 33 Roland Gardens SW7) ⊖ Gloucester Road. Singles & small twins £165, doubles £240-325, suites from £515. For classic style, one of your first choices in London should be Blakes: five Victorian houses knocked into one and decked out with four-poster beds, rich fabrics and antiques on stripped hardwood floorboards.

Five Sumner Place (☎ 7584 7586, fax 7823 9962, e reservations@sumnerplace.com, w www .sumnerplace.com, 5 Sumner Place SW7) ⊖ South Kensington. Singles/doubles & twins/ triples £85/130/152. On a quiet, leafy street just off Old Brompton St, this hotel has 14 comfortable and well-equipped rooms (all with bathroom, TV, phone, drinks cabinet and more), and there's an attractive conservatory and courtyard.

London Lodge Hotel (☎ 7244 8444, fax 7373 6661, w www.londonlodgehotel.com, 134-36 Lexham Gardens W8) ⊖ Earl's Court. Singles/ doubles £119/149. This hotel with 28 individually decorated rooms is a serene place and has everything you need. Its downstairs restaurant and bar, **Stephanie's**, has a good reputation.

Number Sixteen (☎ 7589 5232, fax 7584 8615, e reservations@numbersixteenhotel.co.uk, w www.numbersixteenhotel.co.uk, 16 Sumner Place SW7) ⊖ South Kensington. Singles £85-120, doubles & twins £145-170, suites from £195. Number Sixteen has all the attributes of the almost-opposite Five Sumner Place – and then some. It's a stunning hotel with a cosy drawing room, library, lounge and garden. We love all the extra touches too – news magazines in the rooms, radios tuned to Classic FM and so on.

Kensington & Knightsbridge (Map 5)

The theme of top-end hotels in this part of London seems to be antiques – particularly the Victorian variety.

Basil St Hotel (☎ 7581 3311, fax 7581 3693, e reservations@thebasil.com, w www.thebasil .com, Basil St SW3) ⊖ Knightsbridge. Singles/ doubles from £128/190, 2-room, 1-bath family suite from £260. This antique-stuffed 80-room hideaway in the heart of Knightsbridge is perfectly placed for carrying back the shopping from Harrods or Harvey Nichols.

The Gore (☎ 7584 6601, fax 7589 8127, e reservations@gorehotel.co.uk, w www.gore hotel.co.uk, 189 Queen's Gate SW7) ⊖ High Street Kensington/Gloucester Road. Singles £120-155, doubles & twins £155-265. This splendid 54-room hotel is a veritable palace of polished mahogany, Turkish carpets, antique-style bathrooms, potted aspidistras and portraits and prints (some 4500 of them). The attached **Bistrot 190** is a fine place for brunch, or a drink before/after a trip to the nearby Royal Albert Hall.

Bayswater & Notting Hill (Map 5)

You'll get more for your pound at top-end places in these two areas than you would to the south and east.

Abbey Court Hotel (☎ 7221 7518, fax 7792 0858, e info@abbeycourthotel.co.uk, w www.abbey courthotel.co.uk, 20 Pembridge Gardens W2) ⊖ Notting Hill Gate. Singles £105-145, doubles & twins £155-175, triples £190. The Abbey Court has 22 individually decorated rooms, some with fine views over the rooftops. The breakfast room with an old Victrola phonograph and garden courtyard view is particularly fine.

Miller's Residence (☎ 7243 1024, fax 7243 1064, e enquries@millersuk.com, w www.millersuk .com, 111a Westbourne Grove, enter from Hereford Rd W2) ⊖ Bayswater/Notting Hill Gate. Doubles £140-165, including breakfast. More a five-star B&B than a hotel, Miller's is a real find for the well heeled. The Victorian-style drawing room has to be seen to be believed (preferably by candlelight).

Portobello Hotel (☎ 7727 2777, fax 7792 9641, e info@portobello-hotel.co.uk, w www.porto bello-hotel.co.uk, 22 Stanley Gardens W11) ⊖ Notting Hill Gate. Singles/doubles/twins £150/195/225. This beautifully appointed 24-room place is in a great location and one of the most attractive hotels in London. It has an exclusive feel to it; most people consider prices for rooms to be money well spent.

Queen's Park Hotel (☎ 7229 8080, fax 7792 1330, e reservations@queensparkhotel.com, 48 Queensborough Terrace W2) ⊖ Bayswater. Singles £97.50, doubles £125-135. With 99 rooms, the Queen's Park is a functional top-end place popular with groups, but the rates are good for the location. Discounts are available in winter.

Marylebone (Maps 5 & 6)

Bryanston Court (☎ 7262 3141, fax 7262 7248, w www.bryanstonhotel.com, 56-60 Great Cumberland Place W1) **Map 5** ⊖ Marble Arch. Singles/doubles & twins/triples with private bath £95/120/135. This 60-room hotel has a somewhat formal feel with leather armchairs and sepia-toned lighting.

Durrants Hotel (☎ 7935 8131, fax 7487 3510, e info@durrantshotel.co.uk, w www.durrants hotel.co.uk, George St W1) **Map 6** ⊖ Marble Arch. Singles £92.50-110, doubles & twins £145-165, suites from £285. This luxurious, sprawling hotel, behind the Wallace Collection and well placed for Oxford St, was, amazingly, once a country inn and still retains the feel of a gentleman's club. The rooms are comfortable and it is one of London's last privately owned hotels.

East End & the Docklands (Map 9)

The arrival of our man Terence Conran in East London has increased the top-end pickings in this part of town by a third.

Great Eastern Hotel (☎ 7618 5010, fax 7618 5011, e reservations@great-eastern-hotel.co.uk, w www.great-eastern-hotel.co.uk, Liverpool St EC2) ⊖ Liverpool Street. Singles/doubles £225/260-325, suites from £385. A three-year, £70 million refurbishment has turned this 19th-century Victorian pile above Liverpool Street station into a 267-room modernist palace. Its Conran-inspired outlets get good reviews but the seriously superstitious may think twice about staying here: it sits on the site of what was the Bethlehem Royal Hospital (more commonly known as Bedlam) for more than 400 years from the middle of the 13th century.

Thistle Tower Hotel (☎ 7481 2575, fax 7488 4106, w www.thistlehotels.com, St Katharine's Way E1) ⊖ Tower Hill. Singles £190, doubles £211-270 but rates depend, depending on availability. Just beyond the limits of the Square Mile, this 801-room place has a superb waterside position in St Katharine's Dock. It's a dreadful eyesore of a building, though, marring the architectural harmony of its neighbours, the Tower of London and

If a bunk on the *Golden Hinde* doesn't grab you, the marvelous view from the Tower Thistle might.

Tower Bridge, but you're not going to see much of the outside from within, are you?

PLACES TO STAY – DELUXE

Some of central London's hotels are so luxurious and well established that they are tourist attractions in their own right. Despite their often 'olde-worlde' splendour, which can lean towards eye-poppin' Baroque and rococo just this side of bad taste, all are geared for the needs of modern travellers. Be advised that many hotels in this category do not include the government value-added tax (VAT; 17.5%) in their rates.

Brown's (☎ 7493 6020, fax 7493 9381, e browns hotel@brownshotel.com, w www.brownshotel .com, 30 Albemarle St W1) **Map 7** ⊖ Green Park. Singles & doubles £270-380, triples/quads £410/435, suites from £450. A stunner of a five-star number, this 118-room hotel was created in 1837 from 11 houses joined together and is London's longest-operating deluxe hotel. It was also the first hotel in London to have a lift, a telephone and electric lighting. Service is tip-top.

Claridges (☎ 7629 8860, fax 7499 2210, e info@claridges.co.uk, w claridges.co.uk, Brook St W1) **Map 6** ⊖ Bond Street. Singles/ £315-345, doubles & twins £370-450, suites from £515. Claridges, with 203 rooms, is one of the greatest of London's five-star hotels, a cherished reminder of a bygone era. Many of the Art Deco features of the public areas and suites were designed in the late 1920s and some of the 1930s-vintage furniture once graced the staterooms of the decommissioned SS *Normandie*.

The Connaught (☎ 7499 7070, fax 7495 3262, e reservation@the-connaught.co.uk, w www .the-connaught.com, Carlos Place W1) **Map 6** ⊖ Green Park. Singles £280-345, doubles & twins £315-425, suites from £495. As always, the Connaught refuses to cut its clothes to suit this year's fashion and concentrates instead on a tried-and-tested style appropriate to a hotel that has one of the best restaurants in London. (It has, however, woken up to the trends of the 1970s and recently put in a new fitness centre.) The rooms are similarly old-fashioned in that stately home kind of way.

Covent Garden Hotel (☎ 7806 1000, fax 7806 1100, e covent@firmdale.com, w www.firm dale.com, 10 Monmouth St WC2) **Map 8** ⊖ Covent Garden/Tottenham Court Road. Singles/from £190, doubles & twins from £220-280, suites from £325. As now as the new millennium

but in a reserved, British sort of way, this 58-room hotel prefers to use antiques (don't miss the marquetry desk in the drawing room), gorgeous fabrics and a 'theatreland' theme to stake out its individuality. There's a good bar/restaurant just off the lobby called **Brasserie Max**.

The Halkin (☎ 7333 1000, fax 7333 1100, e res@halkin.co.uk, w www.halkin.co.uk, 5 Halkin St SW1) **Map 6** ⊖ Hyde Park Corner. Singles & doubles £285-360, suites from £425. The 41-room Halkin is for business travellers of a minimalist bent: lots of burlwood, marble and round glass things. Bedrooms are wood-panelled and stylishly uncluttered; staff strut about in Armani uniforms.

Hampshire (☎ 7839 9399, fax 7930 8122, e reshamp@radisson.com, w www.radisson edwardian.com, 31-36 Leicester Square WC2) **Map 8** ⊖ Leicester Square. Singles £305, doubles & twins £335-399, suites from £450. This centrally located hotel attracts rich, retired Americans and top-flight businesspeople.

The Hempel (☎ 7298 9000, fax 7402 4666, e hotel@the-hempel.co.uk, w www.the-hempel .co.uk, 31-35 Craven Hill Gardens W2) **Map 5** ⊖ Lancaster Gate/Queensway. Singles & doubles £255-295, suites from £440. We've visited, inspected and/or stayed in lots and lots of hotels in our day, but we've never – ever – seen anything quite like the 47-room Hempel, a minimalist symphony in white and natural tones where Kyoto meets *2001: A Space Odyssey* and puts a spin on it. We can only say 'Wow!' at the design and, frankly, we feel cool for just having walked through the door. The **I-Thai**, serving a fusion of Italian and Thai cuisine, is one of London's more unusual (and successful) restaurants, and the new **H Bar** on the ground floor fits in like the last piece in a designer's jigsaw puzzle.

Kingsway Hall (☎ 7309 0909, fax 7309 9696, e kingswayhall@compuserve.com, w www .kingswayhall.co.uk, Great Queen St WC2) **Map 8** ⊖ Holborn. Singles £230-245, doubles £240-255, suites from £325. This stylish new kid on the block has 170 rooms and is convenient for Covent Garden. Weekend rates are cheaper.

Meridien Waldorf (☎ 0870 400 8484, fax 7836 7244, w www.lemeridien-hotels.com, Aldwych WC2) **Map 8** ⊖ Temple/Covent Garden/Charing Cross. Singles £275, doubles & twins £275-350, suites from £370. Now part of the Meridien chain, the Waldorf is another grand old dame glorying in her Edwardian splendour, which is typified by the wonderful **Palm Court**, the splendid lounge where Lonely Planet authors are known to have taken their mothers to the weekend tea dance.

The Metropolitan (☎ 7447 1000, fax 7447 1100, ⓔ sales@metropolitan.co.uk, ⓦ www.metro politan.co.uk, 19 Old Park Lane W1) **Map 6** ↔ Hyde Park Corner. Singles £240-265, doubles £300-335, studios £370-445, suites from £545. In the same stable as The Halkin, the 155-room Metropolitan is another minimalist hotel – 'stripped of nonessentials' (as they say) and decorated in shades of cream and muesli – that attracts a super-trendy, well-heeled crowd. More rock star than royal, really. The hotel's Japanese restaurant, *Nobu*, consistently gets rave reviews (more for the diners than the dinners, we suspect), and the *Met Bar* remains one of the more popular night spots for the glitterati, both local and imported.

One Aldwych (☎ 7300 1000, fax 7300 1001, ⓔ reservations@onealdwych.co.uk, ⓦ www .onealdwych.co.uk, 1 Aldwych WC2) **Map 8** ↔ Covent Garden/Charing Cross. Singles/ £275-335, doubles £295-355, suites from £445. What was once an Art Nouveau newspaper office is now a minimalist, 105-room hotel with modern art everywhere the eye rests and a merry, upbeat atmosphere. There's no sign outside but the smell of money will lead you to the door.

Park Lane Hotel (☎ 7499 6321, fax 7499 1965, ⓔ reservations_centrallondon@sheraton.com, Piccadilly W1) **Map 6** ↔ Green Park. Singles £323-381, doubles & twins £346-405, suites from £440/464. Most of the 305 rooms, which require triple-glazing to keep the noise of the outside world outside, have been refurbished in a light, modern style, and the hotel is now part of the Sheraton group. Though there's vintage Art Deco on display in the *Palm Room*, the main entrance remains one of the least impressive in London.

The Ritz (☎ 7493 8181, fax 7493 2687, ⓔ enquire @theritzhotel.co.uk, ⓦ www.theritzlondon .com, 150 Piccadilly W1) **Map 6** ↔ Green Park. Singles £295, doubles & twins £345-415, suites from £485. What can you say about a hotel that has lent its name to the English lexicon? Arguably London's most celebrated hotel, the ritzy Ritz has a spectacular position overlooking Green Park and is supposedly the royal family's 'home away from home'. The *Palm Court*, where tea is now being served, madam, and the *Ritz Restaurant*, where the food is said to have been recently dragged into the 21st century, are decked out like rococo boudoirs.

St Martin's Lane (☎ 7300 5500, fax 7300 5501, 45 St Martin's Lane) **Map 8** ↔ Leicester Square. Singles £255-280, doubles & twins

DENNIS JOHNSON

Putting on the Ritz: the epitome of West End sophistication

£275-300, suites from £1200/1400. London's newest designer hotel provides what it calls a 'slice of New York urban chic' just a stone's throw from Covent Garden. But why should they be so modest when serving up the biggest three-decker attitude sandwich in town? Posy, with star-struck staff and so 'minimalist' it has neither a hotel brochure nor a rate card, this glass box is definitely the place to check into if you want to bump into supermodels in the lift.

Savoy (☎ 7836 4343, fax 7872 8901, ⓔ info@ the-savoy.co.uk, ⓦ www.savoy-group.co.uk, Strand WC2) **Map 8** ↔ Charing Cross. Singles £290-335, doubles & twins £345-425, suites from £465. This hotel stands on the site of the old Savoy Palace, which was burned down during the Peasants' Revolt of 1381. The 207 rooms are so comfortable and have such great views that some people have been known to take up permanent residence. The forecourt is the only street in the British Isles where motorists drive on the right.

PLACES TO STAY

If you want to stay in the heart of the action, you won't get more central than the West End...

LONG-TERM RENTALS
Serviced Apartments

Families or groups may prefer to rent a flat rather than stay in a hotel or B&B. Several agencies can help you. Apartment Services London (☎ 7388 3558, fax 7383 7255, e apserltd@aol.com), 2 Sandwich St WC1 (⊖ King's Cross St Pancras/Euston); Aston's Budget & Designer Studios (☎ 7590 6000, fax 7590 6060, e sales@astons-apartments .com, w www.astons-apartments.com), 31 Rosary Gardens SW7 (⊖ Gloucester Road); and London Holiday Accommodation (☎ 7485 0117, e saleslondonholiday.co.uk, w www.londonholiday.co.uk), 16 Chalk Farm Rd NW1, have a range of flats for rent.

Citadines Apart'hotels (☎ 7766 3800, fax 7766 3766, e reslondon@citadines.com, w www.citadines.com), the French chain of studios for one to two people and apartments for up to four people, has crossed the Channel and counts four properties in London.

Citadines Barbican (☎ 7566 8000, fax 7566 8130, 7-21 Goswell Rd EC1) **Map 9** ⊖ Barbican. Studios £96-115, apartments £148-165, per night for up to 6 nights; studios £85-99, apartments £131-153, for 7 or more nights.

Citadines Holborn/Covent Garden (☎ 7395 8800, fax 7395 8799, 94-99 High Holborn WC1) **Map 8** ⊖ Holborn. Studios £105-125, apartments £157-179, per night for up to 6 nights; and studios £94-114, apartments £141-159, for 7 or more nights.

Citadines South Kensington (☎ 7543 7878, fax 7584 9166, 35a Gloucester Rd SW7) **Map 10** ⊖ Gloucester Road. Studios £110-135, apartments £165-182, per night for up to 6 nights ; studios £104-124, apartments £150-165, for 7 or more nights.

... though you may have trouble sleeping when the fair descends on Leicester Square.

PAUL BIGLAND

Citadines Trafalgar Square *(☎ 7766 3700, fax 7766 3766, 18-21 Northumberland Ave WC2)* **Map 6** ✆ Embankment/Charing Cross. Studios/ apartments £114-135, apartments £171-199, per night for up to 6 nights; studios £104-124, apartments £153-179, for 7 or more.

One of the more popular places outside the West End and the City is the following:

130 Queen's Gate *(☎ 7581 2322, fax 7823 8488,* e *onethirty@compuserve.com,* w *www.one thirty.co.uk, 130 Queen's Gate SW7)* **Map 10** ✆ South Kensington. Studio/1-bedroom/2-bedroom apartments £861.50/1193.50/1522.50 per week. This place, with 54 apartments available year-round, is ideal for anyone wanting to spend a lot of time shopping in Knightsbridge and visiting the museums and attractions in South Kensington.

Finding a Flat

At the bottom end of the rental market, bed-sits are single furnished rooms, usually with a shared bathroom and kitchen, although some have basic cooking facilities. The next step up is a studio, which normally has a separate bathroom and kitchen; one-bedroom flats are more expensive again. Shared houses and flats generally offer the best value. Most landlords demand a security deposit (normally one month's rent) plus a month's rent in advance.

Rents vary dramatically according to the part of the city you're considering – one of the best ways to get an idea of current prices is to look in a paper such as *Loot*, which has a huge selection of small ads. Rooms, flats and flat-shares are also advertised in *TNT*, *Time Out*, the *Evening Standard* (including the *Homes & Property* supplement on Wednesday), the *Pink Paper* and *Boyz*. You might also try W www.thegumtree.com, an online community for Australians, New Zealanders and South Africans based in London, which gets up to 50 flat-share postings per day.

Capital Flat Share is a free service run by Capital Radio (☎ 7484 8000), which collects lists of people willing to share their flats (deadline: 6pm Monday) and publishes the list in *The Guide*, an entertainment listings magazine that comes with the *Guardian* on Saturday. Free copies are available in the foyer of Capital Radio, at 29–30 Leicester Square WC2 (⊖ Leicester Square).

If you prefer to use an agency, make sure that it doesn't charge fees to tenants. The Jenny Jones Agency (☎ 7493 4801), 40 South Molton St W1 (⊖ Bond Street), charges the landlord.

Also watch out for rogue rental agencies that illegally charge potential customers a huge fee just for looking at their list of available properties.

Places to Eat

London is the UK's undisputed culinary capital, and the growth in the number of restaurants – some 8500 at last count, representing 70 different cuisines – has made the city much more international. No matter what you fancy eating, there's bound to be a restaurant serving it.

Yes, things have improved remarkably since the 1970s, and why shouldn't they? There was no way but up from caffs serving greasy fried breakfasts and fish and chips deep-fried in rancid-smelling oil.

In recent years food in all its guises has become the new sex in London, and everyone wants a piece of the action. Just don't count on value for money. We can't remember the number of times we've eaten over-refined Italian food or the ubiquitous Modern European, dropped £35 or £40 per head and wondered why we'd bothered. For that kind of money, this would be inconceivable in cities such as New York (US$47–54), Paris (€55–63) or Sydney (A$90–103). On the other hand we've had Pakistani food in Whitechapel, Turkish in Dalston and Malaysian in Paddington that has made our hearts sing, our tastebuds zing and our wallets only slightly lighter.

ASA ANDERSSON

The way to the heart... trendy restaurants and global fare make this a capital to love.

Eating out in London can be a real hit-or-miss affair. What we've done in this chapter is separate the wheat from the chaff. The restaurants, pubs and cafes appearing below range from pretty good (convenient location, cheap price, unusual cuisine) to fantabulous (worth a big splurge or a lengthy journey). Hopefully this list will lead you in the right direction and you won't walk out wondering why *you* bothered. *Bon appétit!*

Restaurants and other eateries in London have extremely varied opening hours. Many in Soho are closed on Sunday, for example, and in the City for the entire weekend. We have tried to note when restaurants stray from the standard 'open daily for lunch and dinner', but it's always safest to call and check first.

Of the many guides to London restaurants, Lonely Planet's annual *Out to Eat – London* includes a selection of almost 400 of the city's best eateries. Useful Web sites include: **W** www.londonrestaurantreview .co.uk and **W** www.where-to-eat.co.uk.

FOOD
Cuisines

London is the capital of a nation that gave the world beans on toast, mushy peas and chip butties (French fries between two slices of buttered – and untoasted – white bread). But that's hardly the whole story and with the emergence of Modern British cuisine it will get even longer (see the later boxed text 'Eels, Liquor & Spotted Dick: English Food in Perspective').

London has a considerable population of immigrants from former British colonies and protectorates as well as refugees from around the globe, so a wide variety of ethnic food is now consumed by everyone – from the tandooris of the Indian subcontinent and the kebabs of Turkey and Cyprus to the chicken Kievs of Ukraine and the noodles and dim sum of China. Pizza and pasta are the staples of every London high street, and curry remains the takeaway of choice.

Eels, Liquor & Spotted Dick: English Food in Perspective

English food will never win any awards on the world culinary stage, but when well prepared – be it a Sunday lunch of roast beef and Yorkshire pudding (light batter baked until fluffy and eaten with gravy) or a cornet of fish and chips eaten on the hoof – it can have its moments.

Pubs generally serve low-cost traditional dishes of varying quality such as pies – pork pies, Cornish pasties (scallop-shaped pastry filled with minced beef or mutton, diced potatoes and onions) and steak and kidney pie. (Shepherd's pie, on the other hand, has no crust but is a baked dish of minced lamb and onions topped with mashed potatoes.) On a pub menu you'll also usually find bangers and mash (sausages served with mashed potatoes and gravy), sausage rolls (sausage meat cooked in pastry) and the ploughman's lunch (thick slices of bread served with Cheddar or Cheshire cheese, chutney and pickled onions). The catalogue of calorific desserts includes bread and butter pudding, steamed pudding (a cake that contains beef suet, a key ingredient) served with treacle (molasses) or jam, and the frighteningly named spotted dick, a steamed suet pudding with currants and raisins that has now been re-christened 'Spotted Richard' by the supermarket giant Tesco for reasons, it says, of propriety.

The most English of dishes, though, is fish and chips: cod, plaice or haddock dipped in batter, deep-fried and served with chips (French fries) doused in vinegar and sprinkled with salt. With the arrival of American-style fast-food joints, authentic 'chippies' are becoming rarer, but we still like the Rock & Soul Plaice in Covent Garden, the North Sea Fish Restaurant in Bloomsbury and Geales in Notting Hill.

From the middle of the 19th century until just after WWII the staple lunch for many Londoners was a pie filled with spiced eel (then abundant in the Thames) and served with mashed potatoes and liquor, a parsley sauce. Nowadays the pies are usually meat-filled and the eel served smoked or jellied as a side dish. The best places to try this are Manze's near Bermondsey Market, R Cooke Eel & Pie Shop in Waterloo, Castle's in Camden Town and Goddards Pie House in Greenwich.

Many so-called gastropubs and trendy restaurants now serve what is called Modern British cuisine. Though it can sometimes be difficult telling the difference between it and Modern European food, Modern British is a lot more than 'staples like bangers and mash with the grease removed', as one philistine describes it. Modern British food includes traditional staples such as root vegetables, smoked fish, shellfish, game and other meats and even things like bangers and black pudding, and combines them in ways that accentuate their flavour. Dishes can be anything from game served with a traditional vegetable, such as Jerusalem artichoke, and smoked Norfolk eel with little buckwheat pancakes to seared scallops with orange-scented black pudding and roast pork with chorizo on rosemary mash.

Vegetarian Food

Vegetarianism is an accepted part of London's restaurant scene and most places offer at least a couple of dishes for those who do not eat meat. Listings in this chapter include many vegetarian places, but the following is a reliable chain.

Cranks (☎ 7631 3912, 9-11 Tottenham St W1) **Map 6** ⊖ Goode Street; *(☎ 7836 5226, 17-19 Great Newport St WC2)* **Map 8** ⊖ Leicester Square; *(☎ 7495 1340, 23 Barrett St W1)* **Map 6** ⊖ Bond Street. Breakfast £2.25, starters £1.95-3, mains £2-4. This vegetarian eatery serves cheap and wholesome stir-fries, chillies and bakes.

Kosher Food

Searching for a kosher meal in central London can be a joyless task, with one single exception. Otherwise, the best places to look are Golders Green, Stamford Hill and much farther afield in places such as Edgware (Middlesex) and Ilford (Essex).

The following is a short list of kosher-supervised restaurants accessible by tube.

Carmelli (☎ 8455 2074, 128 Golders Green Rd NW11) ⊖ Golders Green. Filled bagels £1.20-1.60, kosher pizza £1.30. Closed Fri evening, Sat till dinner. Here real kosher bagels, *challah*, dark rye bread (pumpernickel) and onion *platzels* are available as well as cakes, pastries and savoury snacks.

Kaifeng (☎ *8203 7888, 51 Church Rd NW4*) ✪ Hendon Central. Mains £5.95-17.95. It's Chinese and it's kosher but really not worth the trip unless you have to.

Reubens (☎ *7486 0035, 79 Baker St W1*) Map 5 ✪ Baker Street. Deli dishes £3-8, mains £9.95-18.95. Closed after lunch Fri, all day Sat. This central cafe-restaurant has all the Ashkenazi favourites: gefilte fish, *latkes* (potato pancakes) and sandwiches as well as more complicated (and filling) main courses.

Solly's (☎ *8455 2121, 8455 0004, 148a Golders Green Rd NW11*) ✪ Golders Green. Dishes £8.50-14, 4-course set dinner £20. Closed for dinner Fri, lunch Sat. Middle Eastern/Sephardic dishes such as *felafel*, North African *merguez* sausage and *tahini* are served in the cafe downstairs, while the huge upstairs does full meals.

If you require further details contact the London Beth Din Kashrut Division (☎ 8343 6255, fax 8343 6254, **e** info@kosher.org .uk, **w** www.kosher.org.uk), which publishes a guide to kosher food throughout the UK called *The Really Jewish Food Guide*.

DRINKS

In general, off-licences and pubs have an impressive range of lagers, bitters, ales and stouts (see the boxed text 'Beer: The National Drink' in the Entertainment chapter). Cider, a fermented drink as strong as beer and not the unfiltered apple juice it is in the USA, also has its fans. The most common brands are Scrumpy Jack and the drier Strongbow and Woodpecker, but there are wonderful 'boutique' ciders available in some pubs from presses in Norfolk and Kent.

Good wine – of whatever nationality – is widely available in London and very reasonably priced (except in pubs and restaurants). In supermarkets an ordinary but quite drinkable bottle can still be found for under £5.

The most popular nonalcoholic drink in the UK has traditionally been tea – whether casually drunk from a mug or ceremoniously taken at 'high tea' (see the boxed text 'On the High Teas' later). But judging from the preponderance of US-style coffee-shop chains such as Aroma, Caffè Uno, Costa and the Seattle Coffee Company, that allegiance might be shifting.

TRAFALGAR SQUARE (Maps 6 & 8)

You won't find a tremendous number of eateries directly on the square, but there are a couple of cafes within striking distance and **Crivelli's Garden** (☎ *7747 2869, 1st floor, Sainsbury Wing, National Gallery*) gets good reviews.

International

Café in the Crypt (☎ *7839 4342, St Martin-in-the-Fields, Duncannon St WC2*) Map 8 ✪ Charing Cross/Embankment. Soups £2.25, mains £3.95-6.50. The food in this atmospheric crypt is good, with plenty of offerings for vegetarians, but the place can be hectic and very noisy at lunch time.

ICA Café (☎ *7930 8619, Institute for Contemporary Arts, The Mall SW1*) Map 6 ✪ Charing Cross. Mains £8.80-11.80. You can lunch well at this bohemian magnet, but it's considerably more expensive in the evening. There are lots of vegetarian dishes, and it's licensed to serve alcohol until 1am. For details of day passes see the Institute for Contemporary Arts section in the Things to See & Do chapter.

WESTMINSTER & PIMLICO (Map 11)

With MPs fed and watered in the Houses of Parliament's subsidised restaurants, there's a dearth of eateries in Westminster. Pimlico, on the other hand, has a wide assortment of restaurants.

Modern British

Grumbles (☎ *7834 0149, 35 Churton St SW1*) ✪ Victoria. Dishes £6.95-12.95, 2-/3-course lunch £11.95/13.95. This pleasant wine bar, around since 1964, serves, among other things, stuffed aubergine (£6.95), fish pie (£8.75) and sirloin steak (£10.95).

French

La Poule au Pot (☎ *7730 7763, 231 Ebury St SW1*) ✪ Sloane Square. Starters £5.50-8.50, mains £13.75-19. Some Londoners claim the 'Chicken in the Pot' is the best country-style French restaurant in town. The *al fresco* front terrace is a lovely spot in the warmer months.

PLACES TO EAT

On the High Teas

Given the important role that tea has always played in English culture, it should be no surprise that going out for 'afternoon tea' is something dear to the heart of many Londoners. In most circles these days, however, it's more of a special occasion than a daily routine.

A traditional set tea comes with a selection of delicate sandwiches (cucumber and smoked salmon are favourites), scones with cream and jam, and rich desserts. Oh, and lots and lots of tea.

The following are some of the best and most atmospheric places to go for afternoon tea:

Brown's Hotel (☎ 7493 6020, 30 Albemarle St W1) **Map 7** ✪ Green Park. Brown's dispenses tea in the Drawing Room 3pm to 6pm daily (from 2.30pm at the weekend), with a pianist to soothe away any lingering stress from the bustling streets outside. A sizeable tea will set you back £23 per person (£33 with a glass of champagne).

Claridges (☎ 7629 8860, Brook St W1) **Map 6** ✪ Bond Street. This landmark hotel serves tea in its grand 18th-century foyer from 3pm to 5.30pm daily. It will cost you £22 per head for a set tea or £30 if you want champagne thrown in.

Fortnum & Mason (☎ 7734 8040, 181 Piccadilly W1) **Map 7** ✪ Piccadilly Circus. This celebrated retailer serves afternoon tea in its 4th-floor restaurant, St James, from 3pm to 5.45pm Monday to Saturday for £17.50 or £19.50 with champagne.

Orangery (☎ 7938 1406, Kensington Palace W8) **Map 5** ✪ Queensway. This graceful park cafe in Kensington Gardens is a superb place to have a relatively affordable set tea; prices range from £7.95 with cucumber sandwiches or scones to £12.95 with champagne. It opens 10am to 6pm daily March to October (10am to 5pm the rest of the year).

The Ritz (☎ 7493 8181, 150 Piccadilly W1) **Map 6** ✪ Green Park. Probably the best-known place in London to take tea, the Ritz requires booking at least six weeks in advance. Afternoon tea costs £27 per person and is served daily at two sittings (3.30pm and 5pm). A strict dress-code applies. Avoid jeans and trainers/sneakers.

Savoy (☎ 7836 4343, Strand WC2) **Map 8** ✪ Covent Garden/Charing Cross. The Savoy serves tea in its enormous Thames Foyer from 3pm to 5.30pm daily. From Monday to Saturday there's a resident pianist; tea costs £22 on weekdays and £25 on Saturday. On Sunday there's a tea dance (£28). The dress code is smart casual.

Waldorf Meridien (☎ 7836 2400, Aldwych WC2) **Map 8** ✪ Temple/Covent Garden/Charing Cross. Tea here is served in the splendid Palm Court from 3pm to 5.30pm Monday to Friday for £21 and £28 (with champagne). From 2.30pm to 5.30pm on Saturday and 4pm to 6.30pm on Sunday you can take part in the old-fashioned ritual of tea dancing (£25/28), but you must book ahead.

Roussillon (☎ 7730 5550, 16 St Barnabas St SW1) ✪ Sloane Square. Set menu £29-42. This is one of the best independently owned French restaurants in London and the service is as seamless as everything that emerges from the kitchen. Encore.

Italian

O Sole Mio (☎ 7976 6887, 39 Churton St SW1) ✪ Victoria. Starters £1.50-5.90, mains £8.70-12.50, pizzas & pastas £5.70-6.90. This is a standard, good-value Italian restaurant, which has a good range of pizzas and pastas on offer.

Olivo (☎ 7730 2505, 21 Eccleston St SW1) ✪ Victoria. Starters £5.50-8, mains £8.50-13.50, 2-/3-course set lunch £15/17. This Mod-

ern Italian place produces unfussy pastas and main dishes such as grilled swordfish or tuna with rocket (£13). Colourful surroundings along with well-priced set lunches make it a real winner.

Oliveto (☎ 7730 0174, 49 Elizabeth St SW1) ✪ Victoria/Sloane Square. Starters £2-6.50, mains £6.50-11.50. This is Olivo's smaller and cheaper branch with mainly pizzas on the menu. Its stylish, minimalist decor makes it feel more up to date than Olivo.

Uno 1 (☎ 7834 1001, 1 Denbigh St SW1) ✪ Victoria. Starters £1.50-7.90, mains £10.30-13.90, pizzas & pastas £5.50-10.90. Pasta is a speciality in this cheery dining room decorated in reds and yellows and there's a good choice of vegetarian dishes.

Asian

Jenny Lo's Tea House (☎ 7259 0399, 14 Eccleston St SW1) ✪ Victoria. Dishes £5-6.95, side dishes £2.50-5. This simple place, started up by the daughter of the late Chinese food supremo Ken Lo, serves soups, fried noodles and rice dishes.

Ken Lo's Memories of China (☎ 7773 7734, 67-9 Ebury St SW1) ✪ Victoria; (☎ 7603 6951, 353 Kensington High St W8) **Map 5** ✪ High Street Kensington. Starters £5.80-10.80, mains £11.50-29.50. Ken Lo brought Chinese food to new levels in London, and the service and decor of the place reflects that position.

Mekong (☎ 7630 9568, 46 Churton St SW1) ✪ Victoria. Starters £3.20-4.90, mains £3-9.50, set meal £13 (2-person minimum). Mekong is a small and intimate neighbourhood Vietnamese restaurant that also offers a sprinkling of Thai.

ST JAMES'S & MAYFAIR (Maps 6 & 7)

This is an expensive part of London and not well stocked with budget eateries, though there are a few exceptions.

English

Stockpot (☎ 7839 5142, 40 Panton St SW1) **Map 7** ✪ Piccadilly Circus; (☎ 7287 1066, 18 Old Compton St W1) **Map 7** ✪ Leicester Square; (☎ 7589 8627, 6 Basil St SW3) **Map 5** ✪ Knightsbridge; (☎ 7823 3175, 273 King's Rd SW3) **Map 10** ✪ Sloane Square. Dishes £4-7.20. This old stand-by, with five branches in central London, does a long list of basic dishes (including a number of vegetarian options) such as spaghetti bolognese (£4) and fish and chips (£4.50).

Modern European

Quaglino's (☎ 7930 6767, 16 Bury St SW1) **Map 7** ✪ Piccadilly Circus. Starters £6-12, mains £9.95-18.50, set lunch & dinner (5.30pm-6.30pm) £12.50/15. Quaglino's, a Conran fixture, has remained popular over the years. The food is average and outdone by the atmosphere and decor, which is fun and relatively glam.

American

Hard Rock Café (☎ 7629 0382, 150 Old Park Lane W1) **Map 6** ✪ Hyde Park Corner. Starters £5.75-7.45, mains £7.95-13.95, salads £6.25-8.95 This, the original Hard Rock Café, has been here since 1971 and is as popular as ever – just check out the queues that form every day of the

year (no bookings taken). It serves for the most part a tried-and-tested diet of burgers and fries (£7.25 to £9.95), including veggie ones.

Indian

Cinnamon Club (☎ 7222 2555 or 7517 9898, Old Westminster Library, 30 Great Smith St W1) **Map 6** ✪ St James's Park. Starters £5.25-7.50, mains £9-17.50. This is India with a difference: a club-like restaurant serving high-quality tiffin fit for a rajah.

Rasa W1 (☎ 7629 1346, 6 Dering St W1) **Map 6** ✪ Bond Street. Starters £4.25-4.50, curries & mains £6.25-10.95. This is a larger, posher and more expensive branch of the South Indian vegetarian restaurant Rasa in Stoke Newington. See the Stoke Newington, Finsbury Park & Dalston section for details.

THE WEST END: PICCADILLY, SOHO & CHINATOWN (Maps 7 & 8)

These days Soho is London's gastronomic heart, with numerous restaurants and cuisines to choose from. The liveliest streets tend to be Greek, Frith, Old Compton and Dean Sts. Gerrard and Lisle Sts are chock-a-block with Chinese eateries.

English/Modern British

Franx Snack Bar (☎ 7836 7989, 192 Shaftesbury Ave WC2) **Map 8** ✪ Tottenham Court Road. Dishes £2.50-4. Franx is as authentic a London caff as you'll find in these parts, with eggs and bacon and other one-plate specials.

The Ivy (☎ 7836 4751, 1 West St WC2) **Map 8** ✪ Leicester Square. Starters £6.75-14.75, mains £10.75-21.75. With its liveried doorman and celebrity clientele, The Ivy is a showbizzy event in itself. The English menu includes dishes such as shepherd's pie (£10.75), steak tartare (£7.75), potted shrimps (£9.95) and kedgeree (£7.50).

International/Modern European

Atlantic Bar & Grill (☎ 7734 4888, 20 Glasshouse St W1) **Map 7** ✪ Piccadilly Circus. Starters £6.50-12.50, mains £11.50-18.50, 2-/3-course set lunch & pre-theatre dinner £14.50/16.50. This buzzy and atmospheric place boasts high ceilings, a large Art Deco dining area and two bars.

Eco Lab Organic (☎ 7439 3900, 57 Poland St W1) **Map 7** ✪ Oxford Circus/Tottenham Court Road. Mains £2.95, 3-course set lunch £7.50.

A nation of tea drinkers? Coffee culture hits Soho.

This rather sterile lunchtime place, which also dibble-dabbles in beauty products, nevertheless produces some decent-quality organic dishes.

Garlic & Shots (☎ *7734 9505, 14 Frith St W1*) **Map 7** ⊖ Tottenham Court Road. Mains £8.75-11.75. Open 5pm-midnight Sun-Wed, 6pm-1am Thur-Sat. Whether or not you'll want to risk eating at this place depends on your tolerance for garlic – and your plans for later in the evening. Everything, including the cheesecake, ice cream and vodka, is spiked with the stuff.

Mezzo (☎ *7314 4000, 100 Wardour St W1*) **Map 7** ⊖ Piccadilly Circus. Starters £5.50-13.50, mains £12.50-16.50. Another of Terence Conran's ventures that attracts London's media crowd and media wannabes, Mezzo is so big you might lose your way coming back from the loo. The main restaurant in the basement is a fun, very modern place to eat. *Mezzonine* is a more casual, cheaper eatery on the ground floor. Small dishes cost from £4.50 to £5.75, large go for £7.50 to £10.95.

New Piccadilly (☎ *7437 8530, 8 Denman St W1*) **Map 7** ⊖ Piccadilly Circus. Starters £1.50, mains £4-6. Entering the New Piccadilly is a step back in time. Apart from the prices virtually nothing has changed since the New Piccadilly opened in the 1950s, and even those haven't increased by as much as you'd expect:

pastas and pizzas cost around £4.50, chicken and steaks come in at around £5.50.

Quo Vadis (☎ *7437 9585, 26-9 Dean St W1*) **Map 7** ⊖ Tottenham Court Road. Starters £8.50-12.50, mains £13.50-32, 2-/3-course set lunch £14.50/17.50 (also available 5.30pm-6.45pm). The French menu here is inventive and memorable and the prices aren't too stratospheric for the location. Karl Marx lived upstairs in two small rooms from 1851 to 1856.

Soup (☎ *7287 9100, 1 Newburgh St W1*) **Map 7** ⊖ Oxford Circus. Cup/1L container £2.95/9.50. Another of those upmarket 'soup kitchens' that have found their way to London via New York, Soup has a wide variety of choices – from pea and mushroom claret to Indonesian crab *laksa*. They also do organic porridge (80p to £2) and wraps (£2.75).

Soup Works (☎ *7439 7687, 9 D'Arblay St W1*) **Map 7** ⊖ Oxford Circus. Soups £1.50-5, salads £1.80-3.20. This place, which deals in (and serves up) the 'Alchemy of Soup', is now a popular lunchtime place.

Star Café (☎ *7437 8778, 22 Great Chapel St W1*) **Map 7** ⊖ Tottenham Court Road. Starters £2.60-5.25, mains £4.95-6.95. Open 7am-4pm Mon-Fri. This reliable cheapie dating from the '30s serves bangers and mash, breakfasts (£1.80 to £2.50) and sandwiches (£2.60 to £3.80).

Sugar Club (☎ *7437 7776, 22 Warwick St W1*) **Map 7** ⊖ Oxford Circus. Starters £6.50-10.50, mains £13.80-19.90. This popular place concentrates on Pacific Rim dishes – grilled scallops with sweet chilli sauce, roast duck on wok-fried black beans – that cleverly mix and match traditions of east and west. It has a sister restaurant, Bali Sugar (see the Notting Hill, Bayswater & Paddington section later for details).

American

Planet Hollywood (☎ *7287 1000, London Trocadero, 13 Coventry St W1*) **Map 7** ⊖ Piccadilly Circus. Mains £6.50-16.95. Be prepared to queue at this international favourite for standard American and Californian fare (eg, burgers, Cajun salmon and so on).

Rainforest Café (☎ *7434 3111, 20 Shaftesbury Ave W1*) **Map 7** ⊖ Piccadilly Circus. Salads £8.45-9.45, pastas £8.95-11.95, mains £10.95-12.95. A Hard Rock Café for kids, with live birds and animatronic wild beasts roaring and hooting, waterfalls cascading and thunder crashing among larger-than-life (alas, fake) banyan trees, the Rainforest Café serves American food such as burgers (£8.95) with a splash of Tex-Mex and Caribbean. It's frenetic but the kids are going to love it.

Sports Café (☎ 7839 8300, 80 Haymarket SW1) **Map 7** ⊖ Piccadilly Circus. Mains £7.95-14.95. There's no escaping sport at this restaurant with a dance floor, mini basketball court, pool tables and arcade games. Indeed, some 140 table-side TVs and four big screens keep you occupied with the latest games, matches and races while you await your burger and chips (from £7.95).

French

The Criterion (☎ 7930 0488, 224 Piccadilly W1) **Map 7** ⊖ Piccadilly Circus. Starters £7.95-18.50, mains £12.50-22.50, 2-/3-course set lunch or dinner (5.30pm-6.30pm) £14.95/17.95. This place right on Piccadilly Circus has a spectacular interior – all chandeliers, mirrors, marble and sparkling mosaics – that one breathless wag has compared to the inside of a Fabergé egg. The menu offers fashionable Modern French food (eg, sautéed goat's cheese and roasted peppers), but there are also some English classics such as fish and chips.

L'Odéon (☎ 7287 1400, 65 Regent St W1) **Map 7** ⊖ Piccadilly Circus. Mains £14.50-21, 2-/3-course set lunch & dinner (5.30pm-7pm) £15.50/19.50. This upmarket restaurant is worth a visit just for the views of Regent St from its lofty windows. The food also gets good reports, especially if you go for the set lunch or dinner.

Italian

Kettners (☎ 7734 6112, 29 Romilly St W1) **Map 7** ⊖ Leicester Square. Dishes £6.95-10.25. If you fancy something with fewer links than the Pizza Express chain, Kettners serves pizzas (£7.95 to £10.25) and burgers (£6.95 to £8.85) of a similar standard and price but in a wonderful atmosphere of gently fading grandeur with a piano tinkling softly in the background.

Pizza Express (☎ 7439 8722, 10 Dean St W1) **Map 7** ⊖ Tottenham Court Road. Pizzas £4.95-7.75. This branch of the huge pizza chain is unusual: at street level you get cheap, good-quality pizzas to the sound of Soho traffic; downstairs you can eat to the accompaniment of excellent jazz (see the Entertainment chapter).

Pollo (☎ 7734 5917, 20 Old Compton St W1) **Map 7** ⊖ Leicester Square. Pizzas & pastas £3.30-3.90, mains £4.70-7.75. This budget eatery attracts a student crowd with its pastas, pizzas and fish dishes. Oddly, given the restaurant's name, there isn't a chicken dish to be seen.

Spiga (☎ 7734 3444, 84-6 Wardour St W1) **Map 7** ⊖ Tottenham Court Road. Pizzas & pastas £6-9, mains £12.50-14. This is where to

head if you want authentic pizza, pasta or an Italian main dish in sleek, pleasant surroundings but don't want to pay the earth for it.

Zilli Fish (☎ 7734 8649, 36-40 Brewer St W1) **Map 7** ⊖ Piccadilly Circus. Starters £6.90-10.90, mains £11.90-22. This place serves passable Italian-inspired seafood dishes but, as is so often the case in London, it's more about the surrounds (buzzy) and your fellow diners (minor celebs and media hounds) than the food.

Hungarian

Gay Hussar (☎ 7437 0973, 2 Greek St W1) **Map 7** ⊖ Tottenham Court Road. Starters £3.80-6.50, mains £11.85-16.75. This is Soho of the 1950s, when dining was done in the grand style in rooms with brocade and sepia prints on the walls. And they serve portions only the Hungarians can: try roast duck (£16.50) with all the trimmings or the 'Gypsy quick dish' of pork medallions, onions and green peppers (£13.90). You won't need to eat again for a while.

Indian

Gopal's of Soho (☎ 7434 0840, 12 Bateman St W1) **Map 7** ⊖ Leicester Square/Tottenham Court Road. Starters £2.95-4.75, mains £6.50-10.95. Gopal's offers reasonably authentic food at affordable prices in a (at long last) recently renovated restaurant. *Thalis* (set meals served on circular metal trays) are good value: £11.95 for vegetarian and £1 more for the meat equivalent.

Chinese

If you're with several people and want a proper sit-down meal, head for Chinatown (⊖ Leicester Square), where you'll be spoiled for choice in terms of both quality and cost. A particularly good way to sample the best of Chinese cuisine is to try Cantonese dim sum where you select numerous small dishes and wash them down with a pot of jasmine tea.

1997 (☎ 7734 2868, 19 Wardour St W1) Mains £6.20-9. Open 24-hrs daily. If you've got a craving for Peking duck (£9.50 for half) or comforting soup noodles (£4.20 to £5) at 4am, head here; it's open 24 hours a day.

Chuen Cheng Ku (☎ 7437 1398, 17 Wardour St W1) Soups £1.90-5, starters £4-7.50, mains £6.50-9. This place is ideal for the uninitiated as all the dim sum and other dishes (dumplings, noodles, paper-wrapped prawns and so on) are trundled around on trolleys.

Gerrard's Corner (☎ 7437 0984, 30 Wardour St WC2) Soups £1.90-6, mains £5.80-9.50. This is one of the more reliable Chinese restaurants in Chinatown, both for quality and good value.

Jen (☎ 7287 8193, 7 Gerrard St W1) Starters £2-6, mains £5-38. Primarily a hotpot restaurant, Jen does scores of other Chinese dishes (both old favourites and more innovative dishes) and is always packed with Chinese diners.

London Hong Kong (☎ 7287 0324, 6-7 Lisle St WC2) Soups £2.50-5.50, noodle & rice dishes £5.50-8.80, mains 6-8.50. This place serves some of the best dim sum in London

Mr Wu (☎ 7839 6669, 6-7 Irving St WC2) **Map 8** ⊖ Leicester Square; (☎ 7287 3885, 26 Wardour St W1) **Map 7** ⊖ Tottenham Court Road; *Mr Au* (☎ 7437 7472, 47-49 Charing Cross Rd WC2) **Map 8** ⊖ Leicester Square. Ten-course buffet £4.50. These two almost identical places offer the same deal: all-you-can-eat Chinese buffet at lunch or dinner. You get what you pay for: it's cheap but of very low quality.

Poons (☎ 7437 4549, 26-7 Lisle St WC2) **Map 8** Dishes £4.40-8.20. This hole-in-the-wall caff is where the upmarket Poons empire started. It offers OK food at very good prices and specialises in wind-dried duck and pork (£4.40 per plate). Be prepared to queue at busy times and to be hustled out again pretty quickly.

Japanese

Ikkyu of Chinatown (☎ 7439 3554, 7-9 Newport Place WC2) **Map 8** ⊖ Leicester Square. Sushi £1.45-2.50, noodle dishes £4.50-7.50, set meals £7.70-11, dinner/Sunday buffet £13.50/11.50. This Chinese-owned restaurant with Japanese cooks has a la carte sushi, sashimi and noodle dishes, but the great draws for budget travellers are the four different set lunches and the all-you-can-eat Japanese buffet at dinner (5pm to 10pm) and on Sunday (12.30pm-5pm).

Kulu Kulu (☎ 7734 7316, 76 Brewer St W1) **Map 7** ⊖ Piccadilly Circus. Sushi £1.20-3. This place is generally believed to serve the best conveyor-belt sushi in London.

Satsuma (☎ 7437 8338, 56 Wardour St W1) **Map 7** ⊖ Leicester Square. Sushi £1.10-1.90, noodle dishes £5.40-6.80, set meals £5.20-15.50. This place is similar to Soba but a wee bit more upmarket.

Soba (☎ 7734 6400, 38 Poland St W1) **Map 7** ⊖ Oxford Circus. Noodle & rice dishes £5.30-5.80. Soba is an excellent choice for an easy (and cheap) bowl of Japanese noodles.

Tokyo Diner (☎ 7287 8777, 2 Newport Place WC2) **Map 8** ⊖ Leicester Square. Soup noodles £5.10, set meals £5.90-8.20, bento-box meals £8.30-12.90. The Tokyo Diner is a good-value place to stop for a quick bowl of noodles or a plate of sushi before the cinema or theatre.

Wagamama (☎ 7292 0990, 10a Lexington St W1) **Map 7** ⊖ Piccadilly Circus; (☎ 7836 3330, 1 Tavistock St) **Map 8** ⊖ Covent Garden; (☎ 7736 2333, 4a Streatham St WC1) **Map 8** ⊖ Tottenham Court Road; (☎ 7409 0111, 101a Wigmore St W) **Map 6** ⊖ Oxford Circus; (☎ 7428 0800, 11 Jamestown Rd NW1) **Map 3** ⊖ Camden Town. Noodle dishes £6-8.50, rice dishes £6-7.25, curries £5.25-6.50, set menus £8.50-9.95. This brash and spartan place does decent Japanese (sort of) food but is hardly the place for a quiet dinner. You have to share long tables and, having queued to get in, may feel pressured to move on again quickly.

Yo! Sushi (☎ 7287 0443, 52 Poland St W1) **Map 7** ⊖ Oxford Circus; (Selfridges, ☎ 7318 3944, 400 Oxford St W1) **Map 6** ⊖ Oxford Circus; (5th floor, Harvey Nichols, ☎ 7201 8641, Brompton Rd SW1) **Map 5** ⊖ Knightsbridge. Sushi £1.50-3.50. Ever-expanding Yo! Sushi is one of London's livelier sushi bars, where diners sit around the bar and the dishes come to

Oodles of noodles can be found at the Tokyo Diner in Leicester Square.

Swish sushi restaurants set the trend in the West End.

them on a 60m-long conveyor belt (drinks, on the other hand, are served by tiny robots). The Poland St branch has a popular bar with snacks called *Yo! Below* (☎ *7439 3660*).

Zipangu (☎ *7437 5042, 8 Little Newport St WC2*) **Map 8** ⊖ Leicester Square. Noodle dishes £3.90-5.30, rice dishes £4.20-7.80. This is another budget choice for Japanese food, with similar fare to that of the Tokyo Diner.

South-East Asian

C & R (☎ *7434 1128, 3-4 Rupert Court W1*) **Map 7** ⊖ Leicester Square. Dishes £5-7.50. This little Singaporean/Malaysian place in the heart of Soho serves authentic dishes such as *sambal udang* (£7) and bans smoking.

Cam Phat (☎ *7437 5598, 12 Macclesfield St W1*) **Map 7** ⊖ Leicester Square. Starters £3.50-6, mains £4.50-12. Cam Phat is a cheap and cheerful Sino-Vietnamese place that serves well-prepared dishes such as roast pork with vermicelli noodles (£4.50) and *pho* (£4.50), the Vietnamese soup staple of beef and noodles in a stock flavoured with lemon grass.

Chiang Mai (☎ *7437 7444, 48 Frith St W1*) **Map 7** ⊖ Tottenham Court Road. Soups & starters £4.50-6.20, noodle & rice dishes £6.90-8.20, set lunch £9.90. A relatively pricey Thai restaurant (it's a branch of the Thai Bistro in Chiswick – see that section for details), Chiang Mai has a separate vegetarian menu and a wide range of soups on offer. They also have set vegetarian or meat and fish menus.

Melati (☎ *7437 2745, 21 Great Windmill St W1*) **Map 7** ⊖ Piccadilly Circus. Mains £5.95-7.85. This Indonesian/Malaysian/Singaporean restaurant has decent food and a respectable range of vegetarian options. There are various noodle and rice dishes and the fish in chilli sauce is excellent.

Middle Eastern

Gaby's (☎ *7836 4233, 30 Charing Cross Rd WC2*) **Map 8** ⊖ Leicester Square. Dishes £4.20-9. This snack bar beside Wyndham's Theatre has been here forever and attracts queues for staples such as hummus and felafel (£4.20) and couscous royale (£9).

Momo (☎ *7434 4040, 25 Heddon St W1*) **Map 7** ⊖ Piccadilly Circus. Starters £6.50-11.50, mains £9.75-16, 2-/3-course set lunch £12/15. The kasbah comes to the West End at this trendy and expensive Moroccan restaurant, with couscous (£9.75 to £16) and *tajines* (£11 £15.50). *Mô Bazaar*, the popularly priced 'salad bar, tearoom and bazaar' next door, is a cheaper,

more relaxed place, with a plate of four vegetarian/meat specialities costing £4.95/5.80.

Vegetarian

Govinda's (☎ *7437 4928, 9 Soho St W1*) **Map 7** ⊖ Tottenham Court Road. Dishes £1.75-3.50, lunch/dinner (7pm-8pm) buffet £4.99/3.99. Govinda's serves purely vegetarian food cooked with love and devotion (the latter to Krishna, to whom the temple next door is dedicated). Don't expect high quality at these prices.

Mildred's (☎ *7494 1634, 58 Greek St W1*) **Map 7** ⊖ Tottenham Court Road. Starters £1.75-3.50, mains £5.40-7.50. Mildred's is so small and popular that you may have to share a table. It's worth it, however, because the vegetarian food – including stir-fried vegetables and bean-burgers – is good, well priced and large.

Red Veg (☎ *7437 3109, 95 Dean St W1*) **Map 7** ⊖ Tottenham Court Road. Dishes £2.35-2.95. This fast-food place is where to head if you want vegetarian chilli, felafel and burgers.

Cafes

Bar Italia (☎ *7437 4520, 22 Frith St W1*) **Map 7** ⊖ Leicester Square. Sandwiches £3.50-5. This great favourite is open round the clock and has a wonderful 1950s decor. It's always packed and buzzing (from the caffeine, no doubt); your best chance for a seat might be after 1am.

Maison Bertaux (☎ *7437 6007, 28 Greek St W1*) **Map 7** ⊖ Tottenham Court Road. Cakes about £3. Bertaux has been turning out confections for 130 years, and they're still as exquisite as ever. There's a tearoom on the 1st floor.

Monmouth Coffee Company (☎ *7645 3560, 27 Monmouth St WC2*) **Map 7** ⊖ Tottenham Court Road/Leicester Square. Essentially a shop selling beans from just about every coffee-growing country in the world, Monmouth has seating for about a dozen people where you can sample their blends: from Nicaraguan and Guatemalan to Kenyan and Ethiopian.

Old Compton Café (☎ *7439 3309, 34 Old Compton St W1*) **Map 7** ⊖ Tottenham Court Road/Leicester Square. Sandwiches £2.65-3.25, crepes £2.75-4.50. Open 24-hrs daily. This friendly, sometimes frantic place is one of just a handful of places open round the clock in London. It has a seemingly endless choice of sandwiches as well as salads and some hot dishes.

Pâtisserie Valerie (☎ *7437 3466, 44 Old Compton St W1*) **Map 7** ⊖ Tottenham Court Road/Leicester Square; (☎ *7823 9971, 215 Brompton Rd SW3*) **Map 10** ⊖ Knightsbridge. Cakes £1.80-3, sandwiches £3.50-5.95. You cannot beat this Soho institution (established 1926) for coffee or tea and something sweet, though you'll be lucky to get a seat. It also does filled croissants and club sandwiches and has four other branches in central London.

COVENT GARDEN & THE STRAND (Map 8)

Right beside Soho and technically part of the West End, Covent Garden is also densely packed with places to eat.

English

Porters (☎ 7836 6466, 17 Henrietta St WC2) ⊖ Covent Garden. Starters £3.25, mains £8.95. Porters specialises in pies, long a staple of English cooking but not regularly found on modern menus. There are unusual ones such as lamb and apricot or chicken and broccoli and faves such as steak and kidney pudding as well as fish and chips (all £8.95).

Rock & Sole Plaice (☎ 7836 3785, 47 Endell St WC2) ⊖ Covent Garden. Mains £6-13. This no-nonsense fish and chips shop has basic Formica tables and delicious cod or haddock in batter with chips (from £4.50 with chips) on the ground floor and more elaborate seating downstairs.

Rules (☎ 7836 5314, 35 Maiden Lane WC2) ⊖ Covent Garden. Starters £6.96-10.95, mains £16.95-22.50. This very posh, very British (and rather stuffy) place has a wonderful Edwardian interior and waiters dressed in starched white aprons. The menu is inevitably meat-oriented but fish dishes are also available. Puddings are traditional: trifles, pies and an abundance of custard.

Simpson's-in-the-Strand (☎ 7836 9112, 100 Strand WC2) ⊖ Covent Garden. Starters £5.95-11.50, mains £9.95-23.95, lunchtime roasts £14.50. For traditional English roasts, Simpson's is where to go – it's been dishing up hot meats in a fine panelled dining room since 1848 (when it was called Simpson's Divan and Tavern). They serve up dishes such as steak and kidney pudding (£14.50), lamb with red currant jelly (£19.50) and pigeon with red cabbage (£16.50). The more popularly priced dining area called **Simply Simpson's** has two-/three-course set lunches for £10/15.50.

American

Joe Allen (☎ 7836 0651, 13 Exeter St WC2) ⊖ Covent Garden. Starters £4.50-7, mains £7.50-14.50, 2-/3-course set meal at lunch £12/14 and pre-theatre dinner (5pm-6.45pm Mon-Fri) £13/15. This long-established American-style eatery is a theatre-star-spotter's paradise. There's a real buzz here and it gets crowded, so book. Starters and main dishes (lamb chops, grilled halibut and so on) are varied, with some vegetarian choices.

French

Café des Amis du Vin (☎ 7379 3444, 11-14 Hanover Place WC2) ⊖ Covent Garden. Starters £5.50-7.95, mains £8.50-16.95, 2-/3-course set lunch £12.50/15, 2-course pre- or post-theatre dinner £10.50. This brasserie is handy for pre- or post-theatre meals with good (and affordable) French fare.

Italian

Orso (☎ 7240 5269, 27 Wellington St WC2) ⊖ Covent Garden. Starters £5-9, mains £5, 2-/3-course set lunch £15/17, pre-theatre dinner £13/15. This established Italian eatery is very popular with media types.

Middle Eastern

Sarastro (☎ 7836 0101, 126 Drury Lane WC2) ⊖ Covent Garden. Starters £4-8.50, mains £8.50-14.50, 2-course lunch & pre-theatre dinner £10, opera cabaret dinner Sun & Mon £20. Any place that bills itself as 'The Show after the Show' has got to be more concerned with gimmicky entertainment than food, but Sarastro, with its Turkish and European dishes, Baroque decor and opera music makes for a night to remember.

Other Cuisines

Belgo Centraal (☎ 7813 2233, 50 Earlham St WC2) ⊖ Covent Garden. Starters £4.95-5.95, mains £8.95-16.95, set lunch/dinner £5/14.95. Taking the lift down to the basement and walking through the kitchens is all part of the fun at Belgo, where the waiters dress up as 16th-century monks. This being a Belgian restaurant, *moules et frites* (mussels and chips/french fries) and spit roasts are the specialities and beer (100 different flavoured Pilsners) is the drink. The set dinner comprises a salad starter, mussels and chips and a beer or soft drink. On weekdays (5pm to 8.30pm) you can try the 'Beat the Clock' menu with one of three main courses and a beer, glass of wine or soft drink – the time you sit down decides the price you pay for your main dish (take a seat at 6.15pm and you pay £6.15, with the minimum charge, of course, being £5).

Hankering for the vegetarian option?
Then head for Neal's Yard.

Café Pacifico (☎ *7379 7728, 5 Langley St)* ⊖ Covent Garden. Starters £4.50-8.95, mains £7.80-9.95. Pacifico serves Mexican food and great margaritas in a cheerful dining room.

Calabash (☎ *7836 1976, The Africa Centre, 38 King St WC2)* ⊖ Covent Garden. Starters £2-2.95, mains £4.75-7.75. This simple eatery in the Africa Centre serves food from all over Africa and has a menu for the uninitiated describing each dish. Typical dishes are *egusi*, a Nigerian meat stew with tomatoes and spices (£6.95), and *yassa*, chicken marinated with lemon juice and peppers, hailing from Senegal. There are also beers from all over Africa and wines from Algeria, Zimbabwe and South Africa.

La Perla (☎ *7240 7400, 28 Maiden Lane WC2)* ⊖ Covent Garden. Starters £2.95-5.25, mains £8.95-12.50. This place serves well-prepared Mexican and Tex-Mex food, with an unusual emphasis on fish.

Mongolian Barbecue (☎ *7379 7722, 12 Maiden Lane WC2)* ⊖ Leicester Square; *(☎ 7581 8747, 61 Gloucester Rd SW7)* **Map 10** ⊖ Gloucester Road. Before 7pm & all day Mon/dinner £7/12.95. At this 'All you Khan eat' place (their joke, not ours) you choose the meat, fish and vegetables, add the sauces and spices and watch it being stir-fried.

Vegetarian

There's a cluster of enjoyable New Age cafes – most of them vegetarian – in Neal's Yard and nearby, including those listed below. All offer a similar diet of wholesome dishes such as cheese breads and home-made noodles in pleasing surroundings, but space fills up quickly. Lunch in any of these places should cost only about £5 to £6 if you choose carefully.

Food for Thought (☎ *7836 0239, 31 Neal St WC2)* Dishes £2.80-5.50. This tiny, no-smoking vegetarian cafe features dishes such as *gado-gado* (£3.90), Indonesian salad with peanut dressing; quiches (£2.80 to £5) and vegetable stir-fries with brown rice (£3.60).

Neal's Yard Salad Bar (☎ *7836 3233, 2 Neal's Yard WC2)* Mains £5.50-6.50. This place can get rather expensive unless you order carefully.

World Food Café (☎ *7379 0298, 1st floor, 14 Neal's Yard WC2)* Mains £5.95-7.95. This place serves vegetarian dishes from all over the world, including Middle Eastern meze, African stews with brown rice and Egyptian felafel.

FITZROVIA & MARYLEBONE (Maps 6 & 7)

In recent years, many restaurants and cafes have crossed the 'Berlin Wall' that is Oxford St and set up shop in Fitzrovia or even farther west into Marylebone.

International/Modern European

Back to Basics (☎ *7436 2181, 2a Foley St W1)* **Map 6** ⊖ Oxford Circus. Starters £3.50-5.50, mains £12.95-14.95. This superb corner restaurant (as close as you'll find to a Parisian *restaurant du quartier* in London) serves excellent seafood dishes and is staffed by a bevy of affable young Poles.

French

Villandry (☎ *7631 3131, 170 Great Portland St W1)* **Map 6** ⊖ Great Portland Street. Starters £5.25-8.50, mains £11.50-17.25. This excellent French restaurant has an attractive market/delicatessen and bar too.

Italian

Spighetta (☎ *7486 7340, 43 Blandford St W1)* **Map 6** ⊖ Baker Street. Pizzas & pastas £6.90-9.90, mains £10.90. Spiga's sister branch is smaller and slightly cheaper.

SIMON BRACKEN

SIMON BRACKEN

**Cooking up a storm: behind the scenes
at a London restaurant**

Spanish

Costa Dorada *(☎ 7636 7139, 47-55 Hanway St
W1)* **Map 7** ⊖ Tottenham Court Road. Starters
£3.50-6.90, mains £8.50-14.50. This is one of a
couple of decent Spanish eateries with tapas (£2
to £6.95) that tourists never get to on Hanway St,
a narrow street running north off Oxford St. This
one has decent vegetarian paella (£10) and fla-
menco show nightly from Monday to Saturday.

Indian

Rasa Samudra *(☎ 7637 0222, 5 Charlotte St W1)*
Map 7 ⊖ Goodge Street. Starters £4.20-7.50,
curries £6-6.50, other mains £9.95-18.95. This
shockingly pink place just north of Oxford St is
from the same people who gave you the South
Indian vegetarian restaurants Rasa in Stoke
Newington and Rasa W1 in Mayfair (see the
Stoke Newington & Finsbury Park and St
James's & Mayfair sections), but here they've
moved on from catering for just veggies and
serve seafood too.

Korean

Han Kang *(☎ 7637 1985, 16 Hanway St W1)*
Map 7 ⊖ Tottenham Court Road. Barbecue
£6-15. With *bulgogi* (literally 'fire meat', usually marinated beef slices) and *kalbi* (ribs) grills
and spicy *kimchee* (hot pickled cabbage), Han
Kang is as authentic a Korean restaurant as
you'll find in the West End. Try the *pibimbap*,
a rice, meat and vegetable concoction that gets
stirred together with a raw egg.

South-East Asian

Archipelago *(☎ 7383 3346, 110 Whitfield St
W1)* **Map 6** ⊖ Warren Street. 2-/3-course set
meal £32.50/38.50. The food here my not be
overwhelming but we lurrve the camp 'island
tropical' theme and decor.

Bam-Bou *(☎ 7323 9130, 1 Percy St W1)* **Map 7**
⊖ Goodge Street. Starters £4.25-7.20, mains
£8.75-13.75. This chichi place serves Vietnamese food with a modern (mostly French) twist:
sauté de bœuf with lime, caramelised ginger
chicken, barbecued pork ribs with lemongrass.

Middle Eastern

Dish Dash *(☎ 7637 7474, 57-9 Goodge St W1)*
Map 6 ⊖ Goodge Street. Starters £1.50-4.50,
mains £6.50-13.50. This pleasant place serves
such 'Persian' dishes as Iraqi lamb shank. It's
good and Persian restaurants are thin on the
ground in London.

Ozer *(☎ 7323 0505, 5 Langham Place W1)*
Map 6 ⊖ Oxford Circus. Starters £3.95-8.50,
mains £7.50-17.50, set menu £8. This 'Ottoman'
restaurant, part of the shrinking Sofra Group, is
really just fancy Turkish but worth a try.

Vegetarian

Woodlands *(☎ 7486 3862, 77 Marylebone Lane
1 W1)* **Map 6** ⊖ Bond Street; *(☎ 7839 7258,
37 Panton St SW1)* **Map 7** ⊖ Piccadilly Circus.
Starters £2.95-3.95, mains £3.95-13.50. This
South Indian vegetarian restaurant, whose rallying cry is 'Let Vegetation Feed the Nation'
sets out to prove that South Indian vegetarian
food can be as inventive as any meat-based
cuisine and does a pretty convincing job of it.

BLOOMSBURY (Maps 4, 6 & 8)

Though usually dismissed as B&B land,
Bloomsbury has a fair number of restaurants
as well, many of them reasonably priced.

English

North Sea Fish Restaurant *(☎ 7387 5892, 7-8
Leigh St WC1)* **Map 4** ⊖ Russell Square.
Starters £3.10-3.95, mains £6.85-16.95. The
North Sea sets out to cook fresh fish and potatoes – a simple ambition in which it succeeds
admirably. Look forward to jumbo-sized plaice
or halibut steaks, deep-fried or grilled, and a
huge serving of chips (£10.95 or £13.95).

Italian

Mille Pini *(☎ 7242 2434, 33 Boswell St WC1)*
Map 6 ⊖ Russell Square/Holborn. Starters £2-
4.50, pizzas & pastas £4.50-5.50, mains £6.50-
9.50, 3-course lunch £6. This well-regarded
place just off delightful Queen's Square is a
true, old-fashioned Italian restaurant and pizzeria with reasonable prices. You'll waddle out
but will only have spent about a few quid.

PLACES TO EAT

Asian

Abeno *(☎ 7405 3211, 47 Museum St WC1)* **Map 8** ⊖ Tottenham Court Road. Rice & noodle dishes £6.95-8.75, mains £5.20-13.80. This understated little Japanese restaurant specialises in *okonomi-yaki*, a kind of Japanese omelette that is combined with the ingredients of your choice and cooked at the table.

Thai Garden Café *(☎ 7323 1494, 32 Museum St WC1)* **Map 8** ⊖ Tottenham Court Road. Soups & starters £3.45-3.95, mains £5.45-6.95. What was once the popular Garden Café has now become a so-so Thai restaurant, but one that happens to be very convenient for those visiting the British Museum.

Vegetarian

Greenhouse *(☎ 7637 8038, Drill Hall Theatre, 16 Chenies St WC1)* **Map 6** ⊖ Goodge Street. Dishes £2.50-4.50. In the basement of the Drill Hall, the Greenhouse is popular and very busy, so expect to share a table. They serve vegetable bakes (£4.20), casseroles (£4.20) and quiches (£2.50).

Cafes

If you're visiting the British Museum it's worth knowing that Museum St is packed with cafes and simple lunch places where you'll get better value for your money than in the museum cafe.

Coffee Gallery *(☎ 7436 0455, 23 Museum St WC1)* **Map 8** ⊖ Tottenham Court Road. Pastas £4.50, sandwiches £3.50-4. This popular non-smoking place serves pasta dishes, salads, sandwiches and afternoon tea (about £4) in a bright, cheerful room with modern paintings on the walls.

Ruskins Café *(☎ 7405 1450, 41 Museum St WC1)* **Map 8** ⊖ Tottenham Court Road. Dishes £2.95-3.50. This place does soup and filled jacket potatoes.

HOLBORN & CLERKENWELL (Maps 4 & 6)

Holborn has a few restaurants and night spots to recommend it but is generally pretty quiet after dark. On the other hand, Clerkenwell has well and truly arrived on the eating-out map. These places are accessible from Farringdon tube station unless stated otherwise.

English/Modern British

Ferrari's Cafe *(☎ 7236 7545, 8 West Smithfield EC1)* **Map 6** Breakfast £1.40-2.10, dishes £3.80, sandwiches £1.50-2.50. This 24-hour greasy spoon opposite the market at Smithfield has fry-ups substantial enough to keep the market folk going through the morning.

Rudland & Stubbs *(7253 0148, 35-7 Greenhill Rents, off Cowcross St EC1)* **Map 6** Starters £3.95-7.75, mains £8.95-11.95. This 'oyster bar & dining room' serves up the freshest of the bivalves and local fish such as Cornish hake. It's jammed at lunch with City folk but quietens down at night.

St John *(☎ 7251 0848, 26 St John St EC1)* **Map 6** Starters £4-7.20, mains £11-16.50. This unadorned former warehouse is the place to come if you fancy sampling old-fashioned British dishes in new guises such as whelks with pickled shallots (£5), duck leg with carrots (£13.80) and rabbit offal with bacon and mash (£11.80). While there are some fish dishes, this place is all about meat, and offal in particular (after all, it is right next to Smithfield Market).

Modern European

Smiths of Smithfield *(☎ 7236 6666, 67-77 Charterhouse Square EC1)* **Map 6** Starters £7.50-11, mains £15-22, 3-course Sunday brunch £25. SOS, opposite Smithfield meat market, has a bar and cafe on the ground floor, a suity bar on the 1st floor and a brasserie and dining room on the second, which serves excellent dishes prepared with top-quality British meat and organic produce.

American

Tinseltown *(☎ 7689 2424, 44-6 St John's St EC1)* **Map 6** Starters £2-3.99, mains £5.99-8.99. Open 24-hrs daily. This American-style basement diner serves average pizza, pasta, burgers and grills, but is a great place for blotting the alcohol after clubbing in Clerkenwell.

French

Le Café du Marché *(☎ 7608 1609, 22 Charterhouse Square, Charterhouse Mews EC1)* **Map 6** 3-course set lunch & dinner £24.95. Tucked away in a tiny alleyway near Smithfield Market, this rustic and very romantic place serves gutsy French fare and has live jazz on the first floor.

Club Gascon *(☎ 7796 0600, 57 West Smithfield EC1)* **Map 6** Portions £3.80-17.10. Right next to glorious St Bartholomew's-the-Great (of *Four Weddings and a Funeral* and *Shakespeare* *in Love* fame), Club Gascon does things differently, serving starter-sized portions (only) of south-west French cuisine. Order from about four of the portions; the food is inventive and very good.

Maison Novelli (☎ *7251 6606, 31 Clerkenwell Green EC1*) **Map 4** Starters £6.50-12.50, mains £16-22.50. This is the sole survivor of the restaurant empire of chef Jean-Christophe Novelli. It continues to serve excellent Modern French food in a serene upstairs restaurant overlooking Clerkenwell Green.

Italian

Spaghetti House (☎ *7405 5215, 20 Sicilian Ave WC1*) **Map 6** ⊖ Holborn. Starters £3.05-8.65, pastas & pizzas £5.95-8.75, mains £8.75-14.95. This branch of a chain of Italian eateries serves basic pizza and pasta dishes in a pedestrianised street between Southampton Row and Vernon Place. It has outside seating in warm weather.

Spanish

Gaudí (☎ *7608 3220, 63 Clerkenwell Rd EC1*) **Map 6** Starters £10-12, mains £16.75-17.50, 2-course set lunch Mon-Fri £15. This restaurant takes its cue from the Catalan architect's designs to provide a backdrop for a classy restaurant specialising in what has been dubbed New Spanish cuisine. Fish plays a big, if not exclusive, role here and there's a good Spanish wine list.

Moro (☎ *7833 8336, 34-6 Exmouth Market N1*) **Map 4** Starters £4.50-6, mains £10.50-14.50. As its name implies, this place (run by husband and wife Sam and Sam Clark) serves 'Moorish' cuisine, a fusion of Spanish, Portuguese and North African flavours. Try the crab *brik*, a crispy deep-fried packet served with piquant *harissa* or the wood-roasted red mullet with sharp Seville orange.

Jewish

Knosherie (☎ *7242 5190, 12-13 Greville Rd*) **Map 6** Sandwiches & filled bagels 90p-£2.90, mains £3.90-7.90. Not kosher but kosher-style, this cafe-restaurant owned by the former director of Bloom's in Whitechapel has all the favourites: salt beef, cholent and rollmops.

Asian

Cicada (☎ *7608 1550, 132-6 St John St EC1*) **Map 4** Starters £4.50-6, mains £6.50-10. Cicada is a lovely, modern restaurant that mingles Asian tastes and flavours with great success. It's always popular.

East One (☎ *7566 0088, 175-9 St John St EC1*) **Map 4** Starters £3.50-7, mains £9.95-14.50. East One is composed of two sections: an a la carte dining room and a another of those Asian do-it-yourself places, where they offer all-you-can-eat stir-fries for lunch (£12) and dinner (£16.50).

Other Cuisines

My Old Dutch (☎ *7242 5200, 131-2 High Holborn WC1*) **Map 8** ⊖ Holborn. Dishes £3.95-7.95. This long-lived restaurant serves over 100 sweet and savoury pancakes and waffles.

Vegetarian

The Greenery (☎ *7490 4870, 5 Cowcross St EC1*) **Map 6** Salads £1.50-3.50, pizzas £2.20-2.80. This small vegetarian cafe, still hanging on amid all the gentrification of Clerkenwell, has salad platters and vegetarian pizzas.

THE CITY (Maps 6 & 9)

The City can be an irritating place in which to try to find a decent, affordable restaurant that stays open after office hours. The following are the pick of the crop.

English

Sweeting's (☎ *7248 3062, 39 Queen Victoria St EC4*) **Map 9** ⊖ Mansion House. Starters £4.95-10.95, mains £8.25-20.50. Open 11.30am-3pm Mon-Fri. Sweeting's is an old-fashioned lunch (only) place, with a mosaic floor and waiters in white aprons standing behind narrow counters serving up all sorts of traditional fishy delights. There are dishes such as wild smoked salmon (£8.95) and oysters in season from September to April

Ye Olde Cheshire Cheese (☎ *7353 6170, Wine Office Court, off Fleet St EC4*) **Map 6** ⊖ Blackfriars. Starters £2.95-5.95, mains £7.25-9.95. Rebuilt shortly after the Great Fire of 1666 and popular with Dr Johnson, Thackeray, Dickens and the visiting Mark Twain, the Cheshire Cheese is touristy but the traditional Chop Room is a good place to take visitors.

International/Modern European

Searcy's (☎ *7588 3008, Level 2, Arts Centre Building, Barbican Centre EC2*) **Map 9** ⊖ Barbican. Starters £6.50-13.50, mains £16.50-23, 2/3-course set meal £18.50/21.50. This brasserie in the bowels of the Barbican is a great place for a pre- or post-performance meal. It has ugly views of the ugly Barbican, though.

Ye Olde Cheshire Cheese, a magnet for literary types through the ages

RICHARD I'ANSON

Wine Library (☎ 7481 0415, 43 Trinity Square EC3) **Map 9** ⊖ Tower Hill. Buffet £11.95. Open for lunch only 11.30am-3pm Mon-Fri. This is a great place to go if you want a light but boozy lunch. Buy a bottle of wine retail (no mark-up; £3.50 corkage fee) from the large selection on offer and then snack on patés, cheeses and salads. It's a good idea to book.

Italian & Pizza

Caravaggio (☎ 7626 6206, Bankside House, 107-12 Leadenhall St EC3) **Map 9** ⊖ Aldgate/Bank. Starters £7.25-10.25, mains £13.50-18. Caravaggio probably wouldn't rate a listing if it were anywhere else, but relatively authentic Italian food is not easy to find in the City. It's very posh.

Da Vinci (☎ 7236 3938, 42-4 Carter Lane EC4) **Map 6** ⊖ Blackfriars/St Paul's. Starters £2.40-6.95, pastas £6.50-7.95, mains £8.60-13.50, 2-course set lunch £8.95. Here's a rare bird indeed: an affordable neighbourhood Italian place in the City.

Indian

Cafe Spice Namaste (☎ 7488 9242, 16 Prescot St E1) **Map 9** ⊖ Tower Hill. Starters £3.95-5.95, mains £6.50-14.75. One of our favourite Indian

restaurants in London, the Namaste serves Goan and Keralan cuisine (with South-East Asian hints) in an old courthouse that has been decorated in 'carnival' colours. Try *frango piri-piri* (£7.95), a fiery hot chicken *tikka* marinated in red *masala*. There are plenty of vegetarian side and main dishes too.

Asian

Dim Sum (☎ 7236 1114, 5-6 Deans Court EC4) **Map 6** ⊖ Blackfriars/St Paul's. Starters £4.50-6.50, mains £7.50-9.50, rice & noodle dishes £4-7.50, 2-course set lunch £9.99. A budget traveller's delight and convenient to St Paul's and the City of London YHA hostel, Dim Sum serves Peking and Szechuan dishes but the best deal is the all-you-can-eat weekday buffet (four person minimum; 6pm to 10.30pm, Monday to Friday) at £12.99.

Vegetarian

Place Below (☎ 7329 0789, St Mary-le-Bow Church, Cheapside EC2) **Map 9** ⊖ St Paul's/Mansion House. Mains £5.80-7. Open for lunch 7.30am-2.30pm, for drinks & snacks 7.30am-4pm Mon-Fri. This vegetarian restaurant in a church crypt serves salads, pasta and soup.

BERMONDSEY (Map 9)

This area's culinary highlights include Terence Conran's gastronomic palaces at Shad Thames, but there are several other places of note.

Modern British

Butlers Wharf Chop House (☎ 7403 3403, Butlers Wharf Building, 36e Shad Thames SE1) ⊖ Tower Hill. Mains £12-30, 2-/3-course set meal £19.75/23.75 (dining room), mains £8.50-22, 2-/3-course set meal £8/10 (bar). Designer and restaurateur Terence Conran, who set up the Design Museum in the little enclave called Shad Thames, also located some of his excellent, though expensive, restaurants nearby. This one serves lamb, beef and its signature steak, kidney and oyster pudding.

Honest Cabbage (☎ 7234 0080, 99 Bermondsey St SE1) ⊖ London Bridge. Starters £4-6, mains £7-14. This Bohemian restaurant with an ever-changing blackboard menu offers everything from soups, salads, sandwiches and pies to mains such as monkfish with star anise and sweet chilli (£13).

Modern European

Blue Print Café (☎ 7378 7031, Design Museum, Butlers Wharf SE1) ⊖ Tower Hill. Starters £5-6.50, mains £11-16.50. Modern European fare is the order of the day at this flagship Conran place. There are spectacular river views too.

Le Pont de la Tour (☎ 7403 8403, Butlers Wharf Building, 36d Shad Thames SE1) ⊖ Tower Hill. Starters £7-22, mains £8.95-27, 3-course set lunch £28.50. Another Conran venue, where you can lunch or dine on French-ish food, peruse the seemingly endless wine list and enjoy the river setting, as movers and shakers such as Prime Minister Tony Blair have done before you.

Italian & Mediterranean

Cantina del Ponte (☎ 7403 5403, Butlers Wharf Building, 36c Shad Thames SE1) ⊖ Tower Hill. Starters £3.95-6.95, mains £11.95-14.95, 2-/3-course set lunch & dinner Mon-Fri £10/12.50. This is a more affordable riverside Conran restaurant serving Italian/Mediterranean food such as pizzas (£6.95 to £7.95) and pastas (£8.95 to £11.50). There's fabulous outside seating in warm weather and live music on Tuesday and Thursday evenings.

SOUTHWARK (Maps 2 & 9)

Options in this part of town range from workers' caffs and pie and mash shops to some more exotic – and expensive – choices.

English/Modern British

Borough Café (☎ 7407 5048, 11 Park St SE1) **Map 9** ⊖ London Bridge. Breakfast £1.60-2, meals £2-4. Open 4am-3pm Mon-Fri, 4am-11am Sat. Close to Borough Market, this is the quintessential London market caff, where you can eat a full (and filling) meal for less than £4.

Fish! (☎ 7836 3236, Cathedral St SE1) **Map 9** ⊖ London Bridge; (☎ 7234 3333, 3b Belvedere Rd SE1) **Map 6** ⊖ Waterloo. Starters £3.95-6.95, mains £8.50-16.95. Situated in an all-glass Victorian pavilion overlooking Borough Market and Southwark Cathedral, Fish! serves fresher-than-fresh fish and seafood prepared simply: steamed or grilled swordfish, cod, skate, squid (or whatever is ticked off on the placemat) served with one of five sauces.

Manze's (☎ 7407 2985, 87 Tower Bridge Rd SE1) **Map 2** ⊖ London Bridge. Dishes from £2. This pie shop, one of the oldest still trading in London, has been going strong for over a century and is handy for Bermondsey Market. In its pleasantly tiled interior you'll find jellied eels, pie and mash and liquor.

Other Cuisines

Fina Estampa (☎ 7403 1342, 150 Tooley St SE1) **Map 9** ⊖ Tower Hill/London Bridge. Starters £4.50-9.50, mains £7.95-12.95. Come here for solid, home-cooked Peruvian fare – and lots of it. Try *cebiche*, white fish marinated in lemon juice (£5.95), to start and either *seco* (lamb or chicken in coriander sauce; £10.95) or *carapulcra* (dried Peruvian potatoes served with pork, chicken and yucca; £10.95). The *pisco* cocktails (£3.50) are deadly.

WATERLOO & LAMBETH (Maps 2 & 6)

This part of south London is not immediately attractive as a place for eating out, although the cafes and restaurants in the Royal Festival Hall, the Royal National Theatre and the National Film Theatre are popular places to meet, with reasonable food.

CHARLOTTE HINDLE

The catch of the day: Livebait is one of London's fish-toting eateries.

English

R Cooke Eel & Pie Shop (☎ 7928 5931, 84 The Cut SE1) **Map 6** ✪ Southwark/Waterloo. Dishes £1.60-3.40. Open 10.30am-2.30pm Tues-Sat. Geezers and luvvies tuck into excellent pies (£1.60) and eel and mash (£2.35) in a lovely old cafe.

Marie's Café (☎ 7928 1050, 90 Lower Marsh SE1) **Map 6** ✪ Waterloo. Dishes £1.30-3.20. Marie's is a typical caff with above-average fry-ups (including great mushrooms) as well as – wait for it – Thai dishes.

International/Modern European

Bar + Kitchen (☎ 7928 5086, 131 Waterloo Rd SE1) **Map 6** ✪ Southwark/Waterloo. Starters £4-6, mains £8-14. Bar + Kitchen is just that – a small boozer and quiet and comfortable restaurant with a 'global' (ie, a bit from everywhere) menu, wooden tables and modern art on the walls.

Bistrot 2 Riverside (☎ 7498 8200, 2nd floor, Barge House St SE1) **Map 6** ✪ Waterloo. 2-course set meal £20. If you can't get into the Oxo Tower restaurant there's always this cheaper option on the 2nd floor. You won't get much of a view though.

Livebait (☎ 7928 7211, 43 The Cut SE1) **Map 6** ✪ Southwark/Waterloo; (☎ 7836 7161, 21 Wellington St WC2) **Map 7** ✪ Covent Garden. Starters £4.95-8.50, mains £13.25-28, 2-/3-course set lunch Mon-Fri, pre- & post-theatre Mon-Sat £12.95/15.95. This tiled green-and-white restaurant, which is trying to look more proletarian than it really is, serves up fresh fish and shellfish dishes in all their many guises. The service is so casual it borders on the cavalier.

Oxo Tower Restaurant & Brasserie (☎ 7803 3888, 8th floor, Barge House St SE1) **Map 6** ✪ Waterloo. Starters £8-14, mains £15-21.50, 3-course set lunch £27.50. The conversion of the old Oxo Tower on the South Bank into housing with this restaurant on the 8th floor helped spur much of the restaurant renaissance south of the river. The food – a bit Mediterranean, a bit French, some Pacific Rim – is satisfactory but you're really here for the views (and they are fabulous).

People's Palace (☎ 7928 9999, Level 3, Royal Festival Hall) **Map 6** ✪ Waterloo. Mains £12-16.50. Easy to miss inside the Royal Festival Hall and boasting some enviable fine views of the Thames and the City, this rather deceptively named restaurant serves such delights as beetroot *tart Tatin* and roast rabbit.

Chic dining accompanied by fine views at the Oxo Tower Restaurant

French

RSJ (☎ 7928 4554, 13a Coin St SE1) **Map 6** ✪ Waterloo. Starters £6.50-8.25, mains £13.95-17.95, 2-/3-course set meal £14.95/16.95. This rather industrially named place (most Britons known as RSJ as a 'rolled steel joist') nonetheless serves comforting Modern British dishes such as pan-fried scallops with black pudding (£8.25) and roast haddock with bubble and squeak (£13.95).

Italian

Gourmet Pizza Company (☎ 7928 3188, Gabriel's Wharf, 56 Upper Ground SE1) **Map 6** ✪ Waterloo. Mains £5.25-9.90. It may not look like much, but there are always queues here waiting for such unusual toppings as Thai chicken (£8.25) and Cajun chicken with prawns (£8.75) along with the more usual cheese and tomato (£5.25) and Italian sausage (£7.70).

Pizzeria Castello (☎ 7703 2556, 20 Walworth Rd SE1) **Map 2** ✪ Elephant & Castle. Mains £4.50-10. Ask any south Londoner to direct you to the best pizzeria on this side of the Thames and you'll find yourself here. Castello has been going for years, is family owned, friendly and prices are low. Book or count on a long wait.

Other Cuisines

Cubana (☎ 7928 8778, 48 Lower Marsh SE1) **Map 6** ✪ Waterloo. Tapas £3.45-4.45, mains £6.25-10.45, 2-/3-course set lunch £5.95/7.95. This popular (though hardly authentic) theme restaurant has tapas, main courses with three vegetarian choices (£6.45), plenty of rum cocktails (£3.75 to £4.95) and live salsa Friday and Saturday evenings, with free lessons from 5pm to 6pm Sunday.

PLACES TO EAT

CHARLOTTE HINDLE

Ooh la la! Cubana brightens up Waterloo with
a taste of Latin America.

Mesón Don Felipe (☎ *7928 3237, 53 The Cut
SE1)* **Map 6** ✆ Southwark/Waterloo. Tapas £3-
5. This tapas-only place gets recommended
more often than most for its wide choice,
affordability and attractive decor.

Cafes

Konditor & Cook (☎ *7620 2700, 66 The Cut
SE1)* **Map 6** ✆ Southwark/Waterloo. Breakfast
£1.75-6.95, mains £3.50-7.85. Open for meals
8.30am-8pm Mon-Fri, 10.30am-8pm Sat. This
place at the Young Vic Theatre serves light meals
but we come here for the pastries and cakes
(£1.95 to £2.75) made by Konditor & Cook, arguably the best bakery in London, with a nearby
branch (☎ *7261 0456, 22 Cornwall Rd SE1).*

BATTERSEA (Map 10)

This part of south London, with its lovely
park and expensive mansion blocks, tends
to have more upmarket restaurants than
areas to the east and west. South of
Clapham Junction, Battersea Rise is a street
of restaurants.

Modern British

Buchan's (☎ *7228 0888, 62-4 Battersea Bridge
Rd SW11)* ✆ Sloane Square/Bus No 19, 49,
239, 319 or 345. Starters £4.25-6.25, mains
£10.95-16.95. This wine bar and restaurant
specialises in Scottish fare such as haggis
(£4.95/8.95 as starter/main course) and the
accompanying neeps and tatties, smoked salmon and so on. But with the range of Caledonian dishes being fairly limited, it ventures into
the Modern British arena too.

Ransome's Dock (☎ *7223 1611, 35-7 Parkgate Rd
SW11)* ✆ Sloane Square/Bus No 19, 49, 239,
319 or 345. Starters £4-9.50, mains £9.50-19.50.
Diners flock here not because it's on a narrow
inlet of the Thames but for the superbly prepared Modern British food: smoked Norfolk eel
with buckwheat pancakes and *crème fraîche*
(£8.75), noisettes of English lamb (£17.50) and
melt-in-your-mouth calf's liver with Italian
bacon and field mushrooms (£14.25).

CLAPHAM, WANDSWORTH & PUTNEY (Maps 1 & 2)

Visitors wouldn't normally stray this far
south for a meal, but there's at least one
reason for doing so.

Italian

Del Buongustaio (☎ *8780 9361, 283 Putney Bridge Rd SW15)* **Map 2** ✆ East Putney. Mains £10-14. People constantly sing the
praises of this Italian local eatery with southern specialities and a menu that changes each
month. Top marks for the welcoming, professional service too.

Eco (☎ *7978 1108, 162 Clapham High St SW4)*
Map 2 ✆ Clapham Common; (☎ *7738 3021, 4
Market Row, Electric Lane SW9)* **Map 15**
✆ Brixton. Starters £1.40-6.50, mains £5.20-
10.50. This Clapham institution, with an equally
celebrated branch in Brixton Market, has some
of the best pizzas (£4.50 to £7.50) and pasta
dishes in south London.

Portuguese

Café Portugal (☎ *7587 1962, 5a-6a Victoria
House, South Lambeth Rd SW8)* **Map 2**
✆ Vauxhall/Stockwell. Starters £1-4.50, mains
£6.50-12.50. Arguably the classiest option in
Little Portugal (ie, the Stockwell neighbourhood), Café Portugal serves Lusitanian favourites such as *porco à Alentejana*, a tasty casserole
of pork and clams, and *arroz de marisco*
(seafood rice), with the occasional nod to big
brother Spain.

PLACES TO EAT

Indian

The Bombay Bicycle Club (☎ 8673 6217, 95 Nightingale Lane SW12) **Map 1** Station: Wandsworth Common/⊖ Clapham South. Starters £4.50-9.50, mains £6.50-12. Those in the know tell us that the this place has the best Indian food south of the river and we can't argue – the chicken *murgh mangalore* tasted authentic enough.

Ma Goa (☎ 8780 1767, 242-4 Upper Richmond Rd SW15) **Map 2** Station: Putney. Starters £3-4.50, mains £6.50-9.50. As its name suggests, this place serves the subtle cuisine of Portugal's erstwhile colony on the western coast of India. Specialities include the owners' special spicy sausages and *Konkan gallina aur baigan* (chicken cooked with aubergine; £8.50).

CHELSEA, SOUTH KENSINGTON & EARL'S COURT (Map 10)

These three areas boast an incredible array of eateries – from Michelin-starred restaurants and upmarket 24-hour burger joints to Polish cafes and French *pâtisseries* – to suit all budgets. While in Chelsea, check out the **Sundance Market** (☎ 7351 4477, 250 King's Rd SW3, ⊖ Sloane Square), which has a number of eateries as well as stalls selling organic produce, vitamins, cosmetics and so on. It opens 9am to 8pm Monday to Saturday and 11am to 5pm Sunday.

Modern British

Bibendum (☎ 7581 5817, 81 Fulham Rd SW3) ⊖ South Kensington. Mains £15-23, 2-/3-course lunch £24/28 Mon-Fri, 3-course lunch £28 Sat & Sun. This Conran establishment graces one of London's finest settings for a restaurant, the Art Nouveau Michelin House (1911). The popular Bibendum Oyster Bar (£7.50 to £8 per half-dozen), on the ground floor, is where you really feel at the heart of the architectural finery. Upstairs is lighter and brighter.

Foxtrot Oscar (☎ 7352 7179, 79 Royal Hospital Rd SW3) ⊖ Sloane Square; (☎ 7481 2700, 16 Byward St EC3) **Map 10** ⊖ Tower Hill. Starters £4-6.25, mains £7.75-10. This place – bar first, restaurant second – serves passable dishes, but the desserts (about £4) are noteworthy.

International/Modern European

Aubergine (☎ 7352 3449, 11 Park Walk SW10) ⊖ Sloane Square/South Kensington. 2-/3-course set lunch £20/25, 3-course set dinner £48, 7-course *dégustation* £65. One of the most popular restaurants in Chelsea, Aubergine serves impeccable Modern European cuisine as set meals only.

Benjy's (☎ 7373 0245, 157 Earl's Court Rd SW5) ⊖ Earl's Court. Breakfast £3.20-4.20, lunch & dinner £3.70-4.20. Though Benjy's is nothing more than a fairly traditional caff, it's always busy and the food is cheap and filling. Serious breakfasts come with as much tea or coffee as you can drink.

Blanco's (☎ 7370 3101, 314 Earl's Court Rd SW5) ⊖ Earl's Court. Starters £1.55-3.50, tapas £2.85-5.95, mains £4.25-11.50. Blanco's is a lively and authentic tapas bar with good Spanish beer.

Chelsea Kitchen (☎ 7589 1330, 98 King's Rd SW3) ⊖ Sloane Square. Starters £1-2.80, mains £2.80-5.60, 3-course set meal £6.40. This spartan place, part of the Stockpot empire (see St James's & Mayfair earlier in this chapter), has some of the cheapest food in London.

The Collection (☎ 7225 1212, 264 Brompton Rd SW3) ⊖ South Kensington. Starters £4.75-11.75, mains £10.75-18.50 (restaurant) & £4.50-10.50 (bar). The Collection has a wonderful location in a converted gallery, with the main restaurant on a balcony overlooking the bar – great for people-watching.

Gordon Ramsay (☎ 7352 4441, 68-9 Royal Hospital Rd SW3) ⊖ Sloane Square. 3-course set lunch £30, 3-course set meal £60, 7-course *dégustation* £75. The reputation of the eponymous chef/owner proceeds him, but he sure can cook – especially his signature dishes of lobster pasta and a salad of scallops and new potatoes.

Oriel (☎ 7730 2804, 50-1 Sloane Square SW1) ⊖ Sloane Square. Starters £4.50-9, mains £7-14. With its comfortable wicker chairs and mirrors, and tables overlooking Sloane Square, Oriel makes the perfect place to meet before going shopping in King's Rd or Sloane St. There are mains such as grilled tuna steak (£10.25) and lighter fare including pasta and Thai salads (£8.25).

Troubadour (☎ 7370 1434, 265 Old Brompton Rd SW10) ⊖ Earl's Court. Full breakfast £4.95, starters £2.75-3.50, mains £4.95-9.50. Boasting an illustrious past as a coffee shop and folk-music venue, the Troubadour has hosted Bob Dylan, Eric Clapton, John Lennon and the Stones, among others. These days it still occasionally has bands, a wonderful garden for sunny days plus good-value food such as pasta and salads (£3.50), bangers and mash (£5.75) and the infamous (and huge) Troubadour omelette (£5.50).

PLACES TO EAT

American

Cactus Blue *(☎ 7823 7858, 86 Fulham Rd SW3)*
⊖ South Kensington. Starters £3.95-6.95, mains £9.95-14.95. This lovely south-western (let's just call it fancy Cal-Mex) restaurant has an impressive list of tequilas and Mexican wine as well as great fajitas and quesadillas.

Henry J Bean's *(☎ 7352 9255, 195 King's Rd SW3)* ⊖ Sloane Square/South Kensington. Starters £4.50-6.50, mains £5.50-7.95. This popular American bar and restaurant has a garden complete with fans and heaters.

French

A large number of French people live in South Kensington, and you'll find a lot of French-operated businesses there, particularly on and around Bute St (SW7), just south-west of South Kensington tube station including:

Bonne Bouche *(☎ 7584 9839, 22 Bute St)* Prices £1-3. Fine cakes, sweets and baguettes are available here to take away.

Brasserie de l'Institut *(☎ 7589 5433, French Institute, 17 Queensberry Place SW7)* Starters £3.75-5.50, mains £4.95-9.95. The French Institute's brasserie serves, among other dishes, salads (£5 to £6) and sandwiches (£2.50 to £3).

FrancoFill *(☎ 7584 0087, 1 Old Brompton Rd SW7)* Meals £8-12. Around the corner from Bute St is this delightful cafe-restaurant.

La Grande Bouchée *(☎ 7589 8346, 31 Bute St)* Sandwiches £1.50-2.10. This is a well-stocked delicatessen that also serves sandwiches and baguettes.

Rôtisserie Jules *(☎ 7584 0600, 6-8 Bute St)* Starters £2.75-4.90, mains £4.95-9.75. A simple French-style cafeteria with flame-roasted chicken (£4.95 to £9.75) and *gigot d'agneau* (leg of lamb).

Italian & Mediterranean

Daphne's *(☎ 7589 4257, 112 Draycott Ave SW3)* ⊖ South Kensington. Starters £4.75-10.50, mains £7.50-19. This place, popular with celebrities and their followers, is small enough to be intimate but large enough not to be claustrophobic. It serves delicious Mediterranean-style meat and fish as well as pasta and risotto dishes.

Pizza Express *(☎ 7351 5031, 152-4 King's Rd SW3)* ⊖ Sloane Square. Starters £1.60-3.40, pizzas £4.75-7.55. This branch of the chain is worth a visit just to have a look at its location: it's in the Pheasantry building, with an ornate facade and portico dating from the mid-18th century.

Pizza Organic *(☎ 7589 9613, 20 Old Brompton Rd SW7)* ⊖ South Kensington. Starters £2.60-5.95, mains £4.75-14.95, set lunch £5.95 noon-4.30pm Mon-Fri. This place, on a busy corner of South Kensington, has a huge selection of pizzas (£4.75 to £7.60) and pastas (£6.60 to £7.85).

Spago *(☎ 7225 2407, 6 Glendower Place SW7)* ⊖ South Kensington. Starters £2.80-5.20, mains £4.60-9.80. This excellent-value restaurant with a good range of pastas and pizzas is convenient for the South Kensington museums. There is live music on Friday evening.

Asian

Krungtap *(☎ 7259 2314, 227 Old Brompton Rd SW10)* ⊖ Earl's Court. Starters £2.75-3.95, mains £4.25-6.25. Krungtap (the Thai name for Bangkok) is a busy, friendly cafe with karaoke from 7pm to midnight Friday to Sunday.

Mr Wing *(☎ 7370 4450, 242-4 Old Brompton Rd SW5)* ⊖ Earl's Court. Starters £4.95-7.50, mains £6.50-14. This is one of London's more interesting Chinese restaurants, with jungle decor and fish tanks in the basement and live jazz at 8.15pm Thursday to Saturday.

New Culture Revolution *(☎ 7352 9281, 305 King's Rd SW3)* ⊖ Sloane Square; *(☎ 7267 2700, 43 Parkway NW1)* **Map 3** ⊖ Camden Town; *(☎ 7833 9083, 42 Duncan St N1)* **Map 4** ⊖ Angel. Starters £2.20-5.50, mains £4.50-6.90. This is a trendy, good-value dumpling and noodle bar.

Other Cuisines

Daquise *(☎ 7589 6117, 20 Thurloe St SW7)* ⊖ South Kensington. Starters £2.50-4, mains £5.50-12.50, set lunch £6.80. This place is a real dinosaur – but a loveable little tyrannosaurus indeed – and close to the museums. It's a rather shabby-looking Polish cafe-diner, with a good range of vodkas and extremely reasonably priced food. Expect dishes such as the 'hunter's stew' called *bigosz* (£6.50) or *golabki* (pork knuckle; £9.50).

Nando's *(☎ 7259 2544, 204 Earl's Court Rd SW5)* ⊖ Earl's Court; *(☎ 7424 9040, 57 Chalk Farm Rd NW1)* **Map 3** ⊖ Camden Town. Dishes £2.45-4.95, set meals £4.75-6.95. This almost-fast-food chain, with branches on virtually every high street, serves Portuguese-style flame-grilled chicken *piri-piri* (£2.45 to £4.95). There's a quarter-/half-chicken with coleslaw and rice or chips (£4.75/6.95) and vegetarian burgers/pitas (£3.10/3.80).

Eating on a Budget

London restaurant prices may look terrifying – and they are – but there are still ways to eat without breaking the bank.

The best way to keep prices down, of course, is to cater for yourself. If you're staying in a hostel you will probably have access to cooking facilities, but – weather permitting – London's parks and open spaces also provide excellent picnic sites. Beware of some of the smaller grocer's shops where prices are marked up considerably; look instead for a **Tesco** or the smaller **Tesco Metro** branches, Britain's most successful supermarket chain, with outlets at 311 Oxford St; 21 Bedford St in Covent Garden; opposite Liverpool Street station at 156 Bishopsgate; in the City at 80 Cheapside; in Notting Hill at 224 Portobello Rd; and at Canada Square in Canary Wharf. Branches of **Safeway**, **Asda** and **Sainsbury's**, which are found throughout the city, are equally competitively priced. **Waitrose** is more upmarket and expensive.

If breakfast is not included in your hotel or hostel and you're within striking distance of Oxford St W1 (Maps 6 & 7), the department stores there do big, sustaining breakfasts for very reasonable prices. **Bhs** (1st floor, 252-58 Oxford St) serves a breakfast of six items (£2.45) and one with eight items (£2.99) 9.30am to 11.30am. Nearby **Debenhams** (2nd floor, 334-48 Oxford St) does a six-item breakfast (£1.95) 9.30am till 11am Monday to Saturday.

In the restaurant and cafe listings in this chapter, the International, English and/or Vegetarian invariably include budget options, with individual prices (or at least a range) listed. Also check the listings for the various international cuisines; Indian (around Brick Lane and in Drummond St near Euston) and Chinese (especially in Soho) are always safe bets. Japanese-style noodle bars, where you can eat for about £5, are becoming a way of life in London. Be on the lookout too for a new breed of budget eatery: upmarket soup kitchens such as Soup near Oxford Circus.

KENSINGTON & KNIGHTSBRIDGE (Maps 5, 6 & 10)

The restaurants, cafes and bars in these posh 'villages' of west and south-west London cater for a very well-heeled clientele, but there's always something good and more affordable just off the high streets.

International/Modern European

Arcadia (☎ 7937 4294, 35 Kensington Court W8) **Map 5** ↔ High Street Kensington. Starters £3.95-5.95, mains £9.50-15.95, 1-/2-/3-course set lunch £8.95/12.95/15.95. Arcadia is one of the more interesting of a cluster of restaurants in Kensington Court. Its interior, with a pair of macaws preening and showing off amid the mirrors and murals, is classy and distinctive, and the menu features dishes such as rack of lamb with sautéed spinach, best sampled via the set lunch.

Fifth Floor (☎ 7823 1839, Harvey Nichols, 109-25 Knightsbridge SW1) **Map 5** ↔ Knightsbridge. Starters £8.50-15.50, mains £19.50-24, 2-/3-course set lunch £20/24.50. This restaurant, bar and cafe is the perfect place to drop after you've shopped.

Launceston Place (☎ 7937 6912, 1a Launceston Place W8) **Map 10** ↔ High Street Kensington. Starters £6-9, mains £16.50-17.50, 2-/3-course set lunch £15.50/18.50. Sister restaurant to Kensington Place in Notting Hill (see the following section) but as different from it as night from day, Launceston Place is tucked away in the quiet back streets of Kensington. It's a pretty, subdued, intimate restaurant, ideal for couples.

American

Sticky Fingers (☎ 7938 5338, 1a Phillimore Gardens W8) **Map 5** ↔ High Street Kensington. Starters £3.75-5.95, mains £6.95-14.95. Sticky Fingers is where ex-Rolling Stone Bill Wyman has chosen to hang up his gold discs and other memorabilia, but it's still a rather good place serving burgers (£7.95 to £10.95), salads (£6.95 to £9.95) and sandwiches (£6.95 to £8.95).

French

Parisienne Chophouse (☎ 7590 9999, 3 Yeoman's Row SW3) **Map 10** ↔ South Kensington. Starters £5-10.50, mains £11.50-14.50, 2-course set lunch £9.95 (£13.50 Sun). *Enfant terrible*

Marco Pierre White is at it again trying to change the face of Londoners' eating habits. This time he sets out to create unpretentious, unfused French food and succeeds marvellously.

Italian

Bellini's (☎ 7937 5520, 47 Kensington Court W8) **Map 5** ✪ High Street Kensington. Starters £1.60-5.95, mains £5.95 13.75, 2-/3-course set lunch till 7pm £7.25/8.75. This stylish restaurant has a few pavement tables and views of a flower-bedecked alley.

Pizza on the Park (☎ 7235 5273, 11 Knightsbridge SW5) **Map 6** ✪ Hyde Park Corner. Main courses £6.50-11. This place is as popular for its nightly jazz in the basement as for its pizza. There's also a spacious restaurant upstairs and, if you're lucky, a few tables overlooking Hyde Park. Breakfast is available all day from 8.15am and afternoon tea starts at 3.15pm.

Zafferano (☎ 7235 5800, 15-16 Lowndes St SW1) **Map 10** ✪ Knightsbridge. 2-/3-course set lunch £18.50/21.50, 2-/3-/4-course set dinner £29.50/35.95/39.50. This glamorous place, sparkling with diamonds and wall-to-wall with perma-tans, serves excellent seasonal and inspired Italian dishes that succeed every time.

Polish

Ognisko Polskie (☎ 7589 4635, 55 Prince's Gate SW7) **Map 10** ✪ South Kensington. Mains £7.90-13.90, 3-course set meal £8.50. The 'Polish Hearth' is the Poland of another world and time, with reasonably priced food served in a clubby dining room filled with portraits, chandeliers and mirrors.

Wódka (☎ 7937 6513, 12 St Alban's Grove W8) **Map 5** ✪ High Street Kensington. Mains £8.90-13.90, 2-/3-course lunch menu £10.90/13.50. This Polish place lies in a quiet residential area away from the hustle and bustle of Kensington High Street. There are *blinis* (filled pancakes; £5.50-11.90) and a large array of clear and flavoured vodkas (£2.25 to £2.75 per shot).

Asian

Vong (☎ 7235 1010, Berkeley Hotel, Wilton Place SW1) **Map 5** ✪ Knightsbridge. Starters £7.50-13, mains £16-32.50, 2-/3-course lunch menu £18.50/21, selection of starters pre- or post-theatre £18.50-22.50. This super-trendy Thai restaurant is a place to be seen, though most people will find the food, with its French accents, as enjoyable and memorable as the decor is spartan.

NOTTING HILL, BAYSWATER & PADDINGTON (Map 5)

Notting Hill has all sorts of interesting places to eat, and there are literally dozens of eateries lining Queensway and Westbourne Grove, with everything from cheap takeaways to good quality restaurants.

English/Modern British

Geales (☎ 7727 7528, 2 Farmer St W8) ✪ Notting Hill Gate. Starters £3.25-11.50, mains £7.25-11.50. This popular fish restaurant established in 1939 prices everything according to weight and season. Fish and chips costs about £9.25, and it's worth every penny.

Sausage & Mash Café (☎ 8968 8898, 268 Portobello Rd W10) ✪ Ladbroke Grove. Starters £3.50, mains £5.75-7. Under the elevated Westway, this is just the ticket if you're looking for cheap English stodge in upbeat surroundings.

Veronica's (☎ 7229 5079, 3 Hereford Rd W2) ✪ Bayswater. Starters £4.50-8.45, mains £12.50-16.95, 2/3-course set menu 13.50/17.50 (lunch Mon-Fri, dinner Mon-Thur). This place is doing its best to establish that England does have a culinary heritage, with some fascinating dishes dating back to as early as the 14th century.

International/Modern European

Bali Sugar (☎ 7221 4477, 33a All Saints Rd W11) ✪ Westbourne Park. Starters £4.50-11.50, mains £13.10-17.20. Bali Sugar has moved into where its parent restaurant, the Sugar Club (see the earlier West End section), used to be. The food is fantastic Asian/Mediterranean fusion and the decor spare but elegant.

Kensington Place (☎ 7727 3184, 201-207 Kensington Church St W8) ✪ Notting Hill Gate. Starters £5-9.50 mains £11-18.50, 3-course lunch £16. This restaurant has an impressive glass frontage, a design-driven interior and consistently good food, but seating seems cramped and the acoustics are bad.

Italian

L'Accento (☎ 7243 2201, 16 Garway Rd W2) ✪ Bayswater. Starters £5-8, mains £12-14, 2-course set menu £12.50. This simply decorated restaurant's set menu could include mussel stew in white wine with fresh herbs, followed by roast leg of lamb with balsamic vinegar. Once you step away from this menu, though, L'Accento becomes a lot more expensive

Assagi (☎ 7792 5501, 39 Chepstow Place W2) ✪ Notting Hill Gate. Starters £7.95-10.95, mains £15.95-18.95. Assagi, a posh neighbourhood

JULIET COOMBE

After mooching around Portobello Rd Market, sit back and relax with a cuppa.

Italian place above the Chepstow pub, serves elaborate starters but pared down main courses such as veal liver *(fegato di vitello)*, roast lamb and sea bass.

Est Est Est (☎ 7221 1110, 147-9 Notting Hill Gate W11) ✆ Notting Hill Gate. Starters £2.75-5.90, pizzas & pastas £5.50-6.95. This branch of a cheap (but cheerful) Italian chain of eateries is a good bet for pasta or pizza, especially between noon and 6pm when they cost a uniform £4.95.

Osteria Basilico (☎ 7727 9372, 29 Kensington Park Rd W11) ✆ Notting Hill Gate/Ladbroke Grove. Starters £6-7.50, mains £6-14.50. Osteria Basilico offers a good mix of Italian rustic charm and west London chic, with an authentic menu and a lively, relaxed atmosphere. The tables by the window are best, but you will need to book. The pasta (£6 to £7) and fish dishes (£12 to £14.50) are recommended. There's also pizza (£6.50 to £8).

Greek & Middle Eastern

Costas Fish Restaurant (☎ 7229 3794, 12-14 Hillgate St W8) ✆ Notting Hill Gate. Starters £1.80-2.60, mains £3.90-6.50. This reliable Greek eatery has a huge array of fresher-than-fresh fish dishes at market prices (eg, haddock £6.50), which some maintain is better than at its closest competitor, Geales (see earlier in this section). Salads (£2 to £6.50) are also good.

Kalamaras Greek Taverna (☎ 7727 5082, 66 Inverness Mews W2) ✆ Bayswater. Starters £1.90-4.90, mains £3.90-6.50. The surroundings aren't anything special, but the food is worth a trip to this Greek spot in a quiet mews off Queensway.

Manzara (☎ 7727 3062, 24 Pembridge Rd W11) ✆ Notting Hill Gate. Starters £2.65-3.45, mains £5.45-7.45 This simple place offers cheap but fresh and well-prepared Turkish food, with great *pides* (£5.45 to £7.95), daily specials and a lots of vegetarian options.

Indian

Khan's (☎ 7727 5420, 13-15 Westbourne Grove W2) ✆ Bayswater. Starters £1.45-2.75, mains £3.70-6.75. Khan's is a vast and popular Indian restaurant where diners eat amid palms and pillars and get out quickly. It's fairly authentic and it's good value but Khan's is really just for a quick curry. There are vegetarian dishes (£2.70) and a selection of meat and seafood curries (£3.20 to £6.75).

Modhubon (☎ 7727 3399, 29 Pembridge Rd W11) ✆ Notting Hill Gate. Starters £1.95-4.95, mains £3.95-11.95, set lunch £4.50, daily all-you-can-eat buffet £7.95. This place has been recommended for its inexpensive Indian food and its budget-saving buffet.

Standard (☎ 7229 0600, 21-23 Westbourne Grove W2) ✆ Bayswater. Mains £4-7. A neighbour of Khan's, the Standard serves excellent and good-value Indian food.

Asian

Inaho (☎ 7221 8495, 4 Hereford Rd W2) ✆ Bayswater. Starters £2.50-4.50, mains £6.80-10.50, set lunch £8.50-12, set dinner £20-24. This tiny but inviting Japanese restaurant has good value set meals such as *tempura* (£20) and *teriyaki* (£24) as well as rice and noodle dishes (£4 to £6) and *tonkatsu* (pork chop; £7.30).

PLACES TO EAT

Mandalay (☎ 7258 3696, 444 Edgware Rd W2) ↔ Edgware Road. Starters £1.20-5, mains £3.90-6.90. This unbelievably good-value place, which looks like a cross between a down-at-heel solicitor's office and a fortune teller's, is London's only Burmese restaurant. Try the spicy mokhingar soup with noodles redolent of shrimp paste and fish sauce.

Mandarin Kitchen (☎ 7727 9468, 14-16 Queensway W2) ↔ Bayswater/Queensway. Mains £5.95-25. This highly regarded Cantonese restaurant specialises in seafood.

Satay House (☎ 7723 6763, 13 Sale Place W2) ↔ Edgware Road/Paddington. Mains £4.50-9.50. The only time we ventured into Paddington was to catch the Heathrow Express until we discovered Satay House. It serves probably the most authentic Malaysian food in north London.

Tawana (☎ 7229 3785, 3 Westbourne Grove W2) ↔ Bayswater/Royal Oak. Starters £4.50-4.75, mains £5.50-5.75, set lunch £6.50. Tawana is a well-presented Thai place with a large selection of dishes.

Other Cuisines

Belgo Zuid (☎ 8982 8400, 124 Ladbroke Grove W11) ↔ Ladbroke Grove. Starters £3.95-6.95, mains £8.50-15.95. The spectacular interior of this branch of Belgo Centraal (see the earlier Covent Garden & the Strand and later Camden Town section) opposite the tube station is worth a visit in itself.

Burritos (☎ 7727 7000, 19 Westbourne Grove W2) ↔ Bayswater/Royal Oak. Dishes £2.95. This basic place serves better-than-average Tex-Mex and Mexican dishes such as burritos, fajitas and tacos to eat-in or takeaway.

Mandola (☎ 7229 4734, 139-141 Westbourne Grove W2) ↔ Bayswater. Starters £2.90-5.25, mains £4.75-10.50. Mandola offers something entirely different: vegetarian Sudanese dishes such as tamia (£4.75), a kind of felafel, and fifilia (£8.95), a vegetable curry. Meat dishes such as chicken halla cost around £9.50. Try the unusual shorba fule (£3.45), a meat and peanut soup.

Cafes

Café Grove (☎ 7243 1094, 253a Portobello Rd) ↔ Ladbroke Grove. Breakfast £4.50-8.50, lunch £4.95-7.25. Open 9.30-4.30 Mon-Fri, 9.30am-6pm Sat, 10.30am-5pm Sun. Head here for gigantic and imaginative breakfasts (chilli sausages, pints of cappuccino) as well as cheap and cheerful vegetarian. The large balcony overlooking the market is great for watching all the action on a weekday or Satur day morning.

Churrería Española (☎ 7727 3444, 177-9 Queensway W2) ↔ Bayswater. Dishes £3-6. This unexpected cafe serves a variety of cheap dishes, including a good selection of vegetarian ones and paella (£6). They also do cooked English breakfasts (£3.95).

MAIDA VALE (Map 5)

Little Venice, a rather ambitiously named area of Maida Vale, not far from St John's Wood, is nonetheless charming and holds a couple of secret 'finds' that food lovers will love.

Modern European

Jason's (☎ 7286 6752, Jason's Wharf, opposite 60 Blomfield Rd W9) ↔ Warwick Avenue Starters £3.95-8.25 mains £11.95-19.75, 2-/3 course set meal £17.95/21.50. While boating along the Grand Union Canal you might just want to stop for lunch at Jason's, which serves superb fresh fish dishes with French, Mauritian and Creole slants. There's outside seating too.

Italian

Green Olive (☎ 7289 2469, 5 Warwick Place W9) ↔ Warwick Avenue. 2-/3-course set lunch £20.50/23.50 & dinner £23/26.50. This neighbourhood Italian place has creative Italian food and comes highly recommended by the Maida Vale cognoscenti.

Get into the groove at Café Grove, another slice of Portobello Rd charm.

EUSTON (Map 3)

While 'Euston' and 'good food' do not usually a valid phrase make, a street just southwest of the station is a mecca for veggies looking for a little bite in their *legumes*.

Vegetarian

Drummond St (⊖ Euston Square or Euston) has a number of good South Indian vegetarian restaurants.

Chutneys (☎ 7388 0604, 124 Drummond St) Mains £2.30-6.10, all-you-can-eat lunch buffet £5.45. The lunch buffet here is better than Diwana's and it's available all day on Sunday.

Diwana (☎ 7387 5556, 121 Drummond St) Starters £2.30, mains £2.80-6.20, all-you-can-eat lunch buffet £5.10. The first (and some say still the best) of its kind on the street, specialises in Bombay-style *bel poori* (a kind of 'party mix' snack) and *dosas*.

Ravi Shankar (☎ 7388 6458, 133-5 Drummond St) Starters £1.95-2.70, mains £3.50-6.95. Chutneys' cousin in the same chain is perhaps the best choice of this trio for an evening meal.

CAMDEN, KENTISH TOWN & HIGHGATE (Maps 3 & 12)

Camden High Street is lined with good places to eat, although to watch the Sunday day-trippers snacking on takeaway sausages and chips you'd hardly believe it.

English

Castle's (☎ 7485 2196, 229 Royal College St NW1) Map 3 ⊖ Camden Town. Dishes £1.75-3.55. Castle's is another member of that almost extinct species: a real live pie and mash caff with Formica tables and plastic chairs. You can get pies with liquor and mash (£1.75) and jellied eels (£1.80).

International

The Highgate (☎ 7485 8442, Highgate Studios, 53-79 Highgate Rd NW5) Map 12 ⊖ Kentish Town. Starters £2.50-6.50, mains £6.50-7.50. A welcome new addition to this gastronmically challenged area of north-west London, The Highgate offers a frequently changing menu of hearty, global dishes to lithesome young locals in its sleek upstairs bar and downstairs restaurant (agorophobics should steer clear of the latter).

Ruby in the Dust (☎ 7485 2744, 102 Camden High St NW1) Map 3 ⊖ Camden Town. Starters £2-6, mains £6.95-9.95. This atmospheric, cheerful branch of a bar/cafe chain has Mexican snacks, soup (£3.25) and main courses such as bangers and mash or burgers (£6.95).

SauCe (☎ 7482 0777, 214 Camden High St NW1) Map 3 ⊖ Camden Town. Starters £2.75-4.95, mains £5.95-12.25, all-day breakfast £6.50. This basement cafe/restaurant serves dishes prepared only with ingredients certified by the UK and the EU as organic (with a few exceptions). Try the crab cakes with sweet chilli sauce (£4.25) or even the hamburgers (£6.95).

French

Café Delancey (☎ 7387 1985, 3 Delancey St NW1) Map 3 ⊖ Camden Town. Starters £4-6.55, mains £8.15. The granddaddy of French-style brasseries in London, Café Delancey offers the chance to get a decent cup of coffee with a snack or a full meal in relaxed European-style surroundings complete with newspapers. Wine starts at £7.50 for a half-bottle. The cramped toilets, bickering staff and Charles Aznavour crooning in the background seem suitably Parisian *aussi*.

Italian

Marine Ices (☎ 7482 9003, 8 Haverstock Hill NW3) Map 3 ⊖ Chalk Farm. Dishes £5.20-6.30. As its name suggests, Marine Ices started out as a Sicilian ice-cream parlour but these days it does some savoury dishes, including pizzas (£5.20 to £6.30) and pastas (£5.60 to £5.95). Try some of the excellent ice cream and sundaes (eat in £2.40 to £5.55, takeaway £1.20 to £3.50).

Pizza Express (☎ 7267 0101, 187 Kentish Town Rd NW5) Map 3 ⊖ Kentish Town. Starters £1.55-3.10, salads £4.95-7.20, pizzas £4.45-7.45. This is a Pizza Express branch with a difference: a converted university building with a balcony bar overlooking a large dining room and an open kitchen. Pizzas average around £6. There's sometimes live jazz at weekends.

Spanish

Bar Gansa (☎ 7267 8909, 2 Inverness St NW1) Map 3 ⊖ Camden Town. Breakfast £3.95, set lunches £4.50 noon-4.30pm Mon-Fri, mains £6.50-7.95. This arty bar/cafe has tapas (£2.50 to £4) and more elaborate Spanish mains. Service is good and the Spanish staff are friendly.

El Parador (☎ 7387 2789, 245 Eversholt St NW1) Map 3 ⊖ Mornington Crescent. Starters £3.30 tapas, £3.50-5, mains £4-6. El Parador is a quiet

Spanish place where the excellent selection of vegetarian dishes and tapas includes *empanadillas de espinacas y queso* (a spinach and cheese dish; £4), with meat and fish dishes just a little more expensive (£4.80).

Asian

Asakusa (☎ 7388 8533, 265 Eversholt St NW1) **Map 3** ⊖ Mornington Crescent. Mains £3-6.30, set meals £5.70-9.60. Open 6pm-11.30pm Mon-Sat. For affordable Japanese – not necessarily an oxymoron – in Camden Town, head for Asakusa where they serve set menus such as prawn tempura with *miso* soup and rice. Sushi costs £1 to £2 per piece and an assorted small/large dish costs £5/8.50.

Lemongrass (☎ 7284 1116, 243 Royal College St) **Map 3** ⊖ Camden Town. Starters £2.60-4.30, £4.80-7.90, set meals £14 (2-person minimum). Open 7pm-10.30pm Mon-Sat. The cuisine at Lemongrass is Cambodian influenced rather than classic Khmer, which makes many dishes indistinguishable from their Thai counterparts. But it's quite good and the staff are keen to please. Smoking is not permitted.

Silks & Spice (☎ 7267 5751, 28 Chalk Farm NW) **Map 3** ⊖ Camden Town; (☎ 7636 2718, 23 Foley St W1) **Map 6** ⊖ Oxford Circus. Starters £4-5, mains £5-12, lunch £4.95-6.20. The Camden branch of the Thai/Malaysian restaurant chain does cheap express lunches and 'beat-the-clock' dinner from 5pm to 8pm (eg, eat at 5.30pm and pay £5.30).

Taste of Siam (☎ 7380 0665, 45 Camden High St NW1) ⊖ Mornington Crescent. Starters £3.30-5.50, mains £5.75-6.75. This place serves passable Thai cuisine from a central location.

Thanh Binh (☎ 7267 9820, 14 Chalk Farm Rd NW1) **Map 3** ⊖ Camden Town. Starters £2.80-7.30, mains £4-7.80, takeaway lunchboxes £3.80. A quiet eatery opposite Camden Market, Thanh Binh serves decent Vietnamese dishes.

Other Cuisines

Belgo Noord (☎ 7267 0718, 72 Chalk Farm Rd NW1) **Map 3** ⊖ Chalk Farm. Starters £3.95-6.95, mains £8.95-15.95. This branch of the Belgo chain has almost exactly the same design and food as its cousins in Covent Garden and Notting Hill. See the earlier Covent Garden & the Strand and Notting Hill, Bayswater & Paddington sections.

Lemonia (☎ 7586 7454, 89 Regent's Park Rd NW1) **Map 3** ⊖ Chalk Farm. Starters £2.80-4.50, mains £7.25-13.50, set lunch £7.95 (Mon-Fri). This upmarket and very popular Greek

restaurant offers good-value food and a lively atmosphere. They serve meze (£13.50 per person) and both the vegetarian and meat *moussaka* (£8) are particularly tasty.

Trojka (☎ 7483 3765, 101 Regent's Park Rd NW1) **Map 3** ⊖ Chalk Farm. Starters £2.50-3.70, mains £5.50-8.50. Trojka serves good-value Eastern European/Russian dishes such as herrings with dill sauce (£3.20), Polish *bigosz* (a cabbage 'stew' with mixed meats; £4) and salt beef (£6.50) in an attractive, sky-lit restaurant. It has a house wine but it's also BYO (£3 corkage).

African & Caribbean

Cottons Rhum Shop, Bar & Restaurant (☎ 7482 1096, 55 Chalk Farm Rd NW1) **Map 3** ⊖ Chalk Farm. Starters £4.55-6.25, mains £11.25-19.95, lunch menu £4.25-7.95. Come to Cottons for authentic Caribbean favourites such as jerk chicken and curried goat (£11.25 to £11.85), but beware of those potent rum-based cocktails (£4 to £85); they'll knock your socks – and most everything else – off.

Mango Room (☎ 7482 5065, 10 Kentish Town Rd NW1) **Map 3** ⊖ Camden Town. Starters £3.70-3.80, mains £8-11. Mango Room is a more upmarket and refined choice than Cottons for island food, with delightful starters like fluffy crab and potato balls (£3.70) and main courses such as a platter of cooked vegetables (£9) including *ackee*, a yellow-skinned Jamaican fruit that has an uncanny resemblance to scrambled eggs, and curried goat with hot pepper and spices (£8).

Cafes

Curly Dog Café (☎ 7483 0433, 75a Gloucester Ave NW1) **Map 3** ⊖ Camden Town. Breakfast £3.70, lunch £1.95-4. This cosy little place near the Engineer pub (see the Entertainment chapter) is great for breakfast, lunch, tea or a quick snack.

ISLINGTON (Maps 2 & 4)

Islington is an excellent place for a night out. At the last count there were more than 60 cafes and restaurants between Angel and Highbury Corner, with most of the action on Upper St.

Modern European

Duke of Cambridge (☎ 7359 9450, 30 St Peter's St N1) **Map 4** ⊖ Angel; *Crown Organic* (☎ 8981 9998, 223 Grove Rd E3) **Map 2** ⊖ Mile End/

Bus: No 8 or 277. Starters £4.50-7.50, mains £8.50-12.50. The UK's first 100% organic gastropub has spawned a lot of imitators but is still way out ahead.

Granita *(☎ 7226 3222, 127 Upper St N1)* **Map 4** ⊖ Angel/Highbury & Islington. Mains £10-14.50, 2-/3-course set Sunday lunch £12.50/14.95. Minimalist to the point of sterility, Granita remains one of the best restaurants in Islington, with well-prepared Mediterranean-inspired (but not exclusively so) food.

Lola's *(☎ 7359 1932, The Mall, Camden Passage, 359 Upper St N1)* **Map 4** ⊖ Angel. Starters £5.50-7.50, mains £12-15. This award-winning restaurant is celebrated for its lovely decor, changing menu and popular Sunday brunch with live jazz.

French

Le Mercury *(☎ 7354 4088, 140a Upper St N1)* **Map 4** ⊖ Angel/Highbury & Islington. Starters £3.25, mains £5.95. 2-/3-course meals £5.45/6.95 till 6pm Mon-Sat. With all the starters and main courses the same low prices (though there are occasional main courses specials for £7 to £10) this three-floor French eatery is a boon for budget travellers.

Le Sacré Coeur Bistro *(☎ 7354 2618, 18 Theberton St N1)* **Map 4** ⊖ Angel. Starters £3.50-5.20, mains £7.75-11.50, 2-/3-course set meals £5.50/6.95 Mon-Fri & £6.95/8.50 Sat & Sun. This cramped little restaurant has very reliable French food, including tempting *moules-frites* (£6.50).

Tartuf *(☎ 7288 0954, 88 Upper St N1)* **Map 4** ⊖ Angel. Dishes £2.80-6.50, 2-course set meals £3.90 & £5.90. We label this one French but, well, it's Alsatian to be precise. This cosy, little place serves *tartes flambées* (or *flammekuchen* in Alsatian), a filling dish that is a thin layer of pastry topped with cream, onion, bacon and sometimes cheese or mushrooms and cooked in a wood-fired oven.

Italian

Cantina Italia *(☎ 7226 9791, 19 Canonbury Lane N1)* **Map 4** ⊖ Highbury & Islington/Angel. Starters £4-8.50, mains £9-14. This Sardinian-owned trattoria has some excellent (and usual mains) but we usually come here for the pizza and the pasta.

Pizzeria Oregano *(☎ 7288 1123, 18-19 St Alban's Place N1)* **Map 4** ⊖ Angel. Starters £4.95-5.95, mains £6.95-11.95, pizza £4.75-£8.25, pasta £6.95-7.95. This cheerful little place, down a small lane not far from Islington's Business

Design Centre, serves mostly pizzas cooked in wood-fired ovens though there are usually main-course choices on offer as well.

Primos Lounge *(☎ 7354 5717, 54 Islington Park St N1)* **Map 4** ⊖ Highbury & Islington/Angel; *(☎ 7626 5009, 19 Bevis Marks EC3)* **Map 4** ⊖ Aldgate. Starters £4-8.50, mains £8.50-12.50, pizza £7.50-9.50, pasta £7.50-10.50. This gem of a place serves some of the best Italian food in London (and not just the standard pasta and pizza but superb maintoo). The decor is modern and upbeat, the front bar always lively and the service seamless.

Solo Stefano *(☎ 7700 6040, 207 Liverpool Rd N1)* **Map 4** ⊖ Angel/Highbury & Islington. Starters £3.85-5.90, mains £4.95-16.95, lunch specials £6.50. What was once a Turkish place has metamorphosed into a stylish Italian restaurant decorated with modern paintings and carvings. Try the veal in lemon and white wine (£8.40) or the chicken breast stuffed with garlic butter and mushrooms (£8.20).

Middle Eastern

Angel Mangal *(7359 7777, 139 Upper St N1)* **Map 4** ⊖ Angel/Highbury & Islington. Mains £6-8.50. No longer a branch of the similarly named establishments in Dalston (see the following section) and we're not saying why as family business is the family's business, Angel Mangal serves some of the best Turkish meze, grilled lamb chops and pigeon and salads in north London.

Other Cuisines

Afghan Kitchen *(☎ 7359 8019, 35 Islington Green N1)* **Map 4** ⊖ Angel. Mains £5.50-6. This tiny, budget place serves up such Afghan delights as *dogh*, a yoghurt and mint concoction, and lamb cooked with spinach.

Cuba Libre *(☎ 7354 9998, 72 Upper St N1)* **Map 4** ⊖ Angel. Starters £4.25-5.70, mains £7.25-11.75. This place has tapas and other, more filling, dishes such as *moros y christianos* (beans and rice). There's a popular bar with extended hours at the back (see Islington under Pubs & Bars in the Entertainment chapter) where you can have six tapas for £6.95 or lunch for £5.

Yellow River Café *(☎ 7354 8833, 206 Upper St N1)* **Map 4** ⊖ Highbury & Islington/Angel. Mains £5.50-9.50. This is a branch of a popular, upbeat chain serving eclectic Asian cuisine under the watchful gaze (in every sense) of American TV chef Ken Hom.

Vegetarian

Ravi Shankar (☎ 7833 5849, 422 St John St EC1)
Map 4 ⊖ Angel. Starters £1.95-2.75, mains
£3.50-4.30. This small, inexpensive restaurant
has some of the best Indian vegetarian food in
London. There's another branch near Euston
station (see the Euston section earlier in this
chapter).

STOKE NEWINGTON, FINSBURY PARK & DALSTON (Maps 1 & 2)

A cosmopolitan area of north-east London,
Finsbury Park has a good mix of restaurants at very reasonable prices. Stoke Newington Church St is lined with an array of
ethnic restaurants.

Italian

La Porchetta (☎ 7281 2892, 147 Stroud Green Rd
N4) **Map 1** ⊖ Finsbury Park; (☎ 7288 2488,
141 Upper St N1) **Map 4** ⊖ Angel/Highbury
& Islington. Starters £2.10-4.70, mains £4-8. La
Porchetta serves such tasty home-made pizzas
and pastas that there's invariably a queue at the
door in the evenings. The branch in Islington is
less cosy and more frenetic.

Middle Eastern

Mangal (☎ 7275 8981, 10 Arcola St E8) **Map 2**
Station: Dalston Kingsland/Bus: No 67, 76, 149
or 243. Starters £2.50-6, mains £6-8.50. This
hole-in-the-wall Turkish eatery is London's
worse-kept little secret 'find'. It serves the
freshest kebabs and other grilled food cooked
over a smoking *ocakbasi* (wood-fired brazier)
and served with excellent salads. It's BYO only
(though there's an off-licence around the
corner).
Mangal II (☎ 7254 7888, 4 Stoke Newington Rd
N16) **Map 2** Station: Dalston Kingsland/Bus:
No 67, 76, 149 or 243. Mains £5.50-11. Mangal's more upmarket (and expensive) sister
restaurant a short distance away has plates of
mixed meze (£4), kebabs and other main dishes
such as *yoghurtlu* (grilled lamb chucks with
bread and yoghurt).

Vegetarian

Rasa (☎ 7249 0344, 55 Stoke Newington Church
St N16) **Map 1** Station: Stoke Newington/
Bus: No 73. Mains £3.50-5.50. This South
Indian vegetarian restaurant gets rave reviews
(and attracts queues) for dishes not often seen
(or tasted) outside private homes. Smoking is
not allowed.

HAMPSTEAD (Map 12)

Hampstead, the well-to-do 'village' south-
west of Hampstead Heath, has loads of
good restaurants within easy walking distance of Hampstead tube station.

Italian

La Gaffe (☎ 7794 7526, La Gaffe Hotel, 107-11
Heath St NW3) Lunch £4.75-8.50, dinner starters
£3.50-8.75, mains £10-17.75. This comfortable,
family-run restaurant, in an 18th-century cottage
that is now a hotel, has been going forever.
Pizza Express (☎ 7433 1600, 70 Heath St NW3)
Mains £4.75-7.75. If you want your pizza a bit
more industrial, head southwards from La Gaffe
to this fancy branch of the popular chain.
There's live jazz on Friday evenings.

Other Cuisines

Al Casbah (☎ 7435 7632, 45 Hampstead High St
NW3) Starters £4.70-5.75, mains £11.50-14.90.
Al Casbah is a friendly Moroccan place serving
couscous and tajines (£11.50 to £14.90).
Giraffe (☎ 7435 0343, 46 Rosslyn Hill NW3)
Map 12 ⊖ Hampstead; (☎ 7359 5999, 29-31
Essex Rd N1) **Map 4** ⊖ Angel. Breakfast/mains
£2.75-7/7-9 (£6.50 5pm-7pm Mon-Fri). This
colourful, upbeat place with CDs for sale as well
is the culinary equivalent of world music, with
everything from sashimi salads and smoked
salmon omelettes (£6.95) to Moroccan tea.
Jin Kichi (☎ 7794 6158, 73 Heath St NW3) Set
dishes £7.90-12.70. A lot of Japanese live in
Hampstead and this cramped little place is
where many of them dine out; some say it's the
best Japanese restaurant in north London.
Lalibela (☎ 7284 0600, 137 Fortress Rd NW5)
⊖ Tufnell Park. Starters £3.50, mains £5.95-
12. Lalibela serves pungent Ethiopian dishes
such as *tibs*, chunks of tender lamb cooked with
onions and tomatoes, and *minchet abish*, a rich
minced beef concoction, which are eaten on a
platter-sized piece of soft but slightly elastic
injera bread.

Cafes

Café Base (☎ 7431 3241, 70-71 Hampstead High
St NW3) Lunch £3-8, dinner mains £9-12. This
bright and clean cafe has unusual ciabattas and
wraps with unusual fillings (£3 to £5) and salads and pastas (£2.95 to £3.95).
Coffee Cup (☎ 7435 7565, 74 Hampstead High St
NW3). Sandwiches £2.50-5, mains £5-6.50. If
you prefer greasy fried breakfasts (£6.50) and
indifferent pasta dishes (£5), as served in the
1950s, head next door to this old-style caff.

EAST END & THE DOCKLANDS (Maps 2, 4 & 9)

From the Indian and Bangladeshi restaurants of Brick Lane to the trendy European/Modern British eateries of Hoxton and Shoreditch, the East End has finally made it onto London's culinary map. Even the Docklands, once the domain of expense accounts and quick lunches, is experiencing a renaissance around West India Quay.

American

Arkansas Café (☎ 7377 6999, Unit 12, Spitalfields Market, 107b Commercial St E1) **Map 9** ⊖ Liverpool Street/Aldgate East. Mains £4-12.50. Open noon-2.30pm Mon-Fri, noon-4pm Sun. This no-frills barbecue run by America Bubba Helberg produces some of the finest American-style grills in London: steaks, chicken, sausage, ribs. At least one Lonely Planet author has had a party catered by the Arkansas so what better recommendation do you need?

Babe Ruth's (☎ 7481 8181, 172-176 The Highway E1) **Map 9** ⊖/DLR: Shadwell. Starters £2.99-5.99, mains £6.95-16.99. Babe Ruth's is a remarkably popular sports restaurant/bar with an American theme and American food (huge but relatively expensive pizzas, pastas, burgers, steaks and so on). Kids will love the miniature basketball court, pool tables and video games.

French

Les Trois Garçons (☎ 7613 1924, 1 Club Row E1) **Map 4** ⊖ Old Street/Liverpool Street. Starters £7.50-14, mains £12.50-19. Walk through the door of this enormous erstwhile pub and your jaw will drop open: giraffe heads stick out from the wall at a right angle, stuffed swans wear tiaras and the mirrors are listed. The food – classic French – is good if not excellent and at least one of the eponymous 'three boys' is always on hand to meet and greet. Truly a night out to be remembered.

Italian

Great Eastern Dining Room (☎ 7729 0022 or 7613 4545, 54-6 Great Eastern St EC2) **Map 4** ⊖ Old Street/Liverpool Street. Mains £8-11. This is a prime example of the new breed of eateries in London – especially in trendy places such as Hoxton and Clerkenwell. It's smallish – two-rooms converted from an old shop – and serves Italianesque food in a new and extremely fresh fashion.

Try Brick Lane for Indian and Bangladeshi restaurants (plus the best bagels in London).

Il Bordello (☎ 7481 9950, 75 Wapping High St E1) **Map 9** ⊖ Wapping. Starters £3.95-6.95, mains £10.50-16.95. Because of the dearth of quality restaurants in the Wapping area, this neighbourhood Italian place is always crammed with happy diners. If you're drinking at the Captain Kidd or Prospect of Whitby (see Wapping & Docklands under Pubs & Bars in the Entertainment chapter), it's a convenient blotter stop for above-average pizzas (£7.25 to £9.50), pasta (£7.25 to £12.95) and meat and fish main courses (£10.50 to £16.95).

Greek

The Real Greek (☎ 7739 8212, 15 Hoxton Market N1) **Map 4** ⊖ Old Street. Starters £7.20-9.30, mains £15-16.90. This place serves what almost could be called Modern Greek food – eg, hotpot of kid with dandelion and leek fricassee (£16.70) – to an appreciative boho crowd.

Spanish

Mesón Los Barriles (☎ 7375 3136, 8a Lamb St E1) **Map 9** ⊖ Liverpool Street. Tapas £2-5.90, main dishes £3.50-18.90. Open 11am-11pm Mon-Fri, noon-4pm Sun. This Spanish tapas bar/restaurant in Spitalfields Market is one of just a few places that welcomes night-time diners around Liverpool Street station and market-goers on Sunday. It has an excellent selection of tapas and fish and seafood main courses.

Indian

Brick Lane E2 (⊖ Aldgate East/Shoreditch) in what has come to be called Bangla Town is lined wall to wall with cheap Indian and

PLACES TO EAT

NEIL SETCHFIELD

Bangladeshi restaurants – not all of them very good – that are popular with City lads and ladettes. Among the better places are:

Aladin (☎ *7247 8210, 132 Brick Lane*) **Map 9** Starters £1.40-1.95, mains £2.90-6.50. This place is said to be a favourite of Prince Charles. It is unlicensed but you can BYO.

Saliques (☎ *7377 2137, 32 Hanbury St E2*) **Map 9** Starters £1.95-3.50, mains £4.95-9.99. Some people swear by this place. It does curries (£4.75) and tandoori and balti dishes (both from £4.95).

Le Taj (☎ *7247 4210, 134 Brick Lane*) **Map 9** Starters £2-3.95, mains £3.50-8.95. This place is more upmarket and expensive than most others on the street. It has both an Indian and a Bengali menu, with a good choice of vegetarian dishes.

Ambala (☎ *7247 8569, 55 Brick Lane*) **Map 9** Cakes & sweets per piece £1.50-2, kilo £5-6.50. Ambala is one of the many bakeries and pastry shops sprinkled along Brick Lane. It sells luridly coloured, sickly sweet cakes and confectionery.

If you want more authentic subcontinental food, give Brick Lane and its drunken denizens the brush-off and head southwards to Whitechapel (⊖ Whitechapel).

Lahore Kebab House (☎ *7488 2551, 2 Umberston St E1*) **Map 9** Starters £2.50, mains £4.50-6. This very simple place, popular with the local community and white-collar workers alike, serves great food and has a good selection of various lamb kebabs.

New Lahore (☎ *7791 0112, 218 Commercial Rd E1*) **Map 9** Starters 60p-£2.75, mains £2.50-4.75. This tiny place with a couple of tables is basically for takeaway, with spicy lamb kebabs (£3) the dish of choice.

New Tayyab (☎ *7247 9543, 83 Fieldgate St E1*) **Map 9** Mains £4-9. Open 5pm-midnight daily. This place has some of the most authentic Indian and Pakistani food this side of Delhi and Karachi. Choose your *seekh* kebabs, lamb chops or one of several *karahi* (a small wok) dishes, then add a vegetable and one of several *dahls*. It's BYO only.

Vietnamese

Green Papaya (☎ *8985 5486, 191 Mare St E8*) **Map 2** Station: London Fields/Bus: D6, 253 or 277. Mains £4.50-6.95. This positive oasis just south of the Hackney Empire (see the Theatre section of the Entertainment chapter) serves

what could almost de described as Modern Vietnamese food of very high quality. The staff are enthusiastic and willing and able to help.

Viet Hoa (☎ *7729 8293, 70-72 Kingsland Rd E2*) **Map 4** Bus: No 67 or 242. Starters £2-4.70, mains £4.15-6.70. This simple canteen-style eatery serves excellent and authentic Vietnamese dishes. It's always full.

Other Cuisines

Little Georgia (☎ *7249 9070, 2 Broadway Market E8*) **Map 2** ⊖ Bethnal Green/Station: Cambridge Heath. Starters £3-4.50, mains £8-12. This place, while somewhat far-flung, is on a lovely old market street and a great introduction to the cuisine of Georgia (as in Tbilisi, not Atlanta or midnight trains). For the uninitiated, it's slightly Greek-ish, with a little Turkish thrown in and they use a lot of walnuts.

Vegetarian

The Quiet Revolution (☎ *7253 5556, 49 Old St EC1*) **Map 4** ⊖ Old St. Mains £3.95-5.95. The food at this large and bright cafe is not 100% vegetarian (there are a couple of meat and fish dishes lurking about) but it is all-organic.

Whitechapel Art Gallery Cafe (☎ *7522 7888, 80-82 Whitechapel High St E1*) **Map 4** ⊖ Aldgate East. Starters/mains £2/4. Open 11am-4.35pm Tues, Thur-Sun, 11am-6.30pm Wed. This vegetarian place upstairs from the gallery serves dishes such as spinach Florentine and salad (£4.65) and soups.

Cafes

Brick Lane Beigel Bake (☎ *7729 0616, 159 Brick Lane E2*) **Map 4** ⊖ Shoreditch. Open 24-hrs daily. Prices 45p-£2.10. More of a delicatessen than a cafe, the Beigel Bake is at the Bethnal Green Rd end of Brick Lane. You won't find fresher or cheaper bagels anywhere in London – just ask any taxi driver or your humble author who ate them for lunch for almost two years while writing up Lonely Planet guides in an office round the corner. Filled bagels are a snip (45p to 95p), the salmon and cream cheese version is a whopping 95p and a salt beef bagel is £1.60. Note that the Beigel Bake is not kosher.

Evering Bakery Bagel Shop (☎ *7729 0826, 155 Brick Lane E2*) **Map 4** ⊖ Shoreditch. Prices 40p-£2.10. We're going to get it in the neck for this, but just between you and me and the lamppost, this bakery just next door has better fillings than the Beigel Bake but not as good bagels and bread.

GREENWICH (Map 14)

Beautiful Greenwich has both old-style eateries and trendy new restaurants to choose from. The Cutty Sark DLR station is convenient for all the following recommendations unless noted otherwise.

English

Goddards Pie House (☎ 8293 9313, 45 Greenwich Church St SE10) Prices 90p-£2.50. Open 10am-6.30pm Mon-Thur, 10am-9.30pm Fri-Sun. Goddards, the city's oldest pie shop (1890), is truly a step back into the past: a real London caff with wooden benches and things like steak and kidney pie (£2.50) with liquor and mash, and shepherd's pie (£2.40) with beans or peas and a rich brown gravy. Sweet pies cost from 95p.

International/Modern European

Beachcomber (☎ 8853 0055, 34 Greenwich Church St SE10) Starters £1.90-6.95, mains £9.90-14.90. This old stalwart festooned with flower baskets and potted plants is a very pleasant place on a sunny afternoon. Daily specials come in at around £4 to £12.

North Pole (☎ 8853 3020, 131 Greenwich High Rd SE10) DLR/Station: Greenwich. Starters £3.80-7.50, mains £8.50-13.75. This pleasant place has a bar on the ground floor and an excellent, if somewhat formal, restaurant on the 1st floor. There's a decent Sunday breakfast (9.30am to noon; £5.50) and brunch (noon to 6.30pm) and a 10 to 15% discount on dinner Monday to Thursday.

Asian

Noodle Time (☎ 8293 5263, 10-11 Nelson Rd SE10) Dishes £2.80-4. Come to this simple place for cheap Japanese noodles and rice dishes.

Vietnam (☎ 8858 0871, 18 King William Walk SE10) Starters £2.50-5.80, mains £3.80-12.50. Along with lunch and dinner, Vietnam serves inexpensive dim sum (from £1.60) from noon to 5pm.

Cafes

Greenwich Church St has a few decent and inexpensive cafes, which include the following:

Meeting House Café (☎ 8305 0403, Shop No 8 Greenwich Market) Prices £3.95-4.50. Open 9am-4.30pm daily. You'll find ploughman's lunches and quiches, as well as milkshakes (£1.50) here.

CHARLOTTE HINDLE

Fill up on some proper English fare in one of the capital's pie houses.

Peter de Wit's (☎ 8305 0048, 21 Greenwich Church St) Prices £1.40-5. This place serves cream teas (£5) and has outside seating in a courtyard in the warmer months.

BRIXTON (Map 15)

If you're coming to Brixton for its market (⊖ Brixton), don't restrict yourself to the eateries in the covered market itself. The surrounding streets (eg, Atlantic Rd, Coldharbour Lane and so on) have a number of excellent places.

Modern European

Helter Skelter (☎ 7274 8600, 50 Atlantic Rd SW9) Starters £4.80-6.20, mains £9.80-12.80. With its bright designer decor (excluding the original ceramic tiles on the walls) and Modern European specialities on the menu, Helter Skelter is something of an oasis in the greater area of Brixton Market.

Other Cuisines

Brixtonian Havana Club (☎ 7924 9262, 11 Beehive Place SW9) Starters £4.50, mains £14. When in Rome... This Caribbean-inspired eatery blends West Indian, French, British and African influences to produce dishes such as roast pepper and ginger soup (£4.59) and baked ham with sweet sorrel sauce (£14).

Satay Bar (☎ 7326 5001, 447-50 Coldharbour Lane SW9) Starters £3.25-6.15, mains £4.50-8.25, set *rijstafel* meal £13.95 per person (minimum 2). A favourite with Brixton trendies, the Satay Bar serves surprisingly authentic Indonesian food: *rendang ayam* (beef cooked with coconut; £5.95), laksa (soup noodles with seafood; £5.25), mixed satays (£5.95)

PLACES TO EAT

and *sambal udang* (prawn cooked with chillies; £6.75). Even more authentic are all the doors that open on to the busy street – you could easily be in a *warung* in Yogyakarta.

Vegetarian

Bah Humbug (☎ 7738 3184, St Matthew's Church, Brixton Hill SW2) Starters £3.50-4.70, mains £7.30-12.70. In the crypt of St Matthew's Methodist Church, Bah Humbug is one of the best vegetarian restaurants in London, with quite a global range – from Thai vegetable fritters (£3) to Cantonese mock duck and masala curry (£6.50).

HAMMERSMITH & FULHAM (Maps 1 & 10)

Hammersmith is not an especially inviting borough, though we can think of much worse ways of spending a sunny afternoon than sipping at one of the riverside pubs along the Upper Mall. Fulham is more agreeable, with Fulham Road in particular a good place for a meal and a night out on the town.

English/Modern British

Chelsea Bun (☎ 7352 3635, 9a Lamont Rd SW10) **Map 10** ⊖ Fulham Broadway/Earl's Court. Starters £2.35-4.30, mains £5.50-7.80. This London version of an American diner is a great-value place in the relatively well-heeled area known as World's End. Breakfast (£1.65 to £6.30) is served all day, and there's seating on an upstairs veranda.

Ed's Easy Diner (☎ 7352 1956, 362 King's Rd SW3) **Map 10** ⊖ South Kensington; *(☎ 7287 1951, Old Compton St W1)* **Map 7** ⊖ Leicester Square/Tottenham Court Road. Mains £3.95-5.95. If you prefer your diner to be more New World-ish, check out Ed's, one of several branches of a diner chain whose telephone numbers and decor all place them back in the 1950s.

International/Modern European

Bluebird (☎ 7559 1222, 350 King's Rd SW3) **Map 10** ⊖ Fulham Broadway. Mains £10-24, 2-/3-course set lunch £12.50/16.50. Another Conran venture, Bluebird is a large complex with a vast, fantastically expensive, restaurant and bar above an upmarket food hall, flower market and cafe, which is one of the few eateries in London to welcome dogs.

Shoeless Joe's (☎ 7610 9346, 555 King's Rd SW6) **Map 10** ⊖ Fulham Broadway; *(☎ 7240 7865, Temple Place WC2)* **Map 6** ⊖ Temple. Dishes £4.50-10, 2-/3-course meal £15/20. This sport-themed bar (half-price happy hour: 5pm to 8pm Monday to Friday) and grill does meat and fish mains. It has a more imaginative approach than is usual at this sort of place.

Vingt-Quatre (☎ 7376 7224, 325 Fulham Rd SW10) **Map 10** ⊖ South Kensington, then bus No 14 or 211. Starters £4.25-6.75, mains £7.95-11.50. Open 24-hrs daily. This popular place is where to go if you're looking for a late-night meal. It has a proper menu at lunch and dinner but also serves more basic dishes such as burgers (£6.95), steak and chips, and salads after midnight (at which time the bar closes).

Italian

River Café (☎ 7381 8824, Thames Wharf, Rainville Rd W6) **Map 1** ⊖ Hammersmith. Starters £9-14.50, mains £21-28. The buzzy, see-and-be-seen River Café owes its fame as much to the cookbooks it has spawned as to the food actually served, but it does have very good Modern Italian cuisine. You're unlikely to have much change from £50 per person once you've added dessert and wine to your meal.

Greek

Wine & Kebab (☎ 7352 0967, 343 Fulham Rd SW10) **Map 10** ⊖ South Kensington, then bus No 14 or 211. Starters £2.95-3.95, mains £7.50-9.50. The Wine & Kebab sounds like a takeaway place but there's more to it than that. It's an attractive, very pleasant Greek restaurant with starters such as *avgolemono* (lemon and egg-drop soup), *dolmades* (stuffed grape-vine leaves; £7.50) and large mixed meze platters (£29 for two).

Indian

The two upmarket Indian places in this neck of the woods are a lot more expensive than your run-of-the-mill curry houses but worthwhile. If you've got a rich uncle or aunt in town, consider them.

Chutney Mary's (☎ 7351 3113, 535 King's Rd SW10) **Map 10** ⊖ Fulham Broadway/Bus: No 11 or 22. Starters £4.50-7.75, mains £9.25-16.50, 2-course lunch £11 Mon-Fri. Mary's does regional Indian and Anglo-Indian food and hosts a great jazz brunch on Sunday (£15).

Vama (☎ 7351 4118, 438 King's Rd SW10) **Map 10** ⊖ Fulham Broadway/Bus: No 11 or 22. Starters £5.50-13.50, mains £6.25-12.50, weekday lunch £7.95. Vama serves unusual dishes from the North-West Frontier and other regions of India in a lovely dining room that feels like an upmarket Italian restaurant (as it was in a previous life). There's also a Sunday buffet (£12.50) with jazz.

Asian

Jim Thompson's (☎ 7731 0999, 617 King's Rd SW6) **Map 10** ⊖ Fulham Broadway; *(☎ 8788 3737, 408 Upper Richmond Rd SW15)* Station: North Sheen. Starters £3.65-4.75, mains £6.25-8.95, rice & noodle dishes £1.95-5.75. Named after the American who kick-started the mass production of silk in Thailand after WWII and then mysteriously vanished in Malaysia's Cameron Highlands, Jim Thompson's offers mixed South-East Asian fare – from Burma to Singapore – rather than straightforward Thai food. What with the dense greenery and swathes of Thai silk, you could easily imagine yourself in some Bangkok *soi*. Food won't be as good as it would be there, though.

Tiger Lil's (☎ 7376 5003, 500 King's Rd SW10) **Map 10** ⊖ Fulham Broadway; *(☎ 7226 1118, 270 Upper St N1)* **Map 4** ⊖ Highbury & Islington/Angel. Unlimited plates adults/children aged under 10 £12.50/5.50, starter platter (for 2) £7.50, set weekday lunch £5 (Upper St branch). At this Asianesque restaurant chain you can create your own meal by selecting from 16 ingredients and taking them to the energetic chefs, who cook them for you in a gigantic wok. The food is so-so but you won't go away hungry.

Blue Elephant (☎ 7385 6595, 4-6 Fulham Broadway SW6) **Map 10** ⊖ Fulham Broadway. Starters £5.50-9.75, mains £9.50-16.50, set brunch £19.50 noon-4pm Sun, multicourse Royal Thai Banquet £32-36. This Fulham institution serves upmarket (and very pricey) Thai food in jungle-like surroundings – you can't see the trees for the forest. The best time to come is for the fab Sunday brunch.

Bonjour Vietnam (☎ 7385 7603, 593-9 Fulham Rd SW6) **Map 10** ⊖ Fulham Broadway. All-you-can-eat lunch/dinner buffet £10/14. This place serves passable a la carte Vietnamese dishes but it's the buffet that pulls most people in.

Vegetarian

Gate (☎ 8748 6932, 51 Queen Caroline St W6) **Map 1** ⊖ Hammersmith. Starters £3.50-6, mains £7.50-10. This may be the place to convert your carnivorous counterparts to the kinder, gentler world of vegetarianism. It has beautifully presented, unusual modern vegetarian mains, such as butternut squash gnocchi and goat's cheese and pear salad (about £5).

CHISWICK

Chiswick High Rd and lovely Turnham Green Terrace are happy hunting grounds for eateries. There are restaurants and cafes to suit all purses and purposes and a wide assortment of cuisines are on offer.

International/Modern European

Chiswick (☎ 8994 6887, 131 Chiswick High Rd W4) ⊖ Turnham Green. Starters £4.50-9, mains £8.50-14.25, 2-/3-course set lunch £9.50/12.95 and dinner (7pm-8pm) £12.95/15.50. Despite its unimaginative name and rather spartan decor, the Chiswick offers decent Modern European dishes such as artichokes stuffed with goat's cheese and herbed monkfish with curry sauce.

French

La Trompette (☎ 8747 1836, 5-7 Devonshire Rd W4) ⊖ Turnham Green. Set lunch/dinner £19.50/25. This flawless Art Deco-inspired place serves *la cuisine française* of a very high standard and boasts an impressive wine list.

Asian

Thai Bistro (☎ 8995 5774, 99 Chiswick High Rd W4) ⊖ Turnham Green. Mains £4.95-7.95. This was one of London's first Thai restaurants and owner Vatcharin Bumichitr has drawn up the main and vegetarian menus from his own cookbooks, including the seminal *The Taste of Thailand*. It is a basic, canteen-style place but worlds apart from all those shared-table eateries in Soho, with its stylishly simple black and white decor and authentic dishes such as *tom ka gai* (chicken in spicy coconut broth) and *pad thai* (Thai-style vermicelli noodles).

Other Cuisines

Coyote Café (☎ 8742 8545, 2 Fauconberg Rd W4) ⊖ Chiswick Park/Gunnersbury. Starters £4.50-6.95, mains £7.95-13. This little local is head and shoulders above most Mexican eateries in London, with 'real' margaritas (£5.95), nachos (£5.95) and fajitas (£8.95).

Springbok Café (☎ 8742 3149, 42 Devonshire Rd W4) ⊖ Turnham Green. Starters £4.50-6.50, mains £11.50-16.50. Fancy a little game? This colourful restaurant will do you zebra in a syrupy red wine sauce (£16.50), chargrilled ostrich and *kobelj*, a fish not unlike sea bass – among, of course, the more usual offerings. It's got a good South African wine list as well.

KEW

A short distance from Kew Gardens tube stop and the wonderful gardens themselves is a popular Modern European restaurant and a historic cafe.

Modern European

Glasshouse (☎ 8940 6777, 14 Station Parade) ✆ Kew Gardens. 2-/3-course set lunch £15/ 21.50, dinner £19.50/25. This little gem, hard by the wonderful gardens, has a short but interesting menu and excellent service.

Cafe

Newens Maids of Honour (☎ 8940 2752, 288 Kew Rd) ✆ Kew Gardens. Set tea £5.25. Open 9.30am-6pm Tues-Sat. This old-fashioned tearoom, which wouldn't seem out of place in a Cotswold village, owes its fame to the 'maid of honour', a special dessert supposedly concocted by Henry VIII's second wife, the ill-fated Anne Boleyn, from puff pastry, lemon, almonds and curd cheese.

RICHMOND (Map 16)

There are several places to eat along Richmond's high street, which runs south-westwards from the train/tube station towards the river, but many of the more interesting places are clustered together around Hill Rise, just east of Richmond Bridge.

French

Chez Lindsay (☎ 8948 7473, 11 Hill Rise) ✆ Richmond. Starters £2.70-8.75, mains £10-16, 2-course set lunch £5.99, 3-course set dinner £10.99. An inviting French restaurant, Chez Lindsay specialises in crepes (£3 to £8) chased with dry cider, as is done in Brittany, the home of the flat, savoury or sweet filled pancakes.

Other Cuisines

Kozachok (☎ 8948 2366, 10a Red Lion St) ✆ Richmond. Starters £3.95-5.50, mains £8.50-9.75. Open 6.30pm-11.15pm Tues-Sat. We can't vouch for the authenticity of the food, but Kozachok serves an array of Russian and Ukrainian dishes – from borscht (£3.95) and blinis (£4.95 to £11.50) to *tabaka* (spring chicken with sour cream and garlic; £9.85). There are more than two dozen different clear and flavoured vodkas on offer – from apricot to *zubrówka* (flavoured with bison's grass).

Entertainment

LISTINGS

To find out what's on in London, buy a copy of the comprehensive entertainment listings magazine *Time Out* (£2.20), which is published every Wednesday (though available Tuesday) and covers a week of events to the following Wednesday. For some sorts of entertainment, *Hot Tickets*, free with the *Evening Standard* newspaper on Thursday, is a better source – briefer and more eclectic. Other newspapers publish their own entertainment supplement, such as *The Guide*, which appears with the *Guardian* on Saturday.

Alternatively you can use the London Tourist Board's London Line (☎ 09068 663344). See Tourist Offices in the Facts for the Visitor chapter for details. Useful Web sites include: Ⓦ www.clubinlondon .co.uk, Ⓦ www.latenightlondon.co.uk and Ⓦ www.crushguide.com.

PUBS & BARS

Pubs are perhaps the most distinctive contribution the English have made to social life, and little can compare to a really good one. What that constitutes beyond a wide range of beers (see the boxed text 'Beer: The National Drink') is very subjective and almost indefinable: a warm welcome, a sense of bonhomie, the feel of a 'local' (ie, assorted characters from the neighbourhood – and not just a bunch of faceless transients and tourists – patronise the place) and so on.

Pubs have complex opening hours, but in general they open 11am to 11pm Monday to Saturday and noon to 10.30pm on Sunday. Some neighbourhood and country pubs still close in the afternoon (which used to be the law) between 3pm and 7.30pm, especially on Sunday. That may change during the life of this book, however, with a bill to be presented before Parliament that would allow pubs and bars to choose their opening hours in a bid to discourage last-minute 'binge drinking' before last orders are called.

These days really traditional pubs can be thin on the ground in London. In many areas spruced-up chain pubs – look for the

Beer: The National Drink

In a public house – otherwise known as a 'pub' – it is usually possible to order a glass of wine or even a simple cocktail. The *raison d'être* of such an establishment, however, is first and foremost to serve beer – be it lager, ale or stout in a glass or a bottle. On draught it is served in a pint (570mL) or half-pint (285mL) glass. The percentage of alcohol (minimum: 2%) can reach a (lurching and staggering 8%.

Most beers are made from malted barley and flavoured with hops. The term lager refers to the amber-coloured bottom-fermented beverage found the world over. In general lagers are highly carbonated, of medium hop flavour and drunk cool or cold. In London, the best known home brews are Tennent's and Carling, but there's nothing special about either of them.

Ale is a top-fermented beer whose flavours can run the gamut from subtle to robust; proponents of 'real ale' (ie, beer made according to traditional recipes and methods) use the language of oenologists to describe them. Ales can be very slightly gassy or completely still, have a strong hop flavour and are drunk at slightly above room temperature (seldom colder). Real ale is sometimes pulled from barrels. Among the multitude of ales on offer in London pubs, London Pride, Courage Best, Burton Ale, Adnam's, Theakston (in particular Old Peculier) and Old Speckled Hen are among the best. If in doubt, just ask for 'a bitter' and you'll be served the house ale. Stout, the best known of which is Irish Guinness, is a slightly sweet, dark beer whose distinct flavour comes from malt that is roasted before fermentation.

omnipresent words 'slug', 'lettuce', 'rat', 'firkin', 'parrot' and 'moon' in their names – have taken over the role of the local. American-style bars, with bottled beer, designer cocktails (the sake-based 'saketini' is flavour of the season) and bar staff who expect a tip, have arrived as have DJ bars, with a resident disk-spinner somewhere in the corner playing tunes all night (usually till late).

Sampling a range of pubs and bars is part of the fun of visiting London but be careful: there are more than 3700 of them. The following list includes most of our favourites, but there's no substitute for individual research. For more suggestions of traditional and historic pubs visit **W** www.pubs.com.

Trafalgar Square (Map 8)

Sherlock Holmes (☎ 7930 2644, 10 Northumberland St WC2) ⊖ Charing Cross. Tucked away just off Northumberland Ave, this cosy pub filled with Holmes memorabilia doesn't get quite as busy as it otherwise might and is not touristy.

Westminster & Pimlico (Maps 6 & 11)

The Orange Brewery (☎ 7730 5984, 37-9 Pimlico Rd SW1) **Map 11** ⊖ Sloane Square. This place, with a microbrewery in the basement churning out all-natural pints of ale and stout, is for serious aficionados of the amber liquid. You can also take a 30- to 40-minute tour of the brewery (£5), but you have to call and book ahead.

Westminster Arms (☎ 7222 8520, 9 Storey's Gate SW1) **Map 6** ⊖ Westminster. Full of atmosphere, this pleasant place is great for a quick one after an exhausting tour of Westminster Abbey, just across the road. Think of the convenience.

St James's & Mayfair (Map 6)

Che (☎ 7747 9380, 23 St James's St W1) ⊖ Green Park. This cigar bar below a trendy restaurant has an enviable collection of vintage rums, tequilas and whiskies and a floor-to-ceiling humidor with more than 70 different cigar types.

I Am the Only Running Footman (☎ 7499 2988, 5 Charles St W1) ⊖ Green Park. This unusually named pub is an olde worlde place that has been extensively refitted. The eponymous running footman – the guy employed by wealthy 18th-century gentlemen to run in front of his carriage, lighting the way and shifting any obstacles (including people) – wouldn't recognise it.

Windows on the World (☎ 7493 8000, Hilton Hotel, 28th floor, Park Lane W1) ⊖ Hyde Park Corner. Anyone not suffering from vertigo might like to have a drink (cocktails £7.95-9.95) at one of the highest-perched bar in London and enjoy the views over the whole city.

West End: Soho & Piccadilly (Maps 7 & 8)

Coach & Horses (☎ 7437 5920, 29 Greek St W1) **Map 7** ⊖ Leicester Square. The Coach is a small, busy pub with a regular clientele of soaks, writers (would-be and otherwise) and the odd tourist. It was made famous by the alcoholic *Spectator* columnist Jeffrey Bernard, who spent a lot of time here, and eventually drank himself to death.

AKA (☎ 7836 0110, 18 West Central St W1) **Map 8** ⊖ Holborn. This popular late-night DJ bar joins together with its neighbour, The End (see the Clubs section later in this chapter), till 7am on Saturday.

Freedom Brewing Co (☎ 7240 0606, 41 Earlham St WC2) **Map 8** ⊖ Covent Garden. This pub serves rather expensive pints of its own in-house brews, including Freedom Organic.

French House (☎ 7437 2799, 49 Dean St W1) **Map 7** ⊖ Leicester Square. The French House was the meeting place of the Free French Forces during WWII and De Gaulle is said to have drunk here often (as have writers such as Dylan Thomas and Brendan Behan and actors like Peter O'-Toole). Beer is served by the half-pint only.

Lupo (☎ 7434 3399, 50 Dean St W1) **Map 7** ⊖ Leicester Square. This place looks small and cramped from the outside, but enter and you'll discover the comfortable rooms that go on forever behind. It's a great escape in Soho.

O Bar (☎ 7437 3490, 83-5 Wardour St W1) **Map 7** ⊖ Piccadilly Circus; (☎ 7935 6121, 21a Devonshire St W1) **Map 3** ⊖ Baker Street/Regent's Park. This upbeat bar has two main drinking floors with a DJ downstairs nightly (£3/5 after 11.30pm Monday to Thursday/after 11pm Friday and Saturday). It also serves half-price pitchers of cocktails till 8pm.

Point 101 (☎ 7379 3112, 1st & 2nd floors, 101 New Oxford St WC1) **Map 7** ⊖ Tottenham Court Road. The Point is a spartan but popular spot on two floors below that skyscraping monstrosity called Centre Point. The *Bite Me@ Point 101* on the ground floor is lively at lunchtime.

The Salisbury (☎ 7836 5863, 90 St Martin's Lane WC2) **Map 8** ⊖ Leicester Square. Brave the crowds at this centrally located pub, established

That's the way to do it: watch the street performers in Covent Garden from this well-placed bar.

CHARLOTTE HINDLE

in 1898, just to see the beautifully etched and engraved windows and other Victorian features that have somehow escaped the developer's hand.

Scruffy Murphy's *(☎ 7437 1540, 15 Denman St W1)* **Map 7** ✆ Piccadilly Circus. This little spot, one of our favourites, is a pretty authentic Irish pub, with brogues, Guinness and drunks, just up from Piccadilly.

Waxy O'Connors *(☎ 7287 0255, 14-16 Rupert St W1)* **Map 7** ✆ Leicester Square. This large, multilevel place is too glitzy to work as an 'Irish theme pub' but it's big enough to get lost in.

Covent Garden & the Strand (Map 8)

Cork & Bottle Wine Bar *(☎ 7734 7807, 44-6 Cranbourn St WC2)* ✆ Leicester Square. Hidden downstairs on the left as you head to Leicester Square from the tube station, the Cork & Bottle is always packed to the hilt after work, but the wine list is commendable (no beer here), the food surprisingly good and there are several hideaway alcoves.

Freud *(☎ 7240 9933, 198 Shaftesbury Ave WC2)* ✆ Covent Garden. Freud is a small basement bar/cafe/gallery, with the sort of beige walls that could look just plain dirty but there are purposefully arty pictures to detract any scrutiny. It also attracts an arty crowd and the food and bar snacks are a cut above.

Gordon's Wine Bar *(☎ 7930 1408, 47 Villiers St WC2)* ✆ Embankment/Charing Cross. This atmospheric wine bar (no beer) in ancient vaults

beneath the street is as close as you'll get to drinking in the London Dungeon.

Lamb & Flag *(☎ 7497 9504, 33 Rose St WC2)* ✆ Covent Garden. Everyone's 'find' in Covent Garden and therefore always jammed, the pleasantly unchanged Lamb & Flag was once known as the Bucket of Blood because of the fighters who favoured it as a local. In 1679 the poet John Dryden was attacked outside for having written less-than-complimentary verses about Charles II's mistress, the duchess of Portsmouth. That'll teach him.

Punch & Judy *(☎ 7379 0923, 40 The Market WC2)* ✆ Covent Garden. Inside Covent Garden's central market hall itself, this two-level pub is another very busy option, but it has a balcony that lets you look down on St Paul's Church and the buskers.

Fitzrovia (Maps 6 & 7)

This area north of Oxford St and south of Euston Rd is also known as Noho, an impossible acronym meant to come from 'North of Soho'.

Goodge *(☎ 7436 9448, 62 Goodge St W1)* **Map 6** ✆ Oxford Circus. This narrow bar is celebrated for its fruity cocktails but good luck trying to fight your way to the front.

Ha Ha! Bar & Canteen *(43-51 Great Titchfield St W1)* **Map 7** ✆ Oxford Street. This canteen-like bar is a bit of an oasis just up from Oxford St that also does nibbles and 'proper food'.

Drop in and chill out at one of London's many boozers.

Mash (☎ 7637 5555, 19-21 Great Portland St W1) **Map 7** ⊖ Oxford Circus. Mash is another in-house brewery decorated to resemble how some imaginative designer in the 1960s may have envisaged the 21st century. There's a decent restaurant upstairs.

Bloomsbury (Maps 6 & 8)

Lamb (☎ 7405 0713, 94 Lamb's Conduit St WC1) **Map 6** ⊖ Russell Square. The Lamb is unprepossessing from the outside, but the interior is full of Victorian mirrors, old wood and snugs.

Museum Tavern (☎ 7242 8987, 49 Great Russell St WC1) **Map 8** ⊖ Tottenham Court Road. After a hard day's work in the British Museum Reading Room, Karl Marx used to retire to this once-capacious pub, where you can now sup your pint in a narrow bar and reflect on dialectical materialism if so inclined.

The Queen's Larder (☎ 7837 5627, 1 Queen Square WC1) **Map 6** ⊖ Russell Square. Overlooking a lovely square south-east of Russell Square, the Queen (1710) is a handy retreat, with outside benches and the fine *Queen Charlotte* restaurant upstairs.

Swan (☎ 7837 6223, 7 Cosmo Place WC1) **Map 6** ⊖ Russell Square. This younger (c.1753) neighbour of the Queen is less authentic but has a good selection of beers.

Holborn & Clerkenwell (Maps 4, 6 & 7)

Al's Bar Café (☎ 7837 4821, 11-13 Exmouth Market EC1) **Map 4** ⊖ Farringdon. The main draw at Al's is the outside seating area, overlooking Exmouth Market, that is heated in the chillier months.

Bleeding Heart Tavern (☎ 7242 8238, 7404 0333, Bleeding Heart Yard, 19 Greville St EC1) **Map 6** ⊖ Chancery Lane. Just off the jewellers' row of Hatton Garden, this pub/brasserie has a good range of beers, excellent food and a lot of history.

The Castle (☎ 7553 7621, 34 Cowcross St EC1) **Map 6** ⊖ Farringdon. This less-than-salubrious boozer has one claim to fame: it is the only pub in London that is also a licensed pawnbroker's (look for the symbol of the three gold balls hanging above the bar inside). This dual function dates from a time when George IV was in urgent need of a float to pay off his gambling debts and got one from the innkeeper in exchange for some bauble.

Cock Tavern (☎ 7248 2918, East Poultry Ave EC1) **Map 6** ⊖ Farringdon. Unlike most others, this pub will serve you a pint between 6.30am and 10.30am when it waters and feeds the workers and porters from Smithfield Market.

Dust (☎ 7490 0537, 27 Clerkenwell Rd EC1) **Map 6** ⊖ Farringdon. This is a classy DJ bar open late at the weekend.

Eagle (☎ 7837 1353, 159 Farringdon Rd EC1) **Map 4** ⊖ Farringdon. The Eagle was the first of the new-style gastropubs to arrive on the scene and now serves so-so Mediterranean-inspired food but has a good range of beers.

O'Hanlon's (☎ 7278 7630, 8 Tysoe St EC1) **Map 4** ⊖ Angel. Come here for house-brewed beer and an eclectic range of distressed seats and sofas under a skylight.

Princess Louise (☎ 7405 8816, 208 High Holborn WC1) **Map 8** ⊖ Holborn. This Grade II-listed pub has some smashing Victorian decor, with fine tiles, etched mirrors, plasterwork and a stunning central bar.

Three Kings of Clerkenwell (☎ 7253 0483, 7 Clerkenwell Close EC1) **Map 4** ⊖ Farringdon. A friendly pub near Clerkenwell Green, the Three Kings is festooned with papier-mache models, including a giant rhino head above the fireplace.

Viaduct Tavern (☎ 7606 8476, 126 Newgate St EC1) **Map 6** ⊖ Holborn. This period piece opened the same year as the Holborn Viaduct (1869) just opposite and retains many of its original features. It's the closest pub to the Old Bailey so mind your Ps and Qs.

Vic Naylor (☎ 7608 2181, 38-42 St John St EC1) **Map 6** ⊖ Farringdon. This perennial favourite, housed in an old meat storage, still draws in punters for its exuberance and good food served in a side restaurant.

ENTERTAINMENT

Ye Olde Mitre (☎ 7405 4751, 1 Ely Court, off Hatton Garden EC1) **Map 6** ⊖ Chancery Lane. One of our absolute favourites, the Mitre is one of London's oldest and most historic pubs, founded in 1546, but the 18th-century-sized rooms can be a bit tight for 21st-century punters.

The City (Maps 6 & 9)

The City is a notorious black spot at weekends, when the suits are off mowing their suburban lawns or watering themselves at pubs closer to home. Some of the following places can oblige, however.

The Counting House (☎ 7283 7123, 50 Cornhill EC3) **Map 9** ⊖ Bank. This award-winning pub in the former headquarters of NatWest attracts suits on the loose after the market closes. Like most pubs in the City you'll find it open weekdays only.

El Vino (☎ 7353 6786, 47 Fleet St EC4) **Map 6** ⊖ Blackfriars. This institution with a strict dress code (jacket and tie for men) on Fleet St has one of the better wine lists in the City.

Hamilton Hall (☎ 7247 3579, Unit 32, Liverpool Street Station, Bishopsgate EC2) **Map 9** ⊖ Liverpool Street. Despite the refurbishment of the Great Eastern Hotel, this warehouse of a

Are you being served? London offers a tempting bevy of bevvies.

JULIET COOMBE

public house remains intact. It started life as the hotel ballroom and bits remain: plaster cherubs, gilt mirrors and shelves of old books lining the turquoise- and gold-coloured walls.

Jamaica Wine House (☎ 7626 9496, .12 St Michael's Alley EC3) **Map 9** ⊖ Bank. Not a wine bar at all but an historic Victorian pub, the 'Jam Pot' stands on the site of what was the first coffee house in London (1652); such places were often just fronts for brothels.

Liberty Bounds (☎ 7481 0513, 15 Trinity Sq EC3) **Map 9** ⊖ Tower Hill. Down by Tower Hill, the Liberty Bounds is a large sterile Wetherspoon pub but has great views of the Tower and Tower Bridge.

Ye Olde Cheshire Cheese (☎ 7353 6170, Wine Office Court, 145 Fleet St EC4) **Map 6** ⊖ Blackfriars, The entrance to this historic pub is via a picturesque alley. Cross the threshold and you'll find yourself in a wood-panelled interior (the oldest bit dates from the mid-17th century) with sawdust on the floor and divided up into various bars and eating areas (see The City section in the Places to Eat chapter).

Rotherhithe to Wandsworth

Rotherhithe (Map 9) This is the place to go if you want to enjoy a pint while watching the Thames flow by.

The Famous Angel (☎ 7237 3608, 101 Bermondsey Wall East SE16) ⊖ Rotherhithe/Bermondsey. There has been a pub here since the 15th century (though the present building is early 17th century). Captain Cook supposedly prepared for his trip to Australia from here and Samuel Pepys quenched his thirst after gorging on fruit in Cherry Gardens to the south-west. Just opposite in Cathay St are the remains of Edward III's Moated Manor House built in 1361.

The Mayflower (☎ 7237 4088, 117 Rotherhithe St SE16) ⊖ Rotherhithe/Canada Water. This 15th-century pub was originally called The Shippe but was renamed after the ship that took the Pilgrims to America in 1620 because it set sail from Rotherhithe, and the captain supposedly charted out its course here while supping schooners. It also serves good-value Thai food.

Spice Island (☎ 7394 7108, 163 Rotherhithe St SE16) ⊖ Rotherhithe/Canada Water. This enormous place, a stone's throw west of Rotherhithe YHA hostel, has a large bar on the ground floor, a restaurant above and a large heated terrace overlooking the river. Of the three pubs listed here, it's got the least history but the best views.

ENTERTAINMENT

Southwark (May 6 & 9) Southwark is home to some historic pubs.

The Anchor Bankside (☎ 7407 1577, 34 Park St SE1) Map 9 ⊖ London Bridge. This 18th-century place, just east of the Globe Theatre, has superb views across the Thames from its terrace and is the nicest (and most popular) riverside pub in London. Samuel Johnson (1709–84), whose brewer friend owned the joint, is said to have written part of his dictionary here.

Doggetts Coat & Badge (☎ 7633 9057, 1 Black-friars Rd SE1) Map 6 ⊖ Blackfriars. Just to the west of Blackfriars Bridge you'll find this pub named after Thomas Doggett, an 18th-century Irish comedian and theatre owner who set up what is believed to be the oldest rowing competition in the world in 1715. Ever since then, six men have set out from London Bridge to race down river to Chelsea Bridge every July. The winner is rewarded with a red coat and a silver badge.

The George Inn (☎ 7407 2056, Talbot Yard, 77 Borough High St SE1) Map 9 ⊖ Borough/London Bridge. The George is a rare bird indeed – a National Trust pub. It's London's last surviving galleried coaching inn, dates from 1676 and is mentioned in Charles Dickens' *Little Dorrit*. Here too is the site of the Tabard Inn (thus the Talbot Yard address), where the pilgrims gathered in Chaucer's *Canterbury Tales* before setting out well lubed, no doubt.

The Royal Oak (☎ 7357 7173, 44 Tabard St SE1) Map 9 ⊖ Borough. This authentic Victorian place owned by a small independent brewery is a short distance from the church of St George the Martyr, where Little Dorrit (aka Amy) got married.

Waterloo & Lambeth (Map 6) The following pubs are convenient if you're coming from the Imperial War Museum or just stepping off the train from Paris.

The Fire Station (☎ 7620 2226, 150 Waterloo Rd SE1) ⊖ Waterloo. This immensely popular gastropub is in a part of town that was once a culinary desert. It's always jammed and has great real ales.

Wellington (☎ 7928 6083, 81-3 Waterloo Rd SE1) ⊖ Waterloo. An acceptable alternative if the Fire Station is full (as it will be), the Wellington is a veritable shrine to the eponymous duke and enough to make any French person arriving on the Eurostar across the road go apoplectic upon entry.

Wandsworth (Map 2) This may be a bit far to travel but Wandsworth has a popular riverside pub.

The Ship (☎ 8870 9667, 41 Jew's Row SW18) Station: Wandsworth Town. Though the Ship is right by the Thames, the views aren't spectacular (unless you're partial to retail parks and workaday bridges). Still, the outside area is large, the summertime barbecues a real treat and the conservatory bar fun in any weather.

Chelsea, South Kensington & Earl's Court (Map 10)

The Antelope (☎ 7730 7781, 22-4 Eaton Terrace SW1) ⊖ Sloane Square. This charming pub has been around longer than any of its neighbouring buildings, and it's music-free so a perfect place for a tete-a-tete. There's a good selection of real ales and the central bar is original.

Chelsea Potter (☎ 7352 9479, 119 King's Rd) ⊖ Sloane Square. Once the bastion of King's Rd punks, this grungy pub still has a great party atmosphere and tends to attract bohemian types.

Cooper's Arms (☎ 7376 3120, 87 Flood St SW3) ⊖ Sloane Square/South Kensington. This 'find', just off the King's Rd, has stuffed critters as 'decorative' items, newspapers to read and excellent food.

King's Head & Eight Bells (☎ 7352 1820, 50 Cheyne Walk) ⊖ Sloane Square. This attractive corner pub, pleasantly festooned with flower baskets in summer, has a wide range of beers and was a favourite of the painter Whistler and the writer Carlyle, who lived nearby at 24 Cheyne Row.

Prince of Teck (☎ 7373 3107, 161 Earl's Court Rd SW5) ⊖ Earl's Court. This is a convivial pub with an Australian theme in the very heart of Kangaroo Valley. But didn't they get that vowel wrong? Avoid it whenever Australia is playing anyone at anything (unless you are of that persuasion, of course).

Kensington, Knightsbridge & Holland Park (Maps 5 & 10)

The Churchill Arms (☎ 7727 4242, 119 Kensington Church St W8) Map 5 ⊖ Notting Hill Gate. This traditional English pub is renowned for its Winston memorabilia, chamber pots suspended from a great height and highly recommended Thai food (around £6) served in a lovely conservatory.

Star Tavern (☎ 7235 3019, 6 Belgrave Mews West SW1) Map 11 ⊖ Knightsbridge/Sloane Square. This cheery place has welcomed Elizabeth

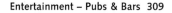

The Market Bar is in the perfect spot for checking out the Notting Hill vibe.

Taylor, Christine Keeler and John Profumo in the trysting days and the Great Train Robbers, who are said to have planned their outrageous crime here.

Windsor Castle (☎ 7243 9551, 114 Campden Hill Rd W11) **Map 5** ✪ Notting Hill Gate. The Windsor has one of the nicest walled gardens of any pub in London and it even has heaters for the chillier months (such as July).

Notting Hill & Bayswater (Map 5)

Beach Blanket Babylon (☎ 7229 2907, 45 Ledbury Rd W11) ✪ Notting Hill Gate. This crazy place boasts extraordinary Gothic decor and is great for observing Notting Hill trendies by day and night.

The Cow (☎ 7221 5400, 89 Westbourne Park Rd W2) ✪ Westbourne Park/Royal Oak. This Irish-themed pub owned by Tom Conran, son of restaurateur Sir Terence, remains wildly popular and for good reason. The fresh oysters with Guinness are a speciality.

Ion Bar (☎ 8960 1702, 161-5 Ladbroke Grove W11) ✪ Ladbroke Grove. This is a very large and popular Afro-Caribbean bar but it's a bit of a fishbowl with the huge front windows.

Market Bar (☎ 7229 6472, 240a Portobello Rd W11) ✪ Ladbroke Grove. Convenient for the Portobello Road Market, this place has an interesting, eclectic decor and an entertaining crowd but it can get mobbed later in the evening. There's jazz from 4pm to 7pm on Sunday and upstairs you'll find – what else? – Thai food.

The Westbourne (☎ 7221 1332, 101 Westbourne Park Villas W2) ✪ Royal Oak/Westbourne Park. The Westbourne is another place where the Notting Hill crowd congregates. The large forecourt is great place to sit in summer.

Maida Vale (Maps 2 & 5)

Bridge House (☎ 7432 1361, 13 Westbourne Terrace Rd W2) **Map 5** ✪ Warwick Avenue. This is in a lovely location just opposite the Grand Union Canal. The Canal Café comedy club is upstairs (see the Comedy section).

The Warrington Hotel (☎ 7266 3134, 93 Warrington Crescent W9) **Map 2** ✪ Warwick Avenue. This former hotel and brothel is now an ornate Art Nouveau pub with heaps of character and a very laid-back atmosphere. There's seating outside in the courtyard and a Thai-run (gratefully) Thai restaurant upstairs.

Camden (Map 3)

Crown & Goose (☎ 7485 8008, 100 Arlington Rd NW1) ✪ Camden Town. This pub feels more like a cafe and attracts a trendy-scruffy youngish crowd. It also does no-nonsense food.

The Engineer (☎ 7722 0950, 65 Gloucester Ave NW1) ✪ Chalk Farm. This is a pretty Victorian pub that has been converted into a highly successful gastropub. It attracts a groovy north London set and boasts a great garden bar.

Oh! Bar (☎ 7383 0330, 111-113 Camden High St NW1) ✪ Camden Town. This DJ bar is a popular spot on the high street and stays open till late.

Pembroke Castle (☎ 7483 2927, 150 Gloucester Ave NW1) ✪ Chalk Farm. We love this light, airy retro place with lovely stained glass and a refined, sportsman's theme.

Spread Eagle (☎ 7267 1410, 141 Albert St NW1) ✪ Camden Town. This place, with its stained glass, frescoed ceiling, real ales and outside seating attracts a mixed crowd of students, suits and the occasional Brit-pop star.

Bar Vinyl (☎ 7681 7898, 6 Inverness St NW1) ⊖ Camden Town. This laid-back bar with an LP theme has a DJ spinning disks most nights.

World's End (☎ 7482 1932, 174 Camden High St NW1) ⊖ Camden Town (☎ 7376 8946, 459 King's Rd SW10)* **Map 10** ⊖ Fulham Broadway. This cavernous place claims to sell a million pints of beer a year, and having seen regulars, we tend to believe them. The main bar, which has a glass roof, has three smaller bars running off it.

Islington (Map 4)

Bierodrome (☎ 7226 5835, 173-4 Upper St N1) ⊖ Highbury & Islington. Another incarnation of the Belgo chain, the people who introduced London to mussels and chips with mayonnaise, pays homage to beer: over 200 types are available.

Cuba Libre (☎ 7354 9998, 72 Upper St N1) ⊖ Angel. The lively bar at the back of the restaurant has exotic cocktails, samba and stays open late. See also the Places to Eat chapter.

The Dove Regent (☎ 7813 4478, 65 Graham St N1) ⊖ Angel. This former gay bar, with special music nights and dancing on Saturday, now attracts a mixed, fairly cool crowd.

King's Head (☎ 7288 2666, 115 Upper St N1) ⊖ Angel. This late-night pub is also a theatre, with some well-received productions. It also serves decent South Indian food at lunchtime during the week and all day at the weekend.

Medicine Bar (☎ 7704 9536, 181 Upper St N1) ⊖ Highbury & Islington. This minimalist boozer is one of the cooler spots on Upper St, which is becoming a weekend playground for young out-of-towners. It plays world music and some funk too.

Old Queen's Head (☎ 7354 9273, 44 Essex Rd N1) ⊖ Angel. Loud, popular and packed to the rafters with merrymakers, the Old Queen's Head was the first pub to introduce the stripped-down, open-plan look to Islington. It still works.

Old Red Lion (☎ 7837 7816, 418 St John St N1) ⊖ Angel. The theatre at this basic boozer and the proximity to Sadler's Wells attracts an arty crowd.

Walkabout Inn (☎ 7359 2097, 56 Upper St N1) ⊖ Angel. A branch of the Aussie/Kiwi chain, this place gets rowdy after the sun goes (and the sundowners go) down.

Stoke Newington (Map 1)

Bar Lorca (☎ 7275 8659, 175 Stoke Newington High St N16) Bus: No 73. This lively tapas bar has good dance music and extended hours.

Hampstead & Highgate (Map 12)

The Flask (☎ 7435 4580, 14 Flask Walk NW3) ⊖ Hampstead. The Flask is a friendly local handy to the tube, with high ceilings, Victorian trimmings, real ale and traditional English food.

The Flask (☎ 8348 7346, 77 Highgate West Hill N6) Bus: No 214. Confusing, we know, but this identically named pub across Hampstead Heath to the north-east in Highgate is even more enjoyable, with a labyrinth of small rooms and snugs and an excellent range of beers.

The Hollybush (☎ 7435 2892, 22 Holly Mount NW3) ⊖ Hampstead. Formerly stables, until it was turned into a pub in the early 1800s, the Hollybush is tucked away in a cul-de-sac above Heath St (reach it via Holly Bush Steps). It has a good selection of beers.

Jack Straw's Castle (☎ 7435 8885, North End Way NW3) ⊖ Hampstead. This ramshackle 1960s-style pub is a favourite with ramblers around Hampstead Heath.

Spaniard's Inn (☎ 8731 6571, Spaniards Rd NW3) ⊖ Hampstead, then bus No 210. This pub dates from 1585 and is associated with the outlaw Dick Turpin. Dickens, Shelley, Keats and Byron also bent their elbows here so you're in good company. In winter you can warm up around an open fire; in summer you'll enjoy the garden.

East End
Hoxton & Shoreditch (Maps 4 & 9)

This nouveau trendy part of the city offers some stylish and chilled choices.

Barley Mow (☎ 7729 0347, 127 Curtain Rd EC2) **Map 4** ⊖ Old Street/Liverpool Street. If you're tired of trying to elbow your way to the bar at the Bricklayers Arms or dozing on the sofa at Home (see later in this section), try this discreetly trendy pub just off the beaten track.

Bricklayers Arms (☎ 7739 5245, 63 Charlotte Rd EC2) **Map 4** ⊖ Old Street. Just up from Cantaloupe, this fairly ordinary pub is where the renaissance of Hoxton and Shoreditch began and continues to be something of a hang-out for artists, artistes and their hangers-on.

Cantaloupe (☎ 7613 4411, 35-43 Charlotte Rd EC2) **Map 4** ⊖ Old Street/Liverpool Street. This was one of the first kids on the block when Hoxton and Shoreditch started to get trendy, and it still manages to feel arty without being overwhelming. There's a decent restaurant.

Charlie Wright's International Bar (☎ 7490 8345, 45 Pitfield St N1) **Map 4** ⊖ Old Street. This is a useful address if you want to carry on after

Echoes of the buccaneering life at the Captain Kidd, named after the swashbuckling pirate

usual pub hours. The clientele is a mixed bag (as far as we can remember).

Home (☎ 7684 8618, 100-106 Leonard St EC2) **Map 4** ⊖ Old Street/Liverpool Street. This rather louche-feeling downstairs place with 'distressed' sofas and armchairs, great cocktails and shots, and a fine restaurant on the ground floor can be so laid-back it's nearly comatose.

Katabatic (☎ 7739 5173, 89 Great Eastern St EC2) **Map 4** ⊖ Old Street. This popular downstairs bar with late opening hours is the Hoxton hotspot of the moment.

Liquid Lab (☎ 7920 0372, 20 City Rd EC1) **Map 4** ⊖ Old Street. This ultra-cool watering station with a medical/dental theme defies description (it offers cocktails such as Blood Clot and Sperm Bank).

Shoreditch Electricity Showrooms (☎ 7739 6934, 39a Hoxton Square N1) **Map 4** ⊖ Old Street. Much edgier than Home (see earlier in this section), this place serves up everything with a lot of attitude.

Vibe Bar (☎ 7377 2899 or 7426 0491, The Brewery, 91-5 Brick Lane E1) **Map 9** ⊖ Shoreditch/ Aldgate East. In a former brewery in trendy Brick Lane, this watering hole has late opening hours at the weekend.

Wapping & Docklands (Maps 9 & 13)

For watering holes with a history look no further than this area.

Captain Kidd (☎ 7480 5759, 108 Wapping High St E1) **Map 9** ⊖ Wapping/Tower Hill. The Kidd, with its large windows, fine beer-garden and mock scaffold recalling the hanging of the eponymous pirate in 1701, is a favourite riverside pub on the northern bank of the Thames.

Dickens Inn (☎ 7488 2208, Marble Quay, St Katharine's Way E1) **Map 9** ⊖ Tower Hill. Overlooking St Katharine's Dock near the Tower of London, this 18th-century wooden-framed brewery was uncovered when a warehouse was being demolished to make way for new houses. The facade, bedecked with flower boxes, is a modern replica but the interior is still full of character.

The Grapes (☎ 7987 4396, 76 Narrow St E14) **Map 13** ⊖ DLR: Westferry. At least one Lonely Planet author's favourite boozer in east London, The Grapes has history (there's been a pub here since 1583), a fine fish restaurant upstairs and a great riverfront terrace.

Prospect of Whitby (☎ 7481 1095, 57 Wapping Wall E1) **Map 9** ⊖ Wapping. Farther afield than the Kidd (see earlier in this section), the Whitby dates from 1520 and is one of London's oldest surviving drinking houses, once known as the Devil's Tavern. It's firmly on the tourist trail, but there's a terrace overlooking the Thames, a decent restaurant upstairs and open fires in winter. Check out the pewter bar – Samuel Pepys once sidled up to it.

ENTERTAINMENT

JULIET COOMBE

SIMON BRACKEN

Pulling in punters with pints: the Westminster Arms serves an assortment of guest real ales.

Greenwich (Map 14)

Trafalgar Tavern (☎ *8858 2437, Park Row SE10*) DLR: Cutty Sark. This cavernous pub with big windows looking onto the Thames and the ill-fated Millennium Dome (at least for the moment) has a lot of history. Dickens knocked back a few here (the Trafalgar is mentioned in *Our Mutual Friend*) and prime ministers Gladstone and Disraeli used to dine on the pub's celebrated whitebait (£5.95) when the whitebait fishery at Greenwich was so famous that Parliament would suspend sitting for the day to feast on the little fishies.

Brixton (Map 15)

Bug Bar (☎ *7738 3184, St Matthew's Church, Brixton Hill SW2*) ✚ Brixton. In the crypt of St Matthew's Methodist Church, this place hosts everything from bands and DJs to comics.

Junction (☎ *7738 4000, 242 Coldharbour Lane SW9*) ✚ Brixton. This cool DJ bar attracts an eclectic crowd and stays open late at the weekend.

Hammersmith (Map 1)

Hammersmith is a fine place to go on a warm spring or summer day, where you can enjoy a pint – if you can manage to get to the bar – and watch Old Man River slowly roll along.

Blue Anchor (☎ *8748 5774, 13 Lower Mall W6*) ✚ Hammersmith/Ravenscourt Park. This is a nautical-themed place close to Hammersmith

Bridge where Gustav Holst (1905–34), who taught at St Paul's Girls' School on Brook Green to the north-east, supposedly wrote his *Hammersmith Suite* between pints.

The Dove (☎ *8748 5405, 19 Upper Mall W6*) ✚ Ravenscourt Park. The Dove, the oldest of this trio, is a small 17th-century building close to the river and popular with rowers for its good range of real ales.

Old Ship (☎ *8748 2593, 25 Upper Mall W6*) ✚ Ravenscourt Park. The Ship, bright and modern, is enviable for the large stretch of grass just outside for sitting, sipping, sunning and/or sleeping.

Fulham (Map 10)

The Atlas (☎ *7385 9129, 16 Seagrave Rd SW6*) ✚ West Brompton. This old-style pub attracts a younger crowd with its real ales, excellent food and small garden bar.

Havana (☎ *7381 5005, 490 Fulham Rd SW6*) ✚ Fulham Broadway. You could hardly miss this place even if you did blink: it's a neon-bright blue-and-ochre-tiled bar/restaurant with zebra-striped and leopard-spotted seating. Rum cocktails cost £4.75 and half-price happy hour is from 5pm to 7pm daily.

Chiswick (Map 1)

Tabard (☎ *8994 3492, 2 Bath Rd W4*) ✚ Turnham Green. This place was designed in 1880 by Norman Shaw as part of Bedford Park, London's first garden suburb. Despite restoration after a fire in 1971 it still boasts panels of William Morris wallpaper and tiles by William de Morgan and Walter Crane.

City Barge (☎ 8994 2148, 27 Strand on the Green W4) ✪ Gunnersbury. The Barge was built in 1484 and is perched dramatically close to the river's edge. A scene from The Beatles' film *Help!* was shot here.

Bull's Head (☎ 8994 1204, 15 Strand on the Green W4) ✪ Gunnersbury. This is another riverside choice, with a good-value Sunday lunch and a Cromwell connection; he is said to have escaped royalist pursuers by using a secret tunnel from the pub to Oliver's Island in the middle of the Thames.

Richmond & Isleworth

White Cross (☎ 8940 6844, Water Lane, Richmond) ✪ Richmond. The riverside location, good food and fine ales make the Cross a winner. When the river's at its highest tide, riverside Cholmondeley Walk floods and the pub is out of bounds to those not willing to paddle.

London Apprentice (☎ 8560 1915, 62 Church St, Isleworth) Station: Isleworth. If you're really into sunning along the Thames, you may want to venture north-west of Richmond, to this riverside pub dating from the 17th century that boasts its own Hogarth drawings on the walls.

CLUBS

Though the majority of London's pubs close at 11pm, there are clubs where you can carry on partying, although you'll have to pay to get in and the drinks are always fairly expensive.

Late-night venues often have a 'club' licence, which means you have to be a member to enter. In practice, they usually include the membership fee in the admission price. Many venues have clubs that only operate one night a week and cater for a specific crowd, such as techno-heads or salsa aficionados.

Admission prices vary from £2 to £5 between Sunday and Thursday and £6 to £12 on Friday and Saturday, but not all clubs charge a cover. Opening hours vary widely. The most happening clubs don't kick off until after midnight and stay open until 4am, 5am or 6am at the weekend. Dress can be smart (no suits) or casual; for some places, the more outrageous you look – within reason – the better the chance you have of getting in. Avoid trainers/sneakers.

West End: Soho & Piccadilly (Maps 7 & 8)

Bar Rumba (☎ 7287 2715, 36 Shaftesbury Ave W1) **Map 7** ✪ Piccadilly Circus. Open 5pm-3.30am Mon-Thur, 5pm-4am Fri, 7pm-6am Sat, 8pm-1am Sun. A small club in the heart of Soho with a loyal following. Tuesday is a Rumba Pa'ti, Saturday is Garage City and Sunday is Bubblin' Over, with ghetto soul and rap.

Emporium (☎ 7734 3190, 62 Kingly St W1) **Map 7** ✪ Oxford Circus. Open 10pm-4am Thur & Fri, 9pm-5am Sat. Very popular with the beautiful set, tourists and assorted trash, Emporium is at the posh end of the scale.

Hanover Grand (☎ 7499 7977, 6 Hanover St W1) **Map 7** ✪ Oxford Circus. Open 10pm-3.30am Wed, 10pm-4am Thur & Fri, 10pm-4.30pm Sat. This split-level venue with a strict dress code is worth glamming up and queuing for. Friday night is Independence, featuring US garage and house.

Salsa! (☎ 7379 3277, 96 Charing Cross Rd WC2) **Map 8** ✪ Leicester Square. Open 5.30pm-2am Mon-Sat. Bar/club combo in the centre of everything, with Latino music guaranteed to get you grooving.

Syndrome (☎ 7437 6830, 53-4 Berwick St W1) **Map 7** ✪ Oxford Circus. Open 10pm-4am daily. Newcomer with '60s, '70s and '80s disco at Blow-up on Saturday.

Velvet Room (☎ 7734 4687, 143 Charing Cross Rd WC2) **Map 7** ✪ Tottenham Court Road. Open 10pm-3am Mon & Thur, 10.30pm-3am Tues, 10pm-2.30am Wed, 10pm-4am Fri & Sat. An intimate, low-lit club swathed in red velvet.

Holborn & Clerkenwell (Maps 6 & 8)

The End (☎ 7419 9199, 18 West Central St WC1) **Map 8** ✪ Holborn. Open 10pm-3am Mon, 10pm-4am Thur, 10pm-7am Fri & Sat. This is a postmodern club with a modern industrial decor on a West End back street. For serious clubbers who like dance music at the hard end of the scale.

Fabric (☎ 7336 8898 or 7490 0444, 77a Charterhouse St EC1) **Map 6** ✪ Farringdon. Open 10pm-5am Fri & Sun, 10pm-7am Sat. This feather in Clerkenwell's well-plumed cap boasts three dance floors in a converted meat coldstore, a 24-hour music licence and capacity for 2500 groovers. Come Friday for Live and Sunday for DTPM.

Turnmills (☎ 7250 3409, 63 Clerkenwell Rd EC1) **Map 6** ✪ Farringdon. Open 6pm-midnight Tues, 10.30pm-7.30pm Fri, 9pm-5am Fri, 10am-6pm Sun. Large, long-running Turnmills does big weekend nights, including a gay after-hours institution called Trade (see the Gay & Lesbian Venues section).

Elephant & Castle (Map 9)

Ministry of Sound (☎ 7378 6528, 103 Gaunt St SE1) ✆ Elephant & Castle. Open 10.30pm-6am Fri, midnight-9am Sat. This cavernous place, arguably London's most famous club (though well past its finest hour, they say), attracts hardcore clubbers and boozers with, among other things, its excellent sound system.

Kensington, Knightsbridge & Holland Park (Map 5)

Cuba (☎ 7938 4137, 11-13 Kensington High St) ✆ High Street Kensington. Open noon-2am Mon-Sat, 2pm-10.30pm Sun. A downstairs bar with salsa lessons, a live band or DJ nightly, dancing till 2am and great mojito cocktails.

Notting Hill & Ladbroke Grove (Map 5)

Notting Hill Arts Club (☎ 7460 4459, 21 Notting Hill Gate W11) ✆ Notting Hill Gate. Open 6pm-1am Tues-Sun. Cosy, funky club whose jewel in the crown is Sunday night's Lazy Dog.

Subterania (☎ 8960 4590, 12 Acklam Rd W10) ✆ Ladbroke Grove. Open 9pm-2am Wed, 10pm-3am Fri & Sat. Atmospheric place directly under the Westway that showcases up-and-coming hip-hop acts, as well as reggae, dub and funk.

Camden & Kentish Town (Map 3)

Camden Palace (☎ 7387 0428, 1a Camden High St NW1) ✆ Mornington Crescent. Open 10pm-2.30am Tues, 8pm-3am Thur, 10pm-6am Fri, 10pm-7am Sat. A multilevel monster of a place thick with sweaty boppers and laser lights.

The Verge (☎ 7267 9452 or 7485 2781, 147 Kentish Town Rd NW5) ✆ Kentish Town. Open 8pm-late daily. Neighbourhood club with a smallish dance floor and a good seating area. Party where the locals do.

WKD (☎ 7267 1869, 18 Kentish Town Rd NW1) ✆ Camden Town. Open noon-2am Mon-Thur, noon-3am Fri & Sat, noon-1am Sun. Smallish club downstairs with varied canned music nightly.

Islington & King's Cross (Map 4)

Bagleys Studios (☎ 7278 2777, King's Cross Freight Depot, York Way N1) ✆ King's Cross St Pancras. Open 9pm-6am Fri, 10pm-7am Sat.

This place is a huge converted warehouse with five dance floors, four bars and an outside area in the summer. It hosts big weekend parties.

Bar Latino (☎ 7704 6868, 145 Upper St N1) ✆ Angel. Open 8pm-2am Mon-Thur, 6pm-2am Fri & Sat. The only dance bar open late in Upper St, Bar Latino is where you'll find nearly everyone in Islington who wants to party after the pubs shut down.

The Cross (☎ 7837 0828, Goods Way Depot, York Way N1) ✆ King's Cross St Pancras. Open 10.30pm-5am Fri & Sat, 10.30am-4pm Sun. This is one of London's leading venues, hidden under the arches off York Way, completely renovated and with brilliant DJs. Come on a Friday for Fiction, with soulful funk and garage.

Scala (☎ 7833 2022, 275 Pentonville Rd N1) ✆ King's Cross. Open 9pm-3am Tues-Thur & Sun, 10pm-5am Fri, 11pm-6am Sat. Excellent hip-hop and breakbeats nights are the speciality at this converted cinema.

East End: Hoxton & Shoreditch (Maps 4 & 9)

333 (☎ 7739 5949, 333 Old St EC1) Map 4 ✆ Old Street. Open 8pm-2am Mon-Thur, 10pm-5am Fri & Sat, 10pm-4am Sun. This distressed-looking venue in Hoxton has everything from breakbeats and techno to funk.

93 Feet East (☎ 7247 3293, 150 Brick Lane E2) Map 9 ✆ Shoreditch/Aldgate East. Open 6pm-11pm Mon-Wed, 8pm-2am Thur-Sat, noon-10.30pm Sun. This former multilevel warehouse in the heart of Bangla Town has lots of Asian underground and electronic sounds in its Bad Magic Main Room and Nucamp Balearic Bar.

The Aquarium (☎ 7251 6136, 256-260 Old St EC1) Map 4 ✆ Old Street. Open 10pm-4am Fri-Sun. This converted gym has its own cool pool and Jacuzzi. Friday night is Naughty, with funky disco house. The Aquarium opens most Sundays too.

Brixton (Map 15)

Dogstar (☎ 7733 7515, 389 Coldharbour Lane SW9) ✆ Brixton. Open noon-1am Mon-Thur, noon-3am Fri & Sat, noon-11pm Sun. As casual as you'd expect from a converted pub so dressing to kill is not imperative. Big parties are held at the weekend.

The Fridge (☎ 7326 5100, 1 Town Hall Parade, Brixton Hill SW2) ✆ Brixton. Open 10pm-6am Fri & Sat. The Fridge offers a wide variety of club nights in an excellent venue that is not too

ASA ANDERSSON

Shake your bootie at one of London's top clubbing spots.

big, not too small. It's still one of the best clubs in London.

MASS (☎ 7737 1016, St Matthew's Church, Brixton Hill SW2) ⊖ Brixton. Open 10pm-2am Thur, 10pm-6am Fri, 9pm-6pm Sat. This appropriately named place in St Matthew's Church, with vaulted ceilings, pews and frescoes, resounds to hard house, trance and a bit of industrial. Friday night is Fetish Night.

Hammersmith (Map 1)

Po Na Na Hammersmith (☎ 8600 2300, 242 Shepherd's Bush Rd W6) ⊖ Hammersmith. Open 10pm-3am Fri & Sat. This place is at the forefront of school uniform parties; you want in, you'd better be dressed up.

GAY & LESBIAN VENUES

The London gay scene has changed considerably over the past few years. From having just a couple of huge discos (eg, Heaven), the odd bar such as Brief Encounter and a few pub once-a-weekers, London now boasts gay and (to a lesser extent) lesbian venues throughout the city.

The best starting point is to pick up the free *Pink Paper*, a relatively serious publication in a new magazine format, *Boyz*, which is more geared toward entertainment,

and the similar *QX*. Both are available from most gay cafes, bars and clubs. Magazines such as *Gay Times* (£2.95) and the lesbian *Diva* (£2.25) also have listings. The four-page gay section of the weekly *Time Out* is another excellent source of information. The London Lesbian & Gay Switchboard (☎ 7837 7324) answers calls 24 hours a day. Useful Web sites include 🅦 www.rainbow network.com for gay men and 🅦 www .gingerbeer.co.uk for lesbians.

London's bars and clubs cater for every predilection, but there's a growing trend towards mixed gay and straight clubs. There are also men- or women-only nights; check the press for details. A lot of the activity is centred in Soho but not all of it by any means; you'll find pubs, cafes and clubs in every direction.

Soho

In the 'gay village' of Soho (⊖ Leicester Square or Piccadilly Circus, unless noted otherwise) – particularly along Old Compton St – bars and cafes are thick on the ground.

Cafes There are a few friendly cafes that are worth checking out.

Balans (☎ 7437 5212, 60 Old Compton St W1) **Map 7** This is a popular and moderately priced, continental-style cafe.

First Out (☎ 7240 8042, 52 St Giles High St WC2) **Map 8** ⊖ Tottenham Court Road. This long-established, friendly place is a mixed lesbian-gay cafe that serves vegetarian food. Girl Friday (8pm to 11pm Friday) is for women only.

Freedom Café-Bar (☎ 7734 0071, 60-6 Wardour St W1) **Map 7** Around the corner from Balans, you'll find this upbeat place serving food and drink to a mixed clientele.

Pubs & Bars From buzzing to laid-back, Soho has gay pubs and bars to suit all tastes.

Brief Encounter (☎ 7552 9851, 42 St Martin's Lane WC1) **Map 8** ⊖ Charing Cross/Embankment. Towards Trafalgar Square and attached to the oh-so chichi St Martin's Lane hotel, Brief Encounter is a cruisy pub with a ground floor bar and a sticky one in the basement.

Candy Bar (☎ 7494 4041, 23-4 Bateman St W1) **Map 7** The venue of choice among the London clitorati, Candy Bar is open till late most nights and always packed.

Compton's of Soho (☎ 7479 7961, 53-5 Old Compton St W1) **Map 7** This eternally busy place is home to skin clones and their followers. It's a good place to start the evening.

Retro Bar (☎ 7321 2811, 2 George Court WC2) **Map 8** ✚ Charing Cross/Embankment. This is a friendly bar, tucked away down a small lane off the Strand, with a host of theme nights in the upstairs bar during the week.

Rupert Street (☎ 7292 7141, 50 Rupert St W1) **Map 7** Situated on a corner with large glass windows for looking, being looked at, looking at being looked at, and so on, Rupert Street is London's trendiest gay bar.

Village Soho (☎ 7434 2124, 81 Wardour St W1) **Map 7** This two-level bar is a good choice for an early evening drink.

West Central (29-30 Lisle St WC2) **Map 8** Situated in the heart of Chinatown, this place has a cruisy gay bar on the ground and 1st floors and a mixed club in the basement with alternating club nights.

The Yard (☎ 7437 2652, 57 Rupert St W1) **Map 7** This relaxed place has a pleasant courtyard where you can drink in the warmer months.

Clubs These are the most popular gay clubs in Soho.

Astoria (☎ 7434 9592, 7434 6963, 157 Charing Cross Rd WC2) **Map 8** Open 10.30pm-4am Mon & Thur, 11pm-4am Fri, 10.30am-4.30am Sat. This dark, sweaty and atmospheric club has gay nights throughout the week. There's a cheap (all senses) gay night on Monday called **G.A.Y** ('good as you'), Thursday night is Music Factory and Friday night is Camp Attack.

Heaven (☎ 7930 2020, Under the Arches, Villiers St WC2) **Map 8** ✚ Charing Cross. Open 10.30pm-3am Mon & Wed, 10.30pm-6am Fri, 10pm-5am Sat. Long-standing and perennially popular gay club with some mixed nights.

North London

There are gay places around King's Cross and in Camden and Hampstead.

Black Cap (☎ 7428 2721, 171 Camden High St NW1) **Map 3** ✚ Camden Town. A late-night bar famous for its drag shows and beer garden.

Central Station (☎ 7278 3294, 37 Wharfdale Rd N1) **Map 4** ✚ King's Cross. This ever-popular place has a bar and club with special one-nighters and the UK's only gay sports bar.

King William IV (☎ 7435 5747, 77 Hampstead High St NW3) **Map 12** ✚ Hampstead. This friendly place is the oasis to head for after a look around the heath.

South London

Brixton and popular Vauxhall are south London's gay centres.

Substation South (☎ 7737 2095, 9 Brighton Terrace SW9) **Map 15** ✚ Brixton. This place is sleazier than its Soho sibling, with a healthy mix of cruising (Y-Front underwear party on Monday, Boot Camp on Wednesday) and dance nights (Queer Nation on Saturday).

The Vauxhall Tavern (372 Kennington Lane SE11) **Map 2** ✚ Vauxhall. This is a long-running gay pub open every night and with different themes.

East London

Turnmills (☎ 7250 3409, 63 Clerkenwell Rd EC1) **Map 6** ✚ Farringdon. Open 4am Sat-1pm Sun. Trade at Turnmills remains *the* gay superclub; breakfast is served at 6am.

White Swan (☎ 7780 9870, 556 Commercial Rd E14) **Map 2** DLR: Limehouse. If you're interested in barrow boys (some real, most *faux*) with buzz cuts, check out the East End's friendliest, cruisiest pub/club (especially BJ's, 10pm to 3am Saturday).

West London

The west's gay area is centred around Earl's Court (Map 10; ✚ Earl's Court) and, despite being overshadowed by Soho, it still has a few places of interest.

Balans West (☎ 7244 8838, 239 Old Brompton Rd) Breakfast £2.25-4.95 Mon-Fri, £4.25-6.95 Sat & Sun, starters £2.50-5.50, mains £5.75-9.95. This is a branch of Balans, the popular, continental-style Soho cafe, with modern decor and something for everyone. Two-for-one happy hour is 4pm to 7pm.

Bromptons (☎ 7370 1344, 294 Old Brompton Rd SW5) Open 4pm-2am Mon-Sat, 1pm-midnight Sun. This is a busy and cruisy place with a pub upstairs and dancing below.

Coleherne (☎ 7244 5951, 261 Old Brompton Rd SW5) This is one of London's oldest pubs and patrons' tastes veer towards leather.

COMEDY

Central London plays host to a number of clubs whose *raison d'être* is comedy; there are even more venues – especially pubs – that set aside specific nights for stand-up comedy acts. The place to look for day-to-day details is *Time Out*, but the following are very popular venues:

Banana Cabaret *(☎ 8673 8904, Bedford Arms, 77 Bedford Hill SW12)* ✪ Balham. Touted as the finest pub comedy club in south London. Two acts run simultaneously on Saturday night.
Canal Café *(☎ 7289 6054, Bridge House, 13 Westbourne Terrace Rd W2)* **Map 5** ✪ Warwick Avenue. This popular comedy venue above a canal-side pub in Little Venice has shows most nights.
Comedy Café *(☎ 7739 5706, 66-8 Rivington St EC2)* **Map 4** ✪ Old Street. There's something for everyone at this colourful and cracking club in Hoxton, just off Shoreditch High St. Wednesday is Try Out Night when you can give it a go yourself.
Comedy Store *(☎ 7344 4444, Haymarket House, 1a Oxendon St SW1)* **Map 7** ✪ Piccadilly Circus. London's longest-established comedy club, now approaching its fourth decade, hosts big acts nightly except Monday, with a double bill on Friday and Saturday.
Jongleurs *(☎ 7564 2500, 49 Lavender Gardens SW11)* **Map 2** Station: Clapham Junction; *(221 Grove Rd, Bow Wharf E3)* **Map 2** ✪ Mile End/Bus: No 8; **Dingwalls** *(11 East Yard, Camden Lock NW1)* **Map 3** ✪ Camden Town. This is a popular chain, serving comedy-lite by the litre glass.
Lee Hurst's Backyard Comedy Club *(☎ 7739 3122, 231-7 Cambridge Heath Rd E2)* **Map 2** ✪ Bethnal Green. Comic Lee Hurst's very own club in a converted textile factory attracts some of the best comics in London. Shows on Friday and Saturday nights.

ROCK & POP

London boasts a wide range of rock and pop venues and you can hear everything from megastars at Wembley, Earl's Court or the London Arena and similar hangar-sized arenas to hot new bands at any number of more intimate places around town.

Both Ticketmaster (☎ 7344 4444, **W** www.ticketmaster.co.uk) and Ticketweb (☎ 7771 2000, **W** www.ticketweb.co.uk)

Game for a laugh at Jongleurs, Camden's comedy club

have 24-hour credit-card booking lines and you can buy tickets online as well. Tickets are also available from Tower Records, the Britain Visitor Centre (Map 7; 1 Regent St SW1; ✪ Piccadilly Circus) and from the London Tourist Board centres at Victoria and Liverpool Street train stations and in the Heathrow Terminals 1, 2, 3 Underground station concourse.

Here are some big-ticket addresses you're likely to need:

Astoria *(☎ 7434 0044)* **& Mean Fiddler** *(☎ 7434 9592,* **W** *www.meanfiddler.com, 157-65 Charing Cross Rd WC2)* **Map 7** ✪ Tottenham Court Road. These massive venues, recently acquired by the Mean Fiddler Group, stage all sorts of concerts – from middle of the road and pop to indie.
Brixton Academy *(☎ 7771 2000,* **W** *www.brixton-academy.co.uk, 211 Stockwell Rd SW9)* **Map 15** ✪ Brixton. Enormous and very popular venue with a good atmosphere and lots of bars.
Earl's Court Exhibition Centre *(☎ 7385 1200 or 0870 903 9033, Warwick Rd SW5)* **Map 10** ✪ Earl's Court. This is one of London's venues for blockbuster concerts – the type that sell out well in advance – but has bad acoustics.

The Forum (☎ *7344 0044*, **W** *www.meanfiddler .com, 9-17 Highgate Rd NW5*) **Map 12** ⊖ Kentish Town. Just a few doors down from the Bull and Gate (see later in this section) this is an excellent roomy venue for all kinds of rock concerts.

Garage (☎ *7607 1818*, **W** *www.meanfiddler.com, 20-2 Highbury Corner N5*) **Map 4** ⊖ Highbury & Islington. Good venue for indie rock from both sides of the Atlantic.

Hackney Ocean (☎ *8533 0111*, **W** *www.ocean .org.uk, 270 Mare St E8*) **Map 2** ⊖ Bethnal Green/Station: Hackney Central. Brand-new multipurpose venue with three halls for 'music making waves' in a renovated old library. Worth the trip for the acoustics alone.

London Arena (☎ *7538 1212*, **W** *www.london arena.co.uk, Limeharbour, Isle of Dogs E14*) **Map 13** DLR: Crossharbour & London Arena. This is a renovated venue for huge capacity gigs.

Roundhouse (☎ *7424 9991*, *Chalk Farm Rd NW1*) **Map 3** ⊖ Chalk Farm. This renovated 1960s music venue, built in 1847 to house the turntable at the terminus of the London to Birmingham Railway, holds a motley assortment of events – from rock concerts and exhibitions to circuses – in a theatre and concert hall seating 2400 people.

Shepherd's Bush Empire (☎ *7771 2000*, **W** *www .shepherds-bush-empire.co.uk, Shepherd's Bush Green W12*) **Map 2** ⊖ Shepherd's Bush. Once a BBC TV building, this is one of the best venues in London.

Wembley Arena (☎ *8902 0902*, *Empire Way, Wembley*) **Map 2** ⊖ Wembley Park. This huge (capacity: 12,500) venue has very little to recommend it bar its high profile.

Smaller places that have a more club-like atmosphere and are worth checking for up-and-coming bands include the following:

Barfly@the Monarch (☎ *7691 4244, 7691 4245*, **W** *www.barflyclub.com, Monarch, 49 Chalk Farm Rd NW1*) **Map 3** ⊖ Camden Town. This small club, which has moved from the Camden Falcon to the Monarch, gives a succession of small-time artists their big break.

Borderline (☎ *7734 2095*, **W** *www.borderline.co .uk, Orange Yard, off Manette St W1*) **Map 7** ⊖ Tottenham Court Road. Borderline is a small, relaxed venue with a reputation for quality new bands.

Bull and Gate (☎ *7485 5358*, *389 Kentish Town Rd NW5*) **Map 12** ⊖ Kentish Town. This

'almost Camden' venue is small, smoky and lines up three acts a night.

Cargo (☎ *7739 3440*, *83 Rivington St EC2*) **Map 4** ⊖ Old Street. This popular venue in Hoxton has live music every night.

Dingwalls (☎ *7267 1577*, *11 East Yard, Camden Lock Place NW1*) **Map 3** ⊖ Camden Town. Dingwalls hosts indie acts from Sunday to Thursday and comedy acts at weekends (see Jongleurs in the Comedy section). The upstairs terrace bar looks onto Camden Lock.

Rock Garden (☎ *7240 3961*, **W** *www.rockgarden .co.uk, The Piazza, Covent Garden WC2*) **Map 8** ⊖ Covent Garden. Small basement venue, often packed with tourists, that hosts mostly local bands.

The Spitz (☎ *7392 9032*, *109 Commercial St E1*) **Map 9** ⊖ Aldgate East/Liverpool Street. This super-relaxed venue backing onto Spitalfields Market hosts everything and anything, from Indian-style breakbeats and Anglo-Cuban music to jazz dance.

Underworld (☎ *7482 1932*, *174 Camden High St NW1*) **Map 3** ⊖ Camden Town. Beneath the World's End pub, Underworld is a small venue that features new bands and has club nights too.

JAZZ

London has always had a thriving jazz scene and, with its recent resurgence thanks to acid-jazz, hip-hop, funk and swing, it's stronger than ever.

100 Club (☎ *7636 0933*, **W** *www.the100club .co.uk, 100 Oxford St W1*) **Map 7** ⊖ Oxford Circus. Admission £7-15, free lunchtime sessions noon-3pm Friday. Legendary London venue that now concentrates on jazz, but once showcased the Stones and was at the centre of the punk revolution.

Jazz Cafe (☎ *7916 6060*, **W** *www.jazzcafe .co.uk, 5 Parkway NW1*) **Map 3** ⊖ Camden Town. Admission £8-20 advance bookings, £10-22 at the door. Very trendy restaurant venue with eclectic offerings; it's best to book a table.

Pizza Express Jazz Club (☎ *7439 8722*, **W** *www.pizzaexpress.co.uk, 10 Dean St W1*) **Map 7** ⊖ Tottenham Court Road. Admission £12.50-15. A small basement venue beneath the main chain restaurant.

Pizza on the Park (☎ *7235 5273*, *11-13 Knightsbridge SW5*) **Map 6** ⊖ Hyde Park Corner. Nightly jazz in the basement.

Ronnie Scott's (☎ *7439 0747*, **W** *www.ronniescotts .co.uk, 47 Frith St W1*) **Map 7** ⊖ Leicester Square. Admission members £5-9, non-members

£15-20, students & under 26s Mon-Wed £9. Operating since 1959, Ronnie Scott's is a classic venue that hosts all the heavyweights and then some, but is expensive if you're not a member (£50 per year).

Spice of Life (☎ 7437 7013, 6 Moor St W1) **Map 8** ↔ Tottenham Court Road/Leicester Square. The Backstage Bar in this perennial pub just off Cambridge Circus hosts jazz sessions from 8pm on Monday and Wednesday.

FOLK & WORLD MUSIC
Places well worth checking out for other types of music in London include:

Africa Centre (☎ 7836 1973, W www.africacentre .org.uk, 38 King St WC2) **Map 8** ↔ Covent Garden. The centre offers African music concerts most Friday nights and one-offs on other nights of the week.

Cecil Sharp House (☎ 7485 2206, 2 Regent's Park Rd NW1) **Map 3** ↔ Camden Town. This headquarters of the English Folk Dance and Song Society, this is *the* venue for English folk music (an acquired taste, it must be said), especially at 8pm on Tuesday when the folk club meets.

Soundtrack to the city: a busker plays the blues.

The Swan (☎ 7978 9778, W www.theswan stockwell.com, 215 Clapham Rd SW9) **Map 15** ↔ Stockwell. There's traditional Irish music most nights at the Swan.

CLASSICAL MUSIC
London is a major classical-music capital, with four world-class symphony orchestras, two opera companies, various smaller ensembles, brilliant venues, reasonable prices and high standards of performance.

There's so much on that you may have trouble deciding what to pick. On any night of the year the choice will range from traditional crowd-pleasers to new music and 'difficult' composers. Opera can be more problematic because it's costly to produce and consequently tickets tend to be pricey.

South Bank Centre (Map 6)
Royal Festival Hall, Queen Elizabeth Hall & Purcell Room (☎ 7960 4242, W www.rfh.org .uk, Belvedere Rd SE1) ↔ Waterloo. Tickets £5-60; box office open 10am-9pm daily. These are three of London's premier venues for classical concerts – from symphonies to chamber groups. Prices vary depending on who's performing and where you sit, but they are usually in the £15 to £30 range.

Wigmore Hall (Map 6)
Wigmore Hall *(☎ 7935 2141, W www .wigmore-hall.org.uk, 36 Wigmore St W1)* ↔ Bond Street. Tickets £8-23; box office open 10am-8.30pm Mon-Sat, 10.30am-8pm Sun, 10.30am-5pm daily Nov-Mar. This Art Nouveau hall, one of the best concert venues in London, offers a great variety of concerts and recitals. The recitals at 11.30am on Sunday are particularly good (£9 to £10). There are lunchtime concerts at 1pm on Monday (adults/seniors £8/6).

Barbican (Map 9)
Barbican *(☎ 7638 8891, W www.barbican .org.uk, Silk St EC2)* ↔ Barbican. Tickets £8-30, stand-by tickets (students & over-60s on day of performance only £6-9). Home to the London Symphony Orchestra, the Barbican is not everyone's favourite venue: it's an architectural monstrosity and

ELLIOT DANIEL

ENTERTAINMENT

finding your way around is a little bit of hell on earth. But its list of monthly concerts is mammoth and the halls' acoustics are great.

Royal Albert Hall (Map 5)

Royal Albert Hall (☎ 7589 8212, W www .royalalberthall.com, Kensington Gore SW7) ✪ South Kensington. Tickets £5-40, Proms tickets £3-70; box office at door No 7 & pre-paid ticket collection at door No 9 open 9am-9pm daily. This is a splendid-looking Victorian concert hall that hosts all kinds of performances. From mid-July to mid-September it stages the Proms – one of the world's biggest and most democratic classical-music festivals. The real Prom experience means queuing for one of the thousand or so standing (or 'promenading') tickets that go on sale one hour before the start of each concert for £3 each. You can choose to be in the gallery or the arena; there are two separate queues.

Kenwood House (Map 12)

Kenwood House (☎ 7413 1443, Hampstead Lane NW3) ✪ Archway/Golders Green, then bus No 210. Admission £14.50-20. A highlight of a sunny summer is to go to an outdoor concert in the grounds of Hampstead Heath's Kenwood House. People sit on the grass or on deck chairs, eat strawberries, drink chilled white wine and listen to classical music on a number of weekend evenings in July and August.

Church Venues

Many churches host evening concerts or lunchtime recitals year-round or during the summer months. Sometimes they are free, with a suggested donation requested; at other times there is a charge. A few of the city's redundant churches now serve as concert halls.

All Hallows-by-the-Tower (☎ 7481 2928, Byward St EC3) Map 9 ✪ Tower Bridge. Organ recitals at 1.15pm; donation requested.
All Souls, Langham Place (☎ 7580 3522, Langham Place W1) Map 6 ✪ Oxford Circus. Evening concerts at 7.30pm on Monday; adults/ seniors & students £6/4.

St Bride's, Fleet St (☎ 7353 1301, Fleet St EC4) Map 6 ✪ Blackfriars. Concert at 1.15pm on Tuesday and Friday; collection taken.
St George's Bloomsbury (☎ 7405 3044, Bloomsbury Way WC1) Map 8 ✪ Tottenham Court Road/Holborn. Concerts (usually at 1.10pm on Tuesday but phone ahead); donation requested.
St James's Piccadilly (☎ 7734 4511, 197 Piccadilly W1) Map 7 ✪ Piccadilly Circus. Concerts at 1.10pm on Monday, Wednesday and Friday; donation requested. Evening concerts at 7.30pm (days vary); £7.50-17.
St John's, Smith Square (☎ 7222 1061, Smith Square SW1) Map 2 ✪ Westminster. Concerts at 1pm on Monday; £6.
St Lawrence Jewry (☎ 7600 9478, Gresham St EC2) Map 9 ✪ Bank. Piano recitals on Monday, organ recitals on Tuesday at 1pm.
St Martin-in-the-Fields (☎ 7839 8362, Trafalgar Square WC2) Map 8 ✪ Charing Cross. Concerts at 1.05pm on Monday, Tuesday and Friday; donations requested. Evening concerts by candlelight Thursday to Saturday at 7.30pm; £6-20.
St Mary-le-Bow (☎ 7248 5139, Cheapside EC2) Map 9 ✪ Mansion House. Concerts at 1.05pm on Thursday; donations requested.
St Paul's Cathedral (☎ 7236 4128, New Change EC4) Map 9 ✪ St Paul's. Organ recitals at 5am on Sunday; £6.
St Sepulchre-without-Newgate (☎ 7248 3826, Giltspur St EC1) Map 6 ✪ Chancery Lane. Lunchtime concerts on Tuesday, Wednesday and Thursday (times vary); donation requested.
Southwark Cathedral (☎ 7367 6703, Montague Close SE1) Map 9 ✪ London Bridge. Organ recitals at 1.10pm on Monday; other concerts at 1.10pm on Tuesday.
Westminster Abbey (☎ 7222 5152, Dean's Yard SW1) Map 6 ✪ Westminster. Concerts at 6.30pm alternate Tuesdays late June to August; adults/students & seniors £7.50/5.

CINEMAS

During the 1950s and 1960s many of London's great Art Deco cinemas shut down. The late 1980s saw the arrival of the first American-style multiplex cinemas and they just keep coming. Although these cinemas offer more choice of films at one site and much more comfortable seating arrangements, they also tend to be expensive and serve up primarily Hollywood fare; the best places to look are in and around Leicester Square for this genre. Although full-price

Head for Leicester Square if you want to gape at the latest film spectacular.

Night Fever: indulging in 1970s kitsch in the West End

tickets can cost from £8 to £10 for a first-run film, afternoon shows are usually cheaper on weekdays (£4.50 to £5), and on Monday several places offer half-price tickets all day.

For less mainstream fare, try any of the following:

Barbican (☎ 7382 7000, Silk St EC2) ✆ Barbican

Everyman Hampstead (☎ 7431 1818, 5 Holly Bush Vale NW3) ✆ Hampstead

Gate (☎ 7727 4043, 87 Notting Hill Gate W1) ✆ Notting Hill Gate

ICA (☎ 7930 3647, Nash House, The Mall SW1) ✆ Charing Cross

Renoir (☎ 7837 8402, Brunswick Centre, Brunswick Square WC1) ✆ Russell Square

Rio (☎ 7254 6677 or 7241 9410, 107 Kingsland High St E8) Station: Dalston Kingsland

Ritzy (☎ 7737 2121, Brixton Oval, Coldharbour Lane SW2) ✆ Brixton

Screen on Baker St (☎ 7935 2772, 96 Baker St NW1) ✆ Baker Street

Screen on the Green (☎ 7226 3520, 83 Upper St N1) ✆ Angel

Screen on the Hill (☎ 7435 3366, 203 Haverstock Hill NW3) ✆ Belsize Park

Repertory and art-house cinemas include:

Ciné Lumière (☎ 7838 2144, W www.institut .ambafrance.org.uk, 17 Queensberry Place SW7) **Map 10** ✆ South Kensington. For French-language films, visit this cinema at the French Institute.

Electric Cinema (☎ 7229 8688, 191 Portobello Rd W11) **Map 5** ✆ Notting Hill. An ambitious refurbishment of this Edwardian building, the oldest purpose-built cinema in the UK, has created a new three-storey annexe with 200 comfy seats, a bar and a bookshop.

Lux (☎ 7684 0201, W www.lux.org.uk, 2-4 Hoxton Square N1) **Map 4** ✆ Old Street. This favourite plays to the trendies of Hoxton and Spitalfields.

National Film Theatre (NFT; ☎ 7928 3232, W www.bfi.org.uk/nft, South Bank SE1) **Map 6** ✆ Embankment/Waterloo. This is Britain's national repository of film and is often doing retrospectives.

Prince Charles (☎ 7437 8181, Leicester Place WC2) **Map 7** ✆ Leicester Square. This is central London's cheapest cinema, with low-price tickets (£2 to £3.50) for recent releases. It shows several films daily so check the programme.

Riverside Studios (☎ 8237 1111, Crisp Rd W6) **Map 1** ✆ Hammersmith. This is a good (if far-flung) choice for films not normally on the circuit.

THEATRE

London is arguably the world's greatest centre for theatre, and there's a whole lot more here than just *Les Miserables*, *Phantom of the Opera* and *Chicago*. With some 160 venues, and tickets so plentiful and reasonably priced, it would be a shame not to take in at least one of the best productions during your stay.

For a comprehensive look at what's being staged, pick up a copy of the free pamphlet *The Official London Theatre Guide* or visit W www.officiallondontheatre.co.uk.

Booking Agencies

You can book tickets through Ticketmaster (☎ 7344 4444, W www.ticketmaster.co.uk)

The Dos & Don'ts of Buying Theatre Tickets

The Society of London Theatre (SOLT; ☎ 7836 0971) offers the following advice for people buying theatre tickets while in London:

- Find out the normal prices for the show first.
- Ask the agent what the ticket's face value is *and* how much commission is being added.
- Ask to be shown where you'll be sitting on a seating plan.
- Do not pay for the ticket until you've actually seen them and checked the face value.
- Don't agree to pick the tickets up later or have them sent to you.
- Purchase tickets only from agents who are members of the Society of Ticket Agents and Retailers (STAR; ☎ 0870 603 9011, W www.s-t-a-r.org.uk). Ask to see proof of STAR membership.
- Never, ever, buy tickets from individuals in the street. Ticket touts are unfortunately still common around London's Theatreland. You will almost certainly be ripped off and might be sold an invalid ticket.

or First Call (☎ 7420 0000, W www.first call.co.uk) or directly through the theatre's box office. Most box offices open around 10am to 8pm Monday to Saturday but almost never on Sunday, when theatres are dark. If the production is sold out you may be able to buy a returned ticket on the day of the performance, although for something really popular you might need to start queuing before the returns actually go on sale.

On the day of performance *only* you can buy half-price tickets for West End productions from the ticket booth in the clocktower on the south side of Leicester Square (Map 7; ↔ Leicester Square). It is run by the nonprofit Society of London Theatre (SOLT) and wholly legitimate; be wary of commercial ticket agencies nearby, particularly those along Cranbourn St, which advertise half-price tickets without mentioning the large commission added to the price. The tkts booth opens 10am to 7pm Monday to Saturday and noon to 3pm on Sunday and levies a £2.50 service charge per ticket. Payment is by cash or credit/debit card (Visa, Mastercard, American Express, Switch).

Student stand-by tickets are sometimes available on production of identity cards one hour before the performance starts. Phone the Student Theatre Line on ☎ 7379 8900 for more details.

Royal National Theatre

Royal National Theatre (☎ 7452 3000, W www.nationaltheatre.org.uk, South Bank SE1) Map 6 ↔ Waterloo. Britain's flagship theatre showcases classic and contemporary plays and hosts appearances by the world's best companies. It has three auditoriums:

Olivier & *Lyttleton* Tickets adult/student & under-18s/senior £10-28/10/15, same-day performance £15, adult/student stand-by tickets £16/8, evening performance £10-32.50; matinee performance Mon-Thur & Sat. Visitors to the box office can sometimes buy one or two tickets for same-day performances and stand-by (or returned) tickets are sometimes available two hours before the performance, students however must wait until just 45 minutes before the curtain goes up to purchase tickets. Registered disabled visitors are eligible for discounts.

Cottesloe Tickets £18-22, restricted-view seats £12, adult/student stand-by tickets £16/8. The Cottesloe stages smaller, more cutting-edge productions than the other two.

Behind the scenes tours (£5) of the theatre are available at 10.15am, 12.15pm (or 12.30pm) and 5.15pm (or 5.30pm) Monday to Saturday. Ring ☎ 7452 3400 for details.

Barbican

Barbican (☎ 7638 8891, W www.barbican .org.uk, Silk St EC2) Map 10 ↔ Barbican. Midweek matinee performance Barbican

Theatre £6-28, Pit £8-10, other times £18-28, £12-15. This is the London home of the Royal Shakespeare Company, with two auditoriums: the Barbican Theatre and the smaller Pit. Tickets are half-price for anyone aged under 25 on the fourth night of performance if booked in advance. There are also price reductions for anyone aged over 60 and students at matinees and Wednesday evening performances.

Royal Court

Royal Court (☎ 7565 5000, [W] www.royal courttheatre.com, Sloane Square SW1) Map 9 ⊖ Sloane Square. Tickets 10p-£24.50, Mon £5. The Royal Court has returned to its home with two stages on the eastern side of Sloane Square following a four-year, £25 million refurbishment, during which time the company operated out of two West End theatres. It tends to favour the new and the anti-establishment.

Globe Theatre

Shakespeare's Globe (☎ 7401 9919, [W] www .shakespeares-globe.org, 21 New Globe Walk SE1) Map 9 ⊖ London Bridge. Standing/seated tickets £5/9-27. Come to the Globe, a replica of William Shakespeare's 'Wooden O' that opened in 1997, for a thoroughly different theatrical experience. Although there are wooden-bench seats in tiers around the stage, many people emulate the 17th-century 'groundlings' who stood in front of the stage, shouting and cajoling as the mood took them.

The Globe makes few concessions to modern sensibilities. With no roof, it is open to the elements, although the seated part is covered; you may have to wrap up warmly, although no umbrellas are allowed (cheap macs are available to buy at the theatre). Performances of plays by Shakespeare and his contemporaries and at least one new work are staged from May to September only. Two pillars holding up the stage canopy (the 'Heavens') obscure much of the view in section D; you'd almost do better to stand. In winter, plays are staged in the new indoor *Inigo Jones Theatre*, a replica of a Jacobean playhouse at the Globe.

West End Theatres

Every summer the West End theatres stage a new crop of plays, musicals and other performances. For full details, consult *Time Out*. Addresses and box-office phone numbers of the theatres are given below.

Adelphi (☎ 7344 0055, Strand WC2) **Map 8** ⊖ Charing Cross
Albery (☎ 7369 1740, 85 St Martin's Lane WC2) **Map 8** ⊖ Leicester Square
Aldwych (☎ 0870 400 0805, 49 Aldwych WC2) **Map 8** ⊖ Holborn
Apollo (☎ 7494 5070, 39 Shaftesbury Ave W1) **Map 7** ⊖ Piccadilly Circus
Cambridge (☎ 7494 5080, Earlham St WC2) **Map 8** ⊖ Covent Garden
Comedy (☎ 7369 1731, Panton St SW1) **Map 7** ⊖ Piccadilly Circus
Criterion (☎ 7413 1437, Piccadilly Circus W1) **Map 7** ⊖ Piccadilly Circus
Dominion (☎ 0870 607 7400, 268-9 Tottenham Court Rd W1) **Map 7** ⊖ Tottenham Court Road
Duke of York (☎ 7836 4615, St Martin's Lane WC2) **Map 8** ⊖ Leicester Square
Fortune (☎ 7836 2238, Russell St WC2) **Map 8** ⊖ Covent Garden
Garrick (☎ 7494 5085, 2 Charing Cross Rd WC2) **Map 8** ⊖ Charing Cross
Gielgud (☎ 7494 5065, 33 Shaftesbury Ave W1) **Map 7** ⊖ Piccadilly Circus
Her Majesty's (☎ 7494 5400, Haymarket SW1) **Map 7** ⊖ Piccadilly Circus
London Palladium (☎ 7494 5020, 8 Argyll St W1) **Map 7** ⊖ Oxford Circus
Lyceum (☎ 7420 8100, 21 Wellington St WC2) **Map 8** ⊖ Covent Garden
Lyric (☎ 7494 5045, Shaftesbury Ave W1) **Map 7** ⊖ Piccadilly Circus
New Ambassadors (☎ 7369 1761, West St WC2) **Map 8** ⊖ Leicester Square
New London (☎ 7405 0072, Drury Lane WC2) **Map 8** ⊖ Holborn
Palace (☎ 7434 0909, Shaftesbury Ave W1) **Map 8** ⊖ Leicester Square
Phoenix (☎ 7369 1733, 110 Charing Cross Rd WC2) **Map 8** ⊖ Tottenham Court Road
Piccadilly (☎ 7478 8800, Denman St W1) **Map 7** ⊖ Piccadilly Circus
Prince Edward (☎ 7447 5400, 30 Old Compton St W1) ⊖ Leicester Square
Prince of Wales (☎ 7839 5987, 31 Coventry St W1) **Map 7** ⊖ Piccadilly Circus
Queen's (☎ 7494 5040, Shaftesbury Ave W1) **Map 7** ⊖ Piccadilly Circus
St Martin's (☎ 7836 1443, West St WC2) **Map 8** ⊖ Leicester Square

ENTERTAINMENT

Shaftesbury (☎ 7379 5399, 210 Shaftesbury Ave WC2) **Map 8** ⊖ Tottenham Court Road/ Holborn

Savoy (☎ 7836 8888, Savoy Court, Strand WC2) **Map 8** ⊖ Charing Cross

Strand (☎ 7836 4144, Aldwych WC2) **Map 8** ⊖ Covent Garden

Theatre Royal Drury Lane (☎ 7494 5060, Catherine St WC2) **Map 8** ⊖ Covent Garden

Theatre Royal Haymarket (☎ 0870 901 3356, Haymarket SW1) **Map 7** ⊖ Piccadilly Circus

Whitehall (☎ 7321 5400, 14 Whitehall SW1) **Map 8** ⊖ Charing Cross

Wyndham's (☎ 7369 1736, Charing Cross Rd WC2) **Map 8** ⊖ Leicester Square

Other Theatres

Open Air Theatre (☎ 7486 2431, W www .open-air-theatre.org.uk, Inner Circle, Regent's Park NW1) **Map 3** ⊖ Baker Street. Tickets £5-23. From June to early September it's fun to take in a Shakespearean play or musical at this outdoor theatre.

And as if all of that wasn't enough, at any time of the year London's many off-West End and fringe-theatre productions offer a selection of the amazing, the boring, the life-enhancing and the downright ridiculous. Some of the better venues include:

Bridewell Theatre (☎ 7936 3456, 14 Bride Lane, off Fleet St EC4) **Map 6** ⊖ Blackfriars

Donmar Warehouse (☎ 7369 1732, 41 Earlham St WC2) **Map 8** ⊖ Covent Garden

Drill Hall (☎ 7307 5060, 16 Chenies St WC1) **Map 4** ⊖ Goodge Street

Greenwich Theatre (☎ 8858 7755, Crooms Hill SE10) **Map 13** DLR: Greenwich

Hackney Empire (☎ 8985 2424, 291 Mare St E8) **Map 2** Station: Hackney Central

Hampstead Theatre (☎ 7722 9301, 98 Avenue Rd NW3) **Map 2** ⊖ Swiss Cottage

King's Head (☎ 7226 1916, 115 Upper St N1) **Map 4** ⊖ Highbury & Islington

Old Vic (☎ 7928 7616, Waterloo Rd SE1) **Map 6** ⊖ Waterloo

Young Vic (☎ 7928 6363, 66 The Cut SE1) **Map 6** ⊖ Waterloo

OPERA

As well as the following venues, Holland Park Theatre (see the Ballet & Dance section) stages opera performances in summer.

Royal Opera House

Royal Opera House (☎ 7304 4000, W www .royaloperahouse.org, Covent GardenWC2) **Map 7** ⊖ Covent Garden. Tickets £6-150, midweek matinees £6.50-50. Following a £213 million redevelopment, this has re-opened and has welcomed home the peripatetic Royal Opera and Royal Ballet (see Ballet & Dance below). As a result of the makeover, it has become much more proletarian: the renovated Floral Hall is now open to the public during the day, with free lunchtime concerts at 1pm on Monday, exhibitions and daily tours. For the best seats, you'll still need to consider a second mortgage, though.

London Coliseum

London Coliseum (☎ 7632 8300, W www .eno.org, St Martin's Lane WC1) **Map 8** ⊖ Leicester Square/Charing Cross. Tickets £3-58. The home of the English National Opera is a lot more reasonably priced than the Royal Opera House and presents its opera in English. From 10am on the day of performance, balcony (restricted view)/ dress circle seats go on sale for £3/29; expect a long queue. Stand-by tickets are available to students for £12.

BALLET & DANCE

London is home to five major dance companies and a host of small and experimental ones. The Royal Ballet, the best classical-ballet company in the land, is based at the Royal Opera House in Covent Garden; the London Coliseum (see the previous section) is another venue for ballet at Christmas and in summer.

The annual contemporary dance event in London is Dance Umbrella (see Special Events in the Facts for the Visitor chapter). For more information about dance in the capital visit the London Dance Network's Web site at W www.londondance.com.

Holland Park Opera Theatre (☎ 7602 7856, W www.operalondon.com, Holland Park, off Kensington High St W8) **Map 5** ⊖ Kensington High Street. This 720-seat theatre hosts ballet and opera performances for 10 weeks in summer.

The Royal Opera House, Covent Garden, is the sophisticated seat of opera and ballet in London.

Peacock Theatre (☎ 7863 8222, Ⓦ www .sadlers-wells.com, Portugal St WC2) **Map 8** ⊖ Holborn. Tickets £8.50-35. 'Sadler's Wells in the West End' is a smaller venue, hosting more popular dance fare and less established companies.

The Place (☎ 7387 0031, Ⓦ www.the place.org.uk, 17 Duke's Rd WC1) **Map 3** ⊖ Euston. This is another important address for contemporary dance and home to the Richard Alston Dance Company.

Riverside Studios & ICA (see the Cinemas section earlier in this chapter) These are the most important venues for small experimental and avant-garde dance companies.

Royal Opera House (☎ 7304 4000, Ⓦ www .royaloperahouse.org, Covent Garden WC2) **Map 8** ⊖ Covent Garden. Tickets £6-65. The Royal Ballet has ended its nomadic existence and has now returned to its refurbished (and resplendent) home.

Sadler's Wells (☎ 7863 8000, Ⓦ www.sadlers-wells.com, Rosebery Ave EC1) **Map 4** ⊖ Angel. Tickets £8.50-40. This venue, which reopened in 1998 after a total refurbishment, has been associated with dance ever since Thomas Sadler set up a 'musick house' next to his medicinal spa in 1683. Its new, ultramodern theatre attracts contemporary and classical-dance troupes from around the world. The smaller *Lilian Baylis Theatre* here stages studio productions.

ORGANISED ENTERTAINMENT

Inevitably there are a few places where you can do the full tourist thing over a themed dinner, with entertainment, food and drink all laid on for one all-inclusive price. Here are a few of the better ones:

Talk of London (☎ 7405 0072, New London Theatre, Parker St, off Drury Lane WC2) **Map 8** ⊖ Holborn. Cabaret £15-25, dinner & cabaret £42.50, 8pm Mon-Thur, 7pm & 10pm Fri & Sat. This place stages the kinds of cabarets where the women wear two beads and a feather (or was that two feathers and a bead?) and the guys all look like hoods.

Beefeater Medieval Banquet (☎ 7480 5353, Ⓦ www.medievalbanquet.com, Ivory House, St Katharine's Dock E1) **Map 9** ⊖ Tower Hill. Fancy a five-course medieval banquet, with jesters, minstrels, chivalrous knights-a-jousting and buxom wenches-a-serving? Doors open at 7.45pm daily and the banquet and show (£38.50 to £39.50 depending on the night, £22 for kids aged 4 to 14) begins a half-hour later.

It's also possible to go on a lunch or dinner cruise on the Thames, complete with dancing and live music:

Bateaux London (☎ 7695 1803, departures from Embankment Pier) **Map 6** This company offers one-hour lunch cruises at 12.15pm Monday to Saturday for £20.50 and 2¾-hour dinner-dance cruises daily at 7.15pm for £57.

City Cruises (☎ 7740 0400, Ⓦ www.city cruises.com, departures from Westminster Pier) **Map 6** This company offers a London Showboat dinner cruise (£48) at 7pm and returning at 10.30pm from Wednesday to Sunday, early

ENTERTAINMENT

April to October. Cruises leave on Friday and Saturday only November to early April.

Thames Cruises (☎ 7928 9009, departures from Westminster Pier) **Map 6** This company offers a four-hour evening disco cruise at 7pm weekdays and at 8pm on Saturday. It costs £17.80/ 12.80 with/without food.

SPECTATOR SPORTS

London plays host to countless sporting events year-round. As always the entertainment weekly, *Time Out*, is the best source of information on fixtures, times, venues and ticket prices.

Football

North-west London's Wembley Stadium, where the English national side has traditionally played international matches and the FA Cup Final has taken place (mid-May), closed in 2000 and the building, dating from 1923 with its two landmark towers, was to be demolished. The plan was to replace it with a state-of-the-art, 80,000-seat national stadium to be used for football, rugby league and athletics, but at the time of writing everything was on hold, and major football matches were being played at stadiums outside London.

There are a dozen league teams in London and usually around six enjoy the big time of the Premier League, meaning that on any weekend of the season, from August to mid-May, quality football is just a tube or train ride away – if you can manage to get hold of a ticket.

The following are the current Premiership teams in and around London, although tickets for most matches are usually sold out well in advance:

Arsenal (☎ 7413 3366, **W** www.arsenal.com, Avenell Rd N5) **Map 1** ⊖ Arsenal. Tickets £10-39.

Charlton Athletic (☎ 8333 4010, **W** www.cafc.co.uk, The Valley, Floyd Rd SE7) **Map 1** Station: Charlton. Usually season ticket-holders only (£120-480) but call ahead.

Chelsea (☎ 7385 5545, ticketline ☎ 7386 7799, **W** www.chelseafc.co.uk, Stamford Bridge Stadium, Fulham Rd SW6) **Map 10** ⊖ Fulham Broadway. Tickets £11-40. Tours (☎ 0870

603 0005; adult/senior & child £8/5) take place at 11am, 1pm and 3pm daily. See Chelsea World of Sport in the Things to See & Do chapter.

Fulham (☎ 7893 8383, ticketline 7384 4710 **W** www.fulhamfc.co.uk, Craven Cottage, Stevenage Rd SW6) **Map 2** ⊖ Putney Bridge. Tickets £6-26.

Tottenham Hotspur (☎ 8365 5000, ticketline 08700 112222 **W** www.spurs.co.uk, White Hart Lane N17) **Map 1** Station: White Hart Lane. Tickets £11-55.

West Ham United (☎ 8365 5000, ticketline 8548 2700, **W** www.westhamunited.co.uk, Boleyn Ground, Green St E13) **Map 1** ⊖ Upton Park. Tickets £26-46.

Cricket

Cricket continues to flourish, despite the dismal fortunes of the England team. Test matches take place at two cricket grounds: Lord's and the Oval. Tickets are expensive (£20 to £50) and tend to go fast; you're better off looking out for a county fixture (£8 to £10) between April and September.

Lord's (☎ 7432 1066, **W** www.lords.org, St John's Wood Rd NW8) **Map 3** ⊖ St John's Wood. Middlesex plays at Lord's. For details of tours of Lord's, see Lord's Cricket Ground in the Things to See & Do chapter.

The Oval (☎ 7582 7764, **W** www.surrey ccc.co.uk, Kennington Oval SE11) **Map 2** ⊖ Oval. Surrey plays at The Oval.

Rugby Union & Rugby League

For rugby union fans, south-west London is the place to be, with a number of good-quality teams such as Harlequins, Wasps and London Welsh playing from August to May. Between January and March England, Scotland, Wales, Ireland, France and Italy compete in the Six Nations Championship.

Twickenham Rugby Stadium (☎ 8892 2000, **W** www.rfu.com, Rugby Rd, Twickenham) **Map 1** ⊖ Hounslow East, then bus No 281/Station: Twickenham. You're guaranteed two or three big matches a year at this shrine of English rugby union. For details of tours of the stadium and its museum, see the Richmond & Twickenham in the Things to See & Do chapter.

London Broncos (☎ 8853 8001, **W** www. londonbroncos.co.uk, The Valley, Floyd Rd SE7) **Map 1** Station: Charlton. This is the only rugby league side in southern England.

Tennis

Tennis and Wimbledon in south-east London are almost synonymous.

Wimbledon (☎ *8944 1066, 8946 2244,* W *www.wimbledon.org, Church Rd SW19)* **Map 1** ⊖ Southfields/Wimbledon Park. The All England Lawn Tennis Championships have been taking place here in late June/early July since 1877. But the queues, exorbitant prices, limited ticket availability and cramped conditions may have you thinking Wimbledon is just a – well – racket. Although a limited number of seats for the Centre Court and Court Nos 1 and 2 go on sale on the day of play, the queues is painfully long. The nearer to the finals it is, the higher the prices; a Centre Court ticket that costs £25 a week before the final will cost twice that on the day. Prices for the outside courts cost under £10 and are reduced after 5pm.

Between 1 September and 31 December each year there's a public ballot for tickets for the best seats at the following year's tournament. Between those dates, you can try your luck by sending a stamped addressed envelope to the All England Lawn Tennis Club, PO Box 98, Church Rd, Wimbledon SW19 5AE.

Athletics

Crystal Palace National Sports Centre (☎ *8778 0131,* W *www.crystalpalace.co .uk, Ledrington Rd SE19)* **Map 1** Station: Crystal Palace. Athletics and swimming meetings attracting major international and domestic stars take place here regularly throughout the summer.

Horse Racing

There are plenty of top-quality racecourses within striking distance of London for those who want to have a flutter. The flat racing season runs from April to September.

In June **Ascot** (☎ *01344-622211,* W *www .ascot.co.uk)* in Berkshire can be nice if a bit posy with all those outrageous hats. Also in June, Derby Day at **Epsom** (☎ *01372-470047,* W *www.epsomderby.co.uk)* in Surrey is much more down-to-earth. **Sandown Park** (☎ *01372-463072,* W *www .sandown.co.uk),* also in Surrey, is generally considered to be the finest racecourse in the south-east. **Windsor** (☎ *01753-865234,* W *www.windsorracing.co.uk),* by the castle, is an idyllic spot for a day at the races.

Greyhound Racing

If you're looking for a cheap and – it must be said – somewhat cheesy night out, consider going to the dogs. Greyhound racing, in which with six to eight dumb mutts chase a mechanical rabbit around an oval track, costs as little as £1.50 to £5 for 12-race meeting and it is Britain's second most popular sport after football. A few small flutters will guarantee excitement, and you'll rub shoulders with a London subculture that's welcoming and more than a little shady:

Catford Stadium (☎ *8690 8000, Adenmore Rd SE6)* **Map 1** Station: Catford Bridge
Walthamstow Stadium (☎ *8531 4255,* W *www .wsgreyhound.co.uk, Chingford Rd E4)* **Map 1** Station: Highams Park
Wimbledon Stadium (☎ *8946 8000,* W *www .wimbledondogs.co.uk, Plough Lane SW17)* ⊖ Wimbledon Park

Shopping

Napoleon described Britain as a nation of shopkeepers, but as faceless chain stores decimate small shops along the high streets, it would be more accurate to say that it's now a nation of shoppers. Nowhere is that more apparent than in London; indeed, shopping is one of the capital's most popular recreational pastimes.

WHAT TO BUY

London is a mecca for shopaholics from the UK and continental Europe, and if you can't find it here, it probably doesn't exist.

If you're looking for something with a British 'brand' on it, eschew the Union Jack-emblazoned kitsch of Carnaby and Oxford Sts and Covent Garden and go for things that the Brits themselves know are of high quality, sometimes stylish and always solid: Dr Marten boots and shoes, Burberry raingear, tailor-made shorts and suits from Jermyn St and Saville Row, Royal Doulton glass and china, and costume jewellery (be it for the finger, wrist, nose, eyebrow or navel). London's bookshops are celebrated on the street and in literature; many cater for the most obscure tastes. And the word 'antique' is not always prefaced by 'priceless'; you'll find any number of interesting and affordable curios and baubles at the Antiquarius Antiques Centre in Chelsea and Bermondsey Market, for example.

Root around Kensington's antique shops for curios from bygone times.

In general, shops open from 9am or 10am to about 6pm or 6.30pm Monday to Saturday, with the usual 'late night' (normally to 8pm) on Thursday. A growing number of larger stores open on Sunday, most typically from noon to 6pm but sometimes from 10am to 4pm. Shoppers who can't get enough should buy the annual *Time Out Shopping Guide* (£7.99), with details of virtually every shopping opportunity in the capital.

Antiques

Antique hunters may find something worthwhile at the Saturday antiques market along Portobello Rd, but better pickings are to be had at Camden Passage or Bermondsey Market (see the special section 'To Market, to Market').

Antiquarius Antiques Centre (☎ 7531 5353, 131-41 King's Rd SW3) **Map 10** ⊖ Sloane Square. Open 10am-6pm Mon-Sat. Antiquarius is packed with 120 stalls and dealers selling everything from top hats and corkscrews to old luggage and jewellery. It's definitely worth a look though crammed with tourists.

Chelsea Old Town Hall (☎ 01225-723894, King's Rd SW3) **Map 10** ⊖ Sloane Square. Open 11am-5.30pm Sunday (monthly). Built on King's Rd in 1886, this solid pile is the venue for a popular antiques fair held one Sunday a month. Call for more information and the exact dates.

London Architectural Salvage & Supply Company (☎ 7749 9944, ☒ www.lassco.co.uk, St Michael's Church, Mark St EC2, enter from Leonard St) **Map 4** ⊖ Old Street. Open 10am-5pm Mon, Wed-Sat, 10am-8pm Tues. This place is a recycler's dream come true, with everything from slate tiles and oak floorboards to enormous marble fireplaces and garden follies. Its location, in an old church, is worth the trip alone.

London Silver Vaults (☎ 7242 3844, Chancery House, 53-63 Chancery Lane WC2, enter from Southampton Buildings) **Map 6** ⊖ Chancery Lane. Open 9am-5.30pm Mon-Fri, 9am-1pm Sat. The 40 subterranean shops collectively known as the London Silver Vaults form the largest collection of silver under one roof in the world. The shops sell anything and everything made from silver – from jewellery and picture frames to candelabra and tea services for a dozen people. Though everything is for sale, you might just want to ogle at some of the merchandise and wonder which over-the-top stately home it came from.

Sean Arnold Sporting Antiques (☎ 7221 2267, 1 Pembridge Villas W2) **Map 5** ⊖ Bayswater. This specialist antique shop stocks pricey old toys for grown-up boys.

Books

General For those who read the book or saw the film *84 Charing Cross Road*, Charing Cross Rd (Maps 7 & 8; ⊖ Tottenham Court Road/Leicester Square) will need no introduction. This is where to go when you want reading material old or new. For antiquarian books, you should also try the little alleyways (Cecil Court and St Martin's Court) linking Charing Cross Rd and St Martin's Lane.

Blackwell's (☎ 7292 5100, **W** www.bookshop .blackwell.co.uk, 100 Charing Cross Rd WC2) **Map 8** ⊖ Tottenham Court Road. This shop is primarily for academic titles but stocks general books as well.

Borders (☎ 7379 8877, **W** www.bordersstores .com, 120 Charing Cross Rd WC2) **Map 8** ⊖ Tottenham Court Road; (☎ 7292 1600, 203 Oxford St W1) **Map 7** ⊖ Oxford Circus. This branch of the American chain has a good selection of general titles as well as academic ones. The bigger Oxford St store has four floors of books, magazines, newspapers from around the world and CDs, tapes and DVDs. There's a coffee shop/bar on the 2nd floor.

Foyle's (☎ 7437 5660, **W** www.foyles.co.uk, 113-9 Charing Cross Rd WC2) **Map 8** ⊖ Tottenham Court Road. This is the biggest and by far the most confusing bookshop in London, but it often stocks titles you may not find elsewhere.

Waterstone's (☎ 7434 4291, **W** www.waterstones .co.uk, 121 Charing Cross Rd WC2) **Map 7** ⊖ Leicester Square; (☎ 7851 2400, 203-6 Piccadilly W1) **Map 7** ⊖ Piccadilly Circus; (☎ 7636 1577, 82 Gower St WC1) **Map 6** ⊖ Goodge Street. This chain, which transformed book buying for Londoners with its knowledgeable staff, organised shelves and serene surrounds, keeps on growing, with over 30 branches in greater London. The megastore on Piccadilly is the biggest bookshop in Europe.

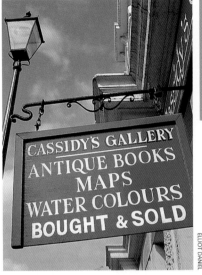

ELLIOT DANIEL

For mighty tomes and ancient maps head down river to Greenwich.

Specialist There are plenty of specialist bookshops on or around the famous Charing Cross Rd (Map 8), including the following:

Helter Skelter (☎ 7836 1151, **W** www.skelter .demon.co.uk, 4 Denmark St WC2) This excellent shop just off Charing Cross Rd has very helpful staff and specialises in books about popular music.

Murder One (☎ 7734 3485, 71-3 Charing Cross Rd WC2) Head for Murder One if crime fiction, science fiction and romance light your candle.

Sportspages (☎ 7240 9604, **W** www.sports pages.co.uk, 94-6 Charing Cross Rd) The sorts of books, magazines and fanzines sold here are self-explanatory.

Zwemmer Art & Architecture (☎ 7240 4158, **W** www.zwemmer.com, 24 Litchfield St WC2; ☎ 7240 4157, 80 Charing Cross Rd WC2) Zwemmer stocks all kinds of art and architecture books, as you may have guessed. The branch opposite and facing Charing Cross Rd specialises in books on photography and the cinema.

For other specialist bookshops, you'll have to travel farther afield.

Books for Cooks (☎ *7221 1992*, **W** *www.books forcooks.com, 4 Blenheim Crescent W11*) **Map 5** ⊖ Ladbroke Grove. This shop has an enormous collection of cookery books; there's also a small cafe with a test kitchen where you can sample some of the recipes.

French Bookshop (☎ *7584 2840*, **W** *www.frenc hbookshop.com, 28 Bute St SW7*) **Map 10** ⊖ South Kensington. Head here for books *en français* and about France.

Garden Books (☎ *7792 0777, 11 Blenheim Crescent W11*) **Map 5** ⊖ Ladbroke Grove. This bookshop, on the same street as Books for Cooks and the seminal Travel Bookshop, is where to head for books on gardening.

Gay's the Word (☎ *7278 7654*, **W** *www.gays theword.co.uk, 66 Marchmont St WC1*) **Map 4** ⊖ Russell Square. This shop stocks guides and literature for, by and about gay men and women.

Grant & Cutler (☎ *7734 2012*, **W** *www.grant andcutler.com, 55-7 Great Marlborough St W1*) **Map 7** ⊖ Oxford Circus. This is positively the best foreign-language bookshop in London, with books in or on everything from Arabic to Zulu.

Ian Allen's Transport Bookshop (☎ *7401 2100, 45-6 Lower Marsh SE1*) **Map 6** ⊖ Waterloo. The train spotter in you won't be able to resist this shop which specialises in transport and defence: aircraft, motor vehicles and, of course, those choo-choo trains.

The major chains are adequate sources of local guidebooks and maps, but there are also several specialist travel bookshops.

Daunt Books (☎ *7224 2295, 83-84 Marylebone High St W1*) **Map 6** ⊖ Baker Street. Daunt has a wide selection of guides and books in a beautiful old sky-lit shop in Marylebone.

Stanford's (☎ *7836 1321*, **W** *www.stanfords.co .uk, 12-14 Long Acre WC2*) **Map 8** ⊖ Covent Garden; (*Britain Visitor Centre*, ☎ *7808 3891, 1 Regent St SW1*) **Map 7** ⊖ Piccadilly Circus; (*British Airways Travel Shop* ☎ *7434 4744, 156 Regent St W1*) **Map 7** ⊖ Piccadilly Circus. Stanford's main shop has one of the largest selections of maps, guides and travel literature in the world. Other branches have limited stock.

Travel Bookshop (☎ *7229 5260*, **W** *www.travel bookshop.co.uk, 13 Blenheim Crescent W11*) **Map 5** ⊖ Ladbroke Grove. London's best 'boutique' travel bookshop has all the new travel guides as well as out-of-print and antiquarian gems.

Second-hand There are several second-hand bookshops along Charing Cross Rd (Map 8) and a used book market south of the river.

Riverside Walk Market (*Riverside Walk SE1*) **Map 6** ⊖ Waterloo/Embankment. Open 10am-5pm Sat & Sun. One of the best places for cheap second-hand books long out of print is this book market on the South Bank under the arches of Waterloo Bridge. Some of the 20-odd dealers open sporadically during the week.

Camping & Backpacking Equipment

London is a great place to search for gear destined for use in the great outdoors.

Blacks (☎ *7404 5681*, **W** *www.blacks.co.uk, 10-11 Holborn WC1*) **Map 6** ⊖ Holborn. This is just one of six branches of the national chain that sells tents and other camping equipment.

Nomad Traveller's Store & Medical Centre (☎ *8889 7014*, **W** *www.nomadtravel.co.uk, 3-4 Wellington Terrace, Turnpike Lane N8*) ⊖ Turnpike Lane. This shop stocks all the bits and bobs a traveller could possibly want or need (mosquito netting, moneybelts and so on) along with more serious outdoor gear.

Outdoors (☎ *7329 8757, 41 Ludgate Hill EC4*) **Map 6** ⊖ Blackfriars; (☎ *7834 6007, 27 Buckingham Palace Rd SW1*) **Map 11** ⊖ Victoria. This rebrand of the Camping & Outdoor Centres chain has two branches in London: one in the City and another in Pimlico.

YHA Adventure Shop (☎ *7938 2948*, **W** *www .yhaadventure.co.uk, 174 Kensington High St W8*) **Map 5** ⊖ High Street Kensington; (☎ *7233 6500, 120 Victoria St SW1*) **Map 11** ⊖ Victoria; (☎ *7025 1900, 152-60 Wardour St W1*) ⊖ Tottenham Court Rd. This is an excellent place to stock up on all sorts of camping and walking gear.

Clothing

Designer Fashion Any international designer worth his or her threads has at least one outlet in London, often in Sloane or Bond Sts or in Knightsbridge. But watch out for classic British designers such as Alexander McQueen (who also does a range of cool sunglasses), Amanda Wakeley, Vivienne Westwood, Paul Smith and

Optical emporiums dot the city if you want designer shades or fancy frames.

Nicole Farhi as well as newcomers Roland Mouret, Scott Henshall, Tracey Mulligan and Liza Bruce, who mix formal design with hip streetwear.

The following designer shops are always window-shoppable even if you can't avoid their fripperies (which, you won't be surprised to learn, comes from the Old French *frèpe* for 'rag').

Amanda Wakeley (☎ 7590 9105, 80 Fulham Rd SW3) ❹ South Kensington. Classic foundation pieces and accessories from the upholder of the twin set and pearls.

Betty Jackson (☎ 7589 7884, 311 Brompton Rd SW3) ❹ South Kensington. Fashionable – but not overly so – linen, suede and knit pieces.

Nicole Farhi (☎ 7499 8368, 158 New Bond St W1) ❹ Bond Street. You'll also find this designer's line at Harrods, Harvey Nichols and Selfridges.

Paul Smith (☎ 7379 7133, 40-4 Floral St WC2) ❹ Covent Garden. The recently knighted designer has both a men's and a women's line.

Prada (☎ 7647 5000, 16-18 Old Bond St W1) ❹ Piccadilly Circus/Green Park. Classic sportswear and casuals that never go out of fashion.

Ralph Lauren (☎ 7535 4600, 1 New Bond St W1) ❹ Piccadilly Circus/Green Park. Simple but elegant dresses, tunics and tops.

Tomasz Starewski (☎ 7244 6138, 14 Stanhope Mews West SW7) ❹ Gloucester Road. Mix and match separates for the young at heart.

Vivienne Westwood (☎ 7629 3757, 6 Davies St W1) ❹ Bond Street. The punk-generation designer still shocks, stocks and sells.

Street Fashion Carnaby St, south-east of Oxford Circus tube station, was the centre of the fashion world in the swinging 1960s but no more. Nowadays you'd be better off checking out the shops on or around the King's Rd and Kensington High St and the stalls in Portobello Rd and Camden markets.

Ad Hoc (☎ 7376 8829, 153 King's Rd SW3) **Map 10** ❹ Sloane Square. A good choice for such items as fetish gear, leather boots and lace-up tops.

CM Store (☎ 7351 9361, 121 King's Rd SW3) **Map 10** ❹ Sloane Square. Mostly mainstream labels, with Ts for the boys and denim for the girls.

Dispensary (☎ 7721 9290, 25 Pembridge Rd W11) **Map 5** ❹ Notting Hill Gate. This place sells similar merchandise to Ad Hoc.

French Connection UK (☎ 7629 7766, 396 Oxford St W1) **Map 6** ❹ Oxford Circus. FCUK, the in-your-face chain with the aggressive PR department, still leads in style and quality in the street-chic department.

High Jinks (☎ 7240 5580, Thomas Neal Centre, Earlham St WC2) **Map 8** ❹ Covent Garden. Large streetwear emporium crammed with street fashion by struggling young designers, who are more than a little keen to sell their imaginative glad rags.

Pineapple (☎ 7836 4006, 6a Lanley St WC2) **Map 8** ❹ Covent Garden. This is one of many trendy shops for women's clothing in the Covent Garden area.

Zara (☎ 7534 9500, 118 Regent St W1) **Map 7** ❹ Piccadilly Circus/Oxford Street. Head here for fashionable throwaways that are here today and gone tomorrow.

Retro & Second-hand Among the better places for second-hand and retro gear (beaded flapper-dresses from the 1920s, 1950s prom dresses, Nehru jackets from the 1960s and so on) are the following:

Blackout II (☎ 7240 5006, 51 Endell St WC2) ✪ Covent Garden. Designer retro gear for men and women from the '50s to the '80s.

Cornucopia (☎ 7828 5752, 12 Upper Tachbrook St SW1) ✪ Victoria. This shop stocks mostly women's apparel and accessories from the 1940s.

Delta of Venus (☎ 7387 3037, 151 Drummond St NW1) ✪ Euston. The speciality here is clothing and other bits and bobs from the 1960s.

Yesterday's Bread (☎ 7287 1929, 29-31 Foubert's Place W1) ✪ Oxford Circus. Here's everything a hipster would need to look cool in the 1970s.

Raingear Not surprisingly in this wet town, raincoats and umbrellas can be stylish and of high quality.

Aquascutum (☎ 7675 8200, 100 Regent St W1) **Map 7** ✪ Piccadilly Circus. Come here for coats, especially retro-inspired pea jackets and storm coats.

Burberry (☎ 7839 5222, 21-3 New Bond St SW1) **Map 6** ✪ Bond Street/Oxford Circus. Head here for that most London of articles of clothing – the macintosh – in its distinctive tartan pattern.

James Smith & Sons (☎ 7836 4731, 53 New Oxford St WC1) **Map 8** ✪ Tottenham Court Road. No-one makes and stocks umbrellas (along with canes and walking sticks) like James Smith. The shop's exterior is a museum piece.

Underwear *Marks & Spencer* (see the Department Stores section later in this chapter) is celebrated from Hong Kong to Hammersmith for its high-quality yet affordable 'smalls', but there are a couple of specialist shops worth peeping at.

Agent Provocateur (☎ 7439 0229, 6 Broadwick St W1) **Map 7** ✪ Oxford Circus; (☎ 7235 0229, 16 Pont St SW1) **Map 5** ✪ Knightsbridge. For women's knickers to die for (or over, or in), check out this place. Both branches are decidedly window-shoppable.

Ann Summers (☎ 7434 2475, 79 Wardour St W1) **Map 7** ✪ Piccadilly Circus. Lingerie for show rather than comfort is the speciality here.

Rigby & Peller (☎ 7589 9293, 2 Hans Rd SW3) **Map 10** ✪ Knightsbridge. This old-fashioned

place's claim to fame is that it makes the queen's bras. Both off-the-peg and made-to-measure bras, corsets and swimwear are available.

Food & Drink

Run-of-the-mill food shops are 10 a penny all over London, but the food halls at *Harrods*, *Selfridges* and *Fortnum & Mason* (see under Department Stores later in this chapter) are attractions in themselves. It's also worth tracking down some of the smaller specialist stores.

Cheese *International Cheese Centre* (☎ 7628 6637, 3b West Mall, Liverpool Street Station EC2) **Map 9** ✪ Liverpool Street. This minichain, with branches in Marylebone and Victoria stations, has hundreds of varieties of cheese both local and continental.

Neal's Yard Dairy (☎ 7240 5700, 17 Shorts Gardens WC2) **Map 8** ✪ Covent Garden. This is the place to go to sample some of the British Isles' better (and more esoteric) cheeses.

Paxton & Whitfield (☎ 7930 0259, 93 Jermyn St SW1) **Map 7** ✪ Piccadilly Circus. London's oldest cheesemonger (since 1797) claims to stock 200 different varieties.

Meat *Simply Sausages* (☎ 7329 3227, 341 Central Markets, Smithfield Market, Cnr Charterhouse & Farringdon Sts) **Map 6** ✪ Farringdon. This is a great place to stock up for a barbecue. Among the many sausages on sale are ones made with duck, apricots and oranges, as well as Thai, beef and Guinness, and vegetarian mushroom and tarragon sausages.

Sugar & Spice *Dugan's Chocolates* (☎ 7354 4666, 149a Upper St N1) **Map 4** ✪ Angel. This hole-in-the-wall shop has a surprisingly large selection of chocolate.

The Hive (☎ 7924 6233, 93 Northcote Rd SW11) ✪ Clapham South. This shop boasts a choice of more than 40 different types of honey, plus a cutaway section through a hive so you can see the bees going about their buzzy business. It also carries royal jelly, beeswax candles and other apiarian products.

Jane Asher Party Cakes (☎ 7584 6177, 22-4 Cale St SW3) **Map 10** ✪ South Kensington/Sloane Street. Jane Asher, actress and cookery book writer best known for her liaison with erstwhile Beatle Paul McCartney in the 1960s, has the

CHRISTOPHER WOOD

The big 'British' cheese wafts its way through London... you can smell it from Covent Garden.

cake-decorating market cornered in London. Check out and/or try her offerings here.

Konditor & Cook (☎ 7261 0456, *22 Cornwall Rd SE1*) **Map 6** ⊖ Waterloo; (☎ 7407 5100, *Borough Market, 10 Stoney St SE1*) **Map 9** ⊖ London Bridge. This is arguably the best 'bespoke bakery' in London.

Rococo (☎ 7352 5857, *321 King's Rd SW3*) **Map 10** ⊖ Sloane Square. Chocoholics will have a field day in this shop, with everything from Belgian Godiva to French Valrhona, the champagne of chocolate.

Spice Shop (☎ 7221 4448, *1 Blenheim Crescent W11*) **Map 5** ⊖ Ladbroke Grove. This shop has a dizzying selection of spices, herbs and aromatic essential oils.

Coffee & Tea

Algerian Coffee Stores (☎ 7437 2480, *52 Old Compton St W1*) **Map 7** ⊖ Leicester Square. This is *the* place to go to buy all sorts of tea and coffee, including Maragogype (aka the Elephant Bean), the biggest coffee bean in the world.

Angelucci Coffee Merchants (☎ 7437 5889, *23b Frith St W1*) **Map 7** ⊖ Tottenham Court Rd. This nearby shop is friendlier, has a wide selection, and its own blend (Mokital) is excellent.

The Tea House (☎ 7240 7539, *15a Neal St WC2*) **Map 8** ⊖ Covent Garden. This place has a range of teas and tisanes plus pots to brew them in.

Alcohol ***Gerry's*** (☎ 7734 4215, *74 Old Compton Rd W1*) **Map 7** ⊖ Leicester Square. This place stocks a frightening array of alcohol garnered from far-flung parts. Come here if you just can't manage without a bottle of Peruvian *pisco*, Polish *zubrówka*, Stoli Razberi or 70% absinthe.

Milroy's of Soho (☎ 7437 9311, *3 Greek St W1*) **Map 7** ⊖ Tottenham Court Road. This shop nearby stocks over 500 whiskies, including 350 malts and 30 Irish whiskeys.

Furnishings & Household Goods

Conran Shop (☎ 7589 7401, *Michelin House, 81 Fulham Rd SW3*) **Map 10** ⊖ South Kensington. This is the brainchild of Terence Conran, who created Habitat (see below) and many upmarket London restaurants. Now his New York minimalist and Asian-inspired furniture, kitchenware and cutlery are available more exclusively – with prices to match. The shop's great appeal lies partly in its setting (see Michelin House in the Things to See & Do chapter).

Habitat (☎ 7631 3880, *196 Tottenham Court Rd W1*) **Map 6** ⊖ Goodge Street; (☎ 7351 1211, *208 King's Rd SW3*) **Map 10** ⊖ Sloane Square. The chain that brought design into British homes has furniture as well as great home accessories. There are Habitat branches throughout London, including one in Chelsea.

Heal's *(☎ 7636 1666, 196 Tottenham Court Rd W1)* **Map 6** ✪ Goodge Street; *(☎ 7349 8411, 224 King's Rd SW3)* **Map 10** ✪ Sloane Square. This long-established furniture store has classy designs and a great kitchenware section.

Kitschen Sync *(☎ 7497 5129, 7 Earlham St WC2)* **Map 8** ✪ Covent Garden. For something unusual, head for a shop with a cringeworthy name selling 'trashy trinkets' (their words) and groovy retro kitchenware such as shocking-pink kettles and polka-dot plastic chairs.

Royal Doulton *(☎ 7734 3184, 154 Regent St W1)* **Map 7** ✪ Piccadilly Circus. Try this place for classic English bone China and cut glassware.

Jewellery

If you're after a pair of common-or-garden variety studs, you'll be able to pick them up at any market or at stalls in the main-line stations. If it's classic (read old-fashioned) settings and unmounted stones you want, stroll along Hatton Garden EC1 (Map 6; ✪ Chancery Lane); it's chock-a-block with gold, diamond and jewellery shops at the southern end. For more up-to-date baubles, head for **Portobello Green** (see the special section 'To Market, to Market'), an arcade in Portobello Rd Market that is home to some cutting-edge jewellery designers.

Into You *(☎ 7253 5085, 144 St John St EC1)* **Map 4** ✪ Farringdon. If you want to get some – any, really – part of your body pierced or tattooed, this place will oblige. It also stocks lots of interesting body jewellery.

ASA ANDERSSON

If swanky boutiques set your heart racing take a stroll down Bond St.

For the sorts of trinkets you'll need to win the lottery to afford, the following are your best bets:

Asprey & Garrard *(☎ 7493 6767, 165-9 New Bond St W1)* **Map 7** ✪ Bond Street/Green Park. This place dripping in opulence also stocks less-expensive novelty items.

Cartier *(☎ 7493 6962, 175-6 New Bond St W1)* **Map 6** ✪ Green Park. This long-established house has supplied the royal family with their baubles since 1902.

Mappin & Webb *(☎ 7734 3801, 170 Regent St W1)* **Map 7** ✪ Oxford Circus/Piccadilly Circus. This shop has been in the business since 1774, but designer watches are a more recent addition.

Tiffany & Co *(☎ 7409 2790, 25 Old Bond St W1)* **Map 7** ✪ Green Park. Tiffany is a bit more affordable than most of the other top-end jewellers in London.

Music

For the largest collections of CDs, DVDs, tapes and games in London check out any of the following Goliath-sized megastores, all in the West End (Map 7):

HMV *(☎ 7631 3423, 150 Oxford St W1)* ✪ Oxford Circus. Open 9am-8pm Mon-Wed, Fri & Sat, 9am-9pm Thur, noon-6pm Sun. There are three floors with stock appealing to every taste.

Tower Records *(☎ 7439 2500, 1 Piccadilly Circus W1)* ✪ Piccadilly Circus; *(☎ 7424 2900, 162 Camden High St NW1)* **Map 3** ✪ Camden Town. Open 8.30am-midnight Mon & Sat, 9am-midnight Tues-Fri, noon-6pm Sun. Though this store stocks a lot of everything, the jazz and folk music sections are particularly extensive. The Picadilly Circus shop is enormous.

Virgin Megastore *(☎ 7631 1234, 14-30 Oxford St W1)* ✪ Tottenham Court Road. Open 9.30am-10pm Mon-Sat, noon-6pm Sun. This is the largest of the megastores, with four floors and massive Top 40 displays.

London also has a wide range of excellent music shops specialising in everything from jazz and big band to world music. Worth trying are:

Blackmarket *(☎ 7437 0478, 25 D'Arblay St W1)* **Map 7** ✪ Oxford Circus. A small and cramped place with six turntables but *the* venue for dance music.

Dub Vendor (☎ *7223 3757, 274 Lavender Hill SW11)* Station: Clapham Junction. This place specialises in reggae music.

Honest Jon's (☎ *8969 9822, 276-278 Portobello Rd W10)* **Map 5** ⊖ Ladbroke Grove. Two adjoining shops with jazz, soul and reggae.

Mole Jazz (☎ *7278 8623, 311 Gray's Inn Rd WC1)* **Map 4** ⊖ King's Cross. Probably the best shop for traditional jazz and second-hand CDs.

Ray's Jazz Shop (☎ *7240 3969, 180 Shaftesbury Ave WC2)* **Map 8** ⊖ Tottenham Court Road. This quiet, serene shop in the heart of frenetic Soho has knowledgeable, helpful staff.

On the Beat (☎ *7637 8934, 22 Hanway St W1)* **Map 7** ⊖ Tottenham Court Road. Retro (mostly '60s and '70s) music shop with helpful staff.

Reckless Records (☎ *7437 4271, 26 & 30 Berwick St W1)* **Map 7** ⊖ Oxford Circus. These two shops are where to come for second-hand soul, punk and new dance music.

Rough Trade (☎ *7229 8541, 130 Talbot Rd W11)* **Map 5** ⊖ Ladbroke Grove/Notting Hill Gate. This long-time survivor does indie better than most.

WHERE TO SHOP

Some of London's bigger stores are tourist attractions in their own right; very few visitors leave the city without having popped into **Harrods** and **Fortnum & Mason**, even if only to browse around. And the cult TV series *Absolutely Fabulous* has made **Harvey Nichols** (known as 'Harvey Nicks' locally) another must-see attraction.

Although most things can be bought anywhere in London, some streets are known

for their own specialities. Tottenham Court Rd, for example, is full of electronics and computer shops, while Charing Cross Rd is the place to go for books. Cecil Court has antiquarian bookshops and Denmark St has musical instruments, sheet music and books

Harrods' horse and carriage can still be seen trotting around Knightsbridge.

JULIET COOMBE

about music. Hanway St is great for used records. These streets are on Maps 6 & 7.

Some shopping streets casually rest on their laurels, their claim to fame having more to do with their past than what they have to offer today (eg, Carnaby Street). Covent Garden (Map 7), the vegetable market of the West End for a century and a half, was redeveloped in the 1980s; the twee shops and stalls inside the old market hall in the centre tend to be pricey and tourist-oriented, but the streets running off it remain a happy hunting-ground for shoppers, with Neal St and Neal's Yard in particular offering an interesting range.

Oxford St (Map 7) can be a great disappointment. *Selfridges* is up there with Harrods as a place to visit, *John Lewis* claims to be 'never knowingly undersold' and the flagship *Marks & Spencer* at the Marble Arch (western) end of the thoroughfare has its fans. But the farther east you go, the tackier and less interesting it gets. Regent St, with *Liberty* and *Hamleys*, the world's greatest toy store, is much more upmarket.

Nipping out for a loaf of bread? You could always try the food halls in Harrods.

Kensington High St (Map 5) is a good alternative to Oxford St. In the City, check out the lovely boutiques in Bow Lane (Map 8), between Cheapside and Cannon St.

Many museums and other tourist attractions have shops selling good-quality souvenirs: war books and videos at the *Imperial War Museum*; designer fans at the *Fan Museum*; William Morris-designed rugs at the *William Morris Gallery* and so on. Buying from these shops also contributes towards the buildings' maintenance.

Department Stores

The biannual sales at London's department stores, when every tourist, local and their grandmother seem to be queuing up outside Harrods, take place in January and July.

Harrods (☎ 7730 1234, W www.harrods.com, 87-135 Brompton Rd SW1) **Map 5** ✆ Knightsbridge. Open 10am-7pm Mon-Sat. This well-known store is truly unique: it can even lay claim to having installed the world's first escalator in 1898. There are the downsides, though: Harrods is almost always crowded, there are more rules than at an army training camp and it's hard to find what you're looking for. But the toilets are fab, the food halls will make you swoon, and if they haven't got what you want, it probably ain't worth having.

Harvey Nichols (☎ 7235 5000, W www.harveynichols.com, 109-25 Knightsbridge SW1) **Map 5** ✆ Knightsbridge. Open 10am-7pm Mon, Tues & Sat, 10am-8pm Wed-Fri, noon-6pm Sun. This is London's temple of high fashion. It has a great food hall on the 5th floor, an extravagant perfume department and jewellery worth saving up for. But with all the big names (from Versace to Alexander McQueen) and a whole floor of up-to-the-minute menswear, it's fashion that Harvey Nichols really does better than the rest.

Fortnum & Mason (☎ 7734 8040, W www.fortnumandmason.co.uk, 181 Piccadilly W1) **Map 7** ✆ Piccadilly Circus. Open 10am-6.30pm Mon-Sat. Fortnum & Mason is noted for its food hall on the ground floor, but it also carries plenty of fashion wear on the six other floors. All kinds of unusual foodstuffs can be purchased here along with the famous food hampers. This is where Scott stocked up before heading off to the Antarctic.

John Lewis (☎ 7629 7711, W www.johnlewis.co.uk, 278-306 Oxford St W1) **Map 6** ✆ Oxford Circus. Open 9.30am-7pm Mon-Wed

Mock Tudor with an Art Nouveau pedigree: free yourself in Liberty on Regent St.

& Fri, 10am-8pm Thur, 9am-6pm Sat. Part of the same group as Peter Jones in Chelsea, John Lewis is the London institution to know about if you're planning the sort of extended stay that requires stocking up with quality household goods.

Liberty (☎ 7734 1234, W www.liberty-of-london.com, 210-20 Regent St W1) **Map 7** ✪ Oxford Circus. Open 10am-6.30pm Mon-Wed, 10am-8pm Thur, 10am-7pm Fri & Sat, noon-6pm Sun. Almost as unique and with as much history as Harrods, Liberty was born at the turn of the century out of the Arts & Crafts movement, and in Italy Art Nouveau is still called Stile Liberty after the store. Liberty has high fashion, great modern furniture, a wonderful luxury fabrics department and those inimitable Liberty silk scarves.

Marks & Spencer (☎ 7935 7954, 458 Oxford St W1) **Map 6** ✪ Marble Arch. Open 9am-8pm Mon-Fri, 9am-7pm Sat, noon-6pm Sun. Marks & Spencer is almost as British as fish and chips, beans on toast and warm beer. It carries the full range of fashion goods, but most people shop here for underwear, well-made affordable clothes such as cashmere sweaters, and ready-made meals.

Peter Jones (☎ 7730 3434, Sloane Square SW1) **Map 10** ✪ Sloane Square. Open 9.30am-7pm Mon-Wed & Fri, 10am-7pm Thur, 9am-6pm Sat. Peter Jones, which caters for a more well-heeled clientele than its sister (well, perhaps brother) store John Lewis due to its location, has been described as the 'best corner shop in Chelsea'. But that would hardly start to describe the wide range of goods on sale here: from electrical goods through china and glass to bedding. Some departments are located in a temporary annexe on Draycott Ave to the west until renovations at the main store are finished in 2004.

Selfridges (☎ 7629 1234, 400 Oxford St W1) **Map 6** ✪ Bond Street. Open 10am-7pm Mon-Wed, 10am-8pm Thur & Fri, 9.30am-7pm Sat, noon-6pm Sun. Arguably the grandest department store on Oxford St and the one with the longest history, Selfridges' main magnet are the food halls (enter from Orchard St on the west side), which are much less confusing, cramped and crowded than the ones at Harrods.

Speciality Stores

Benjamin Pollock's Toy Shop (☎ 7379 7866, 1st floor, 44 The Market, Covent Garden WC2) **Map 8** ✪ Covent Garden. Fancy taking home a cardboard model of a Victorian theatre or a handmade puppet? This toy shop can oblige.

Botanicals (☎ 7637 1610, 12 Great Portland St W1) **Map 8** ✪ Oxford Circus. This wonderful and spacious shop sells handmade organic Czech products – from candles and soaps to herbal vinegars and teas.

Compendia (☎ 8293 6616, Shop 10, Greenwich Market) **Map 14** DLR: Cutty Sark. This shop is piled high with board and other games, including a good selection of travel-themed ones.

Daisy & Tom (☎ 7352 5000, 181-3 Sloane St SW3) **Map 10** ✪ Sloane Square. Gorgeous (and pricey) kids' clothes, shoes and toys are available here, with a marionette show and carousel rides to keep the terrors occupied.

Davidoff of London (☎ *7930 3079, 35 St James's St SW1*) **Map 6** ⊖ Green Park. This is the shop for pipes, pipe equipment and, of course, cigars.

DR Harris (☎ *7930 3915, 29 St James's St SW1*) **Map 6** ⊖ Green Park. Operating as chemists and perfumers since 1790, this shop stocks such esoteric goods as moustache wax, tiny beard-combs and DR Harris Crystal Eye Drops to combat the visual effects of late nights, early starts and jetlag. Best of all it has its own hang-over cure – a bitter herbal concoction called DR Harris Pick-Me-Up. If it works for us, it will work for you.

Gosh! (☎ *7636 1011, 39 Great Russell St WC1*) **Map 8** ⊖ Tottenham Court Road. Try this place for comics, cartoons and playing cards with everything imaginable on the reverse. The London Cartoon Gallery in the basement has books on the subject.

Hamleys (☎ *7494 2000, 188-96 Regent St W1*) **Map 7** ⊖ Oxford Circus. This is an Aladdin's cave of toys and games, but its prices can be high. The ***Lego Café*** on the top floor is a great place for kids.

Kite Store (☎ *7836 1666, 48 Neal St WC2*) **Map 8** ⊖ Covent Garden. This shop stocks at least 100 different types of kites – from the very traditional to the unrecognisable.

Nauticalia (☎ *7480 6805, Ivory House, St Katharine's Dock E1*) **Map 9** ⊖ Tower Hill. Head straight here if you know someone who'd like a ship's clock or a ship's bell or even a jig-saw of HMS *Victory*.

Papier Marché (☎ *7253 7438, 53 Clerkenwell Close EC1*) **Map 4** ⊖ Farringdon. Located in the Clerkenwell Visitors Centre, this is the place to come for all manner of birds and animals made out of papier-mache.

Taylor of Old Bond St (☎ *7930 5321, 74 Jermyn St SW1*) **Map 7** ⊖ Green Park. For the well-groomed male in your life, check out this shop, which has every sort of razor, shaving brush and flavour of shaving soap imaginable, from lavender to mint.

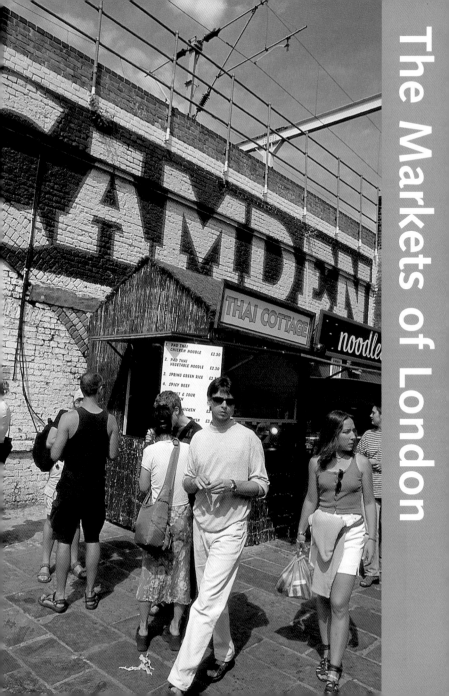

The Markets of London

Believe it or not, London has more than 350 markets selling everything from antiques and curios to flowers and fish. For a more complete run-down, get hold of *The London Market Guide* (Metro Publications; £5.99) by Andrew Richard Kershman and Ally Ireson, which also gives details of smaller local markets and ones farther afield (eg, those in Shepherd's Bush, Swiss Cottage, Walthamstow and Wembley). A prettier but less useful title is *Antique and Flea Markets of London and Paris* (£12.95) by Rupert Thomas and Egle Salvy.

Bermondsey

Bermondsey Market *(Bermondsey Square)* **Map 9** ⊖ Borough/Bermondsey. Open 5am-1pm Fri. This is the place to come if you're after old opera glasses, bowling balls, hatpins, costume jewellery, porcelain or any other 'antique' (read: curio). The main market on Friday takes place outdoors on the square though adjacent warehouses shelter the more vulnerable furnishings and bric-a-brac. Most of the action is over by 8am. Nearby Tower Bridge Rd is also good for antiques.

Berwick St

Berwick St Market *(Berwick St W1)* **Map 7** ⊖ Piccadilly Circus/Oxford Street. Open 8am-6pm Mon-Sat. South of Oxford St and running parallel to Wardour St, this city fruit and vegetable market has managed to hang on to its prime location since 1830; check out the lovely row of Georgian houses to the west at Nos 46 to 58 Broadwick St. This is a great place to put together a picnic or shop for a prepared meal and to hear Cockney accents straight out of Central Casting.

Billingsgate

Billingsgate Fish Market *(Trafalgar Way)* **Map 13** DLR: West India Quay. Open 5am-8.30am Tues-Sat. This wholesale fish market is open to the public, and you'll hear lots of colourful Cockney banter from the market porters, but you'll have to be up at the crack of dawn. People will tell you to buy in bulk here but most vendors are prepared to do a deal.

SIMON BRACKEN

Title Page: Taking in the atmosphere at Camden Market (Photograph by Doug McKinlay)

Bottom: The pick of the crop at Brick Lane Market

JULIET COOMBE

Borough

Borough Market *(Cnr Borough High & Stoney Sts SE1)* **Map 9** ⊖/Station: London Bridge. Open 9am-6pm Fri, 9am-4pm Sat. There has been a fruit and vegetable market on this site since at least the 13th century. Until recently it served only the wholesale trade, but now retailers from around the country sell edibles – ranging from English farm cheeses and specialist sausages to gourmet patisserie and fresh fish – to the public. The best day is the third Saturday of the month.

Brick Lane

Brick Lane Market *(Brick Lane E2)* **Map 9** ⊖ Shoreditch/Aldgate East. Open 8am-1pm Sun. This market is more fun than the nearby one on Petticoat Lane but the recent revival of Spitalfields Market has left it in the dust. There's a mix of stalls spreading from Brick Lane along Bethnal Green Rd that sell clothes, fruit and vegetables, household goods, paintings, bric-a-brac and cigarettes imported from the Continent.

Brixton

Brixton Market *(Reliance Arcade, Market Row, Electric Lane & Electric Ave SW9)* **Brixton Map** ⊖ Brixton. Open 8am-6pm Mon, Tues & Thur-Sat, 8am-3pm Wed. This market is a cosmopolitan treat that mixes everything from the Body Shop and reggae to slick Muslim preachers, South American butcher shops and exotic fruits. On Electric Ave and in the covered Granville Arcade you can buy wigs, unusual foods such as tilapia fish and Ghanaian eggs (really a type of vegetable), unusual spices and homeopathic root cures.

Camden

Camden Market *(w www.camdenlock.net/markets)* **Map 3** ⊖ Camden Town. This market stretches north from Camden Town tube station to Chalk Farm Rd and is composed of several separate markets. It's busiest at weekends, especially on Sunday, between 10am and 6pm.

Camden Market (Cnr Camden High & Buck Sts NW1) Open 9am-5.30pm Thur-Sun. This covered market houses stalls for fashion, clothing, jewellery and tourist tat.

Camden Canal Market (Cnr Chalk Farm & Castlehaven Rds NW1) Open 10am-6pm Sat & Sun. Farther north and just over the canal

Top: Something fishy at Brixton Market

bridge, Camden Canal Market has bric-a-brac from around the world. Inside on the left, and beyond the comparatively new indoor market, is the small section where the market originated.

Camden Lock Market *(Camden Lock Place NW1)* Open 10am-6pm Sat & Sun (indoor stalls 10am-6pm daily). This area, right next to the canal lock, houses a diverse range of food, ceramics, furniture, oriental rugs, musical instruments, designer clothes and so on.

The Stables *(Chalk Farm Rd opposite Hartland Rd NW1)* Open 8am-6pm Sat & Sun. Just beyond the Railway Arches, the Stables is the best part of the market, with antiques, Asian artefacts, rugs and carpets, pine furniture, and 1950s and '60s clothing.

Camden Passage

Camden Passage *(Camden Passage N1)* **Map 4** ⊖ Angel. Open 7am-2pm Wed, 8am-4pm Sat. At the junction of Upper St and Essex Rd, Camden Passage is a cavern of four arcades with antique shops and stalls that has nothing to do with Camden Market. The stalls sell pretty much everything to which the moniker 'antique' or 'curio' could reasonably be applied, and the stallholders know their stuff so real bargains are rare. Wednesday is the busiest day but it's worth coming along on Sunday for Islington Farmers Market between 10am and 2pm.

Chapel Market

Chapel Market *(Chapel Market N1)* **Map 4** ⊖ Angel. Open 9am-3.30pm Tues & Wed, Fri & Sat, 9am-1pm Thur & Sun. There's an all-day fruit and vegetable market in the Islington street called Chapel Market just off Liverpool Rd.

Church St

Church St Market *(Church St NW8)* **Map 5** ⊖ Edgware Road. Open 8am-6pm Mon-Sat. The reason to come to this food market is to visit **Alfie's Antiques Market** (☎ 7723 6066, *13-25 Church St NW8)*, home to some 200 dealers who specialise in decorative antiques, garden paraphernalia and design.

LIZ BARRY

Bottom: Flower power at Columbia Rd Market

Columbia Rd

Columbia Rd Market *(Columbia Rd E2)* **Map 4** ⊖ Bethnal Green/ Station: Cambridge Heath/Bus No 26, 48 or 55. Open 7am-1pm Sun. Although visitors may have little need of geraniums or pelargoniums, a stroll up to the flower market on Columbia Rd (between Gosset St and the Royal Oak pub) is a fun way to spend a Sunday morning. Along with the flower stalls, a few arty shops throw open their doors.

Covent Garden

While the shops in the Covent Garden Piazza are open daily, several markets also take place here.

Apple Market (Covent Garden Piazza, North Hall WC2) **Map 8** ⊖ Covent Garden. Open 9am-5pm daily. This touristy market sells handicrafts and curios.

Jubilee Market (Jubilee Hall, Cnr Covent Garden & Southampton St WC2) **Map 8** ⊖ Covent Garden. Open 9am-3pm Mon, 9am-5pm Tues-Sun. Monday is for antiques and collectables, Tuesday to Friday for general tat, and Saturday and Sunday for quality crafts.

Greenwich

Greenwich Market *(College Approach SE10)* **Map 14** DLR: Cutty Sark. Open 9am-5pm Thur, 9.30am-5.30pm Fri-Sun. Greenwich hosts an antiques market on Thursday and an arts and crafts market Wednes-day and Friday to Sunday; it lies between King William Walk and Greenwich Church St, but you can also enter from College Approach. It's an excellent place for decorated glass, rugs, prints and wooden toys.

Top left: Roll with it: baked delights at Spitalfields

Top right: Mirrors and ceramics at Covent Garden

Village Market Antiques Centre (Cnr Stockwell St & Greenwich High Rd SE10) **Map 14** DLR: Cutty Sark. Open 10am-5pm Fri & Sat, 10am-6pm Sun. This small market opposite St Alfege Church has the usual mix of second-hand clothes, jewellery, plants and bric-a-brac.

JULIET COOMBE

Leadenhall

Leadenhall Market *(Whittington Ave, off Gracechurch St EC1)* **Map 9** ⊖ Bank. Open 7am-4pm Mon-Fri. This market serves food and drink to busy City folk as well as fresh fish, meat and cheese. The selection is excellent for an urban market, and the Victorian glass-and-iron market hall, designed by Horace Jones in 1881, is an architectural delight.

Leather Lane

Leather Lane Market *(Leather Lane EC1)* **Map 6** ⊖ Chancery Lane/ Farringdon. Open 10.30am-2pm Mon-Fri. This market south of Clerkenwell Rd and running parallel to Hatton Garden attracts local office workers with its suspiciously cheap videos, tapes and CDs, household goods and clothing sold by archetypal Cockney stallholders.

Petticoat Lane

Petticoat Lane Market *(Middlesex & Wentworth Sts E1)* **Map 9** ⊖ Aldgate/Aldgate East/Liverpool Street. Open 8am-2pm Sun, Wentworth St only 9am-2pm Mon-Fri. This is east London's long-established Sunday market on the border between the City and Whitechapel. These days, however, it's full of run-of-the-mill junk and tourists.

Portobello Rd

Portobello Rd Market *(Portobello Rd W10)* **Map 5** ⊖ Notting Hill Gate/ Ladbroke Grove. Open 8am-6pm Mon-Wed, 9am-1pm Thur, 7am-7pm Fri & Sat, 9am-4pm Sun. After Camden Market this is London's most famous street market. Starting near the Sun in Splendour pub in Notting Hill, it wends its way northwards to just past the Westway flyover.

Antiques, jewellery, paintings and ethnic stuff are concentrated at the Notting Hill Gate end of Portobello Rd. The stalls dip downmarket as you move north (fruit and veg, second-hand clothing, household goods, bric-a-brac). Beneath the Westway a vast tent covers yet more stalls selling cheap clothes, shoes and CDs, while the Portobello Green arcade is home to some cutting-edge clothes and jewellery designers.

Though shops and stalls open daily, the busiest days are Friday, Saturday and Sunday. There's an antiques market on Saturday, and a flea

Top: These boots were made for walking, so pick up a pair at Brick Lane Market.

market on Portobello Green on Sunday morning. Fruit and veg are sold all week at the Ladbroke Grove end, with an organic market on Thursday.

Ridley Rd

Ridley Rd Market *(Ridley Rd E8)* **Map 2** Station: Dalston Kingsland/Bus No 149 or 242 from Liverpool St. Open 8.30am-6pm Mon-Sat. In many ways the Caribbean/African/Turkish market along Ridley Rd is more colourful than the one in Brixton, and it's certainly less touristy. You'll find more types of Turkish delight and Caribbean tubers than you'll know what to do with.

Roman Rd

Roman Rd Market *(Roman Rd E3)* **Map 2** ⊖ Mile End/Bus No 8 or 277. Open 8am-4pm Tues, Thur & Sat. The market along Roman Rd between St Stephen's and Parnell Rds has pretty standard fare on offer though some people rave about the discount fashion clothes on sale.

Smithfield

Smithfield Market *(West Smithfield EC1)* **Map 8** ⊖ Farringdon. Open 4am-10am Mon-Fri. This is central London's last surviving meat market, and a vision of hell itself for vegetarians. Though the eastern end has been restored to its 1868 original design (by Horace Jones, who also designed Tower Bridge), it is still unclear whether the market will be forced to move out of central London.

Spitalfields

Spitalfields Market *(Commercial St E1)* **Map 8** ⊖ Liverpool Street. Open 9.30am-5.30pm Sun. This market, in a Victorian warehouse (between Brushfield and Lamb Sts), has a great mix of arts and crafts, organic fruit and veg, stylish and retro clothes, and second-hand books, with ethnic shops ringing the central area. Most of the market opens 10.30am to 5pm weekdays too. There's an organic market on Friday.

Bottom: Fresh chicken at Portobello Rd Market

JULIET COOMBE

Excursions

As Britain is a relatively small country and its transport systems generally fan out from London, almost nowhere (at least in England) is impossibly far away. There are a few places within a 60-mile radius of London that can be visited on a day-trip. These include places as diverse as Windsor Castle; the university towns of Oxford and Cambridge; the medieval pilgrimage site of Canterbury; and Brighton, a top seaside town.

This chapter assumes you'll be returning to London the same day. There are plenty of other places within easy reach of London – from Bath to Stonehenge, Waltham Abbey to St Albans. For details of these places and where to spend the night, consult Lonely Planet's *England* or *Britain* guide. Staff at most TICs can book accommodation (for a nominal fee) and members of the YHA or HI can stay at hostels in Oxford, Cambridge, Canterbury, Brighton and Windsor. For membership details and contact numbers, see YHA Hostels in the Places to Stay chapter.

For bus timetables ring National Express (☎ 0870 580 8080, W www.gobycoach .com), the country's largest coach network. Green Line (☎ 0870 608 7261, W www .greenline.co.uk) is an umbrella group of bus companies who operate from the Green Line bus station at Victoria Place shopping centre (Map 11), just south of Victoria train station on Bulleid Way. For train information and the numbers to ring for phone bookings, which differ according to the train operator, phone the 24-hour National Rail Enquiries line on ☎ 0845 748 4950. See the Getting There & Away chapter for more on travel services.

If you're planning to do a lot of rail travel in south-east England, a Network Railcard valid for a year is worth considering. It costs £20 and covers all the destinations in this chapter. Discounts of 34% apply to up to four adults travelling together, provided one is a card-holder. Children pay a flat fare of £1. Travel is permitted only after 10am on weekdays and at any time at weekends.

ORGANISED TOURS

If you're pressed for time, there are several companies that organise excursions.

The Adventure Travel Centre (Map 9; ☎ 7370 4555, W www.topdecktravel.co.uk), 125 Earl's Court Rd SW5 (☻ Earl's Court), does Sunday day-trips departing at 8.30am, which are aimed at (but not limited to) Australasian travellers. Each trip takes in two destinations (Oxford and Blenheim Palace, say, or Leeds Castle and Canterbury) and costs £12. They also do longer festival trips (eg, Ladies Day at Ascot, or the Edinburgh Tattoo). Prices are from £169 for four days.

Another company worth trying is Astral Travels (☎ 0700 078 1016 or 0870 902 0908, W www.astraltravels.co.uk), 72 New Bond St W1, whose day-tours (£47 to £49, including entrance fees) in mini-coaches (some of which run on eco-friendly LPG) cover one or several of the following: Bath, the Cotswolds, Oxford, Salisbury, Stonehenge, Avebury, Glastonbury and Stratford-upon-Avon. Students and YHA/HI members are eligible for a 20% discount on some tours and everyone gets a 5% discount if they book online.

Commercial outfits such as Golden Tours (☎ 7233 7030, W www.goldentours.co.uk) offer both half- and full-day excursions, with pick-ups from 65 London hotels. The morning trip to Windsor and Runnymede costs £27.50/24 (adult/child aged 3-16), including admission to Windsor Castle. Hotel pick-ups begin at about 7.30am daily April to October and on Monday, Wednesday, Thursday, Saturday and Sunday from November to March. The afternoon trip to Leeds Castle costs £29.50/25 (adult/child) and leaves from the tour office at 4 Fountain Square, 123–151 Buckingham Palace Rd SW1 at 12.50pm on Wednesday, Saturday and Sunday April to October (Wednesday and Saturday only November to March).

Evan Evans Tours (☎ 7950 1777, W www .evanevans.co.uk) and Big Value Tours. (☎ 7233 7797, W www.bigvaluetours.com) offer similar excursions.

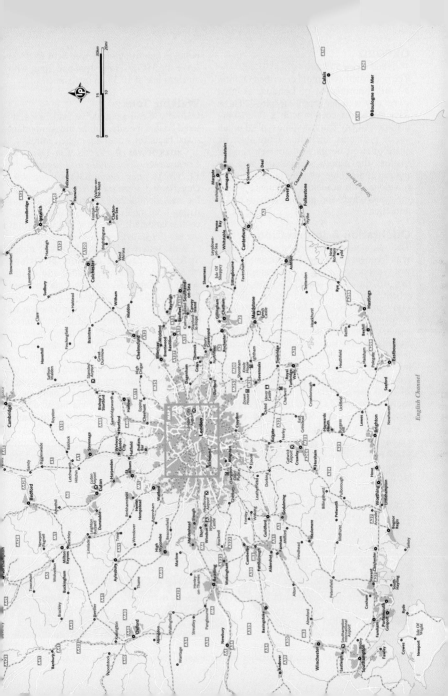

OXFORD

☎ 01865 • pop 115,000

The poet Matthew Arnold described Oxford, 57 miles north-west of London, as 'that sweet city with her dreaming spires'. These days the spires coexist with a flourishing commercial city that has some typical urban social problems, including more than its share of street beggars in summer. But for visitors the superb architecture and the unique atmosphere of the colleges – synonymous with academic excellence – and their courtyards and gardens remain major attractions.

Orientation & Information

The train station is to the west on Botley Rd, with frequent buses to the centre, or you can walk (about half a mile). The bus station is just off the green-less Gloucester Green, where you'll also find the tourist information centre (TIC; ☎ 726871, fax 240261, ⓦ www.visitoxford.org, The Old School House). It opens 9.30am to 5pm Monday to Saturday and 10am to 3.30pm on Sunday from April to September. Staff here can book accommodation in Oxford for a £2.50 fee (plus 10% deposit) or farther afield for £4 (plus deposit); they'll also sell you the useful *Welcome to Oxford* booklet (£1) and *Oxford City Centre Street Map & Guide* (75p). Two-hour guided walking tours of the colleges (adults/children aged 6-16 £5.85/3) leave the TIC at 11am, 1pm and 2pm, with an extra one at 10.30am in summer.

Walking Tour

Oxford's 36 colleges and five 'halls' are scattered around the city, but the most important – and beautiful – ones are in the centre.

Carfax Tower *(☎ 792653, Cnr Queen & Cornmarket Sts; adult/child aged 6-16 £1.20/60p; open 10am-5.30pm daily Apr-Oct, 10am-3.30pm daily Nov-Mar)*, part of the now demolished Church of St Martin dating from medieval times, makes a useful central landmark. There's a fine view from the top (99 steps).

Walk southwards from the tower along St Aldate's, past the **Museum of Oxford** *(☎ 815559, St Aldate's; adult/senior & student/child/family £2/1.50/50p/5; open 10am to 4pm Mon-Fri, 10am-5pm Sat, noon-4pm Sun)*, which offers an easy introduction to the city's long history, and **Christ Church** *(☎ 276150; adult/child £4/3; open 9am-5pm Mon-Sat, 1pm-5.30pm Sun)*, the grandest of the colleges and founded in 1525. The main entrance is below Tom Tower, the top of which was designed by Sir Christopher Wren in 1682, but the visitors' entrance is farther down St Aldate's via the wrought-iron gates of the Memorial Gardens and Broad Walk, which faces Christ Church

JON DAVISON

Oxford has inspired minds for centuries and continues to thrive as a top-class seat of learning.

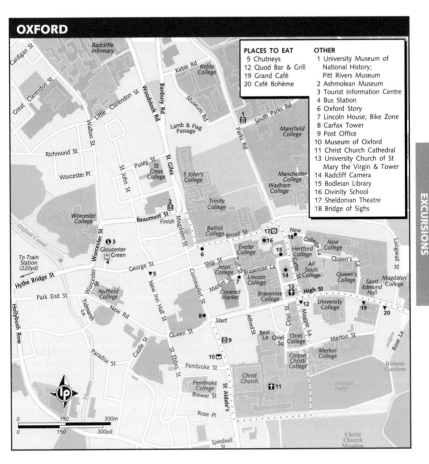

OXFORD

PLACES TO EAT
5 Chutneys
12 Quod Bar & Grill
19 Grand Café
20 Café Bohème

OTHER
1 University Museum of
  National History;
  Pitt Rivers Museum
2 Ashmolean Museum
3 Tourist Information Centre
4 Bus Station
6 Oxford Story
7 Lincoln House; Bike Zone
8 Carfax Tower
9 Post Office
10 Museum of Oxford
11 Christ Church Cathedral
13 University Church of St
   Mary the Virgin & Tower
14 Radcliff Camera
15 Bodleian Library
16 Divinity School
17 Sheldonian Theatre
18 Bridge of Sighs

Meadow. The college chapel, **Christ Church Cathedral**, is the smallest cathedral in the country and a wonderful example of late-Norman architecture.

From Broad Walk continue eastwards then turn left (north) up Merton Grove to Merton St. On your right is **Merton College** (☎ 276310; open 2pm-4pm Mon-Fri, 10am-4pm Sat & Sun), founded in 1264. In the 14th-century **Mob Quad** is the oldest medieval library still in use in the UK. **Corpus Christi College** is on the left of Merton St.

Head northwards up Magpie Lane to High St. Just opposite, at the corner of High and

Catte Sts, is the **University Church of St Mary the Virgin** (☎ 279112, **W** www.university-church.ox.ac.uk; tower admission adult/child £1.60/80p; open 9am-7pm daily Jul-Aug, 9am-5pm daily Sept-Jun). Its 14th-century tower offers views of the city's spires. From St Mary's, walk east along the High St, with its fascinating mix of architectural styles, to **Magdalen College** (*maud-len;* ☎ 276000, adult/child £2/1 Apr-Sept, free Oct-Mar; open noon-6pm daily mid-June–Sept, 2pm-dusk daily rest of year) on the River Cherwell. Magdalen is one of the richest colleges and has huge grounds, including a deer park.

If you retrace your steps and walk northwards up Catte St, you'll come to the circular, Palladian-style **Radcliffe Camera** (1749), a reading room for the **Bodleian Library** (☎ 277000), just to the north across the courtyard (enter via the Great Gate on Catte St). The Radcliffe Camera is closed to the public, but the library and Divinity School, a masterpiece of 15th-century English Gothic architecture, open 9am to 5pm weekdays and 9am to 12.30pm on Saturday. The Bodleian Exhibition Room opens 9.30am to 4.45pm weekdays and 9.30am to 12.30pm on Saturday. Guided tours (☎ 277224; £3.50), which should be booked at least an hour in advance at busy times, depart at 10.30am, 11.30am (March to October only), 2pm and 3pm on weekdays and at 10.30am and 11.30am on Saturday.

Continue northwards along Catte St, passing the **Bridge of Sighs**, a 1914 copy of the famous one in Venice, that spans New College Lane. When you reach Broad St you have one of two options. Walking north along Parks Rd for some 500m will bring you to the **University Museum of Natural History** (☎ 272950, **W** www.ashmol.ox .ac.uk/oum, Parks Rd; admission free; open noon-5pm daily), famous for its dinosaur and dodo skeletons, and the renovated **Pitt Rivers Museum** (☎ 270927, **W** http://units .ox.ac.uk/departments/prm, Parks Rd; admission free; open 1pm-4.30pm Mon-Sat, 2pm-4.30pm Sun), crammed to overflowing with everything from a sailing boat to a collection of South American shrunken heads.

If you go west along Broad St, you'll pass Sir Christopher Wren's first major work (1667), on your left, the **Sheldonian Theatre** (information ☎ 798600; adult/child £1.50/1; open 10am-12.30pm & 2pm-3.30pm Mon-Sat). This is where important ceremonies, including graduations, take place. On the right is **Trinity College**, founded in 1555, and next to it, at the corner with Magdalen St, is **Balliol College**. The wooden doors between the inner and outer quadrangles still bear scorch marks from when Protestant martyrs were burned at the stake in the mid-16th century. Opposite the college is a hokey, 40-minute romp through Oxfordiana, the multimedia

Oxford Story (☎ 728822, **W** www.oxford story.co.uk, 6 Broad St; adult/senior, student & child/family £6.10/4.90/£15-18.50; open 9.30am-5pm daily Jul-Aug, 10am-4.30pm Mon-Sat & 11am-4.30pm Sun Sept-Jun).

A short distance northwards up Magdalen St to St Giles is the **Ashmolean Museum** (☎ 278000, **W** www.ashmol.ox.ac.uk; Beaumont St; admission free; open 10am-5pm Tues-Sat, noon-5pm Sun). Opened to the public in 1683, the Ashmolean is Britain's oldest museum and houses extensive displays of European art and Middle Eastern antiquities.

Punting

There's no better way to soak up Oxford's atmosphere than to take to the river in a punt. **Magdalen Bridge Boathouse** (☎ 202643, Magdalen Bridge; £10 per hour, £30 deposit) hires them from March to October. If you're not up to punting yourself, try a chauffeured boat for up to five people (£20) with a bottle of wine thrown in.

Places to Eat

In addition to the places listed below, there are lots of ethnic eateries – from Indian and Jamaican to Lebanese – along Cowley Rd, which leads off the High St south-east of Magdalen College.

Café Bohème (☎ 245858, 73 High St) Sandwiches £4.50-6, salads £4-8.50, mains £6.50-15. This French-ish cafe with real, live French staff does decent breakfasts as well as upmarket sandwiches and salads.

Café Coco (☎ 200232, 23 Cowley Rd) Starters £2.50-3.35, pizzas £5.35-7.50, salads £6.95-8.65. Come here for a pizza or a salad and a buzzy, nontouristy atmosphere.

Chutneys (☎ 724241, New Inn Hall St) Starters £1.85-2.80, mains £4.10-6.45, lunchtime buffet £7.50. This mostly vegetarian south Indian brasserie attracts customers as much by its brightly coloured exterior as its affordable and tasty fare.

Grand Café (☎ 204463, 84 High St) Sandwiches £5.90-7.50, lunches £4.95-8.75, teas £6.50-12.50. This museum piece of a cafe, on the site of England's first coffee house (1650), is a wonderful place to break during a tour of Oxford.

King's College and its chapel (centre), one of England's finest examples of Gothic architecture

Quod Bar & Grill (☎ 202505, 92-4 High St) Starters £3.85-4.85, pizzas £6.95-7.95, pasta dishes £4.95-8.50, mains £7.35-12.95. This is an incredibly popular place with locals for its stylish Italian cuisine and comfortable surroundings.

The *covered market* in Golden Square, on the northern side of the High St near Carfax Tower, opens 8am to 5.30pm Monday to Saturday. There's also a *farmers market* in Gloucester Green from 9am to 3pm on the first Thursday of every month.

Getting There & Around
Oxford Tube buses (☎ 772250, **W** www.stagecoach-oxford.co.uk) go from Victoria Coach station every 10 to 20 minutes from 6am to 10.30pm and then every 30 to 60 minutes throughout the night via Marble Arch, Notting Hill Gate and Shepherd's Bush (1½ hours). A return ticket, valid till the next day, costs £8/6.50/22 (adult/senior, student & child/family). Oxford Express (☎ 785400, **W** www.oxfordbus.co.uk) has bus departures almost as frequently to/from Victoria Coach station for the same fares. There are frequent trains from Paddington (one to 1½ hours, £14.60 day return).

*Guide Friday (☎ 790522, **W** www.guidefriday.com)* runs a hop-on, hop-off city bus tour of Oxford every 15 minutes from 9.30am to 6pm daily, mid-June to late September and till 5pm or 5.30pm the rest of the year. Tickets cost £8.50/7/2.50/19.50

(adult/senior & student/child aged 5-14/family). **Bikezone** *(☎ 728877)*, in historic Lincoln House at 6 Market St, rents bikes for £10/20 per day/week plus £100 deposit. It opens 9am to 5.30pm Monday to Saturday.

CAMBRIDGE
☎ 01223 • pop 88,000
The university at Cambridge, 54 miles north of London, was founded in the 13th century, several decades later than Oxford. There is a fierce rivalry between the two cities and their universities, and an ongoing debate over which is the best and most beautiful. One thing is for sure: Cambridge is far wealthier, with assets of more than £1.2 billion against Oxford's £800 million, according to a *Times of London* survey in 2001.

If you have time, you should visit both. But if you only have time for one and – this is an important caveat – the colleges are open, choose Cambridge. Oxford draws far more tourists and sometimes seems like a provincial city that happens to have a university. Cambridge, an architectural treasure-trove, always feels like just what it is: an English university town.

Orientation & Information
The centre of Cambridge lies in a wide bend of the River Cam. The best-known section of river bank is the Backs, which combines lush scenery with superb views of half a dozen colleges. The other 25 colleges are scattered throughout the city.

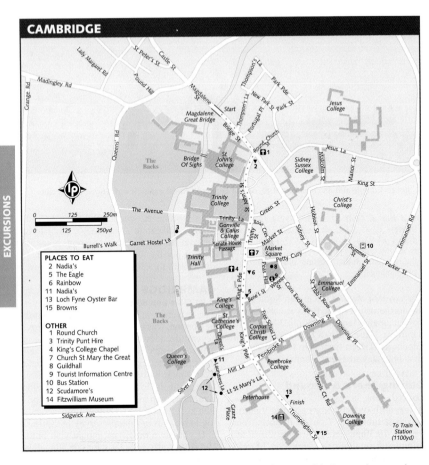

CAMBRIDGE

PLACES TO EAT
2 Nadia's
5 The Eagle
6 Rainbow
11 Nadia's
13 Loch Fyne Oyster Bar
15 Browns

OTHER
1 Round Church
3 Trinity Punt Hire
4 King's College Chapel
7 Church St Mary the Great
8 Guildhall
9 Tourist Information Centre
10 Bus Station
12 Scudamore's
14 Fitzwilliam Museum

The bus station is in the centre on Drummer St, but the train station is a 1-mile walk to the south-east. Sidney St is the main shopping street but changes its name several times to the north and the south.

The TIC (☎ 322640, fax 457549, ⓦ www .cambridge.gov.uk), on Wheeler St just south of Market Square, opens 10am to 6pm weekdays, 10am to 5pm on Saturday and 11am to 4pm on Sunday April to September. It opens 10am to 5.30pm Monday to Saturday the rest of the year. TIC staff can also arrange accommodation in town for £3. Contact the TIC for up-to-date information on college opening

times before you visit. It organises two-hour walking tours at 1.30pm year-round, with more during the summer. Tours cost £6/4 (adult/child aged 12-17) or £7/4 including King's College. Guided walks (☎ 311602) from the Round Church departing at 2.30pm on Sunday and 11am on Wednesday are free though, donations are welcome.

Walking Tour

Starting at Magdalene Great Bridge to the north, walk south-eastwards along Bridge St until you reach the **Round Church** (Church of the Holy Sepulchre; ☎ 518218, Cnr

Round Church & Bridge Sts; open 10am-5pm daily summer, 1pm-4pm daily winter), built in 1130 to commemorate its namesake in Jerusalem. Turn right down St John's St to **St John's College** (☎ 338676, St John St; open 10am-5pm daily). On the other side of the gatehouse (1510) are three beautiful courtyards, the second and third dating from the 17th century. From the third court, the picturesque **Bridge of Sighs**, a replica of the one in Venice, spans the Cam. Stand in the centre and watch the punts float by.

Just south of St John's, **Trinity College** (☎ 332500, Trinity Lane; adult/senior, student & child aged 12-17 £2/1; open 10am-5pm daily) is one of the largest and most attractive colleges. It was established in 1546 by Henry VIII, whose statue peers out from the top niche of the great gateway (he's holding a chair leg instead of the royal sceptre as students kept stealing it). The **Great Court**, the largest structure of its kind in the world, incorporates some fine 15th-century buildings. Beyond the Great Court are the cloisters of Nevile's Court and the dignified **Wren Library** (open noon-2pm Mon-Fri, 10.30am-12.30pm Sun), built by Sir Christopher in the 1680s.

Next comes Gonville and Caius (pronounced keys) College and **King's College** and its chapel (☎ 331100, King's Parade; adult/senior & child aged 12-17 £3.50/2.50; open 9.30am-4pm daily), one of the most sublime buildings in Europe. The chapel was begun in 1446 by Henry VI and completed around 1516. Henry VI's successors, notably Henry VIII, added the intricate fan vaulting and elaborate wood-and-stone carvings of the interior. The chapel comes alive when the choir sings and there are services during term-time and in July. Evensong is at 5.30pm, Monday to Saturday (men's voices only on Wednesday), and at 3.30pm on Sunday. There's a choral service at 9.30am on Sunday as well.

Continue southwards on what is now King's Parade to Trumpington St and the **Fitzwilliam Museum** (☎ 332923, Ⓦ www.fitzmuseum.cam.ac.uk, Trumpington St; admission free; open 10am-5pm Tues-Sat,

2.15pm-5pm Sun), which houses ancient Egyptian sarcophagi and Greek and Roman art in the lower galleries and a wide range of paintings upstairs. Guided tours of the museum at 2.30pm on Sunday cost £3.

Punting

Taking a punt along the Backs is great fun, but it can also be a wet and hectic experience, especially on a busy weekend. The cheapest boats are those at **Trinity Punt Hire** (☎ 338483, Garret Hostel Lane; £6 per hour plus £25 deposit). Trinity also does chauffeured tours of the river (£6 to £8 per person). Another company **Scudamore's** (☎ 359750, Grant Place; £12 per hour plus £60 deposit) has punts for hire and chauffered rides for £10 per person. From April to October you can keep punts overnight for £60 (plus £60 deposit).

Places to Eat

In addition to the places listed below, a number of cheap Indian and Chinese eateries can be found where Lensfield Rd meets Regent St in the direction of the train station.

Browns (☎ 461655, 23 Trumpington St) Starters £2.95-6.95, pasta dishes & salads £6.85-8.95, mains £7.35-13.95, set lunch £5.95 (noon-4pm Mon-Fri). This lovely restaurant, once the outpatient department of a hospital built in 1914, is full of plants and light and boasts excellent pies.

The Eagle (☎ 505020, Bene't St) Lunch about £5.59. Just down from the TIC, this pub, where American airmen left their signatures on the ceiling of the back bar during WWII, is the place to head for a pub lunch.

Loch Fyne Oyster Bar (☎ 362433, The Little Rose, Trumpington St) Starters £3.95-7.95, mains £6.95-34.95. This cosy place serves all types of seafood but oysters (£5.95 to £7.45 per half-dozen) are its speciality.

Nadia's (☎ 568336, 11 St John's St or ☎ 568335, 16 Silver St) Filled bagels & baps £1.85-2.35. A small, local chain of excellent-value take-away bakeries, this place offers sandwiches and cakes.

Rainbow (☎ 321551, 9a King's Parade) Soups £2.75, salads £4.25, mains £6.75 (all). Across the road from King's College and down a narrow passageway is a good vegetarian and gluten-free restaurant that serves dishes such as Thai green vegetarian curry and mushroom and nut crumble.

Punting for Punters

Punting looks fairly straightforward, but we've landed in the drink, heels over head, enough times to say unequivocally that it is *not*. Still, that shouldn't deter anyone who isn't afraid of getting a little wet.

Here are a half-dozen basic tips on how to move the punt forward and, in doing so, not fall in the water.

- Standing at the end of the punt, lift the pole out of the water at the side of the punt.
- Allow the pole to slide through your hands and touch the bottom of the river.
- Tilt the top of the pole forward (ie, in the direction you're headed) and push down to propel the punt forward.
- Twist the pole to free the end from the mud at the bottom of the river.
- Let the pole float up and trail behind the punt; you can then use it as a rudder to steer with.
- If you've not fallen in (yet), raise the pole out of the water and into the vertical position to begin the cycle again.

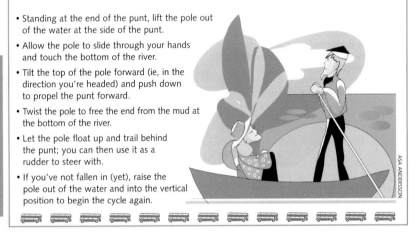

ASA ANDERSSON

The *market* in Market Square opens 9am to 5pm Monday to Saturday.

Getting There & Around

National Express runs hourly shuttle buses from London to Cambridge (£8 day return, two hours). There are trains every 30 minutes from King's Cross and Liverpool Street stations (£14.50 day return, 55 minutes).

There is a free, gas-powered shuttle service (☎ 423554) making its way round Cambridge every 15 minutes from 9am to 5pm Monday to Saturday. Bus No 1 links the train station with the town centre. *Guide Friday* (☎ 362444) runs hop-on, hop-off tour buses round the city that also call at the train station. Tours operate year-round and cost £8.50/7/2.50/19.50 (adult/senior & student/child aged 5-14/family). Bikes can be hired from **Geoff's Bike Hire** (*☎ 365629*), 65 Devonshire Rd, not far from the train station, for £8/15 per day/week (deposit £25). It opens 9am to 6pm daily April to September and 9am to 5.30pm Monday to Saturday from October to March.

CANTERBURY
☎ 01227 • pop 39,000

Canterbury, in Kent, is 56 miles south-east of London and makes a relatively easy day-trip from the capital. Its greatest treasure is its magnificent cathedral, the successor to the church St Augustine built, which was after he began converting the English to Christianity in AD 597. Following the martyrdom of archbishop Thomas à Becket in 1170, the cathedral became the focus of one of Europe's most important medieval pilgrimages, which was immortalised by Geoffrey Chaucer in *The Canterbury Tales*.

Today Canterbury is one of Britain's most impressive and evocative cathedrals and a World Heritage Site. The bustling city centre is atmospheric and lively.

Orientation & Information

The lozenge-shaped centre is enclosed by a medieval city wall and a modern ring road. The TIC (☎ 766567 or 767744, fax 459840, **W** www.canterbury.co.uk), 34 St Margaret's St, opens 9.30am to 5.30pm Monday to

Saturday and 10am to 4pm on Sunday April to October, 9.30am to 5pm Monday to Saturday and 10am to 4pm Sunday in November and December and 9.30am to 5pm Monday to Saturday only from January to March. Guided walks last 1½ hours and leave the TIC at 2pm April to September, with another tour at 11.30am in July and August. Tours cost £3.50/3/8.50 (adult/senior, student & child/family).

Canterbury Cathedral

Like most great cathedrals, Canterbury Cathedral (☎ 762862, 🅦 www.canterbury-cathedral.org, Sun St; adult/child aged 5-16 £3/2; open 9am-6.30pm Mon-Sat, 12.30pm-2.30pm & 4.30pm-5.30pm Sun Easter-Sept, 9am-5pm Mon-Sat, 12.30pm-2.30pm & 4.30pm-5.30pm Sun Oct-Easter) evolved over the centuries and reflects several architectural styles. Since treasures are tucked away in corners and there are a trove of associated stories, a one-hour guided tour costing £3.50/2.50/1.50/6.50 (adult/senior & student/child/family) is recommended. It leaves at 10.30am, noon and 2.30pm Monday to Saturday from Easter to September, and 10.30am, noon and 2pm the rest of the year. If the crowd looks daunting, you can take a 30-minute audioguide tour costing £2.95/1.95 (adult/child).

The traditional approach to the cathedral is along narrow Mercery Lane, which used to be lined with small shops selling souvenirs and votive offerings to pilgrims, to Christ Church Gate. Once inside the gate, turn right and walk eastwards to get an overall picture.

St Augustine's original cathedral burned down in 1067. The first Norman archbishop began construction of a new cathedral in 1070, but only fragments remain. In 1174 most of the eastern half of the building was again destroyed by fire, but the magnificent crypt beneath the choir survived.

The fire presented the opportunity to create something in keeping with the cathedral's new status as England's most important pilgrimage site. In response, William of Sens created the first major Gothic construction in England, a style now described as Early Eng-

lish. Most of the cathedral east of Bell Harry tower dates from this period.

In 1391, work began on the western half of the building, replacing the south-west and north-west transepts and nave. The new perpendicular style was employed, and work continued for over a century, culminating in 1500 with the completion of Bell Harry.

The main entrance is through the **south-west porch**, built in 1415 to commemorate the English victory at Agincourt. From the centre of the nave there are impressive views eastwards down the length of the church, with its ascending levels, and westwards to the **window** with glass dating from the 12th century.

From beneath **Bell Harry**, with its beautiful fan vaulting, more impressive stained glass that somehow survived the idol-smashing Puritans of the Commonwealth (1649–59) is visible. A 15th-century screen,

DENNIS JOHNSON

**Evocative Canterbury Cathedral
dominates the town.**

EXCURSIONS

featuring six kings, separates the nave from the choir.

Thomas à Becket is believed to have been murdered in the north-west transept; a modern **altar and sculpture** mark the spot. The adjoining **Lady Chapel** has beautiful perpendicular fan vaulting. Descend a flight of steps into the Romanesque crypt, the main survivor of the Norman cathedral.

The **Chapel of Our Lady** at the western end of the crypt has some of the finest Romanesque carving extant in England. St Thomas was entombed in the Early English eastern end until 1220. This is where Henry II allowed himself to be whipped in penance for having provoked Becket's murder with the infamous words 'Who will rid me of this turbulent priest?', and is said to be the site of many miracles. The **Chapel of St Gabriel** features 12th-century paintings, while the **Black Prince's Chantry** is a beautiful perpendicular chapel, donated by the prince in 1363.

In the south-west transept the **Chapel of St Michael** includes a wealth of tombs, including that of archbishop Stephen Langton, who helped persuade King John to seal the Magna Carta in 1215. The superb **12th-century choir** rises in stages to the **High Altar** and Trinity Chapel. The screen around the choir stalls was erected in 1305 and evensong has been sung here every day for more than 800 years. **St Augustine's Chair**, dating from the 13th century, is used to enthrone archbishops.

The stained glass in **Trinity Chapel** is mostly 13th century and celebrates the life of St Thomas à Becket. On either side are the tombs of Henry IV, buried with his wife Joan of Navarre, and of the Black Prince, with its famous effigy that includes the prince's shield, gauntlets and sword.

Opposite **St Anselm's Chapel** is the **tomb of Archbishop Sudbury** who, as Chancellor of the Exchequer, was held responsible for a hated poll-tax. He was beheaded by a mob during the Peasants' Revolt of 1381; his body lies here but his head is in a church in Suffolk.

Walk around the eastern end of the cathedral and turn right into Green Court, which is surrounded on the eastern (right) side by the Deanery and on the northern side (straight ahead) by the early-14th-century Brewhouse and Bakehouse. In the north-western corner (far left) is the much celebrated **Norman Staircase** (1151).

Choral evensong is at 5.30pm on weekdays, and at 3.15pm at the weekend.

Other Attractions

The Canterbury Tales (☎ 454888 or 479227, St Margaret's St; adult/senior, student & child/family £5.90/4.90/18.50; open 9.30am-5.30pm daily Apr-Oct, 9.30am-4.30pm Nov-Mar) is an automated historical recreation of Chaucer's famous stories.

Canterbury's only remaining city gate, **West Gate**, dates from the 14th century and survived because it was used as a prison; it now houses a small **museum** (☎ 452747; adult/child £1/65p; open 11am-12.30pm, 1.30pm-3.30pm Mon-Sat) with collections of arms and armour.

Canterbury Heritage Museum (☎ 452747, Stour St; adult/child £1.90/1.20; open 10.30am-5pm Mon-Sat, 1.30-5pm Sun June-Oct, 10.30am-5pm Mon-Sat Nov-May) in a converted 14th-century building gives good, but rather dry, coverage of the city's history. The building, once the Poor Priests' Hospital, is worth visiting in its own right.

Places to Eat

Flap Jacques (☎ 781000, 71 Castle St) Crepes £2.75-6.50. This is a small, inexpensive French bistro serving Breton-style savoury and sweet pancakes.

Il Vaticano (☎ 765333, 33-5 St Margaret's St) Pasta dishes £4.50-8.50. This place has a wide range of pastas and a lovely courtyard.

Thomas Becket (☎ 464384, Best Lane) Lunch £4-6. This is the place to come for traditional pub food, especially their Sunday roast.

Getting There & Away

National Express operates shuttle buses (£9 day return, one hour 50 minutes, up to 16 daily) between London and Canterbury. Canterbury has two train stations: Canterbury East is accessible from Victoria, and Canterbury West is for trains to/from Charing Cross and Waterloo. The journey takes

BRYN THOMAS

The Royal Pavilion: follow in the Prince Regent's footsteps and take an Indian summer in Brighton.

1¾ hours and a day return costs £12.50/16 to Canterbury East/Canterbury West.

BRIGHTON
☎ 01273 • pop 188,000
Just 51 miles south of London, Brighton, with its heady mix of seediness and a certain amount of sophistication, is London's favourite seaside resort.

The town's character essentially dates from the mid-1780s when the dissolute, music-loving Prince Regent (later George IV) began indulging in lavish parties by the sea. Brighton still has some of the hottest clubs and venues outside London as well as a vibrant student population, excellent shopping, a thriving arts scene, and countless restaurants, pubs and cafes.

Orientation & Information
The TIC (☎ 0906 711 2255, fax 292694, W www.visitbrighton.com, 10 Bartholomew Square), a short distance north-west of the bus station, opens 9am to 5.30pm weekdays, 10am to 5pm on Saturday and 10am to 4pm on Sunday March to October. During the rest of the year it opens 9am to 5pm weekdays and 10am to 5pm on Saturday. They sell the useful *Brighton Town Centre Map & Visitor's Guide* (£1).

Royal Pavilion
Indian palace on the outside and over-the-top chinoiserie inside – the Royal Pavilion *(☎ 290900, Pavilion Parade; adult/senior & student/child aged 5-15/family £5.20/3.75 /3.20/13.60; open daily 10am-6pm June-Sept, 10am-5pm Oct-May)* is an extraordinary folly. It began with a seaside affair, when the Prince Regent, the future George IV, came here in the late 18th century to hang out with his wayward uncle, the duke of Cumberland. He fell in love with both the seaside and a local beauty by the name of

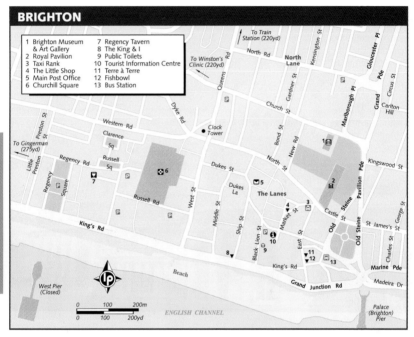

BRIGHTON

1 Brighton Museum & Art Gallery
2 Royal Pavilion
3 Taxi Rank
4 The Little Shop
5 Main Post Office
6 Churchill Square
7 Regency Tavern
8 The King & I
9 Public Toilets
10 Tourist Information Centre
11 Terre à Terre
12 Fishbowl
13 Bus Station

ENGLISH CHANNEL

Maria Fitzherbert, and decided that this was the perfect place to party.

The first pavilion, built in 1787, was a classical villa. It wasn't until the early 19th century, when things Asian became all the rage, that the current confection began to take shape. The final Mogul-inspired design was produced by John Nash, architect of Regent's Park and its surrounding crescents, and was built between 1815 and 1822. George is said to have cried when he first saw the Music Room, with its nine lotus-shaped chandeliers and Chinese murals in vermilion and gold. It was badly damaged by arson in 1975 and again in 1987 by the great storm, but has since been lovingly restored.

The entire over-the-top edifice, which Queen Victoria – who found Brighton 'far too crowded' – sold to the town in 1850, is not to be missed, but have a good look at the Long Gallery, the Banqueting Room (with its domed and painted ceiling), the superb Great Kitchen and the restored Music room

on the ground floor and the South Galleries and Queen Victoria's Apartments (including her water closet) on the 1st floor. Keep an eye out for Rex Whistler's humorous painting *HRH The Prince Regent Awakening the Spirit of Brighton* (1944) in which the overweight (and all-but-naked) prince is rousing a nubile 'Brighton' with a lascivious look in his eye. It's in the Adelaide Corner on the 1st floor just before the entrance to the Queen Adelaide Tearoom.

Tours of the Royal Pavilion (£1.25) leave at 11.30am and 2.30pm daily, with additional departures at 1pm and 1.30pm at the weekend in summer. Free summer band concerts take place in the restored Pavilion Gardens at 3pm on Sunday from late June to early September.

Other Attractions

Originally designed as an indoor tennis court, the **Brighton Museum & Art Gallery** (☎ 290900, Church St; admission free; open 10am-5pm Mon, Tues, & Thur-Sat, 2pm-5pm

Sun), which has been undergoing a £10 million redevelopment for three years, houses a quirky collection of Art Deco and Art Nouveau furniture, archaeological finds, surrealist paintings and costumes.

The **Palace Pier** *(W www.brightonpier .co.uk, Madeira Drive; admission free; open daily)*, known locally as Brighton Pier, with amusement rides such as the Helter Skelter, takeaway food and penny arcades, is the very essence of Brighton. This is the best spot to buy sticks of the famous boiled sweet called Brighton Rock.

Places to Eat
Brighton is jam-packed with decent eateries. Wander around the Lanes, a maze of alleyways crammed with shops and restaurants just north of the TIC, or head down to Preston St, which runs back from the seafront near the disused and crumbling West Pier (1866) and has a lot of ethnic restaurants.

Fishbowl (☎ 777505, 74 East St) Starters £1.45-5.50, mains £4.95-7.95. This small and groovy place serves everything from satay to paella.

Gingerman (☎ 326688, 21a Norfolk Square) 1-/2-/3-course set lunch £9.95/12.95/14.95, 2-/3-course set dinner £21/23.50. This small but stylish restaurant serves seasonal and contemporary food. It's among the top places in Brighton so book ahead.

The King & I (☎ 773390, 2 Ship St) Starters £4.25-4.95, mains £5.65-7.95. This place by the waterfront serves decent Thai food and has a lunchtime special for £4.95.

The Little Shop (☎ 325594, 48a Market St). Sandwiches £1.75-3.95. Visit this hole-in-the-wall for its award-winning sandwiches and filled baguettes.

Regency Tavern (☎ 325652, 32 Russell Square) Lunch £4.95. This unprepossessing place from the outside hides what looks like a room from the Royal Pavilion: striped wallpaper, cameo portraits and brass palm trees.

Terre à Terre (☎ 729051, 71 East St) Starters £4.45-5.95, mains £11.50. A gourmet vegetarian restaurant is not a misnomer; we discovered some of the most inventive meatless dishes ever at this very popular eatery.

Getting There & Around
National Express runs a shuttle service at least hourly from London (£8 day return,

one hour 50 minutes). There are some 40 fast trains a day from Victoria train station (£13 day return, 50 minutes) and slightly slower Thameslink trains from Blackfriars, London Bridge and King's Cross.

Guide Friday (☎ 294466, W www.hopon hopoff.com) runs bus tours every 20 minutes from 10am to 5pm or 5.30pm daily mid-June to August and every half-hour till 3.30pm or 4.30pm the rest of the year. Tours cost £6.50/5.50/2.50/15.50 (adult/senior & student/child aged 5-14/family)

WINDSOR
☎ 01753 • pop 31,000
Windsor Castle is one of the nation's finest tourist attractions and, since it is only 23 miles west of central London and easily accessible by rail and road, it crawls with tourists in all seasons. If possible, avoid visiting at weekends and during the peak months of July and August. Across the River Thames from Windsor is Eton and its celebrated college.

Orientation & Information
Windsor Castle overlooks the Thames, with the town of Windsor fanning out to the west. Eton is essentially a small village linked to Windsor by a pedestrian bridge over the Thames.

Central train station is on Thames St, and directly opposite the entrance gate to Windsor Castle. Riverside train station is near the bridge over to Eton.

The TIC (☎ 743900, fax 743904, W www .windsor.gov.uk), 24 High St, opens 10am to 5pm Monday to Saturday and 10am to 4.30pm on Sunday April to June and September and October, 9.30am to 6pm daily in July and August and 10am to 4pm daily November to March.

Windsor Castle
Standing on chalk bluffs overlooking the Thames, home to British royalty for over 900 years, Windsor Castle *(☎ 869898 or 831118 for opening times, W www.the-royal-collection.org.uk; adult/senior/child aged 5-16/family £11/9/5.50/27.50 or £5.50/4.50/2.70/13.70 when State Apartments are*

closed; public areas open 9.45am-5.15pm daily Mar-Oct, 9.45am-4.15pm daily Nov-Feb) is one of the greatest surviving medieval castles in the world. It started out as a wooden motte-and-bailey castle in 1070, was rebuilt in stone in 1165 and successively extended and rebuilt right through to the 19th century.

In May and June, weather (and other events) permitting, the changing of the guard takes place at 11am Monday to Saturday. It takes place on alternate days from Monday to Saturday the rest of the year. St George's Chapel, a prime attraction, keeps the same hours as the other public areas of the castle from Monday to Saturday *only*; Sunday is reserved for worshippers.

State Apartments & Other Areas The State Apartments are a combination of formal rooms and museum-style exhibits. In 1992, a fire badly damaged St George's Hall and the adjacent Grand Reception Room. Restoration work costing £37 million was completed in 1998.

Like other parts of the castle, the State Apartments have gone through successive reconstructions and expansions, most notably under Charles II, who added lavishly painted ceilings by Antonio Verrio and delicate woodcarvings by Grinling Gibbons. Further modifications were made under George IV and William IV in the 1820s and 1830s.

After the Waterloo Chamber, created to commemorate the Battle of Waterloo and still used for formal meals, and the Garter Throne Room, the **King's Rooms** begin with the King's Drawing Room, also known as the Rubens Room, after the three paintings hanging there. The King's State Bedchamber has paintings by Gainsborough and Canaletto, but Charles II actually slept in the King's Dressing Room next door. Some of Windsor's finest paintings hang here including works by Holbein, Rembrandt, Rubens and Dürer. The King's Closet was used by Charles II as a study and contains works by Canaletto, Reynolds and Hogarth.

From the King's Rooms you come to the **Queen's Rooms**. The Queen's Ballroom has a remarkable collection of paintings by Van Dyck. Only three of the 13 Verrio ceiling paintings from Charles II's time survive, one of them in the Queen's Audience Chamber. Gobelins tapestries and another Verrio ceiling can be found in the Queen's Presence Chamber.

Queen Mary's Doll's House was the work of architect Sir Edwin Lutyens and was built on a 1:12 scale in 1923. It's complete in every detail, right down to running water in the bathrooms.

St George's Chapel One of Britain's finest examples of late-Gothic architecture, the chapel was begun by Edward IV in 1475 but not completed until 1528.

The nave is a superb example of the perpendicular style, with beautiful fan vaulting arching out from the pillars. The chapel contains **royal tombs**, including those of George V and Queen Mary, George VI and Edward IV. The wooden **oriel window**, built for Catherine of Aragon by Henry VIII, is a fine example of the Tudor style. The **Garter Stalls** are the chapel's equivalent of choir stalls. Dating from the late 15th century, the banner, helm and crest above each stall indicates the current occupant. Plates carry names of earlier knights who have occupied the stalls since the 14th century.

Between the Garter Stalls, the **Royal Vault** is the burial place of George III, George IV and William IV. Another vault between the stalls contains the remains of **Henry VIII**, his favourite wife Jane Seymour, and **Charles I**, reunited with his head, which had been removed after the Civil War in 1649.

From the chapel you enter the Dean's Cloister and the adjacent **Albert Memorial Chapel**. This originated in 1240 and became the first chapel of the Order of the Garter in 1350 but fell into disuse when St George's Chapel was built. It was completely restored after the death of Prince Albert in 1861.

Eton College

Cross the River Thames by the pedestrian Windsor Bridge to reach another enduring symbol of Britain's class system: Eton College (☎ *671177*, Ⓦ *www.etoncollege.org.uk*,

Baldwins Shore; adult/child £3/2; open to visitors term-time 2pm-4.30pm daily, Easter & summer holidays 10.30am-4.30pm daily). This famous public (ie, private) school has educated no fewer than 18 prime ministers and princes William and Harry. Several buildings date from the mid-15th century when Henry VI founded the school. One-hour tours cost £4/3 (adult/child) and take place at 2.15pm and 3.15pm daily.

Other Attractions

On High St beside Castle Hill, Windsor's fine **Guildhall** was built between 1686 and 1689, its construction completed under Sir Christopher Wren's supervision. The central columns in the open area don't actually support the 1st floor; the council insisted upon them despite Wren's conviction that they were unnecessary. Wren left a few centimetres of clear space (still visible) to prove his point.

Some of the oldest parts of Windsor lie along the cobbled streets behind the Guildhall, including **Queen Charlotte St**, the shortest road in Britain. The visibly leaning **Market Cross House** is next to the Guildhall. Nell Gwyn, Charles II's favourite mistress, lived at 4 Church St (now a restaurant).

The 1920-hectare **Windsor Great Park** *(☎ 860222; admission free; open 8am-dusk daily)*, where in 1999 Elizabeth II's consort, the Byzantine Prince Philip, had an avenue of ancient trees beheaded because they got in the way of his horse and buggy (or because he was jealous of their crowns), extends from behind the castle almost as far as Ascot.

Places to Eat

Peascod St and its extension St Leonard's Rd are worthwhile hunting grounds for restaurants.

Crooked House *(☎ 857534, 51 High St)* Sandwiches £5-7. From the tiny, precarious-looking Market Cross House, this cafe turns out excellent but expensive sandwiches and French sticks.

Crosses Corner *(☎ 862867, 73 Peascod St)* Lunch £5.25-6. This pub pulls in the crowds with its cheap lunches.

Eton College has educated a host of famous figures.

Francesco's *(☎ 863773, 53 Peascod St)* Pizzas & pasta dishes £5-15, 3-course lunch £6.95. This is a very popular pizza and pasta place.

Ha! Ha! Bar & Canteen *(☎ 770111, Windsor Royal Station)* Snacks £4-4.50, meals £6.50-10. This branch of a London chain in the old Royal railway station is the place to be seen at the moment in Windsor.

The Viceroy *(☎ 858 005, 49-51 St Leonard's Rd)* Starters £2.10-7.75, mains £5.50-11.95, adult/child Sunday buffet £8.50/4.99. This place serves great Indian food but the service can be (in a word) cavalier at times.

Getting There & Around

Green Line buses to Windsor depart from Victoria Coach station on Bulleid Way, between five and 10 times a day from 7.45am (on Saturday from 9am, on Sunday from 9.40am) to about 2pm. The last return bus leaves at around 8.45pm. Day-return tickets cost £7.50/4 (adult/child aged 5-15) and the journey takes one hour.

DAVID WALL

Leeds Castle (confusingly not in Leeds) is one of Britain's most enchanting palaces.

Trains run from Waterloo to Riverside station every 30 minutes (hourly on Sunday) and take around 55 minutes. Services from Paddington to Central station require a change at Slough, five minutes from Windsor, but only take about half an hour. The fare is £6 day return on either route.

Guide Friday (☎ 01789-294466, W www .hoponhopoff.com) has open-top double-decker bus tours of Windsor costing £6.50/ 5.50/2.50/15.50 (adult/senior & student/ child aged 5-14/family). *French Brothers (☎ 851900, W www.boat-trips.co.uk)* operates boat trips between Windsor and Runnymede. A 30-minute trip costs £5.25/7 one-way/return (half-price for children).

LEEDS CASTLE

Some 43 miles south-east of London and justly famous as one of the world's most beautiful palaces, is Leeds Castle *(☎ 01622-765400 or 0870 600 8880, W www .leeds-castle.co.uk, Maidstone, Kent; castle, park & gardens admission adult/senior & student/child aged 4-15 years/family £10/ 8.50/6.50/29, park & gardens admission adult/child aged 4-15 £8.50/5.20; open 10am-7pm, last admission 5pm, daily Mar-Oct; 10am-5pm, last admission 3pm, daily rest of year)*. Like something from a fairy tale, it stands on two small islands in a Kentish lake surrounded by rolling wooded hills. The building dates from the 9th century, but

Henry VIII transformed it from a fortress into a palace.

National Express has a daily direct service that takes 1¼ hours from Victoria Coach Station, leaving at 9am daily and returning in the late afternoon. Tickets cost £10/8/5 (adult/senior & student/child aged 5-15) or £14/11 (adult/child) including castle admission. It must be prebooked. Green Line has a similar inclusive deal costing £14/8 (adult/child), with buses departing at 9.35am Monday to Friday, returning at 4pm. The nearest train station is Bearsted; a combined rail-travel, coach-transfer and admission ticket from either Victoria or Charing Cross train station with Connex Rail (☎ 0870 603 0405 or 0870 580 8080) costs £20.50/10.30 (adult/child).

HEVER CASTLE

Some 35 miles from central London, is idyllic Hever Castle *(☎ 01732-865224, W www .hevercastle.co.uk, Hever, near Edenbridge, Kent; castle & gardens admission adult/ senior & student/child/family £8/6.80/4.40/ 20.40, gardens only £6.30/5.40/4.20/16.80; castle open noon-6pm daily, gardens 11am-6pm daily Mar-Nov)*. The moated castle was the childhood home of Anne Boleyn, mistress and then doomed queen to Henry VIII. It was built in the 13th and 15th centuries and restored in the early 20th century by William Waldorf Astor. The exterior remains unchanged from Tudor times, but the interior now has superb Edwardian woodwork. The castle is surrounded by a garden, again the creation of the Astors, that incorporates a formal Italian garden with classical sculpture. Jousting tournaments in full regalia are staged here at weekends in August.

The closest train station is at Hever, about 1 mile from the castle. Day-returns from Victoria station via Oxted cost £7.10.

DOWN HOUSE

Charles Darwin, the great Victorian evolutionary theorist, lived for over 40 years at Down House (☎ 01689-859119, W www.english-heritage.org.uk, Luxted Rd, Downe, near Orpington, Kent; adult/senior & student/child aged 5-15 years £5.50/4.10/2.80; open 10am-6pm Wed-Sun mid-Apr-Sept, 10am-5pm Wed-Sun Oct, 10am-4pm Wed-Sun Nov-Mar). The stunning Victorian interior of this fine Georgian house has been restored to show his study, where he wrote the seminal On the Origin of Species (1859). Temporary exhibitions are housed upstairs, and you can explore the garden.

Though it has a Kent postal address, Down House is in south-east London. To get there take a train from Victoria to Bromley South and then catch bus No 146 (hourly from Monday to Saturday only). Alternatively, take the train to Orpington and catch bus No R2 (hourly from Monday to Saturday only). A taxi from Orpington station should cost about £8.

KNOLE HOUSE

For the most part dating from 1456, Knole (☎ 01732-462100 or 450608, W www.nationaltrust.org.uk, Sevenoaks, Kent; house admission adult/child/family £5/2.50/12.50, park admission free; house open noon-4pm Wed-Sat & 11am-5pm Sun Mar-Oct, park open year-round) is not as old as some of the great country houses that incorporate medieval fortresses but is more coherent in style. It seems as if nothing has changed since the early 17th century, something for which the Sackville family, who have owned it since 1566, can take credit.

The writer Vita Sackville-West was born here in 1892, and her friend Virginia Woolf based her novel Orlando on the history of the house and family. It is a vast complex, with seven courtyards, 52 staircases and 365 rooms, so the excellent guidebook on sale here is recommended.

Knole is to the east of Sevenoaks, 24 miles south-east of London. Sevenoaks train station is a 1½-mile walk from the house; there's a connecting bus service (☎ 0845 748 4950 for information). A day return from Charing Cross (35 minutes) costs £6.20.

CHARTWELL

Sir Winston Churchill bought Chartwell (☎ 01732-868381 or 866368, W www.nationaltrust.org.uk; Westerham, Kent; house admission adult/child aged 5-16/family £5.80/2.90/14.50, garden & studio only adult/child £2.90/1.45; open 11am-5pm Wed-Sun Apr-Jun, Sep & Oct, 11am-5pm Tues-Sun Jul & Aug), a large country house just north of Edenbridge, some 21 miles south-east of London, in 1922. It remained the family home until his death in 1965.

To get here take a train to Bromley South from Victoria and then catch bus No 246.

Lonely Planet Guides by Region

Lonely Planet is known worldwide for publishing practical, reliable and no-nonsense travel information in our guides and on our Web site. The Lonely Planet list covers just about every accessible part of the world. Currently there are 16 series: Travel guides, Shoestring guides, Condensed guides, Phrasebooks, Read This First, Healthy Travel, Walking guides, Cycling guides, Watching Wildlife guides, Pisces Diving & Snorkeling guides, City Maps, Road Atlases, Out to Eat, World Food, Journeys travel literature and Pictorials.

AFRICA Africa on a shoestring • Botswana • Cairo • Cairo City Map • Cape Town • Cape Town City Map • East Africa • Egypt • Egyptian Arabic phrasebook • Ethiopia, Eritrea & Djibouti • Ethiopian Amharic phrasebook • The Gambia & Senegal • Healthy Travel Africa • Kenya • Malawi • Morocco • Moroccan Arabic phrasebook • Mozambique • Namibia • Read This First: Africa • South Africa, Lesotho & Swaziland • Southern Africa • Southern Africa Road Atlas • Swahili phrasebook • Tanzania, Zanzibar & Pemba • Trekking in East Africa • Tunisia • Watching Wildlife East Africa • Watching Wildlife Southern Africa • West Africa • World Food Morocco • Zambia • Zimbabwe, Botswana and Namibia
Travel Literature: Mali Blues: Traveling to an African Beat • The Rainbird: A Central African Journey • Songs to an African Sunset: A Zimbabwean Story

AUSTRALIA & THE PACIFIC Aboriginal Australia & the Torres Strait Islands •Auckland • Australia • Australian phrasebook • Australia Road Atlas • Cycling Australia • Cycling New Zealand • Fiji • Fijian phrasebook • Healthy Travel Australia, NZ & the Pacific • Islands of Australia's Great Barrier Reef • Melbourne • Melbourne City Map • Micronesia • New Caledonia • New South Wales • New Zealand • Northern Territory • Outback Australia • Out to Eat – Melbourne • Out to Eat – Sydney • Papua New Guinea • Pidgin phrasebook • Queensland • Rarotonga & the Cook Islands • Samoa • Solomon Islands • South Australia • South Pacific • South Pacific phrasebook • Sydney • Sydney City Map • Sydney Condensed • Tahiti & French Polynesia • Tasmania • Tonga • Tramping in New Zealand • Vanuatu • Victoria • Walking in Australia • Watching Wildlife Australia • Western Australia
Travel Literature: Islands in the Clouds: Travels in the Highlands of New Guinea • Kiwi Tracks: A New Zealand Journey • Sean & David's Long Drive

CENTRAL AMERICA & THE CARIBBEAN Bahamas, Turks & Caicos • Baja California • Belize, Guatemala & Yucatán • Bermuda • Central America on a shoestring • Costa Rica • Costa Rica Spanish phrasebook • Cuba • Cycling Cuba • Dominican Republic & Haiti • Eastern Caribbean • Guatemala • Havana • Healthy Travel Central & South America • Jamaica • Mexico • Mexico City • Panama • Puerto Rico • Read This First: Central & South America • Virgin Islands • World Food Caribbean • World Food Mexico • Yucatán
Travel Literature: Green Dreams: Travels in Central America

EUROPE Amsterdam • Amsterdam City Map • Amsterdam Condensed • Andalucía • Athens • Austria • Baltic States phrasebook • Barcelona • Barcelona City Map • Belgium & Luxembourg • Berlin • Berlin City Map • Britain • British phrasebook • Brussels, Bruges & Antwerp • Brussels City Map • Budapest • Budapest City Map • Canary Islands • Catalunya & the Costa Brava • Central Europe • Central Europe phrasebook • Copenhagen • Corfu & the Ionians • Corsica • Crete • Crete Condensed • Croatia • Cycling Britain • Cycling France • Cyprus • Czech & Slovak Republics • Czech phrasebook • Denmark • Dublin • Dublin City Map • Dublin Condensed • Eastern Europe • Eastern Europe phrasebook • Edinburgh • Edinburgh City Map • England • Estonia, Latvia & Lithuania • Europe on a shoestring • Europe phrasebook • Finland • Florence • Florence City Map • France • Frankfurt City Map • Frankfurt Condensed • French phrasebook • Georgia, Armenia & Azerbaijan • Germany • German phrasebook • Greece • Greek Islands • Greek phrasebook • Hungary • Iceland, Greenland & the Faroe Islands • Ireland • Italian phrasebook • Italy • Kraków • Lisbon • The Loire • London • London City Map • London Condensed • Madrid • Madrid City Map • Malta • Mediterranean Europe • Milan, Turin & Genoa • Moscow • Munich • Netherlands • Normandy • Norway • Out to Eat – London • Out to Eat – Paris • Paris • Paris City Map • Paris Condensed • Poland • Polish phrasebook • Portugal • Portuguese phrasebook • Prague • Prague City Map • Provence & the Côte d'Azur • Read This First: Europe • Rhodes & the Dodecanese • Romania & Moldova • Rome • Rome City Map • Rome Condensed • Russia, Ukraine & Belarus • Russian phrasebook • Scandinavian & Baltic Europe • Scandinavian phrasebook • Scotland • Sicily • Slovenia • South-West France • Spain • Spanish phrasebook • Stockholm • St Petersburg • St Petersburg City Map • Sweden • Switzerland • Tuscany • Ukrainian phrasebook • Venice • Vienna • Wales • Walking in Britain • Walking in France • Walking in Ireland • Walking in Italy • Walking in Scotland • Walking in Spain • Walking in Switzerland • Western Europe • World Food France • World Food Greece • World Food Ireland • World Food Italy • World Food Spain **Travel Literature:** After Yugoslavia • Love and War in the Apennines • The Olive Grove: Travels in Greece • On the Shores of the Mediterranean • Round Ireland in Low Gear • A Small Place in Italy

Lonely Planet Mail Order

Lonely Planet products are distributed worldwide. They are also available by mail order from Lonely Planet, so if you have difficulty finding a title please write to us. North and South American residents should write to 150 Linden St, Oakland, CA 94607, USA; European and African residents should write to 10a Spring Place, London NW5 3BH, UK; and residents of other countries to Locked Bag 1, Footscray, Victoria 3011, Australia.

INDIAN SUBCONTINENT & THE INDIAN OCEAN Bangladesh • Bengali phrasebook • Bhutan • Delhi • Goa • Healthy Travel Asia & India • Hindi & Urdu phrasebook • India • India & Bangladesh City Map • Indian Himalaya • Karakoram Highway • Kathmandu City Map • Kerala • Madagascar • Maldives • Mauritius, Réunion & Seychelles • Mumbai (Bombay) • Nepal • Nepali phrasebook • North India • Pakistan • Rajasthan • Read This First: Asia & India • South India • Sri Lanka • Sri Lanka phrasebook • Tibet • Tibetan phrasebook • Trekking in the Indian Himalaya • Trekking in the Karakoram & Hindukush • Trekking in the Nepal Himalaya • World Food India **Travel Literature:** The Age of Kali: Indian Travels and Encounters • Hello Goodnight: A Life of Goa • In Rajasthan • Maverick in Madagascar • A Season in Heaven: True Tales from the Road to Kathmandu • Shopping for Buddhas • A Short Walk in the Hindu Kush • Slowly Down the Ganges

MIDDLE EAST & CENTRAL ASIA Bahrain, Kuwait & Qatar • Central Asia • Central Asia phrasebook • Dubai • Farsi (Persian) phrasebook • Hebrew phrasebook • Iran • Israel & the Palestinian Territories • Istanbul • Istanbul City Map • Istanbul to Cairo • Istanbul to Kathmandu • Jerusalem • Jerusalem City Map • Jordan • Lebanon • Middle East • Oman & the United Arab Emirates • Syria • Turkey • Turkish phrasebook • World Food Turkey • Yemen **Travel Literature:** Black on Black: Iran Revisited • Breaking Ranks: Turbulent Travels in the Promised Land • The Gates of Damascus • Kingdom of the Film Stars: Journey into Jordan

NORTH AMERICA Alaska • Boston • Boston City Map • Boston Condensed • British Columbia • California & Nevada • California Condensed • Canada • Chicago • Chicago City Map • Chicago Condensed • Florida • Georgia & the Carolinas • Great Lakes • Hawaii • Hiking in Alaska • Hiking in the USA • Honolulu & Oahu City Map • Las Vegas • Los Angeles • Los Angeles City Map • Louisiana & the Deep South • Miami • Miami City Map • Montreal • New England • New Orleans • New Orleans City Map • New York City • New York City City Map • New York City Condensed • New York, New Jersey & Pennsylvania • Oahu • Out to Eat – San Francisco • Pacific Northwest • Rocky Mountains • San Diego & Tijuana • San Francisco • San Francisco City Map • Seattle • Seattle City Map • Southwest • Texas • Toronto • USA • USA phrasebook • Vancouver • Vancouver City Map • Virginia & the Capital Region • Washington, DC • Washington, DC City Map • World Food New Orleans **Travel Literature:** Caught Inside: A Surfer's Year on the California Coast • Drive Thru America

NORTH-EAST ASIA Beijing • Beijing City Map • Cantonese phrasebook • China • Hiking in Japan • Hong Kong & Macau • Hong Kong City Map • Hong Kong Condensed • Japan • Japanese phrasebook • Korea • Korean phrasebook • Kyoto • Mandarin phrasebook • Mongolia • Mongolian phrasebook • Seoul • Shanghai • South-West China • Taiwan • Tokyo • Tokyo Condensed • World Food Hong Kong • World Food Japan **Travel Literature:** In Xanadu: A Quest • Lost Japan

SOUTH AMERICA Argentina, Uruguay & Paraguay • Bolivia • Brazil • Brazilian phrasebook • Buenos Aires • Buenos Aires City Map • Chile & Easter Island • Colombia • Ecuador & the Galapagos Islands • Healthy Travel Central & South America • Latin American Spanish phrasebook • Peru • Quechua phrasebook • Read This First: Central & South America • Rio de Janeiro • Rio de Janeiro City Map • Santiago de Chile • South America on a shoestring • Trekking in the Patagonian Andes • Venezuela **Travel Literature:** Full Circle: A South American Journey

SOUTH-EAST ASIA Bali & Lombok • Bangkok • Bangkok City Map • Burmese phrasebook • Cambodia • Cycling Vietnam, Laos & Cambodia • East Timor phrasebook • Hanoi • Healthy Travel Asia & India • Hill Tribes phrasebook • Ho Chi Minh City (Saigon) • Indonesia • Indonesian phrasebook • Indonesia's Eastern Islands • Java • Lao phrasebook • Laos • Malay phrasebook • Malaysia, Singapore & Brunei • Myanmar (Burma) • Philippines • Pilipino (Tagalog) phrasebook • Read This First: Asia & India • Singapore • Singapore City Map • South-East Asia on a shoestring • South-East Asia phrasebook • Thailand • Thailand's Islands & Beaches • Thailand, Vietnam, Laos & Cambodia Road Atlas • Thai phrasebook • Vietnam • Vietnamese phrasebook • World Food Indonesia • World Food Thailand • World Food Vietnam

ALSO AVAILABLE: Antarctica • The Arctic • The Blue Man: Tales of Travel, Love and Coffee • Brief Encounters: Stories of Love, Sex & Travel • Buddhist Stupas in Asia: The Shape of Perfection • Chasing Rickshaws • The Last Grain Race • Lonely Planet ... On the Edge: Adventurous Escapades from Around the World • Lonely Planet Unpacked • Lonely Planet Unpacked Again • Not the Only Planet: Science Fiction Travel Stories • Ports of Call: A Journey by Sea • Sacred India • Travel Photography: A Guide to Taking Better Pictures • Travel with Children • Tuvalu: Portrait of an Island Nation

LONELY PLANET

ON THE ROAD

Travel Guides explore cities, regions and countries, and supply information on transport, restaurants and accommodation, covering all budgets. They come with reliable, easy-to-use maps, practical advice, cultural and historical facts and a rundown on attractions both on and off the beaten track. There are over 200 titles in this classic series, covering nearly every country in the world.

 Lonely Planet Upgrades extend the shelf life of existing travel guides by detailing any changes that may affect travel in a region since a book has been published. Upgrades can be downloaded for free from **www.lonelyplanet.com/upgrades**

For travellers with more time than money, **Shoestring** guides offer dependable, first-hand information with hundreds of detailed maps, plus insider tips for stretching money as far as possible. Covering entire continents in most cases, the six-volume shoestring guides are known around the world as 'backpackers bibles'.

For the discerning short-term visitor, **Condensed** guides highlight the best a destination has to offer in a full-colour, pocket-sized format designed for quick access. They include everything from top sights and walking tours to opinionated reviews of where to eat, stay, shop and have fun.

CitySync lets travellers use their Palm™ or Visor™ hand-held computers to guide them through a city with handy tips on transport, history, cultural life, major sights, and shopping and entertainment options. It can also quickly search and sort hundreds of reviews of hotels, restaurants and attractions, and pinpoint their location on scrollable street maps. CitySync can be downloaded from **www.citysync.com**

MAPS & ATLASES

Lonely Planet's **City Maps** feature downtown and metropolitan maps, as well as transit routes and walking tours. The maps come complete with an index of streets, a listing of sights and a plastic coat for extra durability.

Road Atlases are an essential navigation tool for serious travellers. Cross-referenced with the guidebooks, they also feature distance and climate charts and a complete site index.

ESSENTIALS

Read This First books help new travellers to hit the road with confidence. These invaluable predeparture guides give step-by-step advice on preparing for a trip, budgeting, arranging a visa, planning an itinerary and staying safe while still getting off the beaten track.

Healthy Travel pocket guides offer a regional rundown on disease hot spots and practical advice on predeparture health measures, staying well on the road and what to do in emergencies. The guides come with a user-friendly design and helpful diagrams and tables.

Lonely Planet's **Phrasebooks** cover the essential words and phrases travellers need when they're strangers in a strange land. They come in a pocket-sized format with colour tabs for quick reference, extensive vocabulary lists, easy-to-follow pronunciation keys and two-way dictionaries.

Miffed by blurry photos of the Taj Mahal? Tired of the classic 'top of the head cut off' shot? **Travel Photography: A Guide to Taking Better Pictures** will help you turn ordinary holiday snaps into striking images and give you the know-how to capture every scene, from frenetic festivals to peaceful beach sunrises.

Lonely Planet's **Travel Journal** is a lightweight but sturdy travel diary for jotting down all those on-the-road observations and significant travel moments. It comes with a handy time-zone wheel, a world map and useful travel information.

Lonely Planet's eKno is an all-in-one communication service developed especially for travellers. It offers low-cost international calls and free email and voicemail so that you can keep in touch while on the road. Check it out on **www.ekno.lonelyplanet.com**

FOOD & RESTAURANT GUIDES

Lonely Planet's **Out to Eat** guides recommend the brightest and best places to eat and drink in top international cities. These gourmet companions are arranged by neighbourhood, packed with dependable maps, garnished with scene-setting photos and served with quirky features.

For people who live to eat, drink and travel, **World Food** guides explore the culinary culture of each country. Entertaining and adventurous, each guide is packed with detail on staples and specialities, regional cuisine and local markets, as well as sumptuous recipes, comprehensive culinary dictionaries and lavish photos good enough to eat.

LONELY PLANET

OUTDOOR GUIDES

For those who believe the best way to see the world is on foot, Lonely Planet's **Walking Guides** detail everything from family strolls to difficult treks, with 'when to go and how to do it' advice supplemented by reliable maps and essential travel information.

Cycling Guides map a destination's best bike tours, long and short, in day-by-day detail. They contain all the information a cyclist needs, including advice on bike maintenance, places to eat and stay, innovative maps with detailed cues to the rides, and elevation charts.

The **Watching Wildlife** series is perfect for travellers who want authoritative information but don't want to tote a heavy field guide. Packed with advice on where, when and how to view a region's wildlife, each title features photos of over 300 species and contains engaging comments on the local flora and fauna.

With underwater colour photos throughout, **Pisces Books** explore the world's best diving and snorkelling areas. Each book contains listings of diving services and dive resorts, detailed information on depth, visibility and difficulty of dives, and a roundup of the marine life you're likely to see through your mask.

OFF THE ROAD

Journeys, the travel literature series written by renowned travel authors, capture the spirit of a place or illuminate a culture with a journalist's attention to detail and a novelist's flair for words. These are tales to soak up while you're actually on the road or dip into as an at-home armchair indulgence.

The range of lavishly illustrated **Pictorial** books is just the ticket for both travellers and dreamers. Off-beat tales and vivid photographs bring the adventure of travel to your doorstep long before the journey begins and long after it is over.

Lonely Planet **Videos** encourage the same independent, tough-minded approach as the guidebooks. Currently airing throughout the world, this award-winning series features innovative footage and an original soundtrack.

Yes, we know, work is tough, so do a little bit of deskside dreaming with the spiral-bound Lonely Planet **Diary** or a Lonely Planet **Wall Calendar**, filled with great photos from around the world.

TRAVELLERS NETWORK

Lonely Planet Online. Lonely Planet's award-winning Web site has insider information on hundreds of destinations, from Amsterdam to Zimbabwe, complete with interactive maps and relevant links. The site also offers the latest travel news, recent reports from travellers on the road, guidebook upgrades, a travel links site, an online book-buying option and a lively traveller's bulletin board. It can be viewed at **www.lonelyplanet.com** or AOL keyword: lp.

Planet Talk is a quarterly print newsletter, full of gossip, advice, anecdotes and author articles. It provides an antidote to the being-at-home blues and lets you plan and dream for the next trip. Contact the nearest Lonely Planet office for your free copy.

Comet, the free Lonely Planet newsletter, comes via email once a month. It's loaded with travel news, advice, dispatches from authors, travel competitions and letters from readers. To subscribe, click on the Comet subscription link on the front page of the Web site.

LONELY PLANET

You already know that Lonely Planet produces more than this one guidebook, but you might not be aware of the other products we have on this region. Here is a selection of titles that you may want to check out as well:

Out to Eat London 2002
ISBN 1 74059 205 0
US$14.99 • UK£7.99

London City Map
ISBN 1 86450 008 5
US$5.95 • UK£3.99

London Condensed
ISBN 1 86450 043 3
US$9.95 • UK£5.99

England
ISBN 1 86450 194 4
US$21.99 • UK£13.99

Scotland
ISBN 1 86450 157 X
US$16.99 • UK£10.99

Wales
ISBN 1 86450 126 X
US$15.99 • UK£9.99

Edinburgh
ISBN 1 86450 378 5
US$12.99 • UK£8.99

Britain
ISBN 1 86450 147 2
US$27.99 • UK£15.99

Western Europe
ISBN 1 86450 163 4
US$27.99 • UK£15.99

Walking in Britain
ISBN 1 86450 280 0
US$21.99 • UK£13.99

Cycling Britain
ISBN 1 86450 037 9
US$19.99 • UK£12.99

British Phrasebook
ISBN 0 86442 484 1
US$5.95 • UK£3.99

Available wherever books are sold

Index

Text

A

Abbey Road 35
Abney Park Cemetery 212
accommodation 247–68, *see also* Places to Stay index
apartments 268
B&Bs 253–7
booking offices 248
camping 248
deluxe 264–8
guesthouses 253–7
hotels 253–7
long-term rentals 266
mid-range 257–60
student accommodation 252–3
top end 260–4
activities, *see* individual entries
Adam, Robert 40
Admiralty Arch 138
air travel 94–7
Africa 97
airlines 97
airports 106–109
Asia 97
Australia 96–7
Canada 96
continental Europe 94, 96
Ireland 94
New Zealand 96–7
USA 96
within UK 94
Albert Bridge 197
Albert Memorial 202
Albert, Prince 21
ale 303
Alexander Fleming Laboratory 241
Alexandra Palace 215–16
Alexandra Park 215–16
Alfred the Great 50
All Hallows-by-the-Tower 181
All Souls, Langham Place 149
Allies memorial 149
Apsley House 205–6
architecture 38–41
athletics 327

auction houses 335
Australia House 169

B

BA London Eye 192
ballet 34–5, 324–5
Bank 173–4
Bank of England Museum 174
Bankside 185–90
Bankside Gallery 190
Bankside Power Station 128
Banqueting House 138
Barbican 162–3, 319–20, 322–3
Barbican Gallery 163
bars 303–13
Battersea 194–5
Battersea Bridge 197
Battersea Park 194–5
Battersea Power Station 194
Bayswater, *see* Notting Hill & Bayswater
Bazalgette, Sir Joseph 20, 54
Bedford Square 155
Beefeaters, *see* Yeoman Warders
beer 303
Berkeley Square 146
Bermondsey 182–3
Bethnal Green Museum of Childhood 220
bicycle travel 102, 117–18
rental 117
Big Ben 140
Blackheath 228
Blair, Tony 24–5
Blitz, the 22
Bloomsbury 154–9
Bloomsbury Group 21
blue plaques 118
boat travel 102–4, 118–20
Belgium 104
canal trips 119–21
France 103–4
Germany 104
Ireland 102–3
Netherlands 104
river shuttle 118–19
Scandinavia 104
Spain 104

books 75–6, *see also* literature
Borough Market 341
Boudicca 10
statue 139
Bouverie House 168
Bow Street Runners 19
Bramah Museum of Tea & Coffee 183
Brentford, *see* Isleworth, Brentford & Ealing
Brick Lane Market 341
bridges 120
Albert Bridge 197
Battersea Bridge 197
Millennium Bridge 189
Tower Bridge 181–2
Brighton 357–9, **358**
Britain at War Experience 184–5
British Broadcasting Corporation (BBC) 22
British Library 210–11
British Museum 155–8
Great Court 129
Britten, Benjamin 35
Brixton 231–2, **Map 15**
Broadcasting House 149
Broadgate Centre 218
Broadwick House 129
Brompton Oratory 198
Brunel's Engine House 241
bubonic plague 12
Buckingham Palace 144–5
ticket office 127
Buddhapadipa Temple 232–3
Burgh House 214–15
Burlington Arcade 148
bus travel 97–8, 112–13
continental Europe 98
within UK 98
Bush House 169
business hours 89

C

Cabinet War Rooms 138–9
Cabot Square 223
Cambridge 351–4, **352**
Camden & Kentish Town 212–13
Camden Market 212–13, 341–2
Camden Passage 342

Bold indicates maps.

Bold indicates maps.

Bold indicates maps.

Places to Stay

Places to Eat

Boxed Text

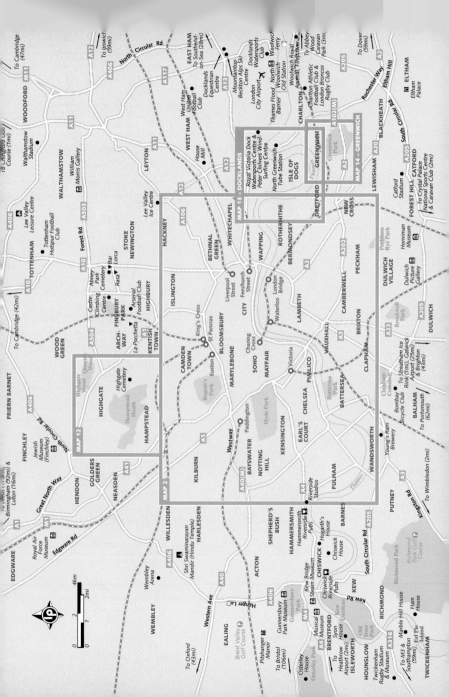

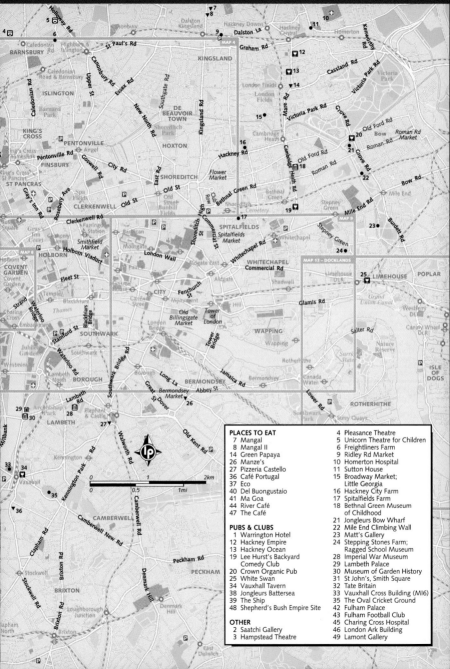

MAP 2

PLACES TO EAT
7 Mangal
8 Mangal II
14 Green Papaya
26 Manze's
27 Pizzeria Castello
36 Café Portugal
40 Del Buongustaio
41 Ma Goa
44 River Café
47 The Café

PUBS & CLUBS
1 Warrington Hotel
12 Hackney Empire
13 Hackney Ocean
19 Lee Hurst's Backyard
   Comedy Club
20 Crown Organic Pub
25 White Swan
34 Vauxhall Tavern
38 Jongleurs Battersea
39 The Ship
48 Shepherd's Bush Empire Site

OTHER
2 Saatchi Gallery
3 Hampstead Theatre

4 Pleasance Theatre
5 Unicorn Theatre for Children
6 Freightliners Farm
9 Ridley Rd Market
10 Homerton Hospital
11 Sutton House
15 Broadway Market;
   Little Georgia
16 Hackney City Farm
17 Spitalfields Farm
18 Bethnal Green Museum
   of Childhood
21 Jongleurs Bow Wharf
22 Mile End Climbing Wall
23 Matt's Gallery
24 Stepping Stones Farm;
   Ragged School Museum
28 Imperial War Museum
29 Lambeth Palace
30 Museum of Garden History
31 St John's, Smith Square
32 Tate Britain
33 Vauxhall Cross Building (MI6)
35 The Oval Cricket Ground
42 Fulham Palace
43 Fulham Football Club
45 Charing Cross Hospital
46 London Ark Building
49 Lamont Gallery

MAP 3

PLACES TO STAY
42 St Christopher's Inn Camden;
    Belushi's Bar
48 St Pancras YHA Hostel
50 Euston Travel Inn Capital
52 Jenkins Hotel
53 Cresent Hotel; Euro Hotel
55 John Adams Hall Student Residence
56 Passfield Hall Student Residence
60 Hotels
64 International Students House

PLACES TO EAT
2   Lemonia
3   Trojka
5   Marine Ices
6   Belgo Noord
7   Nando's
8   Cotton's Rum Shop,
    Bar & Restaurant
10 Silks & Spice
11 Thanh Binh
14 Wagamama
16 SauCe
18 Pizza Express
19 Lemongrass
20 Castle's
23 Mango Room
25 Bar Gansa
27 Curly Dog Café
32 New Culture Revolution
39 Ruby in the Dust
41 Café Delancey
43 Taste of Siam
45 Asakusa
46 El Parador
61 Diwana
62 Ravi Shankar
63 Chutneys

PUBS, BARS & CLUBS
4   Pembroke Castle
9   Barfly@the Monarch
13 Dingwalls; Jongleurs Camden Lock
17 The Verge
22 WKD
26 The Engineer
28 Cecil Sharp House
30 Spread Eagle
33 Bar Vinyl Café
34 Jazz Café
35 World's End; Underworld
37 Black Cap
38 Crown & Goose
40 Oh! Bar

OTHER
1   Freud Museum
13 London Waterbus Company
15 Waterside Cafe; Jenny Wren Cruises
21 Sainsbury's Supermarket
24 Camden Market
29 Jewish Museum
31 Forco Laundrette
36 Tower Records
44 Camden Palace
47 Camley St Natural Park
49 STA Travel
51 The Place
54 St Pancras New Church
57 Petrie Museum of Egyptian Archaeology
58 University College Student
    Residences Office
59 University College Hospital
65 Open Air Theatre
66 London Central Islamic
    Centre & Mosque
67 Entrance to London Zoo
68 Abbey Rd Zebra Crossing

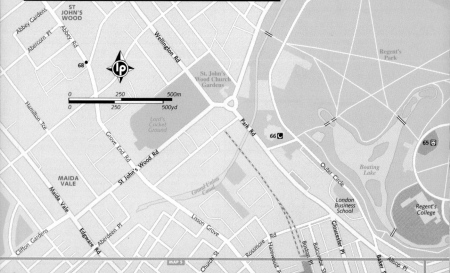

PLACES TO STAY
36 Alhambra Hotel
39 Ashlee House
43 The Generator
51 Rosebery Avenue Student Hall
61 Finbury Residences
67 London City YMCA

PLACES TO EAT
3 Cantina Italia
4 Yelllow River Café
5 Primos Lounge
9 Tiger Lil's
13 La Porchetta
14 Le Mercury
15 Angel Mangal
16 Solo Stefano
18 Granita
19 Le Sacré Coeur Bistro
23 Giraffe
24 Tartuf
25 Pizzeria Oregano
26 Cuba Libre
28 Afghan Kitchen
30 Lola's
31 New Culture Revolution
40 North Sea Fish Restaurant

46 Ravi Shankar
53 Moro
57 Maison Novelli E1
63 Cicada
65 The Quiet Revolution
75 Great Eastern Dining Room
84 The Real Greek
86 Viet Hoa
89 Les Trois Garçons
90 Brick Lane Beigel Bake;
   Evering Bakery Bagel Shop

PUBS, BARS & CLUBS
1 Garage
7 Medicine Bar
9 Bierodrome
12 Bar Latino
20 King's Head
22 Old Queen's Head
27 Walkabout Inn
29 Duke of Cambridge
34 Central Station
35 Bagleys Studios;
   The Cross
37 Scala
48 Old Red Lion

49 Dove Regent
52 O'Hanlon's
54 Al's Bar Café
55 The Eagle
59 Three Kings of Clerkenwell
68 Liquid Lab
70 The Aquarium
71 Charlie Wright's
   International Bar
72 Katabatic
74 Home
76 Cantaloupe
77 Cargo
78 Comedy Café
79 Barley Mow
80 Bricklayers Arms
81 333
82 Shoreditch Electricity
   Showrooms

OTHER
2 Estorick Collection of
   Modern Italian Art
8 Upper St Laundrette
10 Islington Town Hall
11 Dugan's Chocolates
17 Little Angel Theatre

21 Criterion Auctioneers
32 Chapel Market
33 London Canal Museum
38 Mole Jazz
41 Cyberg@te
42 Gay's the Word
44 Red & White Laundrette
45 Dickens' House
47 Crafts Council
50 Sadler's Wells;
   Lilian Baylis Theatre
56 Clerk's Well
58 Karl Marx Memorial Library
60 Papier Marché;
   Clerkenwell Visitor Centre
62 Into You
66 Ironmonger Row Baths
69 John Wesley's House;
   Chapel & Museum
   of Methodism
73 PLondon Architectural Salvage
   & Supply Company (LASCO)
83 White Cube²
85 Lux Cinema
87 Geffrye Museum
88 Columbia Road
   Flower Market

MAP 5

PLACES TO STAY

22 Wigmore Court Hotel
23 Bryanston Court Hotel
24 Glynne Court Hotel
25 Edward Lear Hotel
30 Pavillion Hotel
32 Gresham Hotel
33 Balmoral House Hotel
34 Europa House Hotel
35 Balmoral House Branch
36 Cardiff Hotel
37 St David's Hotel
39 Elysée Hotel
42 Lancaster Hall Hotel YMCA
43 Oxford Hotel; Sass House Hotel
44 The Hempel; I-Thai; H Bar
45 Queen's Park Hotel
46 Quest Hotel; Royal Hotel
47 Hyde Park Hostel
48 Inverness Court Hotel
58 Garden Court Hotel
60 Miller's Residence
61 Leinster Inn
77 Portobello Gold Hotel; Buzz Internet Bar
78 Portobello Hotel
79 Gate Hotel
81 Abbey Court Hotel
82 Manor Court Hotel
v86 Hillgate Hotel
95 Abbey House; Vicarage Hotel
103 Basil St Hotel
108 The Gore; Bistrot 190
121 Holland House YHA Hostel

PLACES TO EAT

2 Belgo Zuid
4 Sausage & Mash Café
6 Café Grove
8 Bali Sugar
12 Green Olive
16 Mandalay
21 Reubens
31 Satay House
49 Mandarin Kitchen
50 Kalamaras Greek Taverna
53 Churrería Española
54 Tawana
55 Khan's
56 Burritos
57 The Standard
59 L'Accento
62 Inaho
63 Veronica's
64 Assagi; The Chepstow Pub
66 Mandola
75 Osteria Basilico
80 Modhubon
87 Manzara
89 Est Est Est
90 Costas Fish Restaurant
91 Geales
92 Kensington Place
96 The Orangery
101 Vong
104 Stockpot
109 Wódka
112 Arcadia; Bellini's
119 Sticky Fingers

PUBS & CLUBS

1 Ion Bar
5 Subterania
7 Market Bar
9 The Cow
10 The Westbourne
14 Bridge House; Canal Café Comedy Club
67 Beach Blanket Babylon
85 Notting Hill Arts Club
93 The Churchill Arms
94 Windsor Castle
111 Cuba

OTHER

3 Honest Jon's
11 Jason's Canal Trips; Jason's Restaurant
13 British Waterways Office
15 London Waterbus Company
17 Church St Market
18 Sherlock Holmes Museum
19 Transport for London's Lost Property Office
20 Madam Tussaud's; London Planetarium
26 Marble Arch
27 Speaker's Corner
28 Tyburn Tree Site
29 Tyburn Convent
38 Hyde Park Stables
40 Sandwich Bar Laundrette
41 Drifters Travel
51 Laundrette Centre
52 Porchester Spa
65 Sean Arnold Sporting Antiques
68 Award Winning Toilets
69 Rough Trade
70 Electric Cinema
71 Spice Shop
72 Books for Cooks
73 Garden Books
74 Travel Bookshop
76 Portobello Rd Market
83 Airbus Stop
84 Airbus Stop
88 Dispensary
97 Bandstand
98 Peter Pan Statue
99 Serpentine Gallery
100 Serpentine Lido
102 Harvey Nichols; Fifth Floor
105 Bonhams
106 Royal Geographical Society
107 Albert Memorial
110 Leith's School of Food & Wine
113 easyEverything
114 usit Campus; YHA Adventure Shop
115 Linley Sambourne House
116 Snow + Rock
117 Trailfinders (Branch)
118 Trailfinders (Main Office)
120 Commonwealth Institute

ELLIOT DANIEL

The big frieze: the splendidly decorated Albert Hall

Unwind in Hyde Park's tranquil rose garden in summer or...

DOUG MCKINLAY

... romp through leaves on an autumnal day.

DENNIS JOHNSON

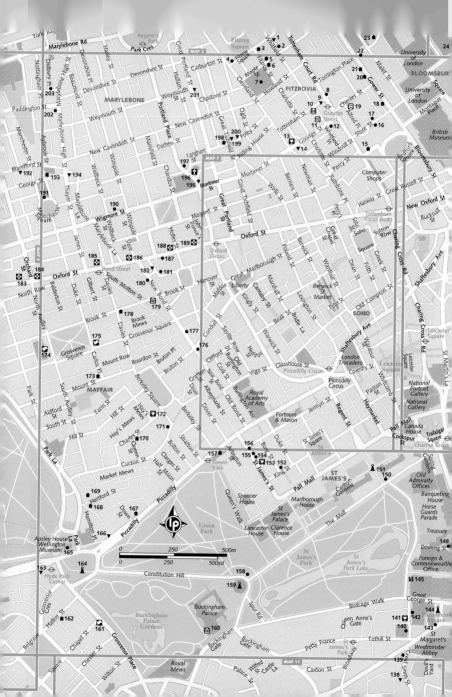

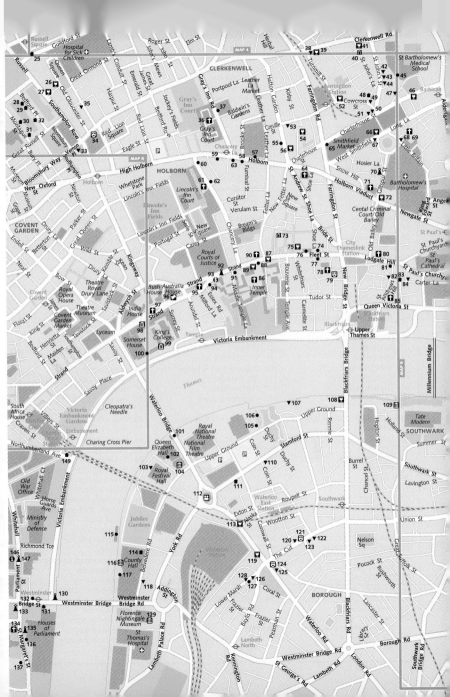

MAP 6

PLACES TO STAY

- 3 Indian Student YMCA
- 5 Ramsay Hall
- 6 Carr-Saunders Hall
- 15 My Hotel
- 18 Academy Hotel
- 20 Jesmond Hotel; Ridgemount Hotel
- 21 Hotel Cavendish; Arran House Hotel
- 23 Quaker International Centre
- 24 Royal National Hotel; Contiki Travel
- 25 Celtic Hotel
- 28 St Margaret's Hotel
- 29 Repton Hotel
- 30 Ruskin Hotel
- 31 Museum Inn
- 32 Haddon Hall
- 48 The Rookery
- 83 City of London YHA Hostel
- 111 King's College Student Hall
- 114 County Hall Travel Inn Capital
- 149 Citidines Trafalger Square
- 157 The Ritz
- 162 The Halkin
- 167 Park Lane Hotel
- 168 The Metropolitan; Nobu; Met Bar
- 169 Hilton Hotel; Windows of the World Bar
- 170 Chesterfield
- 173 The Connaught
- 178 Claridges
- 193 Durrants Hotel
- 198 Langham Court Hotel

PLACES TO EAT

- 1 Archipelago
- 9 Cranks
- 14 Dish Dash
- 33 Spaghetti House
- 35 Mille Pini
- 38 Gaudí
- 42 Tinseltown
- 43 Vic Naylor
- 44 St John
- 47 Le Café du Marché
- 49 The Greenery
- 50 Rudland & Stubbs
- 51 Smiths of Smithfields
- 53 Knosherie
- 67 Ferrari's Café
- 68 Club Gascon
- 82 Da Vinci
- 84 Dim Sum
- 103 People's Palace
- 107 Oxo Tower Restaurant & Brasserie; Bistrot 2 Riverside
- 110 RSJ
- 118 fish!

- 120 R Cooke Eel & Pie Shop
- 122 Livebait
- 123 Mesón Don Felipe
- 125 Bar + Kitchen
- 126 Cubana
- 128 Marie's Café
- 138 Cinnamon Club
- 163 Pizza on the Park
- 166 Hard Rock Café
- 182 Rasa W1
- 192 Spighetta
- 194 Woodlands
- 195 Özer
- 199 Silks & Spice
- 200 Back to Basics
- 201 Villandry

PUBS & CLUBS

- 13 Goodge
- 26 The Queen's Larder
- 27 The Swan
- 39 Turnmills
- 41 Dust
- 46 Fabric
- 52 The Castle
- 54 Bleeding Heart Tavern
- 56 Ye Olde Mitre
- 66 Cock Tavern
- 72 Viaduct Tavern
- 75 Ye Olde Cheshire Cheese
- 87 El Vino
- 89 Ye Olde Cock Tavern
- 108 Doggetts Coat & Badge
- 113 The Wellington
- 119 The Fire Station
- 141 Westminster Arms
- 153 Che
- 172 I Am the Only Running Footman

CHURCHES

- 36 Gray's Inn Court Chapel
- 61 Lincoln's Inn Court Chapel
- 64 St Andrew Holborn
- 69 St Bartholomew-the-Great
- 71 St Sepulchre-without-Newgate
- 78 St Brides, Fleet St
- 80 St Martin-within-Ludgate
- 85 St Andrew-by-the-Wardrobe
- 86 Temple Church
- 90 St Dunstan-in-the-West
- 95 St Clement Danes
- 97 St Mary-le-Strand
- 134 St Margaret's; Westminster
- 196 All Souls Church; Langham Place

THEATRES

- 19 Drill Hall Theatre; The Greenhouse

- 34 Cochrane Theatre
- 79 Bridewell Theatre
- 121 Young Vic; Konditor & Cook Café
- 124 Old Vic

OTHER

- 2 Well Women Centre
- 4 Red & White Laundary
- 7 Telecom Tower
- 8 Heal's; Habitat
- 10 Pollock's Toy Museum
- 11 Cyberia
- 12 STA Travel
- 16 STA Travel
- 17 Imagination Building
- 22 Waterstone's
- 37 Terrance Higgins Trust
- 40 St John's Gate; Order of St John Museum
- 45 Charterhouse
- 55 Jewelers
- 57 Prudential Assurance Building
- 58 Blacks
- 59 Kinko's
- 60 Typing Overload
- 62 London Silver Vaults
- 63 Staple Inn
- 65 Simply Sausages
- 70 Great Fire Memorial
- 73 Dr Johnson's House
- 74 Salisbury Court
- 76 Peterborough Court (Formerly Daily Telegraph Building)
- 77 Reuters Building
- 81 Outdoors
- 88 Wig & Pen Club
- 91 Prince Henry's Room
- 92 Griffin (Temple Bar Site)
- 93 Lloyds Bank
- 94 Twinings
- 96 Australian High Commission
- 98 Courtauld Gallery
- 99 Gilbert Collection
- 100 Hermitage Rooms
- 101 Riverside Walk Book Market
- 102 Purcell Room
- 104 Hayward Gallery
- 105 London Bicycle Tour Company
- 106 Gabriel's Wharf; Gourmet Pizza Company
- 109 Bankside Gallery
- 112 London IMAX Cinema
- 115 BA London Eye
- 116 Dali Universe
- 117 London Aquarium
- 127 Ian Allen Bookshop
- 129 Florence Nightingale Museum

130 Queen Boudicca Statue
131 Big Ben
132 New Parliament Building
133 Winston Churchill Statue
135 Cromwell Statue
136 St Stephen's Entrance
137 Jewel Tower
139 Trade Partners UK
140 Westminster Central Hall
142 Office of the European Commission
143 Middlesex Guildhall
144 Abraham Lincoln Statue
145 Cabinet War Rooms
146 Foreign & Commonwealth Information Centre
147 Cenotaph
148 No 10 Downing St
150 Institute for Contemporary Arts; ICA Café
151 Duke of York Column
152 Christies
154 DR Harris
155 Thomas Cook (Main Office)
156 Davidoff of London
158 Buckingham Palace Ticket Office (Summer Only)
159 Queen Victoria Memorial
160 Queens Gallery
161 Irish Embassy
164 Wellington Arch
165 Apsley House (Wellington Museum)
171 Kinko's
174 US Embassy
175 Canadian High Commision
176 Burberry
177 Sotheby's
179 Handel House Museum
180 Phillips
181 Chinese Contemporary Gallery
183 Marks & Spencer
184 Selfridges
185 French Connection
186 Debenhams; Thomas Cook Branch
187 Tesco Metro
188 John Lewis
189 BHS
190 Wigmore Hall
191 Wallace Collection
197 Broadcasting House
202 Daunt Books
203 Childminders

CHARLOTTE HINDLE

Stately Banqueting House is the only surviving remnant of the Tudor Whitehall Palace.

MAP 7

PLACES TO STAY
3 Charlotte Street Hotel
32 Hazlitt's
41 Oxford St YHA Hostel
104 Manzi's Hotel
112 Thistle Piccadilly
119 Regent Palace Hotel
125 Brown's Hotel

PLACES TO EAT
4 Rasa Sumudra
5 Bam-Bou
8 Han Kang
10 Costa Dorada
17 Soba
20 Star Café
21 Red Veg
22 Govinda's; Krishna Temple
31 Gay Hussar
33 Pizza Express; Jazz Club
40 Soup Works
45 Soup
46 Yo! Sushi; Yo! Below
47 Eco Lab Organic
49 Quo Vadis
50 Mildred's
53 Garlic & Shots
54 Gopal's of Soho
55 Chiang Mai
57 Bar Italia;
   Angelucci Coffee
   Merchants
58 Old Compton Café
60 Pollo; Stockpot
61 Ed's Easy Diner
63 Kettners
64 Pâttisserie Valerie
66 Mezzo; Mezzonine
68 Spiga
69 Freedom Café Bar
71 Satsuma
77 Jen
78 Cam Phat
82 Melati
83 Zilli Fish
84 Wagamama
90 Sugar Club
91 Momo
93 Kulu Kulu
96 New Piccadilly
100 Gerrad's Corner
101 London Hong Kong
102 Fung Shing
105 Chuen Cheng Ku
106 1997
107 C & R

109 Rainforest Café
115 Planet Hollywood
120 Atlantic Bar & Grill
131 L'Odéon
135 The Criterion
139 Stockpot
140 Woodlands
144 Sports Café
149 Quaglino's

PUBS & CLUBS
1 Ha! Ha! Bar & Canteen
11 100 Club
13 Mash
19 Syndrome
26 Astoria
27 Velvet Room
29 Borderline
44 Hanover Grand
52 Candy Bar
56 Ronnie Scott's
62 Coach & Horses; Maison
   Bertaux
70 Village Soho; O Bar
73 Balans
74 Compton's of Soho
75 French House Pub & Dining
   Room
76 Lupo
80 Rupert Street
81 The Yard
86 Emporium
95 Scruffy Murphy's
108 Bar Rumba
111 Waxy O'Connor's
114 Comedy Store

THEATRES
24 Dominion
34 Soho Theatre
43 London Palladium
59 Prince Edward
79 Queen's
94 Piccadilly
97 Lyric
98 Apollo
99 Gielgud
113 Prince of Wales
134 Criterion
141 Comedy
142 Theatre Royal Haymarket
143 Her Majesty's

OTHER
2 Kinko's
6 Computer Shops

7 easyEverything
9 On the Beat
12 HMV
14 Botanicals
15 Borders
16 Global Visa's
18 usit Campus
23 Virgin Megastore
25 Centre Point; Point 101;
   Confederation of British
   Industry
28 Waterstone's
30 Milroy's of Soho
35 Webshack Cybercafé
36 Agent Provocateur
37 Reckless Records
38 Reckless Records
39 Blackmarket
42 Grant & Cutler
48 Broadwick House
51 Trax
65 Algerian Coffee Stores
67 Ann Summers
72 Gerry's
85 Mappin and Webb
87 Hamley's
88 British Airways Travel Shop;
   Stanford's
89 Royal Doulton
92 Zara
103 Prince Charles Cinema
110 Internet Exchange
116 HMV
117 Rock Circus
118 London Pavilion
121 Aquascutum
122 Allies Statue
123 Asprey & Garrard
124 Faraday Museum
126 Cartier
127 Tiffany & Co
128 Ralph Lauren
129 St James's Piccadilly
130 Waterstones
132 Tower Records
133 Eros Statue
136 Virgin Megastore
137 Horses of Helios
   Fountain
138 American Express
145 New Zealand House; High
   Commision
146 Britain Visitor Centre;
   Stanfords
147 Paxton & Whitfield
148 Taylor of Old Bond St

MAP 8

PLACES TO STAY
1 Morgan Hotel
10 Citadines Holborn/Covent Garden
18 High Holborn Student Hall
21 Kingsway Hall Hotel
31 Covent Garden Hotel; Brasserie Max
40 Fielding Hotel
63 Waldorf Meridian
66 One Aldwych
104 Hampshire
111 St Martin's
117 Strand Palace
119 The Savoy
134 Trafalgar Hilton

PLACES TO EAT
3 Thai Garden Café
5 Ruskins Café
6 Coffee Gallery
7 Abeno
9 My Old Dutch
25 Franx Snack Bar
32 World Food Café
33 Monmouth Coffee Company
34 Neal's Yard Salad Bar
36 Rock & Sole Plaice
39 Sarastro
42 Food for Thought
54 Belgo Centraal
56 Café Pacifico
58 Café des Amis du Vin
68 Livebait
69 Orso
70 Joe Allen
82 The Ivy
90 Ikkyu
91 Poons
93 Toyko Diner
94 Zipangu
95 Mr Au
96 Cranks
102 Gaby's
106 Mr Wu
112 Porters
113 La Perla
114 Mongolian Barbeque
115 Rules
116 Wagamama
118 Simpson's-in-the-Strand

PUBS, BARS & CLUBS
4 Museum Tavern
12 Princess Louise
13 The End; AKA
16 First Out
24 Freud
43 Freedom Brewing Co
49 Salsa!
73 Rock Garden
75 Punch & Judy
80 Lamb & Flag
83 Spice of Life; Backstage Bar
92 West Central
98 Cork & Bottle Wine Bar
101 The Salisbury
110 Brief Encounter
123 Retro Bar
137 Sherlock Holmes
138 Heaven
139 Gordon's Wine Bar

THEATRES
17 Shaftesbury
22 New London; Talk of London
29 Phoenix
38 Peacock Theatre
44 Donmar Warehouse
51 New Ambassadors
52 St Martin's
53 Cambridge
60 Fortune
61 Theatre Royal Drury Lane
62 Aldwych
64 Strand
67 Lyceum
84 Palace
99 Wyndham's
100 Albery
107 Garrick
108 Coliseum; English National Opera
109 Duke of York
120 Savoy Theatre
121 Adelphi
141 Whitehall Theatre

OTHER
2 Gosh!; London Cartoon Gallery
8 St George's Bloomsbury
11 Sainsbury's
14 James Smith & Sons
15 Jessops
19 Bikepark Bicycle Rental
20 Sir John Soane's Museum
23 Oasis Sports Centre
26 Helter Skelter
27 Borders
28 Foyle's
30 Ray's Jazz Shop
35 Neal's Yard Dairy
37 Old Curiosity Shop
41 Kite Store
45 High Jinks
46 STA Travel
47 Kitschen Sync
48 Blackwell's
50 Sportspages
55 Pineapple
57 The Tea House
59 Church of Scotland Crown Court; Globetrotters
65 Courtauld Gallery
71 London's Transport Museum
72 Theatre Museum
74 Internet Exchange
76 Benjamin Pollock's Toyshop
77 St Paul's Church
78 Africa Centre; Calabash
79 The Sanctuary
81 Stanford's
85 Cambridge Circus
86 Zwemmer Art & Architecture
87 Zwemmer Books
88 Murder One
89 Silver Moon
97 Photographer's Gallery
103 tkts
105 Westminster Central Library Reference
122 Zimbabwe House
124 St Martin-in-the-Fields; Cafe in the Crypt
125 Handicraft Market
126 Trafalgar Square Post Office
127 Edith Cavell Memorial
128 George Washington Statue
129 South Africa House; High Commission
130 easyEverything
131 Empty Plinth
132 Nelson's Column
133 Canada House
135 British Council
136 Charles I Statue
140 Embankment Place Building

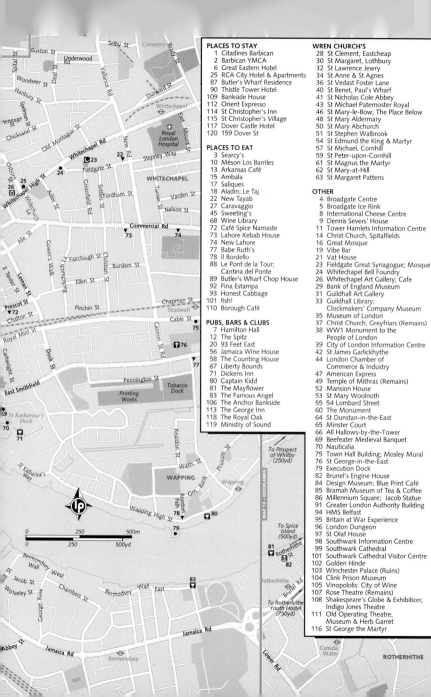

PLACES TO STAY
1 Citadines Barbican
2 Barbican YMCA
6 Great Eastern Hotel
25 RCA City Hotel & Apartments
87 Butler's Wharf Residence
90 Thistle Tower Hotel
109 Bankside House
112 Orient Exppresso
114 St Christopher's Inn
115 St Christopher's Village
117 Dover Castle Hotel
120 159 Dover St

PLACES TO EAT
3 Searcy's
10 Méson Los Barriles
13 Arkansas Café
15 Ambala
17 Saliques
18 Aladin; Le Taj
22 New Tayab
27 Caravaggio
45 Sweeting's
68 Wine Library
72 Café Spice Namaste
73 Lahore Kebab House
77 New Lahore
77 Babe Ruth's
78 Il Bordello
88 Le Pont de la Tour;
    Cantina del Ponte
89 Butler's Wharf Chop House
92 Fina Estampa
93 Honest Cabbage
101 fish!
110 Borough Café

PUBS, BARS & CLUBS
7 Hamilton Hall
12 The Spitz
20 93 Feet East
56 Jamaica Wine House
58 The Counting House
67 Liberty Bounds
71 Dickens Inn
80 Captain Kidd
81 The Mayflower
83 The Famous Angel
106 The Anchor Bankside
113 The George Inn
118 The Royal Oak
119 Ministry of Sound

WREN CHURCH'S
28 St Clement, Eastcheap
30 St Margaret, Lothbury
32 St Lawrence Jewry
34 St Anne & St Agnes
36 St Vedast Foster Lane
40 St Benet, Paul's Wharf
41 St Nicholas Cole Abbey
43 St Michael Paternoster Royal
46 St Mary-le-Bow; The Place Below
48 St Mary Aldermary
50 St Mary Abchurch
51 St Stephen Walbrook
54 St Edmund the King & Martyr
57 St Michael, Cornhill
59 St Peter-upon-Cornhill
61 St Magnus the Martyr
62 St Mary-at-Hill
63 St Margaret Pattens

OTHER
4 Broadgate Centre
5 Broadgate Ice Rink
8 International Cheese Centre
9 Dennis Severs' House
11 Tower Hamlets Information Centre
14 Christ Church, Spitalfields
16 Great Mosque
19 Vibe Bar
21 Vat House
23 Fieldgate Great Synagogue; Mosque
24 Whitechapel Bell Foundry
26 Whitechapel Art Gallery; Cafe
29 Bank of England Museum
31 Guildhall Art Gallery
33 Guildhall Library;
    Clockmakers' Company Museum
35 Museum of London
37 Christ Church, Greyfriars (Remains)
38 WW1 Monument to the
    People of London
39 City of London Information Centre
42 St James Garlickhythe
44 London Chamber of
    Commerce & Industry
47 American Express
49 Temple of Mithras (Remains)
52 Mansion House
53 St Mary Woolnoth
55 54 Lombard Street
60 The Monument
64 St Dunstan-in-the-East
65 Minster Court
66 All Hallows-by-the-Tower
69 Beefeater Medieval Banquet
70 Nauticalia
75 Town Hall Building; Mosley Mural
76 St George-in-the-East
79 Execution Dock
82 Brunel's Engine House
84 Design Museum; Blue Print Café
85 Bramah Museum of Tea & Coffee
86 Millennium Square; Jacob Statue
91 Greater London Authority Building
94 HMS Belfast
95 Britain at War Experience
96 London Dungeon
97 St Olaf House
98 Southwark Information Centre
99 Southwark Cathedral
101 Southwark Cathedral Visitor Centre
102 Golden Hinde
103 Winchester Palace (Ruins)
104 Clink Prison Museum
105 Vinopolis: City of Wine
107 Rose Theatre (Remains)
108 Shakespeare's Globe & Exhibition;
    Indigo Jones Theatre
111 Old Operating Theatre,
    Museum & Herb Garret
116 St George the Martyr

MAP 5

HOLLAND
PARK

Melbury Rd

Holland Rd

Addison Rd

Holland Park Rd

Kensington High St

Edwardes Sq

Pembroke Gardens

Pembroke Rd

Pembroke Sq

Pembroke Villas

Logan Place

Earls Court Rd

Stratford Rd

Abingdon Villas

Scarsdale Villas

Marloes Rd

Lexham Gardens

Stanford Rd

Cornwall Gardens

Gloucester Rd

Victoria Grove

Launceston Pl

Launceston Pl

Grenville Pl

Cornwall Gardens

Kensington
(Olympia)

Olympia

Earls Court Sq

Redfield La

Kenway Rd

Templeton Pl

Earls Court Rd

West Cromwell Rd

Longridge Rd

Trebovir Rd

Nevern Sq

Philbeach Gardens

Penywern Rd

Warwick Rd

Old Brompton Rd

EARL'S
COURT

Cromwell Rd

SOUTH
KENSINGTON

Gloucester Roa

Courtfield Gardens

Collingham Rd

Collingham Pl

Courtfield Rd

Harrington Gardens

Wetherby Gardens

Bina Gardens

The Boltons

Earl's Court Exhibition Centre

Eardley Crescent

WEST
BROMPTON

West Brompton

Finborough Rd

Ifield Rd

Redcliffe Gardens

Redcliffe Gardens

Hollywood Rd

Fawcett St

Cathcart Rd

Tregunter Rd

Harcourt Terrace

Westgate Terrace

Gunter Grove

Hortensia Rd

Fernshaw Rd

Cremorne Rd

Sedlescombe Rd

Ongar Rd

Lillie Rd

Seagrave Rd

Halford Rd

Anselm Rd

Racton Rd

Farm La

Walham Grove

Vanston Place

Fulham Rd

Fulham Broadway

FULHAM
BROADWAY

Barclay Rd

Effie Rd

King's Rd

Moore Park Rd

Waterford Rd

Britannia Rd

Harwood Rd

Maxwell Rd

Imperial Rd

New King's Rd

Wandsworth Bridge

Bagley's La

Harwood Terrace

Imperial Rd

WALHAM
GREEN

Parsons
Green

Eel Brook Common

Musgrave Crescent

Fulham Rd

Basuto Rd

Favart Rd

Brompton Cemetery

Chelsea Village, Chelsea Football Club & Chelsea World of Sport

Fulham Broadway

West Brompton

PLACES TO STAY

4 Citadines South Kensington
6 London Lodge Hotel; Stephanie's
8 Amber Hotel
8 Shelbourne Hotel
10 Barmy Badger Backpackers
17 Merlyn Court Hotel
18 Curzon House Hotel
19 St Simeon Hotel
20 Windsor House; Regency Court Hotel
21 London Town Hotel
22 York House Hotel
23 Philbeach Hotel; Wilde about Oscar
25 Boka Hotel
33 Earl's Court YHA Hostel
34 Swiss House Hotel
35 Hotel 167
37 130 Queen's Gate
46 Five Sumner Place
47 Number Sixteen
51 Imperial College Student Hall
61 Blakes
70 Annandale House Hotel

PLACES TO EAT

3 Launceston Place
12 Benjy's
14 Nando's
27 Troubadour
29 Balans West
30 Krungtap
31 Mr Wing
32 Blanco's
40 La Grande Bouchée
42 Bonne Bouche
43 Rôtisserie Jules
44 Spago
45 Pizza Organic
48 FrancoFill
49 Daquise
50 Ognisko Polskie
53 Pâtisserie Valerie
54 Parisienne Chophouse
56 Daphne's
57 The Collection
60 Cactus Blue
62 Vingt-Quatre
63 Aubergine
64 Wine & Kebab
66 Chelsea Kitchen
68 Oriel
74 Foxtrot Oscar
75 Gordon Ramsey
81 Ransome's Dock
82 Buchan's
83 Pizza Express
92 Henry J Bean's
94 Stockpot
94 Bluebird
95 New Culture Revolution

97 Ed's Easy Diner
98 Vama
100 Chelsea Bun
102 Tiger Lil's
103 Chutney Mary's
104 Shoeless Joe's
105 Jim Thompson
108 Blue Elephant
109 Bonjour Vietnam

PUBS & CLUBS

13 Prince of Teck
24 The Atlas
26 Bromptons
28 Coleherne
67 The Antelope
76 Cooper's Arms
78 King's Head & Eight Bells
84 Chelsea Potter
101 World's End
110 Havana

OTHER

1 Board of Inland Revenue
2 Leighton House
7 Cromwell Hospital
9 Bobo's Bubbles Laundrette
11 Top Deck Travel; Vaccination Clinic; Rapid Visa Worldwide
15 Callshop
16 Internet Lounge
36 STA Travel
38 Wash & Dry Laundrette
39 French Institute; Ciné Lumière; Brasserie de l'Institut
41 French Bookshop
52 Brompton Oratory
55 Rigby & Peller
58 Michelin House; Bibendum; Conran Shop
59 Royal Marsden Hospital
65 Jane Asher Party Cakes
69 Royal Court Theatre
71 Chapel
72 Great Hall
73 National Army Museum
77 Carlyle's House
79 Chelsea Old Church
80 Peace Pagoda
85 Antiquarius Antiques Centre
86 CM Store
87 Ad Hoc
88 Heal's; Habitat
89 Chelsea Farmers Market
90 Sundance Market
91 Daisy & Tom
96 Rococo
99 Cremorne Launderers
106 Bikepark Chelsea
107 Pippa Pop-Ins

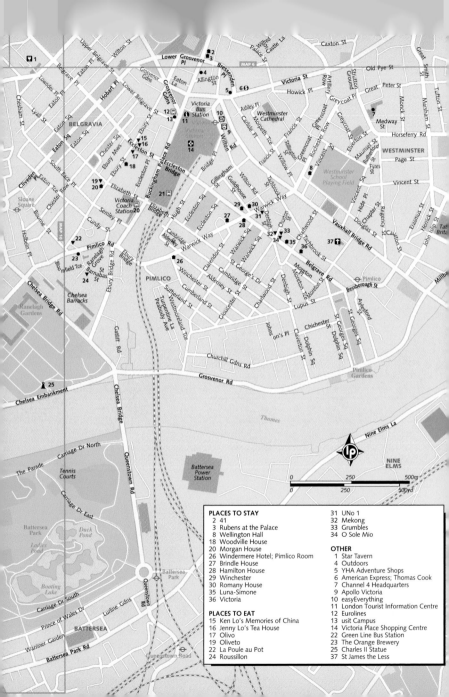

PLACES TO STAY
2 41
3 Rubens at the Palace
8 Wellington Hall
18 Woodville House
20 Morgan House
26 Windermere Hotel; Pimlico Room
27 Brindle House
28 Hamilton House
29 Winchester
30 Romany House
35 Luna-Simone
36 Victoria

PLACES TO EAT
15 Ken Lo's Memories of China
16 Jenny Lo's Tea House
17 Olivo
19 Oliveto
22 La Poule au Pot
24 Roussillon

31 UNo 1
32 Mekong
33 Grumbles
34 O Sole Mio

OTHER
1 Star Tavern
4 Outdoors
5 YHA Adventure Shops
6 American Express; Thomas Cook
7 Channel 4 Headquarters
9 Apollo Victoria
10 easyEverything
11 London Tourist Information Centre
12 Eurolines
13 usit Campus
14 Victoria Place Shopping Centre
22 Green Line Bus Station
23 The Orange Brewery
25 Charles II Statue
37 St James the Less

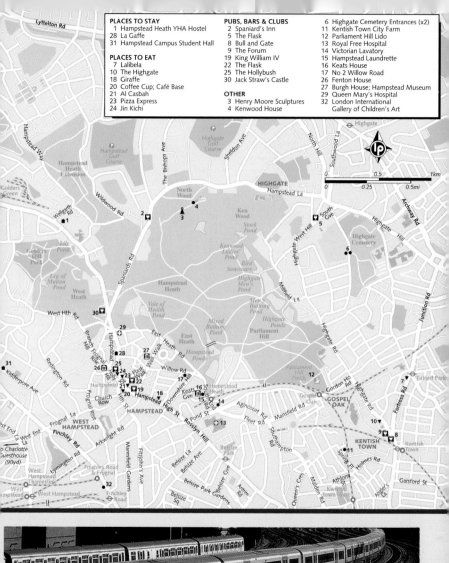

PLACES TO STAY
1 Hampstead Heath YHA Hostel
28 La Gaffe
31 Hampstead Campus Student Hall

PLACES TO EAT
7 Lalibela
10 The Highgate
18 Giraffe
20 Coffee Cup; Café Base
21 Al Casbah
23 Pizza Express
24 Jin Kichi

PUBS, BARS & CLUBS
2 Spaniard's Inn
5 The Flask
8 Bull and Gate
9 The Forum
19 King William IV
22 The Flask
25 The Hollybush
30 Jack Straw's Castle

OTHER
3 Henry Moore Sculptures
4 Kenwood House

6 Highgate Cemetery Entrances (x2)
11 Kentish Town City Farm
12 Parliament Hill Lido
13 Royal Free Hospital
14 Victorian Lavatory
15 Hampstead Laundrette
16 Keats House
17 No 2 Willow Road
26 Fenton House
27 Burgh House; Hampstead Museum
29 Queen Mary's Hospital
32 London International
   Gallery of Children's Art

High-speed trains dash across England... well, you have to hope.

PAUL BIGLAND

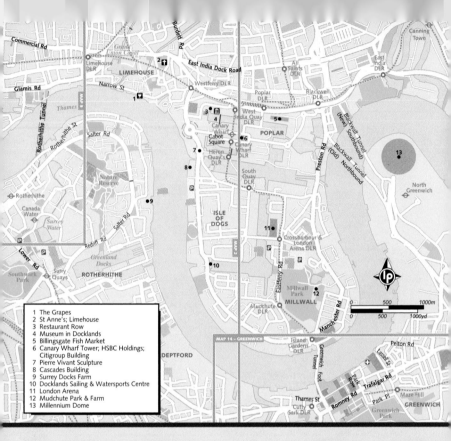

1 The Grapes
2 St Anne's; Limehouse
3 Restaurant Row
4 Museum in Docklands
5 Billingsgate Fish Market
6 Canary Wharf Tower; HSBC Holdings;
   Citigroup Building
7 Pierre Vivant Sculpture
8 Cascades Building
9 Surrey Docks Farm
10 Docklands Sailing & Watersports Centre
11 London Arena
12 Mudchute Park & Farm
13 Millennium Dome

Sitting on the dock of the Thames: spacious abodes and fine dining typify the Docklands today.

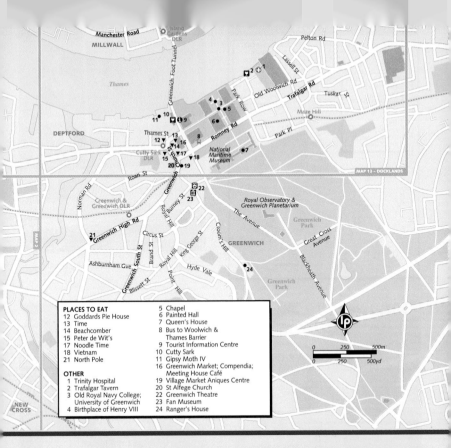

PLACES TO EAT
12 Goddards Pie House
13 Time
14 Beachcomber
15 Peter de Wit's
17 Noodle Time
18 Vietnam
21 North Pole

OTHER
1 Trinity Hospital
2 Trafalgar Tavern
3 Old Royal Navy College;
  University of Greenwich
4 Birthplace of Henry VIII

5 Chapel
6 Painted Hall
7 Queen's House
8 Bus to Woolwich &
  Thames Barrier
9 Tourist Information Centre
10 Cutty Sark
11 Gipsy Moth IV
16 Greenwich Market; Compendia;
  Meeting House Café
19 Village Market Aniques Centre
20 St Alfege Church
22 Greenwich Theatre
23 Fan Museum
24 Ranger's House

The view from Greenwich as the sun sets on the City.

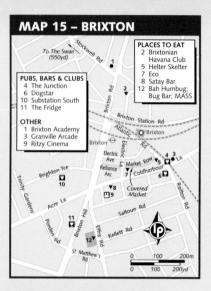

MAP 15 – BRIXTON

PLACES TO EAT
2 Brixtonian Havana Club
5 Helter Skelter
7 Eco
8 Satay Bar
12 Bah Humbug; Bug Bar; MASS

PUBS, BARS & CLUBS
4 The Junction
6 Dogstar
10 Substation South
11 The Fridge

OTHER
1 Brixton Academy
3 Granville Arcade
9 Ritzy Cinema

To The Swan (550yd)
Stockwell Rd
Brixton Rd
Brixton Station Rd
Atlantic Rd
Brixton
Electric Rd
Electric Ave
Market Row
Coldharbour
Railton Rd
Brighton Tce
Trinity Gardens
Reliance Arc
Covered Market
Acre La
Saltoun Rd
Brixton Hill
Effra Rd
Kellett Rd
Porden Rd
St Matthew's Rd

JULIET COOMBE

Brixton station: the wait isn't usually that bad...

JULIET COOMBE

JULIET COOMBE

Fresh produce galore at Brixton's bright and lively fruit and veg market on Electric Avenue

Richmond Park is the perfect place for a lazy Sunday stroll.

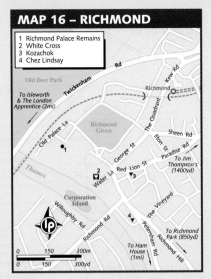

MAP 16 – RICHMOND

1 Richmond Palace Remains
2 White Cross
3 Kozachok
4 Chez Lindsay

Laidback Richmond, with its fine Georgian architecture, is but a boat ride away from central London.

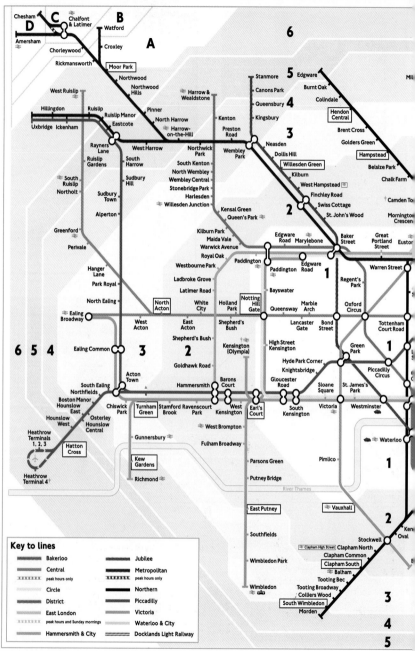

© Transport for London

High Barnet
Cockfosters
Epping
Totteridge & Whetstone
Oakwood
Theydon Bois
Loughton
Debden
Woodside Park
Southgate
Buckhurst Hill
6
West Finchley
Arnos Grove
Finchley Central
Bounds Green
Roding Valley † Chigwell †
East Finchley
Wood Green
Woodford
5 Grange Hill †
Highgate
Turnpike Lane
4
Hainault
Archway
Manor House
Tottenham Hale ≷ Blackhorse Road ≷
South Woodford
Fairlop
Tufnell Park
Seven Sisters
Walthamstow Central ≷
Newbury Park
Barkingside
Upminster
Finsbury Park ≷
Redbridge
Snaresbrook
Wanstead Gants Hill
Upminster Bridge
Kentish Town ≷
Arsenal
Holloway Road
3
Leytonstone
Hornchurch
Caledonian Road
Dagenham East
Elm Park
King's Cross St. Pancras ≷
Highbury & Islington ≷
Leyton
Dagenham Heathway
Angel
≷ Stratford
Upney
Becontree
Farringdon Barbican
Old Street
2
Barking ≷
Russell Square
Liverpool Street
Bethnal Green
Mile End
East Ham
Moorgate
Shoreditch †
Pudding Mill Lane
Upton Park
Chancery Lane ★
St. Paul's
Bow Road
Bromley-by-Bow
Plaistow
West Ham
1
Aldgate East
Stepney Green Whitechapel
Bow Church
Devons Road
3
4 5 6
Bank
Aldgate
2
All Saints
East India
Bus to London City Airport
vent Garden
Shadwell Westferry
Poplar
Canning Town ≷
ster
† ≷ Cannon Street
Limehouse
Blackwall
Royal Victoria
Mansion House
Monument Tower Hill
Wapping West India Quay
Custom House for ExCeL
≷ Fenchurch Street
Tower Gateway
Prince Regent
Royal Albert
Blackfriars
Canary Wharf
Beckton Park
Temple ★
River Thames
North Greenwich
Cyprus
Gallions Reach
ankment ring Cross
London Bridge
Rotherhithe
Beckton
Bermondsey
Canada Water
Heron Quays
outhwark Waterloo East
South Quay Crossharbour & London Arena
Lambeth North
Borough
Surrey Quays
Mudchute
Island Gardens
Elephant & Castle
≷ New Cross Gate
New Cross ≷
Cutty Sark for Maritime Greenwich
Greenwich ≷
Deptford Bridge
Elverson Road
Lewisham ≷

MAP LEGEND

BOUNDARIES

.... International
.... Provincial, State
.... Regional, Suburb

HYDROGRAPHY

.... Coastline
.... River, Creek
.... Lake
.... Canal

.... Building
.... Hotel

ROUTES & TRANSPORT

.... Freeway
.... Highway
.... Major Road
.... Minor Road
.... Unsealed Road
.... City Freeway
.... City Highway
.... City Road
.... City Street, Lane

.... Pedestrian Mall
.... Tunnel
.... Train Route & Station
.... Underground & Station
.... Tramway & Tram Stop
.... Cable Car or Chairlift
.... Path
.... Walking Tour
.... Ferry Route & Terminal

AREA FEATURES

.... Park, Gardens
.... Cemetery

.... Market
.... Pedestrian

MAP SYMBOLS

�*/ **LONDON** .... National Capital
● **Colchester** .... City or Large Town
● Biggleswade .... Town or Village

● .... Point of Interest

■ .... Place to Stay
▲ .... Camp Site

▼ .... Place to Eat
🍺 .... Pub or Bar

✈ .... Airport
...... Ancient or City Wall
🏛 .... Archaeological Site

♦ .... Bank
🚌 🚏 ...... Bus Stop, Station
🏰 .... Castle or Fort
⛪ ...... Church or Cathedral
🎬 .... Cinema
🏢 ... Embassy or Consulate
⛲ .... Fountain
⛳ .... Golf Course
✚ .... Hospital
🖥 .... Internet Cafe
☼ .... Lookout
⚱ .... Monument
☪ .... Mosque
🏛 .... Museum
→ .... One Way Street

🏰 .. Palace or Stately Home
🅿 .... Parking
⛽ .... Petrol Station
🚓 .... Police Station
✉ .... Post Office
🛒 .... Shopping Centre
🏊 .... Swimming Pool
✡ .... Synagogue
🚕 .... Taxi
☎ .... Telephone
🎭 .... Theatre
🚻 .... Toilet
ℹ ...... Tourist Information
🚍 .... Transport
🐾 .... Zoo

Note: not all symbols displayed above appear in this book

LONELY PLANET OFFICES

Australia
Locked Bag 1, Footscray, Victoria 3011
☎ 03 8379 8000 fax 03 8379 8111
email: talk2us@lonelyplanet.com.au

USA
150 Linden St, Oakland, CA 94607
☎ 510 893 8555 TOLL FREE: 800 275 8555
fax 510 893 8572
email: info@lonelyplanet.com

UK
10a Spring Place, London NW5 3BH
☎ 020 7428 4800 fax 020 7428 4828
email: go@lonelyplanet.co.uk

France
1 rue du Dahomey, 75011 Paris
☎ 01 55 25 33 00 fax 01 55 25 33 01
email: bip@lonelyplanet.fr
www.lonelyplanet.fr

World Wide Web: www.lonelyplanet.com *or* AOL keyword: lp
Lonely Planet Images: lpi@lonelyplanet.com.au